Handbook of Restorative Justice

Handbook of Restorative Justice

Edited by

Gerry Johnstone
and
Daniel W. Van Ness

WILLAN
PUBLISHING

Published by

Willan Publishing
Culmcott House
Mill Street, Uffculme
Cullompton, Devon
EX15 3AT, UK
Tel: +44(0)1884 840337
Fax: +44(0)1884 840251
e-mail: info@willanpublishing.co.uk
website: www.willanpublishing.co.uk

Published simultaneously in the USA and Canada by

Willan Publishing
c/o ISBS, 920 NE 58th Ave, Suite 300
Portland, Oregon 97213-3644, USA
Tel: +001(0)503 287 3093
Fax: +001(0)503 280 8832
e-mail: info@isbs.com
website: www.isbs.com

First published 2007

Paperback
ISBN-13 978-1-84392-150-9
ISBN-10 1-84392-150-2

Hardback
ISBN-13 978-1-84392-151-6
ISBN-10 1-84392-151-0

British Library Cataloguing-in-Publication Data

A catalogue record for this book is available from the British Library

Project management by Deer Park Productions, Tavistock, Devon
Typeset by GCS, Leighton Buzzard, Beds
Printed and bound by T.J. International, Padstow, Cornwall

Contents

List of abbreviations

ACT	Australian Capital Territory
ADR	alternative dispute resolution
AVP	Alternatives to Violence Project
BARJ	Balanced and Restorative Justice
BJS	Barangay Justice System
BJSS	Barangay Justice Service System
CASEL	Collaborative for Academic Social and Emotional Learning
CRE	conflict resolution education
CSC	Correctional Services of Canada
DfES	Department for Education and Skills
FGC	family group conference (conferencing)
JRC	Justice Research Consortium
MCC	Mennonite Central Committee
NCDRO	National Coalition of Dispute Resolution Organizations
NGO	non-governmental organization
NICPRO	National Institute for Crime Prevention and the Reintegration of Offenders
NSJS	non-state justice system
OAS	Organization of American States
OJJDP	Office of Juvenile Justice and Delinquency Prevention
OVC	Office of Victims of Crime

PMC	people's mediation council
PRAWA	Prisoners Rehabilitation and Welfare Action
PRC	People's Republic of China
PRI	Penal Reform International
PSR	pre-sentence report
RCMP	Royal Canadian Mounted Police
RGC	restorative group conference
RISE	Re-integrative Shaming Experiments
RJ	restorative justice
RR	Restorative Resolutions
SACRO	Scottish Association for Safeguarding Communities and Reducing Offending
SAJJ	South African Juvenile Justice/South Australian Juvenile Justice
TRC	truth and reconciliation commission
VOM	victim–offender mediation
VORP	Victim Offender Reconciliation Program
YJB	Youth Justice Board
YOP	youth offender panel
YOT	youth offending team

Notes on contributors

Gordon Bazemore is Professor of Criminology and Criminal Justice and Director of the Community Justice Institute at Florida Atlantic University. His research has focused on juvenile justice and youth policy, restorative justice, crime victims, corrections and community policing. He is the author of *Juvenile Justice Reform and Restorative Justice: Building Theory and Policy from Practice* (with Mara Schiff), and two edited books, *Restorative Juvenile Justice: Repairing the Harm of Youth Crime* (co-edited with Lode Walgrave) and *Restorative and Community Justice: Cultivating Common Ground for Victims, Communities and Offenders* (co-edited with Mara Schiff).

Christopher Bennett is Lecturer in Philosophy at the University of Sheffield. He has published on forgiveness, retribution and issues concerning the communicative theory of punishment, as well as on other areas of moral and political philosophy. He is currently working on a book that examines the nature of apology, its connection with ideas of individual responsibility and its potential role in a justice system.

Jonathan Burnside is Lecturer in Law at the School of Law, University of Bristol. He pioneered 'relational justice' at the Relationships Foundation, Cambridge, in the early 1990s and co-edited *Relational Justice: Repairing the Breach*. He has written extensively on the Jewish and Christian roots of restorative and relational thinking. He is the author of *The Signs of Sin: Seriousness of Offence in Biblical Law* and *My Brother's Keeper: Faith-based Units in Prisons* (with Nancy Loucks, Joanna R. Adler and Gerry Rose). He is currently preparing a textbook on biblical law for Cambridge University Press titled *Jewish Justice in the Bible*.

Dobrinka Ivanova Chankova is Associate Professor of Criminology and Human Rights Protection at South-Western University, Blagoevgrad, Bulgaria. She is also the Executive Director of the Institute for Conflict Resolution in Sofia, has served as an expert on the Council of Europe Committee on

Mediation in Penal Matters (1995–7) and as a Permanent Secretary of Bulgaria in the EU Subcommittee on Approximation of Bulgarian Legislation to the EC Law (1996–7). She has played a pioneering role in introducing restorative justice practices to Bulgaria's criminal justice system and in increasing public awareness of the benefits of restorative justice. Her latest book is *Mediation: An Innovation in Criminal Justice*.

Chris Cunneen holds the NewSouth Global Chair in Criminology, Law Faculty, University of New South Wales. He has published widely in the areas of restorative justice, juvenile justice and indigenous legal issues.

Kathleen Daly is Professor of Criminology and Criminal Justice at Griffith University, Brisbane. Since 1995, she has directed a programme of research on restorative justice, indigenous justice, and the race and gender policies of new justice practices in Australia, New Zealand and Canada.

Xiaohua Di is Professor of Law at Nanjing University, People's Republic of China, and Director of the Institute of Crime Prevention and Control at the University. He specializes in research into the theory and practice of criminal punishment. He has conducted research and taught in the areas of criminology, criminal physiology, penology, criminal procedure, restorative justice, community rehabilitation, jail rehabilitation and juvenile justice. He has researched a number of projects at both provincial and ministerial level, and has produced over 10 books as sole author, co-author, editor or translator, as well as having written over 60 papers.

James Dignan is Professor of Criminology and Restorative Justice at the Centre for Criminological Research, University of Sheffield. He has conducted research in the fields of restorative justice and community mediation and has written on a variety of theoretical, practical and policy issues relating to the development and implementation of restorative justice. His other main research interests encompass comparative penal policy and youth justice. His recent publications include *Understanding Victims and Restorative Justice* and (with Michael Cavadino) *Penal Systems: A Comparative Approach* and *Penal Systems: An Introduction* (4th edn). Other works include *Restorative Justice for Northern Ireland: A Comparative Review* and (with Tony Bottoms) 'Youth justice in Great Britain' (published in *Crime and Justice: A Review of Research*, Vol. 31).

Lori Elis is Assistant Professor of Criminology and Criminal Justice at Florida Atlantic University. Her research interests include developmental theories of crime, domestic violence and the impact of restorative justice programmes on female offenders. Her publications have appeared in *Public Organization Review*, *Criminology* and the *Journal of Research in Crime and Delinquency*.

Jan Froestad is Associate Professor at the Department of Administration and Organization Theory, University of Bergen. He has written extensively on disability issues, with an emphasis on historical and cross-national studies, using this approach to criticize aspects of the Norwegian and Scandinavian modernization process. Latterly, his interest has been on the role of trust in social processes, especially on the conditions necessary for generalizing trust in developing countries. He is currently involved in several projects concerned with identifying the design principles for the governance of security in Africa, with a focus on the need to mobilize local knowledge and capacity in poor communities as an essential element to creating innovative and just conditions for good governance.

Simon Green is Lecturer in Community Justice and Criminology at the University of Hull. He is currently co-editing a text entitled *Addressing Offending Behaviour* for Willan Publishing and co-authoring a new edition of *Understanding Crime Data* for the Open University Press *Crime and Justice* series. His research interests are in the fields of social and criminological theory, victimology, probation and community studies. He is currently Hull University's Programme Director for the Diploma in Probation Studies and is in the process of developing an online MA in restorative justice with Gerry Johnstone.

Hennessey Hayes is Senior Lecturer in the School of Criminology and Criminal Justice, Griffith University, Brisbane. He has been researching and writing in the area of restorative justice, youthful offending and recidivism for nearly a decade. His current work includes a major qualitative study of young offenders in youth justice conferences with a focus on what young people understand about restorative justice processes and how such knowledge impacts future behaviour.

Carolyn Hoyle is Lecturer in Criminology, and Fellow of Green College, University of Oxford. Her recent research has been on restorative justice, including four years of research into restorative cautioning in the Thames Valley; a national evaluation of restorative justice schemes for juveniles; a comparative study of traditional and restorative measures for resolving complaints against the police by the public; and, most recently, a resanctioning study, assessing the impact of restorative cautioning on offending. In addition to publishing widely in this area, she teaches a course on restorative justice to MSc students studying criminology at Oxford.

Gerry Johnstone is Professor of Law at the University of Hull, where he has taught since 1989 and is currently Head of the Law School. He is the author of *Restorative Justice: Ideas, Values, Debates* and editor of *A Restorative Justice Reader*. He has also written on other aspects of penal policy, including a book on *Medical Concepts and Penal Policy*. He is currently working on a book on the legal construction of crime and a series of essays on the theme 'the power of restorative conferencing'.

Jennifer Larson Sawin is Program Associate at Central Virginia Restorative Justice based in Charlottesville, Virginia, where she manages juvenile cases from area courts and community agencies. Jennifer has consulted in restorative justice programme networking in Northern Ireland and the Republic of Ireland, and in restorative justice programme promotion in South Africa. She has a background in marketing and also holds an MA in conflict transformation from Eastern Mennonite University in Harrisonburg, Virginia.

Jennifer Llewellyn is Associate Professor of Law at Dalhousie University, Canada. She worked with the South African Truth and Reconciliation Commission in 1997 and was a member of the Research Initiative on the Resolution of Ethnic Conflict (RIREC) at the Joan B. Kroc Institute for International Peace Studies, University of Notre Dame (2002–4). She is currently Academic/Policy Adviser to the Nova Scotia Provincial Restorative Justice Program. She recently served as a member of the Assembly of First Nations' Expert Task Group on Compensation for Abuses in Indian Residential Schools (2004) and continues to advise AFN on issues related to truth and reconciliation. She has published extensively on restorative justice theory and practice and in the area of restorative justice, truth commissions and transitional contexts.

Christopher D. Marshall is St John's Senior Lecturer in Christian Theology at the Religious Studies Department, Victoria University of Wellington, New Zealand. Among his many publications is the award-winning *Beyond Retribution: A New Testament Vision of Justice, Crime and Punishment*, generally considered to be the benchmark study on justice, punishment and restorative justice themes in the Bible. He was recipient of an International Community Justice Award in 2004 in recognition of his involvement in the promotion and practice of restorative justice.

Gabrielle Maxwell, previously Director of the Crime and Justice Research Centre at Victoria University of Wellington, New Zealand, is now an associate at the Institute of Policy Studies, School of Government. She is well known for her research and writing on youth and restorative justice. Her most recent books are two edited volumes: one with Allison Morris (*Restorative Justice for Juveniles: Conferencing, Mediation and Circles*) and one with T. Wing Lo and Dennis Wong (*Alternatives to Prosecution*). A major study on 'Achieving effective outcomes in youth justice in New Zealand' was published by the Ministry of Social Development, Wellington, in 2004.

David Miers is Professor of Law at Cardiff University Law School. He has a long-standing research interest in the position of the victim in the criminal justice system, in particular in the law governing the compensation of victims of crime and, more recently, restorative justice. He has completed two major research projects for the Home Office concerning restorative justice provision schemes in England and Wales, and in Europe. The latter was published in 2001 (*An International Review of Restorative Justice*) and an updated version was published in 2004 by the European Forum for Restorative Justice,

Belgium. He is a member of the European Commission's COST Action A21, *Restorative Justice Developments in Europe*.

Brenda Morrison is a research Fellow at the Centre for Restorative Justice at the Australian National University, and is currently seconded to the Jerry Lee Center of Criminology at the University of Pennsylvania. The study of restorative justice and responsive regulation in schools has been her main area of work and is the focus of her forthcoming book, *Restoring Safe School Communities: A Whole School Response to Bullying, Violence and Alienation*. The study of juveniles transitioning from residential placements back to schools and communities is also a focus of her work in Philadelphia.

George Pavlich is Professor of Law and Sociology at the University of Alberta. He has written extensively on social and legal theory, critical criminology and governmental studies. Widely considered to be a leading critical analyst of community mediation and restorative justice, he is the author of *Governing Paradoxes of Restorative Justice*, *Justice Fragmented* and *Critique and Radical Discourses on Crime*. He has co-edited collections entitled *Law, Society and Governance* (with Gary Wickham), *Sociology for the Asking* and *Questioning Sociology* (with Myra Hird). He is currently working on an analysis of criminal accusation.

Kay Pranis is an independent trainer and facilitator for peacemaking circles. From 1994 to 2003 she served the Minnesota Department of Corrections as the Restorative Justice Planner. She worked with leaders in corrections, police, courts, neighbourhood groups, faith communities and education to develop a comprehensive response to crime and conflict based on restorative justice. Kay has been involved in the development of circle processes in criminal justice, schools, neighbourhoods, families and the workplace. She is a co-author of the book (with B. Stuart and M. Wedge) *Peacemaking Circles: From Crime to Community* and author of the *Little Book of Circle Processes: A New/Old Approach to Peacemaking*.

Linda Radzik is Associate Professor of Philosophy at Texas A&M University. She is a moral theorist, who has written on such topics as the justification of punishment, collective responsibility and the moral obligations of wrongdoers. She is currently at work on a manuscript that investigates the proper role of atonement in morality, law and politics.

Barbara E. Raye (MBA) is the Executive Administrator for the international Victim Offender Mediation Association. She is also Executive Director of the Center for Policy, Planning and Performance. The centre provides consulting services and project management to public and non-profit organizations committed to social justice. It has offices in Minnesota, Kenya and Romania. Barbara received her basic mediation training at CDR Associates, co-wrote a curriculum for restorative group conferencing produced by BARJ and VOMA, and helped establish the Restorative Justice Council on Sexual Misconduct in Faith Communities. She has published and trained on race, gender and cultural bias in mediation and on the restorative justice movement. She began her restorative justice work creating programmes for domestic violence victims and offenders and as the Director of Victim Services at the MN Department of Corrections where she helped establish the first restorative justice planner in a US department of corrections.

Ann Warner Roberts (MSc) is a Senior Fellow in Restorative Justice at the University of Minnesota, School of Social Work, and an independent consultant. She has provided training and technical assistance for the Center for Restorative Justice and Peacemaking, the National Institute of Corrections, BARJ and other government and non-governmental organizations both nationally and internationally (including the UK, Kenya and Romania). Ann is the author of a number of articles and book chapters, and was a co-founder of the Restorative Justice Consortium UK. For seven years Ann served as a board member and as co-chair of the international Victim Offender Mediation Association.

Declan Roche has a PhD from the Australian National University and, between 2001 and 2005, was Lecturer in Law at the London School of Economics. He has published widely in the field of restorative justice, including *Accountability in Restorative Justice*, which was awarded the British Society of Criminology's Book Prize for 2003. He is also the editor of the collection *Restorative Justice*, published by Ashgate. He now works for the Australian Government Solicitor, where he is a senior lawyer, specializing in litigation. The views expressed in his chapter are his own, and do not represent those of the Australian Government Solicitor.

Mara Schiff is currently Associate Professor of Criminology and Criminal Justice at Florida Atlantic University. She has had over 25 years' experience in criminal and juvenile justice research, planning, evaluation and teaching. Her research and publications focus on restorative and community justice, substance abuse and juvenile justice, and her work has appeared in a variety of academic journals. In addition, she has completed two edited volumes on restorative justice, and recently published a new book, *Juvenile Justice and Restorative Justice: Building Theory and Policy from Practice* (with Gordon Bazemore).

Pedro Scuro is Director of Centro Talcott of Law and Justice, Brazil. He pioneered the use of restorative processes as components of evidence-based policies aimed at increasing the clarity of norms and the consistency of rule enforcement, reinforcing appropriate behaviour, and improving individual conduct and the relations between institutions and communities. He has written extensively on legal sociology and individual compliance to norms, and is currently involved with the application of restorative justice methods and principles to industrial relations.

Makubetse Sekhonyane is senior Researcher in the Crime and Justice Programme at the Institute for Security Studies (a leading African human security research institution) in Pretoria, South Africa. His background includes work as a researcher at the Human Rights Committee of South Africa, where he examined state policies and legislation to ensure state compliance with the constitution and international human rights treaties.

Susan Sharpe, PhD, is Adjunct Professor in the School of Criminology at Simon Fraser University, British Columbia. She has worked in the restorative justice field since 1994, as a victim–offender mediator and as an independent writer and consultant, and currently serves on the board of the international Victim Offender Mediation Association. She is the author of *Restorative Justice: A Vision for Healing and Change*. She lives in Seattle, where she is at work on a book about justice.

Clifford Shearing is Professor of Criminology and Director of the Institute of Criminology, Faculty of Law, University of Cape Town. His research focuses on developments in governance and regulation which he explores through the window of security. Recent books include *Governing Security: Explorations in Policing and Justice* (with Les Johnston) and *Imagining Security* (with Jennifer Wood). His forthcoming book is *Policing* (with Michael Kempa).

Ann Skelton obtained her BA LLB degree from the University of Natal in 1985, and her LLD (on restorative justice) from the University of Pretoria in 2005. She was employed by Lawyers for Human Rights for 11 years, and directed a technical assistance project for the UN on child justice for four years. Ann has played a leading role in child law reform in South Africa, and has published widely on the issue of children's rights and restorative justice. She is currently co-ordinating a children's litigation project at the Centre for Child Law, University of Pretoria.

Julie Stubbs is Associate Professor and Deputy Director of the Institute of Criminology, University of Sydney. Her research and publications deal primarily with violence against women (including homicide, self-defence, battered woman syndrome and child contact in the context of post-separation domestic violence) and restorative justice.

Daniel W. Van Ness is Executive Director of the Center for Justice and Reconciliation at Prison Fellowship International in Washington, DC. He has practised law, lobbied for changes in sentencing laws and for victim rights in the USA, and taught. For over twenty years he has explored the public policy implications and possibilities of restorative justice. He is the author (with Karen Heetderks Strong) of *Restoring Justice: An Introduction to Restorative Justice* (3rd edn) and is the general editor of www.restorativejustice.org.

Lode Walgrave is Emeritus Professor of Criminology at the Katholieke Universiteit Leuven, and Director of the Research Group on Youth

Criminology which researched on youth crime, prevention, juvenile justice and restorative justice. He chaired the International Network for Research on Restorative Justice. Among his recent publications is *Restorative Justice and the Law*.

King Hung Wan is Chief Officer at Prison Fellowship Hong Kong. His doctoral dissertation was on 'Assessing the effectiveness of respondent complainant mediation at Mediation Services of Winnipeg and the Community Mediation Centre of Singapore'. Since then, he has collaborated closely with Nanjing University and the China University of Political Science and Law, where he has helped promote restorative justice theory and practice among the judiciary and university law students. He has co-edited a book entitled *Walking through Prison Life*.

Ping Wang is Associate Dean and Professor of the School of Criminal Justice at the China University of Political Science and Law (CUPL) in Beijing, and Director of the Centre for Restorative Justice at CUPL. He has written extensively on criminal law, criminology, corrections and restorative justice. Widely considered to be a leading scholar on corrections and restorative justice in his country, he is the author of 'Chinese prison reform and its modernization' (the first doctoral dissertation addressing corrections in the People's Republic of China), and has edited the *Forum on Restorative Justice* annually from 2005. He has recently organized the Restorative Justice Library project, which will translate and publish leading English-language restorative justice books in Chinese.

Jolien Willemsens is Executive Officer of the European Forum for Restorative Justice. She studied criminology at the Catholic University of Leuven (Belgium) and has also obtained a masters degree in European criminology. She has written a number of articles on restorative justice, and co-edited the book (with D. Miers), *Mapping Restorative Justice: Developments in 25 European Countries*. She was also a co-editor of the book (with I. Aertsen, R. Mackay, C. Pelikan and M. Wright), *Rebuilding Community Connections – Mediation and Restorative Justice in Europe*.

Martin Wright was a founder member of Mediation UK, and of the European Forum for Restorative Justice. He is Vice-Chair of the Restorative Justice Consortium, and a volunteer mediator in Lambeth, south London. Publications include *Making Good: Prisons, Punishment and Beyond, Justice for Victims and Offenders: A Restorative Response to Crime* (2nd edn) and *Restoring Respect for Justice*, as well as conference papers in several European countries. Previously he was Director of the Howard League for Penal Reform, and Policy Officer for Victim Support. He holds an honorary fellowship of the Institute of Conflict Resolution, Sofia, Bulgaria.

Howard Zehr is author of numerous books, including *Changing Lenses: A New Focus for Crime and Justice*, one of the foundational texts that defined the theoretical framework of restorative justice. In their recent book, *Restoring*

Justice, Daniel W. Van Ness and Karen Heederks Strong cite Howard as the 'grandfather of restorative justice'. He lectures and consults internationally on restorative justice and victim–offender conferencing, which he helped pioneer. He is also Professor of Sociology and Restorative Justice and Co-director of the Center for Justice and Peacebuilding at Eastern Mennonite University in Harrisonburg, Virginia.

Margarita Zernova is a postdoctoral research Fellow in the Institute of Applied Ethics, University of Hull. Her doctoral research involved an examination of aspirations of proponents of restorative justice and experiences of participants in family group conferences. She is currently researching the ethics of restorative justice.

Preface

The idea of restorative justice emerged over a quarter of a century ago. Since the 1990s it has become a central topic in debates about the future of criminal justice. In recent years, the concept has also become prominent in debates about how we might respond to wrongdoing and conflict in schools, workplaces and everyday life, and in discussions of how we should handle gross violations of human rights. Hundreds of restorative justice schemes are being developed around the world and they are attracting more and more attention from academics, professionals and policy-makers.

Advocates of restorative justice argue that traditional ways of responding to wrongdoing tend to leave the needs of victims, perpetrators and communities unmet and leave the harm caused by wrongdoing unrepaired. They advocate alternative approaches designed to make wrongdoers aware of the nature and magnitude of the harm they cause to other people and of their obligation to atone for that harm through constructive and reparative gestures and deeds. Such reparative action, they suggest, can pave the way to forgiveness and reconciliation, the reintegration of wrongdoers into the community and the healing of victims' trauma. But achieving these goals, they argue, requires a more participatory approach than is traditional. Wrongdoers and their victims, when willing, should ideally meet face to face in a safe and supportive environment and play an active role in discussion and in decision-making. A core idea of restorative justice is that the people most affected by a problem decide among themselves how it should be dealt with.

The rise of restorative justice has been accompanied by the development of a large, diverse and increasingly sophisticated body of research and scholarship. This has now reached the stage where a comprehensive, reliable and accessible survey of the field is possible and necessary. The *Handbook of Restorative Justice* is intended to provide such a survey. Aimed at students, practitioners, policy-makers, researchers – and, indeed, anybody curious about restorative justice and the future of criminal justice – the Handbook:

- explains how the campaign for restorative justice arose and developed into the influential global social movement it is today;
- elucidates and discusses the key concepts and principles of restorative justice;
- analyzes the relationship of restorative justice to more conventional concepts of criminal justice;
- discusses the roots of restorative justice in ancient approaches to conflict resolution, aboriginal justice, religious texts and the victims' movement;
- examines issues of gender and race as they are dealt with within the field of restorative justice;
- describes the variety of restorative justice practices, explains how they have developed in various places and contexts, and critically examines their rationales and effects;
- identifies and examines the various ways by which restorative justice is being (and might be) integrated into mainstream responses to crime and strategies of regulation and the various contexts in which restorative justice has been developed;
- summarizes the results so far of empirical evaluations of restorative justice and looks critically at the assumptions and methods of these studies;
- outlines the global development and appeal of restorative justice;
- critically examines the rhetoric, practices and policies of restorative justice and discusses its future.

It was clear to us from the outset that, in order to provide such a survey of the field of restorative justice, we would need to commission the sharpest and most illuminating writers in the field – both emerging and well established and from around the globe – and get them not only to write chapters on predefined topics, but also to provide comprehensive and even-handed coverage of these topics. We have been fortunate in persuading so many excellent writers to agree to such a task and then to stick to the topic and style asked of them (not to mention meeting our demanding deadlines).

Now that we are at the end – rather than in the middle – of the mammoth task of compiling this Handbook, we are very grateful to Brian Willan for coming up with the idea and for asking us to take it on. As anybody familiar with the field will know, Willan Publishing has led the way in encouraging and providing an outlet for research and scholarly writing about restorative justice, and we are proud to be chosen to edit this particular contribution to Willan's much-admired *Handbook* series. During the planning stages, we benefited significantly from a number of thoughtful reviews of our plans. We would like to thank these reviewers: Adam Crawford, Russ Immarigeon, George Pavlich, Brian Williams and Howard Zehr. Finally, on a more personal note, we thank our families for their encouragement, support and understanding during this project.

Gerry Johnstone and Daniel W. Van Ness, October 2006

Part I

The Idea of Restorative Justice

Gerry Johnstone and Daniel W. Van Ness

Part 1 opens with six chapters explaining and discussing the basic ideas of restorative justice. In the first chapter, we set the scene by looking at what it is that people who promote restorative justice are actually trying to bring about. There is widespread agreement among proponents that the goal is to transform the way contemporary societies view and respond to crime and related forms of troublesome behaviour. However, there are a range of views as to the precise nature of the transformation sought. These are to some extent in tension with one another, suggesting that restorative justice is best understood as a deeply contested concept. We outline three different but overlapping conceptions of restorative justice: the *encounter* conception, the *reparative* conception and the *transformative* conception. We suggest that rather than pushing one of these forward as the true or primary meaning of restorative justice, or trying to gloss over disagreements among proponents, the most fruitful way forward for the restorative justice movement is to keep debating the meaning of the concept but to conduct this debate in a manner consistent with the principles of restorative justice.

The following chapters explore particular conceptions of restorative justice in more detail. In Chapter 2, Susan Sharpe explores what it means to redress wrongdoing by repairing the harm resulting from it. Whereas the notion of repairing harm is often presented as if it required little further elaboration, Sharpe presents a reflective account of the forms reparation can take, what it can accomplish and optimal conditions for achieving those results. From there, she goes on to discuss some of the key issues facing those who propose repair of harm as an alternative to seeking redress through vengeance and retribution: must reparation be onerous for those undertaking it? How important is the principle of proportionality when it comes to reparation? Should those who point to the need for wrongdoers to repair harm also push for perpetrators of systemic injustices to undertake reparation?

Jennifer Larson Sawin and Howard Zehr consider a rather different but equally important aspect of the idea of restorative justice: the idea that those most directly affected by crimes and other wrongful acts should be engaged and empowered in the process by which it is decided what should be done to put things right. In Chapter 3, after illustrating this idea by an account of the now classic 'Kitchener experiment', Larson Sawin and Zehr explore in depth why, for restorative justice advocates, engagement and empowerment are essential to the achievement of justice in the aftermath of crime, and what it means (and what it does not mean) to be engaged and empowered in a justice process. Importantly, they then go on to look at the challenges faced by those who seek to put these ideas into practice – i.e. how in practice does one determine precisely who needs to be engaged and empowered in any particular restorative justice process and how does one ensure that key stakeholders are in fact engaged and empowered?

Increasingly, restorative justice proponents are referring to values as a key means of distinguishing restorative justice from other approaches to crime and wrongdoing. In Chapter 4, Kay Pranis examines how the values of restorative justice are expressed in the literature. Crucially, counter to a recent tendency to draw a sharp distinction between a 'process' conception of restorative justice and a 'values' conception (a tendency described in Chapter 6), Pranis shows that the discussion of restorative values in the literature is primarily about 'process values'. That is to say, those who think of restorative justice primarily as a process – whereby parties affected by criminal wrongdoing come together to resolve collectively what should be done about it – are trying to identify and define values which should guide and constrain such processes, thereby ensuring that what happens within them and as a result of them can properly be described as 'restorative'. These attempts to guide and constrain 'restorative processes' raise an important question: are those who are promoting restorative justice now imposing upon people whom they claim to be empowering a set of values which are in fact 'foreign' to those people? Pranis, drawing upon her extensive practical work with those developing justice circles in a wide range of settings, suggests not. In her experience, while people do not always behave according to restorative values, they do tend to affirm those values as ones which they should follow.

In Chapter 5, Declan Roche looks at one of the key debates in current restorative justice literature: that concerning the relationship between retributive and restorative justice. He shows how an early and persisting assumption that retributive and restorative justice are polar opposites has been challenged by a number of writers for a variety of reasons. He reviews the work of contributors to this debate such as Kathleen Daly, who argues that the depiction of conventional justice as 'retributive' and restorative justice as lacking retributive elements is vastly mistaken and misleading, and the rather different arguments of philosopher Antony Duff, whose position is that our aim in responding to crime should indeed be restoration, but that this should be achieved through a form of retributive punishment (although not necessarily the harsh exclusionary sanctions which other proponents of restorative justice tend to associate with the idea of retribution). For

Roche, the more sophisticated understanding of restorative justice that has emerged from this debate has important implications for thinking about the possible dangers of (well intentioned) restorative interventions and the need for checks and balances – issues which are taken up in a number of later chapters in the *Handbook*.

The final chapter of Part 1, by Margarita Zernova and Martin Wright, returns to the theme of diversity and conflict within the restorative justice movement over how restorative justice could be conceptualized and practised. This chapter examines closely specific debates between proponents over how restorative justice should be understood and implemented. Zernova and Wright show that, for some, restorative justice should be conceived as a process outside the criminal justice system to which appropriate cases can be diverted if the parties agree. Others would want to include, within the restorative justice tent, alternative sentencing practices within criminal justice, in which offenders are ordered to undertake reparative deeds rather than to undergo more traditional forms of punishment. Another debate which Zernova and Wright elucidate is that between those who think restorative justice should aim primarily at reforming our response to crime (whether by creating alternatives to conventional criminal justice or changing the criminal justice system) and those who think that the project of restorative justice is incoherent and impractical unless it also and perhaps primarily aims to bring about much deeper and wider social changes designed to ensure social justice. Similar to our own position in Chapter 1, Zernova and Wright conclude, not by calling for a more unified vision of restorative justice and the elimination of diversity and conflict, but for an acceptance that differences within a social movement – if discussed in an appropriate way – can be source of strength, keeping the movement open and fluid.

Chapter 1

The meaning of restorative justice

Gerry Johnstone and Daniel W. Van Ness

Introduction

The restorative justice movement is a global social movement with huge internal diversity. Its broad goal is to transform the way contemporary societies view and respond to crime and related forms of troublesome behaviour. More specifically, it seeks to replace our existing highly professionalized systems of punitive justice and control (and their analogues in other settings) with community-based reparative justice and moralizing social control. Through such practices, it is claimed, we can not only control crime more effectively, we can also accomplish a host of other desirable goals: a meaningful experience of justice for victims of crime and healing of trauma which they tend to suffer; genuine accountability for offenders and their reintegration into law-abiding society; recovery of the social capital that tends to be lost when we hand our problems over to professionals to solve; and significant fiscal savings, which can be diverted towards more constructive projects, including projects of crime prevention and community regeneration.

However, there is no agreement on the actual nature of the transformation sought by the restorative justice movement. For instance, some regard restorative justice as a new social technique or programme which can be used within our criminal justice systems. Others seek ultimately to abolish much of the entire edifice of state punishment and to replace it with community-based responses that teach, heal, repair and restore victims, perpetrators of crime and their communities. Still others apply the vision of healing and restoration to all kinds of conflict and harm. In fact, the ultimate goal and primary focus, they suggest, should be on changing the way we view ourselves and relate to others in everyday life (Sullivan and Tifft 2001). What all proponents of restorative justice seek is something better than that which exists, and also something better than the various other alternatives (such as penal treatment) which have been tried, with limited success, in the past.

It is in fact only recently that the restorative justice movement has achieved widespread prominence. Writing in 1998, the founders of the

Contemporary Justice Review stated: 'there still remain a considerable number of people involved in the administration of criminal justice and even many who teach about justice issues at the university level, for whom issues of restorative justice, even the term itself, remain quite foreign' (Sullivan *et al.* 1998: 8). Today, by contrast, one seldom encounters people involved in the administration or study of criminal justice who are not familiar with the term.[1] Indeed, the concept of restorative justice is already cropping up in other discourses, including those of school discipline, workplace management, corporate regulation, political conflict resolution and transitional justice.

Yet, despite its growing familiarity in professional and academic circles, the meaning of the term 'restorative justice' is still only hazily understood by many people. The main goal of this chapter, therefore, is to explore what people who advocate 'restorative justice' are actually promoting. This is by no means a straightforward task. The term 'restorative justice' appears to have no single clear and established meaning, but instead is used in a range of different ways. Some who have attempted to clarify the meaning of restorative justice have tended to conclude, often with some hint of despair, that 'restorative justice' means 'all things to all people' (Roche 2001: 342). Moreover, it is not simply that people use the term in different ways in different contexts. Rather, some proponents of restorative justice assert or imply that their use of the concept is the only proper one, and that to use the concept in a different way is to create confusion or to adulterate the concept of restorative justice by applying it to practices or agendas which are not restorative. These assertions can be made with such passion that they take on 'the tone of a weird inter-faith squabble in an obscure religious sect' (Bazemore and Schiff 2004: 51; cf. McCold 2004a).

Why so much passion? As we hope to show, it is because restorative justice is not simply a persistently vague concept; it is in fact a deeply contested concept.

What sort of a concept is 'restorative justice'?

In what follows, in order to explain why 'restorative justice' is so profoundly contested, we will undertake a brief examination of the *type* of concept which restorative justice is.[2]

An appraisive concept

Most of those who use the term restorative justice consider it to be a constructive and progressive alternative to more traditional ways of responding to crime and wrongdoing. Hence, for its proponents, the judgement about whether a particular practice or situation is properly characterized as 'restorative justice' is not simply a matter of taxonomy, it is a matter of evaluation. The question is whether a particular practice or agenda meets the *standards* of restorative justice. The appraisive nature of the quest for a definition is brought out explicitly by Declan Roche:

In the same way that counterfeit goods may tarnish the good reputation of a manufacturer's brand label, programs that are called restorative when they are not can tarnish the concept ... restorative justice should seek to prevent counterfeiters from benefiting from the good name of restorative justice. One way to do this is to continually clarify the meaning of restorative justice so that judgments can be made about how restorative a program or practice really is (2001: 343).

An internally complex concept

Not every constructive and progressive alternative to traditional interventions into crime and wrongdoing can be described as restorative justice. For such an alternative to be credibly described as restorative justice, it will usually have one or more of the following ingredients, which are presented in no particular order of importance:

1 There will be some relatively informal process which aims to involve victims, offenders and others closely connected to them or to the crime in discussion of matters such as what happened, what harm has resulted and what should be done to repair that harm and, perhaps, to prevent further wrongdoing or conflict.

2 There will be an emphasis on empowering (in a number of senses) ordinary people whose lives are affected by a crime or other wrongful act.

3 Some effort will be made by decision-makers or those facilitating decision-making processes to promote a response which is geared less towards stigmatizing and punishing the wrongdoer and more towards ensuring that wrongdoers recognize and meet a responsibility to make amends for the harm they have caused in a manner which directly benefits those harmed, as a first step towards their reintegration into the community of law-abiding citizens.

4 Decision-makers or those facilitating decision-making will be concerned to ensure that the decision-making process and its outcome will be guided by certain principles or values which, in contemporary society, are widely regarded as desirable in any interaction between people, such as: respect should be shown for others; violence and coercion are to be avoided if possible and minimized if not; and inclusion is to be preferred to exclusion.

5 Decision-makers or those facilitating decision-making will devote significant attention to the injury done to the victims and to the needs that result from that, and to tangible ways in which those needs can be addressed.

6 There will be some emphasis on strengthening or repairing relationships between people, and using the power of healthy relationships to resolve difficult situations.

Few would deny the applicability of the concept of restorative justice to an intervention which clearly has all these ingredients. Quite often, however, interventions will possess some of these ingredients, but not others.[3] Whether or not a person defines such an intervention as 'restorative justice' will then depend on how important he or she regards any particular ingredient as being. For example, those who regard the first two ingredients as essential to restorative justice will be reluctant to apply the concept to an intervention which lacks them, even if it clearly possesses the other four. Moreover, they may be willing to apply the concept to an intervention which clearly has the first two ingredients even if some of the others are barely present.

An open concept

New and unforeseen developments can affect the way we use the concept of restorative justice. For instance, in the 1970s and 1980s, the concept was most commonly used in the context of North American experiments with victim–offender mediation and reconciliation (Peachey 2003). These programmes rarely included more participants than the victim, the offender and the facilitator. The facilitator was typically a trained community volunteer. Then, in the early 1990s, new 'conferencing' approaches to crime emerged from New Zealand and Australia, and were subsequently identified as a form of restorative justice (Zehr 1990: 256–62). In these, much larger groups of people, including the friends and family of the victim and offender, are brought together to discuss and decide a much wider range of issues. Furthermore, criminal justice officials, such as police, may participate in the conferences and even serve as facilitators. Several years later, peacemaking circles of the First Nations peoples in North America began to be recognized by some criminal courts as a way to resolve criminal matters. Circles include not only victims, offenders and their 'communities of care', but interested members of the surrounding community as well. The involvement of criminal justice officials also expanded, with prosecutors and judges participating. These developments, unforeseen in the late 1980s, had a profound impact upon the usage of the concept of restorative justice. It came to be understood by some as an approach that places high value on bringing together as many stakeholders affected by a crime as possible. Furthermore, the initial assumption that only community volunteers have sufficient neutrality to facilitate restorative processes has given way in some jurisdictions to an assumption that following best practice standards is sufficient to assure that criminal justice officials can provide the neutral setting necessary for authentic participation by offenders.

These are just two examples of how the generally accepted understanding of restorative justice in the 1970s and 1980s shifted because of developments that few would have anticipated in advance. In fact, those shifts were initially resisted by some as departures from restorative justice principles and values (Umbreit and Zehr 1996: 24–9; Pranis 1997; McCold 2004b).

In sum, we suggest that restorative justice is an appraisive, internally complex and open concept that continues to develop with experience, and that this helps explain why it is so deeply contested.

Conceptions of 'restorative justice'

One of the significant implications of viewing restorative justice as a deeply contested concept is that there is not likely ever to be (indeed perhaps should not be) a single accepted conception of restorative justice. Instead, we must acknowledge the differing and indeed competing ideas about its nature. To ignore or gloss over these differences misrepresents the character of the restorative justice movement, presenting it as more unified and coherent than it actually is. Just as importantly, doing this presents it as a more limited and more impoverished movement than it truly is. In an effort to avoid such shortcomings, we will review three conceptions of restorative justice.[4]

The *encounter* conception of restorative justice

In recent years a set of new processes has been devised, developed and employed in social responses to incidents of criminal behaviour, processes such as victim–offender mediation, conferencing and circles (Johnstone 2003: part C; Van Ness and Strong 2006: ch. 4). What is most distinctive about these processes is that, rather than remaining passive while professionals discuss their problem and decide what to do about it, victims, offenders and others affected by some crime or misconduct meet face to face in a safe and supportive environment and play an active role in discussion and in decision-making. For instance, with the assistance of a facilitator, they speak openly but respectfully to each other about what happened, express their feelings and have a say in what is to be done about the matter. Such meetings are intended to be democratic experiences in which the people most affected by a problem decide among themselves how it should be dealt with (O'Connell *et al.* 1999: 17). Rather than being the chief decision-makers, professionals and state officials remain more in the background, making it possible for the stakeholders themselves to make the decisions (Christie 2003).

Many people refer to such processes as 'restorative justice' (Robinson 2003: 375). Indeed, this is probably the most common way of using the term. That is to say, 'restorative justice' is most commonly used as if it were interchangeable with mediation, conferencing, etc.[5] We will refer to this way of defining restorative justice as the *encounter* conception, a term which captures one of the central ideas of the movement: that victims, offenders and other 'stakeholders' in a criminal case should be allowed to encounter one another outside highly formal, professional-dominated settings such as the courtroom.

In order to understand this encounter conception what we need to ask, of course, is *why* encounters are thought to be better than 'courtroom' responses to crime. One possible answer could be that people who are most directly affected by a discussion and decision have a *right* to be meaningfully involved in the discussion and decision-making process. Adherents to this position might argue that this right must be respected even if doing so disturbs the efficient running of the justice machinery, and even if it results in 'solutions' to problems which strike professionals as unenlightened, wrong, absurd and not even in the best interests of the parties involved.[6]

There are some traces of the above rationale for encounter processes in the discourse of restorative justice. Significantly, however, this is not the main way in which proponents of restorative justice tend to argue for encounters. Rather, the more common argument is that such processes are useful for achieving a whole range of beneficial outcomes. This raises the question of how to characterize encounter processes which clearly fail to achieve such beneficial results: are these examples of restorative justice that have failed, or are they not examples of restorative justice? In order to explore this issue, it will be helpful if we provide a brief account of the beneficial effects typically attributed to encounter processes.

Proponents of encounter processes tend to argue that, when they are used in appropriate cases and properly conducted, a number of beneficial results can emerge. Some of these are familiar within the criminal justice system: rehabilitation (changing offenders' attitudes makes them less likely to commit new crimes), deterrence (it is difficult for offenders to meet with their victims, and to do so in the presence of family and friends) and reinforcement of norms (the process and the people involved underscore the importance of the norm that the offender has violated). Other benefits are new in the context of criminal justice: it offers victims avenues for receiving restitution, gives them the opportunity to be involved in decisions in the aftermath of the crime, can contribute to reduced fear and an increased sense of safety, and may help them understand offenders' circumstances that led to commission of the crimes (Robinson 2003: 375–6).

This transformative potential has led some to use encounters to allow the parties to achieve personal growth even if they do not settle claims that victims have against offenders. Umbreit (2001; see also Johnstone 2002: 140–50) contrasts settlement-driven mediation with what he calls humanistic mediation. In humanistic mediation the presenting conflict will receive some attention, but the focus is on helping the parties reach inner resolution through mediated dialogue. This begins with empowerment of the parties and a process of mutual recognition of the other's humanity:

> Through recognition, 'the parties voluntarily choose to become more open, attentive, [and] responsive to the situation of another, thereby expanding their perspective to include an appreciation for another's situation.' Whether an actual settlement occurs is quite secondary to the process of transformation and healing that occurs in their relationship
> ...
> One of the most powerful and perhaps most controversial expressions of the transformative qualities of empowerment and recognition has been consistently observed in the small but growing application of mediation and dialogue between parents of murdered children and the offender. After lengthy preparation by the mediator, involving multiple individual meetings, the parties frequently, through a genuine dialogue about what happened and its impact on all involved, get beyond the evil, trauma, and inconsistencies surrounding the event to achieve an acknowledgement of each other's humanity and a greater sense of closure (Umbreit 2001: 8–9, citations omitted).

Crucially, however, meetings of stakeholders may not turn out to be transformative or even restorative. They can be conducted in non-restorative ways and arrive at non-restorative results (see Young 2003) such as a now infamous conference which ended with the decision that the young offender should publicly wear a T-shirt emblazoned with 'I am a thief' (Braithwaite 2000). The encounter process alone is not enough to assure the desired results. The question then arises: does such an encounter that does not yield the desired results fall within the definition of restorative justice? Roche raises this issue starkly when he suggests that if we adhere to a strict encounter conception of restorative justice, it is difficult to explain why an encounter which resulted in such a decision should not count as an example of restorative justice. Indeed, he suggests: 'Viewed simply in process terms, any punishment meted out by a victim on an offender, such as lynching and stoning, may potentially satisfy the definition of restorative justice' (2001: 344).

It is important to be clear about what is going on here. Ambiguity over whether encounter processes are important in their own right (because they enable those affected by crime to meet and be involved in the process of deciding what is to be done about it) or are valued mainly because of the desirable outcomes that they can achieve (but will also fail to achieve) manifests itself in uncertainty over whether encounters which are conducted in 'non-restorative' ways and fail to deliver restorative outcomes fall within or outside the *definition* of restorative justice.

Recently, efforts have been made to resolve this issue by focusing as much upon the distinctive *values* of restorative justice as upon its distinctive *processes*. In these efforts, restorative justice becomes redefined, or perhaps we should say more sharply defined, as an encounter process which is guided and constrained by certain values. For instance, Braithwaite (2003: 9–13) suggests that there are three sorts of values to attend to: values that *constrain the process* to prevent it from becoming oppressive (he mentions the values of non-domination, empowerment, respectful listening and equal concern for all stakeholders, among others); values that *guide the process* and that can be used to measure the success of the process (values such as restoration of property, emotional restoration, restoration of dignity, compassion, social support and so forth); and values that *describe certain outcomes of the process* that may, but also may not, emerge from a successful restorative process (values such as remorse, apology, censure of the act, forgiveness and mercy).

Others have proposed alternative sets of values, and it will be necessary for adherents to the values-based encounter conception to continue refining and defining the values that must be present in a restorative process (see, for example, Braithwaite and Strang 2001: 12; Roche 2001: 347; Boyack *et al.* 2004: 1–12 Supp.). It will also be necessary for them to address the question of where these values come from and what their status is. For instance, what needs to be explained is the precise relationship, if any, between the values being proposed by leading advocates of restorative justice (who tend, after all, to be professionals) and the values adhered to by typical lay participants in encounters. And, to the extent that there are tensions between these two different sets of values, it needs to be made clear how these tensions are to be resolved. Important initial efforts to do just that are discussed in more detail by Kay Pranis in her contribution to this handbook.[7]

The reparative conception of restorative justice

There are many, however, who use the concept of restorative justice in a markedly different way; it is a distinctive state of affairs that we should attempt to bring about in the aftermath of criminal wrongdoing, and which might be said to constitute 'justice'. Those who use the concept in this way share, with adherents to an encounter conception, the goal of revolutionizing our response to offending and wrongdoing (cf. Wachtel 1997). However, their ideas about what this project entails are considerably different. For them, it involves a radical break with certain widely accepted 'wisdoms' about what needs to be done to re-establish just relationships when somebody commits a crime against another person (or persons).

Conventionally, we assume that if a person commits a serious wrong against another, a state of injustice arises which needs to be corrected. It tends to be further assumed that, in order to correct this state of injustice, the perpetrator of the wrong must undergo pain or suffering in proportion to the seriousness of the offence. Once the offender has suffered, according to his or her just deserts, the equilibrium has been restored and justice prevails.

Proponents of what we will call a reparative conception of restorative justice reject this way of thinking almost entirely. To be precise, they do agree that if a person commits a serious wrong against another an injustice arises which needs to be put right. However, they insist that simply imposing pain upon offenders is neither necessary nor sufficient to make things right. They argue that the imposition of pain upon offenders, while it occasionally provides us with a slight and short-lived sense that justice has been done, generally fails to deliver a rich and enduring experience of justice.[8] In order to create such an experience, other things need to happen. In particular, the harm which the crime has caused to people and relationships needs to be repaired. This is a very complex process, involving a wide range of things an offender might do to repair the material and symbolic harm he or she has caused to his or her victim(s) (see Chapters 2 and 14, this volume; also Zehr 1990). Some adherents to this reparative conception of restorative justice suggest further that reparation of harm is a *sufficient* ingredient of justice – i.e. in order to achieve justice it is not necessary that the offender undergoes pain or suffering.

What we want to explore briefly now is how this reparative conception of restorative justice relates to the encounter conception outlined earlier. At first sight, the two seem barely distinguishable, since it tends to be argued that in order to achieve the goal of repair of harm, encounter processes are almost indispensable. This argument is based upon a number of ideas. In particular, it is suggested that one of the chief ways in which victims are harmed by crime is that they lose their sense of personal power (Zehr 1990: 27). According to Zehr, one of the reasons why crime is so traumatic for its victims is that it upsets their belief in personal autonomy (1990: 24).

Hence, for the harm of crime to be repaired, this sense of personal power needs to be returned to them. However, when the case is then dealt with by conventional criminal justice processes, in which victims are largely neglected and expected to play a passive role while professionals make all the key decisions, the victim's sense of personal power is further damaged rather than repaired. For repair to take place, victims 'need a sense of control or involvement in the resolution of their own cases' (1990: 28). Other things that victims need in order to recover from the trauma of crime, according to Zehr and others, are answers to questions that only 'their' offenders can answer (and perhaps can only answer convincingly in face-to-face meetings) and the opportunity to express the way they feel about what happened to them and to have their feelings (such as anger, pain and fear) validated by others (1990: ch. 2). For these things to happen, an encounter process is virtually essential.

Turning to offenders, one of the key contributions of the restorative justice movement (broadly conceived) is to argue that, quite apart from any harm they may have suffered in the past (offenders often being the victims of past injustices), they too are harmed by their criminal wrongdoing, since this often has the affect of alienating them – or further alienating them – from their own community.[9] If this harm is to be repaired (i.e. if offenders are to be reintegrated into the community), things need to happen to repair this breach (Burnside and Baker 1994). One thing that can contribute to repair, indeed that may be necessary if repair is to take place, is for the offender to demonstrate genuine repentance and a willingness to make amends for his or her wrongdoing (see Chapter 11, this volume). One significant way in which offenders can do this is to meet with those harmed, listen respectfully to them, answer any questions they may have, apologize and agree to reasonable reparative actions which they suggest. Again, this all points to encounter processes.

An important question, however, is: what happens if such a process is not possible? What if the parties are unwilling or unable to meet? Those who adhere to the reparative conception of restorative justice argue that even then the justice system should respond in a way that repairs, rather than adds to, the harm resulting from crime. A simple example is a sentence of restitution rather than a fine or imprisonment (unless there are overriding considerations of public safety, for example). Under this conception, restorative principles would become a profound reform dynamic affecting all levels of the criminal justice system, whether or not the parties to particular crimes eventually choose to meet. This would revolutionize the justice system, yielding a range of new, restorative responses to all kinds of crimes and circumstances:

While these responses might differ greatly in the case of, say, a minor property crime by a first-time offender and a serious violent crime (based in part on the level of restrictiveness imposed on an offender according to the threat imposed to public safety or to individual victims), restorative interventions would be carried out according to what must become widely understood basic principles and familiar processes (Bazemore and Walgrave 1999: 45–74, 64).

The important point here is that adherents to a reparative conception of restorative justice, while they express a strong preference for encounter processes, also envisage the possibility of *partially* restorative solutions to problems of crime emerging outside such processes, including through reparative *sanctions* ordered and administered by professionals employed by the formal criminal justice system (Van Ness and Strong 2006). Those strongly committed to an encounter conception of restorative justice, on the other hand, have difficulty in seeing how interventions such as these can be properly included within the definition of restorative justice. They lack what, for adherents to an encounter conception, are the most crucial elements of restorative justice – i.e. meetings of key stakeholders to discuss what happened and to agree on what should be done about it (McCold 2004a). Even if they have repair of harm as one of their official goals, such reparative sanctions appear to strong adherents of the encounter conception as professionally imposed measures masquerading as restorative justice in order to benefit from its good name (see the quotation from Roche, earlier in this chapter).

We saw earlier that adherents to an encounter conception of restorative justice have turned to 'restorative values' to provide guidance in order to counter certain problems with a pure encounter conception. In a similar vein, adherents to a reparative conception have turned to 'restorative principles' in order to ensure that the wide range of reparative interventions that they would include within the definition of restorative justice do not veer into becoming punitive and purely offender oriented. Principles are general guidelines that point from normative theory to specific application (see Chapter 21, this volume). They offer policy guidance to those designing systems or programmes that increases the likelihood that the result will be restorative.

These principles have been expressed in different ways. One useful collection, prepared by Zehr and Mika (Zehr 2002: 40), is called 'restorative justice signposts' and takes the form of ten indicators that work being done is actually restorative. Two examples of these indicators are 'show equal concern and commitment to victims and offenders, involving both in the process of justice', and 'encourage collaboration and reintegration rather than coercion and isolation'.

Bazemore and Walgrave (1999: 65) offer three principles to inform the government's role in restorative justice.[10] First, it would seek to ensure that all parties are treated with *equity*, meaning that they and others in similar circumstances will feel that they are treated similarly. Secondly, it would seek the *satisfaction* of the victim, offender and community. Thirdly, it would offer *legal protection* of individuals against unwarranted state action.

Van Ness and Strong (2006) identify three alternative principles on which a restorative system might be constructed:

First, justice requires that we work to heal victims, offenders and communities that have been injured by crime. Second, victims, offenders and communities should have the opportunity for active involvement in the justice process as early and as fully as possible. Third, we must rethink the relative roles and responsibilities of government and community: in promoting justice, government is responsible for preserving a just order, and community for establishing a just peace.

Just as the values espoused in the encounter conception need continuing refinement and definition, so too do principles proposed to guide the reparative conception. Nevertheless, both serve a similar function within their respective conception: to increase the likelihood that what actually takes place in the new processes and justice structures is actually restorative.

The *transformative* conception of restorative justice

The restorative justice movement has tended to focus its efforts upon changing social responses to crime and wrongdoing. Its initial energies were focused upon revolutionizing societal responses to behaviour which we classify as crime and which is regarded as serious enough to warrant intervention by criminal justice agencies such as the police and correctional institutions. For the most part, this remains the main focus of the restorative justice movement, although it has also been applied to forms of misconduct which, although defined as rule-breaking, are usually not classified or handled as criminal offences, such as misconduct in schools (see Chapter 18, this volume) or in workplaces.

Others, however, go further still and suggest that both the initial and the ultimate goal of the restorative justice movement should be to transform the way in which we understand ourselves and relate to others in our everyday lives (Sullivan and Tifft 2001; cf. Ross 1996 and some of the essays in Strang and Braithwaite 2001). The argument appears to be: (1) that, in the absence of such transformations, any efforts to change specific practices, such as our social responses to crime, are unlikely to succeed and can even have effects quite different from those intended; and (2) that even if such changes do succeed, they can make only a peripheral contribution to the goal of achieving a just society – achieving that goal requires much deeper and more far-reaching transformations.

Such goals entail a conception of restorative justice significantly different from those we have described so far. Under this *transformative* conception, restorative justice is conceived as a way of life we should lead. For its proponents, among the key elements of this way of life is a rejection of the assumption that we exist in some sort of hierarchical order with other people (or even with other elements of our environment). Indeed, it rejects the very idea that we are ontologically separate from other people or even from our physical environment. Rather, to live a lifestyle of restorative justice, we must abolish the self (as it is conventionally understood in contemporary society) and instead understand ourselves as inextricably connected to and identifiable with other beings and the 'external' world.

This has implications in the way we use language (Ross 1996: ch. 5), the way we regard and treat other people and the environment, and the way in which we allocate resources – which should be on the basis of need rather than right or desert and with the recognition that the needs of all are equally important (Sullivan and Tifft 2001). In such a context, we would probably not make sharp distinctions between crime and other forms of harmful conduct, but simply respond to all harmful conduct (from crime, to economic exploitation, to the use of power in everyday life) in much the same way – by identifying who has been hurt, what their needs are and how things can be put right (cf. Zehr 2002: 38).

It is vision that animates and guides this conception. Restorative justice seems to evoke a passion and commitment among its adherents that cannot be explained by rational cost/benefit calculations. Stories are repeated of dramatic changes in attitude in which the victim and offender recognize within the other a common humanity, empathy develops and inner resolution takes place. But what animate proponents are not simply the transformations taking place in others; they are also, and equally importantly, the transformations they begin to experience inside themselves. Sullivan and Tifft (2005: 154–60) describe this as a transformation of the 'power-based self' to the true self, a 'being, a consciousness, of peace and gentleness' (p. 155). This does not happen automatically, but instead takes place through a discipline of self-criticism that leads eventually to self-transformation.

For those who come to see restorative justice as a way of life, this recognition that the most profound changes 'out there' require (and may generate) inner transformation has political implications. Quinney observes:

> All of this is to say, to us as criminologists, that crime is suffering and that the ending of crime is possible only with the ending of suffering. And the ending both of suffering and of crime, which is the establishing of justice, can come only out of peace, out of a peace that is spiritually grounded in our very being. To eliminate crime – to end the construction and perpetuation of an existence that makes crime possible – requires a transformation of our human being ... When our hearts are filled with love and our minds with willingness to serve, we will know what has to be done and how it is to be done (1991: 11–12).

Overlaps and tensions

Earlier attempts to explore disagreements over the meaning of restorative justice include exchanges over the 'purist' and the 'maximalist' models (cf. Bazemore and Walgrave 1999; McCold 2000; Walgrave 2000; Chapter 6, this volume) and over whether community justice can appropriately be considered part of restorative justice (cf. the entire issue of *Contemporary Justice Review*, 2004, Vol. 7, no. 1). We, of course, have the benefit of insights those controversies have generated. We have suggested in this chapter that the differences are more than a dispute over models, but not so profound as to conclude that any of the perspectives is outside the restorative justice movement. The differences are over alternative *conceptions* of restorative justice.

All three conceptions embrace encounter, repair and transformation. The difference between them is where the emphasis is placed. The restorative emphasis of the *encounter conception* is that the parties to a crime should be offered an opportunity to meet and decide the most satisfactory response to that crime. The restorative nature of that process is guided by values which constrain and guide the process and which help describe its desired results. The restorative emphasis of the *reparative conception* is that the response to crime must seek to repair the harms resulting from crime. The restorative nature of that reparation is guided by principles which constrain and guide justice processes and outcomes designed to bring healing. The restorative emphasis of the *transformative conception* is the restorative insight that fundamentally we are relational beings connected through intricate networks to others, to all humanity and to our environment. The restorative nature of those relationships is guided by a vision of transformation of people, structures and our very selves.

Clearly, there are considerable overlaps between these three conceptions. In fact, there is sufficient common ground to regard advocates of each conception as members of the same social movement, rather than as members of quite different social movements which have somehow become entangled. Yet, there are also considerable tensions between them which are not easy to dissolve.

For example, many adherents to an encounter conception do, in fact, share a commitment to the broad approach to crime espoused by those who hold to a reparative conception. However, practice is in many ways more limited and in other ways more extensive than that emerging from the reparative conception. The encounter conception is more limited in that it has no response when the parties to the crime are unable or unwilling to meet. It is more extensive in that its adherents use processes to address harm, conflict or problems that do not involve lawbreaking, or for purposes other than to repair the harm resulting from the lawbreaking.

Furthermore, adherents to both the encounter and reparative conceptions are attracted to and motivated by the vision of transformation.[11] They may apply what they learn from restorative justice to other dimensions of their lives. But they are more likely to explain this in terms of new skills or growing spiritual insight than as necessary elements of doing restorative justice. In other words, restorative justice is considered more limited in application than adherents of the transformative conception claim. It is either a profound and useful process or it is an improved and hopeful way of addressing wrongdoing, but it is not an all-encompassing way of looking at life and relationships.

The overlaps help explain why it has been difficult to arrive at a common definition of restorative justice; we suggest that it will be impossible to do so, for reasons that we might explain using the metaphor of a three-storey home.

Imagine a home built on a gentle hillside with three storeys. Because of the grade of the hill, it is possible to enter the house from outside into each of the three floors. Because of porches and decks on the two top floors, and additions made to the first floor, each floor is a different size. The first floor is the largest, while the two upper floors are offset, so that areas of the third floor are directly above the second, but other areas are only above the first floor, creating a porch for those on the second floor. Similarly, some parts of the building are only two storeys high, which offers a deck area for the third floor.

The house stands for the restorative justice movement. The first floor represents the transformative conception, whose application of restorative justice is the most expansive of the three. The second and third floors represent the encounter and reparative conceptions, each of which overlaps the other in some matters but not all, as we have seen. Reflecting on this house suggests at least four reasons for internal disagreement over the meaning of restorative justice.

First, the people who disagree spend most of their time on different floors of the house. As long as we are talking about a restorative process in the context of dealing with crime, people on all floors agree that this is restorative justice. But a process used for purposes other than dealing with a rule violation (for example, helping neighbours find a solution to a problem) will be embraced more by people on the encounter and transformative floors, and either resisted or only half-heartedly accepted by those on the reparative floor. Restitution commitments that emerge from a restorative process are viewed as restorative by all; those that are ordered by a judge are accepted only by people on the reparative and transformative floors. Organizing community members in an economically deprived neighbourhood to oppose a proposed action by City Hall that would harm them is understood to be restorative only by people on the transformative floor.

A second reason for lack of agreement is that there are internal stairs connecting the three floors. This means, for example, that an encounter proponent might walk up to the reparative floor to consider matters like the needs and interests of victims, even though that person would not agree with reparative proponents that all measures to meet those needs and interests are restorative.

A third reason also stems from the fact that people are able to move easily from floor to floor: sometimes they forget what floor they are on, and as a result may wander into areas that do not fall within their conception. This can happen because they haven't thought through the areas of agreement and disagreement they have with people on other floors. Other times it is because of the topic being discussed. For example, reparative adherents might meet with encounter proponents, to discuss how restorative values are shaping encounters that lie outside the reparative conception, such as in peace-making circles convened to address neighbourhood conflicts.

A fourth reason is that there are a number of points of entry into the building. The 'normal' entry, then, could actually be any of the floors, depending on how the person approaches the building. So political perspectives, life experiences, employment and other factors contribute to a person's perspective as to which floor is the obvious or self-evident floor that should be the ground floor for restorative justice.

Conclusion

There are a number of ways in which its proponents and critics might answer the question: 'What does restorative justice mean?' For some it is principally an encounter process, a method of dealing with crime and injustice that involves the stakeholders in the decision about what needs to be done. For others it is an alternative conception of the state of affairs that constitutes justice, one that seeks to heal and repair the harm done by crime rather than to ignore that harm or try to impose some sort of equivalent harm on the wrongdoer. Still others would answer that it is a distinctive set of values that focus on co-operative and respectful resolution of conflict, a resolution that is reparative in nature. Others argue that it calls for the transformation of structures of society and of our very way of interacting with others and our environment. For many it is a vision that things can be made better, that it is possible to aspire to more than fair processes and proportionate punishment in the aftermath of crime, that out of tragedy can come hope and healing if we seek it.

These are different but related conceptions. We have argued that these differences are the consequence of the nature of the concept 'restorative justice' itself: it is a deeply contested concept. As a consequence, work to understand the meaning of restorative justice should not have as its goal the resolution of those differences, but instead a deeper appreciation of the richness of the concept and perhaps new insights about how to apply restorative measures to make things better than they are now. The intensity of discourse about those disagreements reveals areas in which proponents have moved from common ground to disputed territory.

How, then, might restorative advocates deal with the tensions that arise from working with people who hold to different conceptions? Restorative justice itself offers some guidance. Encounters are important, and when possible disputes should be explored in safe environments in which disagreeing parties are able to listen and speak. Apology is a useful way to make amends, when that becomes necessary. Conflict is not something to avoid or solve, necessarily; it can be a valued possession for those who are in conflict, and wrestling with that can become the occasion for inner growth and personal transformation.

Above all, allow restorative values to inform conversation and discourse. Zehr and Toews (2004: 403) have distilled these into two words: *humility* and *respect*. Humility includes, but is more than, the idea of not taking more credit than one should. It also means having such a profound awareness of the limitations of one's knowledge and understanding that it is possible to remain open to the truth that others' life realities are not the same as one's own, and that therefore they may have insights one does not yet possess. Respect means not only treating all parties as persons with dignity and worth, but also as people with wisdom and other valuable contributions to offer.

We make one final suggestion: it would be useful to adopt names for the different conceptions to avoid disputes that arise because of misunderstanding and to increase collaboration. We have proposed the 'encounter conception', the 'reparative conception' and the 'transformative conception'. It may be that there are other and better names. But it does seem sensible, if we cannot settle on a single meaning of restorative justice, to become more adept at articulating its contested meanings.

Acknowledgements

We would like to thank a number of people who commented on earlier drafts of this chapter: Gordon Bazemore, Paul McCold, Kay Pranis, Karen Heetderks Strong, Dennis Sullivan, Lode Walgrave and Howard Zehr. Some of the ideas which have found their way into this chapter were presented in a paper at the British Criminology Conference, Leeds, 12–14 June 2005; we are grateful for the feedback received from participants.

Notes

1   At least in Europe, North America, the Pacific and Africa. Interest in restorative justice is growing in Asia and Latin America, but these are early days. On the international development and global appeal of restorative justice, see Part 6 of this handbook.

2   This analysis is influenced by an important essay published in the 1950s by the philosopher W.B. Gallie on 'essentially contested concepts' and the work of the political theorist William Connolly, who has developed Gallie's ideas and applied them in the domain of political discourse (Gallie 1962; Connolly 1993). We believe that these classic works have very important lessons for the restorative justice movement, although in the space available here it is not possible to discuss these theoretical sources or to indicate how we have utilized them.

3   Given the nature of these characteristics, the question is usually to what extent are they present, rather than a simple are they or are they not present. See Van Ness (2003) on the need to think in terms of *degrees* of restorativeness.

4   We wish to emphasize that, while distinguishing these three conceptions is (in our view) useful for analysing debates about the meaning of restorative justice, we are not suggesting that any actual use of the concept of restorative justice can be neatly matched to a particular conception. Also, we are by no means suggesting that these three conceptions are *totally* distinct from one another; to the contrary we will point to numerous points of overlap.

5   Although there are some disputes over whether all these processes are properly called restorative justice, or over which of them is the purest form of restorative justice.

6   Analogously, one of the key arguments for democratic governance is that people have the right to govern themselves, even if they do so in what a minority (or outsiders) consider to be an unenlightened manner.

7   While our goal in this chapter is to introduce various ways of conceiving restorative justice, rather than to discuss particular issues in any detail, we do think it necessary to make one suggestion: that efforts to articulate a set of distinctive restorative justice values and to think through their status would be significantly advanced by a prior effort to describe with more sophistication than usual the range of values which underlie conventional criminal justice processes.

To describe these processes – as is often done – as being underpinned simply by a desire to get even with those who hurt us or to respond to the hurt of crime with the hurt of punishment is too crude. A more fruitful starting point might be to recognize that conventional criminal justice practices tend to embody a wide range of values, and can be better understood as shaped by passionate struggles over which values should predominate in the penal realm, rather than being shaped by one particular set of values (see Garland 1990 for an account of the competition to shape the field of penal practices, in line with particular values and commitments, and of how this results in a highly complex institution which embodies and gives expression to a wide range of values, many of them contradictory). Also, we would go so far as to suggest that, rather than engage in wholesale rejection of traditional criminal justice values in favour of restorative justice values, the restorative justice movement might commit itself to devising responses to crime which incorporate the best of both. For instance, we might conceive of restorative justice as a process which enables people affected by crime to devise responses which meet *their* local needs and which are closely in keeping with *their* ethical ideals. We could then recognize that such a response needs to be bounded by broad values more often associated with the idea of the rule of law than with restorative justice. As Braithwaite elegantly puts it, restorative justice (the 'justice of the people') needs to be constrained by the 'justice of the law' (2003: 14–16).

8   See Zehr (1990) for a rich and sophisticated account of this position. We have relied heavily upon Howard Zehr's work in this section because we regard it as one of the most cogent expositions of, and arguments for, restorative justice available, and because of its influence on the restorative justice movement (Zehr is often referred to as 'the grandfather of restorative justice – see Zehr 2002: 76). Just a few of the other works worth consulting in this context are Braithwaite (2002), Cayley (1998), Consedine (1999), Graef (2000), Johnstone (2002), Marshall (2001), Ross (1996), Sullivan and Tifft (2001), Wright (1996) and Van Ness and Strong (2006).

9   These ideas are explored in more depth in Johnstone (2002) and Van Ness and Strong (2006).

10   They call these 'values'.

11   Stories of transformation abound. The most spectacular stories, told with an air of wonder, are those in which a restorative encounter leads to transformation of the victim, the offender and ultimately of their relationship. Out of evil, something good has come, something far better than could be expected from contemporary criminal justice, and in some ways something better than existed before the crime.

There is almost a mythic dimension in these stories, one that emerges in arguments for restorative justice as well. The themes of rebirth and renewal that recur in mythology and in religion have their place as well in restorative justice. Within the death and destruction of crime lies the possibility of resurrection and new life. This may not be realized in all, or even in most, cases. But the possibility is there, and is realized frequently enough to give reason for hope.

References

Bazemore, G. and Schiff, M. (2004) 'Paradigm muddle or paradigm paralysis? The wide and narrow roads to restorative justice reform (or, a little confusion may be a good thing)', *Contemporary Justice Review*, 7: 37–57.

Bazemore, G. and Walgrave, L. (1999) 'Restorative juvenile justice: in search of fundamentals and an outline for systemic reform', in G. Bazemore and L. Walgrave (eds) *Restorative Juvenile Justice: Repairing the Harm of Youth Crime.* Monsey, NY: Criminal Justice Press, 45–74.

Boyack, J., Bowen, H. and Marshall, C. (2004) 'How does restorative justice ensure good practice?', in H. Zehr and B. Toews (eds) *Critical Issues in Restorative Justice.* Monsey, NY: Criminal Justice Press and Cullompton: Willan Publishing.

Braithwaite, J. (2000) 'Standards for restorative justice.' Paper presented at the ancillary meetings of the Tenth United Nations Congress on the Prevention of Crime and Treatment of Offenders, Vienna, Austria, 10–17 April.

Braithwaite, J. (2002) *Restorative Justice and Responsive Regulation.* New York, NY: Oxford University Press.

Braithwaite, J. (2003) 'Principles of restorative justice', in A. von Hirsch *et al.* (eds) *Restorative Justice and Criminal Justice: Competing or Reconcilable Paradigms.* Oxford: Hart Publishing.

Braithwaite, J. and Strang, H. (2001) 'Introduction: restorative justice and civil society', in H. Strang and J. Braithwaite (eds) *Restorative Justice and Civil Society.* Cambridge: Cambridge University Press.

Burnside, J. and Baker, N. (eds) (1994) *Relational Justice: Repairing the Breach.* Winchester: Waterside Press.

Cayley, D. (1998) *The Expanding Prison: The Crisis in Crime and Punishment and the Search for Alternatives.* Cleveland, OH: Pilgrim Press.

Christie, N. (2003) 'Conflicts as property', in G. Johnstone (ed.) *A Restorative Justice Reader: Texts, Sources, Context.* Cullompton: Willan Publishing (originally published in *British Journal of Criminology* (1977) 17: 1–15).

Connolly, W.E. (1993) *The Terms of Political Discourse* (3rd edn). Oxford and Cambridge, MA: Blackwell.

Consedine, J. (1999) *Restorative Justice: Healing the Effects of Crime* (revised edn). Lyttelton, New Zealand: Ploughshares.

Gallie, W.B. (1962) 'Essentially contested concepts', in M. Black (ed.) *The Importance of Language.* Englewood Cliffs, NJ: Prentice Hall (originally published in *Proceedings of the Aristotelian Society*, 1955–6, 56).

Garland, D. (1990) *Punishment and Modern Society: A Study in Social Theory.* Oxford: Clarendon Press.

Graef, R. (2000) *Why Restorative Justice? Repairing the Harm Caused by Crime.* London: Calouste Gulbenkian Foundation.

Johnstone, G. (2002) *Restorative Justice: Ideas, Values, Debates.* Cullompton: Willan Publishing.

Johnstone, G. (ed.) (2003) *A Restorative Justice Reader: Texts, Sources, Context.* Cullompton: Willan Publishing.

Marshall, C.D. (2001) *Beyond Retribution: A New Testament Vision for Justice, Crime, and Punishment.* Green Rapids, MI and Cambridge: Eerdmans.

McCold, P. (2000) 'Toward a holistic vision of restorative juvenile justice: a reply to the maximalist model', *Contemporary Justice Review,* 3: 357–414.

McCold, P. (2004a) 'Paradigm muddle: the threat to restorative justice posed by its merger with community justice', *Contemporary Justice Review,* 7: 13–35.

McCold, P. (2004b) 'What is the role of community in restorative justice theory and practice?', in H. Zehr and B. Toews (eds) *Critical Issues in Restorative Justice.* Monsey, NY and Cullompton: Criminal Justice Press and Willan Publishing.

O'Connell, T., Wachtel, B. and Wachtel, T. (1999) *Conferencing Handbook: The New Real Justice Training Manual.* Pipersville, PA: Piper's Press.

Peachey, D.E. (2003) 'The Kitchener experiment', in G. Johnstone (ed.) *A Restorative Justice Reader: Texts, Sources, Context*. Cullompton: Willan Publishing (originally published in M. Wright and B. Galaway (eds) (1989) *Mediation and Criminal Justice*. London: Sage).

Pranis, K. (1997) 'Restoring community: the process of circle sentencing.' Paper presented at the conference *Justice without Violence: Views from Peacemaking, Criminology, and Restorative Justice*, 6 June 6.

Quinney, R. (1991) 'The way of peace: on crime, suffering and service', in H.E. Pepinsky and R. Quinney (eds) *Criminology as Peacemaking*. Bloomington: Indiana University Press.

Robinson, P.H. (2003) 'The virtues of restorative processes, the vices of "restorative justice"', *Utah Law Review*, 1: 375–88.

Roche, D. (2001) 'The evolving definition of restorative justice' *Contemporary Justice Review*, 4: 341–53.

Ross, R. (1996) *Returning to the Teachings: Exploring Aboriginal Justice*. Toronto: Penguin.

Strang, H. and Braithwaite, J. (eds) (2001) *Restorative Justice and Civil Society*. Cambridge: Cambridge University Press.

Sullivan, D. and Tifft, L. (2001) *Restorative Justice: Healing the Foundations of Our Everyday Lives*. Monsey, NY: Willow Tree Press.

Sullivan, D., Tifft, L. and Cordella, P. (1998) 'The phenomenon of restorative justice: some introductory remarks', *Contemporary Justice Review*, 1: 7–20.

Umbreit, M. (2001) *The Handbook of Victim Offender Mediation: An Essential Guide to Practice and Research*. San Francisco, CA: Jossey-Bass.

Umbreit, M.S. and Zehr, H. (1996) 'Restorative family group conferences: differing models and guidelines for practice', *Federal Probation*, 60: 24–9.

Van Ness, D.W. (2003) 'Creating restorative systems', in G. Johnstone (ed.) *A Restorative Justice Reader: Texts, Sources Context*. Cullompton: Willan Publishing (originally published in Walgrave, L. (ed.) (2002) *Restorative Justice and the Law*. Cullompton: Willan).

Van Ness, D.W. and Strong, K.H. (2006) *Restoring Justice* (3rd edn). Cincinnati, OH: Anderson.

Wachtel, T. (1997) *Real Justice: How We can Revolutionize our Response to Wrongdoing*. Pipersville, PA: Piper's Press.

Walgrave, L. (2000) 'How pure can a maximalist approach to restorative justice remain? Or can a purist model of restorative justice become maximalist?', *Contemporary Justice Review*, 3: 415–32.

Wright, M. (1996) *Justice for Victims and Offenders: A Restorative Response to Crime* (2nd edn; 1st edn. published by Open University Press, 1991). Winchester: Waterside Press.

Young, R. (2003) 'Just cops doing "shameful" business? Police-led restorative justice and the lessons of research', in G. Johnstone (ed.) *A Restorative Justice Reader: Texts, Sources, Context*. Cullompton: Willan Publishing (originally published in Morris, A. and Maxwell, G. (eds) (2001) *Restorative Justice for Juveniles*. Oxford: Hart Publishing).

Zehr, H. (1990) *Changing Lenses: A New Focus for Crime and Justice*. Scottdale, PA: Herald Press.

Zehr, H. (2002) *The Little Book of Restorative Justice*. Intercourse, PA: Good Books.

Zehr, H. and Toews, B. (eds) (2004) *Critical Issues in Restorative Justice*, Monsey, NY: Criminal Justice Press.

Chapter 2

The idea of reparation

Susan Sharpe

A former soldier asked a Buddhist nun how to atone for the destruction he had caused during the war. She said, 'If you blow up a house, then you build a house. If you blow up a bridge, then you build a bridge' (Thomas 2004: 18). This basic prescription – the simple fairness of replacing what one has taken or destroyed – is the essential idea of reparation.

The word 'reparation' stems from 'repair' meaning to fix or mend. It overlaps with a cluster of other related concepts, including restitution, compensation, atonement, damages and remedies (Weitekamp 1999: 75; Teitel 2000: 119). Reparation is a kind of recompense, which means to give back or give something of equivalent value. Often the term is used in reference to making amends or paying damages.[1] In all these senses, reparation is a mechanism for redress – i.e. a way of correcting or remedying a situation. Redress is not specific to the context of justice; one might speak of redressing a troubling economic trend, for example. But in human affairs, redress often has the connotation of correcting a wrong.

As such, redress is linked to reciprocity, which William Ian Miller identifies as a fundamental mechanism by which human beings maintain stable social relationships. He says that reciprocity is triggered whenever we receive something from others: 'Both the good and the ill received oblige the other to make a return' (1993: 5). While we need not repay every kindness or injury, we typically do not accept many of either before finding a way to reciprocate or at least to prevent the imbalance from growing.

Keeping our social accounts in relative balance appears to be a basic human drive. Honour, Miller says, is 'rooted in a desire to pay back what we owe, both the good and the evil. The failure to reciprocate, unless convincingly excused, draws down our accounts of esteem and self-esteem' (1993: x). He says that we 'feel bound to return kindness and we feel frustrated when we are prevented from returning wrongs' (p. 6). Thus reciprocity gives rise not only to social obligations, but also to our drive for justice.

This chapter begins with a look at basic ways of redressing injustice and then at the nature of reparation – forms it can take, what it can accomplish and optimal conditions for achieving those results. From there, the chapter turns to a discussion of several key issues related to reparation in restorative justice.

Ways of redressing wrong

Philosopher Peter French points out that 'we have certain attitudes toward those who do not treat us with goodwill and respect or esteem or who act toward us with contempt, indifference, or, especially, malevolence' (2001: 81). When such things happen, he says, our attitudes about them reflect the way we perceive ourselves to be treated as measured against a standard of expectations related to our concepts of right and wrong. One of these attitudes is resentment: 'When we perceive or recognize that someone has injured or slighted us or failed to render to us what we regard as proper respect, we resent the offender' (French 2001: 81). A second attitude occurs when resentment is felt vicariously on behalf of people with whom we have some affinity, or when it is generalized in response to the way other people are treated; the attitude in that case is indignation. A third attitude occurs 'when one turns one's moral scrutiny on oneself and recognizes or perceives oneself to be morally wanting. In such cases, the feeling is neither resentment nor indignation. It is either guilt or shame' (p. 81).

French goes on to explain that 'the reactive attitudes, especially resentment, indignation, and shame, trigger the response mechanisms that give the moral qualities of actions causal power in human affairs' (2001: 82). In other words, the moral judgements we make – our 'recognition of the moral qualities of both action and actor' (p. 82) – are rooted in these primary attitudes. Taking French's work a step further, we can see these three attitudes underlying the primary ways by which humans redress injustice: vengeance, retribution and repair. Redress is crafted by the victim when it takes the form of vengeance, by a responsible authority when the form is retribution and by the offender in the case of repair.

Vengeance – i.e. revenge, or retaliation – repays like for like, reciprocating injury with injury. Vengeance essentially says 'You have wronged me and I will not stand for it. I will do to you as you did to me.' Taking revenge is primarily a personal act, triggered by the attitude of resentment that comes of feeling oneself (or someone with whom one's identity is closely linked) to be the target of insult or injury. Martha Minow says this 'is the impulse to retaliate when wrongs are done. Through vengeance, we express our basic self-respect' (1998: 10). We commonly associate vengeance with violence, but revenge is not always extreme. As Robert Solomon says, 'The more usual act of revenge is a negative vote in the next department meeting, a forty-five minute delay in arriving to dinner, or a hurtful comment or letter' (1990: 276).

Retribution, the second form of redress, also repays injury with injury but in this case the motivating attitude is indignation on behalf of others. Blameworthiness is expressed and responsibility is indicated (Walgrave 2004: 55) for the sake of asserting moral truth (Hampton 1988: 137). The goal,

Minow says, is not 'the vengeful, self-help response of tit-for-tat, [but rather] the deliberate, retributive use of governmentally administered punishment to vindicate the victim's value' (1998: 151, n. 13). The potential destructiveness of vengeance is 'curbed by the intervention of someone other than the victim and by principles of proportionality and individual rights' (Minow 1998: 12). Whatever punishment is administered through retribution, the offender is expected to accept it as appropriate and the victim is expected to accept it as sufficient.

Repair, the third primary way of redressing injustice, does something for the victim rather than to the offender. As with vengeance and retribution, a basic aim is to reduce the inequity created by injustice. But here the strategy is to decrease suffering for the victim rather than increase suffering for the offender. This form of redress also has a different source. Whereas revenge and retribution both originate in a judgement that someone else's behaviour has been wrong, repair originates in a recognition that one's own behaviour has been wrong. The judgement comes from within.[2] Redressing injustice through repair says, 'I created a situation you should not have to bear, and I regret it. I cannot undo my behaviour, but I want to minimize the damage it caused.'

Each of these forms of redress – vengeance, retribution and repair – is an effort to reduce the inequity created when one person gains something at the expense of another. A victim can retaliate by repaying the offender in kind, an authority can impose some kind of equivalent suffering or an offender can give back as much as possible of what was taken from the victim. (Or redress may take more than one form. As noted later in this chapter, many people believe that repair alone is insufficient in cases of willful harm.) Reparation has a role both in retribution and in repair, although its role and its effect can be quite different in the two. Before turning to those differences, it will help to look at the basic nature of reparation.

The nature of reparation

Reparation has been a vehicle for justice throughout human history. Ancient societies, recognizing that retaliation could lead to costly cycles of mutual destruction, turned to restitution or some form of compensation as their primary form of redress (Weitekamp 1999: 76, 79; Johnstone 2002: 40). As societies grew more complex, they began developing legal codes that identified appropriate reparation for various kinds of harm (Weitekamp 1999: 83–9), including limits on what could reasonably be demanded (Zehr 1990: 103; Brunk 2001: 39).

Reparation still has a role in contemporary legal systems. In Western civil law, which deals with individuals' offences against one another, the focus is on the monetary value of an injury or loss, and reparation takes the form of financial compensation (Johnstone 2003: 11). Reparation has had a smaller role in Western criminal justice, which deals with behaviour classified as offences against the state and operates primarily from a retributive philosophy. However, reparation has become more common in recent decades as a judicial sentencing option (Bazemore 1998: 773; Van Ness and Strong 2002: 86).

Reparation also has a role in the political arena, when governments make amends for hostilities against other nations or for policies that are harmful to their own people. Brownlie defines reparation as 'all measures which a plaintiff may expect to be taken by a defendant state: payment of compensation (restitution), an apology, the punishment of the individuals responsible, the taking of steps to prevent a recurrence of the breach of duty, and any other forms of satisfaction' (2003: 442). An example of such reparation is the US government's payments to the surviving Japanese Americans who were interned during the Second World War.

Types of reparation

Reparation can take many forms. In general, reparations are described as being either material or symbolic, although the two categories overlap to a large extent. Material reparation can have a symbolic function, conveying an acknowledgment of responsibility and thus having the effect of an apology, while symbolic reparation can make a substantial difference in a victim's life. Still, the two differ in terms of their primary function: material reparation generally addresses the specific harms (tangible or intangible) that result from wrongdoing, while symbolic reparation speaks to the wrongness of the act itself.

Material reparation offers something concrete to repair a specific harm or to compensate for the damage or loss associated with that harm. Material reparation may reduce the extent of the harm done by a crime, may reduce the victim's cost for dealing with that harm, or both. This type of reparation often takes the form of goods (e.g. the return of stolen property) or financial payments (such as to cover the cost of medical treatment or psychological therapy). It also can take the form of concrete action, perhaps to repair a damaged structure or to provide a service that reduces the victim's burden (such as delivering groceries while a victim recovers from injuries). These goods or actions might address a crime's primary or most direct harm (Van Ness and Strong 2002: 91), or the secondary harms set in motion by the crime. Thus reparation could include things like counselling, transportation, training, financial assistance, employment, day care, new housing or drug treatment (Herman 2004: 81).

Material reparation often takes the form of restitution or compensation. While each of these terms is sometimes used in other ways, restitution is usually the broader term: 'Restitution is made by returning or replacing property, by monetary payment, or by performing direct services for the victim' (Van Ness and Strong 2002: 85–6). In the larger context of injustice to a people or cultural group, restitution typically means the return of 'wrongly appropriated property, artifacts, and human remains' (Minow 1998: 117). Compensation usually has a narrower meaning, referring to a financial payment (Brownlie 2003: 442) that makes up for property that cannot be returned or repaired, or that acknowledges a fundamental loss such as the violation of human rights. Some use this term specifically in reference to payments made by a government or another third party (e.g. Van Ness and Strong 2002: 85, n.13), such as through victim compensation funds.[3]

As important as material reparation can be in enabling a victim to recover from the effects of a crime, symbolic reparation (sometimes called emotional reparation) can be even more significant. As Heather Strang says: 'Victims studies over the past decade repeatedly show that what victims want most is not material reparation but instead symbolic reparation, primarily an apology and a sincere expression of remorse' (2004: 98).[4]

Apology is the primary form of symbolic reparation, but there are other forms as well. For example, victims may implicitly hear responsibility and remorse during a restorative justice dialogue as an offender explains how and why the crime occurred and respectfully listens to the victim's experience of it (Marshall 2003: 32). Or symbolic reparation might be expressed through actions like buying a gift, providing a service for the victim, donating time or money to a charity of the victim's choice, doing community service or entering treatment in order to address the roots of criminal behaviour (Duff 2002: 90, 94; Johnstone 2003: 11; Marshall 2003: 32; Strang 2004: 102). Partial restitution sometimes is called symbolic reparation because it conveys an offender's willingness to make amends even when full restitution is beyond that person's means.

What reparation can accomplish

Reparation is only one of many factors that may help a victim recover from a crime; healing might also depend on the support of loved ones, on medical or psychological therapy, on the satisfaction of feeling that justice has been served, or even on the effect of time. Yet the role of reparation can be pivotal to recovery because it achieves four things: it can help to repair damage, vindicate the innocent, locate responsibility and restore equilibrium.

Repairing the damage caused by a crime is important for the same reasons it is important to repair damage caused by accident or natural wear: to restore function, to make something safe to use again or to help preserve its value. Whether hit by a hailstone or a hammer, a broken tail-light needs to be fixed – to comply with the law requiring that a car have two functioning brake lights, to prevent being rear-ended, or in order to get a better price when selling the car. Repairing intangibles can be equally important for the same reasons. Therapy can help a victim function well again at school or work, or make it feel safe again to go to sleep at night; an apology might help preserve a relationship that has been important, or strengthen someone's damaged self-worth.

A second function is that reparation can vindicate the innocent, giving victims 'a moral statement to the community that they were right and that the other person was wrong' (Zehr 2003: 75). It gives victims a recognition that the wrong suffered was in fact a wrong (Strang 2004: 102), and that the victim was not somehow at fault (Bazemore and Schiff 2005: 51). Victims might find vindication in the support of other individuals, through expressions of sympathy or assurances that what happened was not acceptable. Or they may find it through the criminal justice system, in that criminal prosecution confirms that certain behaviours are not tolerated by the community (Daly 2002: 62; Duff 2002: 91–2). But vindication is most powerful when it comes from the offender, and reparation helps convey it.

Thirdly, reparation locates responsibility. 'When you commit a crime,' says Howard Zehr, 'you create a certain debt, an obligation, a liability that must be met. Crime creates an obligation – to restore, to repair, to undo' (2003: 79), and reparation meets at least part of that obligation. As Dan Van Ness and Karen Heetderks Strong explain, 'Something given or done to make up for an injury... underscores that the offender who caused the injury should be the active party' in redressing it (2002: 47).

Fourthly, reparation can help victims regain the equilibrium so often lost after a crime. Victims commonly find that their physical, mental or emotional well-being is disrupted; they may be unable to eat or sleep normally and may be preoccupied, anxious or fearful. Susan Herman reports that crime victims suffer a loss of confidence, reduced academic performance and work productivity, and increased rates of mental illness, drug and alcohol abuse, and suicide (2004: 77). By repairing a crime's primary and secondary harms, material reparation can play a significant role in helping victims integrate the trauma and heal its effects, regaining stability and confidence. Symbolic reparation, by acknowledging the wrongness of the behaviour and expressing regret for it, returns to the victim some of the power seized by the offender in committing the crime. Minow says: 'By retelling the wrong and seeking acceptance, the apologizer assumes a position of vulnerability before not only the victims but also the larger community of literal or figurative witnesses' (1998: 114).

The fact that reparation accomplishes these things does not link it exclusively to one form of redress. For reasons discussed in the next section, reparation is most powerful when it reflects a genuine desire to repair. But reparation can also have a role in retribution; a court might require the payment of restitution or compensation in order to punish an offender, irrespective of the victim's needs.

Optimal conditions for reparation

If justice is, as Howard Zehr says, properly rooted in a concern for victims' needs and offenders' obligations (2002: 22–4), and if reparation is the vehicle by which offenders meet those obligations, then it follows that reparation would be most effective under certain circumstances. Those circumstances characterize restorative justice: when the reparation is tailored to meet a victim's particular needs, when the terms of the reparation are chosen by those most directly involved and when it is offered rather than ordered.

Tailored

The point of reparation is to repair damage caused by wrongdoing. Reparation therefore is most effective when it directly addresses the specific harms done in a particular situation. For example, Gerry Johnstone points out that if a youth has damaged a fence, washing police cars would have no relevance to the harm done and thus would constitute punishment more than reparation (2003: 12). Conrad Brunk points out that if a husband wants to make amends for abusing his wife, joining the effort to end domestic violence or raising money for a women's shelter has 'far more psychological, sociological, and moral power in "righting the wrong" or "restoring justice" than does simple financial payment' (2001: 52). The importance of tailoring reparation to address victims' specific needs is just as relevant when a community is the victim. Van Ness and Strong point out that community service is likely to be no more than a rhetorical phrase if the exact harm done to the community has not been defined (2002: 88). They note that this does not mean community service is inappropriate, but 'it does require that we clarify the nature and extent of the harm done to society at large, as well as the most appropriate means for the offender to repair that harm' (2002: 89).

While there are consistencies in the kinds of things victims experience as a result of crime, the particular harms to be repaired cannot reliably be predicted by knowing the nature of the crime; one victim might come out of a crime with post-traumatic stress syndrome, while someone else harmed in the same crime might recover quickly and easily. It also is impossible to predict a victim's priorities for reparation; even victims are often surprised to discover that receiving an apology is more valuable than the restitution they had thought mattered most. Tailoring reparation so that it best meets a victim's needs, therefore, depends first on learning from the victim the full range of harms he or she has experienced and, secondly, on finding ways an offender can at least contribute to the repair of those harms.

Determined by stakeholders

Some repairs are straightforward: a broken window on a new house usually needs to be replaced with an identical one. Other repairs involve choices: the owner of a heritage home might opt to replace a broken window either with new glass, with antique glass or with reproduction glass; replacing the window might be a task the offender could do or help with, or it might require an expert glazier. Regaining a sense of safety after a break-in and assault might require new lighting or it might require therapy; the victim's insurance might cover the cost of that therapy, or it might need to be paid for by the offender. Reparation is most effective when such choices are made by those who have a stake in what the repair involves or how it turns out – primarily the victim, who will live with the outcome, and the offender, who is responsible for the repair, as well as others who might also be affected. There are several reasons why stakeholders' participation is significant to the effectiveness of reparation.

First, as Van Ness and Strong point out, 'Being victimized is by definition an experience of powerlessness – the victim was unable to prevent the crime from occurring' (2002: 38). A victim can regain some sense of control through the experience of describing the harms he or she suffered, identifying what he or she needs as a result, and helping to determine what reparation would be appropriate. Control also is found in having the opportunity to gauge the sincerity of the offender's apology and weigh its strength against the magnitude of the harm. In Minow's view, as important as it is for the offender to take full responsibility for wrongdoing, it is equally important that the victim be granted the power to accept, refuse or ignore the offender's apology. Whichever choice they make, 'The survivors secure a position of strength, respect, and specialness' (1998: 115).

Secondly, an offender who has a voice in the decision is more likely to understand why a given repair is needed and what difference it might make for the victim, and also more likely to follow through on the commitment to make reparation (Schiff 1999: 331; Johnstone 2002: 143). Beyond these practical benefits, there is a deeper reason why reparation is most effective when it is determined by the stakeholders. The primary rationale for putting the decision in their hands takes us, once again, to the primary significance of reciprocity. A crime either changes the relationship between the victim and offender (if they already knew each other) or puts them into relationship with each other (if they had been strangers). And relationships are bound by reciprocity. In order to restore whatever equilibrium they had in relation to each other before the crime, the harm must be reciprocated – either by the victim through some form of vengeance, by others in the form of punishment or by the offender through some kind of repair. Repair initiated by a third party – such as a court or a community justice panel – may achieve partial reparation but it is necessarily limited. Repair that comes from outside the victim–offender relationship cannot meet the requirement of reciprocity. To be effective, it must come from the offender – which can happen even when reparation is ordered by a judge or another third party, if that offender recognizes its importance and feels good about providing it.

Offered

Reparation that is offered by an offender – or at least readily agreed to – can accomplish more for offenders as well as for victims than reparation carried out under duress. Voluntarily assuming responsibility can help an offender develop a more prosocial value system (Van Ness and Strong 2002: 41), and those who take an active helping role in making amends tend to experience more positive behavioural change than those who carry out reparation that is required of them or imposed as punishment (Bazemore and Schiff 2005: 51). Johnstone (2002) explains why this might occur. One factor is that making repairs helps offenders realize the harm they have caused, which is a crucial step towards reintegration (p. 102). More specifically, voluntarily repairing the harm they have caused helps to appease the anger and indignation that victims and the public may feel towards them, perhaps even turning this into respect (p. 102). Drawing on the work of Sir Walter Moberly, Johnstone also argues that repentance and voluntary reparation can help to reverse an offender's own moral degradation and the social harm caused by the crime (2002: 104).

For victims, there are occasions where coerced reparation is as effective as when it is voluntary. The return of a rare art object may be the only way to restore the value of a prized collection, and the victim may not care how the offender feels as long as the object is returned. More often, however, a victim finds more value in an offender's demonstrated willingness to make amends than in receiving the actual reparation, even if the person is unable to follow through and complete the promised reparation (Bazemore and Schiff 2005: 50). What makes the offender's willingness so significant is that this is what constitutes symbolic reparation.

Symbolic reparation can do two things that material reparation cannot. One is that it can help redress harms that cannot be repaired, such as permanent injury or death. Secondly, symbolic reparation can go to a layer underneath specific harms, redressing the injury of injustice itself. Whenever one person gains something at the expense of another – which is what happens in wrongdoing – that gain and loss create an unfair imbalance between the victim and offender. As seen earlier in this chapter, reciprocity demands that proper balance be restored, at least to the extent possible. In expressing one's responsibility and a feeling of remorse, an offender renounces the advantage gained and offers the respect that was denied in the course of the wrongdoing.

Material reparation can be coerced, but symbolic reparation cannot. Someone can be ordered to write a letter of apology, but victims tend to be very good at gauging whether apologies are genuine, and quick to reject those that are not. Reparation delivered reluctantly may be better than none at all. But the reparation that achieves the most is reparation that comes from a true sense of regret.

In general, restorative justice processes facilitate the optimal conditions for effective reparation, insofar as they involve all interested stakeholders, help victims articulate the full range of harms they have experienced and assist offenders in finding ways to make amends. Yet there are issues to consider for anyone offering restorative justice to that end.

Issues related to reparation in restorative justice

Reparation is a simple idea that holds considerable complexity. Within the context of restorative justice, some of that complexity is evident around three issues in particular. Two bear on the practice of restorative justice and a third relates to the breadth of activity found in restorative justice programmes. First, how difficult should reparation be? Secondly, how important is proportionality? Thirdly, must restorative justice concern itself with systemic injustice?

Must reparation be burdensome?

Two arguments have been prominent in restorative justice since this approach began to emerge. On the one hand we insist that restorative justice is fundamentally different from retributive justice with its philosophy of just deserts. At the same time we assure sceptics that being accountable directly to one's victim is anything but soft on crime. How consistent are these claims? Johnstone frames this issue when he says:

> It is important to be clear about the reason for demanding that the offender repair harm in restorative justice. Is our main concern that the harm be repaired, as in the civil law model? Or, is our main concern

that the perpetrator be made to suffer some burden, as in the criminal law model? (2003: 12).

The restorative justice literature is divided in response to this question. Some authors say that if our priority really is to repair harm rather than to punish offenders, then it is irrelevant whether or not that repair is burdensome. Randy Barnett takes this view, arguing for pure restitution over punitive restitution: 'This represents the complete overthrow of the paradigm of punishment... No longer would the criminal deliberately be made to suffer for his mistake. Making good that mistake is all that would be required' (2003: 50).[5] Martin Wright also rejects the notion of punishment in reference to any measure that is primarily intended to help the victim, and which may also help the offender. Wright recognizes that reparative sanctions may involve the loss of liberty or money but says this should occur by consent if possible, rather than being imposed (2003: 7).

Others say that, while outcomes may sometimes feel burdensome to the offender, what matters is the intention behind that choice of outcome. As Walgrave says: 'There is a crucial difference between obligations that are inevitably painful, like paying taxes or compensation, and obligations that are imposed with the purpose of imposing pain, like paying a fine' (2004: 48). Brenda Morrison also focuses on intent rather than on the actual hardship of a sanction. She says: 'School suspensions (as opposed to permanent exclusion), for example, could constitute a restorative justice practice if it is seen as legitimate opportunity, by all involved in the process, to "make things right"' (2001: 203).

Still others believe that punishment has as legitimate a role in restorative justice as repair does. Kathleen Daly argues that retribution and restoration are not the opposites they are often assumed to be. For her, retribution is a clear and important denunciation of wrong, for the sake of vindicating the victim (2002: 72, 84). Similarly, Antony Duff argues that a clearer understanding of the concepts of punishment and restoration would dissolve the apparent conflict between the two. In his view, 'Criminal punishment should aim at restoration, whilst restorative justice programmes should aim to impose appropriate kinds of punishment' (2002: 83). For Duff, punishment is what gives an apology its requisite moral weight:

> The reparation I undertake must be something burdensome – something that symbolizes the burden of moral injury that I laid on my victims and would now like (if only I could) to take on myself; the burden of wrongdoing that I laid on myself; and the burden of remorse that I now feel (2002: 90).

The question of whether reparation must be burdensome is a crucial one in restorative justice because it hinges on the central distinction between retribution and repair as forms of redress. As Johnstone notes, the argument that punitive restitution is more appropriate than pure restitution 'may be inconsistent with the notion that restorative justice is a new *paradigm* in criminal justice' (2003: 22, emphasis in original).

Must reparation be proportionate?

Proportionality is the principle underlying light sentences for minor crimes and progressively harsher sentences for more serious crimes. Barry Feld says that 'As long as the criminal law rests on a moral foundation, the idea of blameworthiness remains central to ascribing guilt and allocating punishment. Penalties proportionate to the *seriousness* of the crime reflect the connection between the nature of the conduct and its blameworthiness' (1999: 32, emphasis in original). Feld also notes that 'Because punishment entails censure for blameworthy choices, the *proportionality* of sentences reflects actors' culpability rather than just the harm their behavior caused' (1999: 33, emphasis in original).

Proportionality aims to achieve fairness in sentencing, such that the severity of a sanction correlates to the severity of a wrong. Clearly it would not be right to punish a shoplifter more severely than an armed robber who hurt and traumatized several victims. For Nigel Walker, though, the chief benefit of proportionality is consistency in sentencing (1991: 104–5) such that two people causing comparable harm would experience the same kind and degree of punishment. But if punishment were not part of the equation – if repair were all that mattered – would proportionality still be important?

Martin Wright and Guy Masters say no. They acknowledge that 'fairness dictates that the reparation should not be excessive, even if a contrite offender agrees to it' (2002: 55), but they do not see proportionality as an appropriate criterion for reparation. In their view, 'Restorative justice aims to reach a conclusion which is satisfactory to a particular victim and offender, which need bear no relation to what is appropriate for any others who may appear similarly placed' (2002: 55). In other words, because crime harms persons and victims' needs are unique, it is appropriate for reparation also to be unique, even if the result is that similar wrongs are dealt with very differently.

This particularity is a strength of restorative justice, focusing as it does on unique needs and tailored repair. Wright says: 'The idea of restorative justice is that any reparative acts by the offender are if possible agreed by the victim and the offender. They therefore are not necessarily proportionate to the seriousness if the victim does not feel this to be necessary' (2003: 11). But this particularity also creates a risk. Wright's claim assumes that the victim and offender both have a good understanding of the harms to be repaired, and each is fully empowered to make a fair agreement with the other. Els Dumortier (2003) points to a number of concerns, based on the experience of juveniles who meet with their victims and then carry out reparation as set out in their agreements. She says, for example, that a focus on material reparation can mean that an offender does more to make up for a minor crime like graffiti than for a more serious crime like break and enter; because older youth often earn higher wages per hour, younger offenders may have to work longer in order to pay an equivalent amount of financial reparation. Too, offenders sometimes accept unreasonable terms for reparation; they do so in order to avoid criminal prosecution, out of ignorance or in response to parental pressure (pp. 200–1). Offenders sometimes end up working more than is deserved, because some victims demand unreasonable damage claims (Braithwaite 2002a: 165; Dumortier 2003: 200).

Because of such concerns, a number of people suggest setting outside boundaries for restorative justice agreements, within which victims and offenders could arrive at whatever terms seem fair to them – whether or not those terms are proportionate and whether or not they are comparable to agreements made by other victims and offenders. Some recommend setting two boundaries, to specify both minimum and maximum outcomes (Crawford 2002: 125; Eliaerts and Dumortier 2002: 210). A minimum threshold might be reassuring to those who want to ensure that community standards are affirmed and that unacceptable behaviours are unequivocally denounced. But might it violate the primacy of the victim's needs as the basis for reparation? Wright and Masters note cases where victims and offenders both felt it was unfair that judges imposed community service after they had agreed that an apology was sufficient. The authors suggest that 'this is another example of retributive thinking undermining the restorative ideal' (2002: 56).

Others recommend setting only an upper limit. For Walgrave, this upper limit should be proportionate – not linking the reparation to the seriousness of the crime, but linking the seriousness and kind of harm to a maximum of reasonable restorative effort (2002: 213). John Braithwaite offers a more traditional view in support of an upper limit. He says: 'Within the social movement for restorative justice, there is and always has been absolute consensus on one jurisprudential issue. This is that restorative justice processes should never exceed the upper limits on punishment enforced by the courts for the criminal offence under consideration' (2002b: 150).

If Braithwaite is right (and I believe he is) that this point is broadly accepted in the restorative justice field, then we may need to examine the implications of linking restorative boundaries to a retributive scale: is it safe to assume that limits on punishment are reasonable limits on repair? Walgrave offers what may be a crucial reminder: 'Due process proportionality and other principles remain respectable, but they must be critically checked as to their meaning in a restorative justice context, and possibly be reformulated, rejected or replaced' (2002: 216).

Must reparation address systemic injustice?

With its emphasis on repairing harm, and on bringing people into dialogue where they deepen their empathy, interdependence, and accountability, restorative justice has been seen as a vehicle for the redress of social as well as criminal injustice (Zehr and Toews 2004: 375–6). At issue is whether the field also has a responsibility to work towards that redress.

Part of this issue is whether or how reparation might contribute to social justice at the individual level – a question that invites taking a broader view of the harms connected to a crime. Van Ness and Strong distinguish contributing injuries – 'those that existed prior to the crime and that prompted in some way the criminal conduct of the offender' – from resulting injuries – 'those caused by the crime itself or its aftermath' (2002: 40). For Morris, restoration requires attention to both kinds of injuries: 'Restoring means that action needs to be taken to address both the factors underlying their offending in the first place and the consequences of that offending' (2002: 605). Braithwaite and Parker similarly caution that the outcomes agreed to in restorative justice processes should be 'grounded in dialogue that takes account of underlying injustices' (1999: 109). Delens-Ravier suggests that well designed reparation can help to accomplish that goal: 'Encounters between adults and young people during the performance of community service represent a form of indirect reparation, constituting a veritable promise by society for youths deprived of human, non-pecuniary relationships' (2003: 155).

A larger part of this issue is what difference restorative justice might be able to make in regard to injustice that occurs on a larger scale – either through egregious wrongs like slavery, genocide and other mass atrocities, or through systemic wrongs that insidiously harm classes of people on an ongoing basis. Chris Cunneen points out that 'perhaps the greatest crimes in the twentieth century causing direct human harm have been committed by governments' (2001: 90), or at least have been supported by state institutions (p. 93). Such crimes include slavery in the USA, and the practice of removing indigenous children from their families and communities in Australia and Canada. When such harms are redressed, reparation usually has an important role in confirming responsibility. 'If unaccompanied by direct and immediate action, such as monetary reparations', Minow says, 'official apologies risk seeming meaningless' (1998: 117). Here in particular, regarding reparations for wrongs that have devastated whole peoples, the simple idea of repairing harm becomes complicated and difficult. As Minow asks, when those most clearly responsible or those most directly harmed are no longer alive, who is in a position to issue a true apology, and to whom? And who is in a position to accept such an apology, or to refuse it (Minow 1998: 112–5)?

Reparation for mass atrocities is not a concern for most restorative justice practitioners or programmes. Yet the effects of such harms may be a regular presence in any restorative justice practice. The fact that marginalized groups are over-represented in the criminal justice system is something that many see as evidence of continuing postcolonial trauma (Behrendt 2002; Blagg 2002; Kelly 2002).

Cunneen points out that family problems are individualized through child welfare or criminal justice casework, and that 'restorative justice advocates can make a real contribution in this area by supporting welfare and justice practices which allow for the deeper meanings of harm and responsibility to emerge' (2001: 96). Discerning those deeper meanings may equip us to tackle something Jeffrie Murphy points to. 'One tends to think that all demands for repentance must be addressed to the criminal. But surely the community, through its patterns of abuse, neglect and discrimination, sometimes creates a social environment that undermines the development of virtuous character and makes the temptations to crime very great' (2003: 54). We might ask what reparation will look like when we decide to redress that wrong.

Conclusion

Reparation, both material and symbolic, has a primary role in redressing wrong. As such, it is central to restorative justice. Restorative justice theory calls for engaging all of what reparation helps to achieve – repair, vindication, the location of responsibility and the restoration of equilibrium – and for keeping them in balance with one another. Too strong an emphasis on repair or vindication could fuel the charge that restorative justice is soft, unable to redress injustice effectively. Too strong a focus on accountability might encourage the co-optation of restorative justice and turn repair into retribution. A preoccupation with restoring equilibrium could accommodate communities or systems whose norms are harmful. But tending to all these functions and keeping them in proportion may help us reduce our reliance on retribution and cultivate greater skill with repair. Doing so may be a crucial step towards transforming our understandings, and thus our experience, of justice.

Selected further reading

• Minow, M. (1998) *Between Vengeance and Forgiveness: Facing History after Genocide and Mass Violence*. Boston, MA: Beacon Press. This book explores the ways that nations have developed for responding to mass atrocities, including trials, truth commissions and reparations. In looking at the complex struggles involved in facing what has happened, holding people accountable for it, and moving beyond it, Minow highlights the personal as well as the social and political challenges that result from the worst of what humans do to one another.

Walgrave, L. (2004) 'Has restorative justice appropriately responded to retribution theory and impulses?', in H. Zehr and B. Toews (eds) *Critical Issues in Restorative Justice*. Monsey, NY: Criminal Justice Press and Cullompton: Willan Publishing. After exploring retribution as an argument for criminal punishment, Walgrave claims its only justification lies in the censure of wrongful behaviour, which he says is more effectively achieved through restoration.

Wright, M. (2003) 'Is it time to question the concept of punishment?', in L. Walgrave (ed.) *Repositioning Restorative Justice*. Cullompton: Willan Publishing. This essay offers a detailed review of arguments that punishment has a role in restorative justice, that sanctions must be punitive and that sentencing can be proportional and fair. Wright concludes with a framework for reducing harm and for responding to it effectively.

Notes

1 The definitions and connotations set out in this chapter are drawn from *The Oxford English Dictionary, New Edition*; *Webster's Third New International Dictionary, Unabridged*; the *Stanford Encyclopedia of Philosophy*; and from the way terms are used in my reading of relevant literature outside as well as inside the restorative justice field. The constructs behind these terms are complex and overlapping, and I do not claim my interpretations as definitive.

2 This distinction between external and internal judgement is a crucial one. As French says, guilt or shame is a feeling that occurs when our own behaviour

falls short of our standards for right and wrong (2001: 81). It does not follow from being told by others that one is morally wanting – as happens when people dispense 'shaming' in ostensibly restorative processes.

3 Some argue that the victim's community has a responsibility to offer compensation. Allison Morris says: 'Full monetary restoration is not always achieved as many offenders have limited resources. However, if we as a community take restorative justice seriously, this type of restoration could, and perhaps should, be a community (state) responsibility' (2002: 604).

This view is also found within the conventional criminal justice system. Van Ness and Strong point out that a British magistrate was the first in modern times to suggest that the state compensate crime victims, arguing that when a government has taken on a responsibility for public order, it also takes on an obligation to compensate victims when it fails to protect them from crime (2002: 85, n. 13). Van Ness and Strong note that 'few governments have been willing to recognize victim compensation as an obligation they owe to victims, but many have implemented victim compensation schemes' (2002: 85, n. 13).

Susan Herman advocates parallel justice, where 'compensating victims for their losses would be a responsibility shared by offenders and society at large. Restorative justice programs should continue to promote the payment of restitution by offenders, but we should also use tax revenue to meet victims' needs' (2004: 80).

4 A victim's hunger for apology can sometimes put that person at risk. Because an apology expresses regret for past choices, an apology – even if sincerely meant – can give a victim false confidence that the offence will not be repeated, leading him or her to re-enter a dangerous situation. This is a pattern in cases of repeated harm that occurs in ongoing relationships, such as in situations of domestic violence (Barnett *et al.* 1997: 237; Herman 1997: 83; Griffing *et al.* 2002: 313).

5 In overthrowing the paradigm of punishment, Barnett would also dispense with the criminal justice system as we know it, replacing it with a purely reparative model based on civil (tort) law.

References

Barnett, O., Miller-Perrin, C. and Perrin, R. (1997) *Family Violence across the Lifespan: An Introduction.* Thousand Oaks, CA: Sage.

Barnett, R. (2003) 'Restitution: a new paradigm of criminal justice', in G. Johnstone (ed.) *A Restorative Justice Reader: Texts, Sources, Context.* Cullompton: Willan Publishing.

Bazemore, G. (1998) 'Restorative justice and earned redemption: communities, victims, and offender reintegration', *American Behavioral Scientist*, 41: 768–813.

Bazemore, G. and Schiff, M. (2005) *Juvenile Justice Reform and Restorative Justice: Building Theory and Policy from Practice.* Cullompton: Willan Publishing.

Behrendt, L. (2002) 'Lessons from the mediation obsession: ensuring that sentencing "alternatives" focus on indigenous self-determination', in H. Strang and J. Braithwaite (eds) *Restorative Justice and Family Violence.* Cambridge: Cambridge University Press.

Blagg, H. (2002) 'Restorative justice and Aboriginal family violence: opening a space for healing', in H. Strang and J. Braithwaite (eds) *Restorative Justice and Family Violence.* Cambridge: Cambridge University Press.

Braithwaite, J. (2002a) *Restorative Justice and Responsive Regulation.* Oxford: Oxford University Press.

Braithwaite, J. (2002b) 'In search of restorative jurisprudence', in L. Walgrave (ed.) *Restorative Justice and the Law*. Cullompton: Willan Publishing.

Braithwaite, J. and Parker, C. (1999) 'Restorative justice is Republican justice', in G. Bazemore and L. Walgrave (eds) *Restorative Juvenile Justice: Repairing the Harm of Youth Crime*. Monsey, NY: Criminal Justice Press.

Brownlie, I. (2003) *Principles of Public International Law* (6th edn). Oxford: Oxford University Press.

Brunk, C. (2001) 'Restorative justice and the philosophical theories of criminal punishment', in M. Hadley (ed.) *The Spiritual Roots of Restorative Justice*. New York, NY: State University of New York Press.

Crawford, A. (2002) 'The state, community and restorative justice: heresy, nostalgia and butterfly collecting', in L. Walgrave (ed.) *Restorative Justice and the Law*. Cullompton: Willan Publishing.

Cunneen, C. (2001) 'Reparations and restorative justice: responding to the gross violation of human rights', in H. Strang and J. Braithwaite (eds) *Restorative Justice and Civil Society*. Cambridge: Cambridge University Press.

Daly, K. (2002) 'Sexual assault and restorative justice', in H. Strang and J. Braithwaite (eds) *Restorative Justice and Family Violence*. Cambridge: Cambridge University Press.

Delens-Ravier, I. (2003) 'Juvenile offenders' perceptions of community service', in L. Walgrave (ed.) *Repositioning Restorative Justice*. Cullompton: Willan Publishing.

Duff, R. (2002) 'Restorative punishment and punitive restoration', in L. Walgrave (ed.) *Restorative Justice and the Law*. Cullompton: Willan Publishing.

Dumortier, E. (2003) 'Legal rules and safeguards within Belgian mediation practices for juveniles', in E. Weitekamp and H. Kerner (eds) *Restorative Justice in Context: International Practice and Directions*. Cullompton: Willan Publishing.

Eliaerts, C. and Dumortier, E. (2002) 'Restorative justice for children: in need of procedural safeguards and standards', in E. Weitekamp and H. Kerner (eds) *Restorative Justice: Theoretical Foundations*. Cullompton: Willan Publishing.

Feld, B. (1999) 'Rehabilitation, retribution and restorative justice: alternative conceptions of juvenile justice', in G. Bazemore and L. Walgrave (eds) *Restorative Juvenile Justice: Repairing the Harm of Youth Crime*. Monsey, NY: Criminal Justice Press.

French, P. (2001) *The Virtues of Vengeance*. Lawrence, KS: University of Kansas Press.

Griffing, S., Ragin, D., Sage, R., Madry, L., Bingham, L. and Primm, B. (2002) 'Domestic violence survivors' self-identified reasons for returning to abusive relationships', *Journal of Interpersonal Violence*, 17: 306–19.

Hampton, J. (1988) 'The retributive idea', in J. Murphy and J. Hampton (eds) *Forgiveness and Mercy*. Cambridge: Cambridge University Press.

Herman, J. (1997) *Trauma and Recovery*. New York, NY: Basic Books.

Herman, S. (2004) 'Is restorative justice possible without a parallel system for victims?', in H. Zehr and B. Toews (eds) *Critical Issues in Restorative Justice*. Monsey, NY: Criminal Justice Press, and Cullompton: Willan Publishing.

Johnstone, G. (2002) *Restorative Justice: Ideas, Values, Debates*. Cullompton: Willan Publishing.

Johnstone, G. (ed.) (2003) *A Restorative Justice Reader: Texts, Sources, Context*. Cullompton: Willan Publishing.

Kelly, L. (2002) 'Using restorative justice principles to address family violence in Aboriginal communities', in H. Strang and J. Braithwaite (eds) *Restorative Justice and Family Violence*. Cambridge: Cambridge University Press.

Marshall, T. (2003) 'Restorative justice: an overview', in G. Johnstone (ed.) *A Restorative Justice Reader: Texts, Sources, Context*. Cullompton: Willan Publishing.

Miller, W. (1993) *Humiliation: And Other Essays on Honor, Social Discomfort, and Violence*. Ithaca, NY: Cornell University Press.

Minow, M. (1998) *Between Vengeance and Forgiveness: Facing History after Genocide and Mass Violence*. Boston, MA: Beacon Press.

Morris, A. (2002) 'Critiquing the critics: a brief response to critics of restorative justice', *British Journal of Criminology*, 42: 596–615.

Morrison, B. (2001) 'The school system: developing its capacity in the regulation of a civil society', in H. Strang and J. Braithwaite (eds) *Restorative Justice and Civil Society*. Cambridge: Cambridge University Press.

Murphy, J. (2003) *Getting Even: Forgiveness and its Limits*. Oxford: Oxford University Press.

Schiff, M. (1999) 'The impact of restorative interventions on juvenile offenders', in G. Bazemore and L. Walgrave (eds) *Restorative Juvenile Justice: Repairing the Harm of Youth Crime*. Monsey, NY: Criminal Justice Press.

Solomon, R. (1990) *A Passion for Justice: Emotions and the Origins of the Social Contract*. Reading, MA: Addison-Wesley Publishing.

Strang, H. (2003) 'Justice for victims of young offenders: the centrality of emotional harm and restoration', in G. Johnstone (ed.) *A Restorative Justice Reader: Texts, Sources, Context*. Cullompton: Willan Publishing.

Strang, H. (2004) 'Is restorative justice imposing its agenda on victims?', in H. Zehr and B. Toews (eds) *Critical Issues in Restorative Justice*. Monsey, NY: Criminal Justice Press, and Cullompton: Willan Publishing.

Teitel, R. (2000) *Transitional Justice*. Oxford: Oxford University Press.

Thomas, C. A. (2004) 'At Hell's gate: a soldier's journey from war to peace', *The Sun*, October, 12–19.

Van Ness, D. and Strong, K. (2002) *Restoring Justice* (2nd edn). Cincinnati, OH: Anderson.

Walgrave, L. (2002) 'Restorative justice and the law: socio-ethical and juridical foundations for a systemic approach', in L. Walgrave (ed.) *Restorative Justice and the Law*. Cullompton: Willan Publishing.

Walgrave, L. (2004) 'Has restorative justice appropriately responded to retribution theory and impulses?', in H. Zehr and B. Toews (eds) *Critical Issues in Restorative Justice*. Monsey, NY: Criminal Justice Press, and Cullompton: Willan Publishing.

Walker, N. (1991) *Why Punish?* Oxford: Oxford University Press.

Weitekamp, E. (1999) 'The history of restorative justice', in G. Bazemore and L. Walgrave (eds) *Restorative Juvenile Justice: Repairing the Harm of Youth Crime*. Monsey, NY: Criminal Justice Press.

Wright, M. (2003) 'Is it time to question the concept of punishment?', in L. Walgrave (ed.) *Repositioning Restorative Justice*. Cullompton: Willan Publishing.

Wright, M. and Masters, G. (2002) 'Justified criticism, misunderstanding, or important steps on the road to acceptance?', in E. Weitekamp and H. Kerner (eds) *Restorative Justice: Theoretical Foundations*. Cullompton: Willan Publishing.

Zehr, H. (1990) *Changing Lenses: A New Focus for Crime and Justice*. Scottsdale, PA: Herald Press.

Zehr, H. (2002) *The Little Book of Restorative Justice*. Intercourse, PA: Good Books.

Zehr, H. (2003) 'Retributive justice, restorative justice', in G. Johnstone (ed.) *A Restorative Justice Reader: Texts, Sources, Context*. Cullompton: Willan Publishing.

Zehr, H. and Toews, B. (2004) 'Introduction to Part VI', in H. Zehr and B. Toews (eds) *Critical Issues in Restorative Justice*. Monsey, NY: Criminal Justice Press, and Cullompton: Willan Publishing.

Chapter 3

The ideas of engagement and empowerment

Jennifer Larson Sawin and Howard Zehr

From the earliest days of the restorative justice movement, advocates have criticized conventional criminal justice, especially as practised in Western societies, for its failure to engage and empower those most directly affected by crime. Indeed, it was argued, those affected by a crime were often excluded almost entirely from the criminal justice process, an exclusion which had very damaging results. Restorative justice emerged, then, as an effort to engage more fully and empower those involved in or affected by criminal wrongdoing.

In recent years, restorative justice has found applications in many arenas including schools, the workplace, even situations of mass violence. However, since its origins were in the criminal justice arena and the restorative justice field is most developed there, the following discussion will focus primarily on the concepts of engagement and empowerment within criminal justice.

Engagement and empowerment: the principles

Origins

The following story is well known in the field of restorative justice.[1] In 1974, in the town of Elmira in the Canadian province of Ontario, two young men pleaded guilty to 22 counts of willful damage, following a drunken Saturday night vandalism spree. Prior to their sentencing, two probation workers, Mark Yantzi and Dave Worth, had been mulling over more creative responses to crime in that town. At some risk to his reputation as a probation officer, Yantzi (who had been assigned to prepare pre-sentence reports for the young men) made a suggestion to the judge that had no basis in law: that it might be valuable for the two young men to meet personally with the victims of their several offences.

One might imagine the judge's reaction. Indeed, the judge's initial response was that he did not think it was possible for him to ask the offenders to do this. But something about this idea must have caught the judge's attention because he was eventually persuaded and ordered a one-month remand to enable the pair to meet the victims and assess their losses, with the assistance of Dave Worth and Mark Yantzi. The two offenders subsequently visited and spoke to all but one of their victims (one had moved) and discovered that they had caused over $2,000 damage, of which half had been recovered through insurance policies. The judge then fined each offender $200 and placed them on probation, with one of the conditions being that they make restitution to their victims. Within a few months of sentencing, the two young men had revisited their victims and had made restitution accordingly.

Strictly speaking, the facilitated encounter approach in this story represents only one expression of restorative justice principles in practice. Moreover, one might point to a number of roots of restorative justice principles and practice; many claim, for example, that the origins of restorative justice are located in indigenous traditions.[2] However, we place the narrative here because it did play a prominent role in the emergence of restorative justice as a field, and it is an illustrative case study of the two restorative principles of engagement and empowerment.

Stakeholders

Nils Christie, a Norwegian criminologist who influenced many early restorative justice theorists, famously describes conflict as property (1977). Christie argues that lawyers and other professionals in our justice system 'steal' the property of conflict and its aftermath from those to whom it should rightly belong. This view of conflict provides an important theoretical basis for the argument that individuals and communities need to be more fully engaged and empowered in justice.

However, in order to discuss engagement and empowerment, we must first introduce the subjects, or *who* is being (dis)engaged and (dis)empowered in any story of justice. The field of restorative justice has adopted the term 'stakeholder' to describe the parties who have been most affected by wrongdoing. It tends to distinguish 'direct' stakeholders – the victim and offender – from 'indirect' stakeholders, such as family members and friends of each, the surrounding community or even members of the judicial system who are drawn into the event by some relationship to the victim and offender. It may be helpful to think of the stakeholder positions as emerging in concentric rings from the pivotal event of wrongdoing that lies at the centre.

If we return to the story from Elmira, direct stakeholders would include victims of the vandalism whose personal property had been destroyed. Of course, the two young men who had offended are also direct stakeholders in that they were personally responsible for the vandalism that took place. Indirect stakeholders in this event may have been family members and perhaps friends of the victims and offenders, and more official figures such as a community youth worker, a sports coach, a schoolteacher, the presiding judge, lawyers for the accused men and an arresting officer. Some have called certain members of this latter group the 'community of care' (McCold and Wachtel 1998), a term that emerged as restorative justice practitioners and theorists sought to identify the appropriate people to include in a restorative conferencing process. This 'community of care' or 'micro-community' is distinguished, by McCold and Wachtel, from the larger community of citizens indirectly affected by the crime (the 'macro-community').

Although early proponents of restorative justice saw it as a way of returning conflicts to the community, the initial practice of restorative justice in the USA tended to engage primarily the victims, offenders and facilitators. Some limited provision was made for involvement of communities of care, especially family members, but the macro-community was supposedly represented by the presence of volunteer facilitators and community-based organizations. Subsequently, new restorative approaches, such as family group conferencing and peace-making circles, emerged, which made more explicit provision for participation by both micro- and macro-community members (Zehr 1990: 256–62).

The Western legal system

Restorative justice advocates have argued not only that the various stakeholders need to be engaged and empowered, but also that the Western criminal justice disengages and disempowers them. The book *Changing Lenses* (Zehr, 1990) was among a group of early reflections on this phenomenon of restorative justice.[3] In this widely cited text, Howard Zehr (co-author of this chapter) sets forth a 'new focus for crime and justice' and invites readers to consider restorative measures rather than retributive ones. He proposes that the current justice paradigm (at least in the West) is preoccupied with identifying the wrongdoer, affixing blame and dispensing an appropriate punishment or pain to the offender.[4] The system, as any organized activity, engages specific people in the pursuit of justice. Police officers are employed to investigate crime, apprehend wrongdoers, interview witnesses, collect evidence and so on. In the trial phase – affixing blame – prosecutors assume the role of victim and craft a case to present the evidence linking the accused to the particular crime. Other lawyers will speak on behalf of the accused and defend them against the charges brought. Crime victims may be invited to testify if the prosecution believes that their testimony will assist the prosecution case. A judge or jury will hear both sides of the story during the trial. If the offender is found guilty, a sentence proceeding will dictate a proportional punishment of prison time, community service, probation or a fine.

In this generalized scenario of criminal wrongdoing, one might ask, '*Who* is engaged?' as well as '*How* are they engaged?' Certainly members of the justice system serve a prominent role in the process, from the first arresting police officer to the probation officer. The offender will appear marginally and will rarely speak on his or her own behalf, unless called to testify. The views of offenders, and the story they would tell about the particular wrongdoing or crime, are almost always filtered by legal professionals through the vocabulary of law and the grammar of relevant statutes. Representation by proxy is the standard, and those who decline counsel and choose to act in their own defence are deemed unwise. The focus of the process is on establishing guilt, and the state has the burden of proof. Moreover, the concept of guilt is highly technical. For these reasons, offenders are often inclined to deny responsibility and the degree of engagement is usually passive or oppositional.

Most glaringly absent from this process are the victims. Since the state is declared the victim in criminal cases, victims are often almost entirely excluded from the process except when needed for testimony. Victim impact statements in some jurisdictions do allow input. However, victims generally are unable to control – and indeed are not informed about – the use to which their statement will be put. More generally, there tends to be a lack of clarity about the relevance of victim impact statements in a process oriented towards retributive justice. Due to the success of the victims' rights/services movement in the past decades (especially in the USA and the UK), victims have been able to obtain increased information, services and rights in many areas. Nevertheless, the fundamental definition of crime – an offence against the state – continues to limit meaningful involvement of victims.

In addition, it is the exception rather than the rule that the community is meaningfully involved in the justice process. While the state occasionally sends a message to the community about a wrongdoing, typically through the media in periodic press statements on progress of the case or rationales for pressing charges, the community rarely has the opportunity to participate directly in the justice-seeking deliberations.

The question of who is engaged in a justice event points to the deeper, sometimes more unsettling, question: 'Whose interests and needs are valued in the process of seeking justice?' If one reviews the above scenario, it is clear from the number of state representatives present that the state interest is paramount. As the ostensible custodian of social order, the state's duty is to denounce the wrong, ensure that the offender receives the 'hard treatment' he or she deserves and take steps to assure that no further harm will be committed. The state carries out this duty by discovering the source of wrongdoing (the offender), condemning the act and extracting assurances that the offences will desist, either through imprisonment, monitoring, treatment or reform. Much of this is done in the name of the larger or macro-community, but rarely is the community actually consulted or involved in any meaningful way.[5] Moreover, the reality that the individual victims are sidelined indicates that their needs and roles have not found a comfortable place in the architecture of justice.

It would seem reasonable to assume that those most affected by wrongdoing should be the ones engaged and empowered to assist in seeking justice; indeed, the restorative justice field has argued that engagement is crucial to meeting the needs of both victims and offenders and to holding offenders accountable. As we have seen of the current justice system, those who have been directly harmed are excluded. As a result, many people – victims in particular – find some of our justice forms and processes bewildering. For instance, with regard to the legal practice of designating criminal cases as 'The Queen versus [the offender]', one Canadian victim's strong reaction was: 'The charges were pressed in the name of the Queen, her Crown and dignity, and I was just a witness. I didn't like that bullshit – this happened to me. It didn't happen to the fucking Queen!' (Zehr 2001: 144).[6] On the other hand, many victims say that if they are included at all in the justice system, they typically experience further harm and disempowerment. Judith Lewis Herman, a specialist in the field of trauma, writes: 'If one set out to design a system for provoking intrusive post-traumatic symptoms, one could not do better than a court of law' (1992: 72).

Yet restorative justice advocates argue that some of the victims' most critical needs cannot be met without genuine engagement and empowerment; these include the need to tell one's story and to obtain authentic information related to the case. A victim may wish to know: why was my loved one hurt? What were his or her final words? Where are the items that were stolen from me? Why were we specifically targeted? Such questions as well as their need for assurance of safety are not particularly relevant to the finding of guilt in a courtroom. They may want to ask: is my home safe now? Who will be on the lookout for my well-being? Besides these practical and physical concerns, one aspect of trauma of crime is that the offence and the offender take away power over one's emotional life. A critical need, then, is for an experience of empowerment.

At least in principle, offenders do have their legal interests represented in that a lawyer may defend them against the case presented by the prosecution. However, offenders will usually lack the power or the encouragement to take full responsibility for their wrongdoing, even if they wish to. While there may be an opportunity to enter a formal plea of no contest or guilt, there is rarely a place or time to apologize meaningfully and there are few mechanisms to make direct amends to the victims. As defined by restorative justice, accountability would encourage offenders to develop understanding of their offence and empathy for the victim, and then take active steps to right the wrong, symbolically or practically. In fact, some argue that real accountability would encourage offenders to have some responsibility in deciding what is needed as an adequate outcome. Clearly the Western legal system does not leave much room for such gestures.

Finally, the absence of an assigned place for the community, both micro- and macro-, in justice proceedings means that it also lacks a full measure of power to serve the victim and offender, to find reassurances of its own well-being or to explore the social and moral issues highlighted by the situation. Of course civic-minded individuals in the community may come to the aid of both victim and offender in significant ways. Neighbourhood Watch programmes can extend a helping hand to someone who has been robbed. A prison ministry may assign a pastor to visit the offender. These moves are important indications of a resilient community where connections between people are valued and cultivated. Yet only in the most exceptional cases is there a place for systematic or institutionalized responses by either micro- or macro-communities to victims and offenders after wrongdoing.

Use of terms

When early theorists began outlining restorative justice, one of the major assertions was that this field would be rooted in principled values rather than strict rules. While the precise list of those values shifts slightly from one theorist or practitioner to the next, engagement and empowerment appear consistently. But what exactly is intended by these terms?

We will begin by mentioning a few basic assumptions in the field. Ted Wachtel proposes that restorative justice is characterized by 'doing things *with* people rather than *to* them or *for* them' (2004). The different prepositions here are critical and allude to collaboration, which requires engagement, and to meaningful contribution, which requires empowerment. In addition, restorative justice theorists would say that that crime – even wrongdoing in general – is a rupture of relationships more than a transgression of law. Those relationships may be extremely close (e.g. between a mother and daughter), somewhat tenuous (e.g. between neighbours) or barely existent (strangers passing on a street). Regardless, those committing the wrong and those harmed by that wrongdoing are the central figures. This view of crime is the starting place for deciding who is engaged and empowered in the wake of wrongdoing and hurt.

What is meant?

While the term 'engagement' is used occasionally in restorative justice literature, the more prevalent, but perhaps less active, bywords have been 'inclusion' or 'involvement'. In societies governed by democratic principles, a basic ethical precept of decision-making is to include in the decision process those who will be most directly affected by it. This principle applies as much to political democracy as to community development and environmental policy. One author in the related field of group facilitation eloquently argues that:

> [I]nclusive solutions are wise solutions. Their wisdom emerges from the integration of everybody's perspectives and needs. These are solutions whose range and vision is expanded to take advantage of the truth held not only by the quick, the articulate, the most powerful and influential, but also of the truth held by the slower thinkers, the shy, the disenfranchised and the weak. As the Quakers say, 'Everybody has a piece of the truth' (Kaner *et al.* 1996: 24).

When it comes to harm in a criminal sense, those most directly affected are victim, the offender and those who care about them. Restorative justice practitioners and theorists argue these parties need to be included in seeking justice. Gordon Bazemore (2000) defines restorative justice as addressing 'all acts related to repairing harm' through a process in which stakeholders are provided the opportunity for active involvement as fully and as often as possible (Bazemore also credits Van Ness and Strong 1997). In this version, he places emphasis on the term 'opportunity' while acknowledging that in some cases not all stakeholders wish or are able to engage in a restorative process (Bazemore 2000: 468).

While most will agree on the principle of engagement, there has been considerably more debate in the field over the term 'empowerment'. In *The Promise of Mediation*, Robert Bush and Joseph Folger write: 'In simplest terms, empowerment means the restoration to individuals of a sense of their own value and strength and their own capacity to handle life's problems' (1994: 2). This definition emerges from the field of mediation and some connotations may not fully apply in restorative justice settings. For example, some crime victims may take umbrage at the presumption that after a particularly traumatic event they should be expected to 'handle life's problems' as they used to. Indeed, the return to a sense of power and control over one's own life may be a long time coming. That achievement is, by and large, an intensely personal journey that takes years for some, and never happens for others. Yet a victim's sense of personal disempowerment, related to the harm and its aftermath, should be the very reason that the process of justice should seek to restore power to the victim. In that respect, the definition by Bush and Folger is helpful. For offenders, many would find it easier to assume responsibility to make things right if they are given a range of options – even if they are limited – rather than being forced down one predetermined path by an external actor.

What is not meant?

To expand the definitions, it may be helpful to delineate what these words do *not* mean in the field of restorative justice.

Engagement does not require that everyone, no matter what the association, should be involved in a restorative justice process. For instance, some in the restorative justice movement find problematic the growing tendency to invite into the process a range of people who are not obviously affected stakeholders. This, they suggest, can have harmful consequences: the process stalls because there are too many decision-makers; the case becomes so high profile that the parties become unwitting poster-children for larger groups of people; the autonomy of the central players is eroded; and the needs of the central figures are not given adequate consideration. While participation by affected people is fruitful, engagement without any criteria or responsibility can be problematic.

Engagement does not necessarily mean a face-to-face encounter between victim and offender. While some may choose this method of engaging the other party, typically after a good deal of preparation, it can be emotionally or practically difficult especially in serious offences. There are meaningful ways outside a personal meeting that offenders and victims can engage with one another and their respective communities of care. Letters, video conferencing, shuttle representation and telephone calls are all varieties of engagement that can meet the needs of the various stakeholders and lead to empowerment. Where an offender is not identified or apprehended, or where a victim may decline to meet with an offender, surrogate arrangements can prove to be restorative forms of engagement. Whether or not any kind of direct or indirect encounter is involved, however, restorative justice assumes that all parties should be provided an opportunity to be engaged and empowered in defining and meeting their own needs, roles and responsibilities.

Even Bush and Folger, who were among the first to take hold of the term empowerment in the context of victims and offenders, admit that the term can be cloudy because of its broad usage. They assert that empowerment does *not* mean that an external actor (such as a facilitator) should mysteriously balance, add to or redistribute power; neither does empowerment mean that the facilitator should control or influence the empowerment process (1994: 95–6). On the contrary, the most rewarding restorative justice processes spur individuals and their communities of care to draw upon *their own resources* to reflect on the wrongdoing, the hurt caused, the obligations created and the ways to meet needs.

One feminist voice, Stephanie Riger (1993), has suggested that the term empowerment is fundamentally problematic. She argues, among other things, that the empowerment concept favours individual actors who strive against one another for self-interest over communal actors who seek co-operation. This arrangement may suit Western cultures that value individualism over collectivism but may be undesirable in cultures where family, religious or ethnic values supersede those of any one person. She also argues that in community facilitation and related fields, the *sense* of empowerment rather than *actual* power is sought and valued. The danger with this discrepancy is that people can be lulled into the illusion of power over self or process and that the structural 'status quo may actually be supported' (p.2). The sorts of questions she prompts include: is the practice of victim–offender mediation in prisons truly empowering to the participants when the punitive prison structure goes unexamined, and when the courts are reluctant to hear the story of the victim? Are we truly empowering people if we do not address the unequal distribution of power in the larger society? Are we in fact perpetuating a larger pattern of structural injustice?

Kay Pranis also addresses some of these issues (2001: 301). She argues that, while the restorative justice movement does have a radical vision of structural change, it cannot by itself correct the troubling power inequities in society. She suggests, however, that restorative justice practitioners can operate in two meaningful ways: on a micro level by bridging social distance, affirming mutual responsibility and helping to level power dynamics; and on a macro level by providing a well tried model for transforming relationships and power across multiple systems and structures. In summary, she links these two levels of activity with the oft-quoted dictum 'think global, act local'.[7]

Working definitions

For the purposes of this chapter, we assume the following definitions: engagement is the voluntary participation of stakeholders in deciding what happens in the wake of wrongdoing and hurt; and empowerment is not only the power to participate but also the ability to draw upon needed resources to make a decision and to follow through on that decision.

Engagement and empowerment: the challenges

We now turn to look at some of the real-world challenges of truly engaging and empowering stakeholders.[8]

Victims

Studies of victim attitudes towards and satisfaction with restorative justice have generally been quite positive. However, with the proliferation of programmes promoting restorative justice, there has been simultaneous criticism, especially in the USA and UK, that the claim of increased victim engagement and empowerment has too often been in name only. A variety of forces are seen to contribute to that failure. These include the offender-centred focus of the justice system; the offender-advocacy backgrounds of many restorative justice practitioners; the unwillingness of practitioners to take seriously the worries and concerns of victims and victim advocates; and the failure to include victim voices in the development and oversight of programmes (Achilles 2004). Victim advocates have also criticized restorative justice programmes for only serving (thus empowering and engaging) victims when offenders have been caught and when offenders are willing to participate; this amounts to a form of offender centredness and victim exclusion (Herman 2004).

Mary Achilles, a state-level victim advocate from Pennsylvania, argues that some programmes have been designed on the assumption that 'one size fits all', that victim voices have too often been excluded from the design and evaluation of programmes, and that victims are engaged only to the extent that they can serve or rehabilitate offenders (Achilles and Zehr 2001: 94). With such warnings in mind, Achilles suggests that any restorative justice process that genuinely seeks to engage and empower victims should do the following:

- Provide victim representation on governing bodies and initial planning committees.
- Ensure that the safety of victims is a fundamental element of programme design.
- View victims and their needs as critical; victims are not expected to aid or rehabilitate the offender unless they so choose.
- Inform victims at every step of the process, offering as much information as possible.
- Protect the level of privacy sought by the victims.
- Offer the widest possible range of choices with flexibility in process and outcome as well as referrals where needed.
- Find ways to engage victims even when offenders are not apprehended or identified.

For some years after restorative justice practice emerged, there was anecdotal but increasing evidence that victims and their supporters were feeling excluded from and disempowered in the expression of this concept and practice. In 1999, a group of researchers and advocates in the USA sought to explore this evidence further. A 'listening project' was designed and carried out in seven states during 1999–2000; its main goals were to 'confront the significant deficiencies of restorative justice practice pertaining to victim participation and impacts for victims, their advocates and victim services generally' (Mika *et al.*, 2002: 3). The research did indeed identify serious concerns among the victim services community around the engagement and empowerment of victims. However, it also identified significant areas of promise and suggested remedies to be taken by both the restorative justice and victim services field in the USA.

Offenders

As noted earlier, from the beginning, a key element of restorative justice was an understanding of accountability that engaged and empowered offenders. However, critics have noted that this was a very constrained understanding of these terms. Moreover, they suggest, the field has focused too exclusively on accountability, neglecting other offender needs, such as their needs to come to grips with their own sense of victimization and their needs for personal growth. What does a restorative approach have to say to such needs, and how do engagement and empowerment fit in?

While there is wide agreement that participation by victims in restorative processes must be voluntary, there has been significant debate as to whether offenders might be coerced to participate. Some programmes claim that the process of engagement is purely voluntary, but this claim is hard to maintain when, for example, a victim–offender conference is being offered as a potential alternative to prosecution or another sentence. The appropriateness, limits and dangers of coercion remain an ongoing issue in the field.

Based on their work with prisoners and ex-prisoners, long-time restorative justice practitioners Jackie Katounas (herself an ex-offender) and Barb Toews have raised significant questions about whether restorative justice has truly been as sensitive as it should to offenders and their perspectives. For instance, they have heard offenders ask: 'If restorative justice is about accountability and empowerment, what can I do when I am not permitted to take any initiative to make amends – e.g. by initiating a victim–offender encounter?' (Most states in the USA require victim-initiated inquiries, even if offenders have interest in meeting their victims.) Similarly, 'If restorative justice is about understanding the crime and people's needs for justice, why am I supposed to understand the victim and community perspectives when my own experiences, needs and perspectives are ignored or minimized'(Toews and Katounas 2004: 115)? They conclude that if offenders are not engaged and empowered in these ways, restorative justice is at risk of becoming an activity 'done to' offenders rather than done with them, ironically duplicating the punitive and retributive measures of the current justice system that it sought to correct. To address this concern, Toews conducted a series of focus groups and seminars in prison and developed a new study book on restorative justice for prisoners that seeks to begin with their concerns and worldviews (Toews 2006).

Community

Most restorative justice advocates see some role for the community in the process. However, there have been heated debates within the field about the definition of community, the actual role of community, and approaches for actually engaging and empowering the community.

For example, Paul McCold outlines the dangers of an ill-defined community in restorative justice (2004). Some approaches would engage and empower the 'community of care' or 'the networks of obligation and respect between an individual [victim or offender] and those who care about him or her the most'. However, he warns that a community justice model could define community as 'local hierarchical formations, structured upon lines of power, dominance, and authority' (p.19). While McCold does not disparage the relevance and appropriate use of such community justice practices in addressing crime and wrongdoing, he urges practitioners to be clear about the underlying theory, definitions and values because these will spring forth the design and implementation of practice itself.

Other criticism is levelled at the too-rosy views of community in restorative justice. Robert Weisberg has written a critical inquiry on the use of the word 'community' and its engagement in the field of restorative justice (2003). He wonders, for example, to what extent the 'sunny harmonious sound' of the term is used to mask more difficult legal and social issues (p.343) as well as the often-fractured views that may exist within a seemingly monolithic and homogeneous group. George Pavlich also warns that advocates of community engagement should be wary of 'totalitarianism [where] rigid formulations of community create simulated divisions that isolate insiders from outsiders' (2004: 174). The danger of such a course, he suggests, is that insiders will feel no obligation or responsibility to engage with those who are considered outsiders. A related question concerns how restorative justice can guard against the possible excesses of community, such as vigilantism.

Still others have been concerned about engaging and empowering the community when its condition is not healthy. First Nation women in Canada, for example, have worried that involving a hierarchical, patriarchal community may only perpetuate or deepen patterns of abuse (Cayley 1998: 119–214). However, others have argued – and case examples such as the Hollow Water community in Canada illustrate – that properly engaged and empowered, restorative processes can lead to healing of communities as well as individuals (Ross 1996; Pranis 2001).

Another debate is around community empowerment and the extent to which it overlaps with concerns about victims. The concern here is that, as the circle of participation grows, and as restorative processes come to be promoted as participatory democracy, the empowerment of the broader community might be pursued at the expense of individual victims, who will be sidelined yet again.

The state

Most theorists in restorative justice would probably admit to a community-centred, or at least a state-decentralized, bias. After all, the state is primarily responsible for the alienation of victim and offender from each other, the separation of the offender from the community in cases of incarceration, and the failure to meet the needs of participants after an offence is committed. In addition, the state also represents the traditional seat of coercive power. Yet Susan Herman argues that the state plays a critical role in marshalling resources. If engaged, the state can meet victim and offender needs, sometimes quite long term, that are sometimes beyond the ability of community to meet: day-care, employment counselling, substance abuse treatment, housing (2004: 78). Herman also asserts that whether ideal or not, the state is in the position of speaking on behalf of society at large. State representatives can be engaged to raise wrongdoing to public awareness, to assure society that the offending action was in breach of a social contract and to acknowledge the hurt of the victim.

Vernon Jantzi (2004: 189) agrees, pointing to New Zealand as the exemplar of a state engaging as the enabler of communities that are empowered, within a formal legal framework, to take responsibility for local wrongdoing. He adds that the state can also engage as resourcer and guarantor of practice standards. In New Zealand, a police officer as a state representative is present in family group conferencing (FGCs) that are now standard practice in the national juvenile justice system. Allan MacRae, manager of FGC Co-ordinators for the Southern Region of New Zealand, explains police engagement this way: 'The FGC process empowers the police to seek appropriate outcomes. They gain ... information about the community which they police [and] build a closer and more effective relationship with youth, their families, and their community' (MacRae and Zehr 2004: 70).

There are some who would dispute the engagement of police in any justice proceeding that purports to be restorative. This would be especially true in contexts where the state has occupied a controversial position in the administration of impartial justice. South Africa and Northern Ireland are the classic examples of this phenomenon. Kieran McEvoy, Professor of Law and Transitional Justice at Queens University in Belfast, believes with co-author Harry Mika that while the state and community restorative justice schemes may eventually merge their respective efforts, a police officer's company – and perhaps the presence of any state representative – would be too coercive in some community-based restorative justice efforts today. The most important aspect of empowerment is that people should 'take control over the *steering* of their own lives without programmes being swallowed up by the state infrastructure' (2002: 556, emphasis in original).

Along a similar line, others would see that the state serves an important, if somewhat passive, function of background coercion with offenders. The mere existence of more retributive measures such as possible incarceration may encourage offenders to engage in restorative processes and help to monitor the follow-through. Braithwaite writes, 'Very few criminal offenders who participate in restorative justice processes would be sitting in the room absent a certain amount of coercion ... No coercion, no restorative justice (in most cases)' (2002: 34). The trick, he later argues, is to keep the explicit threat of formal state-imposed punitive measures – what he terms 'the Sword of Damocles' (p.119) – firmly in the background and never the foreground.

Otherwise, the process may backfire and put the stakeholders in further danger of hurt and failure. McCold agrees that in addition to existing as a less desirable option for offenders, state authority may be invoked when 'the offense is deemed too serious for an informal voluntary response alone' (2000: 394).

Most restorative justice theorists agree that the state has some role and stake in restorative justice. In societies that experience the luxury of the rule of law and a relatively corruption-free environment, many would see the state role as central. Van Ness argues that while it is the community's role to make peace, it is the state's responsibility to maintain order (1989: 20). A crucial role for the state, it might then be argued, is to be engaged as a safeguard and backup for the restorative process, ensuring due process, seeing to it that those responsible for wrongdoing are brought to justice. The design of New Zealand's youth justice system, for example, has most serious offences going to a restorative conference, but with youth court there to ensure it happens and to make decisions that cannot be made in the conference (MacRae and Zehr 2004).

Facilitators

Restorative justice literature has long emphasized who is *being* empowered or engaged. But it has not shed as much light on who is *doing* the empowering or engaging in any given restorative justice event – although early efforts saw the facilitator playing a key role as representative of the community. For some, it seems that the facilitator is erased, perhaps due to Christie's early challenge: 'Let's have as few experts as we dare' (1977: 12). Certainly, use of a talking piece[9] in circle processes would place the facilitator in a less prominent role. Yet the power of invitation, the time spent in preparing and the ability to set the scene all shape the extent to which other stakeholders are engaged and empowered. Most argue that 'encounter forms' of restorative justice require a trained facilitator operating under clear guidelines or principles; debate persists, however, on what those guidelines might be, and how rigidly to adhere to them.[10] As practices become more widespread and on a larger scale, however, the use of professional facilitators is growing, leading to some question as to whether they can adequately represent the community and still remain true to the empowering and engaging spirit of restorative justice. A related concern is whether professionals from allied professions such as law will co-opt the practice as has happened so often in the mediation field (Auerbach 1983).

Kay Pranis has reflected on the relationship between story-telling and empowerment: 'Listening to someone's story is a way of empowering them, of validating their intrinsic worth as a human being' (1998: 23). In any restorative process, the accomplished facilitator would serve a critical role by engaging the victim, offender and loved ones, and inviting each party to articulate a life story, or the story of the wrongdoing itself, in order to assess the impact of the wrongdoing and the needs made plain from that event. If Pranis's assertion holds true, then the very opportunity to be *listened to* might begin to empower the parties and propel them towards healing. Braithwaite offers the example in a nursing home context: 'Wheeling the bed of that ... resident into a room full of fairly important people who listen attentively to her stories of neglect is extraordinarily empowering' (2003: 166). Thus, it can be asserted that the facilitator is a pivotal stakeholder who cultivates the safety and space to engage people in the hearing and telling of stories.

Frontier issues

The preceding sections have provided a sample of some of the concerns and challenges that have emerged in the field around the issue of engagement and empowerment in theory and practice. There is another cluster of issues that we call 'frontier issues' – new areas where the field needs to expand and develop.

Cultural adaptation of restorative justice practice is one theme that looms large. In most settings, relatively little has been done to examine the cultural assumptions that underlie the theory and practice of restorative justice (Jenkins 2004), or to study systematically what forms of empowerment and engagement are appropriate or inappropriate in various cultural settings. In a study of how the Indo-Canadian community interacted with Western victim–offender mediation practice, Bruce Grant (2004) found that there is significant resonance between the traditional processes and victim–offender mediation, but significant modifications are needed in how the encounter is carried out. He examines not only the cultural variations of victim–offender mediation practice that are necessitated for intra-group use (i.e. *within* the Indo-Canadian community) but also intergroup use (i.e. when processes involve more than one culture). New Zealand's statute establishing the youth justice system is unusual in recognizing cultural customization; it mandates that facilitators of conferences work with the parties involved to ensure that the process is culturally appropriate for them (MacRae and Zehr 2004). In some situations, adaptations may require the use of substitute participants or even rule out direct encounter altogether. In many cases in that setting, empowerment and engagement will also require culturally specific rituals to be part of the process.

After the restorative justice concept was used to help shape (or at least explain in retrospect) South Africa's Truth and Reconciliation Commission (TRC), some have begun to debate whether restorative justice might be a framework for informing a justice response to other societal-level wrongdoing and conflict. In the USA, for example, the Greensboro (North Carolina) Massacre of 1979[11] spurred many to work towards restorative justice through a regional TRC modelled explicitly after South Africa. But questions of engagement and empowerment linger. On this scale, with the passage of time, under such public scrutiny, and when so many sectors of society are required for buy-in, how is full engagement by all affected parties possible? How can each party be empowered in a tragedy claimed by so many people? These are but a few of the frontier issues facing restorative justice as it enters into its fourth decade as a field of practice and theory.

Conclusion

Victim–offender encounter processes have often been seen as the primary way to provide opportunities for engagement and opportunities. However, the conceptual framework of restorative justice assumes that these principles should guide the search for justice from the start and throughout – regardless of whether an offender is identified, whether the victim is willing to participate or whether an encounter is possible or appropriate. Zehr has argued, for example, that restorative justice is essentially a set of 'guiding questions' to inform the real-world search for just solutions. The last two of these questions centre on engagement and empowerment: who has a stake in this situation? What is the appropriate process to involve stakeholders in an effort to put things right?

Although significant conceptual and practical issues remain to be resolved, the intertwined concepts of engagement and empowerment have been central in the field since its origins. They remain fundamental to the theory and practice of restorative justice.

Selected further reading

Braithwaite, J. (1989) *Crime, Shame and Reintegration*. New York, NY: Cambridge University Press. In one of the early texts in the field, Braithwaite explores theories on the reasons why people commit crimes. As a way to engage the offender in constructive ways, the author proposes a process of 'reintegrative shaming' (versus stigmatizing shaming), whereby loved ones express social disapproval to the offender for his or her behaviour.

Pranis, K., Stuart, B. and Wedge, M. (2003) *Peacemaking Circles: From Crime to Community*. St Paul, MN: Living Justice Press. Drawing from Native American and other indigenous traditions, the authors outline the peace-making circle – a process that engages and empowers those who have assembled to deliberate on a specific issue or event. Used in communities, schools and correctional settings, the circle calls upon the community's ability to prevent wrongdoing, seek underlying causes and begin healing.

Ross, R. (1996) *Returning to the Teachings: Exploring Aboriginal Justice*. Toronto: Penguin Books. In first-person narrative, Ross details his exploration of 'peace-maker justice' in aboriginal communities of Canada. While the text does not deal explicitly with restorative justice, it does outline the values and vision that give rise to a justice system that has the power to promote healing and respect.

Zehr, H. (1990 and 2005) *Changing Lenses: A New Focus for Crime and Justice*. Scottdale, PA: Herald Press. In this text, one of the first to outline the theoretical framework of restorative justice, Zehr describes our current system as 'retributive justice' and outlines an alternative of 'restorative justice'. While the former sees crime as an offence against the state, the latter views crime as a violation of people and relationships. These two 'lenses' lead to radically different justice responses.

Notes

1   The story is told and analysed in Peachey (1989).

2   Restorative measures in the wake of wrongdoing can be found throughout many cultural practices, especially indigenous forms of justice seeking. See, for example, Rupert Ross (1996) for a review of North American aboriginal justice. A succinct review of restorative-leaning, pre-modern justice and analysis can also be found in Johnstone (2002: ch. 3).

3   See also Van Ness (1986).

4   In his book *Limits to Pain* (1981), Nils Christie uses the term 'pain law' rather than 'penal law' and argues that this legal code is an elaborate mechanism for administering 'just' doses of pain.

5   One might argue that, by political design, democratically elected candidates put forth a criminal justice platform for public consideration (the 'Three Strikes' policy in California is one controversial example). Candidates are then elected into or out of office depending on the public's satisfaction with those policies and the public is thereby 'engaged' in justice proceedings. Yet these policies are written by a small subset of the public, remain relatively abstract, rarely invite genuine community input and do not adequately flex to address specific circumstances of each case. Moreover, the dialogue on these issues is often on a highly symbolic level, usually framed by political and media agendas.

6   Restorative justice advocates generally acknowledge an important role for the government in making sure the needs of the larger community are represented. They argue, however, that this public dimension has overwhelmed the 'private' dimension, and call for a better balance of the two.

7   For more on these dynamics, with an emphasis on practitioner training in structural matters, see Dyck (2000).

8   For a more complete discussion of these issues, see Zehr and Toews (2004).

9   Talking pieces emerge from indigenous traditions where a group, usually seated in a circle, convenes to discuss a matter relevant to the community. The talking piece is passed around the circle, each person speaking only when in possession of the piece. The group is encouraged to speak and listen from the heart and each participant voice is weighed equally.

10 For example, Ross has questioned whether the aboriginal figure of the 'elder' is the ideal figure to assume the role of judge (1996: 223). In addition, while some advocate a scripted proceeding with a trained facilitator (the Real Justice group conferencing model, found at www.realjustice.org/Pages/script.html), most others (including New Zealand's family group conferencing; see MacRae and Zehr 2004) would pursue a less regimented conversation.

11 On the morning of 3 November 1979, a group of organized labour advocates gathered to march in downtown Greensboro against the Ku Klux Klan and Nazi sympathizers. Police were accused of abandoning security measures over a lunchbreak during which KKK and Nazi groups allegedly shot and killed five marchers and injured ten. There were no convictions by all-white juries and the tragedy has shaped much of the racial divide in North Carolina over the last decades. Greensboro TRC commissioners began to hear testimony in January 2005 but no KKK, Nazi sympathizers or police officers have agreed to testify and the mayor and city council members have disapproved of the largely grassroots-inspired TRC.

References

Achilles, M. (2004) 'Can restorative justice live up to its promise to victims?', in H. Zehr and B. Toews (eds) *Critical Issues in Restorative Justice*. Monsey, NY: Criminal Justice Press.

Achilles, M. and Zehr, H. (2001) 'Restorative justice for crime victims: the promise and the challenge' in G. Bazemore and M. Schiff (eds) *Restorative Community Justice: Repairing Harm and Transforming Communities*. Cincinnati, OH: Anderson Publishing.

Auerbach, J. S. (1983) *Justice Without Law?* New York, NY: Oxford University Press.

Bazemore, G. (2000) 'Rock and roll, restorative justice, and the continuum of the real world: a response to "purism" in operationalizing restorative justice', *Contemporary Justice Review*, 3: 459–77.

Braithwaite, J. (2002) *Restorative Justice and Responsive Regulation*. Oxford: Oxford University Press.

Braithwaite, J. (2003) 'Restorative justice and corporate regulation', in E. Weitekamp and H.-J. Kerner (eds) *Restorative Justice in Context: International Practice and Directions*. Cullompton and Portland, OR: Willan Publishing.

Bush, R.A.B. and Folger, J.P. (1994) *The Promise of Mediation: Responding to Conflict through Empowerment and Recognition*. San Francisco, CA: Jossey-Bass.

Cayley, D. (1998) *The Expanding Prison: The Crisis in Crime and Punishment and the Search for Alternatives*. Canada: House of Anasi Press.

Christie, N. (1977) 'Conflicts as property', *British Journal of Criminology*, 17: 1–15.

Christie, N. (1981) *Limits to Pain*. New York, NY: Columbia University Press.

Dyck, D. (2000) 'Reaching toward a structurally responsive training and practice of restorative justice', *Contemporary Justice Review*, 3: 239–65.

Grant, B.W.C. (2004) 'Adapting Western-based restorative justice models to account for cultural distinctiveness.' Unpublished MA thesis, Conflict Analysis and Management, Royal Roads University, Canada (available at http://www.sfu.ca/crj/fulltext/grant.pdf).

Herman, J. L. (1992) *Trauma and Recovery*. New York, NY: Basic Books.

Herman, S. (2004) 'Is restorative justice possible without a parallel system for victims?', in H. Zehr and B. Toews (eds) *Critical Issues in Restorative Justice*. Monsey, NY: Criminal Justice Press.

Jantzi, V. (2004) 'What is the role of the state in restorative justice?', in H. Zehr and B. Toews (eds) *Critical Issues in Restorative Justice*. Monsey, NY: Criminal Justice Press.

Jenkins, M. (2004) 'How do culture, class and gender affect the practice of restorative justice?', in H. Zehr and B. Toews (eds) *Critical Issues in Restorative Justice*. Monsey, NY: Criminal Justice Press.

Johnstone, G. (2002) *Restorative Justice: Ideas, Values, Debates*. Cullompton: Willan Publishing.

Kaner, S. *et al.* (1996) *Facilitator's Guide to Participatory Decision-making*. Gabriola Island, BC: New Society Publishers/Canada.

MacRae, A. and Zehr, H. (2004) *The Little Book of Family Group Conferences, New Zealand Style: A Hopeful Approach when Youth Cause Harm*. Intercourse, PA: Good Books.

McCold, P. (2000) 'Toward a holistic vision of restorative juvenile justice: a reply to the maximalist model', *Contemporary Justice Review*, 3: 357–414.

McCold, P. (2004) 'Paradigm muddle: the threat to restorative justice posed by its merger with community justice', *Contemporary Justice Review*, 7: 13–35.

McCold, P. and Wachtel, B. (1998) 'Community is not a place: a new look at community justice initiatives', *Contemporary Justice Review*, 1: 71–85.

McEvoy, K. and Mika, H. (2002) 'The critique of informalism in Northern Ireland', *British Journal of Criminology*, 42: 534–62.

Mika, H. *et al.* (2002) *Taking Victims and their Advocates Seriously: A Listening Project.* Akron, PA: Mennonite Central Committee Office on Crime and Justice.

Pavlich, G. (2004) 'What are the dangers as well as the promises of community involvement?' in H. Zehr and B. Toews (eds) *Critical Issues in Restorative Justice.* Monsey, NY: Criminal Justice Press.

Peachey, D. (1989) 'The Kitchener experiment', in M. Wright and B. Galaway (eds) *Mediation and Criminal Justice: Victims, Offenders and Community.* London: Sage.

Pranis, K. (1998) 'Engaging the community in restorative justice'. Paper prepared for the Balanced and Restorative Justice (BARJ) Project, funded by the Office of Juvenile Justice and Delinquency Prevention, US Department of Justice (available at http://2ssw.che.umn.edu/rjp/Resources/Documents/cpra98a.PDF).

Pranis, K. (2001) 'Restorative justice, social justice, and the empowerment of marginalized populations', in G. Bazemore and M. Schiff (eds) *Restorative Community Justice: Repairing Harm and Transforming Communities.* Cincinnati, OH: Anderson Press.

Riger, S. (1993) 'What's wrong with empowerment', *American Journal of Community Psychology*, 21: 279.

Ross, R. (1996) *Returning to the Teachings: Exploring Aboriginal Justice.* Canada: Penguin Books.

Toews, B. (2006) *The Little Book of Restorative Justice for People in Prison: Rebuilding the Web of Relationships.* Intercourse, PA: Good Books.

Toews, B. and Katounas, J. (2004) 'Have offender needs and perspectives been adequately incorporated into RJ?', in H. Zehr and B. Toews (eds) *Critical Issues in Restorative Justice.* Monsey, NY: Criminal Justice Press.

Van Ness, D.W. (1986) *Crime and its Victims.* Downers Grove, IL: InterVarsity Press.

Van Ness, D.W. (1989) 'Pursuing a restorative vision of justice', in P. Arthur (ed.) *Justice: The Restorative Vision. New Perspectives on Crime and Justice.* Akron, PA: Mennonite Central Committee Office of Criminal Justice.

Van Ness, D. W. and Strong, H. (1997) *Restoring Justice.* Cincinnati, OH: Anderson Press.

Wachtel, T. (2004) 'From restorative justice to restorative practices: expanding the paradigm.' Paper presented at the 5th International Conference on Conferencing and Circles, 5–7 August 2004, Vancouver (available at www.realjustice.org/library/bc04_wachtel.html).

Weisberg, R. (2003) 'Restorative justice and the danger of "community"', *Utah Law Review*, 2003: 343–74.

Zehr, H. (1990) *Changing Lenses: A New Focus for Crime and Justice.* Scottdale, PA: Herald Press.

Zehr, H. (2001) *Transcending: Reflections of Crime Victims.* Intercourse, PA: Good Books.

Zehr, H. and Toews, B. (eds) (2004) *Critical Issues in Restorative Justice.* Monsey, NY: Criminal Justice Press.

Chapter 4

Restorative values

Kay Pranis

Introduction

Restorative justice as a field flows back and forth between practice that informs philosophy and philosophy that informs practice. As the weaving of practice and philosophy has developed and the variety of practice has grown, it has become increasingly evident that the movement needs unifying concepts that are flexible enough to encompass new practice possibilities, but clear enough to preclude that which is not restorative. Restorative values are emerging as a unifying concept that grounds theory and guides practice.

My lens

Any discussion of values is framed by the personal orientation of the writer. My first exposure within criminal justice to the core values I see embodied in restorative justice was when I read an article by Kay Harris (1987), about a vision of justice based on feminist principles. Kay identified the following as key tenets of feminism and discussed their importance to issues of justice:

- All human beings have dignity and value.
- Relationships are more important than power.
- The personal is political.

These principles are at the centre of what I understand restorative justice represents. The lens through which I view restorative justice is a lens initially influenced by Kay Harris's writing and my own experience as a community activist and a parent. I believe that the restorative emphasis placed on relationships focuses on more than the single relationship between a person who was harmed and the person who caused the harm – it also includes the larger web of relationships in which they live. Furthermore, the harms important to restorative justice include larger social harms as well as individual harms. Crime is embedded in its community context both in terms of harms and responsibilities, and the relatedness of things always makes underlying causes or contexts relevant. It is possible to influence outcomes deliberately within that relatedness.

Over the past nine years my work has focused increasingly on peace-making circles which began in the justice system as a restorative approach called sentencing circles and gradually migrated to other sectors of the community including schools, neighbourhoods, churches and workplaces. I have been involved in the development of justice circle processes for African American, Hmong American, Latino, Native American and Euro American communities in rural, suburban and urban settings. The peace-making circle process has roots in the talking circle, a process common among indigenous people of North America. Consequently, my perspective has also been heavily influenced by Native American and First Nation teachers who emphasize the interconnectedness of all things and the importance of balance in the mental, physical, emotional and spiritual aspects of human experience.

Writing about values is a challenging task for me – like trying to pin down a slippery watermelon seed. What feels obvious slips away when I try to capture it with words. For example, it is difficult to separate clearly values from principles, ideals and beliefs or assumptions. In the book *Peacemaking Circles: From Crime to Community*, my co-authors and I identify a shift from 'justice as getting even' to 'justice as getting well' suggesting that for us true justice is a process of healing (Pranis *et al.* 2003). Is *healing* a value, a principle, an ideal or is 'true justice is *healing*' a statement of a core belief? Is *healing* an outcome? Perhaps it is all the above. But without trying to resolve these questions, let me offer this: when I speak of restorative *values*, I mean those things that feel deeply important to the essence of the restorative impulse and are carried in the spirit of what we do and how we do it.

In this chapter I will highlight restorative justice values identified by other writers, discuss my own experience with values exploration in trainings and identify the practical contribution of a values foundation to the restorative justice movement.

Values associated with restorative justice

Restorative values might be divided into process values and individual values. Process values address the qualities of the restorative processes themselves. Individual values address qualities the processes should nurture within the participating individuals. These are typically the same characteristics people aspire to when they are at their best. Some values, such as respect, appear in both groups. Some, such as honesty, relate primarily to the individual participants while others, such as inclusion, are relevant to the process. The process values encourage or enable the participants to exhibit the individual values. Both are critical for the transformative outcomes sought in restorative interactions.

Process values

The discussion of restorative values in the literature is primarily about process values – those qualities which should characterize any effort in order for it to be restorative. They are embedded in the underlying philosophy and they guide practice, including the design and implementation of the structure and operation of specific processes. Just as there is no single agreed definition of restorative justice, so there is not a single definitive list of values; rather, people have articulated those essential aspects of restorative justice in a variety of ways:

> 'Restorative practices are those which reflect a concern for such values as *respect*, *inclusion* and *self determination*, *equality*, *truth-telling*, *listening* and *understanding*, *humility*, *responsibility*, *safety*, *renewal* and *reintegration*' (Dyck 2004: 275–6, emphasis added).

> Restorative processes 'give expression to key restorative values, such as *respect*, *honesty*, *humility*, *mutual care*, *accountability* and *trust*. The values of restorative justice are those values that are essential to healthy, equitable and just relationships.' In a subsequent section they identify the 'Core Restorative Justice Values' as *participation*, *respect*, *honesty*, *humility* and *interconnectedness* (Boyack *et al.* 2004: 268–70, emphasis added).

> '*Empathy*, *mutual* *understanding*, *restitution* and *accountability* are guideposts of restorative justice. A high priority is placed on maintaining or restoring *individual dignity*' (Herman 2004: 75, emphasis added).

> '*Fairness*, *truth*, *honesty*, *compassion* and *respect for people* are the basic tenets of an acceptable morality that flows from justice and seeks to protect and enhance the common good' (Consedine 1999: 41, emphasis added).

> Restorative justice is *holistic*, *inclusive* and *affirming of the dignity and worth* of every human being (Judah and Bryant 2004: 5, emphasis added).

> The values of restorative justice 'begin with *respect*, seek *reconciliation* and are based on *love*' (Wonshe 2004: 255, emphasis added).

> At its core restorative justice 'seeks to *meet the needs*, not of some, but *of all* those who find themselves in a situation of harm' (Sullivan and Tifft 2004: 387), emphasis added).

> *Non-domination* is a core value of restorative justice. *Equality* and *community* are corollary values required to support non-domination 'because one can never enjoy assurance against domination by others if one lives in poverty' and 'because assurance against domination must be moored in a strong community that will mobilize collective disapproval against the arbitrary exercise of power' (Braithwaite and Parker 1999: 104, emphasis added).

'*Hospitality* is a guiding value for restorative justice. Hospitality connotes inclusiveness and acceptance and engages the sense of mutual obligation of the host and visitors to be in good relationship without requiring long term connection' (Pavlich 2004: 178–80, emphasis added).

'There is wide agreement that restorative justice is fundamentally characterized by certain kinds of values.' These are 'concepts like *inclusion, democracy, responsibility, reparation, safety, healing* and *reintegration*' (Sharpe 2004: 19, emphasis added).

'Restorative values can be distilled to two key underlying values – *humility* and *respect*. Furthermore, we should approach our work with *wonder*' (Zehr and Toews 2004: ix, emphasis added).

'Restorative justice's normative values are informed by a peace-making approach to conflict; its operational values support those normative values. *Peaceful social life* is supported by the operational values of *resolution* and *protection*. *Respect* is supported by the operational values of *encounter* and *empowerment*. *Solidarity* is supported by the operational values of *inclusion, assistance* and *moral education*. *Active responsibility* is supported by the operational values of *collaboration* and *reparation*' (Van Ness, 2004: 8–9, emphasis added).

While these represent multiple ways to express the values of restorative justice, the descriptions above form a consistent and coherent picture. They vary in their starting points but they lead to one another from those various points of departure.

Respect is the most consistently used term. Other key themes are maintaining individual dignity, inclusion, responsibility, humility, mutual care, reparation and non-domination. These process values nurture good relationships in groups and ensure that the group holds individual members in a good way.

These values are similar to those identified by citizens as components of a better way to resolve conflict and harm. For six or seven years one of the main components of my job at the Minnesota Department of Corrections was introducing restorative justice to groups of people ranging in size from half a dozen to several hundred individuals. In the course of that work I engaged in discussions about values with thousands of people from all walks of life and many different cultures, education levels and socioeconomic statuses. I developed a process that elicited key points of a restorative framework from the audience because it was an engaging way to do presentations. One part of that process posed the following question to the audience: *If we had a good process in the community to resolve conflict and harm, what would you want to be the characteristics of that process?* The resulting list always reflected group process values consistent with those given by the writers cited above. For example, the following is a list created by one group while doing the exercise:

An effective community process to resolve conflict and harm should:

- Be egalitarian – everyone has an equal voice
- Involve all interested parties – the community, the victim, the offender and the system
- Be safe for participants both physically and emotionally
- Be clear and understandable
- Produce changes in behaviour
- Promote healing
- Include monitoring of agreement and evaluation of outcomes
- Be voluntary for participants
- Use consensus based decision-making
- Be achievable
- Condemn the behaviour
- Provide opportunities for reintegration
- Focus on repair of the harm
- Provide opportunities for learning
- Provide rewards for positive behaviour
- Hold all participants responsible for their appropriate roles

Why is it significant that members of my audiences and restorative justice writers produce similar lists of values? Because the similarity means that restorative justice processes do not impose a foreign set of values on participants but, instead, create environments in which participants are able to operate according to the values they themselves affirm. It is obvious that people's behaviour does not constantly demonstrate these values (although we and they might be surprised at how often they do). But the values themselves are not foreign to those people, nor do they reject the values; in fact, they affirm them. As I will discuss later in this chapter, I have found that when people do not act according to those values, it is often because they do not feel safe doing so. And this is why there is a need for restorative justice – not to force an alien approach on parties in dispute, but to create a safe environment in which they can apply what they themselves acknowledge to be the best approach.

Individual values

The second level of values important to restorative justice consists of individual values. Those are the values that restorative processes strive to draw out of the participants – the values that represent participants acting out of their best self. Restorative processes are designed to encourage participants to act on those values. The process values of respect, maintaining individual dignity, inclusion and non-domination create a space in which participants are more likely to access the best within themselves. That best self is characterized by values such as respect, honesty, taking responsibility, compassion, patience.

In addition, facilitators seek to model these individual values to the best of their ability. The process design and the facilitator's example create an environment in which value-based behaviour by the participants is more likely. Not all participants will be able to act on those values initially, but the process values will encourage movement in that direction from wherever the participant starts. The individual values are not a list of criteria for involvement, but a vision of the direction in which everyone will try to step from where they are. As with the process values there is some variation in how the individual values may be expressed, but they always include respect and always describe qualities that promote good relationships with others and one's self.

In peace-making circle trainings I do an exercise to elicit individual values, and from those by consensus develop a list of shared values for the group. The exercise asks people what they would hope for in their own behaviour during a difficult family conflict. The exercise was designed to cause people to reflect on who they want to be when they are at their best. The essence of that list has been the same across culture, religion, age, socioeconomic status, education, geography and all other differences. Every group I have ever done that exercise with has a similar sense of what values guide their behaviour when they are at their best. A typical list includes: responsible, fair, open minded, patient, creative, considerate of others' needs, compassionate, loving, respectful, a good listener, able to express my own needs. These core values that support good relationships with others seem to be universal and do not appear to depend upon environmental factors.

Adults often assume that these values must be taught and that young people who get into trouble have not been taught those values, and that they therefore cannot be engaged by appeal to those values. I had the opportunity to do a circle training with 25 youths in the juvenile male correctional facility at Red Wing, Minnesota. In the exercise the youths produced a list similar to every other group. Their list included: respect, open minded, caring, helpful, loving, sharing, courage, honesty, integrity. I have done several trainings in adult prisons. Those groups also produced similar lists to describe who they want to be at their best.

It appears that awareness of and desire for the values that support healthy relationships are profoundly embedded in human nature. It makes sense; humans are communal. Our DNA should carry the information necessary to be successful in community.

However, participants readily acknowledge that the list does not describe how they normally behave, especially in conflicted or difficult situations. The youths were especially clear that there is a gap between how they would like to see themselves and how they actually are. Because I work with processes that aim to bring out the best in people, I find it very important to understand what blocks the impulse towards behaviour that reflects values supporting good relationships with others. When I asked the young people, it became clear that they do not consider the world a safe place to act on their better values. They felt that such behaviour would be taken advantage of, abused or ridiculed. Their life experience has taught them to protect themselves from the sense of vulnerability they associate with acting on those values.

This has huge implications for practice if we wish to bring those deeply buried values to the surface. Safety – emotional, physical, mental and spiritual – becomes paramount to support behaviour based on those values. It is the process values that guide us in creating safe spaces for people to act on their core individual values.

Underlying beliefs

There is another category of concepts closely connected to values – beliefs or assumptions about the nature of the universe and its operation. Because these are sometimes difficult to distinguish from values, I will discuss some of the assumptions of restorative justice that might overlap with values.

The importance of relationships

Restorative justice assumes that humans are profoundly relational. There is a fundamental human need to be in good relationship with others. Restorative approaches recognize and work with that core human need.

Interconnection and interdependence

Restorative justice assumes an interconnected and interdependent universe. Every part of existence is connected to every other part and impacts every other part. Every part of the universe needs every other part. The concepts of interconnection and interdependence engender a deep sense of mutual responsibility. Individuals are responsible for their impact on others and on the larger whole of which they are a part. Communities are responsible for the good of the whole, which includes the well-being of each member. Because all parts of the community are interdependent, harm to one is harm to all – good for one is good for all. This is an ancient understanding of indigenous peoples around the world, and it is one that Western science has recently 'discovered'. Modern physics and biology assert that the universe is an interconnected web and that nothing exists except in relation to something else – that the content of matter is not as important as the relationships between things – the betweenness of existence.

Mutual responsibility between the individual and the community is not just a passive responsibility to do no harm but an active responsibility to support and nurture the well-being of the other in his or her unique individual needs. Consequently, the mutual responsibility between individual and community at the core of restorative justice does not entail the suppression of individuality to serve the group but, rather, attends to individual needs while taking into account the impact on the collective. It seeks to meet the needs of both the individual and the group in a way that serves both, or that at least achieves balance between them (Pranis 2002).

Wisdom resides in each person

Restorative justice assumes that ordinary people have the capacity to figure out what happened, why it happened and what needs to happen to move towards repair and healing. In a restorative approach professional expertise is at the service of the wisdom of the participants rather than the other way around.

Justice is healing

Injustice causes harm – to the person who experiences the injustice, to the community and to the person who commits the injustice. Justice, as a state of healthy balance, requires healing of all those parties. Healing needs are guided by the values of respect, maintaining individual human dignity, non-domination. When all parties feel equal, respected, valued in their individual uniqueness, able to exercise constructive control in their lives and able to take responsibility for their actions, then justice is achieved.

These beliefs are not shared by mainstream systems of justice in Western countries. Consequently, restorative justice represents much more than simply a different or more effective set of techniques. Values are not set by functionality alone. A values framework does not just ask: 'Will this produce what I want?' Instead, it asks: 'Is this the right thing to do? Does this fit my values?' Ends and means must both be consistent with the values.

The contributions of a values foundation in restorative justice

The importance of values is embedded in the philosophy of restorative justice. At the same time the emphasis on values serves pragmatic purposes. Acting on restorative values produces results that serve the well-being of others. Such values guide us in very concrete ways to better relationships. The application of our values helps produce solutions to difficult problems. The emphasis on values in restorative justice serves the vision of the restorative justice movement in numerous ways. For example, acting according to restorative values:

- accesses strengths in participants to resolve very difficult problems;
- bridges differences of culture, age, gender, geography, status, etc., because they are widely understood and endorsed;
- engages people on a spiritual or meaning level as well as mental, physical and emotional levels;
- reinforces healthy relationships and builds community to prevent further harm;
- energizes a long-term commitment in practitioners;
- links practice and practitioner – external work and internal work;
- provides a way to guide and assess practice without becoming prescriptive;
- forms a unifying force across disciplines and circumstances; and
- allows local autonomy while holding a common vision;

And, finally, restorative values guide us in our relationships with those who disagree with us, enabling us to find a way forward without causing harm.

Values access strengths in participants

Participants in restorative processes are sometimes surprised by their own behaviour. In very difficult circumstances they behave better than they expected. The values that are modelled and nurtured in the process allow participants to access the best in themselves, to experience their inner strength. The respect, inclusion and non-domination characteristics of restorative processes also free up creativity because fear and defensiveness are reduced by those process values.

Values bridge differences because they are widely understood and shared

As mentioned earlier, my discussions concerning values with thousands of people in a wide variety of circumstances have brought me to the conclusion that there is substantial agreement among humans about values. Across differences of race, culture, age, education, gender, income levels, geography, political philosophy and occupation, I discovered that every group came up with a similar list. That experience profoundly reshaped my understanding of my work. I found that my role was not to educate, but to uncover and make visible the values and wisdom that were already present in participants.

The common ground of shared values holds enormous potential for effective collective work in addressing the difficulties faced by communities. Discovering shared values reduces the sense of 'other', the social distance between groups or individuals that results in harmful behaviour towards others. The fact that restorative values appear to be so widely understood and affirmed suggests the potential for deep and lasting change through restorative processes.

Values engage people on a spiritual or meaning level

The criminal justice process is a process of mental and physical engagement. But creation of a just world, a non-violent world – a world in which we understand that harm to another is harm to ourselves, a wound to another is a wound to ourselves – is an effort of heart and spirit as much as an effort of mind. Restorative justice engages the emotional and spiritual/meaning aspects of human experience and calls the heart and spirit to a higher level of performance. Participants often transcend their own sense of themselves and their capabilities – and in so doing create a new sense of how they can be in the world and how they can relate to one another differently (Pranis, 2002).

It is the values of restorative justice that engage people on a heart and spirit level. They do so without appeal to religiosity or any faith system. The connection between spirituality and values is described by the Dalai Lama (1999) in his book, *Ethics for the New Millennium*. He defines spirituality as 'concerned with those qualities of the human spirit – such as love and compassion, patience, tolerance, forgiveness, contentment, a sense of responsibility, a sense of harmony – which bring happiness to both self and others' (1999: 22). He suggests that 'spiritual practice according to this description involves, on the one hand, acting out of concern for others' wellbeing. On the other, it entails transforming ourselves so that we become more readily disposed to do so' (p. 23).

Those qualities the Dalai Lama ascribes to spirituality (love, compassion, patience, tolerance, forgiveness) are the kinds of values that people identify in describing their best self. A sense of spirituality is not required to act on those core values, but for many people a spiritual connection motivates and supports acting on those values. Frank Schweigert writes about the peace-making circle process, one of the primary models of restorative practice: 'Participants speak often of unexpected changes of heart, a profound sense of connection, the freeing experience of honesty and humility, unanticipated outbreaks of generosity – as an awareness of a power greater than the individuals present but moving through them' (1999: 2–3).

Harm, conflicts and difficulties have emotional and spiritual/meaning content for participants. Consequently, effective resolutions require exploring the emotional and spiritual content and accessing emotional and spiritual resources. While allowing people to relate from their spiritual understanding through values, restorative justice does not privilege faith of any kind. It isn't necessary. The Dalai Lama notes: 'There is thus no reason why the individual should not develop them [these values] even to a high degree, without recourse to any religious or metaphysical belief system' (1999: 22).

In a cycle of mutual reinforcement the values engage spiritual/meaning connections for many people and spirituality prompts behaviour based on the values.

Values reinforce healthy relationships and build community

Because restorative values emphasize those characteristics that support good relationships, the application of those values continuously strengthens relationships and deepens the connections among people. When people experience respect, equality and mutual care they become more likely to drop defences or protections, which are often the source of destructive or non-cooperative behaviour. They become open to recognizing common ground and acting in the common interest – a critical aspect of community.

Values energize a long-term commitment in practitioners

Values-based practice is more resistant to the ups and downs of funding, leadership, organizational structure and general support. When practitioners are engaged on a values level they do not easily abandon the values component of the practice. They often find a creative way to continue to act on those values even when the visible components of the practice may not be institutionally supported. A school principal who was trained in restorative practices in schools did not feel able to establish a face-to-face dialogue programme, but because of the values he learnt he took the initiative to reach out to students who had been harmed – a practice he did not have previously. At a meeting about potential loss of funding, community volunteers who have been part of a community justice circle programme clearly declared their intention to keep doing circles – even if the circle had to meet in their home. This kind of commitment is a consequence of engagement on a values level.

Living our core values that support good relationships with others is its own reward and has less need of external support to be sustained. Many seasoned veterans in probation have told me that restorative justice has given them renewed energy for their work because it rekindles the value-based reasons that led them to become probation officers in the first place. Several police officers who were ready to retire because of burn-out have stayed with the police force because they became involved in restorative justice. Behaviour supported by internalized values is more flexible, creative and sustainable than behaviour supported by technical competence. Because of the emphasis on values, restorative justice nurtures and strengthens practitioners who want to be acting from those core values, but may in the past have felt alone and without a justifying framework for their intuitive understanding of what to do.

Values link the external work and the internal work of practitioners

In my experience the work in restorative justice calls for inner reflection and inner work as much as it calls us to work with others. The personal and professional do not separate into distinct boxes. This is the wisdom captured in the third tenet of feminism identified by Kay Harris: the personal is political. We cannot have one set of standards for our personal lives and a different set of standards for our public lives. What happens in our private life affects our public life and vice versa (Pranis 2002). The personal and the professional or public selves are inextricably intertwined. The values framework of restorative justice offers a way to make our lives more holistic and integrated in all aspects.

Restorative justice moves from the old paradigm of 'client and service provider', in which there is a clear giver and a taker, to a model in which every participant is presumed to be learning from every other participant – everyone has a gift to offer for the good of the whole. In guiding those who have been hurt and those who have caused harm towards healing, practitioners find they must walk their own healing path. Restorative values integrate those two aspects of our lives and put us on the same playing field with those we work with. In encouraging respect, listening, accountability, self-forgiveness, etc., for others, practitioners are constantly confronted with their own levels of respect, accountability and self-forgiveness in their lives. The same standard – a values standard – operates for everyone – those being helped and those helping. The values apply to everyone and living those values is a struggle for everyone – even the best among us. We all need help to live them.

Values provide a way to guide and assess practice without becoming prescriptive

Values must be the foundation for assessment of practice. That is both a strength and a challenge for the restorative justice movement. Evaluation based on how well values are demonstrated by practice and experienced by those who are affected allows a great deal of freedom to develop creative new ways to achieve restorative ends. It removes the need to define specifically what practitioners do and focuses more on how it is done and how it is experienced by others. This shift is very empowering to practitioners and ultimately to participants. On the other hand, assessing whether the values articulated are translating into values-based experience for participants is not as easy as measuring concrete process steps. It requires a different kind of training for practitioners – one that spends significant time exploring values and the difficulty of applying those values in daily life. A values-based approach to assessment sets out guideposts that do not dictate practice but do help us know when we are outside the path.

For example, restorative justice does not tell communities what they must do, but it does set value limits around community processes. In a restorative framework communities are expected to take into account the interests of all members, not just the majority, to allow all voices to participate in decision-making, and are to respect the dignity of all persons (Pranis 2002). Where communities are not able to act within those parameters the responsibility lies with government to uphold the values and protect those vulnerable to mistreatment by the community.

Values create a unifying framework across disciplines

The language of restorative justice, as developed in the context of criminal justice, often does not resonate with people in other disciplines, though the issues of harm and what to do about harm occur in all human endeavours. In Minnesota educators adopted the language of 'restorative measures' to avoid alienating teachers who did not see themselves as involved in 'justice' or as working with 'victims' or 'offenders'. In dialogue with child welfare practitioners, the Minnesota restorative justice movement discovered similar resistance to the term 'restorative justice', even when talking about the use of New Zealand family group conferencing in child welfare. Agreement on values, on the other hand, was relatively easy. On the basis of shared values, all parties were willing to do the hard work of finding common language and building a collaboration to co-sponsor trainings and conferences. They created introductory training about restorative practices in child welfare, criminal justice, schools, the workplace and communities that begins with a discussion of values.

Cross-disciplinary support and fertilization have been critical to the success of restorative justice in Minnesota. When people in one discipline are feeling discouraged or overwhelmed, there is often a success in another discipline that energizes everyone and feeds hope. I believe that the exciting work in schools in Minnesota has kept folks in criminal justice from becoming disheartened by the difficulty of making change. Emphasis on values made it possible for practitioners to come together across the divide between disciplines.

Values allow local autonomy while holding a shared vision

One of the great strengths of the restorative justice movement is that it is not dependent upon a centralized source of legitimacy or support. The movement is very dispersed in leadership and activity (Pranis, 2004). For example, in the USA, without large amounts of money, high-profile leadership or a marketing plan, the movement has nevertheless spread across the country in justice systems and is now influencing other fields such as education, social services and workplace conflict. There is a remarkable level of coherence and focus in the movement, in spite of the lack of a national voice, infrastructure or financial resources. The organizing force is values.

A clearly articulated vision and values to guide action replace prescribed actions and extensive control mechanisms. Values-guided practice can respond to unique circumstances or unexpected developments in ways that technique-driven practice cannot. If there is agreement on vision and values, there can be an enormous amount of local autonomy for practitioners with local efforts contributing to the larger shared vision. A powerful way to bring change is to think globally and act locally with autonomy. The shared values synergize countless discrete activities happening at the local level into a whole that is greater than the sum of its parts. By avoiding the need for centralized control enormous amounts of energy are freed to be invested in the actual work.

The values that nurture and promote good relationships with others are the foundation of restorative justice. There is no single 'right' way of expressing those values and, even though in my experience those values are similar across different groups, they cannot be assumed for others. Each group must determine the values for themselves and must take responsibility for maintaining them. The struggle to identify the guiding values and to elaborate the meaning of those values in a specific situation creates the foundation supporting a restorative process. This foundation is a living thing like a root system, not inanimate like a concrete foundation. It requires feeding and watering. It is important to return to a discussion of values periodically and to invest energy in them as beacons of desired behaviour. It is also very important to create feedback loops that assess whether participants experience those values in practice. Good intentions are not sufficient; values-based practice must include regular determination of whether the impact aligns with the values.

Values guide our response to those who disagree with us

Restorative justice calls for us to apply these values in all aspects of our lives and in all our relationships – with family, co-workers, neighbours, clients and adversaries. Acting on the basis of restorative values means we will even have respectful relationships with our adversaries. One of the paradoxes of restorative justice is that it is a vision of radical change, but it asks us to make those changes in a gentle way. Restorative justice asks us to create change without attempting to decide for others, because to control them violates the values of restorative justice (Pranis 2001).

This vision is contrary to our usual sense of making social change. The core values of restorative justice call for respectful treatment of all – including those we might deem to be blocking our good work. Restorative justice presumes that harm to one is harm to all; therefore, we create change while proceeding with compassion towards those with whom we disagree.

It is extremely difficult to treat those who oppose our work with respect and compassion. It is the values foundation of restorative work that encourages advocates to hold a place of hospitality even for the adversary.

Conclusion

Values are the foundation of restorative justice, the touchstone to which we return when in doubt about what to do or how to do it, the yardstick for assessing action. Just as there is not a single accepted definition of restorative justice, so there is not a single list of its values. But my experience has been that the values are consistent across the variety of ways of expressing them. Process values of restorative justice – e.g. respect, individual dignity, inclusion, responsibility, humility, mutual care, reparation, non-domination – nurture good relationships in groups and draw out individual values – e.g. respect, honesty, compassion, open-mindedness, patience – from its members.

Because both individual and process values are broadly shared, they provide common ground for dialogue about harm, repair and prevention.

I had an experience recently that illustrated the way values guide restorative work. I attended a week-long intensive workshop with a Native American teacher. Outdoor activities were a part of the programme. One exercise involved blindfolding us and leading us to a place in the woods where a rope line had previously been strung from tree to tree. The rope sometimes went through the Y of a tree, over a fallen tree, under a partially fallen tree, turned at sharp angles, and sometimes ran only a few inches off the ground. Our task was to follow the rope to the end with the blindfold on. It required moving carefully because we could not see obstacles and it required flexibility and responsiveness when we encountered obstacles or unexpected turns. As long as we held on to the rope, we were safe and would get to the end. We did not need to know exactly what the path was or exactly what the destination looked like. We did need to stay connected to the rope and move carefully, attentive to what might be around us.

For me, the rope became a metaphor for the values guiding us in restorative justice work. If we hold on to them and move carefully, we will be okay. When we don't know exactly what to do or when things seem confusing and don't follow the expected path, we can trust those values. To do that we must trust the values, for the rope represents not expertise but, rather, clarity about what the values are and what they call us to do.

Our understanding of values, furthermore, is not static. Our understanding of their meanings grows over time. Understanding the values, living the values to the best of our ability, is a continuing journey – a living process.

A philosophy or guiding vision based on values is rooted in a deep inner truth and does not limit itself to that which can be proven by evidence. Values express our hopes and aspirations, not just our current reality. Articulating and intentionally working from a value-based philosophy matters. The world is not an objective reality that remains the same regardless of what we believe (Kuhn 1962). To a large degree our beliefs shape the world we create with our actions and our energy. Choosing a positive vision expressed through values contributes to creating a more positive world (Pranis 2004).

Selected further reading

Boyack, J., Bowen, H. and Marshall, C. (2004) 'How does restorative justice ensure good practice?', in H. Zehr and B. Toews (eds) *Critical Issues in Restorative Justice*. Monsey, NY: Criminal Justice Press. The authors present the results of a two-year effort by the Restorative Justice Network in New Zealand to develop standards for restorative justice practice that offer both clear direction and flexibility. The network concluded that the optimal approach was to develop values-based guidelines.

Harris, M.K. (1987) 'Moving into the new millennium: toward a feminist vision of justice', *Prison Journal*, Fall–Winter: 27–38. Although this article is dated, it offers a useful example of how clarity about underlying assumptions and values allows one to critique existing practice and identify constructive new approaches.

Pranis, K., Stuart, B. and Wedge, M. (2003) *Peacemaking Circles: From Crime to Community*. St Paul, MN: Living Justice Press. Circles are profoundly values based. This book demonstrates how values have guided the development and use of one of the three key forms of restorative dialogue.

Acknowledgements

I wish to thank the editors for the opportunity to share my thinking about restorative values and I wish to acknowledge that each reader brings great wisdom to this subject as well. My intention is to offer my view for the reader's consideration while recognizing that my view is limited. I also wish to express my gratitude to the many teachers who have supported my journey of exploring restorative values.

References

Boyack, J., Bowen, H. and Marshall, C. (2004) 'How does restorative justice ensure good practice?', in H. Zehr and B. Toews (eds) *Critical Issues in Restorative Justice*. Monsey, NY: Criminal Justice Press.

Braithwaite, J. and Parker, C. (1999) 'Restorative justice is republican justice', in G. Bazemore and L. Walgrave (eds) *Restorative Juvenile Justice: Repairing the Harm of Youth Crime*. Monsey, NY: Willow Tree Press.

Consedine, J. (1999) 'Twin pillars of justice: morality and the law', in H. Bowen and J. Consedine, (eds) *Restorative Justice: Contemporary Themes and Practice.* Lyttelton, NZ: Ploughshares Publications.

Dalai Lama (1999) *Ethics for the New Millennium.* New York: Riverhead Books.

Dyck, D. (2004) 'Are we – practitioner, advocates – practicing what we preach?', in H. Zehr and B. Toews (eds) *Critical Issues in Restorative Justice.* Monsey, NY: Criminal Justice Press.

Harris, M.K. (1987) 'Moving into the new millennium: toward a feminist vision of justice', *Prison Journal,* Fall-Winter: 27–38.

Herman, S. (2004) 'Is restorative justice possible without a parallel system for victims?', in H. Zehr and B. Toews (eds) *Critical Issues in Restorative Justice.* Monsey, NY: Criminal Justice Press.

Judah, E. and Bryant, M. (2004) 'Introduction' in E. Judah and M. Bryant (eds) *Journal of Religion and Spirituality in Social Work: Social Thought,* 23: (1/2).

Kuhn, T. (1962) *The Structure of Scientific Revolutions.* Chicago, IL: University of Chicago Press.

Pavlich, G. (2004) 'What are the dangers as well as the promises of community involvement?', in H. Zehr and B. Toews (eds) *Critical Issues in Restorative Justice.* Monsey, NY: Criminal Justice Press.

Pranis, K. (2001) 'Restorative justice, social justice, and the empowerment of marginalized populations', in G. Bazemore and M. Schiff (eds) *Restorative Community Justice: Repairing Harm and Transforming Communities.* Cincinnati, OH: Anderson Publishing.

Pranis, K. (2002) 'Restorative values and confronting family violence', in H. Strang and J. Braithwaite (eds) *Restorative Justice and Family Violence.* Cambridge: Cambridge University Press.

Pranis, K. (2004) 'The practice and efficacy of restorative justice', in E. Judah and M. Bryant (eds) *Journal of Religion and Spirituality in Social Work: Social Thought,* 23: 133–57.

Pranis, K., Stuart, B. and Wedge, M. (2003) *Peacemaking Circles: From Crime to Community.* St Paul, MN: Living Justice Press.

Schweigert, F. (1999) 'Underlying principles: the spirituality of the circle,' *Full Circle,* 3: 2–4.

Sharpe, S. (2004) 'How large should the restorative justice 'tent' be?', in H. Zehr and B. Toews (eds) *Critical Issues in Restorative Justice.* Monsey, NY: Criminal Justice Press.

Sullivan, D. and Tifft, L. (2004) 'What are the implications of restorative justice for society and our lives?', in H. Zehr and B. Toews (eds) *Critical Issues in Restorative Justice.* Monsey, NY: Criminal Justice Press.

Van Ness, D. (2004) *RJ City.* Prison Fellowship International (available at www. pfijr.org).

Wonshe (2004) 'How does the 'who, what, where, when and how' affect the practice of restorative justice?', in H. Zehr and B. Toews (eds) *Critical Issues in Restorative Justice.* Monsey, NY: Criminal Justice Press.

Zehr, H. and Toews, B. (2004) *Critical Issues in Restorative Justice.* Monsey, NY: Criminal Justice Press.

Chapter 5

Retribution and restorative justice

Declan Roche

Retributive justice has always played an important role in the explanation and promotion of restorative justice. Early proponents – most notably Howard Zehr – defined restorative justice as an alternative to retributive justice. This retributive/restorative justice dichotomy became the standard approach to defining restorative justice, and was widely adopted by critics and supporters alike. In more recent times, however, the contrast has become the subject of extensive critique. Both halves of the contrast are susceptible to criticism: the retributive part misrepresents equally the theory of retributive justice and the diversity of criminal justice practice; while the restorative justice part fails to capture the complexity of punishment processes outside the formal courtroom.

This chapter begins by retracing the origins of this contrast in restorative justice, examining why this dichotomous approach was so widely employed, before going on to consider its shortcomings, and the newer approaches to defining restorative and retributive justice. The final section considers the implications of these debates for practice, in particular the implications for the question of where restorative justice programmes should be located in the criminal justice system and the safeguards and checks and balances that should accompany them.

The retributive/restorative dichotomy in early restorative justice writings

Zehr's *Changing Lenses* (1990) is one of the key texts on restorative justice. Widely read by practitioners and academics, its language and ideas shaped the way many early advocates explained restorative justice. In it, Zehr provides a critique of the modern approaches to criminal justice, which he argues leave victims, offenders and communities injured and unsatisfied, and suggests an alternative approach, which he argues has its roots in both historical approaches to dealing with harm, and in biblical teachings. Zehr uses the label 'retributive justice' to describe current practice, and 'restorative justice' to describe the alternative model of justice he supports. According to Zehr (1990: 184), the retributive approach 'defines the state as victim, defines wrongful relationship as violation of rules, and sees the relationship between victim and offender as irrelevant', whereas a restorative approach 'identifies people as victims and recognizes the centrality of the interpersonal dimensions'. In Table 5.1, Zehr sets out the salient differences between these two models of justice.

Table 5.1 Understandings of crime

Retributive lens	Restorative lens
Crime defined by violation of rules (i.e. broken rules)	Crime defined by harm to people and relationships (i.e. broken relationships)
Harms defined abstractly	Harms defined concretely
Crime seen as categorically different harms from other	Crime recognized as related to other harms and conflicts
State as victim	People and relationships as victims
State and offender seen as primary parties	Victim and offender seen as primary parties
Victims' needs and rights ignored	Victims' needs and rights central
Interpersonal dimensions irrelevant	Interpersonal dimensions central
Conflictual nature of crime obscured	Conflictual nature of crime recognized
Wounds of offender peripheral	Wounds of offender important
Offence defined in technical, legal terms	Offence understood in full context: moral, social, economic, political

Source: Zehr, *Changing Lenses* (1990), 184–5

When *Changing Lenses* was published in 1990, there was little in the way of a restorative justice movement. There had been a number of similar efforts to reform criminal justice systems in the USA, England and, most notably, New Zealand, that gave the people directly affected by crimes, victims, offenders and their families, more say in their resolution, but these programmes operated largely in isolation from one another and lacked a strong theoretical framework. This picture changed dramatically, however, over the course of the 1990s as policy-makers, communities and academics began to visit and compare these new programmes, and writers such as Zehr began to place these ideas within a theoretical and historical context.

Increasingly, people referred to these developments as restorative justice. The adoption of this term was not instantaneous (this can be seen by the fact that a number of writers did not use the term 'restorative justice' to describe these developments – see, e.g. Braithwaite and Mugford 1994; Zedner 1994), but by the second half of the 1990s, the expression 'restorative justice' was gaining popularity and, in 2006, the term is used almost universally. But people did not use just the term 'restorative justice' by itself. Almost always, whenever someone wanted to talk about restorative justice, whether to promote the concept (Van Ness 1993) or to criticize it (e.g. Ashworth 1993), they used the dichotomy between retributive and restorative approaches to criminal justice (e.g. Braithwaite 2002: 5). As John Braithwaite (2002: 10) observes, 'restorative justice is most commonly defined' as an alternative to retribution and rehabilitation. Kathy Daly (2000: 34) argues that this distinction has 'become a permanent fixture in the field', and 'it is made not only by restorative justice scholars, but increasingly, one finds it canonised in criminology and juvenile justice text books'.

Of course, this approach to defining a concept, employing an oppositional concept, is not new. In criminal justice debates, it is familiar as the tactic used by the rehabilitative justice movement, which set itself in opposition to retributive justice in a similar way (see Table 5.2).

Table 5.2 Retributive and rehabilitative justice

Retributive	Rehabilitative
Focuses on the offence	Focuses on the offender
Focuses on blame for past behaviour	Focuses on changing future behaviour
Aim: to punish the offence	Aim: to treat the offender

Source: Daly (2000)

Problems with the restorative/retributive distinction

The distinction drawn between restorative and retributive justice has the virtue of being neat and simple. These virtues should not be underestimated. They make the difficult job of explaining an unfamiliar concept much easier. Restorative justice has only grown as quickly as it has because its promoters have been able to excite the interest of a wide range of people, including police officers, judges, schoolteachers, politicians, juvenile justice agencies, victim support groups, aboriginal elders, and mums and dads. An explanatory tool such as Table 5.1 helps communicate succinctly the important elements of restorative justice to this diverse audience.

However, any such simple, neat distinction runs the risk of oversimplifying and distorting the concepts it purports to explain. In this case, the distinction between restorative and retributive justice suffers such problems, distorting the real meaning of retributive justice, our understanding of what modern criminal justice systems do, and also the meaning of restorative justice.

Retributive justice

Retributive justice has fared badly at the hands of restorative justice writers. In the hands of penal theorists, retributive justice is a duty-based, backward-looking theory approach to justice developed particularly by Enlightenment thinkers Kant and Hegel. According to a retributive theory of justice, wrongdoing 'must be punished simply because the wrongful act merits condemnation and punishment' (Mani 2002: 33).

But you will not find this sort of narrow definition of retributive justice in a discussion about restorative justice. In this context, retributive justice has come to represent much more (and much less) than a theory of justice. This tendency was evident in Zehr's use of the term. Zehr uses the expression 'retributive justice' to describe not just a particular approach to punishment, but the system for delivering punishment, and the underlying view of crime: 'Crime is a violation of the state, defined by lawbreaking and guilt. Justice determines blame and administers pain in a contest between the offender and the state directed by systematic rules' (1990: 181).

More recently, the meaning of restorative justice has only expanded and further distorted. Increasingly, retributive justice is used not just as a synonym for punishment generally, but in the hands of critics, as a type of shorthand for all the numerous faults and failings of punishment practices. To many, 'retributive justice' is a dirty word, not a theory of punishment. The original meaning of retributive justice is further obscured by the tendency to use the terms 'vengeance', 'revenge' and 'retaliation' interchangeably with 'retributive justice'. Bit by bit, 'retributive justice' loses its meaning, and people are left with a stark choice between humane restorative justice on the one hand, and barbaric retaliation on the other. Perhaps the most striking example of this tendency comes from South Africa, where Mandela's government sought to convince the country that the only choices they had were restorative justice, in the form of a truth commission, or vengeance. As the legislation creating the South African Truth and Reconciliation Commission put it: 'there is a need for understanding but not for vengeance, a need for reparation but not for retaliation, a need for ubuntu [humanity to others] but not for victimization' (Promotion of National Unity and Reconciliation Act 1995). The possibility of pursuing retributive justice through formal prosecution and punishment has disappeared from the equation altogether.

Before we are swept too far down this path, we need to stop and reflect. People may disagree with retributive theories of justice but it is inaccurate to reduce them to mere revenge and the law of the jungle. Retributive justice is rooted in the idea that the offender has taken an unfair advantage in committing a crime, which can only be corrected by the administering of a punishment. But this is different from simple revenge; according to retributive justice, punishment must be imposed according to strict limits: only the guilty deserve to be punished, and punishment is justified only if it inflicts the suffering they deserve (Duff and Garland 1994: 7). It is often forgotten that retributive justice – in the guise of the 'just deserts' model – was promoted by liberal reformers in the 1970s as a response to increasing levels of punishment. These new retributivists argued that offenders should receive their 'just deserts': 'that they should suffer fair and determinate punishment proportionate to the seriousness of the crime' (Duff and Garland 1994: 12).

It is understandable why many people would not associate retributive justice and 'just-deserts' with a campaign to reduce sentences, however.

Notwithstanding the intentions of its original advocates, the just deserts model was soon 'hijacked by more conservative forces aiming to increase levels of punishment – especially of punishment' (Duff and Garland 1994: 112). Politicians claimed that new sentencing laws, including those that imposed stiff, mandatory sentences, would give offenders 'their just deserts'. Given these associations, it is perhaps inevitable that that which began its life as a theory to limit punishment would eventually become a synonym for punitive approaches to criminal justice.

One argument for confining the expression 'retributive justice' closer to its original meaning is that we can observe how the restorative tradition has brought to light some inherent problems with retributive justice. In particular, retributive theory is often defended on the basis that the administering of punishment rights the imbalance created by the offender's actions and brings vindication to victims, but restorative justice queries whether punishment achieves these goals in practice. According to Zehr (2002: 59), 'what truly vindicates is acknowledgment of victims' harms and needs, combined with an active effort to encourage offenders to take responsibility, make right the wrongs, and address the causes of their behaviour'.

Another contribution of the restorative justice tradition is to question the article of faith among retributive justice scholars that it is possible to identify some amount of punishment that an offender deserves. Restorative justice questions the link between crime and punishment. Punishment equates to the harm done by crime only in the most general sense that both crime and punishment can be painful experiences to those on the receiving end. But beyond that, how do we decide whether a boy who steals a bike deserves three days, three weeks, or three months' punishment? By contrast, advocates would argue that restorative justice does provide a guide to what should happen to the boy – he should be required to make good the harm he has suffered.

Conventional criminal justice

As well as being unfair to retributive justice theory, the restorative/retributive dichotomy is unfair to mainstream criminal justice practices. If you were to believe restorative justice accounts, mainstream criminal justice practice is uniformly terrible. And although there is a voluminous criminological literature attesting to the many failings of mainstream criminal justice systems, there is no one single, monolithic criminal justice system. Criminal justice systems not only vary considerably from one country to another, but criminal justice institutions within a single country vary considerably, just as do individuals within the same institution.

When we start to look more closely at criminal justice systems in this way we see that it is plainly absurd to suggest that they can all be characterized as pursuing a retributive justice approach. Criminal justice agencies have always applied a mixture of principles but this texture and variation are absent from most restorative justice accounts. For a start, restorative justice accounts have almost completely ignored the influence of the rehabilitative ideal on modern criminal justice systems. This is a mistake and restorative justice could learn much from the older rehabilitation movement about how benevolent ideals can quickly become corrupted (Levrant *et al*. 1999). Eliding retributive justice and modern criminal justice also ignores the existence of juvenile courts, which tend to operate on a more informal basis, with much more emphasis on rehabilitation and reintegration, than on rules. It should be remembered that in many jurisdictions there is a tradition of compensation that predates the restorative justice movement. For example, as Zedner (1994: 240) notes, since 1973 in the UK it has been possible to impose compensation as the sole penalty. It should also be remembered that, despite the upsurge in imprisonment in the USA and the UK, the fine remains the most common penalty in those countries.

Simple characterizations of modern criminal justice systems also gloss over the numerous innovations within police, courts and prisons unrelated to the restorative justice movement, but also designed to promote the goals of offender reintegration and victim reparation. A prominent example is the recent advent of drug courts across the USA that suspend offenders' sentences pending completion of a drug treatment programme. Drug courts vary considerably in quality, but the best ones rely on committed and co-operative criminal justice professionals, including judges, probation workers and district attorneys.

Such a view also gives little, if any, credit to the victims' movement which since its beginnings in the 1960s and 1970s in Europe and the USA, has raised awareness among politicians, legislators and communities of the problems suffered by victims, and has been responsible for introducing many reforms, including the creation of victim support groups, and in the UK, a 'Victim's Charter' (Shapland 1988; Strang 2001). At an international level, the drafters of the International Criminal Court have gone to considerable lengths to design a court that addresses many concerns of victims' groups. This includes giving victims the right to present their views to the court at various stages in the proceedings, and the creation of a victims' trust fund (ICC 2005). Although it is true that many victimologists themselves remain pessimistic about the extent to which things have changed (e.g. Shapland 2000), much restorative justice writing simply ignores the existence of a victim's movement predating the emergence of the restorative justice movement.

Restorative justice

The depiction of informal justice in the restorative/retributive contrast is just as inaccurate, but inaccurate in the opposite direction. The restorative/retributive contrast perpetuates an overly rosy and benign view of informal modes of justice. If you were to believe many restorative justice advocates, state-led criminal justice has only interfered with people's innate desire to reconcile and forgive one another. Of course, this tendency is not attributable solely to the simple restorative/retributive characterization. It runs through much of the restorative justice literature. Restorative justice advocates have consistently challenged the conventional wisdom that justice before the emergence of the nation-state was vengeful and barbaric, arguing that this overlooks numerous examples where informal processes were characterized by an emphasis on negotiation and compensation (e.g. Christie 1977). But one generalization has been replaced with another, as many advocates have presented an air-brushed history of punishment practices before the state assumed control. Zehr (1990: 106) himself is well aware of the dangers of restorative justice, but unfortunately the restorative/retributive justice dichotomy only encourages a dangerous type of binary thinking – restorative justice, good; everything else, bad.

Informal justice poses several inherent dangers to participants. Take for example the central claim of the restorative justice movement that informal processes are more sensitive to victims' interests. As Zehr's table suggests, 'victims' needs and rights [are] central'. In advocating these processes advocates recall that victims used to play a more significant role in the criminal justice system. But the often-intolerable burden this imposed on many victims, for prosecuting, collecting witnesses and even paying court staff, was one of the 'major reasons for the formation of police forces and the establishment of an official prosecuting system' (Shapland et al. 1985: 174). From an offender's perspective, the history of informal justice is a similarly unhappy one. Although it is true that communities sought to defuse hostilities by encouraging reconciliation where parties shared a continuing relationship (through marriage, kinship or economic exchange), where no such relationship existed, parties would often resort to violent self-help (Roberts 1979).

Modern examples inspired by the restorative justice movement also suggest that people's experiences of informal justice are much more complicated than the simple retributive/restorative dichotomy suggests. Those who observed restorative justice conferences, and interviewed participants afterwards, note that far from being oases of reconciliation, conferences also provide opportunities for people to punish and hurt one another. There is evidence that both those doing and those on the receiving end perceive themselves to be involved in a punishment process. Charles Barton (2000: 55) goes as far as to argue that 'punishment and retribution cannot be ruled out by any system of justice'.

Real-life practice raises doubt on whether retribution and restoration can be neatly classified and corralled in the way that restorative justice advocates suggest. Not all people wish to pursue restoration, and some people may pursue a combination of goals in a conference. Daly (2002: 59) argues that, based on her experience observing conferences, participants flexibly incorporated multiple justice aims, which included:

1. some elements of retributive justice (that is, censure for past offences);

2. some elements of rehabilitative justice (for example, by asking, what shall we do to encourage future law-abiding behaviour?); and

3. some elements of restorative justice (for example, by asking, how can the offender make up for what he or she did to the victim?).

But perhaps the most unsettling insight for the restoration/retribution contrast is that, for many victims, retribution may provide a form of restoration – i.e. that what makes a victim feels better is to see the offender suffer. This was true in acephalous societies, where restoration could take forms such as the banishment or spearing of an offender (Finnane 2001), and some observers point to the same tendency, albeit expressed less dramatically, in modern restorative justice programmes (Daly 2000, 2002).

Merging restorative and retributive justice?

There are a variety of restorative justice responses to the points raised above. Many writers would be prepared to concede that modern criminal justice systems are not as uniformly terrible as early restorative justice writings point out. Many would concede that early descriptions had a slightly rhetorical tone that was more about introducing a new idea than it was about faithfully representing current practice. However, restorative justice advocates tend to be more resistant when it comes to acknowledging the shortcomings of informal justice. Some writers and practitioners hold steadfastly to the view that people are inherently good. A variation on this view is that restorative justice processes have a humanizing effect on people. People may come full of anger or defiance but these emotions give way to acceptance, and sometimes even forgiveness when people have had the opportunity to express themselves, and meet the person on the other side. The claim of restorative justice advocates is that meetings encourage victims and offenders alike to become more empathetic and compassionate towards one another. There is some empirical evidence for this as well. For example, the experiment conducted in Canberra comparing conferences with court found that most victims left a conference feeling more forgiving, and less fearful and angry than at the beginning (Strang 2002: 130).

However, all but the most partial restorative justice advocates would also concede that meetings can be very painful experiences for victims and offenders alike. In the light of this fact, does the restorative justice/retributive justice contrast need to be collapsed or at least redrawn? Many restorative justice advocates resist any attempt to do so (e.g. McCold 2000; Walgrave 2003). One leading restorative justice writer argues that the retributive/restorative justice contrast is sound because, although participants may experience meetings as painful, they do not constitute punishment because – unlike court-imposed sanctions – they are not intended to be that way (Walgrave 2002: 198). This resistance is linked to the fact that, for many advocates, restorative justice is not simply a variation on current punishment practices, but a whole 'new paradigm for doing justice', or even a 'different view of society' (Walgrave 2003: 216). In this new world, there is no room for retribution. Braithwaite (2002: 16) speaks for many restorative justice advocates when he argues:

[R]etributive values are more a hindrance to our survival and flourishing than a help. Hence restorative justice should be explicitly about a values shift from the retributive/punitive to the restorative. Retributive emotions are natural, things we all experience and things that are easy to understand from a biological point of view. But, on this view, retribution is in the same category as greed or gluttony; biologically they once helped us to flourish, but today they are corrosive of human health and relationships.

So while Braithwaite is prepared to concede that restorative justice conferences may contain elements of retribution, he is not prepared to concede that retribution is part of restorative justice. Instead he draws an analogy with democratic processes: when the voting public elects a politician who manifests an anti-democratic tendency, we do not expand the definition of democracy to include totalitarianism; rather we continue to reject totalitarian governments, at the same time acknowledging that one of the paradoxes of a commitment to democracy is that it may occasionally produce undemocratic results (Braithwaite and Strang 2000: 207).

Other writers take a more positive view of retribution, arguing that we do not have to make a choice between restorative and retributive justice. They argue that there is a place for retribution in a restorative justice conference (Barton 2000; Daly 2000, 2002; Dignan 2003, Duff 2001, 2003a, 2003b; Von Hirsch *et al.* 2003). Most of these writers have drawn on the work by legal theorist Duff, who has made the most sophisticated attempt to reconcile restorative and retributive justice. Duff argues that the restorative/retributive contrast drawn by restorative justice advocates (and some critics) commits the common error of confusing particular conceptions of punishment for the concept of punishment itself. A critic may reject highly punitive punishment, but this does not mean that he or she need reject the concept of retributive justice, or the even broader concept of punishment. Duff (2003a: 43) argues that 'restoration is not only compatible with retribution: it requires retribution', as it is only retributive punishment that can help bring about restoration. In other words, restorative justice is not an alternative to punishment, but an alternative form of punishment.

This argument depends on the definition of punishment. To Duff, punishment is associated with pain, but can only be understood properly as a communicative act. It is the communication of censure or criticism that transforms the simple administration of pain into punishment. Censure serves a variety of purposes. First it should recognize the harm a victim has suffered. As Duff puts it, 'not to condemn it would be implicitly to deny that it was a wrong, or that its wrongfulness mattered' (2003a: 50). The imposition of this pain, or burden, is done with the aim of reaffirming standards, which includes the more specific aim of persuading offenders not to reoffend, and to strengthen other citizens' commitment not to offend at all. Perhaps less obviously, processes of censure also show respect for an offender. As Duff explains, if offenders are to be treated as members of 'a normative community', this implies that we criticize them for their wrongdoing (and be prepared to accept their criticism for the wrongs we do to them).

In many modern punishment practices, of course, this censure is expressed through the use of formal punitive sanctions, the most extreme forms of which are imprisonment or, in some places, execution, but censure need not be expressed in this form; it can equally be expressed in what Duff (2003a: 53–4) calls 'criminal mediation':

> [Criminal mediation] focuses on the offender and his crime: on what he must do to repair the moral damage wrought by his crime. It is intended to be painful or burdensome, and the pain or burden is to be suffered *for* the crime. The mediation process itself aims to confront the offender with the fact and implications of what he has done, and to bring him to repent it as a wrong: a process which must be painful. The reparation that he is then to undertake must be burdensome if it is to serve its proper purpose. The aim is not just to 'make the offender suffer' for its own sake, but to induce an appropriate kind of suffering – the suffering intrinsic to confronting and repenting one's own wrongdoing and to making reparation for it.

A number of assumptions about how people are held accountable, and how harm is repaired, underlie this argument. In Duff's eyes, these processes must be painful to be effective. This is why civil mediation, where there may not be an admission of guilt, and it may be possible to rectify harm in a way that is not painful to anyone, does not constitute punishment (Duff 2003a: 50).

These views are all variations on the theme that an intervention can both restore and punish. In the mid-nineteenth century, Bentham (1830) recognized the potential for compensation to serve both purposes:

> This compensation, founded upon reasons which have been elsewhere developed, does not at first view appear to belong to the subject of punishments, because it concerns another individual than the delinquent. But these two ends have a real connexion. There are punishments which have the double effect of affording compensation to the party injured, and of inflicting a proportionate suffering on the delinquent; so that these two ends may be effected by a single operation. This is, in certain cases, the peculiar advantage of pecuniary punishments.

Duff's sophisticated version of retribution has allowed supporters and critics of restorative justice to move closer to some sort of common ground. Two such examples are Ashworth and Von Hirsch, one of the leading architects of the just-deserts movement in the 1970s. In their early writings on restorative justice (e.g. Ashworth 1993), both voiced serious, perhaps fundamental, concerns about restorative justice, including that restorative justice failed to deliver retributive punishment. In their most recent writings, however, they (along with Shearing) have suggested a theoretical model along the lines of

Duff's that could potentially satisfy critics and supporters alike (Von Hirsch *et al.* 2003).

Restorative justice advocates have also shifted ground, including Zehr himself, who has recently conceded that the 'polarization [between retributive and restorative approaches] may be somewhat misleading'. Zehr (2002: 59) now sees substantial areas of common ground between the two, namely:

> Both retributive and restorative theories of justice acknowledge a basic moral intuition that a balance has been thrown off by a wrongdoing. Consequently, the victim deserves something and the offender owes something. Both approaches argue that there must be a proportional relationship between the act and the response.

But Zehr maintains that there remains a distinction between the two:

> Retributive theory believes that pain will vindicate, but in practice that is often counterproductive for both victim and offender. Restorative justice theory, on the other hand, argues that what truly vindicates is acknowledgment of victims' harms and needs, combined with an active effort to encourage offenders to take responsibility, make right the wrongs, and address the causes of their behaviour.

But Zehr's distinction misses the point made by retributivists such as Duff who 'do not see pain delivery as an end in itself, nor as a crude form of deterrence, but regard it as an essential component (but only one component) of a more constructive, educative and reintegrative process' (Johnstone 2002: 109). They argue it is not possible to achieve the goals Zehr describes, acknowledgement, taking responsibility, reparation and rehabilitation, without some pain. Daly (2000: 43), another prominent advocate of the view that restoration and retribution are complementary not contrary principles, underlines Duff's argument by pointing to the similarity between his accounts of the elements of punishment and theoretical accounts of the processes in a restorative justice conference, in particular Braithwaite's theory of reintegrative shaming, which calls for the censuring of wrongdoing (but not of wrongdoers) before reintegrating offenders.

This argument is not without its own loose ends, though. The claim that taking responsibility and making reparation will always necessarily be painful is an empirical one. And even if it is true for all people, the painfulness of the process will vary from person to person. Should restorative justice programmes be attempting to administer a consistent level of pain across similar types of offenders? And even if we could reach agreement that this was desirable, how could it be achieved, given that offenders will vary substantially in how painful they find admitting responsibility, and making reparation? For some, the opportunity to ease their conscience and win back the respect of their families and victims may completely overwhelm any painfulness involved.

Implications for practice

Re-examining conventional practices

One implication of collapsing the distinction between restorative justice and retributive justice is that advocates of restorative justice should examine more closely the criminal justice practices glibly lumped together and dismissed as retributive justice to determine which of these practices do in fact promote the goals espoused by restorative justice advocates.

Restorative justice advocates have tended to think in limited terms about the shape of restorative justice. For many advocates, restorative justice necessarily involves some sort of communication between the victim and the offender. But there are other ways in which it may be possible to help repair victims' harm. For example, as I have mentioned, many jurisdictions have victim support programmes, sometimes located within police stations, sometimes outside, which are responsible for assisting victims through the investigative process, and if the matter is taken further, through the processes of prosecution, conviction and, eventually, parole and release. Most Western countries have introduced compensation schemes, and in many jurisdictions there is provision for victims to make a statement to court about their experiences. Of course these innovations have attracted their share of criticism (just as have victim–offender conferencing schemes), but it would pay restorative justice enthusiasts to grapple more seriously with these and other initiatives (see Zedner 2002 for an overview of victim-related developments in the mainstream criminal justice system).

Re-examining restorative practices

While it is unlikely that that consensus will emerge on the role punishment should play in restorative justice, there are greater prospects for more widespread agreement, if not consensus, on what should be done in practice (Braithwaite and Strang 2000: 206). This is because, as I mentioned earlier, regardless of whether people think restorative justice should include punishment, most would concede that things can and do go wrong in restorative justice meetings.

This raises the question of what sort of safeguards should be used to protect participants in restorative justice meetings from excessive punishment. The risk of not recognizing the potential for conferences to punish people (whether it be desired or not) is that the importance of checks and balances can be overlooked. In fact safeguards can come to be viewed as an obstacle to the attainment of restorative justice. As a practitioner overseeing an American restorative justice programme told me: 'Once you take punishment away, you don't need lawyers, their [offenders'] liberty is not at threat. Lawyers just get in the way, and justice delayed is justice denied' (Roche 2003b: 34). But as I and other authors in this volume have tried to demonstrate, there are plenty of things that can go wrong in a restorative justice meeting. In this chapter I have focused on the harm that can be done to offenders, but there are also risks for victims. There are many instances where conferences fail to live up to their goals in the treatment of victims.

One solution is to place limits on participants' discretion. There is considerable discussion about what limits should be placed on restorative justice conferences. My survey (Roche 2003b: 235) of 25 restorative justice programmes showed that:

> regardless of the form of review, agreements are most often left undisturbed. In such cases as those when agreements are overruled, practitioners and judges take different approaches: when practitioners overrule it is to decrease their severity, when judges intervene it is increase it; internal review tends to enforce upper limits, and external review lower ones.

Limits can also be built into the original decision-making processes. I mentioned earlier Braithwaite's analogy with democratic processes in discussing aberrant conference outcomes. Braithwaite also argues that commitment to democratic, deliberative values also provides a solution to the problem of self-defeating outcomes. In the case of the despot, this means campaigning for the election of a genuine democratic at the next vote (Braithwaite and Strang 2000: 207). In the case of a retributive conference, it means having confidence that someone will challenge the retributive sentiment expressed in the conference: 'Welcoming plurality is the best way of guaranteeing that there will be someone who will speak up when domination occurs' (Braithwaite and Strang 2000: 205). This suggested approach is not unproblematic, as it presumes that all victims and offenders have someone who will speak up on their behalf, a claim which is the subject of lively debate (see Roche 2003a: 636 for a discussion of the debate between Johnstone 2002 and Braithwaite 2002 on this point).

If restorative justice is to follow this procedural path, however, it follows that offenders should be entitled to accept more punishment than a judge would otherwise order (just as victims should be entitled to decline to call for offenders' punishment). It would also suggest that the agreement should not turn on its severity or consistency but on the quality of the decision-making process that produced it. Provided deliberations involve those affected by a crime, agreements only need comport with broad parameters. Where problems are detected in the quality of the decision-making process or transgress those limits, agreements should be quashed and participants invited to remake the decision, with the benefit of advice from a judge.

Conclusion

Zehr's *Changing Lenses* is one of the key references in the restorative justice literature, and his retributive/restorative contrast has been repeated on countless occasions. It is easy to see why. In 1990, when *Changing Lenses* was written, restorative justice was almost unheard of, and the retributive/restorative contrast – like the rest of the book – was an elegant and catchy exposition of a certain approach to criminal justice that helped create a global social movement that has had considerable impact on modern debates about criminal justice. But the contrast, as I have attempted to show in this chapter, also had its limits. It is neat but inaccurate. Not only did it fail to represent fairly retributive justice theory, and ignore reforms to modern criminal justice institutions, it also stymied critical thinking about restorative justice. Early restorative justice scholarship and practice were typified by an almost evangelical fervour that was apparently blind to the possible shortcomings of restorative justice. Of course, this tendency cannot be attributed solely to any one writer or any one method of explaining justice, and such faith is not always a bad thing; after all, without it, reform advocates would quickly become discouraged and give up. But in the long run, simple understandings and blind faith are not conducive to the design and implementation of fair and effective systems of justice.

There are signs, however, that restorative justice scholarship has already entered a new phase. Two major elements of this second generation are visible. One is a lively theoretical debate about whether punishment should play any role in restorative justice. As I have described, writers line up on both sides of this question, but it is encouraging to observe the attempts by writers on both sides to bridge the gap, or at least narrow the topics on which they disagree. The second strand to this scholarship is an emerging understanding of restorative justice that is increasingly built on observation of actual processes, rather than on ideal, or biblical or historical images. Based on this understanding, there is an increasing awareness of the dangers posed by restorative justice, and the ways in which restorative justice can depart from its goals. With this awareness comes a growing interest in examining the effectiveness of checks and safeguards in restorative justice programmes.

Both these debates have plenty left to run. One relatively undeveloped area of debate is about the different possible forms of restorative justice. The retributive/restorative contrast has possibly contributed to a tendency to see restorative justice in fixed terms. And while there has been intense debate about the merits of models developed in different countries – mediation, circles, conferences, etc. – these approaches all have more in common than they have differences. A fruitful area of future debate is to contemplate the forms of restorative justice that are compatible with the mainstream institutions of criminal justice, as well as to consider forms of restorative justice that might operate outside the criminal justice system.

Selected further reading

Duff, R.A. (2001) *Punishment, Communication and Community*. Oxford: Oxford University Press. This book presents possibly the most sustained attempt to reconcile the ideas of restorative justice with more conventional penal theory.

Braithwaite, J. (2002) *Restorative Justice and Responsive Regulation*. New York, NY: Oxford University Press. Braithwaite presents a panoramic view of restorative justice across a range of arenas, including criminal justice, corporate regulation and international peace-making. His analysis considers both theoretical and empirical questions alike.

Daly, K. (2002) 'Restorative justice – the real story', *Punishment and Society*, 4: 55–79. Daly is one of the leading restorative justice writers. Her work is particularly valuable because it pays as much attention to demonstrating empirically the strengths of restorative justice as it does to criticizing its weaknesses.

Duff, R.A. and Garland, D. (eds) (1994) *A Reader on Punishment*. Oxford: Oxford University Press. This an excellent place to start for anyone interested in punishment, providing a collection of key writings from leading theorists, with helpful introductions and explanations from the editors.

References

Ashworth, A. (1993) 'Some doubts about restorative justice', *Criminal Law Forum*, 4: 277–99.

Barton, C. (2000) 'Empowerment and retribution in criminal justice', in H. Strang and J. Braithwaite (eds) *Restorative Justice: Philosophy to Practice*. Aldershot: Ashgate.

Bentham, J. (1830) *The Rationale of Punishment*. London: Heward digitized version available at http://www.la.utexas.edu/research/poltheory/bentham/rp/index.html.

Braithwaite, J. (2002) *Restorative Justice and Responsive Regulation*. New York, NY: Oxford University Press.

Braithwaite, J. and Mugford, S. (1994) 'Conditions of successful reintegration ceremonies: dealing with juvenile offenders', *British Journal of Criminology*, 34: 139–71.

Braithwaite, J. and Strang, H. (2000) 'Connecting philosophy and practice', in H. Strang and J. Braithwaite (eds) *Restorative Justice: Philosophy to Practice*. Aldershot: Ashgate.

Christie, N. (1977) 'Conflicts as property', *British Journal of Criminology*, 17: 1–26.

Daly, K (2000) 'Revisiting the relationship between retributive and restorative justice', in H. Strang and J. Braithwaite (eds) *Restorative Justice: Philosophy to Practice*. Aldershot: Ashgate.

Daly, K (2002) 'Restorative justice – the real story', *Punishment and Society*, 4: 55–79.

Dignan, J. (2003) 'Towards a systemic model of restorative justice: reflections on the concept, its context, and the need for clear constraints', in A. Von Hirsch *et al.* (eds) *Restorative Justice and Criminal Justice: Competing or Reconcilable Paradigms*. Oxford: Hart Publishing.

Duff, R.A. (2001) *Punishment, Communication and Community*. Oxford: Oxford University Press.

Duff, R.A. (2003a) 'Restoration and retribution', in A.Von Hirsch *et al.* (eds) *Restorative Justice and Criminal Justice: Competing or Reconcilable Paradigms*. Oxford: Hart Publishing.

Duff, R.A. (2003b) 'Probation, punishment and restorative justice: should altruism be engaged in punishment', *Howard Journal*, 42.

Duff, R.A. and Garland, D. (eds) (1994) *A Reader on Punishment*. Oxford: Oxford University Press.

Finnane, M. (2001) '"Payback", customary law and criminal law in colonised Australia', *International Journal of the Sociology of Law*, 29: 293–310.

ICC (International Criminal Court) http://www.icc-cpi.int/home.html (last accessed 5 May 2005).

Johnstone, G. (2002) *Restorative Justice: Ideas, Values, Debates*. Cullompton: Willan Publishing.

Levrant, S. Cullen, F. Fulton, B. and Wozniak, J. (1999) 'Reconsidering restorative justice: the corruption of benevolence revisited?', *Crime and Delinquency*, 45: 3–27.

Mani, R. (2002) *Beyond Retribution: Seeking Justice in the Shadows of War*. Cambridge: Polity Press.

McCold, P. (2000) 'Toward a holistic vision of restorative juvenile justice: a reply to the maximalist model', *Contemporary Justice Review*, 3: 357–72.

Roberts, S. (1979) *Order and Dispute: An Introduction to Legal Anthropology*. Harmondsworth: Penguin Books.

Roche, D. (2003a) 'Gluttons for restorative justice', *Economy and Society*, 32: 630–44.

Roche, D. (2003b). *Accountability in Restorative Justice*. Oxford: Oxford University Press.

Shapland, J. (1988) 'Fiefs and peasants: accomplishing change for victims in the criminal justice system', in M. Maguire and J. Pointing (eds) *Victims of Crime: A New Deal?* Milton Keynes: Open University Press.

Shapland, J. (2000) 'Victims and criminal justice: creating responsible criminal justice agencies', in A. Crawford and J. Goodey (eds) *Integrating a Victim Perspective within Criminal Justice*. Aldershot: Ashgate.

Shapland, J., Willmore, J. and Duff, P. (1985) *Victims in the Criminal Justice System*. Aldershot: Gower.

Strang, H. (2001) 'The crime victim movement as a force in civil society', in H. Strang and J. Braithwaite (eds) *Restorative Justice and Civil Society*. Cambridge: Cambridge University Press.

Strang, H. (2002) *Repair or Revenge: Victims and Restorative Justice*. Oxford: Oxford University Press.

Van Ness, D. (1993) 'New wine and old wineskins: four challenges of restorative justice', *Criminal Law Forum*, 4: 251–76.

Von Hirsch, A., Ashworth, A. and Shearing, C. (2003) 'Specifying aims and limits for restorative justice: a 'making amends' model?', in A. Von Hirsch *et al.* (eds) *Restorative Justice and Criminal Justice: Competing or Reconcilable Paradigms*. Oxford: Hart Publishing.

Walgrave, L. (2002) 'Restorative justice and the law: socio-ethical and juridical foundations for a systematic approach', in L. Walgrave (ed.) *Restorative Justice and the Law*. Cullompton: Willan Publishing.

Walgrave, L. (2003) 'Imposing restoration instead of inflicting pain', in A. Von Hirsch *et al.* (eds) *Restorative Justice and Criminal Justice: Competing or Reconcilable Paradigms*. Oxford: Hart Publishing.

Zedner, L. (1994) 'Reparation and retribution: are they reconcilable?', *Modern Law Review*, 57: 228–50.

Zedner, L. (2002) 'Victims', in M. Maguire *et al.* (eds) *The Oxford Handbook of Criminology*. Oxford: Oxford University Press.

Zehr, H. (1990) *Changing Lenses*. Scottdale, PA: Herald Press.

Zehr, H. (2002) *The Little Book of Restorative Justice*. Intercourse, PA: Good Books.

Chapter 6

Alternative visions of restorative justice

Margarita Zernova and Martin Wright

Introduction

As restorative justice has grown in popularity, its proponents have developed a number of models of how restorative justice could be conceptualized and practised. It may not be an exaggeration to suggest that each proponent has his or her own vision of restorative justice. The diversity of thinking has led to numerous debates among proponents putting forward their own versions of it and criticizing competing models (McCold 1998). We shall consider two recent debates. The first relates to the implementation of restorative justice and its relationship with the criminal justice system. The second concerns ways of extending its scope: from reform of the criminal justice system, to change at the local community level, to transforming the structure of society.

Implementing restorative justice and its relationship with the criminal justice system

Process and outcome-focused visions of restorative justice

There is no agreement among restorative justice proponents as to how exactly restorative justice should be implemented and what its relationship to the criminal justice system should be (Van Ness 1989, 1993; Bazemore and Walgrave 1999b; Wright 1996, 1999; McCold 2000; Walgrave 1999, 2000; Braithwaite 2002; Van Ness and Strong 2002; Dignan 2002, 2003). Yet it is possible to distinguish at least two major competing models (although most proposals will probably fall somewhere in between the two versions, or will present some combination of them). We shall refer to them as the process-focused and the outcome-focused models.

The process-focused model has been outlined and advocated by McCold (2000) under the label of the 'purist' model of restorative justice. It is 'pure' in the sense that it 'includes only elements of the restorative paradigm and excludes goals and methods of the obedience and treatment paradigms' (McCold 2000: 372–3). It adopts Tony Marshall's definition: 'Restorative justice is a process whereby all the parties with a stake in a particular offence come together to resolve collectively how to deal with the aftermath of the offence and its implications for the future'(1998 cited in McCold 1998: 20).

That is, the fundamental feature of the model is the empowering co-operative problem-solving process which involves victims, offenders and their communities in face-to-face meetings and provides them with an opportunity to solve their problems in a way acceptable to them. Proponents of this model are reluctant to bring legal professionals and authorities into the restorative justice process and argue that co-operative decision-making cannot be accomplished by other people on behalf of primary stakeholders in crime because '[a]uthorities simply cannot compel co-operation, remorse, reconciliation or forgiveness' (McCold 2000: 373, 382).

Because the co-operative empowering process cannot be forced, this model of restorative justice is voluntary in the sense that it rejects judicial coercion (McCold 2000). Although in some situations imposition of 'minimum' force may be necessary, this does not make coercion a restorative practice, even when it is employed with restorative motivation (McCold 2000: 382–3).

In practice, the process-focused model of restorative justice would involve diverting cases from the criminal justice system to victim–offender mediation programmes, community conferences or peace/healing circles. Proponents believe that as more and more cases are diverted from the traditional procedure to restorative justice programmes, restorative processes could gradually permeate the formal justice system (McCold 2000: 387). Eventually the restorative way of dealing with offences would become the norm and traditional punishment an exception. That is, advocates of this version of restorative justice suggest that it should start small and 'pure' and then grow until it transforms the criminal justice system. The long-term ambition is radically to change the system, yet to do so in an incremental, 'bottom-up' fashion.

The outcome-focused model of restorative justice arose out of criticism of Marshall's definition, which is fundamental to the process-focused model. According to advocates of the outcome-focused vision of restorative justice, Marshall's definition is 'at once too broad and too narrow' (Bazemore and Walgrave 1999b: 48). It is too narrow because it limits restorative justice to instances where 'coming together' can take place and excludes from the restorative justice 'tent' situations where a face-to-face meeting between victims, offenders and their communities is either impossible or undesirable. At the same time, these authors believe that the definition is too broad because it does not refer to repairing harm. As a consequence, such a definition 'provides no specific boundaries on the kinds of processes included' (Bazemore and Walgrave 1999b: 48).

The process-focused model of restorative justice has also been criticized on the ground that 'it will be condemned to remain some kind of a "soft ornament" in the margins of "hard core" criminal justice' (Walgrave 1999: 131) and will have no chance to change the criminal justice system. This is because this model is likely to operate by way of diverting cases from the 'traditional' criminal justice system to restorative justice programmes outside the system to enable informal and voluntary restorative justice encounters to take place.

Critics of Marshall's definition propose that '[r]estorative justice is every action that is primarily oriented toward doing justice by repairing the harm that has been caused by a crime' (Bazemore and Walgrave 1999b: 48). This definition serves as the foundation for a model which has become known as 'maximalist' restorative justice (Bazemore and Walgrave 1999b; Walgrave 2000) and which we refer to as the outcome-focused vision. It clearly attaches primary importance to the achievement of restorative outcomes – in particular, reparation of harm caused by crime. Its proponents acknowledge that these can be best achieved through a voluntary and empowering restorative process, but believe that where such a process is either impossible or undesirable it is acceptable to employ judicial coercion. Involvement of crime stakeholders in the restorative process is seen as a means towards restorative outcomes, rather than as an end in itself.

The outcome-focused model ascribes a significant role to legal professionals. In situations where no voluntary reparation of harm occurs judges would order reparation. Also, there will be judicial oversight over the restorative process as a safeguard, and judges will be able to over-rule decisions of stakeholders if they are inconsistent with restorative values (Bazemore and Walgrave 1999b; Walgrave 2000).

The outcome-focused model requires that, in practice, restorative justice should operate by transforming the criminal justice system at once in a 'top-down' fashion. This should be done through reorienting the goals of the criminal justice system away from retributive and towards restorative ones. The aim is 'maximal' transformation of the system.

Subsequent debates about the outcome- and process-focused models

Some other critics have joined the outcome *v.* process-focused models debate. Thus, Braithwaite and Strang claim that 'restorative justice is conceived in the literature in two different ways. One is a process conception, the other a value conception' (2001: 1). The 'process' conception of restorative justice is based on the belief that its distinctive feature is a process which brings together stakeholders in crime. This is essentially McCold's process-focused model (or 'purist' model, using his own terminology). The 'value' conception is an understanding of restorative justice based on the assumption that what is distinctive about restorative justice is the underlying values. The outcome-focused model (or 'maximalist' restorative justice as it is called by Bazemore and Walgrave 1999b and Walgrave 2000) can be viewed as a value conception, given the claim that the model reflects what its proponents argue is the core value of restorative justice (reparation of harm).

The first issue discussed in these debates has been the question of which model presents a more desirable blueprint for the development of restorative justice. Most advocates who have joined the debate have raised doubts about whether restorative justice can present a viable alternative to the existing criminal justice system if it is limited to informal processes (as the process-focused model seems to suggest), at least at this stage in its development:

> if the definition of restorative justice is indeed tied to a particular kind of informal dispute-resolution processing the effect will be to drastically restrict the scope of restorative justice theory and practice. And restorative justice initiatives themselves are likely to remain confined for the most part to diversionary processes that will, at best, have a marginal status at the periphery of the regular criminal justice system. (Dignan 2003: 138).

It was argued that the adoption of a process-oriented concept of restorative justice represents a missed opportunity to bring about broad and far-reaching reforms of the criminal justice system. Instead, restorative justice needs to be conceptualized and developed as a 'fully integrated' part of the criminal justice system, which needs to be 'radically and systematically' reformed in accordance with restorative justice principles (Dignan 2002, 2003).

The second issue was the question of what degree of importance should be attached to restorative processes, as opposed to outcomes. A number of restorative justice proponents criticise the process-focused model of restorative justice because of the danger that focusing on process and maximally empowering stakeholders in crime may well lead to punitive outcomes. The outcome-focused model may avoid this particular danger because it sets explicit criteria as to what the outcome should be: to repair harm caused by the crime. However, it does not pay sufficient attention to the participatory process which is a fundamental element of restorative justice. A number of restorative justice advocates have proposed to combine the process-oriented model with the outcome-oriented one, so that participants in the process are treated in accordance with an independent set of values (Boyes-Watson 2000; Braithwaite and Strang 2001; Roche 2001). So, a process where stakeholders decide 'to boil the offender in oil and criticise the victim for bringing trouble on herself' will not qualify as restorative justice. Neither will a situation where 'a judge makes a non punitive order to help both an offender and a victim to get their lives back together but refuses to hear submissions from them that this is not the kind of help they want' (Braithwaite 2000: 434–5).

The third issue debated in the aftermath of the process-focused/outcome-focused disagreement was whether the respective models represent true alternatives to punishment and treatment paradigms. Advocates of the outcome-focused vision of restorative justice believe that their model has a potential to present a 'fully-fledged systemic alternative intended to replace in the longer term both the rehabilitative and retributive … justice systems' (Walgrave 1999: 131). However, McCold (2000) accused the outcome-focused model of absorbing both the rehabilitative and retributive goals. According to McCold, the model incorporates rehabilitative goals because its proponents argue that restorative justice should 'offer (at a minimum) no fewer opportunities for offender reintegration and rehabilitation than systems grounded in individual treatment assumptions' (Bazemore and Walgrave 1999a: 363–4). At the same time, the model implicitly includes retributive goals because it views the society as a direct victim of crime to which the offender owes direct reparation in addition to – or instead of – individual victims. It allows an obligation to repair '[a]n abstract harm to an abstract entity' to be judicially imposed; therefore it incorporates elements of retributive justice (McCold 2000: 389–90).

Walgrave responded to McCold's criticisms, arguing that judicially imposed reparation does not constitute punishment, because when a reparative obligation is imposed on the offender, the intention is to repair harm, and not to punish the offender (Walgrave 2000, 2001, 2002, 2003; for a similar view, see Willemsens 2003; Wright 1996, 2003). Walgrave also argues that it is important for strategic reasons to distinguish restorative justice from punishment. If the distinction is not maintained, restorative justice will be absorbed into the traditional punitive approach and lost conceptually.[1]

Some questions and critical comments about the process and outcome-focused models

In this subsection we would like to make some critical comments and raise questions concerning the process and outcome-focused models and the debates surrounding them. We shall also attempt to analyse the implications of each model for the development of restorative justice and the potential problems and dangers.

Defining restorative justice

It seems that proponents of each model have felt a pressing need to 'develop a clear and explicit definition and vision of restorative justice … [which] should serve as a unifying focus for reflection and experimentation among practitioners and scientists, and should inform policy makers and the public about what restorative justice is and *is not*' (Bazemore and Walgrave 1999b: 46, emphasis in original). Such 'clear and explicit' definitions serve as foundations for the respective models. It can be argued that the attempt to develop precise definitions and unifying visions of restorative justice is problematic. What appears to underlie the quest for precision and homogeneity is a belief that these are desirable phenomena within the restorative paradigm. It has been suggested, for instance, that a clear definition of restorative justice would help to preserve its good reputation by expelling from the restorative justice realm practices which are not restorative (Bazemore and Walgrave 1999b; Roche 2001).

If this suggestion is grounded on the notion that it may be possible to guarantee this by coming up with a foolproof definition and vision of restorative justice, such an assumption is rather questionable (Pavlich 2002b). But even if it were possible to develop such a perfect definition and vision, they could be misinterpreted or misapplied in practice; as is true of most human ideals. The aim would be to help prevent programmes which are not truly restorative from being described as such, and therefore giving restorative justice a bad name. For example, Miers and colleagues (2001: 2) question whether programmes in which there is little attempt to involve victims can reasonably be called 'restorative' at all. However, some would argue that losses resulting from restricting admission into the restorative justice camp might outweigh benefits in the long term, because imposing strict criteria may stifle creativity, discourage innovation, reduce diversity within the restorative justice field and create a danger of bringing dogmatism into the restorative justice movement.

It appears that a balance needs to be found between establishing a value framework for restorative justice and avoiding rigidity in applying that framework. Some proponents suggest that restorative justice should not be viewed in 'either/or' terms: either something is restorative justice or not. Perhaps it should be a matter of degree. McCold (2000), for example, proposes degrees of restorativeness, and so does Van Ness (2002). Bazemore and Schiff (2005: 32) argue against claiming that restorative justice should be confined to any specific programme (or to having a programme at all); they quote Dignan and Marsh's (2001) view that a response is restorative if it emphasizes the offender's accountability, provides a decision-making process that encourages participation by key participants and aims at putting right the harm.

An alternative to the criminal justice system?

Other questions concern the relationship between restorative justice and the criminal justice system. As noted above, proponents of both the outcome- and process-focused models of restorative justice aspire to create a radical alternative which would challenge the existing criminal justice system. However, they propose different routes towards that end. Outcome-focused writers believe that it could be achieved if restorative justice were incorporated into the criminal justice system as a sentencing option. Process-focused writers argue that an alternative to the criminal justice system could be created by keeping restorative justice informal and voluntary and diverting cases from the criminal justice system into restorative programmes operating outside the system. We would question the potential of both – outcome- and process-focused – models to present a genuine alternative to the state justice system and challenge it.

We have presented the two models as opposites. However, are they really so different from each other and from the 'traditional' response to crime? Both accept the authority of criminal law, both seem to subscribe to a number of assumptions underlying the criminal justice system, neither seems to challenge its broader ideology and structure.

As far as the outcome-focused model is concerned, its proponents suggest that the proposed 'alternative' should develop *within* the criminal justice system, bound by legal formality and implemented by criminal justice practitioners. Is there not a contradiction between something claiming to be an 'alternative' to the system and at the same time essentially accepting – and operating within – the institutional and ideological framework of the system (Pavlich 2005)? Is there not a danger that attempts to implement restorative justice within the criminal justice system will dilute and distort restorative justice philosophy, lead to co-optation of restorative justice, and perpetuate and strengthen the existing system, instead of challenging it?

The potential of restorative justice operating by way of diversion from the criminal justice system – as advocated by the proponents of the process-focused model – to present an alternative is also doubtful. It appears from proposals of the advocates of this vision of restorative justice that their model would be sanctioned by the system and would depend on the system in numerous ways (for example, cases would be referred to restorative programmes only if they satisfied the criteria set by the system; should restorative justice 'fail' in an individual case, the case would be referred back to the unrestorative system). What seems to be proposed is restorative justice operating outside the system, but at the same time under the tutelage of the system, surrounded by law. Whereas outcome-focused writers claim to challenge the system while operating restorative justice within it, the advocates of the process-focused vision aspire to do so while complementing it and leaving it to deal with the cases they cannot handle. Arguably, neither model has a potential to bring about significant changes to the way crime is being responded to.

The issue of coercion

Another issue relates to coercion. The outcome-focused model regards formal judicial coercion as consistent with restorative practice, and neglects the empowerment of stakeholders in the offence. According to proponents of the process-focused model, in doing so, the outcome-focused vision fails to challenge the existing system. In McCold's words, '[r]estorative justice is about a fundamentally different way of doing justice' (2000: 396), but the outcome-focused model, with its judicially imposed sanctions and its neglect of the restorative process, fails to challenge 'business as usual': 'the same laws, the same process, the same coercion, and the same goals – with one addition' (McCold 2000: 396).

The debate appears to have centred on whether judicial coercion should be part of restorative justice, or whether restorative justice should be limited to voluntary informal encounters. An assumption seems to be made by proponents of the process-focused model that restorative justice operating by way of diversion from the criminal justice system can qualify as a voluntary way of 'doing justice'. However, it seems inevitable that at least in some cases the consent of offenders may be motivated by the fear that unless they agree to take part in a restorative justice encounter 'voluntarily', they will be subjected to prosecution and judicial sanctions. Also, should the issue of coercion be limited to judicial coercion? Offenders may be subjected to various informal pressures (for example, from their families or other members of their communities) to participate in restorative justice interventions. These, too, might make offenders' participation in restorative justice encounters less than voluntary.

We suggest that the outcome- and process-focused debate concerning the question of coercion is misleading and ignores some important issues. In particular, it overlooks the fact that completely voluntary restorative justice may be an unrealistic ideal. As long as restorative justice operates in the shadow of the criminal justice system, judicial coercion is present at the background. The process-focused model also fails to view informal pressures as a form of coercion. Besides, it may be too simplistic to think of coercion in either/or terms: the process is either coercive or voluntary. There are degrees of coercion.

The marginalization issue

Our next set of questions relates to the issue of potential marginalization of restorative justice. As has been mentioned above, critics of the process-focused model believe that if restorative justice is conceptualized and practised as a voluntary informal process, it will be marginalized with no chance of influencing events in the criminal justice arena (Bazemore and Walgrave 1999b; Walgrave 1999, 2000; Dignan 2003). Hence it is argued that restorative justice needs to be made an integral part of the criminal justice system, and a 'radical and systemic' reform of the criminal justice system in line with restorative justice principles and values needs to be conducted (Dignan 2002, 2003).

Those who suggest that preserving restorative justice as voluntary and informal is likely to lead to its marginalization may be right. However, would that necessarily be an undesirable development, and is the large-scale state-managed implementation currently taking place in some European countries (Miers and Willemsens 2004) necessarily benefiting restorative justice? First, it can be argued that keeping it low-profile may benefit restorative justice at this stage, because before a large-scale implementation involving radical institutional transformations is attempted, certain fundamental changes in public attitudes and social values need to take place. Thus, arguably, today restorative justice need not be more than a 'sensitizing theory' (Zehr 1990: 227), or a critique which could cause us to think more carefully and critically about our ideologies and actions in the criminal justice arena (and perhaps more generally). Secondly, the idea of grand state-sponsored reforms (with a view to transforming the criminal justice system and thereby avoiding marginalization of restorative justice) has strong authoritarian and totalitarian overtones, and therefore should be treated with great caution (Pavlich 2002b). Thirdly, there are numerous historical examples suggesting that large-scale top-down reforms often backfire, and it may be wise to be suspicious of them.

The conflict behind the debate

What deeper conflict lies behind the outcome- *v.* process-focused models debate? One critic commenting on the distinction between the 'process' and 'value' conceptions of restorative justice has suggested that:

> *the tension is between two competing value commitments:* (i) to a process in which victims and other stakeholders can participate meaningfully in criminal justice proceedings; and (ii) to case dispositions which are designed to further restorative rather than punitive goals. (Johnstone 2004: 12, emphasis in original)

Applying this comment to the debate on outcome- *v.* process-focused models, we suggest that the debate is a consequence of a potential conflict between two restorative justice values. The process-focused model prioritizes the empowerment of stakeholders.[2] However, attaching primary importance to the stakeholder empowerment could increase the risk of non-restorative outcomes, in particular punishment. The outcome-focused model avoids this danger by prioritizing restorative outcomes, imposed if necessary. The consequence is that the empowerment of stakeholders is restricted, as their decisions can be over-ruled or they may be left out of the process. So, arguably, this is a debate resulting from a potential conflict of two restorative justice values – empowering stakeholders and ensuring restorative outcomes.

Is it desirable to resolve this conflict and to declare certain restorative justice values to be superior to others in all circumstances (as the two models seem to be doing)? It can be argued that if some restorative justice values are considered as overarching and universalizable, this can lead to potentially unethical or 'unrestorative' responses in some situations. Maybe a better approach is to weigh up the relevant factors on a case-by-case basis within those general principles without which the process could not properly be called 'restorative'. If restorative justice values seem to conflict in a particular situation, the ethical work needs to be carried out within the complexities of a concrete situation, while balancing such restorative values as, for example, empowerment of stakeholders, repair of harm to the victim, the needs of the offender and the protection of the community.

The scope of restorative justice

Restorative 'reformism' and 'radicalism'

What is now called 'restorative justice' started out as victim–offender mediation and focused on creating programmes aiming to deal with individual offences or disputes by means of dialogue between the victim and the offender, or disputants. As it has evolved, its proponents have raised their aspirations to transformation of the criminal justice system so as to reorient it away from retributive and towards restorative goals. However, today among those who have gathered under the banner of restorative justice not everybody sees this as their primary, or only, objective. Some restorative justice advocates are critical about defining goals so narrowly and propose a much more ambitious agenda (Mika 1992; Harris 1989, 1991, 1998a, 1998b cited in McCold 1998; Dyke 2000; Morris 1995, 2000; Sullivan and Tifft 1998, 2000a, 2000b, 2001). The next debate within the restorative justice movement which we shall describe and analyse relates to the questions: should restorative justice be limited to the reform of criminal justice system, or should it aim at much deeper and wider social changes? Should it be confined to responding to individual instances of behaviour defined as 'criminal' or 'anti-social', or should it become a tool in a struggle against social and economic injustices? We shall use the labels 'reformist' and 'radical', respectively, for the advocates of these two models. We would like to point out, however, that not every proponent clearly falls within either the 'reformist' or the 'radical' camp. Many proposals fall in between.

'Reformist' restorative justice views the transformation of the criminal justice system in accordance with restorative justice principles (but within the existing structural and ideological framework) as its primary – or only – objective. The process and outcome-focused models discussed earlier in this chapter could serve as examples of 'reformist' restorative justice, as their proponents believe that 'restorative justice is about healing responses to crime or wrongdoing and is not a general social justice theory about the distribution of social and/or economic goods' (McCold 2000: 361).

The 'radical' model of restorative justice emerged as a result of criticism of the 'reformist' one, its narrow focus and its desire to preserve much of the existing system. Radical critics are sceptical about the 'reformist' model which 'represents a fundamental unwillingness to break away from the existing paradigm' (Harris 1989: 34). They believe that '[t]rying to patch restorative justice onto the existing fundamentally retributive system is a transplant the social body will reject ... restorative justice without transformation of the roots of social injustice and without dismantling the contours of our present retributive system is *not* enough' (Morris 1995: 288, 291, emphasis in original).

Radical critics argue that the 'reformist' model of restorative justice, like conventional criminal justice, puts responsibility on the individual offender and ignores social-structural pressures towards crime (Harris 1998b cited in McCold 1998). It limits the scope of restorative justice to dealing with harms and injustices labelled 'crimes' by the criminal justice system and, consequently, fails to respond to instances of harm and violence which tend to escape legal definitions of 'crime', or are 'only' white collar crime. This implies an assumption that some categories of harms and instances of violence are acceptable, or matters merely for civil law, while others are unacceptable. It is suggested by proponents of 'radical' restorative justice that the requirements of restorative justice cannot be met, unless the campaign is significantly widened in such a way as to confront not only instances of violence and harm which have been proscribed by criminal law, but also all other instances of violence and injustices at all levels of the social existence, irrespective of whether or not they have been defined as 'crimes' by the criminal justice system (Morris 2000; Sullivan and Tifft 1998, 2000a, 2000b).

On this view restorative approaches should extend their scope beyond criminal justice to other forms of conflict resolving and peace-making. Thus, Braithwaite (2002) argues that the term should include the 'responsive regulation' of industrial relations, mediation in schools and even international conflicts. The method could be applied to breaches of industrial safety laws and corporate frauds which, as Gorringe (2004: 62–3) points out, cause thousands more deaths and injuries, and cost vastly more, than 'street crime'.

Some comments on restorative 'radicalism' and 'reformism'

The 'reformist'/'radical' debate raises questions of what restorative justice should attempt to be: should it be justice for individuals or for society?

Should it be a one-issue campaign aimed at the reform of the criminal justice system, or should it aim at fundamental social changes?

The 'reformist' model focuses on the reform of the criminal justice system. The model accepts the authority of criminal law and operates within the structural and ideological framework of the state justice system. It may well be that its advocates are no less concerned with broader and deeper social problems and reforms, but do not appear to regard them as part of the campaign for restorative justice. 'Radical' restorative justice challenges the fundamental concepts and assumptions underlying the criminal justice system and proposes to operate outside the traditional definitions of 'crime'. It significantly widens the scope of the campaign for restorative justice to include all injustices, harms and violations of some people by others, irrespective of whether or not they have been proscribed by criminal law.

What is behind this debate? Is it likely to be resolved? On one view, the 'radical'/'reformist' debate reflects the deeper philosophical and political persuasions of its proponents. They attempt to ground restorative justice within their broader political and philosophical perspectives and create models of restorative justice that would fit within those perspectives: for instance, Harris attempts to locate restorative justice within radical feminism (1989b cited in McCold 1998), Sullivan and Tifft try to adapt it to anarchist communism (2001), Braithwaite positions it within his 'republican theory' (Braithwaite and Pettit 1990; Braithwaite 2002). Achieving some sort of consensus on the question of what the scope of restorative justice should be and what exactly it should aim to achieve would require no less than proponents radically changing their wider political and philosophical stances – a highly unlikely event.

A different explanation for the reformist/radical debate is that it has to do with the meanings of the word 'justice'. The advocates on the two sides of the argument are talking past each other, because they have different aspects of 'justice' in mind. The radicals use 'justice' to mean social justice. While many proponents of the 'reformist' restorative justice are, no doubt, just as much in favour of social reform as the radicals, they do not appear to include it in their conception of justice. They are thinking of the reactive response: what do we do when person A robs person B in the street? One aspect of justice *is* about street robbery, which can have serious consequences for the person injured (and perhaps some others); the social injustices mentioned are no less real, but of a different kind.

However, irrespective of whether the 'radical'/'reformist' debate is resolved, it is still possible that restorative justice could be extended beyond the confines of criminal justice, even if a less radical route for its development is taken. One possibility, as Braithwaite (2002) suggests, lies in extending the scope of restorative justice beyond conflicts that are conventionally defined as criminal. For example, school peer mediation could be viewed as an aspect of restorative justice because it shares the same basic approach to conflict, putting the repair of harm done to relationships and people above the need for assigning blame and dispensing punishment (Hopkins 2004: 29). In addition to dealing with individual conflicts, this might be a strategy for bringing up generations of children to become citizens who are more likely to respect one another, deal with conflicts in a restorative way and, on the most optimistic view, remodel the society accordingly.

Restorative justice may also extend its effects beyond the confines of criminal justice by pointing to local reforms, although admittedly they are not major structural ones.[3] Information about social conditions can emerge in the course of restorative dialogue, to be used in the formulation of crime reduction policy. In restorative justice a conference could be compared with a small 'truth and reconciliation commission', where the background can be explored. This means that the mediation or conferencing service can build up a picture of factors which tend to lead to crime: not merely security factors such as easy-to-steal goods in supermarkets, but high unemployment, lack of adequate recreational facilities for young people, ethnic minorities denied opportunities because of discrimination and many more. For instance, a member of one youth offending panel was 'so concerned about one of the [local] schools that he has been to speak to the governors and almost issued them with an ultimatum to start putting their house in order' (Crawford and Newburn 2003: 152). A process based on problem-solving can encourage open discussion, from which the community can learn about pressures towards crime and can take preventive action. Writing in the context of peace-making circles, Pranis *et al.* (2003) point out that circles enable participants to realize that crime is a symptom of deeper problems, and '[u]nderstanding this and pulling together to do something about it, participants begin to tackle the larger issues – social, economic, educational, political, racial, philosophical, institutional, governmental, or religious – that cause disharmony and that can culminate in crime' (Pranis *et al.* 2003: 224). The paradigm of restorative justice should, according to Wright (2002), include the responsibility of the mediation agency to feed back findings of this kind to the authorities responsible for social policy, so that remedial action can be taken. It can bring out worthwhile local improvements, even if it does not reform the basic socioeconomic structure of society. Thus, Bazemore and Schiff (2005: 70–7, 271–310) propose that community groups should conduct the conferencing process, and that this in turn would lead to community-building, which could result in more significant changes in the long term than merely dealing with the diverse individual cases. They also give the example of a school where there were hundreds of expulsions and calls to the police each year (2005: 270–1, 298–9): as a result of a restorative initiative, it was transformed into one where children help one another resolve incidents.

It is of course very much to be hoped that these proposals would indeed lead to worthwhile improvements, but radical critics would have some reservations about extending the scope of restorative justice in this way. As far as proposals to expand restorative justice through use of school peer mediation are concerned, it may well be that this innovation may create a generation of people with better communication skills and abilities to achieve peaceful resolutions to their conflicts. However, critics of mediation have argued that resolutions of interpersonal disputes through mediation may mask and perpetuate wider social conflicts, inequalities and oppressions which may have generated a dispute in the first place (Mika 1992; Pavlich 1996; Dyke 2000).

This presents a recurrent dilemma for reformers: should they leave people to suffer bad conditions so as to build up a head of steam to force a thoroughgoing upheaval, or should they alleviate the present suffering at the risk of weakening the pressure for change? Besides, many disputes do not have any obvious roots in socioeconomic injustices but may spring from ordinary human interactions.

As for the suggestion (above) that mediations or conferences could serve as 'small truth and reconciliation commissions', the findings of which could be reported to the 'authorities responsible for social policy', radical critics would be rather sceptical of the potential of such practices to bring about the changes which they consider necessary and desirable for the success of restorative justice. Given that the reforms instigated by restorative processes are to be carried out by the 'authorities responsible for social policy', such reforms are unlikely to be of a kind that will bring about radical social change. They may well mop up some of the failures of the existing system, but are highly unlikely to challenge social injustices and conflicts which may well create the pressures leading to actions defined as 'crime'.

Conclusion

In this chapter we have described and analysed two major debates over how restorative justice should be conceived and practised. Is it possible and desirable to resolve the differences we have identified and discussed? We suggest that attempts to create precise visions of restorative justice, promoting them as superior to competing visions, and to strive towards consensus and unity may present dangerous paths towards elimination of diversity within the movement and stifling innovation. At the same time, deep disagreements among proponents may fragment and weaken the movement.

Writing in the context of feminism and building on works of Foucault, Jana Sawicki develops a concept of a 'politics of difference' (1991). Sawicki accepts that difference could be the source of fragmentation and disunity within a movement. However, it can also be a creative source of resistance and change:

> In a politics of difference one is not always attempting to overcome difference. One does not regard difference as an obstacle to effective resistance. Difference can be a resource insofar as it enables us to multiply the sources of resistance to the many relations of domination that circulate through the social field ... Moreover, if we redefine our differences, discover new ways of understanding ourselves and each other, then our differences are less likely to be used against us. In short, a politics that is designed to avoid dogmatism in our categories and politics, as well as the silencing of difference to which such dogmatism can lead, is a welcome alternative to polarized debate. (Sawicki 1991: 45).

We suggest that the concept of 'politics of difference' could be helpful and applicable to the restorative justice debates. Disagreements and differences among restorative justice advocates may be used either to divide them and damage their cause, or to enrich and benefit their campaign. Maybe it could be beneficial for restorative justice advocates to focus not on developing unified visions and eliminating diversity but on learning to live and struggle with differences. Some may feel that their task is to develop restorative justice as an improvement on criminal justice; others may believe that restorative justice should pursue the larger aim of building a fairer society.

Selected further reading

Bazemore, G. and Walgrave, L. (1999) 'Restorative justice: in search of fundamentals', in G. Bazemore and L. Walgrave (eds) *Restorative Juvenile Justice: Repairing the Harm of Youth Crime.* Monsey, NY: Criminal Justice Press. Outlines the outcome-focused vision of restorative justice.

Harris, M.K. (1989) 'Alternative visions in the context of contemporary realities', in *Justice: the Restorative Vision. New Perspectives on Crime and Justice.* Occasional Papers of the MCC Canada Victim Offender Ministries Program and the MCC US Office on Crime and Justice, 7: 29–38. Criticizes the 'reformist' vision and suggests a different agenda for restorative justice.

McCold, P. (2000) 'Toward a holistic vision of restorative juvenile justice: a reply to the maximalist model', *Contemporary Justice Review*, 3: 357–414. Presents the process-focused model of restorative justice and criticizes the outcome-focused model.

Sullivan, D. and Tifft, L. (2001) *Restorative Justice: Healing the Foundations of our Everyday Lives.* Monsey, NY: Willow Tree Press. Presents an example of the 'radical' vision of restorative justice.

Walgrave, L. (2000) 'How pure can a maximalist approach to restorative justice remain? Or can a purist model of restorative justice become maximalist?', *Contemporary Justice Review*, 3: 415–32. Defends the outcome-focused model from the criticisms put forward by proponents of the process-focused one.

Notes

1 Like Walgrave, Wright (2003: 5–7) distinguishes different forms of punishment, and points out that '[i]f all these are described by the same term, confusion is inevitable'; he suggests identifying them by terms such as 'punitive sanctions', 'reparative sanctions' and so on. The underlying argument is that restorative justice is an alternative to conventional punishment because the intention behind restorative sanction is not to inflict pain. There is opposition to this view within restorative discourse (Barton 2000; Daly 2000, 2002; Dignan 2002; Johnstone 2002; Duff 2002, 2003). Critics argue that whether or not causing pain is the primary intention is immaterial. Restorative justice is not an alternative to punishment. Rather, it is a different form of punishment.

2 However, it needs to be pointed out that the empowering process is prioritized only as long as the stakeholders actually want consensual decision-making, rather than court proceedings, or negotiations with professional representation.

3 The South African Zwelethemba experiment is a practical example (Shearing 2001; Roche 2003): incidents can be reported directly to community conferences, and peace-building committees consider what local improvements could reduce pressures towards crime.

References

Barton, C. (2000) 'Empowerment and retribution in criminal justice', in H. Strang and J. Braithwaite (eds) *Restorative Justice: Philosophy to Practice*. Aldershot: Ashgate/Dartmouth.

Bazemore, G. and Schiff, M. (2005) *Juvenile Justice Reform and Restorative Justice: Building Theory and Policy from Practice*. Cullompton: Willan Publishing.

Bazemore, G. and Walgrave, L. (eds) (1999a) *Restorative Juvenile Justice: Repairing the Harm of Youth Crime*. Monsey, NY: Criminal Justice Press.

Bazemore, G. and Walgrave, L. (1999b) 'Restorative justice: in search of fundamentals', in G. Bazemore and L. Walgrave (eds) *Restorative Juvenile Justice: Repairing the Harm of Youth Crime*. Monsey, NY: Criminal Justice Press.

Boyes-Watson, C. (2000) 'Reflections on the purist and maximalist models of restorative justice', *Contemporary Justice Review*, 3: 441–50.

Braithwaite, J. (2000) 'Decomposing a holistic vision of restorative justice', *Contemporary Justice Review*, 3: 433–40.

Braithwaite, J. (2002) *Restorative Justice and Responsive Regulation*. Oxford: Oxford University Press.

Braithwaite, J. and Pettit, P. (1990) *Not Just Deserts: A Republican Theory of Criminal Justice*. Oxford: Oxford University Press.

Braithwaite, J. and Strang, H. (2001) 'Introduction: restorative justice and civil society', in H. Strang and J. Braithwaite (eds) *Restorative Justice and Civil Society*. Cambridge: Cambridge University Press.

Council of Europe, Committee of Ministers (1999) *Recommendation No. R(99)19 ... to Member States Concerning Mediation in Penal Matters*. Strasbourg: Council of Europe.

Crawford, A. and Newburn, T. (2003) *Youth Offending and Restorative Justice: Implementing Reform in Youth Justice*. Cullompton: Willan Publishing.

Daly, K. (2000) 'Revisiting the relationship between retributive and restorative justice', in H. Strang and J. Braithwaite (eds) *Restorative Justice: Philosophy to Practice*. Aldershot: Ashgate/Dartmouth.

Daly, K. (2002) 'Restorative justice – the real story', *Punishment and Society*, 4: 55–79.

Dignan, J. (2002) 'Restorative justice and the law: the case for an integrated, systemic approach', in L. Walgrave (ed.) *Restorative Justice and the Law*. Cullompton: Willan Publishing.

Dignan, J. (2003) 'Towards a systemic model of restorative justice', in A. von Hirsch *et al*. (eds) *Restorative Justice: Competing or Reconcilable Paradigms?* Oxford and Portland, OR: Hart Publishing.

Dignan, J. and Marsh, P. (2001) 'Restorative justice and family group conferences in England: current state and future prospects', in A. Morris and G. Maxwell (eds) *Restorative Justice for Juveniles: Conferencing, Mediation and Circles*. Oxford: Hart Publishing.

Duff, R.A. (2002) 'Restorative punishment and punitive restoration', in L. Walgrave (ed.) *Restorative Justice and the Law*. Cullompton: Willan Publishing.

Duff, R.A. (2003) 'Restoration and retribution', in A. von Hirsch *et al.* (eds) *Restorative Justice: Competing or Reconcilable Paradigms?* Oxford and Portland, OR: Hart Publishing.

Dyke, D. (2000) 'Reaching toward a structurally responsive training and practice of restorative justice', *Contemporary Justice Review,* 3: 239–65.

Gorringe, T.J. (2004) *Crime.* London: SPCK.

Harris, M.K. (1989) 'Alternative visions in the context of contemporary realities', in *Justice: The Restorative Vision. New Perspectives on Crime and Justice.* Occasional Papers of the MCC Canada Victim Offender Ministries Program and the MCC US Office on Crime and Justice, 7: 29–38.

Harris, M.K. (1991) 'Moving into the new millennium: toward a feminist vision of justice', in H.E. Pepinsky and R. Quinney (eds) *Criminology as Peacemaking.* Bloomington, Indiana University Press.

Harris, M.K. (1998a) 'Reflections of a skeptical dreamer: some dilemmas in restorative justice theory and practice', *Contemporary Justice Review,* 1: 55–69.

Hopkins, B. (2004) *Just Schools: A Whole School Approach to Restorative Justice.* London: Jessica Kingsley.

Johnstone, G. (2002) *Restorative Justice: Ideas, Values, Debates.* Cullompton: Willan Publishing.

Johnstone, G. (2004) 'How, and in what terms, should restorative justice be conceived?', in H. Zehr and B. Toews (eds) *Critical Issues in Restorative Justice.* Monsey, NY: Criminal Justice Press, and Cullompton: Willan Publishing.

McCold, P. (1998) 'Restorative justice: variations on a theme', in L. Walgrave (ed.) *Restorative Justice for Juveniles: Potentialities, Risks and Problems for Research.* Leuven: Leuven University Press.

McCold, P. (2000) 'Toward a holistic vision of restorative juvenile justice: a reply to the maximalist model', *Contemporary Justice Review,* 3: 357–414.

Miers, D., Maguire, M., Goldie, S., Sharpe, K., Hole, C., Netten, A., Uglow, S., Doolin, K., Hallam, A., Enterkin, J., and Newburn, T. (2001) *An Exploratory Evaluation of Restorative Justice Schemes. Crime Reduction Research Series,* Paper 9. London: Home Office Research Development and Statistics Directorate.

Miers, D. and Willemsens, J. (2004) *Mapping Restorative Justice: Developments in 25 European Countries.* Leuven: European Forum for Victim–Offender Mediation and Restorative Justice.

Mika, H. (1992) 'Mediation interventions and restorative justice: responding to the astructural bias', in H. Messmer and H.-U. Otto (eds) *Restorative Justice on Trial. Pitfalls and Potentials of Victim Offender Mediation – International Research Perspectives.* Dordrecht: Kluwer Academic.

Morris, R. (1995) 'Not Enough!', *Mediation Quarterly,* 12: 285–91.

Morris, R. (2000) *Stories of Transformative Justice.* Toronto: Canadian Scholars' Press.

Pavlich, G. (1996) *Justice Fragmented: Mediating Community Disputes under Postmodern Conditions.* London: Routledge.

Pavlich, G. (2002a) 'Deconstructing restoration: the promise of restorative justice', in E.G.M. Weitekamp and H.-J. Kerner (eds) *Restorative Justice: Theoretical Foundations.* Cullompton: Willan Publishing.

Pavlich, G. (2002b) 'Towards an ethics of restorative justice' in L. Walgrave (ed.) *Restorative Justice and the Law.* Cullompton: Willan Publishing.

Pavlich, G. (2005) *Governing Paradoxes of Restorative Justice.* London, Sydney and Portland OR: Glasshouse Press.

Pranis, K., Stuart, B. and Wedge, M. (2003) *Peacemaking Circles: From Crime to Community.* St. Paul, MN: Living Justice Press.

Roche, D. (2001) 'The evolving definition of restorative justice', *Contemporary Justice Review,* 4: 341–53.

Roche, D. (2003) *Accountability in Restorative Justice*. New York, NY: Oxford University Press.

Sawicki, J. (1991) *Disciplining Foucault: Feminism, Power, and the Body*. New York, NY, and London: Routledge.

Shearing, C. (2001) 'Transforming security: a South African experiment', in H. Strang and J. Braithwaite (eds) *Restorative Justice and Civil Society*. Cambridge: Cambridge University Press.

Sullivan, D. and Tifft, L. (1998) 'The transformative and economic dimensions of restorative justice', *Humanity and Society*, 22: 38–54.

Sullivan D. and Tifft, L. (2000a) 'The requirements of just community: an introduction that takes into account the political economy of relationship', *Contemporary Justice Review*, 3: 121–52.

Sullivan, D. and Tifft, L. (2000b) *Restorative Justice as a Transformative Process: The Application of Restorative Justice Principles to Our Everyday Lives*. Voorheesville, NY: Mutual Aid Press.

Sullivan, D. and Tifft, L. (2001) *Restorative Justice: Healing the Foundations of Our Everyday Lives*. Monsey, NY: Willow Tree Press.

Van Ness, D. (1989) 'Pursuing a restorative vision of justice', in *Justice: The Restorative Vision. New Perspectives on Crime and Justice*. Occasional Papers of the MCC Canada Victim Offender Ministries Program and the MCC US Office on Crime and Justice, 7: 11–27.

Van Ness, D. (1993) 'New wine and old wineskins: four challenges of restorative justice', *Criminal Law Forum*, 4: 251–76.

Van Ness, D. (2002) 'The shape of things to come: a framework for thinking about a restorative justice system', in: E.G.M. Weitekamp and H.-J. Kerner (eds) *Restorative Justice: Theoretical Foundations*. Cullompton: Willan Publishing.

Van Ness, D. and Strong, K. (2002) *Restoring Justice*. Cincinnati, OH: Anderson.

Walgrave, L. (1999) 'Community service as a cornerstone of a systematic restorative response to (juvenile) crime', in G. Bazemore and L. Walgrave (eds) *Restorative Juvenile Justice: Repairing the Harm of Youth Crime*. Monsey, NY: Criminal Justice Press.

Walgrave, L. (2000) 'How pure can a maximalist approach to restorative justice remain? Or can a purist model of restorative justice become maximalist?', *Contemporary Justice Review*, 3: 415–32.

Walgrave, L. (2001) 'On restoration and punishment: favourable similarities and fortunate differences', in A. Morris and G. Maxwell (eds) *Restorative Justice for Juveniles: Conferencing, Mediation and Circles*. Oxford and Portland OR: Hart Publishing.

Walgrave, L. (2002) 'Restorative justice and the law: socio-ethical and judicial foundations for a systemic approach', in L. Walgrave (ed.) *Restorative Justice and the Law*. Cullompton: Willan Publishing.

Walgrave, L. (2003) 'Imposing restoration instead of inflicting pain', in A. von Hirsch *et al.* (eds) *Restorative Justice: Competing or Reconcilable Paradigms?* Oxford and Portland, OR: Hart Publishing.

Willemsens, J. (2003) 'Restorative justice: a discussion of punishment', in L. Walgrave (ed.) *Repositioning Restorative Justice*. Cullompton: Willan Publishing.

Wright, M. (1996) *Justice for Victims and Offenders: A Restorative Response to Crime* (2nd edn.) Winchester: Waterside Press.

Wright, M. (1999) *Restoring Respect for Justice*. Winchester: Waterside Press.

Wright, M. (2002) 'The paradigm of restorative justice', *VOMA Connections (Victim/Offender Mediation Association, Minneapolis)* (11), Summer, research and practice supplement.

Wright, M. (2003) 'Is it time to question the concept of punishment?', in L. Walgrave (ed.) *Repositioning Restorative Justice*. Cullompton: Willan Publishing.

Zedner, L. (1994) 'Reparation and retribution: are they reconcilable?', *Modern Law Review*, 57: 228–50.

Zehr, H. (1990) *Changing Lenses: A New Focus for Crime and Justice*. Scottdale, PA: Herald Press.

Part 2

Roots of Restorative Justice

Gerry Johnstone and Daniel W. Van Ness

Part 2 focuses on the intellectual, cultural, political and ethical roots of restorative justice ideas and practices. A common concern of the chapters in this part is to demonstrate the complexity of what are all too often presented as simple links between various social movements (such as the indigenous justice movement, the feminist movement and the victims movement), on the one hand, and the restorative justice movement, on the other.

One claim that frequently appears in the literature of restorative justice is that it draws upon restorative approaches to conflict resolution found in aboriginal communities and in the practices of our ancient ancestors. In Chapter 7, Christopher Cunneen starts by cautioning against uncritical acceptance of such a simplistic view, arguing instead for a conceptualization of current developments in restorative justice within a framework of 'hybridity' that is neither pre-modern nor modern. Using this framework, Cunneen goes on to explore numerous complex issues that need to be understood and addressed in any project which seeks to revive indigenous restorative justice.

Another place to which restorative justice thinkers have looked for alternative models of justice is biblical texts. These, of course, are problematic for those seeking an alternative to 'retributive' teachings on crime and justice since the Bible – or at least the Old Testament or the Hebrew Bible – *seems* to mandate a harsh and often violent response to wrongdoers. The claim of some restorative justice proponents, that biblical justice was restorative, appears to fly in the face of the evidence. In order to clarify the issues, Jonathan Burnside – in Chapter 8 – undertakes a much-needed exploration of the relationship between retribution and restoration in the 'meta-narrative' of the Bible as a whole and in the life of the early church. His conclusion – that rather than seeing retribution and restoration as stark opposites, the biblical tradition treats them as interdependent – is one which chimes well with some current thinking elsewhere in the restorative justice movement (see Chapter 5).

In Chapter 9 Kathleen Daly and Julie Stubbs shift attention from the roots of restorative justice in our past and in indigenous traditions to its links with feminist perspectives on law and justice and with contemporary race and gender politics. Following a succinct account of feminist perspectives on law and justice in general, they go on to review five themes which feminists have focused upon in their engagement with the restorative justice movement: theories of justice; the role of retribution; gender in restorative justice practices; the appropriateness of restorative justice for cases of sexual or family violence; and the politics of race and gender in making justice claims. In the process, they dismiss any simple notion of a natural affinity between feminist perspectives on justice and restorative perspectives. Yet, they do show that despite some scepticism about restorative justice's potential to advance women's, including racialized women's, justice claims, there is some degree of openness within the feminist movement to experimenting with restorative justice practices.

Another social movement which has shown considerable, but again cautious, interest in restorative justice is the victim movement. In Chapter 10, Simon Green explains the victim movement's stance towards restorative justice by describing the wider concerns expressed by the victim movement about the position and treatment of the crime victims in the criminal justice system. The restorative justice movement claims to respond to these concerns by providing an approach to justice that genuinely places the needs of victims at the centre of the justice process, as opposed to exploiting the suffering of victims in an effort to obtain tougher sanctions for offenders. While this is a laudable aim, Green points to voices not only within the victim movement but also within the restorative justice movement itself which warn against over-selling restorative justice as a victim-centred approach to crime capable of meeting all needs of all crime victims. A more realistic goal for restorative justice would be to place much more emphasis on meeting some real needs of some real victims, while also recognizing that – for victims' needs to be more fully met – restorative justice would have to be developed as one part of a wider set of initiatives, many of them outside the justice process. In the meantime, Green urges the restorative justice movement to take seriously its commitment to victims of crime by seeking ways of protecting victims from rhetoric and policies advanced in the name of the victim without actually being for the victim.

We close Part 2 with a chapter (11) by moral theorist Linda Radzik exploring some of the ethical roots of restorative justice theory and practice in everyday social practices through which people seek to make amends for wrongdoing and to repair relationships damaged by misconduct. According to Radzik, criminal wrongdoers often have a capacity, which is seldom recognized or exploited, to undertake positive and constructive acts – such as apology and restitution – to make amends for their wrongdoing. What is interesting about restorative justice, for Radzik, is that, rather than treating offenders as 'things to be manipulated', it recognizes this capacity and seeks to provide processes and forums that facilitate its development and expression. This does raise questions, though, about whether the moral goal of getting offenders to make amends is an appropriate one for the (liberal) state to pursue through coercive interventions into the lives of offenders and about whether the active pursuit of this goal through coercive means actually undermines any moral repair that may take place. Radzik carefully considers these reservations and urges restorative justice theorists to recognize them and take them seriously, while also pointing to ways in which restorative justice can be defended against such objections.

Chapter 7

Reviving restorative justice traditions?

Chris Cunneen

Introduction

I entitled this chapter with a question because of the complexity of the issues involved and the unresolved matters that continue to be debated among restorative justice advocates. Much of the debate over restorative justice 'traditions' centres around claims that restorative justice draws on traditional processes for resolving disputes among indigenous peoples and on processes in the Western world which were eroded from the twelfth century onwards and were gradually supplanted with the modern state. Yet there are serious historical and factual questions that need to be addressed before we can assume an Arcadian past where restorative justice ruled supreme. Are there restorative justice traditions to be revived? And should they be revived? Like most complex matters, a simple answer to these questions is neither possible nor desirable.

The particular development of restorative justice in the later decades of the twentieth century in North America, Australia and New Zealand helps to explain the links made between restorative justice and indigenous societies. Early developments in restorative justice in Australia, New Zealand and Canada based their approaches on connections to indigenous cultures. Family group conferencing in Australia and New Zealand was said to have been inspired by Maori traditions. Sentencing circles began in Canada in the 1990s in response to indigenous demands for more effective sentencing, while American 'peace-making' criminology also drew inspiration from native American traditions.

The search for origins of restorative justice in indigenous traditions provided an important rhetorical tool to distinguish restorative justice traditions from modern state-centred systems of punishment. Similarly, in relation to the development of punishment in the West, it has been argued that the processes for ensuring that offenders made up for wrongdoings through restitution to the victim were eroded as the state assumed a central role in prosecuting and punishing offenders.

The broad argument is that over the longer period of human history the state assumed the function of punishment only relatively recently and that, previously, societies functioned well with restorative forms of sanctioning. Restorative methods of dispute resolution were dominant in non-state, pre-state and early state societies: individuals were bound closely to the social group and mediation and restitution were primary ways of dealing with conflict. Further, these pre-modern, pre-state restorative forms of sanctioning can still be found practised in indigenous communities today.

There are a number of assumptions underpinning this story of restorative justice. Most important for the current discussion are the simple dichotomies: non-state sanctioning is restorative (and, conversely, state-imposed punishment is not) and indigenous societies and pre-modern societies do not use utilize retributive forms of punishment as their primary mode of dispute resolution. Adding to the difficulties of separating fact from fiction have been some grandiose claims made by advocates. For example, John Braithwaite claimed that restorative justice was grounded in traditions of justice from the ancient Arab, Greek and Roman civilizations through to the public assemblies of the Germanic peoples, Indian Hindu, ancient Buddhist, Taoist and Confucian traditions. He concluded that 'restorative justice has been the dominant model of criminal justice throughout most of human history for all the world's peoples' (Braithwaite 1999: 1).

As Daly (2002: 62) has noted, these extraordinary claims need to be seen in a particular context. They are not 'authoritative histories' of justice, but attempts to construct origin myths about restorative justice. If it can be established that the first form of human justice was restorative justice, then advocates can claim legitimacy for contemporary restorative justice alternatives to state-sponsored retributive justice.

Of course, not all claims about the historical origins of restorative justice are so all-encompassing. Johnstone (2002) has noted that proponents do acknowledge some problems with ancient forms of restitution, but emphasize their advantages over systems of state punishment: 'Most importantly, they argue, pre-modern people saw clearly what has become obscured to us: that crime is at its core a violation of a person by another person' (Johnstone 2002: 40). Thus, the primary purpose should be to persuade offenders to acknowledge their responsibility for harm and to make restitution. Although the development of a state-based system of punishment has led to some better outcomes, such as greater equality before the law, it also resulted in the loss of community-based mechanisms of crime control, the neglect of victims and the loss of communally educative, constructive and reintegrative responses to crime and punishment.

The search for restorative justice in indigenous traditions of dispute resolution has also led to claims which grossly oversimplify indigenous cultures. As Daly notes, the 'reverence for and romanticisation of an indigenous past slide over practices that the modern "civilised" Western mind would object to, such as a variety of harsh physical (bodily) punishments and banishment' (2002). Part of the interest in indigenous forms of justice derives from the renewed political assertion of rights by indigenous groups in the former British 'settler' colonies of North America, Australia and New Zealand from the 1970s onwards. Indigenous demands for recognition of customary law and rights brought attention to indigenous modes of social control, and indigenous leaders themselves would often articulate their claims for indigenous law within the language of restorative justice.

The Navajo Nation in the USA provides an example of the rejuvenation of indigenous law. A revival of Navajo justice principles and processes began in the 1980s. The Navajo customs, usages and traditions came to form what has been called the Navajo common law (Yazzie and Zion 1996: 159). The Navajo system is based on peace-making, described as a healing process aimed at restoring good relationships among people. Navajo methods seek to educate offenders about the nature of their behaviours, how they impact on others, and to help people identify their place in the community and reintegrate into community roles: 'Peace-making is based on relationships. It uses the deep emotions of respect, solidarity, self examination, problem-solving and ties to the community' (Yazzie and Zion 1996: 170).

However, indigenous processes for maintaining social order and resolving disputes are diverse and complex. The United Nations estimates there are 300 million indigenous peoples globally, living in 70 nations spread over all continents. One might think that this basic fact should caution claims made about indigenous restorative justice practices. The Yolgnu people of Arnhemland in Australia and the Inuit of the Arctic Circle may have quite similar historical experiences of colonization and subsequent social and political marginalization, but their traditional social processes of resolving disputes are not necessarily 'restorative' simply because they are indigenous peoples.

Given the diversity of indigenous cultures it is not surprising that there are a variety of sanctions used by indigenous peoples within their specific cultural frameworks. Certainly in most cases these sanctions are by definition 'non-state'.[1] However, are they restorative? Not surprisingly, some sanctions are 'restorative', in the sense that a modern proponent of restorative justice would accept, and some, clearly, are not. Indigenous sanctions might include temporary or permanent exile, withdrawal and separation within the community, public shaming of the individual and restitution by the offender and/or his or her kin. Some sanctions may involve physical punishment such as beating or spearing.

There are a number of lessons to draw from this. First, indigenous societies deploy a range of sanctions depending on the seriousness of the offending behaviour. The definition of 'seriousness' will arise from specific cultural frameworks. In terms of traditional sentencing goals we could legitimately characterize these as retribution, deterrence, public denunciation, restitution and reparation. Certainly, restitution to the victim is an important goal but it would be incorrect to see it as the only the goal. Physical punishments seem to display a strong element of retribution.

Secondly, many of the sanctions are based on avoidance rather than confrontation between offender and victim. Temporary or permanent exile of the offender, or enforced avoidance between the offender and the victim, may certainly restore harmony to the community but it is not a process which would normally find favour with restorative justice advocates. It is certainly not a process that is based on a principle of reintegration.

Restorative justice has had a tendency to romanticize indigenous dispute resolution. Blagg (1997: 2001) has argued that this romanticization is a type of Orientalism – a phrase referring to the way the West develops a complex set of representations for constructing and understanding the 'Other'. In this case restorative justice discourses have come to construct indigenous justice mechanisms which are devoid of political and historical contexts:

> 'Through the Orientalist lens, distinctive and historically embedded cultural practices are essentialised, reduced to a series of discrete elements, then reassembled and repackaged to meet the requirements of the dominant culture' (Blagg 2001: 230).

Ironically, the reconstruction and appropriation of idealized indigenous modes of social control and governance by restorative justice advocates may serve further to disempower indigenous political claims for self-determination.

As indigenous people struggle with modern nation-states over fundamental rights to self-governance, restorative justice advocates may see their own agenda for justice reform as more important. From this perspective even the very notion of 'reviving' indigenous traditions may seem patronizing to indigenous groups engaged in long historical struggles to have their rights to land, law and culture respected.

Restorative justice mechanisms and indigenous participation

There are many forms of restorative justice currently being practised in a variety of countries. This section of the chapter will discuss some problems in the interaction between restorative justice practices and indigenous people. It seems clear from the experience in Australia that family group conferencing and youth justice conferencing, as examples of a restorative justice approach, have not always had a beneficial outcome for indigenous people (Cunneen 1997). As Blagg has noted:

> While references to pre-modern forms of dispute resolution liberally embellish the texts of many restorative justice advocates, the actual practices of conferences tend to be highly modernistic in content, privileging established forms of justice discourse, official modes of communicative reasoning, and reflecting non-Indigenous patterns of community association (2001: 231).

Identifying the reasons for lack of indigenous participation in conferencing allows us to explore broader questions about what we might expect from the 'promise' of restorative justice and its capacity to deliver on that promise for indigenous people.

First, there is a need to understand the relationship between indigenous peoples and the state. Although restorative justice advocates argue against state-centred retributivist punishment, in practice, restorative justice is often firmly embedded within the formal justice apparatus. The problem for indigenous people is that the state may be seen to lack legitimacy. A restorative programme initiated and controlled by the state may be viewed with suspicion by indigenous peoples, who see the state in terms of its colonial functions. The state is synonymous with government agencies that forced people on to reservations, denied basic citizenship rights, forcibly removed children, enforced education in residential schools, banned cultural and spiritual practices, and imposed an alien criminal justice system (Zellerer and Cunneen 2001: 246–47).

While the creation of restorative programmes within a legal framework and through centralized government agencies may be seen as an achievement by some restorative justice advocates, it may create specific problems for marginalized indigenous communities who seek to maintain and develop their own justice initiatives. In short, although both indigenous groups and restorative justice advocates may seek to alter traditional state practices of punishment, the political outcomes they are seeking to achieve cannot be assumed to be identical.

Secondly, we need to consider the relationship between culture, subjectivity and identity. There is a tendency in the restorative justice literature to see 'victim' and 'offender' statuses as uncomplicated and homogeneous categories. The assumption is that we all subjectively experience these categories in identical or, at least, similar ways without any inherent complexity. Yet indigenous people, like all people, will subjectively experience the restorative justice process through the lens of their culture. How they conceptualize being a victim or offender will be determined by a range of experiences and cultural understandings.

The fact that some indigenous cultures use separation/banishment between offender and victim suggests that subjective experiences of a restorative justice model will be quite different from non-indigenous participants. Patterns of kinship authority will also play a fundamental role in the way individuals will react and interact within a process like a conference. There is ample evidence of the cultural difficulties and disadvantages indigenous people face in the formal legal process and the same problems may be reproduced in restorative justice programmes (Cunneen 1997). These difficulties partly derive from a range of cultural and communicative (verbal and non-verbal) differences which govern who can speak and when. The failure to understand and respect indigenous structures and processes for interpersonal communication can lead to further 'silencing' of an indigenous voice in the process.

Punishment and postmodern hybridity

The simple dichotomy posed is between a pre-modern, pre-state restorative justice, and a modern state's model of retributive (and rehabilitative) punishment. Perhaps a more useful conceptualization is to see the current developments in restorative justice within a framework of hybridity that is neither pre-modern nor modern.[2] By 'hybridity', I am referring to transformations in punishment, similar to a form of 'fragmented' justice or 'spliced' justice, where traditional legal bureaucratic forms of justice are combined with elements of informal justice and indigenous justice (Blagg 1997; Daly 2002).

Thinking about restorative justice within the context of hybridity provides us with the opportunity to ascertain some of the more complex answers to questions regarding the possibility of 'reviving' restorative justice traditions, particularly as they relate to indigenous peoples, and the forms such revival might take. There are both pessimistic and optimistic accounts of where hybrid forms of restorative justice might lead. I present both arguments below.

A pessimistic view of hybridity

A pessimistic reading of current developments is that in many cases restorative justice programmes have been introduced within frameworks emphasizing individual responsibility, deterrence and incapacitation. Thus, there may be elements of restorative justice, retribution, just deserts, rehabilitation and incapacitation all operating within a particular jurisdiction at any one time. For example, it has been argued that this is a fair characterization of what occurred in the introduction of youth justice conferencing in Australia during the 1990s (Cunneen 1997).

Some form of conferencing operates in all Australian jurisdictions and, along with New Zealand, Australia is regularly upheld as an example of restorative justice programmes in action. Yet, as I have noted elsewhere (Cunneen 2002), during the late 1990s and early 2000 the Australian government was criticized by four United Nations human rights monitoring bodies for possible breaches of international human rights conventions because of the operation of 'three strikes' mandatory sentencing legislation for juveniles, particularly indigenous young people, in a number of Australian jurisdictions. Other research has consistently shown that indigenous young people do not receive the same restorative justice options as non-indigenous young people and are more likely to be processed through interventions of arrest and court appearance (Cunneen 1997; Blagg 2001). A paradoxical outcome, then, is that restorative justice is available to non-indigenous young people while indigenous youth are subject to the formal mechanisms of non-indigenous state punishment.

Some discussions on postmodern penality are useful for contextualizing the relationship of restorative justice to traditional modes of punishment. Pratt (2000), for example, has discussed the return of public shaming and the resurfacing of a pre-modern penal quality. He also notes the development of other phenomena that would seem out of place within a modern penal framework, including boot camps, curfews and the abandonment of proportionality (2000: 131–3). O'Malley (1999) has also discussed the 'bewildering array' of developments in penal policy, including policies based on discipline, punishment, enterprise, incapacitation, restitution and reintegration – policies which are mutually incoherent and contradictory. In this context, state-run restorative justice programmes need to be seen within the totality of policing and criminal justice strategies. These strategies increasingly involve a range of inconsistencies in punishment, from programmes which hark back to a nostalgic past (emphasizing either discipline or 'shaming') while others emphasize individual responsibility (just deserts and incapacitation).

According to O'Malley (1996), state justice programmes which allow 'government at a distance' have been attractive and include a re-emphasis on 'community-based' processes. These have involved apparently indigenous forms of control where they are seen as complementary to the broader aims of government. The attempt is usually made to appropriate certain aspects of indigenous forms of governance and to ignore others seen as irrelevant or inappropriate.

We can understand these processes operating in the context of a greater *bifurcation* of existing justice systems. For example, conferencing models have been introduced in contexts where juvenile justice systems are increasingly responding to two categories of offenders: those defined as 'minor' and those seen as serious and/or repeat offenders. Minor offenders benefit from various diversionary programmes involving restorative justice methods. Serious and repeat offenders are ineligible for diversionary programmes and are dealt with more punitively through sentencing regimes akin to adult models. The paradox for indigenous people is that they are more likely to find themselves on a non-restorative pathway into the justice system.

Pathways into the justice system are increasingly determined by the prediction of risk. Risk analysis and risk prediction become critical for determining how individuals are identified, classified and managed, and whether they are diverted to restorative justice processes like conferencing. Thus, strategies of actuarialism, the prediction of risk and incapacitation (like mandatory imprisonment) can be seen as complementary to restorative justice, and coexisting within a single system of criminal justice. Risk assessment becomes a tool for dividing populations, between those who are seen to benefit from restorative justice practices and those who are channelled into more punitive processes of incapacitation.

Issues of bifurcation and risk assessment are fundamental to understanding indigenous people's experience of restorative justice within state criminal justice systems. The risk assessment tools used in countries like Canada and Australia (such as the Youth Service Level Case Management Inventory) disadvantage indigenous people. There is a strong focus on individual factors to predict risk. Factors such as age of first court order, prior offending history, failure to comply with court orders and current offences are all used to predict risk of future offending. A range of socioeconomic factors are also connected to risk, including education (such as 'problematic' schooling and truancy) and unemployment. The individual 'risk' factors are decontextualized from broader social and economic constraints within which young people live. This is particularly problematic for indigenous people who are among the poorest and most marginalized groups within society.

Not surprisingly, studies of recidivism, using a risk analysis framework, draw the following conclusions: 'Over time, the probability of those juveniles on supervised orders in 1994–95 who are subject to multiple risk factors (eg, male, indigenous, care and protection order) progressing to the adult corrections system will closely approach 100 per cent' (Lynch *et al.* 2003). Like many such studies, the above research identifies the most 'robust' characteristics for predicting repeat offending – and political minority status (in this case being indigenous) is at the forefront. For governmental regimes that attempt to balance imperatives of 'evidence-based' programmes and more punitive law and order policies for recidivists, it means that indigenous young people are seen as the 'problem cases' who are unlikely to respond to the opportunities offered by restorative justice.

An optimistic view of hybridity

An optimistic account of the interaction between indigenous demands for the development of their own justice systems, the work of restorative justice advocates and the changing face of state-controlled punishment is that new positive forms of hybrid justice can be created which are consistent with the principles of restorative justice. In this context, new spaces are created wherein indigenous communities can formulate and activate processes derivative of their own particular traditions and where scepticism about state-imposed forms of restorative justice can be replaced with organically connected restorative justice processes that resonate with indigenous cultures.

What we have is the opening up of 'liminal spaces' (Blagg 1998) where dialogue can be generated, where hybridity and cultural difference can be accepted. This vision of restorative justice is emancipatory in a broader political sense, whereby restorative justice is not only a tool of criminal justice, it is a tool of social justice. As I have stated elsewhere, hybridity can involve a reimagining of new pathways and meeting places between indigenous people and the institutions of the colonizer – a place where the institutions of the colonizer are no longer taken for granted as normal and unproblematic, where the cultural artefacts of the colonizers (i.e. the criminal justice system) lose their pretension to universality. In this context, restorative justice provides an opportunity for decolonization of our institutions and our imaginations and a rethinking of possibilities (Cunneen 2002).

A significant body of research indicates that where Aboriginal community justice initiatives have flourished there have been successes in reducing levels of arrests and detention, as well as improvements in the maintenance of social harmony (for an overview, see Cunneen 2001). The success of these programmes has been acknowledged as deriving from active Aboriginal community involvement in identifying problems and developing solutions. These solutions can be seen within the context of restorative justice. They cover the range of criminal justice practice:

- Offender programmes such as indigenous men's programmes which target family violence.
- Indigenous healing lodges and other culturally specific residential alternatives to prison.
- Alternative court and sentencing processes such as circle sentencing and indigenous courts.

- Alternative policing processes such as night patrols.
- Alternative victim–offender mediation and dispute resolution processes such as community justice groups and elders groups.

The examples provided below will show more fully the hybrid nature of the interaction between indigenous restorative justice processes and the demand of non-indigenous state law. A major area of recent change has been the growth in circle sentencing and indigenous courts, allowing the community to become more actively involved in the sentencing process and, as a result, introduce new ideas about what might constitute an appropriate sentence for an offender. In this sense, community involvement opens the sentencing process up to influences beyond the ideas of criminal justice professionals. This is particularly important for Aboriginal communities who have generally been excluded from legal and judicial decision-making.

Indigenous courts[3] have been established for indigenous adult and juvenile offenders in many jurisdictions in Australia over recent years. The courts typically involve Aboriginal elders or community group members sitting on the bench with a magistrate. They speak directly to the offender, expressing their views and concerns about offending behaviour and provide advice to the magistrate on the offender to be sentenced and about cultural and community issues. Offenders might receive customary punishments or community service orders as an alternative to prison. As one example, consider the Murri Court in Queensland. The elders and community justice group members express their concerns and views directly to the offender. The conditions placed on court orders may involve meeting with elders or a community justice group on a regular basis and undertaking courses, programmes or counselling relevant to their particular needs. A non-indigenous Murri Court magistrate noted the following:

> Orders, particularly probation orders and intensive correction orders, often include conditions requiring attendance on the Justice Group and/ or Elders, attendance at counselling and/or programmes to address specific issues (for example domestic violence and family violence, alcohol or drug abuse), attendance at Indigenous Men's Groups or other support groups ... The extent of compliance required represents what might be considered to be significant punishment and deterrence whilst offering rehabilitation opportunities (Hennessy 2005: 5).

While the non-indigenous courts see traditional sentencing objectives are met, other factors are clearly at play. The magistrate at the Brisbane Children's Court stated:

> The [Youth] Murri Court sessions are intense, emotional occasions with a greater involvement of all parties. I can say that since the Youth Murri Court has been held that there has been a reduction in the number of serious offences committed by young Indigenous persons. There may be a number of reasons for this but I like to think that the Youth Murri

Court, by involving the wider community in the concern for the futures of young Aboriginal and Torres Strait Islander people, has in some way contributed to this result (Pascoe 2005: 7).

The courts are seen to validate a basic tenet of indigenous law and values – the authority and respect for elders of the community:

> The acknowledgment in a public forum of the Elders' authority and wisdom and their role as moral guardians of the community by the Court honours traditional respect for the role of the Elders. The Elders mean business and they make it quite clear to the offenders that they must honour their responsibilities after Court for the community support to be available. Often when addressing offenders, the Elders speak of the 'old people' (ancestors) and what they would have done or seen done to an offender in the 'old days'. This always strikes a chord with offenders – even the toughest (Hennessy 2005: 6).

Other customary actions include banishment from various areas, apologies and reparation. However, it is the role of the community in sanctioning the offender and providing conditional reacceptance that appears most powerful:

> Feedback indicates that the most significant impact on offenders in the Murri Court process is the possibility of reconnection with their local community and the support this offers them. Those who choose to take advantage of the support offered by the elders and the justice group tend to successfully complete their orders and make valuable changes to their lives (Queensland Magistrates Courts 2004: 43).

It is clear that the Murri Court has a powerful effect on participants:

> What cannot easily be explained is the power of the Murri Court process on a spiritual or emotional level. The power of the natural authority and wisdom of the Elders is striking in the courtroom. There is a distinct feeling of condemnation of the offending but support for the offender's potential emanating from the Elders and the Justice group members.
>
> Often similar emotions are expressed by the offender's family members. Declaring private concerns and fears for and about the offender in front of those assembled in court, in a public way, can be very cathartic for the family members (who are often victims of the offending themselves). Orders often need to take intimate family considerations into account in order to tailor orders which are designed not only to punish but also assist the offender address his/her problems with appropriate supports (Hennessy 2005: 5).

Indigenous community justice groups and elders groups have developed in many jurisdictions. In the examples above their work is directly connected to a modified court process. However, the work of these groups extends beyond the role of the courts in passing sentence. They are essentially involved in responding to community problems and restoring community harmony. For example, community justice groups might be involved in developing measures in relation to alcohol and substance abuse and domestic violence in indigenous communities. These strategies might include:

- Elders publicly shaming adults who gave alcohol to children.
- Educative and counselling programmes to address domestic violence and alcohol abuse.
- Banning individuals from purchasing alcohol in response to alcohol abuse problems.
- Sending juveniles to outstations[4] to address petrol and glue sniffing addictions (DATSIPD 1999: 8).

Community justice groups typically employ mediation between individuals and between family groups, which assists in reducing community tensions and provides the opportunity to reduce court matters for minor disputes. Community justice groups may work with and encourage the police to use their discretion in referring individuals to the community justice group to be dealt with through customary law. They may assist in the granting of bail, supervising bail conditions to ensure compliance and organizing accommodation. Regarding sentencing, the community justice groups help courts maximize the use of community-based orders as an alternative to prison by providing local programmes and working to ensure that offenders do not breach orders. This work may involve developing programmes and initiatives on outstations for use as diversionary options.

An assessment of community justice groups found that 'a strong theme in the activities of community justice groups is a desire to strengthen language, culture and customary law in their communities in order to restore a sense of cultural identity and high self-esteem' (DATSIPD 1999: 9). Indigenous people support notions of restorative justice to the extent that it promises an element of self-determination. For example, Nancarrow's interviews with indigenous women found that they supported restorative justice for dealing with family violence as an alternative to the criminal justice system, which they saw 'as a tool of oppression against indigenous people and a facilitator of increased violence against them and their communities' (2006: 8). Indigenous women identified restorative justice strategies as including 'mediation involving extended family members; outstations where elders guide people to achieve a sense of belonging and self worth; families supporting people to stop the violence; and community or family meetings' (Nancarrow 2006: 8).

Importantly, restorative justice provides an avenue for opening up the justice system to greater indigenous control. It is an opportunity to reconfigure the justice system with different values, different processes and different sets of accountability.

Some broader issues in 'reviving' indigenous restorative justice

The question of 'reviving' indigenous restorative justice is complex and there are a number of issues that need to be understood and addressed. These include the state's legal framework within which restorative justice operates, conflicting punishments, conflicting laws and the balancing of rights.

The state's legal framework

The broad legal and political framework within which justice operates critically affects the way indigenous justice develops. For example, the Navajo have been largely able to retain and develop indigenous law because they have the recognized inherent right to exercise jurisdiction over tribal matters. The recognition of the right of tribal sovereignty (limited though it may be) is part of the legal framework of Federal–Indian relations in the USA and derives from important US Supreme Court decisions in the early part of the nineteenth century recognizing Indian tribes as domestic dependent nations. The US Supreme Court affirmed in 1832 that Indian nations retained their inherent right of self-government. Since then they have been entitled to exercise legislative, executive and judicial powers, subject to the powers of the US Federal government.

This situation can be contrasted with Australia where indigenous peoples were not seen to possess laws or customs recognizable by the British. As a result there is no inherent right recognized today whereby indigenous people can develop and exercise their own jurisdiction over legal matters, except in situations where the state permits them to do so as a matter of policy or practice.

Processes like circle sentencing and indigenous courts in Australia and Canada fit within the broader criminal justice framework. If we take the development of circle sentencing in Canada we can see how the sentencing circles are placed within the existing parameters of Canadian law. Circle sentencing arose in Canada in 1992 out of a decision from the Supreme Court of the Yukon in the case of *R* v. *Moses*. The circle is said to be premised on three principles that are part of the culture of the Aboriginal people of the Yukon:

> Firstly, a criminal offence represents a breach of the relationship between the offender and the victim as well as the offender and the community; secondly, the stability of the community is dependent on healing these breaches; and thirdly, the community is well positioned to address the causes of crime (Lilles 2001: 162).

Circle sentencing is part of the court process and it results in convictions and criminal records for offenders (Lilles 2001: 163). Discretion as to whether a sentencing circle is appropriate remains with the judge, as does the ultimate sentencing decision. The judge is still obliged to impose a 'fit' sentence and is free to ignore the recommendations of the sentencing circle. Sentences imposed with the assistance of a sentencing circle are still subject to appellate court sentencing guidelines (Green 1998). Not surprisingly, there may be tensions between community involvement in the circle and the power which the judge retains. While at one level there is an appeal to 'equality' within the circle, it is clear that the circle itself is significantly constrained by the wider power of the non-indigenous criminal justice system.

Canadian case law sets out the criteria for involvement in a sentencing circle. *R* v. *Joseyounen* (1996) set out the following criteria:

1. The accused must agree to be referred to the sentencing circle.
2. The accused must have deep roots in the community in which the circle is held and from which the participants are drawn.
3. There are elders or respected non-political community leaders willing to participate.
4. The victim is willing to participate and has been subjected to no coercion or pressure in so agreeing.
5. The court should try to determine beforehand, as best it can, if the victim is subject to battered woman's syndrome. If she is, then she should have counselling and be accompanied by a support team in the circle.
6. Disputed facts have been resolved in advance.
7. The case is one which a court would be willing to take a calculated risk and depart from the usual range of sentencing (see Green 1998: 76).

Although not 'etched in stone' by the court, the criteria have been widely quoted and applied across Canada (albeit with variations such as whether the victim must attend).

Section 718.2(e) of the Canadian *Criminal Code* is also relevant to understanding the sentencing of Aboriginal offenders in Canada (McNamara 2000). The legislation provides that a court that imposes a sentence shall take into consideration (among a range of other factors) the following principles:

> (e) all available sanctions other than imprisonment that are reasonable in the circumstances should be considered for all offenders, with particular attention to the circumstances of Aboriginal offenders.

The Canadian Supreme Court in *R* v. *Gladue* (1999) confirmed that the unique circumstances of Aboriginal people that judges needed to consider included both the *processes* and *outcomes* of sentencing:

> The background consideration regarding the distinct situation of Aboriginal people in Canada encompass a wide range of unique circumstances, including most particularly:
> (a) the unique systemic or background factors which may have played a part in bringing the particular Aboriginal offender before the courts; and
> (b) the types of sentencing procedures and sanctions which may be appropriate in the circumstances for the offender because of his or her particular Aboriginal heritage or connection (cited in McNamara 2000).

Thus, the Supreme Court of Canada emphasized the importance of restorative justice and circle sentencing as an appropriate sentencing procedure for Aboriginal offenders.

Circle sentencing has been operating for indigenous offenders in a number of areas in New South Wales. Circle sentencing guidelines, procedures and criteria are established through criminal procedure regulations. The objectives of the circle sentencing court are to:

(a) include members of Aboriginal communities in the sentencing process;

(b) increase the confidence of Aboriginal communities in the sentencing process;

(c) reduce barriers between Aboriginal communities and the courts;

(d) provide more appropriate sentencing options for Aboriginal offenders;

(e) provide effective support to victims of offences by Aboriginal offenders;

(f) provide for the greater participation of Aboriginal offenders and their victims in the sentencing process;

(g) increase the awareness of Aboriginal offenders of the consequences of their offences on their victims and the Aboriginal communities to which they belong;

(h) reduce recidivism in Aboriginal communities (Potas *et al.* 2003: 4).

The fundamental premise underlying circle sentencing is that the community holds the key to changing attitudes and providing solutions. The court's deliberations have been typified as power-sharing arrangements: 'It is recognized that if the community does not have confidence that the power-sharing arrangements will be honoured, the prospect that circle sentencing will be successfully implemented is likely to be diminished' (Potas *et al.* 2003: 4).

An evaluation by New South Wales Judicial Commission found that circle sentencing helped break the cycle of recidivism and introduced more relevant and meaningful sentencing options for Aboriginal offenders. The courts improved the level of support for Aboriginal offenders and victims and promoted healing and reconciliation. The courts also increased the confidence and promoted the empowerment of Aboriginal persons in the community (Potas *et al.* 2003: iv).

Conflicting punishments and conflicting laws

A final area of contention in discussions of reviving or recognizing indigenous law is how to handle conflict when it arises between state and indigenous laws and punishments. It was noted at the beginning of this chapter that indigenous systems of sanctioning and punishment may involve inflicting serious physical injury. For example, in Australia, the ceremonial spearing of offenders, though not frequent, does occur as a legitimate tribal punishment.

Aboriginal law could give rise to conflict, for example, with rights and protections established by the United Nations in the Universal Declaration of Human Rights, the International Covenant on Civil and Political Rights, the Convention for the Elimination of All Forms of Discrimination against Women, the Convention on the Rights of the Child and the Convention against Torture and Other Cruel, Inhuman or Degrading Treatment or Punishment.

It is generally accepted that international human rights standards should apply. Article 33 of the draft *Declaration on the Rights of Indigenous Peoples* notes that indigenous peoples have the right to promote, develop and maintain their institutional structures and their distinctive juridical customs, traditions, procedures and practices, in accordance with internationally recognized human rights standards.

Thus, it is an established requirement that indigenous customs, traditions, procedures and practices comply with internationally recognized human rights standards. In Australia, the Aboriginal and Torres Strait Islander Social Justice Commissioner noted that 'all proposals for the recognition of Aboriginal customary law have taken as their starting point that any such recognition must be consistent with human rights standards' (Jonas 2003: 3).

The issues that arise not only refer to punishment but also to basic definitions of what constitutes crime. A recent case in the Northern Territory of Australia shows this complexity. GJ was a 55-year-old traditional Aboriginal man convicted of assaulting and having unlawful sexual intercourse with a 14-year-old Aboriginal girl. When the child was about 4 years of age, in the traditional way of the Aboriginal law of the community, the Ngarinaman Law, the child was promised as a wife to the older man. The 14-year-old was to be his second wife, and his first wife and their children were to remain as part of the household. In sentencing, Judge Martin noted the following:

> This is an extremely difficult case … You believed that traditional law permitted you to strike the child and to have intercourse with her. On the other hand, the law of the Northern Territory says that you cannot hit a child. The law of the Northern Territory also says that you cannot have intercourse with a child …
>
> You and the child's grandmother decided that you would take the child to your outstation. The grandmother told you to take the child and the grandmother told the child that she had to go with you. The child did not want to go with you and told you she did not want to go. The child also asked her grandmother if she could stay. Rather than help the child, the grandmother packed personal belongings for her …
>
> The child later told the police that she was 'at that old man's place for four days', and that she was crying 'from Saturday to Tuesday'. She knew that she was promised to you in the Aboriginal traditional way, but she did not like you. In the words of the child, 'I told that old man I'm too young for sex, but he didn't listen' (Martin CJ, *Queen v. GJ*, Supreme Court of Northern Territory, SCC 20418849, 11 August 2005, at 1–2).

GJ admitted hitting the child with a boomerang and having sexual intercourse with the child. He told police that in Aboriginal culture the child was promised as a wife from the time she was 4 years old and said that it was acceptable to start having sexual intercourse with a girl when she was 14 years old:

> I appreciate that it is a very difficult thing for men who have been brought up in traditional ways which permit physical violence and sexual intercourse with promised wives, even if they are not consenting, to adjust their ways. But it must be done. I hope that by sitting in your community today and saying these words, and I hope that by the sentence that I am going to impose upon you, that the message will get out not just to your community, but to communities across the Territory ...
>
> You have had a strong ceremonial life across widespread communities. You are regarded by the Yarralin Community as an important person in the ceremonial life of the community. You are responsible for teaching young men the traditional ways. I accept that these offences occurred because the young child had been promised to you ...
>
> I have spoken quite a lot about what you believed and how you felt. I must also remind you about how the child felt. She was upset and distressed and I have no doubt that your act of intercourse with her has had a significant effect upon her. The child has provided only a very brief Victim Impact Statement in which she does not speak of any emotional and psychological impact upon her. That is not surprising. This is a child who has been shamed within a community that obviously has very strong male members and strong traditional beliefs. It is not surprising that she would not be prepared to publicly state how she was feeling. I do not know, therefore, the extent of the effects or how long they will last, but I have no doubt that the effects have been significant (Martin CJ, *Queen* v. *GJ*, Supreme Court of Northern Territory, SCC 20418849, 11 August 2005, at 3–4).

The *GJ* case shows that generally accepted international human rights for women and children are in conflict with some indigenous laws and that there is significant conflict between state and indigenous law. It shows that the blending of indigenous law and state law will not always be an easy task. Further, in specific cases it will be indigenous law that needs to change if basic human rights are to be respected. Finally, the case shows that we cannot assume consensus on what constitutes lawful and unlawful behaviour. There is clearly significant support among *GJ*'s community for traditional law to be upheld.

Conclusion

This chapter has shown that simple dichotomies contrasting pre-modern indigenous restorative justice with modern state-centred systems of justice are not necessarily helpful. Indigenous societies were, and are, complex and their processes for dealing with crime and social disorder cover a range of possible responses from the restorative to the retributive.

It has been argued that a context of hybridity is a more useful representation to consider contemporary developments, where new forms of doing justice are developed which merge the restorative in new practices. The flexibility of new justice practices may accommodate indigenous justice demands, but are not necessarily the same as indigenous practices. For example, we can see the movement of circle sentencing from indigenous communities in Canada to indigenous communities in Australia, and from dealing with exclusively indigenous offenders to also including non-indigenous offenders. We can see this as 'reviving' indigenous dispute resolution, but it is also much more transformative than this as it moves across a range of jurisdictional, national and cultural boundaries.

Yet as indicated in this chapter there is also a 'dark' side to a developing hybridity. Restorative justice has found itself a partner to a greater emphasis on individual responsibility, deterrence and incapacitation. Criminal justice systems that bifurcate by dividing offender populations between the minor offenders and serious repeat offenders have only a limited vision of restorative justice, and indigenous and other minorities are likely to be fast-tracked towards the hard end of the system.

There are positive examples of indigenous/state processes merging in a hybrid way and which do respect indigenous claims for greater self-determination and control. In the examples of the indigenous courts and community justice groups we see the justice system reconfigured with different and more restorative values. However, it is also necessary to understand that processes like circle sentencing and indigenous courts exist within a broader state-based legal framework that still prioritize a range of considerations within sentencing. Further, we need to be clear that some indigenous laws and practices do not comply with generally recognized human rights standards. This is not an argument against restorative justice or indigenous justice. It is an argument for considering how we might deal with these conflicts.

Selected further reading

Blagg, H. (2001) 'Aboriginal youth and restorative justice: critical notes from the frontier', in A. Morris and G. Maxwell (eds) *Restorative Justice for Juveniles*. Oxford: Hart Publishing. Blagg provides a critical analysis of the introduction of restorative schemes for juveniles in Australia in relation to their impact on Aboriginal youth.

Green, R.G. (1998) *Justice in Aboriginal Communities: Sentencing Alternatives*. Saskatoon, Saskatchewan: Purich Publishing. The author provides a comprehensive overview of the development of circle sentencing in Canada, including analysis of key cases and particular initiatives such as Hollow Water.

Nancarrow, H. (2006) 'In search of justice for domestic and family violence: indigenous and non-indigenous Australian women's perspectives', *Theoretical Criminology*, 10: 1. Nancarrow discusses her comparative research on indigenous and non-indigenous women's understanding of the role of restorative justice in responding to domestic and family violence.

Zellerer, E. and Cunneen, C. (2001) 'Restorative justice, indigenous justice and human rights', in G. Bazemore and M. Schiff (eds) *Restorative Community Justice: Repairing Harm and Transforming Communities*. Cincinnati, OH: Anderson Press. The authors discuss restorative justice in the context of international human rights standards, particular those applicable to indigenous peoples.

Notes

1 The exception might be in post-colonial societies where the dominant indigenous group ensures state control through exclusion of other minorities (for example, Fiji), but even here it is likely that international pressure will ensure that the state legal system is one at least resembling something workable to the interests of the West (Findlay 1999).

2 It is tempting to argue that the hybridity is *postmodern*. However, there has been an ongoing debate over whether contemporary punishment in Western societies should be conceptualized as late modern or postmodern (Garland 1995; Hallsworth 2002). How the concept of hybridity fits within this debate is an issue in itself.

3 The courts are titled after local indigenous names such as Koori Courts (Victoria), Murri Courts (Queensland) and Nunga Courts (South Australia). New South Wales has adopted the Canadian circle sentencing model for indigenous people in that state.

4 Remote camps on indigenous land which may be used for a range of activities including cultural ceremonies and initiation, and training in traditional skills and work skills.

References

Blagg, H. (1997) 'A just measure of shame', *British Journal of Criminology*, 37: 481–506.

Blagg, H. (1998) 'Restorative visions and restorative justice practices: conferencing, ceremony and reconciliation in Australia', *Current Issues in Criminal Justice*, 10: 5–14.

Blagg, H. (2001) 'Aboriginal youth and restorative justice: critical notes from the frontier', in A. Morris and G. Maxwell (eds) *Restorative Justice for Juveniles*. Oxford: Hart Publishing.

Braithwaite, J. (1999) 'Restorative justice: assessing optimistic and pessimistic accounts', in M. Tonry (ed.) *Crime and Justice: A Review of Research*. Vol. 25. Chicago, IL: University of Chicago Press.

Cunneen, C. (1997) 'Community conferencing and the fiction of indigenous control', *Australian and New Zealand Journal of Criminology*, 30: 292–311.

Cunneen, C. (2001) *The Impact of Crime Prevention on Aboriginal Communities*. Sydney: New South Wales Crime Prevention Division and Aboriginal Justice Advisory Council.

Cunneen, C. (2002) 'Restorative justice and the politics of decolonisation', in E. Weitekamp and H.-J. Kerner (eds) *Restorative Justice: Theoretical Foundations*. Cullompton: Willan Publishing.

Daly, K. (2002) 'Restorative justice : the real story', *Punishment and Society*, 4: 55–79.

DATSIPD (Department of Aboriginal and Torres Strait Islander Policy Development) (1999) *Local Justices Initiatives Program. Interim Assessment of the Community Justice Groups*. Brisbane: Queensland Government.

Findlay, M. (1999) *The Globalisation of Crime. Understanding Transitional Relationships in Context*. Cambridge: Cambridge University Press.

Garland, D. (1995) 'Penal Modernism and Postmodernism', in S. Cohen and D. Blomberg (eds) *Punishment and Social Control*. New York, NY: Aldine.

Green, R.G. (1998) *Justice in Aboriginal Communities: Sentencing Alternatives*. Saskatoon, Canada: Purich Publishing.

Hallsworth, S. (2002) 'The case for postmodern penality', *Theoretical Criminology*, 6: 2.

Hennessy, A. (2005) 'Indigenous justice: indigenous laws at the colonial interface'. Paper presented to *Law Asia Conference*, Bali, March.

Johnstone, G. (2002) *Restorative Justice: Ideas, Values, Debates*. Cullompton: Willan Publishing.

Jonas, B. (2003) Background paper delivered at the expert seminar on *Indigenous Peoples and the Administration of Justice*, Office of the High Commissioner for Human Rights, Madrid, 12–14 November (HR/MADRID.IP/SEM/2003/BP.26).

Lilles, H. (2001) 'Circle sentencing: part of the restorative justice continuum', in A. Morris and G. Maxwell (eds) *Restorative Justice for Juveniles*. Oxford: Hart Publishing.

Lynch, M., Buckman, J. and Krenske, L. (2003) *Youth Justice: Criminal Trajectories. Research and Issues Paper* 4. Brisbane: Crime and Misconduct Commission.

McNamara, L. (2000) 'The locus of decision-making authority in circle sentencing: the significance of criteria and guidelines', *Windsor Yearbook of Access to Justice*, 18: 60–114.

Nancarrow, H. (2006) 'In search of justice for domestic and family violence: indigenous and non-indigenous Australian women's perspectives', *Theoretical Criminology*, 10: 87–106

O'Malley, P. (1996) 'Indigenous governance', *Economy and Society*, 25: 310–26.

O'Malley, P. (1999) 'Volatile and contradictory punishments', *Theoretical Criminology*, 3: 175–96.

Pascoe, T. (2005) 'The youth justice system and the Youth Murri Court.' Paper presented at *Our Shared Future Conference*, Brisbane Youth Detention Centre, 7 June.

Potas, I., Smart, J., Bignell, G., Lawrie, R. and Thomas, B. (2003) *Circle Sentencing in New South Wales. A Review and Evaluation*. Sydney: New South Wales Judicial Commission and Aboriginal Justice Advisory Committee.

Pratt, J. (2000) 'The return of the wheelbarrow men', *British Journal of Criminology*, 40, 127–45.

Queensland Magistrates Courts (2004) *Annual Report 2003–2004*. Brisbane: Office of the Chief Magistrate.

Yazzie, R. and Zion, J. (1996) 'Navajo restorative justice: the law of equality and justice', in B. Galaway and J. Hudson (eds) *Restorative Justice: International Perspectives*. Monsey, NY: Criminal Justice Press.

Zellerer, E. and Cunneen, C. (2001) 'Restorative justice, indigenous justice and human rights', in G. Bazemore and M. Schiff (eds) *Restorative Community Justice: Repairing Harm and Transforming Communities*. Cincinnati, OH: Anderson Press.

Chapter 8

Retribution and restoration in biblical texts

Jonathan Burnside

Introduction

In the early days of the restorative justice movement there was an explicit assumption that retribution and restoration were opposed concepts. Further, it was widely assumed that this opposition was mirrored in the spiritual roots of many of its proponents. In part this was due to the attempt to develop a simple explanation of restorative justice that distinguished it from contemporary criminal justice practice. Howard Zehr, perhaps the most influential proponent of restorative justice in its initial decades, distinguished restorative from retributive justice in trying to explain the new paradigm (e.g. 1990: 63–82, 126–58, and 177–214).

Some advocates still view retribution as the antithesis of restoration. But others have made convincing arguments that this is in fact a false dichotomy; one that presents a misleading view of both retribution and restoration, and hence of restorative justice. Many of these arguments have had philosophical and criminological roots (e.g. Roche, ch. 5) while others have been theologically based (e.g. Marshall 2001). While the debate can hardly be considered settled, Zehr (2002) himself has moved away from his restorative versus retributive dichotomy on the grounds that this concedes to retribution important attributes of restoration.

This chapter explores the question of the relationship between retribution and restoration from a religious perspective. It focuses on the Judaeo-Christian tradition, for several reasons. First, most of the debate has taken place in the context of this tradition.[1] Secondly, the Judaeo-Christian tradition has been highly influential in the development of Western understandings of criminal justice, and it is therefore worth considering conversation within that tradition that challenges or supports those understandings.

The larger part of the chapter will explore this matter by considering the biblical texts themselves. However, rather than doing so from a particular doctrinal perspective, this examination will do so from a historical/literary perspective. It will do so by exploring three main strands: 1) the story or 'meta-narrative' of the Bible as a whole; 2) specific provisions in the biblical legal collections related to this topic; and 3) recommended practice, based on its understanding of these provisions, in the early church.

Finally, we will make observations regarding the relationship between retribution and restoration and concerning the limits of both, and will consider penological applications that can reasonably be derived from this biblical account.

Retribution and restoration in the biblical story

Some restorative justice advocates tend to regard the biblical texts as exclusively retributivist;[2] indeed, Johnstone is able to claim that this is the 'prevailing view' (2003: 106) of biblical justice. On the other hand, some restorative justice advocates have claimed that biblical justice is exclusively restorative. Thus Consedine avers, without qualification, that 'Biblical justice was restorative' (1995 cited in Daly 2002). There is thus a need to look more closely at the biblical texts themselves, which repeatedly and wisely bear witness to the complex relationship between retribution and restoration.

We begin by looking at the relationship between retribution and restoration in the story or 'meta-narrative' of the Bible as a whole. In doing so, we need to make a couple of preliminary points regarding the biblical texts. First, although there is nothing wrong with approaching the Bible (or any other ancient text) with questions to which we seek answers, we must be careful to locate this discussion within the larger world of the text – that is, the biblical story as a whole. The Bible is not presented in the form of a philosophy textbook on the meaning of punishment. It is presented as a story – in particular, the story of the creator God who did not need to create but who made the whole creation out of overflowing and generous love. It tells of a rebellion against love from within that Creation which led to the progressive spoiling of what God had made. The remainder of the story is about how God himself took risky and costly action from within Creation to rescue it from its plight. Without going into too much detail the story then becomes:

> focused on the relationship between this God and the chosen people, Israel; and this, in turn, is focused narrowly and tightly on the one man, Jesus of Nazareth, who was declared by the creator God to be Israel's Messiah through his resurrection from the dead. In this man, and particularly through his death, the justice and peace which the creator God intends for the whole cosmos has been unveiled once and for all, offering renewed humanness for all who give him their allegiance (Wright 1999: 78–9).

The story of history is thus the story of a long search for reconciliation between God and human beings. It is, in other words, the story of restoration that involves retribution.

Secondly, this story is expressed throughout in concrete terms, being about specific people doing specific things at specific times. This makes it exactly the kind of material from which one might derive an ethical approach to punishment (Barton 1998). The downside is that, although we can identify broad themes of retribution and restoration, the sources themselves do not lay the matter out in a systematic fashion. We cannot tidy everything into neat bundles. Thus perhaps the best starting-point for our overview of retribution and restoration is to locate them in the context of biblical claims about justice.

Biblical justice

The Bible proclaims that 'justice' is a characteristic of the God of Israel and that he is its source: 'The Rock, his work is perfect; for all his ways are justice. A God of faithfulness and without iniquity, just and right is he' (*Deuteronomy* 32: 4).[3] If justice is a characteristic of God himself, it follows that justice is something about which God is passionate. God delights in justice because it reflects his character. Through the prophet Jeremiah, God declares: 'I am the LORD who practises steadfast love, justice, and righteousness in the earth; for *in these things I delight*, says the LORD' (*Jeremiah* 9: 23–4, emphasis added). The association of justice with God, and therefore with what is 'good' (including love and righteousness), means that true justice takes sides when it comes to 'good' and 'evil'. Justice is partial in the sense that it always upholds what God defines as 'good' and is opposed to what God defines as 'evil'. Justice is a vigorous virtue. The usual Hebrew term for justice (*mishpat*) can bear a variety of meanings including 'judgement'. Justice is vigorous in this sense as well because it is subject to God's intention to produce it by means of acts of judgement.[4] Here we begin to see the interplay between retribution and restoration. God's delight in good and his opposition to evil provoke a response in the form of retribution. At the same time, God's delight in good and his opposition to evil mean that what is ultimately desired is restoration to the good of God's original creative intent.

If true justice upholds good and opposes evil it follows that there are two sides to justice in the Bible. On the one hand, justice brings down the oppressor and on the other hand it liberates the oppressed. Accordingly, a single act of justice can be experienced differently and have different outcomes depending on whether one is the oppressor or the oppressed. For one person, justice is cause for pain; for another, justice is cause for celebration: 'The LORD watches over the sojourners, he upholds the widow and the fatherless; but the way of the wicked he brings to ruin' (*Psalm* 146: 9; cf. *Psalm* 103: 6). The same act of justice brings oppressors 'to ruin' and 'lifts up those who are bowed down'. The oppressed are typified as the hungry, the blind, those in slavery and those who have no male protector who can act on their behalf in a patriarchal society (*viz.* aliens, widows and the fatherless). Placing retribution and restoration in the context of biblical justice we see that retribution for the oppressors typically brings restoration for the oppressed.

This means that it is misleading to characterize biblical justice as severe, retributive justice. It is more accurate to characterize biblical justice as transformative: a saving action by God that puts things right. This is reflected in actual biblical images of justice. The prophet Amos, speaking roundabout 760 BC, declared 'Let justice roll down like waters, and righteousness like an ever-flowing stream' (*Amos* 5: 24). Justice is here seen as a mighty, surging river, like the River Jordan in full flood. This image indicates that justice is not a static state but an intervening power that brings life to a parched land. Retribution and restoration are held together in this single image of a powerful river that strikes and changes, destroys and heals.

The Exodus

The greatest example of God's justice in the Old Testament (judging oppressors and liberating the weak) is the Exodus of the Hebrew people from Egypt. The book of *Exodus* tells the story of how God destabilized the totalitarian rule of Pharaoh in order to deliver the descendants of Abraham from slavery. The climactic moment occurs when God parts the waters of the 'Yam Suph' ('Sea of Reeds'), Pharaoh's armies are destroyed (retribution) and the Israelites are set free (restoration):

> Then Moses and the people of Israel sang this song to the LORD, saying, 'I will sing to the LORD, for he has triumphed gloriously; the horse and his rider he has thrown into the sea. The LORD is my strength and my song, and he has become my salvation' (*Exodus* 15: 1–2).

In this paradigmatic act of God, justice, punishment, freedom and salvation are inseparable. So too are retribution and restoration.

The 'new Exodus'

In the same vein, the greatest example of God's justice in the New Testament is the crucifixion of Jesus;[5] an event that is expressly characterized as the 'new Exodus'. *The Gospel according to Luke* describes a conversation between Jesus and two famous Old Testament figures (Moses and Elijah), in which the latter 'spoke of his [Jesus'] departure [the Greek word *exodus*], which he was to accomplish at Jerusalem' (*Luke* 9: 31). Jesus' 'departure' refers to his looming crucifixion. Elsewhere, the death of Jesus and baptism[6] in the name of Jesus are likened to the slaughter of the Passover lamb prior to the Exodus from Egypt and the crossing of the Sea of Reeds, respectively (*First Letter to the Corinthians* 5: 7; 10: 2). The death of Jesus[7] is thus explicitly presented as a new and better Exodus.

This is because the New Testament understands the crucifixion of Jesus as the means of overthrowing a far greater oppressor than Pharaoh and also as the means of liberating a far greater number of people. In brief, Jesus saw that the real oppressor of Israel was not the Romans but the Accuser, Satan, 'a quasi-personal source of evil standing behind both human wickedness and large-scale injustice' (Wright 2001: 316), opposed to humanity and to God's purposes. Consequently, the human beings who needed liberation were not only the inhabitants of occupied Israel in the first century AD but all who were enslaved to Satan's power – that is, the entire human race. This indicates a further dimension to the story of oppression and freedom. Humanity is not neutral; it has joined Satan's rebellion against God and thus the cross addresses, head on, personal and corporate sins, rebellions and failures of the captives themselves. As Barth observed: 'only the cross shows us just how abhorrent our actions are' (cited in Holmes 2005: 123). The New Testament claims that the cross was the place where Israel's Messiah won this ultimate victory over evil[8] and that it was here that the Messiah was enthroned (*Mark* 10: 37–40; 15: 27). For our purposes, it is important to note that the apostle Paul describes Jesus' crucifixion – the greatest act of salvation – as a manifestation of God's justice:

> [The crucifixion] was to show God's righteousness [which can also be translated as 'justice'[9]], because in his divine forbearance he had passed over former sins; it was to prove at the present time that he himself is righteous ['just'] and that he justifies him who has faith in Jesus (*Romans* 3: 25–6).

Retribution results in restoration to favour with God: the object of wrath is transformed into a child of God.[10] There is an ultimate restoration, but not one that ignores the need for a penalty.

The cross is thus the ultimate act of God's justice in the Bible because it overthrows the ultimate oppressor and it bestows the ultimate freedom from tyranny (*Hebrews* 2: 14–5). Of course, the cross itself should never be separated from Jesus' resurrection and ascension which together amount to God's 'vindication' of His people and His purposes. Vindication is itself a moment of and the completion of God's redemptive justice.[11] Together, the cross and the Resurrection display the relationship between retribution and restoration. As O'Donovan writes:

> In the light of the resurrection the cross is seen to be a judgement which is, at the same time and completely, an act of reconciliation: an act of judgement, because it effected a separation between right and wrong and made their opposition clear; an act of reconciliation, because by this judgement the way was opened for the condemned to be included in the vindication of the innocent (1996: 256–7).

Between Christ's Resurrection and return

The New Testament closes with the book of *Revelation*, which looks ahead to the return of Christ as Judge who gives the Last Judgement on behalf of God. This raises the question of how the Bible understands the exercise of judgement in the period between Christ's Resurrection and his return. Whole books have been written on single aspects of this complex and fascinating topic; suffice it to say that a key text is *Romans* (13: 3–4):

For rulers are not a terror to good conduct, but to bad. Would you have no fear of him who is in authority? Then do what is good, and you will receive his approval, for he is God's servant for your good. But if you do wrong, be afraid, for he does not bear the sword in vain; he is the servant of God to execute his wrath on the wrongdoer.

The passage recognizes that: 'Society cannot live without judgement – it is precisely for this reason that political authority persists in its functions until Christ's coming' (O'Donovan 1996: 256). This passage reveals that the purpose of the prevailing authorities is judgement ('he [government] is the servant of God to execute his wrath on the wrongdoer'). However, it is wrong to assume that 'judgement' refers simply to retribution. O'Donovan reminds us that: 'judgement in the ancient world always has in mind a decision between two parties' and thus the purpose of the authorities, according to the apostle Paul in *Romans*, is 'to "praise" the party who has acted rightly' (1996: 147). This is in long-range continuity with the biblical vision of justice noted above. Justice is opposed to evil and it upholds the good, about which God is passionate. Within the broader structure of Paul's thought this righteous judgement is 'a restraining element in society which preserves the social order that furthers the spread of the Gospel' (O'Donovan 1996: 148). Again, retribution is harnessed to the purpose of restoration: 'God's servant for your good'.

The Last Judgement

This brings us to the projected end of the biblical story, which is described in the last book of the Bible, the book of *Revelation*. The Last Judgement is presented as an act of divine justice that finally brings the victory of Israel's Messiah on the cross to bear eternally upon the whole of Creation. There is eternal retribution for those who reject God's means of reconciliation through Jesus Christ and eternal restoration for those who choose to accept. As in previous pictures of biblical justice (see above), there is retribution followed by the prospect of restoration for those who have chosen to repent of their rebellion against God and who have chosen to side with God's good purposes. There is retribution and judgement upon evil (the 'lake of fire'; *Revelation* 19: 20–1; 20: 10, 14–5). When all that threatens God's good creation is finally dealt with, it is possible to turn to healing, transformation and restoration. *Revelation* describes the restoration of believers to God in terms of an intimate relationship: 'And I saw the holy city, new Jerusalem, coming down out of heaven from God, prepared as a bride adorned for her husband' (21: 2). Everything that oppresses God's creation is overthrown and everything that seeks freedom from bondage is fully liberated.[12]

It is clear from these examples of God's just acts, first, that retribution has a positive role to play in securing justice (overthrowing the oppressor and liberating the oppressed) and, secondly, that retribution paves the way (at least potentially) for restoration. Throughout the Bible, the interdependence of retribution and restoration reflects the consistent character of a God who remains true to himself by punishing sin, but who also wishes offenders to repent and be reunited to his original good purposes. As Marshall sums up:

> the New Testament looks *beyond retribution* to a vision of justice that is finally satisfied only by the defeat of evil and the healing of its victims, by the repentance of sinners and the forgiveness of their sins, by the restoration of peace and the renewal of hope – a justice that manifests God's redemptive work of making all things new (2001: 284, emphasis in original).

Retribution and restoration in the biblical legal collections

We turn from the role of retribution and restoration in the overall story of the Bible to some specific examples of how they relate in the biblical legal collections. This shows that the relationship between retribution and restoration does not merely function at the level of narrative only, nor is it restricted to divine activity. Retribution and restoration can also be held together at the level of human judgements. Many examples could be given but, to keep length under control, I have selected a few of the primary biblical passages on the subject. Of these, the *lex talionis* (see below) is particularly important because this is commonly, and wrongly, assumed to indicate a purely retributive approach.

Physical assault

First, *Exodus* 21: 18–9 which reads as follows:

> When men quarrel and one strikes the other with a stone or with his fist and the man does not die but keeps his bed, then if the man rises again and walks abroad with his staff, he that struck him shall be clear; only he shall pay for the loss of his time, and shall have him thoroughly healed.

What is interesting about this passage is that it imposes a duty on the perpetrator of a physical assault to see that his victim is 'thoroughly healed'. The retributive penalty (here, a literal 'paying back') aims at restoration in the fullest sense. The perpetrator is to see that the victim is restored to his original position; so far as possible the obligation is not reduced to payment of a fine or damages. Thus if the victim was a farm hand, for example, and unable to work because of the injury, the most natural thing would be for the offender to send his son to farm the land, or else to send someone to look after him. This contrasts with the goal of our modern 'compensation culture' which is to give money *instead of* restoring the situation. The paradigm case in biblical law is not one of calculation of damages because the obligation is one of restoration, not compensation.

Theft

Moving from personal injury to theft, *Exodus* 22: 1–4 prescribes multiple restitution for stealing animals. The sanctions vary according to whether the stolen goods have already been slaughtered or sold and are hence unrecoverable (*Exodus* 22: 1) or whether they are still in the thief's possession (the paradigm, perhaps, of being 'caught in the act'; *Exodus* 22: 4). The advantage of multiple restitution is that it not only puts the victim back in the position he was before the crime (in so far as that is materially possible) but also places him in a financially better position. Again, the retributive penalty (here, a literal 'paying back') aims at restoration.

The lex talionis

Third, we turn to the *lex talionis* ('eye for an eye and a tooth for a tooth') formula.[13] This is important because one of the reasons why some restorative justice practitioners regard retribution in negative terms is due in part to their misconceptions of this biblical teaching. The formula appears in a number of places[14] and has been associated by many with the misuse and overuse of punishment. As Gandhi put it: 'An eye for an eye makes the whole world blind.'[15] However, Gandhi's rejoinder reflects a popular misunderstanding of the text. The word 'for' (*tachat*) can mean 'in the place of' – that is to say, one thing being given in the place of another (Daube 1947: 103–5). Thus 'life for life' (e.g. *Exodus* 21: 23) points towards compensation, the return of a living creature for a dead one, rather than another dead one (Daube 1947: 112–5; Jackson 2000: 289). Thus *talion* may have provided guidance as to the appropriate level of compensation and not just the permissible level of retaliation.[16] This is implicit in the classic statement of the *lex talionis* in *Leviticus* 24: 13–32 (Milgrom 2001: 2128–33). Verse 18 of this unit states: 'He who kills a beast *shall make it good*, life for life'. This is mirrored in Verse 21a: 'He who kills a beast *shall make it good*'. 'Making good' is more consistent with compensation than retaliation. To this extent, once again, retribution and restoration go together.

The only case of *talion* being physically implemented for non-fatal assaults in the Hebrew Bible is found at the beginning of the book of *Judges*:

Adonibezek [a Canaanite king] fled; but they [the men of Judah] pursued him, and caught him, and cut off his thumbs and his great toes. And Adonibezek said, 'Seventy kings with their thumbs and their great toes cut off used to pick up scraps under my table; as I have done, so God has requited me.' And they brought him to Jerusalem, and he died there (Judg. 1: 6–7).

Although there is no compensation in this (rare) example, it is possible to find what Jackson calls 'cognitive equivalences between retaliation and retribution' (Jackson pers. comm.). Daube (1947: 128) writes:

retaliation, roughly, does restore the original proportion of power between the two persons or families concerned. The difference between it and restitution proper is that it restores the original relation in a negative way, by depriving the wrongdoer of the same thing of which he has deprived the person wronged; while restitution is positive and gives back to the person wronged that which the wrongdoer has appropriated.

In the absence of compensation, the 'repayment' of retribution may also be said to have an expressive function: denouncing the offender's act and/or reasserting the victim's right. This may be especially relevant where, as in *Judges* 1: 6–7, the offender's act is 'clearly deliberate' (Jackson pers. comm.). This expressive function may also be restorative in the philosophical sense that it is 'the denial of wrong by the assertion of right' (Bradley cited in Walker 1991: 78). Notably Adonibezek accepts the legitimacy and the justice of his punishment; indeed, he goes so far as to see it as a manifestation of divine punishment.

Retribution and restoration in the early church

We turn from retribution and restoration in ancient Israel, as depicted in the biblical legal collections, to retribution and restoration in the life of the early church, which claimed to be in continuity with ancient Israel as the 'people of God'. In general terms the exercise of judgement in the life of the Christian community was to stand in contrast to the exercise of judgement in the rest of world (as noted above). Once again, the Bible wisely bears witness to the complex relationship between retribution and restoration.

The Gospel According to St Matthew (18: 15–20)

St Matthew's *Gospel* describes the following practice of judgement, aimed at the reconciliation of the offender. The outcome of a successful reconciliation is 'gaining a brother' (v. 15). O'Donovan describes this as 'an institutional commentary on Jesus' parable of the lost sheep'[17] (1996: 150). If restoration fails, the only alternative is retribution which takes the form of expulsion from the community. This is logical because 'the essence of the offence has been to reject God's judgement in the community, and so, in effect, to reject Christ himself' (1996: 150).

The Corinthian correspondence (First and Second Letters to the Corinthians)

This provides an example of recommended practice in the early church when the offender refuses to recognize that a wrong has taken place. Censure and retribution on the part of community are required, and this takes the form of exclusionary punishment.

The offence in question concerned an incestuous relationship between a man and a woman in the church at Corinth (a lively Greek seaport in the Roman Empire). Under Roman law, the punishment for incest was 'exile and the loss of citizenship and property for both parties in the liaison' (Winter

2001a: 6; see also Winter 2001b: 44–57). Upon learning of this offence, the apostle Paul demanded that the Christian community exclude the man involved in a decisive act (presumably the woman involved was not a Christian): 'You are to deliver this man to Satan for the destruction of the flesh, that his spirit may be saved in the day of the Lord Jesus' (*First Letter to the Corinthians* 5: 5). 'Delivering to Satan' probably refers to putting the man outside the church and thus into the realm of the Satan: 'the act of exclusion … was the sign that attempts to reconcile could go no further' (O'Donovan 1996: 259). Winter notes that in this respect 'the Christian community is seen to reflect (however imperfectly) a characteristic of God himself' (2001a: 6). This is because we read later in the same letter that God removed some members of the Corinthian church from the active life of the community either permanently (by death) or temporarily (absence through weakness and illness) (*First Letter to the Corinthians* 11: 30). These, too, are forms of exclusionary punishment.

Exclusionary punishment involves censure and retribution because it recognizes that a wrong has taken place. However, it is also intentionally restorative in the sense that its purpose was to reconcile the offender with the church's judgement that his behaviour was wrong. Judgement:

> served the church's need to make a public distinction between right and wrong, to 'purge out the old leaven' (*First Letter to the Corinthians* 5: 6); but this was to be done by confronting the offender and inviting him in penitence to join the church in making this distinction (O'Donovan 1996: 259).

The goal is restoration: 'that his spirit may be saved in the day of the Lord Jesus.' Once again, retribution aims at restoration.

A further glimpse into the practice of the early church is found in a subsequent letter from the apostle Paul to the same church. In the *Second Letter to the Corinthians* (2: 1–8) the community is taught how to receive back into its fellowship a man who had been excluded from the community, along the lines mentioned above, but who was now repentant. We do not know whether the repentant offender is the incestuous man referred to in the *First Letter to the Corinthians* but, whoever it was, the apostle claims that three things should characterize the community's new relationship with the repentant offender. First, they were to show 'grace' (2: 7) (i.e. do good towards someone who does not deserve it). In this regard, the community shows the justice of the cross noted above. Secondly, they were to encourage the formerly excluded person and help him to re-establish his relationships (2: 7). Interestingly, they were to show 'grace' and encouragement lest 'he may be overwhelmed by excessive sorrow' (2: 7). Thirdly, they were to 'affirm their love' for the person. 'Only then can the person know that the past is the past and that restoration of relationships has been achieved …' (Winter 2001a: 7). Once again we see that 'punishment is meant to be remedial with the ultimate aim of restoring fractured relationships' (2001a: 7).

Some limits to retribution and restoration

Our overview of the relationship between retribution and restoration in the Judaeo-Christian tradition enables us to make some observations regarding their limits.

Limits to retribution

There are limits to retribution in biblical law. *Deuteronomy* 25: 1–3 indicates that offenders deserve to be punished in proportion[18] to their offence, affirming the value the Bible places upon moral autonomy. However, there is an upper limit in the sense that no offender deserves to be degraded. The passage reads:

> If there is a dispute between men, and they come into court, and the judges decide between them, acquitting the innocent and condemning the guilty, then if the guilty man deserves to be beaten, the judge shall cause him to lie down and be beaten in his presence with a number of stripes in proportion to his offence. Forty stripes may be given him, but not more; lest, if one should go on to beat him with more stripes than these, your brother be degraded in your sight.

This is close to what Duff calls 'the central retributivist slogan', namely 'that the guilty should be punished as they deserve and because that is what they deserve' (2002: 96). This is reflected in biblical law – with the important gloss that no one deserves to be degraded. There are limits to retribution. It is perhaps significant that in setting limits to retribution *Deuteronomy* 25: 3 refers to the offender as 'your brother'. 'Brotherhood' is one of the key themes in *Deuteronomy*, a book that 'envisages a society that is quite distinct from every other known society in its world: [one] based on the absolute respect for all its members' (McConville 2003: 189).

A limit to retribution is related to the perceptions of offenders. Perceptions in turn affect attitudes and much is said in biblical law about cultivating the attitude of heart that leads to forbearance from conflict. For example, *Exodus* 23: 1–9 contains a series of prohibitions against the perversion of justice (23: 1–3; 6–9). At the centre of this unit is the following admonition: 'If you meet your enemy's ox or his ass going astray, you shall bring it back to him. If you see the ass of one who hates you lying under its burden, you shall refrain from leaving him with it, you shall help him to lift it up' (*Exodus* 23: 4–5). Commentators have queried the relationship between this 'humanitarian' provision and the surrounding prohibitions. Jackson points out that verses 4 and 5 envisage 'a context of enmity' (2000: 224) specifically between the owner and the person who is obliged to help. Enmity is thus the key to the internal structure of the unit because enmity leads to litigation. By placing the command to assist one's enemy at the heart of a passage concerned with litigation, the Bible is encouraging its hearers to have the attitude of forbearance that makes litigation unnecessary. By limiting litigation and encouraging forbearance the passage also limits retribution.

How does this advice sit with, for example, the *lex talionis* noted above, whether conceived as compensation or physical retaliation? Here we must recognize that it was always possible to transcend even the literal application of the *lex talionis* in biblical law. The fact that a punishment was *permitted* in biblical law did not mean that it *had* to be applied – or even that it *should* be applied. For example, a text from the wisdom literature recommends that *talion* should *not* be exacted: 'Do *not* say, "I will do to him as he has done to me; I will pay the man back for what he has done"' (*Proverbs* 24: 29; emphasis added). Retribution is permitted but it is not mandatory in biblical law. In fact, other parts of the legal collections command that the best response of all is forbearance and love: 'You shall not take vengeance or bear any grudge against the sons of your own people, but you shall love your neighbour as yourself: I am the LORD' (*Leviticus* 19: 18). This reflects the character of God who does not take pleasure in inflicting pain and who sets the greatest value upon reconciliation: 'I have no pleasure in the death of the wicked, but that the wicked turn from his way and live; turn back, turn back from your evil ways; for why will you die, O house of Israel?' (*Ezekiel* 33: 11).

We see similar restraint upon litigation and retribution in the early church. Jesus demands of 'the multitudes' in the *Gospel According to St. Luke*: '... why do you not judge for yourselves what is right? As you go with your accuser before the magistrate, make an effort to settle with him on the way' (12: 57–58). O'Donovan notes that 'reconciliation is itself a form of judgement. Those who avoid the law court by settling the quarrel have in fact judged for themselves' (1996: 259). Here we see the long-range continuity with the attitudes promoted by biblical law: the community established by Jesus is to be characterized by a lack of litigation and vengeance and by forgiveness and love towards the enemy.[19]

Limits to restoration

There are also limits to the goal of restoration in biblical law. At the level of the biblical meta-narrative, it is possible for human beings to choose not to be part of God's planned-for restoration. The book of *Revelation* closes with a picture of the new heavens and the new earth that God has accomplished, but not all human beings choose to be part of this work of restoration. Their tragic and avoidable absence, as the Bible sees it, reflects God's respect for moral autonomy. Moral autonomy sets limits to both retribution and restoration.

There are also some practical limits to restoration in biblical law. In *Exodus* 22: 5, which concerns agricultural delicts, restitution is simply made 'from the best in his [the offender's] own field and in his own vineyard'. There is no guarantee that it will fully compensate the victim for the loss. There may not be full restoration. However, any disparity must be offset by the advantage of resolving the matter quickly and allowing the parties to get on with their lives. Biblical law seems to recognize that there are times when the quest for full restoration is detrimental. It appears that any outstanding injustice must be left, ultimately, with God. There are also limits to restoration to the extent that the parties are unwilling to enter into the attitude of heart towards offenders commended by both the Hebrew Bible and the New Testament (see above). Human nature sets limits to the restorative ideal. Again, the Bible wisely bears witness to the complex relationship between retribution and restoration.

Penological applications

Finally, we turn to the penological applications that can reasonably be derived from this biblical account, particularly for restorative justice.

First, the biblical material shows that there is a role for retribution and challenges those within the restorative justice movement who view retribution and restoration as mutually exclusive. *Deuteronomy* 25: 1–3 reminds us that proportionality is a perfectly sound basis for a responsible sentence. It takes offenders and their choices seriously and is one way of affirming the moral value and dignity of persons.[20] It is both difficult and dangerous to move too far away from this (e.g. mandatory, indeterminate or exemplary sentences). The biblical material also shows that there are limits to retribution and that care must also be taken to avoid degrading the offender. This challenges our perceptions and attitudes towards offenders. Punishment may lower an offender in the eyes of others but not to the extent that he loses dignity as a human person. This has political application given the increasing reliance upon imprisonment around the world. Indeed, some have argued that the institution of mass imprisonment 'depend[s] upon our refusal to comprehend the human beings we so completely condemn' (Garland 2001: 185) and certainly the human consequences can be degrading in the extreme. Nor are we justified in using offenders in a utilitarian fashion as a means to some other (conscious or unconscious) end – for example, as a way of soothing cultural anxieties (Garland 2001: 167–205).

Secondly, the biblical material shows that retribution should aim at restoration, and challenges retributivists outside the restorative justice movement who would deny this. It also reminds us that there are, sadly, limits to restoration. Daly's analysis of data from the South African Juvenile Justice (SAJJ) research which concerned youth justice conferences suggests that there are 'limits on offenders' interests to repair harms and on victims' capacities to see offenders in a positive light' (2003a: 28).

Thirdly, the biblical material helps us to see how retribution and restoration can work together. At both the level of meta-narrative and at the level of specific examples in the biblical legal collections and the life of the early church, it affirms the conclusion that while responses to crime should aim for 'restoration', this is properly achieved through retribution (Duff 2002).

The political application of a biblical vision of justice might inspire a number of policies. The danger lies in isolating one element of an inseparable whole to the exclusion of others. The temptation is to stress, for example, retribution without any thought of restoration (the claim that 'prison works') or restoration without retribution (Richards 1998). Either element, on its own, quickly leads to injustice. The political application of a biblical approach for a given criminal justice process at a given point in time depends on current practices and previous penal history. For this reason Christians in different countries have campaigned at different times to redress quite different imbalances.[21]

Fourthly, the distinction between secular judgement and the church's judgement has major political application. If the purpose of government is to express God's judgements, there is a sense in which political authority may need to recover confidence in its ability to punish justly, which is to say that it may also need to reconnect with what it means to judge with humility. As O'Donovan (1996: 278) writes:

> Christian liberalism taught judges to look over their shoulders when they pronounced on fellow-sinners' crimes. It taught them they were subject to the higher judgement of God, who would judge mercifully those that judged mercifully. Ex-Christian liberalism inherited all the hesitancy; but, no longer grounded in religious humility, it became moral insecurity. From this springs the haunted unease with which the West views its own agents of law ... We have made the detection and punishment of major crime more efficient than any other society, yet we believe in it less.

Finally, the argument of *Romans* chapter 13 suggests that 'Secular justice could not itself effect what church justice set out to achieve, [namely] the repentance and regeneration of the sinner' (O'Donovan 1996: 260). This supports and illuminates von Hirsch's objection that it should not be the business of the state to use censure to try to bring about the repentance of an offender (1993). According to O'Donovan, this is indeed what secular justice cannot do. It is, however, what the church can do as it witnesses to 'the fact of reconciling judgement already given' in the form of the cross (1996: 259).

Conclusion

This chapter challenges perceptions that the Judaeo-Christian tradition represents severe retributive justice and that there is a dichotomy between retribution and restoration. It follows some recent challenges to restorative justice as a whole – namely, a questioning of the assumption that retribution and restoration are fundamentally opposed and a growing recognition that this is, in fact, a false dichotomy. It is hoped that this biblical reappraisal of the spiritual roots of restorative justice will further undermine this dichotomy and provide further grounds for recognizing the necessity of both retribution and restoration to punishing with justice. The Bible indicates that there is an interdependence of retribution and restoration at a number of different levels; not only at the level of the overall biblical story but also in the specific provisions of the biblical legal collections and the recommended practice of the early church. The biblical material also helpfully reminds us of some of the practical limits to both retribution and restoration, and some of the penological applications to which it points. Throughout, the Bible wisely bears witness to the complex relationship between retribution and restoration.

Selected further reading

Burnside, J.P. (forthcoming) *Jewish Justice In the Bible*. Cambridge: Cambridge University Press. An overview of biblical justice from the patriarchal period to the trials of Jesus.

Burnside, J.P. (2005) 'Criminal justice', in M. Schluter and J. Ashcroft (eds) *Jubilee Manifesto*. Leicester: Inter-Varsity Press. A descriptive account of the operation of divine justice in the Bible and of the role of relationships in securing justice, with some implications for contemporary practice.

Jackson, B.S. (2006) *Wisdom-laws: A Study of the Mishpatim of Exodus 21:1–22:16*. Oxford: Oxford University Press. An authoritative investigation of the earliest biblical legal collection, which provides insight into the practical operation of biblical law and biblical justice.

Marshall, C.D. (2001) *Beyond Retribution*. Grand Rapids, MI: Eerdmans. A thorough account of New Testament teaching on justice and punishment from a theological perspective.

O'Donovan, O. (1996) *The Desire of the Nations*. Cambridge: Cambridge University Press. A leading work of political theology, which explores ideas of political authority, justice and punishment from a biblical and theological perspective.

Notes

1 An exception is Hadley (2001), which offers the perspectives of a number of religions.
2 For a critique of retribution as a theoretical construct, and a discussion of the theological considerations that arise, see Marshall (2001: 97–143).
3 Scripture quotations are taken from the Holy Bible, Revised Standard Version, unless otherwise stated.
4 I am grateful to Gordon McConville (pers. comm.) for this observation.
5 As many have noted, this is ironic, because Jesus' execution is the result of human *in*justice. Ultimately, the full meaning of the cross is something that can never be fully comprehended and there is a risk of making it appear one-dimensional in a thumbnail sketch of this kind. See Holmes: 'the cross is a single decisive event that evades ... categorisation precisely because it is so basic to any properly theological account of the nature of true humanity, true justice, true sacrifice, true relationship, or a host of other realities' (2005: 105).
6 Baptism is a religious ceremony which signifies that the person has converted to Christianity.
7 Classic accounts of penal substitution (e.g. by the Swiss reformer John Calvin) '[assume] that sin requires satisfaction [and] that God cannot simply forgive, without some act of reparation taking place' (Holmes 2005: 107). Penal substitution as a way of explaining the efficacy of Christ's work upon the cross has come under heavy fire from some theological quarters (e.g. Marshall 2001: 59–69), yet there remain strong scriptural and exegetical arguments for understanding Christ's sacrifice in substitutionary terms (see Holmes 2005). Penal metaphors are important within the overall meta-narrative noted above because 'they take the reality of sin seriously ... A key element of penal substitution is language of acts of transgression – crimes – and the guilt they bring, which must be dealt with' (Holmes 2005: 123).

8 See *Colossians* (2: 13–15) 'And you, who were dead in trespasses and the uncircumcision of your flesh, God made alive together with him, having forgiven us all our trespasses, having cancelled the bond which stood against us with its legal demands; this he set aside, nailing it to the cross. He disarmed the principalities and powers and made a public example of them, triumphing over them in him.'

9 This is the translation used in the New International Version of the Bible.

10 As the *Gospel According to St John* puts it: 'to all who received him [Jesus], who believed in his name, he gave power to become children of God; 13 who were born, not of blood nor of the will of the flesh nor of the will of man, but of God' (1: 12–13).

11 I owe this observation to Jonathan Chaplin.

12 See Marshall (2001: 175–99) for a general discussion.

13 See Marshall (2001: 78–92) for a general discussion.

14 *Exodus* 21: 23–25, *Leviticus* 24: 18–20 and *Deuteronomy* 19: 21.

15 http://www.quotationspage.com/quotes/Mahatma   Gandhi/,   accessed   22 October 2005.

16 Zehr (1985) rightly recognized that the *lex talionis* could be a means of establishing restitution: 'the value of an eye for the value of an eye.'

17 The parable of the lost sheep is found in the *Gospel According to St Luke* 15: 5–6.

18 The Bible is critical of disproportionate responses (e.g. *Genesis* 4: 23–4).

19 This is part of the reason why the apostle Paul was appalled to hear of a court case between two Christians in Corinth (*First Letter to the Corinthians* 6: 1ff.). There was a contrast between the exercise of judgement by the 'prevailing authorities' noted above and that exercised among the church community (see, generally, Winter 1994: 106–21, 2001b: 64–75). Whereas: 'The secular function in society was to witness to divine judgement by, as it were, holding the stage for it; the church, on the other hand, must witness to divine judgement by no judgement, avoiding litigation and swallowing conflict in forgiveness' (O'Donovan 1996: 259). Where Christians in conflict could not agree together Paul held that church authorities could step in to deliberate on the case (6: 4). But this was not the ideal scenario: it was better to suffer wrong (6: 7). Even in the exceptional case involving church authorities, the church's exercise of judgement would be very different from that of the secular world: 'The sole purpose of the church court was to make the implications of God's judgement clear, by reconciling the contending Christians in a common understanding of God's right' (O'Donovan 1996: 150). It was to be a witness to 'the fact of reconciling judgement already given' (O'Donovan 1996: 259).

20 Cf. Von Hirsch: 'a condemnatory sanction treats the actor as a *person* who is capable of moral understanding … [This] is a matter of acknowledging his dignity as a human being' (1993: 11; emphasis in original).

21 Some of the reform initiatives to which a biblical vision of justice might point are set out elsewhere (Baker and Burnside 1994; Burnside and Baker 2004; Burnside 2005; Burnside with Loucks, Adler and Rose 2005).

References

Baker, N. and Burnside, J. (1994) *Relational Justice: A Reform Dynamic for the Criminal Justice System*. Cambridge: Jubilee Policy Group.

Barton, J. (1998) *Ethics and the Old Testament*. London: SCM.

Burnside, J. (2003) *The Signs of Sin: Seriousness of Offence in Biblical Law. JSOT Supplementary Series*. 364. Sheffield: Sheffield Academic Press.

Burnside, J.P. (2005) 'Criminal justice', in M. Schluter and J. Ashcroft (eds) *Jubilee Manifesto*. Leicester: Inter-Varsity Press.

Burnside, J. and Baker, N. (eds) (2004, repr.) *Relational Justice: Repairing the Breach*. Winchester: Waterside Press.

Burnside, J. with Loucks, N., Adler, J. and Rose, G. (2005) *My Brother's Keeper: Faith-based Units in Prisons*. Cullompton: Willan Publishing.

Burnside, J. and Schluter, M. (1994) 'Relational justice: a reform dynamic for the criminal justice system', *New Life*, 11: 17–30.

Daly, K. (2002) 'Restorative justice: the real story', *Punishment and Society*, 4: 5–79.

Daly, K. (2003) 'Making variation a virtue: evaluating the potential and limits of restorative justice', in E.G.M. Weitekamp and H.-J. Kerner (eds) *Restorative Justice in Context: International Practice and Direction*. Cullompton: Willan Publishing.

Daube, D. (1947) *Studies in Biblical Law*. Cambridge: Cambridge University Press.

Duff, R.A. (2001) *Punishment, Communication and Community*. Oxford: Oxford University Press.

Duff, R.A. (2002) 'Restorative punishment and punitive restoration', in L. Walgrave (ed.) *Restorative Justice and the Law*. Cullompton: Willan Publishing.

Garland, D. (2001) *The Culture of Control*. Oxford: Oxford University Press.

Gorringe, T. (1996) *God's Just Vengeance*. Cambridge: Cambridge University Press.

Hadley, M.L. (ed.) (2001) *The Spiritual Roots of Restorative Justice*. Albany, NY: State University of New York Press.

Holmes, S. (2005) 'Can punishment bring peace? Penal substitution revisited', *Scottish Journal of Theology* 58: 104–23.

Jackson, B.S. (unpublished) '*Lex Talionis:* Revisiting Daube's Classic.'

Jackson, B.S. (2000) *Studies in the Semiotics of Biblical Law. JSOT Supplement Series* 314. Sheffield: Sheffield Academic Press.

Johnstone, G. (ed.) (2003) *A Restorative Justice Reader: Texts, Sources, Context*. Cullompton: Willan Publishing.

Marshall, C.D. (2001) *Beyond Retribution*. Grand Rapids, MI: Eerdmans.

McConville, J.G. (2002) 'Deuteronomy, Book of', In D.T. Alexander and D. W. Baker. (eds) *Dictionary of the Old Testament: Pentateuch*. Leicester: Apollos.

Milgrom, J. (2001) 'Leviticus 23–27', in *Anchor Bible Commentary*. London: Doubleday.

O'Donovan, O. (1996) *The Desire of the Nations*. Cambridge: Cambridge University Press.

Phillips, A. (1973) *Deuteronomy*. Cambridge: Cambridge University Press.

Rex, S. (2001) 'Rethinking community punishment', *Relational Justice Bulletin*, 10: 4–5.

Richards, M. (1998) *Censure without Sanctions*. Winchester: Waterside Press.

Von Hirsch, A. (1993) *Censure and Sanctions*. Oxford: Oxford University Press.

Walker, N. (1991) *Why Punish?* Oxford: Oxford University Press.

Winter, B.W. (1994) *Seek the Welfare of the City*. Grand Rapids, MI: Eerdmans.

Winter, B.W. (2001a) 'Punishment as remedy', *Relational Justice Bulletin*, 12: 6–7.

Winter, B.W. (2001b) *After Paul Left Corinth*. Cambridge: Eerdmans.

Wright, T. (1999) *The Myth of the Millennium*. Glasgow: Azure.

Wright, T. (2001) *Luke for Everyone*. London: SPCK.

Zehr, H. (1985 repr. 2003) 'Retributive justice, restorative justice', in G. Johnstone (ed.) *A Restorative Justice Reader*. Cullompton: Willan Publishing.

Zehr, H. (1990) *Changing Lenses: A New Focus for Crime and Justice*. Scottdale, PA: Herald Press.

Zehr, H. (2002) *The Little Book of Restorative Justice*. Good Books.

Chapter 9

Feminist theory, feminist and anti-racist politics, and restorative justice

Kathleen Daly and Julie Stubbs

Feminist engagement with restorative justice (RJ) takes several forms, and this chapter maps five areas of theory, research and politics.[1] They are: theories of justice; the role of retribution in criminal justice; studies of gender (and other social relations) in RJ processes; the appropriateness of RJ for partner, sexual or family violence; and the politics of race and gender in making justice claims. There is overlap among the five, and some analysts or arguments may work across them. However, each has a particular set of concerns and a different kind of engagement with RJ.

The most developed area of feminist scholarship concerns the appropriateness of RJ for partner, sexual or family violence. It is not surprising that feminist analysts have focused on this area: it is a common context in which women come into contact with the justice system, and the significance of gender is readily apparent. It is also an area in which many RJ advocates are poorly informed. At the same time, there are other domains of feminist engagement with RJ. Before turning to these areas, we give an overview of feminist theory and politics, and different perspectives on law and justice.

Feminist theory and politics

Feminist theory (which comprises many theories) is concerned with the ways in which sex/gender structures social institutions, social life, groups, the self and the body. As importantly, it considers how knowledge is itself gendered, including how authoritative understandings of the world, both feminist and non-feminist, can be evaluated. Feminist researchers work in all domains of knowledge. What is termed the 'second wave' of the women's movement emerged in the 1960s, alongside other social movements such as the civil rights movement in the USA, Indigenous social movements in North America and in Australia and New Zealand, gay and lesbian movements, and many more. These social movements were, at a minimum, calling for extending liberal ideals of citizenship and 'rights' to formerly excluded groups (such as women and people of colour) and more maximally, seeking a transformation of society.

Feminist perspectives on law and justice

Feminist theory and politics have changed over the past four decades, and we depict these developments to contextualize shifts over time in feminist engagement with law and alternative justice practices.

Liberal feminism has been in place for over three centuries as women have sought to secure equality of legal and citizenship rights with men. In the twentieth century, the rights agenda intensified further. In striving to remove barriers to women's access to the public sphere of education, paid work and state entitlements, liberal feminists argued that most (perhaps all) sex-based classifications were wrong. The criminal justice agenda that flows from this stance is that women should have equal treatment and the same opportunities as men. Such an approach may advance women's employment in formerly male-dominated jobs (such as police officers or prison guards), but it may ignore the impact of pregnancy and child care on women's paid work, and affect women adversely in other areas, such as sentencing policy (see Raeder 1993; Daly and Tonry 1997). The major justice question for liberal feminist theorists is: do women have the same rights and opportunities as men, and are they treated the same as men?

Cultural feminism has also been in place for over a century, and it is concerned with the limits of an 'equality with men' agenda. Emphasis is given to bringing women's social, sexual and reproductive experiences to the fore, not to overlook or submerge them. This was (and is) a politically risky move because, in bringing women's specificity or 'difference' from men into public debate, one may end up re-inscribing women's difference as deficiency compared with men. A celebrated twentieth century example of cultural feminism is Carol Gilligan's (1982) research on gender differences in moral thinking. She finds that women's ways of responding to moral problems differ from those of men: girls and women more often use contextual and relational reasoning, whereas boys and men more often use abstract reasoning. She argues that both modes of thinking should be part of mature moral development. The major question for cultural feminist theorists is: how can 'women's ways of knowing' and women's 'difference' be brought more fully into a justice agenda?

Like liberal and cultural feminism, *radical feminism* analyses gender difference, but the arguments focus more forcefully on inequalities and power that construct gender difference. A well-known twentieth century radical feminist, Catharine MacKinnnon, critiqued Gilligan's thesis, saying that the content of the reputedly 'female voice' arose from men's dominance of women, and that women could not currently articulate a different form of power 'because his foot is on her throat' (cited in Dubois *et al.* 1985: 74–5). In MacKinnon's view, we cannot know what women's values or voice are until there is a transformation of gender power relations. Radical feminists examine the routine forms of oppression in women's everyday lives that flow from sex/gender, as this is experienced by female bodies and controlled through heterosexual relations and men's structural domination of women. The major question for radical feminist theorists is: how do we transform sex/gender power relations so that women are not subordinate to men?

These three feminist perspectives dominated the political landscape in the 1960s and 1970s but, during the mid-1980s, they were unsettled by critical race feminism and feminists drawing from postmodern and post-structural social theories. The latter group of feminists retain varying degrees of commitment to the 'liberal-modernist project': some wish to 'reconstruct' it, and others, to 'abandon' it (Hudson 2003: 123).

Liberal, cultural and radical feminists typically focus on one axis of inequality and power – that connected to sex and gender difference – but other feminists are interested in connecting sex/gender to other relations of inequality, such as race and class. During the 1970s and 1980s, there was interest to connect feminist theories of gender (and patriarchy) with Marxist theories of class (and capitalism), a perspective termed *socialist feminism*. Soon after, there was interest to connect gender and class to race and ethnicity (see Daly 1993). *Critical race feminism*, which emerged in the early 1980s, built on these developments, and it challenged those feminist analysts who viewed women's circumstances through the lens of sex and gender alone. At the same time, critical race feminism challenged movements for racial justice, which focused on racialized men's, but not women's, circumstances. This created increasing complexity in making 'rights' claims, especially because the law tended to centre *either* on gender relations *or* on race relations, but not on both together.[2] For critical race feminists, the question is: how can both women's and racialized groups' claims for rights and justice be addressed? Analyses of power became more fractured and conceptualized as interactive or intersectional (Crenshaw 1989; Collins 1990; Wing 1997).

Postmodern and post-structural feminism, emerging at around the same time as critical race feminism, shared similar concerns, but conceptualized multiple identities and fractured justice claims in differing theoretical and political terms. There is considerable variety among this group of thinkers, some of whom see an emancipatory potential within the ideals of a liberal modern society, and others who do not. Informed by social theorists who argued against universalizing claims (whether about 'women' or 'black women', among others), and who wished to engage the problem of 'difference' in philosophical and linguistic terms, postmodern feminist theorists became highly reflexive about the problem of power in theorizing and explaining women's, and gender differences in, social existence. The idea of power relations shifted from conceptualizing the dominance of one group (such as men) over another (such as women) to analysing the legal and social discourses which construct sex/gender relations. Several types of problems emerged. First, within feminist theorizing, the category *woman*, without reference to other social categories, became increasingly untenable. For example, who could speak as 'a woman' about things that mattered to women? Who could speak as 'a black woman'? Secondly, and as important, it was evident to some thinkers that woman and sex/gender relations more generally were caught in a profound structural closure. Specifically, it seemed to many postmodern feminists that the transformative promise of radical and other critical feminisms was doomed. Because the meaning of gender (or other differences) is constructed in binary terms – that is, not 'man' (or not 'white' or not 'heterosexual', etc.) – women are inevitably constructed as 'Other'. Foundational thinking about any social relation (gender, race, class, among others) lost authority. Justice claims became more complex. Not only did they become more contingent and uncertain but, for many social theorists, they became unknowable, deferred or something that could only become. While such developments have been unsettling for some, they have opened up new possibilities for challenging legal and social discourses on gender (and other social categories), rethinking justice and for pursuing justice claims in different terms and on behalf of new coalitions and constituencies.

Theories of justice

A sketch of feminist theorizing about justice, even a highly selective one, is daunting because the term 'justice' has many referents. We limit our discussion to the response to crime, but we recognize that some analysts believe that criminal justice is not possible without social justice. For example, some RJ advocates have a more expansive definition of justice, and embedded within Indigenous justice are sociopolitical aspirations of sovereignty and self-determination that presume a broad social justice agenda.

Contexts of justice claims and practices

Several streams of activism moved the idea of RJ forward, and social movements during the 1950s to 1970s were influential (Daly and Immarigeon 1998). One stream came from critiques of racism in police practices, courts and prisons. In the USA, racial domination by whites was maintained, it was believed, by the over-criminalization and imprisonment of African-Americans and other racial and ethnic minority groups. Indigenous groups in the USA, Canada, Australia, New Zealand and South Africa also challenged extant criminal justice practices as methods of maintaining neocolonial power. These analyses were central to decarceration movements, including prisoners' rights, alternatives to the prison and arguments to abolish the prison; and they challenged the ways in which justice system practices routinely disadvantaged racialized groups. Whereas Indigenous and racial-ethnic minority group challenges to justice system practices focused largely on the experiences and treatment of accused persons and offenders, the women's movement centred attention to violence against women and children, and to the mistreatment of victims in the criminal justice process, although some feminist activism also focused on prisoners' rights campaigns. Although offenders and victims are often viewed as protagonists in the justice system, social movement politics made it possible to see them as having common experiences of unfair and unresponsive treatment although, as we shall see, there are inevitable tensions in making justice claims from a victim's and an offender's (or an accused's) perspective. Paralleling and shadowing social movement activism were research and theory on the possibilities of informal justice (Abel 1982; Merry 1982; Matthews 1988). Victim–offender mediation, community justice, among other alternatives, gave concrete expression to the aspirations of social movement and community development activists; but these were not without feminist critique.

Early feminist thought (1970s and 1980s)

Feminist engagement with alternative justice practices predates RJ's emergence (Daly and Immarigeon 1998). The introduction of a range of informal justice practices such as alternative dispute resolution, coupled with the work of Carol Gilligan (1982), had a large impact on feminist theory and activism.

Different voices

Gilligan's (1982) difference voice construct was hugely popular in the 1980s because, among other reasons, it is a simple dichotomy that seems to respect and honour women's ways of knowing. Gilligan said that girls' (or women's) moral reasoning is guided by an 'ethic of care', which differs from an 'ethic of justice' (the 'male' voice, theorized by others to be at the top of a hierarchy of moral development). The ethic of care centres on moral concepts of responsibility and relationship; it is a concrete and active morality. The ethic of justice centres on moral concepts of rights and rules; it is a formal, universalizing and abstract morality. Gilligan argued that both the male and female voice should have equal importance in moral reasoning, but that women's voices were misheard or judged as inferior to men's. Her ideas had a major impact on feminist thought throughout the disciplines.

In criminology, Frances Heidensohn (1986) and Kay Harris (1987) applied the care/justice dichotomy to the criminal justice system. Heidensohn compares a 'Portia' model of justice, which values rationality and individualism, with a more women-centred 'Persephone' model, which values caring and personal relations. She says that greater attention should be given to the values and concepts of justice associated with a Persephone model. Harris (1987: 32) argues 'for a massive infusion of the values associated with the care/response model of reasoning', although she also believes that it would be mistaken to substitute a justice/rights orientation with a care/response orientation. Daly (1989) challenges the association of justice and care reasoning with male/masculine and female/feminine voices, arguing that this gender-linked association is not accurate empirically, and that it would be misleading to think that an alternative to men's forms of criminal law and justice practices could be found by adding women's voice or reconstituting the system along the lines of an ethic of care. During the 1990s, Gilligan's different voice construct was superseded by more complex and contingent analyses of ethics and moral reasoning. This shift was propelled, in part, by critical race and postmodern feminist influences. However, some RJ advocates have not kept up with these developments in feminist thought. For instance, Guy Masters and David Smith (1998) invoke Gilligan's work in their attempt to compare retributive justice and RJ, and they argue that RJ offers a more caring response to crime (see the critique in Daly 2002a).

Informal justice

Informal justice, along with victim–offender mediation and community conflict resolution, featured in the 1970s and 1980s as precursors to RJ. Although some feminist analysts initially saw mediation as compatible with feminist values, many others thought it was inappropriate when partner violence was present. The mediation or conciliation model (Lerman 1984) was criticized for defining battering (or other offences) as 'disputes', for 'pushing reconciliation', 'erasing victimization' and 'limiting [formal] justice options' (Presser and Gaarder 2000: 180–1). Critiques of mediation were influential in curbing feminist interest in RJ, but mediation and RJ practices are not the same. For example, in their ideal form, RJ practices recognize crime victims and offenders; there is no push to reconcile, nor is victimization erased. Additional support people are present beyond the victim–offender dyad, and a normative stance against partner violence can be articulated by community members, including feminist groups (Braithwaite and Daly 1994).

Later feminist thought (1990s to the present)

Psychoanalytical, postmodern and critical race theories have had a significant impact on theorizing gender differences and differences among women. For example, in characterizing gender difference, some feminists argue that it may not be possible to construct 'woman' except as a lack, an absence or as 'not man'. Thus, the question arises: is the subject of law (or justice) ultimately always masculine, such that woman is 'always and only the Other' (Hudson 2003: 133)? If the answer is yes, then 'there can be no possibility of different but symmetrical (male and female) subjectivities' (Hudson 2003: 133), as Gilligan had posited. In characterizing differences among women, critical race theorists emphasize power differences among women and a racial/ethnic inflection of 'woman' (Wing 1997).

Major debate exists among feminist philosophers concerning the term *woman*. As reviewed by Hudson (2003: ch. 4), scholars such as Iris Marion Young and Seyla Benhabib say that specific identities, such as black woman or lesbian, are formed in advance of encounters with others, and are invoked in 'staking claims to justice'. Others, such as Drucilla Cornell and Judith Butler, say that specific identities are fluid and contingent, based on what occurs in interactions with others. What unites these theorists and critical race feminists is that the category woman is not stable and unified, but inflected by other elements of difference among women. Assuming this is true, then a 'woman's justice' or a 'feminist justice' is not possible because the subject woman (or category women) is too varied or contains hierarchies of difference, which cannot be smoothed over without excluding and oppressing some women.

Hudson builds on feminist and other social theories to conceptualize a post-liberal and post-communitarian justice, which must satisfy certain conditions (2003: 206; see also Hudson 2006). She endorses Habermas's 'liberal ideas of rights and equal respect and equal liberty' and 'his proposals of a communicative ethics', which provide for a 'discursive justice', where multiple views are heard (p. 175). However, she identifies a major weakness in his (or other liberal and communitarian) perspectives on justice: they lack an 'openness to Otherness', to 'alterity' (p. 175) and overlook key insights from recent feminist thought. She proposes that criminal justice should be 'predicated on difference rather than identity' and the major principle of justice should be 'equal respect' (p. 206).

Hudson argues that justice should be 'relational, discursive, plurivocal, rights regarding, and reflective' (p. 206), and she believes that RJ may be able to 'meet these requirements', although she has reservations about whether RJ ideals are implemented in practice. Notwithstanding a stated interest by RJ advocates in balancing the interests of offenders, victims and the community, she believes that there is 'insufficient regard for offenders' interests and moral status' (p. 207); and, despite the promise of a more discursive justice, the potential remains for victims, offenders or both to be dominated by others in RJ encounters. Hudson's contribution to debates about RJ is especially important: rather than asking, does RJ satisfy the justice claims of feminist, critical race or other groups, she outlines a set of ideal justice principles and asks: to what degree does RJ meet these principles? At the same time, she gives passing reference to particular kinds of criminal justice policies and practices, including RJ, and their implications for gender difference and women's situation, or for feminist debates in these areas. It is to these areas that we now turn.

The role of retribution in criminal justice

Feminist engagement with RJ cannot avoid considering the role of criminal law and the aims of punishment in achieving justice. Whereas some believe that 'law can never bring justice into being' (Hudson 2003: 191), others are more hopeful that better laws can achieve a more responsive criminal justice system. There are several major aims of punishment, including deterrence, incapacitation, rehabilitation and retribution. We focus on retribution because it is often used, wrongly in our view, to typify established criminal justice and to make comparisons with RJ.

Feminist debates about retribution are difficult to characterize because commentators presuppose an opposition of retributive and restorative justice (for a critique of this approach, see Daly and Immarigeon 1998; Daly 2000, 2002a). Moreover, retribution is used in varied ways: often it is used negatively to refer to responses that are punitive, degrading and/or involve incarceration; but it can also be used neutrally to refer to censuring harms (e.g. Duff 1996; Hampton 1998; Daly 2000) or deserved punishment in proportion to a harm (von Hirsch 1993), which is decoupled from punitiveness. Finally, commentators mistakenly refer to established criminal justice practices as retributive justice, when a variety of theories of punishment have been and are used.

Some feminists have criticized a feminist over-reliance on the criminal law to control men's violence against women (Martin 1998; Snider 1998).[3] They challenge feminist uses of 'punitive criminalization strategies', which rest on naïve beliefs that criminal law has the capacity to bring about social change and that deterrence promotes safety (Martin 1998: 155, 184), and they raise concerns that feminist reforms have not empowered women and may have been detrimental to racial and ethnic minority group women (Snider 1998: 3, 10).

Jean Hampton has a more positive reading of the 'retributive ethic' in criminal justice. She distinguishes vengeance – a '[wish] to degrade and destroy the wrongdoer' – from retribution – a '[wish] to vindicate the value of the victim' (1998: 39). She asks if it is possible to 'add something to this retributive response in order to express a kind of compassion for the [wrongdoer] in ways that might do him good, and if he has been the victim of injustice, acknowledge and address that injustice' (p. 43).[4] Hampton desires a 'more sophisticated way of thinking about the nature and goals of a punitive response, which incorporates both compassion and condemnation' (p. 37). She anticipates that a 'well-crafted' retributive response should be cognitive, to 'provok[e] thought' in the mind of the wrongdoer (p. 43; see also Duff 1996, 2001). But what form and amount of retributive punishment are appropriate or necessary to vindicate victims? In considering the relationship between RJ and the expressive functions of punishment, Hudson (1998) proposes that censure for an act should be decoupled from the quantum of punishment, and this activity should occur in a context of penal deflation overall.

Annalise Acorn (2004) makes a different case for retribution in her critique of RJ. She believes that expecting compassion from victims in face-to-face RJ encounters is wrong. She conceives of justice as 'some kind of counterbalancing pain for the wrongdoer' (p. 47) and is critical of RJ advocates who 'see these connections between justice and the infliction of pain on the offender as arbitrary' (p. 47). She argues that 'our institutions of retributive punishment put forward measured, state-administered punishment *precisely as a token* in order to prevent outraged victims and communities from going for what they *really* want' (p. 51, emphasis in original). RJ meetings may 'provide an opportunity for the victim to vent or blow off steam' towards an offender, but they do not 'validate or legitimate the victim's desire to see the perpetrator suffer' (p. 53). She thinks that the 'lived experience of relational justice' (defined as 'the personal achievement of relations of repair, accountability, healing, respect, and equality'), which RJ promises, is unlikely to be achieved. Nor does she think that RJ's sense of justice is desirable, even as a utopian vision (p. 162). Acorn is concerned that, in an RJ encounter, 'the compassion we feel for the offender ... often upstages the compassion we feel for the victim. [And] the victim's compassion for the offender overshadows her desire to receive compassion for her own loss' (pp. 150–1).

Acorn is primarily concerned with how victims can be 'used' in an RJ process and how their suffering is too quickly ignored, whereas Hudson is primarily concerned that offenders' interests are not given sufficient weight. Their different views reveal a fault line in feminist engagement with RJ: are analysts more concerned with victims' or offenders' interests? Is it possible to balance both?

In the context of genocide and collective violence, Martha Minow (1998) considers a spectrum of responses from vengeance to forgiveness. She argues that no one path is the right one, and much depends on the contexts of the violence (pp. 133–5); moreover, survivors vary in 'their desires for revenge [and] for granting forgiveness' (p. 135). She distinguishes vengeance from retribution and views retribution as important and necessary to vindicate victims (although it may not be the right path for some nations following a mass atrocity); but at the same time, 'retribution needs constraints' (p. 135). While she sees a role for bounded retribution in the aftermath of collective violence, she distinguishes this path from RJ, which she equates with reparation. Here, she draws on Howard Zehr's (1990) oppositional contrast of retributive and restorative justice.[5]

That RJ is posed as an 'alternative' to established criminal justice can create confusion in debates on the role of retribution. Whereas most assume that the values of RJ are an alternative to the 'retributive ethic' of established criminal justice, or that RJ cannot include retribution (or punishment), there is another way to see the relationship between the two: as deeply entwined. Antony Duff (2003: 58) makes the point in philosophical terms: criminal mediation 'aims … to achieve restoration, but to achieve it precisely through an appropriate retribution'. He argues that the 'retributivist slogan [the guilty deserve to suffer] says nothing about *what* the guilty deserve to suffer' (p. 48, emphasis in original), and he nominates remorse, censure and reparation. By de-coupling retribution from vengeance and vindictiveness, and by not engaging in dichotomous and oppositional thinking about justice practices, it may be possible to deploy the positive and constructive elements of retribution in a restorative process.

Gender (and other social relations) in RJ processes

There are few empirical studies of how gender and other social relations (such as class, race and age) are expressed in RJ practices. Major projects on conferencing, such as the Re-Integrative Shaming Experiments (RISE) in Australia and related research on victims (Strang 2002), have little to say about gender. Gender is not mentioned in key studies of youth justice conferences in New Zealand (Maxwell and Morris 1993; but see Maxwell *et al.* 2004 below), the Thames Valley Police restorative cautions (Hoyle *et al.* 2002) or referral orders and RJ in England (Crawford and Newburn 2003).

Daly (1996) examined class, race, age and gender dynamics in youth justice conferences in the Australian Capital Territory (ACT) and South Australia. From observations of 24 conferences, she finds they are highly gendered events: few offenders were female (15 per cent), women were the majority of the offender's supporters (52 per cent) and victim's supporters (58 per cent), and more mothers than fathers were present at conferences. She finds that 25 per cent of the victims present were treated with disrespect or were revictimized in the conferences; all but one were female. In these cases, the offender did not take responsibility for the act; this occurred when victims did not have supporters or were outnumbered by offenders and their supporters. In New Zealand, Gabrielle Maxwell and Allison Morris (1993: 119) also find that 25 per cent of victims felt worse after attending the conference, but the authors did not indicate the victim's gender.

A second study by Daly of 89 conferences in South Australia finds that the experiences of victims and offenders are conditioned by the gendered contexts of offending and victimization in the larger society (Daly 2002b). Female victims of female assaults were distressed and frightened by the offence and the offender, and female victims of certain property offences perceived a threat of violence, more so than the male victims. Thus, a feminist lens should be broadened to include offences other than male assaults against girls or women. Moreover, any claimed benefits of conferences, especially reductions in victims' fear or the degree to which victims have recovered from offences, need to be qualified by reference to the gender composition and other features of the offence. As for female offenders, they were as self-assured as their male counterparts; they were more defiant and less apologetic for their behaviour.[6]

Maxwell *et al.*'s (2004) study of youth justice conferences in New Zealand shows similar patterns in the gender composition of conferences to Daly's (1996) earlier study. From interviews with 520 youths, the study finds that girls were more likely than boys to report difficulties growing up (such as moving around a lot, experiencing violence and abuse, poor relationships with others and running away from home) and to have been reported for care and protection reasons (58 and 41 per cent, respectively) (p. 73). Girls were less likely to say that the police treated them fairly during the police interview (26 per cent) or the conference (51 per cent) than the boys (44 and 64 per cent, respectively) (p. 151). Although most youths had generally positive experiences of the conference process, the girls were less positive (pp. 150–1). As in Daly's later study (2002b), the girls appear to be less compliant and more challenging of the conference process than the boys.

The findings reported thus far fall within a realist epistemology in that the research has sought to determine whether, by observational or interview data, the experiences of RJ differ for males and females, or for members of dominant and minority racial-ethnic groups. Such information is crucial and not easily obtained or interpreted. None the less, realist approaches need to be supplemented by phenomenological and discursive approaches that, although rarely used in RJ research, offer the potential to deepen our understanding of gender (and other social relations) in RJ practices. For instance, research could take a social constructionist approach to gender and RJ (see Cook 2006); or it could analyse RJ as a gendering strategy (Smart 1992) or through the lens of 'sexed bodies' (Daly 1997; Collier 1998).

The appropriateness of RJ for partner, sexual and family violence

Feminist analysts face dilemmas in addressing the appropriateness of RJ for partner, sexual, and family violence.[7] Many desire a less stigmatizing and less punitive response to crime in general, but we are not sure that RJ, as currently practised, is capable of responding effectively to these offences (see, e.g., contributors to Strang and Braithwaite 2002). The potential problems and benefits of RJ for such offences are highlighted below. Some problems may be more acute for some offences, and potential benefits more likely for others.

Potential problems with RJ

The following potential problems with RJ have been identified:[8]

- *Victim safety*. As an informal process, RJ may put victims at risk of continued violence; it may permit power imbalances to go unchecked and reinforce abusive behaviour.
- *Manipulation of the process by offenders*. Offenders may use an informal process to diminish guilt, trivialize the violence, or shift the blame to the victim.
- *Pressure on victims*. Some victims may not be able to advocate effectively on their own behalf. A process based on building group consensus may minimize or overshadow a victim's interests. Victims may be pressured to accept certain outcomes, such as an apology, even if they feel it is inappropriate or insincere. Some victims may want the state to intervene on their behalf and do not want the burdens of RJ.
- *Role of the 'community'*. Community norms may reinforce, not undermine, male dominance and victim blaming. Communities may not be sufficiently resourced to take on these cases.
- *Mixed loyalties*. Friends and family may support victims, but may also have divided loyalties and collude with the violence, especially in intra-familial cases.
- *Impact on offenders*. The process may do little to change an offender's behaviour.
- *Symbolic implications*. Offenders (or potential offenders) may view RJ processes as too easy, reinforcing their belief that their behaviour is not wrong or can be justified. Penalties may be too lenient to respond to serious crimes like sexual assault.

Critics typically emphasize victim safety, power imbalances, and the potential for re-victimization in an informal process. However, the symbolic implications are also important. Critics are concerned that in not treating serious offences seriously, the wrong messages are conveyed to offenders. They also believe that as an informal process, RJ may 're-privatize' male intimate violence after decades of feminist activism to make it a public issue.

Potential benefits of RJ

The following potential benefits of RJ have been identified:[9]

- *Victim voice and participation.* Victims have the opportunity to voice their story and to be heard. They can be empowered by confronting the offender, and by participating in decision-making on the appropriate penalty.
- *Victim validation and offender responsibility.* A victim's account of what happened can be validated, acknowledging that he or she is not to blame. Offenders are required to take responsibility for their behaviour, and their offending is censured. In the process, the victim is vindicated.
- *Communicative and flexible environment.* The process can be tailored to child and adolescent victims' needs and capacities. Because it is flexible and less formal, it may be less threatening and more responsive to the individual needs of victims.
- *Relationship repair (if this is a goal).* The process can address violence between those who want to continue the relationship. It can create opportunities for relationships to be repaired, if that is what is desired.

Although there is considerable debate on the appropriateness of RJ for partner, sexual or family violence, empirical evidence is sparse. There have been few studies (e.g. Braithwaite and Daly 1994; Lajeunesse 1996; Pennell and Burford 2002; Daly 2002b, 2006; Daly and Curtis-Fawley 2006; see also the discussion of circle sentencing below), but insufficient attention has been paid to the great variation in the contexts and seriousness of these offences.

With the exception of circle sentencing, RJ has been kept off the agenda for partner and sexual violence, in part due to feminist or victim advocacy. New Zealand and South Australia are the only two jurisdictions where RJ is used routinely in youth justice cases of sexual assault. In a New Zealand pilot of RJ as pre-sentence advice for adult cases, partner and sexual violence cases are currently ineligible. The US project, RESTORE, is the first pilot to test RJ in adult cases of sexual violence (Koss *et al.* 2003).

After reviewing 18 conference cases of sexual violence, Daly (2002b: 81–6) concludes that the question of the appropriateness of RJ for these offences may be impossible to address in the abstract. In a more recent study of nearly 400 sexual violence cases finalized in court, by conference or formal caution, Daly (2006) argues that conferences are a better option for victims, if only because there is an admission to the offence and a penalty of some sort. More of the youths at conferences than in court were required to attend an adolescent sex offender counselling programme, and this, in turn, was associated with reductions in reoffending. While the court process may vindicate some victims, nearly half of court cases were dismissed or withdrawn.[10]

Evaluations of RJ must recognize the different kinds of violence experienced by victims in these cases, and whether it is ongoing, as is more likely in partner violence and some family violence cases. Feminist critiques of RJ focus mainly on partner violence, and have raised wellfounded concerns with RJ in these cases. Zehr (2003: 11, 39), a major RJ advocate, now suggests that 'domestic violence is probably the most problematic area of application, and here great caution is advised'. The central place of apology in RJ practices is suspect for partner violence, since 'the skill of contrite apology is routinely practiced by abusers in violent intimate relationships' (Acorn 2004: 73). Acorn also argues that in emphasizing forgiveness and reconciliation, RJ would be inappropriate in cases of sexual violence and is antithetical to vindicating a victim's suffering. While some RJ advocates emphasize forgiveness and reconciliation, and Zehr (2003: 8) suggests that 'this may occur more often' in RJ, he also insists that there is 'no pressure to choose to forgive or to seek reconciliation' and these are not primary goals of RJ (see also Minow 1998). However, some analysts question the assertion that the power to forgive is necessarily a choice freely open to victims; for example, Rashmi Goel (2000: 326–7) suggests there are pressures on women to forgive in circle sentencing.

Debate continues over whether RJ may be more constructive than formal court processes in cases such as historical child sexual abuse, including in institutions (see Julich 2006), sexual violence or certain family violence cases. The use of RJ to divert admitted offenders from court remains controversial for many feminist activists, and specific consideration needs to be given to what is proposed by diversion. For instance, project RESTORE involves prosecutorial (pre-charge) diversion, but requires sex offender treatment and ongoing monitoring of offenders (Koss *et al.* 2003). Much depends on the model used in carrying out RJ. For example, Joan Pennell and Gale Burford (2002) use a 'feminist praxis framework' in conceptualizing RJ responses to family violence; their approach is tailored to the dynamics of partner and family violence in ways that the standard RJ package is not.

Race and gender politics: different justice claims

One of the legacies of the 1960s and 1970s social movement activity is that justice claims for offenders and victims are overlaid by race and gender politics, respectively. Specifically, racial and ethnic minority groups' claims commonly centre on the treatment of suspects and offenders, while feminist claims more likely centre on the treatment of victims. This can create problems in finding common ground.

Indigenous communities often show a willingness to engage with alternative forms of justice, born in part from a critique of the damage wrought by conventional criminal justice, and many are keen to adopt RJ. However, Indigenous aspirations for justice are commonly holistic and are associated with calls for self-determination; these elements are not often acknowledged in alternative modes of justice, nor are Indigenous women's perspectives typically addressed. Claims that RJ is derived from Indigenous practices and or is particularly appropriate for Indigenous communities have been challenged for denying diversity among Indigenous peoples (Cunneen 2003: 188) and for re-engaging a white-centred view of the world (Daly 2002a: 61–4). Critics also say that RJ has been imposed on Indigenous communities, is neocolonialist, not community driven, and is an adjunct rather than an alternative to conventional criminal justice (Tauri 1998).

Circle sentencing is one form of RJ (and Indigenous justice practice)[11] that has been used widely in Canada and adopted more recently in Australia. In Canada, women's experiences with sentencing circles are mixed. Concerns have been raised that the subordination of women in some Canadian First

Nations communities means that they do not enter the circle on an equal basis (Goel 2000; Stewart *et al.* 2001) and that women have sometimes been excluded, silenced or harmed because power relations were not recognized, or gendered violence not taken seriously. Whether in the context of circles or conventional criminal justice, Razack argues that 'culture, community, and colonialization can be used to compete with and ultimately prevail over gender-based harm' (1994: 907). Thus, 'cultural' arguments (such as that sexual violence occurs because the community is coming to terms with the effects of colonialization) may be accepted while 'women's realities at the intersection of racism and sexism' (p. 913) are ignored.

In the Australian context, Melissa Lucashenko (1997: 155–6) suggests that state 'forms of violence against Aboriginal people have been relatively easy for academics and Black spokespeople to see' and 'to point a finger at', by contrast with 'the individual men doing the bashing and raping and child molesting'. She shows the difficult situation in which Indigenous women are placed: 'Black women have been torn between the self-evident oppression they share with Indigenous men – oppression that fits uneasily … into the frameworks of White feminism – and the unacceptability of those men's violent, sexist behaviours toward their families' (p. 156).

How, then, do these race and gender politics relate to RJ? First, there is considerable debate, and no one position. For instance, in Australia, there is support for RJ principles by many Indigenous people and organizations (Aboriginal and Torres Strait Islander Women's Task Force 2000; Behrendt 2003: 188–9). However, the use of RJ to divert men who have been involved in family violence from the criminal justice system is accepted by some communities (Blagg 2002: 200), but resisted by others. Indigenous communities vary culturally, politically and in their access to resources.

Secondly, violence is experienced differently in Indigenous and non-Indigenous communities. 'Family violence' is the commonly preferred term for Indigenous women and encapsulates a broader range of 'harmful, exploitative, violent, and aggressive practices that form around … intimate relations' (Blagg 2002: 193) than what is typically contemplated in feminist approaches to partner or domestic violence. Thus, if RJ-like responses are introduced, they will require significant reconceptualization of what is, ultimately, a white justice model. RJ cannot be prescribed, nor adopted formulaically. Rather it needs to be explored and transformed with due regard to the indigenous principle of self-determination, with reference to existing Indigenous initiatives and with explicit recognition of Indigenous women's interests (Blagg 2002: 199; Behrendt 2003; for Canada, see Stewart *et al.* 2001: 57; for the USA, see Coker 2006). Thirdly, Indigenous and non-Indigenous women may differ in their conceptualization of, and responses to, RJ. For instance, Heather Nancarrow (2006) finds greater support by Queensland Indigenous women than non-Indigenous women for RJ in domestic and family violence cases. Whereas the Indigenous women viewed RJ as a means of potentially empowering Indigenous people, the non-Indigenous women equated RJ with mediation. The non-Indigenous women had greater trust in the criminal justice system, whereas Indigenous women's support for RJ lay, in part, with their distrust of established criminal justice.

Finally, race and gender politics have a particular signature, depending on the country and context examined; and there is considerable debate among and between Indigenous and non-Indigenous women. For example, in contrast to Nancarrow's findings cited above, research by Anne McGillivray and Brenda Comaskey (1999) finds that, among the Canadian Indigenous women they interviewed, who had been long-term victims of partner violence, there is 'overwhelming support for punishment [jail]', although 'they also supported effective treatment programmes' (p. 117). The women held mixed views towards diversion: most thought it was 'worth a try' (p. 127), but they wanted to see conditions met such as 'guarantee[ing] treatment and victims' safety, and be[ing] immune to manipulation by abusers' (p. 133).

Other Canadian studies have not reported a strong preference for criminal justice, and some note disillusionment with, but not necessarily a rejection of, some models of alternative justice. For instance, a review of the justice system in the Canadian province of Nunavut questions whether conferencing and victim–offender mediation meet women's needs and interests (Crnkovich *et al.* 2000). The authors note the potential to reflect 'Inuit values of restoring harmony and peace within the community rather than punishing an individual for a crime committed against the state' (p. 29). However, they are troubled by a lack of uniformity in practice and the potential for victims to be silenced, especially when members of powerful families were implicated as offenders; and an inordinate focus on the offender (p. 31). They also challenge the presumption of choice: 'When the community, including the accused and the victims, are given the choice between the outside Euro-Canadian justice system and their "own," the pressure to choose their own system will be great' (p. 30). They recommend 'developing a process of community involvement that is accountable and community based, representative and sensitive to gender as well as culture' (p. 37). Likewise, Goel (2000) argues that problems with circle sentencing could be addressed by empowering women in their communities to ensure that they enter a circle on a more equal footing.

The Canadian context for contemporary race and gender politics includes 'the 30-year struggle by Aboriginal women for sexual equality rights' (Nahanee 1992: 33; see also McIvor 1996; Cameron 2006), including litigation over the denial of sexual equality to Indian women, and challenges to male-dominated Aboriginal organizations for not representing Indian women's interests. This struggle is commonly characterized as a clash between individual and collective rights. Critics say that certain Indigenous women's organizations were (and are) aligned with feminist interests (an individual rights focus), and by implication not with Aboriginal, communitarian interests. In response, some Indigenous women say that they are being asked to put community interests before their own individual interests – for instance, in the demands by some Indigenous organizations that women's claims for equality should await the attainment of Indian self-government (a collective rights focus). Teressa Nahanee (1992) sees the pursuit of individual rights claims as having brought important gains for Aboriginal women, but she seeks to avoid an oppositional and dichotomous construction of rights by arguing for a recognition of individual rights, and the accommodation of group rights, including those of women and children, 'within the collective' (p. 53). In connecting these debates to criminal justice, Emma LaRocque (1997) asks 'how offenders, more than victims, have come to represent "collective rights"' (p. 81), and she challenges the successes claimed for some alternative justice programmes in Aboriginal communities such as Hollow Water.

Australian debates have a different character and, in the absence of a national bill of rights, constitutional challenges have been less significant than in Canada. None the less, there have been significant political challenges to government and Indigenous organizations for failing to recognize Indigenous women's interests, especially concerning violence against women and children. Although the oppositional contrast between collective and individual rights is not as deeply etched in political debates in Australia as in Canada, a clear example of the interests of Indigenous communities being counterposed with those of Indigenous women in debates about justice arose in the wake of the Royal Commission into Aboriginal Deaths in Custody. Some women reported being silenced in their attempts to raise concerns about violence against women and being told that, if they reported the violence, they put Indigenous men at risk (Greer 1994: 66; Cunneen and Kerley 1995; Marchetti 2005).

Conclusion

Feminist engagement with RJ is recent and evolving. Although there is scepticism about what RJ can do to advance women's, including racialized women's, justice claims, there is some degree of openness to experimenting with a new set of justice practices. Feminist debate on the merits of RJ revolves around those who believe that justice alternatives can offer more options for victims, offenders (or suspects) and communities than established criminal justice; and those who see more dangers than opportunities with informal justice, who are concerned with the symbolic significance of RJ as appearing to be too lenient and who are critical of RJ's overly positive and sentimental assumptions of human nature. Debate about the merits of RJ has been conducted largely in the abstract, with little empirical research on areas that are of particular interest to feminist analysts. There are differences between and among white and racialized women on the degree to which the state and the criminal justice system are viewed as trustworthy and effective sites for responding to violence against women. However, in the light of historic and contemporary experiences of racism in established criminal justice practices, racialized women may be more open to experimenting with alternative justice practices, and for Indigenous women, when such practices are tied to principles of self-determination.

We identified a wide spectrum of theoretical, political and empirical problems for future feminist engagement with RJ. More attention needs to be given to ideal justice principles and to whether RJ measures up to those principles. For instance, greater reflection is required on the roles of retribution and punishment in RJ and mainstream criminal justice, and the potential for RJ across a wider range of offences and in handling broader forms of community conflict. This largely uncharted empirical ground should depict men's and women's experiences of victimization and recovery from crime, as well as their experiences as offenders, using the tools of realist, social constructionist and discursive analyses. We require comparative analyses of feminist debates about RJ in different countries and for different communities, necessitating greater sophistication in comparative work. A fundamental problem for comparative analysis is that the meanings and practices of RJ vary greatly. Among the more contentious areas is the optimal relationship between RJ and established criminal justice, especially for racialized women. Finally, the relationship of RJ to other new justice forms such as Indigenous justice, transitional justice and international criminal justice is a rich, but untapped, area.

Since the late 1980s, feminist analyses of justice have shifted from notions that criminal justice could be reformed by adding 'women's voice' or an 'ethic of care' to a more sobering appraisal of what, in fact, criminal law and justice system practices can do to achieve women's and feminist goals (Smart 1989). During this period, several new justice forms have emerged, among them RJ; as a consequence, we face a far more complex justice field than a decade ago. It is clear that feminist and anti-racist theories and politics must engage with these new developments, at the national and international levels, and with state and community political actors. At the same time, we should expect modest gains and seek additional paths to social change.

Selected further reading

Ptacek, J. (ed.) (2005) 'Feminism, restorative justice, and violence against women', *Violence Against Women*, Special Issue, 11 (5). The contributors to this special issue reflect on what restorative justice might have to offer in response to sexual assault and domestic violence. Several contributions consider the position of racialized women.

Cook, K., Daly, K. and Stubbs, J. (eds) (2006) 'Gender, race and restorative justice', *Theoretical Criminology*, Special Issue 10 (1). This special issue provides a feminist analysis of restorative justice, with a particular focus on gender and race, and brings an international and comparative dimension to theory and research.

Acorn, A. (2004) *Compulsory Compassion: A Critique of Restorative Justice*. Vancouver: UBC Press. A former advocate of restorative justice, Acorn engages critically with key tenets of restorative justice from a feminist perspective, drawing on a wide range of disciplines.

Strang, H. and Braithwaite, J. (eds) (2002) *Restorative Justice and Family Violence*. Cambridge: Cambridge University Press. Advocates and sceptics of restorative justice from several countries analyse the potential of restorative justice as a response to family and sexual violence.

Notes

1 This chapter excerpts from and expands upon Daly and Stubbs (2006).
2 As discussed in the section on race and gender politics, the same problem is evinced in the individual and collective rights debate in Canada.

3   This work has offered a welcome challenge to any naïve reliance on criminalization strategies, but some analysts have failed to acknowledge the diverse responses to violence against women, which include hybrid models that engage advocacy groups, community groups, and criminal justice agents (see Stubbs 2004).

4   The masculine pronoun is used because Hampton is discussing a case that involved male prisoners' rights to vote.

5   Zehr (2003: 58) has since argued that retributive and restorative justice have commonalities of wishing to 'right the balance' in the aftermath of crime, and that the response should be proportional to the offending act.

6   This result is partly a consequence of a high proportion of adolescent 'punch-ups' (fights) in the female offence distribution.

7   Partner violence refers to couple violence, whereas family violence (the preferred term for Australian Indigenous women) refers to a broader array of offences such as child sexual abuse and family fights (Blagg 2002). For youth justice cases, family violence would include sibling assaults and assaults on parents by children.

8   These problems have been identified by Goel (2000), Presser and Gaarder (2000), Shapland (2000), Lewis et al. (2001), Busch (2002), Coker (1999, 2002), Acorn (2004), Hopkins et al. (2004) and Stubbs (1997, 2002, 2004).

9   These benefits have been identified by Braithwaite and Daly (1994), Martin (1998), Koss (2000), Morris and Gelsthorpe (2000), Presser and Gaarder (2000), Daly (2002b), Hudson (1998, 2002), Morris (2002), Pennell and Burford (2002), Koss et al. (2003), Mills (2003), Hopkins et al. (2004), Curtis-Fawley and Daly (2005) and Daly and Curtis-Fawley (2006).

10   In South Australia, RJ can only occur when a youth has admitted the offence to the police or in court. More research is needed to determine whether RJ, as diversion from court, may offer incentives for those who have offended to make admissions.

11   Circles have been identified as a form of RJ and an Indigenous justice practice. Some analysts distinguish between the two, and others do not. In practice, RJ is predominantly a 'white justice' form, which is applied to Indigenous offender cases although, ironically, advocates claim that RJ has its origins in Indigenous practices (see Blagg 1997 on an orientalist appropriation of RJ). Circles are often assumed to reflect Indigenous practices, but this remains controversial. We do not address this matter, with its associated politics, here (but see Cameron 2006).

References

Abel, R. (ed.) (1982) *The Politics of Informal Justice* (2 vols). New York, NY: Academic Press.

Aboriginal and Torres Strait Islander Women's Task Force (2000) *Aboriginal and Torres Strait Islander Women's Task Force on Violence*. Brisbane: Department of Aboriginal and Torres Strait Islander Policy and Development.

Acorn, A. (2004) *Compulsory Compassion: A Critique of Restorative Justice*. Vancouver: UBC Press.

Behrendt, L. (2003) *Achieving Social Justice: Indigenous Rights and Australia's Future*. Annandale: Federation Press.

Blagg, H. (1997) 'A just measure of shame? Aboriginal youth and conferencing in Australia', *British Journal of Criminology*, 37: 481–501.

Blagg, H. (2002) 'Restorative justice and Aboriginal family: opening a space for healing', in H. Strang and J. Braithwaite (eds) *Restorative Justice and Family Violence*. Cambridge: Cambridge University Press.

Braithwaite, J. and Daly, K. (1994) 'Masculinities, violence and communitarian control', in T. Newburn and E.A. Stanko (eds) *Just Boys Doing Business? Men, Masculinities, and Crime*. London: Routledge.

Busch, R. (2002) 'Domestic violence and restorative justice initiatives: who pays if we get it wrong?', in H. Strang and J. Braithwaite (eds) *Restorative Justice and Family Violence*. Cambridge: Cambridge University Press.

Cameron, A. (2006) 'Stopping the violence: Canadian feminist debates on restorative justice and intimate violence', *Theoretical Criminology*, 10: 49–66.

Coker, D. (1999) 'Enhancing autonomy for battered women: lessons from Navajo peacemaking', *UCLA Law Review*, 47: 1–111.

Coker, D. (2002) 'Transformative justice: anti-subordination processes in cases of domestic violence', in H. Strang and J. Braithwaite (eds) *Restorative Justice and Family Violence*. Cambridge: Cambridge University Press.

Coker, D. (2006) 'Restorative justice, Navajo peacemaking and domestic violence', *Theoretical Criminology*, 10: 67–85.

Collier, R. (1998) *Masculinities, Crime and Criminology: Men, Heterosexuality and the Criminal(ised) Other*. London: Sage.

Collins, P.H. (1990) *Black Feminist Thought*. London: HarperCollins Academic.

Cook, K. (2006) 'Doing difference and accountability in restorative justice conferences', *Theoretical Criminology*, 10: 107–24.

Crawford, A. and Newburn, T. (2003) *Youth Offending and Restorative Justice: Implementing Reform in Youth Justice*. Cullompton: Willan Publishing.

Crenshaw, K. (1989) 'Demarginalizing the intersection of race and sex: a black feminist critique of antidiscrimination doctrine, feminist theory, and antiracist politics', *University of Chicago Legal Forum*, 4: 139–67.

Crnkovich, M and Addario, L., with Archibald, L. (2000) *Inuit Women and the Nunavut Justice System*. Canada: Research and Statistics Division, Department of Justice (available online at http://canada.justice.gc.ca/en/ps/rs/rep/2000/rr00-8a-e.pdf).

Cunneen, C. (2003) 'Thinking critically about restorative justice', in E. McLaughlin *et al.* (eds) *Restorative Justice: Critical Issues*. London: Sage.

Cunneen, C. and Kerley, K. (1995) 'Indigenous women and criminal justice', in K. Hazlehurst (ed.) *Perceptions of Justice: Indigenous Encounters with the Criminal Law*. London: Avebury.

Curtis-Fawley, S. and Daly, K. (2005) 'Gendered violence and restorative justice: the views of victim advocates', *Violence Against Women*, 11: 603–38.

Daly, K. (1989) 'Criminal justice ideologies and practices in different voices: some feminist questions about justice', *International Journal of the Sociology of Law*, 17: 1–18.

Daly, K. (1993) 'Class–race–gender: sloganeering in search of meaning', *Social Justice*, 20: 56–71.

Daly, K. (1996) 'Diversionary conferencing in Australia: a reply to the optimists and skeptics'. Paper presented at the American Society of Criminology annual meeting, Chicago, November.

Daly, K. (1997) 'Different ways of conceptualizing sex/gender in feminist theory and their implications for criminology', *Theoretical Criminology*, 1: 25–51.

Daly, K. (2000) 'Revisiting the relationship between retributive and restorative justice', in H. Strang and J. Braithwaite (eds) *Restorative Justice: Philosophy to Practice*. Aldershot: Dartmouth/Ashgate.

Daly, K. (2002a) 'Restorative justice: the real story', *Punishment and Society*, 4: 55–79.

Daly, K. (2002b) 'Sexual assault and restorative justice', in H. Strang and J. Braithwaite (eds) *Restorative Justice and Family Violence*. Cambridge: Cambridge University Press.

Daly, K (2006) 'Restorative justice and sexual assault: an archival study of court and conference cases', *British Journal of Criminology*, 46: 334–56.

Daly, K. and Curtis-Fawley, S. (2006) 'Restorative justice for victims of sexual assault', in K. Heimer and C. Kruttschnitt (eds) *Gender and Crime: Patterns of Victimization and Offending*. New York, NY: New York University Press.

Daly, K. and Immarigeon, R. (1998) 'The past, present, and future of restorative justice: some critical reflections', *Contemporary Justice Review*, 1: 21–45.

Daly, K. and Stubbs, J. (2006) 'Feminist engagement with restorative justice', *Theoretical Criminology*, 10: 9–28.

Daly, K. and Tonry, M. (1997) 'Gender, race, and sentencing', in M. Tonry (ed.) *Crime and Justice: A Review of the Research. Vol. 22*. Chicago, IL: University of Chicago Press.

Dubois, E., Dunlap, M., Gilligan, C., MacKinnon, C. and Menkel-Meadow, C. (1985) 'Feminist discourse, moral values, and law: a conversation', *Buffalo Law Review*, 34: 11–87.

Duff, R.A. (1996) 'Penal communications: recent work in the philosophy of punishment', in M. Tonry (ed.) *Crime and Justice: A Review of Research. Vol. 20*. Chicago, IL: University of Chicago Press.

Duff, R.A. (2001) *Punishment, Communication, and Community*. New York, NY: Oxford University Press.

Duff, R.A. (2003) 'Restoration and retribution', in A. von Hirsch *et al.* (eds) *Restorative Justice and Criminal Justice: Competing or Reconcilable Paradigms?* Oxford: Hart Publishing.

Gilligan, C. (1982) *In A Different Voice*. Cambridge, MA: Harvard University Press.

Goel, R. (2000) 'No women at the centre: the use of Canadian sentencing circles in domestic violence cases', *Wisconsin Women's Law Journal*, 15: 293–334.

Greer, P. (1994) 'Aboriginal women and domestic violence in New South Wales', in J. Stubbs (ed.) *Women, Male Violence and the Law*. Sydney: Institute of Criminology.

Hampton, J. (1998) 'Punishment, feminism, and political identity: a case study in the expressive meaning of the law', *Canadian Journal of Law and Jurisprudence*, 11: 23–45.

Harris, M.K. (1987) 'Moving into the new millennium: toward a feminist vision of justice', *Prison Journal*, 67: 27–38.

Heidensohn, F. (1986) 'Models of justice: Portia or Persephone? Some thoughts on equality, fairness and gender in the field of criminal justice', *International Journal of the Sociology of Law*, 14: 287–98.

Hopkins, C.Q., Koss, M. and Bachar, K. (2004) 'Applying restorative justice to ongoing intimate violence: problems and possibilities', *Saint Louis University Public Law Review*, 23: 289–311.

Hoyle, C., Young, R. and Hill, R. (2002) *Proceed with Caution: An Evaluation of the Thames Valley Police Initiative in Restorative Cautioning*. York: Joseph Rowntree Foundation.

Hudson, B. (1998) 'Restorative justice: the challenge of sexual and racial violence', *Journal of Law and Society*, 25: 237–56.

Hudson, B. (2002) 'Restorative justice and gendered violence: diversion or effective justice?', *British Journal of Criminology*, 42: 616–34.

Hudson, B. (2003) *Justice in the Risk Society*. London: Sage Publications.

Hudson, B. (2006) 'Beyond white man's justice: race, gender and justice in late modernity', *Theoretical Criminology*, 10: 29–47.

Julich, S. (2006) 'Views of justice among survivors of historical child sexual abuse: implications for restorative justice in New Zealand', *Theoretical Criminology*, 10: 125–38.

Koss, M. (2000) 'Blame, shame, and community: justice responses to violence against women', *American Psychologist*, 55: 1332–43.

Koss, M., Bachar, K. and Hopkins, C.Q. (2003) 'Restorative justice for sexual violence: repairing victims, building community and holding offenders accountable', *Annals of the New York Academy of Science*, 989: 384–96.

Lajeunesse, T. (1996) *Community Holistic Circle Healing, in Hollow Water Manitoba: An Evaluation*. Ottawa: Solicitor General of Canada.

LaRocque, E. (1997) 'Re-examining culturally appropriate models in criminal justice applications', in M. Asch (ed.) *Aboriginal and Treaty Rights in Canada: Essays on Law, Equality and Respect for Difference*. Vancouver: UBC Press.

Lerman, L. (1984) 'Mediation of wife abuse cases: the adverse impact of informal dispute resolution on women', *Harvard Women's Law Journal*, 7: 57–113.

Lewis, R., Dobash, R., Dobash, R. and Cavanagh, K. (2001) 'Law's progressive potential: the value of engagement with the law for domestic violence', *Social and Legal Studies*, 10: 105–30.

Lucashenko, M. (1997) 'Violence against Indigenous women: public and private dimensions', in S. Cook and J. Bessant (eds) *Women's Encounters with Violence: Australian Experiences*, London: Sage.

Marchetti, E. (2005) 'Missing subjects: women and gender in the Royal Commission into Aboriginal Deaths in Custody.' PhD, School of Criminology and Criminal Justice, Griffith University.

Martin, D.L. (1998) 'Retribution revisited: a reconsideration of feminist criminal law reform strategies', *Osgoode Hall Law Journal*, 36: 151–88.

Masters, G. and Smith, D. (1998) 'Portia and Persephone revisited: thinking about feeling in criminal justice', *Theoretical Criminology*, 2: 5–27.

Matthews, R. (1988) 'Reassessing informal justice', in R. Matthews (ed.) *Informal Justice?* Newbury Park, CA: Sage.

Maxwell, G., Kingi, V., Robertson, J., Morris, A. and Cunningham, C. (2004) *Achieving Effective Outcomes in Youth Justice: Final Report*. Wellington: Ministry of Social Development.

Maxwell, G. and Morris, A. (1993) *Family, Victims and Culture: Youth Justice in New Zealand*. Wellington: Institute of Criminology, Victoria University of New Zealand.

McGillivray, A. and Comaskey, B. (1999) *Black Eyes All of the Time*. Toronto: University of Toronto Press.

McIvor, S.D. (1996) 'Self government and Aboriginal women', in M. Jackson and N.K. Banks (eds) *Ten Years Later: The Charter and Equality for Women*. Vancouver: Simon Fraser University.

Merry, S. (1982) 'The social organization of mediation in nonindustrial societies: implications for informal community justice in America', in R. Abel (ed.) *The Politics of Informal Justice. Vol. 2*. New York, NY: Academic Press.

Mills, L. (2003) *Insult to Injury: Rethinking our Responses to Intimate Abuse*. Princeton, NY: Princeton University Press.

Minow, M. (1998) *Between Vengeance and Forgiveness: Facing History after Genocide and Mass Violence*. Boston, MA: Beacon Press.

Morris, A. (2002) 'Children and family violence: restorative messages from New Zealand', in H. Strang and J. Braithwaite (eds) *Restorative Justice and Family Violence*. Cambridge: Cambridge University Press.

Morris, A. and Gelsthorpe, L. (2000) 'Re-visioning men's violence against female partners', *Howard Journal of Criminal Justice*, 39: 412–28.

Nahanee, T. (1992) '"Dancing with a gorilla": Aboriginal women, justice and the charter.' Paper prepared for the roundtable, *Justice Issues*, Royal Commission on Aboriginal Peoples, Ottawa (on file with the authors).

Nancarrow, H. (2006) 'In search of justice for domestic and family violence: Indigenous and non-Indigenous Australian women's perspectives', *Theoretical Criminology*, 10: 87–106.

Pennell, J. and Burford, G. (2002) 'Feminist praxis: making family group conferencing work', in H. Strang and J. Braithwaite (eds) *Restorative Justice and Family Violence*. Cambridge: Cambridge University Press.

Presser, L. and Gaarder, E. (2000) 'Can restorative justice reduce battering? Some preliminary considerations', *Social Justice*, 27: 175–95.

Raeder, N. (1993) 'Gender and sentencing: single moms, battered women, and other sex-based anomalies in the gender free world of the federal sentencing guidelines', *Pepperdine Law Review*, 20: 905–90.

Razack, S. (1994) 'What is to be gained by looking white people in the eye? Culture, race, and gender in cases of sexual violence', *Signs*, 19: 894–923.

Shapland, J. (2000) 'Victims and criminal justice: creating responsible criminal justice agencies', in A. Crawford and J. Goodey (eds) *Integrating a Victim Perspective within Criminal Justice: International Debates*. Aldershot: Ashgate.

Smart, C. (1989) *Feminism and the Power of Law*. London: Routledge.

Smart, C. (1992) 'The woman of legal discourse', *Social and Legal Studies*, 1: 29–44.

Snider, L. (1998) 'Toward safer societies: punishment, masculinities and violence against women', *British Journal of Criminology*, 38: 1–39.

Stewart, W., Huntley, A. and Blaney, F. (2001) *The Implications of Restorative Justice for Aboriginal Women and Children Survivors of Violence: A Comparative Overview of Five Communities in British Columbia*. Ottawa: Law Commission of Canada (available online at http://www.lcc.gc.ca/pdf/Awan.pdf).

Strang, H. (2002) *Repair or Revenge: Victims and Restorative Justice*. Oxford: Clarendon Press.

Strang, H. and Braithwaite, J. (eds) (2002) *Restorative Justice and Family Violence*. Cambridge: Cambridge University Press.

Stubbs, J. (1997) 'Shame, defiance, and violence against women: a critical analysis of "communitarian" conferencing', in S. Cook and J. Bessant (eds) *Women's Encounters with Violence: Australian Experiences*. London: Sage.

Stubbs, J. (2002) 'Domestic violence and women's safety: feminist challenges to restorative justice', in H. Strang and J. Braithwaite (eds) *Restorative Justice and Family Violence*. Cambridge: Cambridge University Press.

Stubbs, J. (2004) *Restorative Justice, Domestic Violence and Family Violence. Issues Paper 9*. Sydney: Australian Domestic and Family Violence Clearinghouse (available online at http://www.austdvclearinghouse.unsw.edu.au/PDF%20files/Issues_Paper_9.pdf).

Tauri, J. (1998) 'Family group conferencing: a case study of the indigenisation of New Zealand's justice system', *Current Issues in Criminal Justice*, 10: 168–82.

von Hirsch, A. (1993) *Censure and Sanctions*. New York, NY: Oxford University Press.

Wing, A. (ed.) (1997) *Critical Race Feminism: A Reader*. New York, NY: New York University Press.

Zehr, H. (1990) *Changing Lenses: A New Focus for Crime and Justice*. Scottdale, PA: Herald Press.

Zehr, H. (2003) *The Little Book of Restorative Justice*. Intercourse, PA: Good Books.

Chapter 10

'The victims' movement and restorative justice

Simon Green

Introduction

> What would we say about a movement that apparently forgot to invite most of its professed beneficiaries? What, if we discovered, for example, in the victims 'movement' that victims were, politically, all dressed up but had no place to go? What kind of movement would it be? Would it really be a movement at all? (Elias 1993: 26).

When, over a decade ago, Robert Elias wrote these words, restorative justice was in its infancy and he was essentially commenting on the political manipulation of crime victims in terms of both rights and service provision. You could therefore be forgiven for believing that the restorative justice explosion came in the nick of time, responding to the concerns about victims raised by Elias in the USA and others in the UK and Europe (e.g. Shapland *et al.* 1985; Christie 1977, 1986; Phillips 1988; Walklate 1989). Collectively, these authors expressed concerns about the role of the victim in the criminal justice process; the unequal treatment of different types of victims; and the co-option of victim interests into wider ideological and political agendas. Although during the 1970s and 1980s the idea of victim–offender mediation or victim reparation was already in existence (Blew and Rosenblum 1979; Harding 1982; Marshall and Walpole 1985), it was still a fledgling movement, the jurisdiction of a few key protagonists (for example, Martin Wright, John Harding and Tony Marshall in the UK or Howard Zehr in the USA) and highly localized in predominantly extra-legal projects often run by religious groups or probation services (for an account of these early years, see Rock 2004). Yet despite the success of restorative justice over the last decade the concerns raised by Elias (1990, 1993) still have relevance. To what extent does restorative justice meet the needs of victims? Has restorative justice led to a significant change in the fortunes of the victims of crime? Or have the aspirations of restorative justice led to heightened expectations among victims who are then made the pawns of political expediency?

These questions will be explored in relation to the wider debates and concerns expressed within the victim movement about the position and treatment of the victims of crime in the criminal justice system. To do this consideration will be given to the place of the victim within a restorative framework and the empirical evidence that demonstrates whether or not restorative justice fulfils the needs of victims. The aim is to take a close look at the interaction between victims and restorative justice; the objective is to consider whether this interaction is developing in line with the principles of restorative justice or whether the concerns raised above by Elias (1993) still have relevance to the ways in which victims are represented and included within a seemingly more victim-orientated criminal justice system.

The emergence of victimology and the victims' movement

The exact origins of the victim movement are hard to divine. At what point victim issues began to play a more prominent role in academic or policy discussion depends upon what benchmark is taken. One distinction can be made between academic victimology and the victims' movement. Academic victimology refers to research and theory about victims whereas the victim movement is much more associated with the political pursuit of victim assistance (Goodey 2005). For example, academic victimology is often cited as starting with the ideas of Von Hentig (1948) and Mendelsohn (1974) who introduced the notion of victim precipitation; that is, the level of individual responsibility for victimization. However, these early forays into victim studies have been heavily criticized for victim blaming (Walklate 1989) and are not generally representative of a victims' movement concerned with improving the treatment of victims. In terms of a political movement that began to question the treatment of victims in the criminal justice system, it is more widely accepted that the resurgence of victim interests began during the 1960s and 1970s (Shapland *et al.* 1985; Mawby and Walklate 1994) with the introduction of criminal injuries compensation and the growth of second-wave feminism that led to the spotlight falling on a huge 'dark figure' (Coleman and Moynihan 1996) of sexual and violent crimes committed against women.

Plotting the development of victim-centred initiatives in criminal justice requires discussion of a number of different paradigms and policy directions (van Dijk 1988; Miers 1989, 1990; Walklate 1999, 2003a; Goodey 2005). Further, there is significant variation in the character and focus of victim-centred initiatives depending on which country is studied (Maguire and Shapland 1990; Mawby 2003).

Four aspects of the victims' movement have been described as 'victim aid and assistance, victim experiences with the criminal justice system, State compensation and reparation by the offender' (Shapland *et al.* 1985: 2). These four aspects provide a useful starting point to consider the major trends and shifts in the victims' movement since the 1960s and the introduction of criminal injuries compensation. Goodey (2005: 102) has suggested that the rise of the victims' movement during the late 1960s and 1970s can be attributed to three factors:

1. a rising crime rate and, at the same time, a rejection of the rehabilitative criminal justice model as a response to offending;
2. the emergence of the centre-right in British and North American politics, and, with it, a tough approach to law and order;
3. growth in the feminist movement, and, with this, an emphasis on women and children as victims of interpersonal patriarchal violence.

The accumulation of these factors led to an increased political focus on criminal justice reform that brought to the forefront victim interests, or at least what was perceived as victim interests.

State compensation

Van Dijk (1988: 119) refers to the first wave in the victim movement as 'state compensation and initiatives by probation officers'. During this early stage (1965–75) state compensation schemes for victims were introduced under a broad social welfare ethos (Goodey 2002). The earliest scheme started in New Zealand in 1963 and was soon followed by similar initiatives in England and California. Towards the end of the 1960s and early 1970s more and more US states began to adopt compensation schemes and these were closely followed by similar initiatives in Northern Europe. In the UK and the Netherlands small–scale counselling projects were established to help crime victims come to terms with their experiences and early restitution projects in the USA were introduced. As a result of limited commitment and planning these early essays in victim counselling and restitution were largely unsuccessful (Van Dijk 1988). Conversely, state compensation proliferated and has become a mainstay of most West European and North American countries. Yet it has attracted criticism for the length of time it takes victims to receive compensation and, in England, it has been further criticized for reducing the award depending on the offending history of the victim, whether he or she has contributed to the offence and whether or not he or she co-operated quickly with the police (Maguire and Shapland 1990). As Christie (1986) points out, this assumes a notion of the 'ideal victim' which has little relevance to the realities of criminal victimization. These problems have both disillusioned and frustrated the victims of crime in the UK.

Offender compensation

In a similar vein, compensation from the offender has become a major component in the 'package' of victim-centred options in the UK. First introduced into criminal law in 1972, the compensation order was given priority over state compensation in the Criminal Justice Act 1982. In its early years the compensation order was widely endorsed by the judiciary, and since 1998 it has been required that the judiciary give reasons for not attaching compensation where there is an identifiable victim. Yet, as with state compensation, offender compensation has been met with mixed feelings. On the one hand research has shown that victims appear to prefer compensation from the offender rather than the state (Shapland *et al.* 1985; Hamilton and

Wisniewski 1996) while, on the other, the use of the compensation order has gradually dropped off since the 1990s. One of the main reasons cited for this by Flood-Page and Mackie (1998) was the judiciary's reluctance to employ compensation when the offender had little ability to pay, particularly as the amounts then appear derisory in relation to the victim's experiences. This problem is further exacerbated by the uneven and comparatively small sums that are periodically paid, or not paid, to the victim (Maguire and Shapland 1990).

The victim's experience of criminal justice

A third strand to the victims' movement has been attempts to improve the victim's experiences of criminal justice. Following from a long period of victim disenfranchisement which led Christie (1977) and Shapland *et al.* (1985) to refer to the victim as the non-person of criminal justice, a plethora of reforms within both the USA and UK sought to alleviate victim anxieties and disparities within the criminal justice process. Up until this period there was very little funding or provision to include the victims of crime in the criminal justice process or to take their needs into account (Holstrom and Burgess 1978; Elias 1983; Shapland *et al.* 1985; Shapland 1988; Walklate 1989). Crime was committed by offenders against the state and the victim had little or no role beyond that of witness for the prosecution. Thus in a bid both to address the damaging experiences many victims had of the criminal justice system (in particular the victims of sexual violence) and to improve the probability of these victims reporting crimes, a series of measures were enacted to improve the victim's experiences of criminal justice. In both the USA and the UK this entailed a range of measures intended to improve the responsiveness of criminal justice agencies to victims, including the treatment of rape victims, better scheduling of hearings and the introduction of standards for agencies for keeping victims informed about their cases (Shapland 1988; Kelly 1990). These improvements have been lent weight at the international level by both the United Nations in 1985 and a series of declarations from the Council of Europe during the mid-1980s, which reinforced the need to provide the victims of crime with respect, information, protection and compensation.

More specifically, in the USA, several legislative reforms were enacted that provided the victim with enhanced rights. These included allowing the victim to testify at the plea-bargaining stage; to submit a victim-impact statement; and to be present in the courtroom at key stages of the trial (Kelly 1990). In the UK, improvements have been less focused on formal rights than in the USA (Maguire and Shapland 1990; Strang 2002; Goodey 2005) and more focused on service provision. These have included the introduction of two Victim's Charters (Home Office 1990, 1996) that lay down the responsibilities of the statutory agencies to provide information and advice to victims. Further, there have been attempts to improve the status and support for victims in the courtroom and comparatively recently the introduction of victim personal statements has allowed victims to outline the consequences of their victimization. Finally, at the post-sentence stage, parole boards were required to consider more fully the wishes of the victims when deciding upon early release from prison.

Victim aid and assistance

Victim aid and assistance constitute the final strand of Shapland *et al.*'s (1985) description of the victim movement's influence. There are various types of victim assistance throughout Europe and North America (Mawby 2003) and, although there are a range of differences among nations regarding the exact composition and role of victim assistance agencies, they are generally focused on providing counselling and advice to the victims of crime. In addition to these victim support organizations, the feminist influence on the victims' movement was largely responsible for the establishment of rape crisis centres in both the UK and USA. In the UK, Victim Support is the national charity that takes referrals from the police and provides services to the victims of crime. Unlike some of its European counterparts (e.g. Spain, Belgium and Germany), most of Victim Support's resources are drawn from the voluntary sector. This raises questions about the funding of such services (Mawby and Gill 1987; Gill and Mawby 1990) and the problem of recruiting volunteers, which can be most difficult in the most needed localities (Mawby and Gill 1987). In the USA the National Organization for Victim Assistance is an umbrella organization that provides a similar range of services plus more specialist counselling services for the victims of serious sexual and domestic violence. Mawby (2003: 151) draws broad distinctions between the British, American and European victim assistance programmes, suggesting that:

> In Britain the emphasis has traditionally been placed on a combination of sympathetic support and advice, in the USA 'support' has tended to include a greater emphasis on crisis counselling, with professional therapists seen as a common resource (Young and Stein 1983). In contrast, in much of Western Europe emphasis has been on the provision of legal advice and financial assistance.

This has been a brief, whistle-stop tour through the types of activities usually associated with the victims' movement. Critical issues have only been lightly touched upon and, while there are a host of specific nuances regarding how these trends have emerged in different countries, and while there is a large body of research which questions the effectiveness of particular measures, it would appear that the victims' movement has been busy. Given the extent of victim-orientated reform during the 1960s, 1970s and 1980s, it seems strange that Elias (1990, 1993) should state his concerns about the political manipulation of victims and their continued marginalization within the criminal justice system. Yet, in the USA, Elias (1990, 1993) and, in the UK, Mawby and Walklate (1994) and Williams (1999), have levelled concerns about both the commitment to victim-centred initiatives and the co-option of victim concerns into wider ideological and political agendas. These issues will be returned to in greater depth in the final section of this chapter, where they will be used to consider whether restorative justice represents a real divergence from this issue or whether it too has become, or is becoming, a political tool of the state.

Victim participation in restorative justice

At its heart restorative justice is concerned with addressing the harm caused by a wrongdoing (Baker 1994; Daly and Immarigeon 1998). As this definition implies, restorative justice is not a process only applied to criminal cases. It has been successfully employed in schools, the workplace, neighbourhood disputes (Braithwaite 2003a) and for broader political conflicts such as post-apartheid South Africa (South African Truth and Reconciliation Commission 1998). Yet, in most contemporary criminological debates, it is within the criminal justice jurisdiction that restorative justice is most commonly applied. Restorative justice aims to restore victims, restore offenders and restore the community by 'repairing the breach' caused by criminal behaviour (Burnside and Baker 1994). As such restorative justice represents a shift in focus. No longer are crimes committed against a remote and impartial state but against individuals, specific victims in specific contexts:

> Crime then is at its core a violation of a person by another person, a person who himself or herself may be wounded. It is a violation of the just relationship that should exist between individuals. There is also a larger social dimension to crime. Indeed, the effects of crime ripple out, touching many others. Society too has a stake in the outcome and a role to play. Still these public dimensions should not be the starting point. Crime is not first an offence against society, much less against the state. Crime is first an offence against people, and it is here we should start (Zehr 1990: 182).

Therefore, in restorative justice the victim is promoted to a central actor (Wright 1996; Strang 2002; Zehr and Mika 2003). No longer is the victim relegated to the role of witness or spectator in the unfolding courtroom drama between the offender and the state (Shapland *et al.* 1985). They are crucial. Restorative justice conceives a criminal event as harming relationships between individuals (Baker 1994) which can logically only then be resolved by those same individuals. The victim's participation is fundamental if the process of restoring the harm caused is to occur. As Van Ness (2002) states, the four key components of restorative justice are: encounter, amends, reintegration and inclusion. For these key components to occur the relevant stakeholders need to be present so that the interactive mechanisms by which restorative justice functions can take place. Restorative justice aims to empower victims, providing them with a forum in which their voices are both heard and respected. As Heather Strang (2002, 2004) has noted, these features have long been recognized as important to the victims of crime, and are both a good in themselves and an essential component for restorative processes. Without the participation of the victim it is hard to imagine how restorative outcomes can be achieved as communication between the victim and offender is the primary process by which conflict resolution in reached. Yet participation itself does not ensure restoration occurs, only that a condition for restoration is met. The context, quality and direction of individual projects also have a huge bearing on whether victims have a positive experience of restorative justice.

The victim restored

There is an increasingly large body of empirical evidence that has demonstrated that restorative justice is positively received by victims and operates to their benefit. As a comparatively new phenomenon, research evidence is still emerging regarding the success of restorative schemes around the globe but there have been numerous evaluations of specific projects that seek to assess how well victims have responded to the process. However, before embarking on this review it would be sensible to note that there is significant variation between restorative schemes according to their aims, cultural context and location (Miers 2001; Johnstone 2004). Dignan (2005) points to five broad categories of restorative practice that include: court-based restitutive and reparative measures, victim–offender mediation programmes, conferencing initiatives, community reparation boards and panels, and healing or sentencing circles. Of these five categories the first has least in common with the types of restorative practice outlined here and will therefore be omitted, while the last is usually the remit of indigenous communities in North America and there is little reliable research evidence to discuss. The remaining three categories, while comprising a range of different approaches to restorative justice, all involve some form of victim–offender engagement, and the evaluations of such schemes all draw on similar measures to assess their effectiveness at meeting victim expectations. The aim, therefore, is to review the positive research findings about victim involvement.

Most forms of victim–offender mediation have relied heavily on victim satisfaction measures to determine their success (Kurki 2003; Dignan 2005). Victim satisfaction is usually assessed in terms of the victim's experiences of the restorative process and whether they compare favourably to conventional criminal justice. For example, some early forms of evaluation in the USA demonstrated that in comparison with the more traditional courtroom trial, victims found the restorative process more satisfactory (Umbreit and Coates 1993; Umbreit 1994). Similar patterns of satisfaction have also been documented in Canada (Umbreit 1996) and in the UK (Umbreit and Roberts 1996).

In more recent years these findings have been replicated around the globe. In Australia, Strang (2002) studied the Reintegrative Shaming Experiments (RISE) and found that a greater percentage of victims were satisfied with the restorative conference than with courtroom justice and generally had lower levels of anger towards offenders once they had been through the restorative process. Similarly, Daly (2001, 2003a, 2003b) studied the South Australian Juvenile Justice (SAJJ) project and found that victims had a positive reaction to the process and had a significant reduction in anger towards the offenders, with over 60 per cent recording that they had fully recovered from the offence. In the UK similar patterns of victim satisfaction have been recorded by Hoyle *et al.* (2002) when evaluating the Thames Valley Police initiative on restorative cautioning. In this project, most participating victims (two thirds) felt that the process positively influenced their perceptions of offenders and the vast majority of victims felt that the meeting had been valuable in helping them recover from their experiences. A recent evaluation of the youth justice panels in the UK (Crawford and Newburn 2003: 213) also pointed to some of the benefits to victims:

> Panels received high levels of satisfaction from victims on measures of procedural justice, including being treated fairly and with respect, as well as being given a voice in the process. In addition, there was indication of restorative movement on behalf of victims as a consequence of panel attendance and input.

Crawford and Newburn (2003) consider the motivational factors that lead to victims wishing to participate in a panel and then look at their experiences of participation. What they found was that the reasons for participation and the subsequent experiences of the process varied significantly from person to person. Yet despite these variations there were some overall trends that pointed towards victim satisfaction with the process.

This brief overview of some of the larger studies of restorative practice glosses over the huge range of contextual and practical issues that are relevant when conducting any evaluation of a particular scheme. Yet, despite this gloss, the general conclusion of most restorative justice studies has been that when victims participate in some form of victim–offender mediation the majority find the process helpful. Of course, what is exactly meant by victim satisfaction is open to question, as is whether or not levels of satisfaction are an appropriate benchmark for assessing restorative justice (Braithwaite 1999; Dignan 2005). Satisfaction scales in themselves usually refer to the different stages of the restorative process or to the factors considered important to the victims of crime. Hence, although the findings presented here are largely the broad or aggregate findings of research projects, most studies have demonstrated variable levels of victim satisfaction according to the particular scheme and stage in the process (for a closer discussion of these stages, see Strang 2002 or Crawford and Newburn 2003). There are, of course, other measures that could also contribute to the victim's interests, most notably the ability of restorative justice projects to reduce levels of reoffending. Yet, although a reduction in reoffending may well benefit the population of victims in general, it occurs at a distant point from the restorative process and is therefore much harder to measure directly against victim experiences of the process. What is evident is that the attitudes of victims who take part in the restorative process are largely positive when compared with those of victims whose cases are tried and sentenced in the conventional way. At this level, at least, restorative justice appears to fulfil its promise to the victims of crime – for the first time in recent history they have been given both a role and status in the resolution of their victimization.

The victim neglected

In contrast to the broadly positive findings outlined above there is a growing concern that, despite the laudable aims of restorative justice towards the victims of crime and despite its organizing principles of bringing together the relevant stakeholders to repair the harm caused by a crime, victims still find themselves sidelined (Reeves and Mulley 2000; Achilles and Zehr 2001). Both within and without the restorative camp there exist doubts about the capacity of restorative measures to fulfil the needs of crime victims. Braithwaite (2002) rightly points to the huge unknown quantity of crime that is either not brought to the attention of the authorities or not resolved when it is. This leads to a tiny proportion of criminal acts resulting in the identification of an offender to take part in restorative processes. This obviously leads those victims whose crimes are either never reported or solved without redress to the possible advantages offered by restorative justice. Further, the instigation of a restorative process is still firmly located within the remit of the offender. They have the initial choice as to whether they wish to participate, leaving the victim dependent on the offender's decision (Herman 2004).

In addition to these concerns, Victim Support in the UK and the American National Center for Victims of Crime have argued that the growth of victim–offender mediation had been largely championed by 'penal reformers, offender groups and academics who were persuaded that offenders had been mistreated' (Rock 2004: 291). This suggests that the advancement of restorative justice is predominantly focused around attempts to improve the way in which we treat offenders rather than victims and as a result has been treated with a good degree of wariness by those pursuing victim entitlements. In the UK, Victim Support, under the leadership of Helen Reeves, has been particularly cautious about the increased demands and potential harms that involvement in restorative conferences may have on victims (NAVSS 1984; Reeves and Mulley 2000). Hence, the debate about what restorative justice is for and whom it benefits continues to rage. Much of this controversy stems from a concern that reparation is predominantly an offender-focused provision, designed to encourage desistence from offending and reintegration back into the community. As Johnstone (2002: 81) points out: 'At the heart of these doubts is a suspicion that restorative justice, for all its talk of restoring victims, is still offender-focused and is likely to become more so as it becomes implemented in the criminal justice system'. The concern seems to be that, for all its talk of being victim-centred, restorative justice, while involving the victim, does so primarily to benefit the offender.

What evidence is there to suggest this concern is valid? Of the various empirical studies that attempt to evaluate the effectiveness of restorative justice most have been broadly favourable, suggesting higher levels of victim satisfaction with the process than those going through the court-based system. Yet, recently, more sophisticated studies have begun to question whether satisfaction is a good measure of restorative success and look more closely at the victim's experiences of mediation. Chief among this research has been the work of Kathleen Daly (2001, 2003a, 2003b) who has increasingly begun to point to the 'gap' between the principles and practice of restorative justice. Her research of SAJJ looked at four distinct areas of the restorative experience, including conference process, legal context, outcome and compliance, and conference effects.

Daly's research suggested that only about 60 per cent of conferences were attended by victims, which clearly casts a question mark over the capacity of conferences to work effectively in the remaining 40 per cent of cases. Yet this 60 per cent mark is comparatively high compared with some other victim participation rates. In the UK, Crawford and Newburn (2003) recorded an average victim attendance at a referral panel in only 13 per cent of cases, and the Thames Valley police restorative cautioning scheme found only about 14 per cent of victims attended (Hoyle 2002; Hoyle *et al.* 2002). The predominant reason victims gave for non-attendance was that they did not wish to, with other reasons including inability to attend and no invitation to attend. In the case of SAJJ, non-attendance was further aggravated by a lack of information given to victims regarding the purpose and principles of restorative mediation. Interestingly, Daly (2003a) also found that, contrary to the literature, 36 per cent of victims were not curious to find out what the offender was like, while a further 32 per cent were not interested in finding out why they had been victimized. Yet, more worrying, is Daly's (2003a) finding that only 27 per cent of victims felt that apologies from offenders were sincere, throwing into doubt the capacity of restorative schemes actually to repair the harm caused to relationships. This concern is further demonstrated by the worrying statistic that one in five victims left the SAJJ conference upset by what the offender and the offender's supporters had said.

At later stages of the process, Daly (2003a) records that approximately half of the victims who had attended the conference did not find that the agreed reparation helped repair the harm caused by the offence. Daly (2003a) speculates that this may be due in part to the sense that the reparation undertaken by the offender was not conducted sincerely. Regarding the effect of the conference on victims, Daly (2003a) goes on to show that the majority of victims cited factors such as the passage of time, their own resilience and support from family and friends as the predominant explanations for overcoming the harm caused; with only 30 per cent saying that the conference was the most important factor in their healing process. What this suggests is that, while the conference clearly plays a part in repairing the harm done, there are other personal resources that are at least equally important in helping victims recover from their experiences of crime.

The variable reluctance or inability of victims to attend mediation combined with issues about sincerity begins to cast doubt over the capacity of restorative justice to fulfil the needs of all victims. Daly (2003a) provides one of the most compelling discussions of the inconsistencies between the principles and practice of restorative justice. This leads her to question to what extent 'restorativeness' can be achieved in the majority of cases:

> The nirvana story of restorative justice helps us to imagine what is possible, but it should not be used as the benchmark for what is practical and achievable. The nirvana story assumes that people are ready and able to resolve disputes, to repair the harms, to feel contrite,

and perhaps to forgive others when they may not be ready and able to do any of these things at all. It holds out the promise that these things *should happen most of the time* when research suggests that these things can occur *some of the time* (2003a: 234, emphasis in original).

Although it would be a gross misrepresentation to characterize Daly's (2001, 2003a, 2003b) research as entirely negative about restorative justice, it does raise important questions about the direction in which restorative projects are travelling. Returning to the title of this chapter the concern must be whether or not restorative justice genuinely offers the victims of crime a meaningful forum both to express their needs and have them met. The limited attendance by victims at mediation combined with doubts over the ability to achieve restorative, as opposed to reparative or inclusive, outcomes suggests that this is not demonstrably proven. Many of these issues have been dismissed as largely implementation problems (e.g. Maxwell and Morris 1993), which suggests that they need only refine the process to make it work properly. Daly (2003a) is more cautious, signposting the discrepancy between principles and practice and asking the important question: can restorative justice ever live up to its expectations? To answer this question we need to explore why this gap between principle and practice exists for victims. Is there some problem with how restorative justice understands and incorporates victims, or has the process unwittingly fallen foul of competing and counter priorities in the political and criminal justice realms?

Invoking the victim: manipulation and meaning

As has already been discussed, the victims' movement has led to the introduction of a range of different services and rights for the victims of crime. Yet in the USA, Elias (1993) has claimed that victims are still largely marginalized in the criminal justice system. The basis of his claim lies in a range of different criticisms, including poor implementation and short-term funding as well as shabbily enforced legislation at both the state and federal levels. More fundamentally, he asserts that, despite the plethora of victim and witness schemes, the vast majority of victims do not benefit from such provision. Indeed, Elias (1993) argues that, although it would seem obvious that victims should be the beneficiaries of victim-centred reform, it is those in political power who have really been the winners. In the USA, Elias (1993) points to the Reagan and Bush administrations' support for the victims of crime and argues that their policies have in fact bolstered the status quo, reinforcing orthodox conceptions of criminal victimization and diverting attention away from the arenas in which the majority of victimization occurs: the lower-class minorities. Instead, politically 'safe' victims have been targeted, notably children and the elderly. Essentially, Elias (1993: 48) believes:

The movement may have been co-opted not only by being diffused, but also by being 'used' for reforms that may have little to do with victims.

Yet it allows victims to be manipulated to enhance political legitimacy, government police powers, and an apparent agenda to further civil rights erosion, a symbolic use of politics to convert liberal rhetoric into thin air or conservative ends.

While this argument is specific to the USA, parallel concerns have also been raised in the UK, particularly in relation to the Victim's Charter (Mawby and Walklate 1994) and the focus on the 'ideal' victim rather than those who are most heavily victimized. In this sense, Williams (1999) makes a very similar point to Elias (1993), suggesting that the real beneficiaries of victim reforms have been the politicians who have used such changes to appear tough on crime.

How applicable are these concerns to restorative justice? At one level it seems improbable that restorative justice has also become a symbolic talisman for governments' attempting to show they are tough on crime as it is more often criticized for appearing as a 'soft' option (Morris and Young 2000). Yet, as we have already seen, there are some disturbing trends in the delivery of restorative schemes that suggest they do not always enable high levels of victim participation (Hoyle *et al.* 2002; Johnstone 2002; Crawford and Newburn 2003; Daly 2003a). Some of these problems have often been attributed to implementation failure (Dignan 2005), but there are also other concerns about the capacity of restorative justice fully to deliver victim-centred justice as it becomes increasingly more entwined with established criminal justice systems. Chief among these concerns is the incompatibility between restorative goals and offender-orientated, increasingly administrative criminal justice. Crawford and Newburn (2003), in their analysis of the referral order in the UK, note that the time frame between sentence and initial panel meeting had been given a national standard of 20 days, which suggests an administrative priority that does not sit well with a restorative process designed to be responsive to the needs and demands of victims. Yet, this is clearly not an example of overt political manipulation and more a consequence of the meshing of restorative and criminal justice. However, this presents its own form of manipulation, whereby the principles of restorative justice are diluted as they are absorbed into a criminal justice system that operates on a different set of priorities.

At a wider sociological level, Garland (1996, 2001) explores the underlying tensions that exist within criminal justice and points to a number of different ways in which the state has sought to overcome its inability to control high crime by modifying its responses. Included within these modifications, or adaptations, are strategies of responsibilization which seek to devolve some of the state's responsibility for crime control to other sectors. For Garland (1996), mediation and reparation schemes form part of these responsibilization strategies and are therefore construed as part of the state's response to the crime problem. This implies a different type of manipulation, where the aim is not direct political gain, but a more subtle shift in onus that fulfils a wider governmental strategy designed to paper over the cracks of a spiralling crime rate it is unable to control. This presents an alternative motive behind the increasing adoption of restorative schemes and one which has little to do with the needs of victims. Although this may go some way to help explain why restorative justice has grown in stature it doesn't necessarily lead to the conclusion that it fails to benefit the victims of crime. However, in a similar fashion to the concerns raised by Elias (1993), it does cast doubt over whether the needs of victims are actually being pursued, or whether they simply form part of an expedient tool designed to benefit the state's need to appear to be doing something about crime. If this is the case then the question must be asked: what capacity does restorative justice have to resist these external threats to its principles? One way of answering this question is to consider how restorative justice actually engages with victims and whether this represents any real divergence from orthodox notions of the victim enshrined with popular discourse.

Although restorative justice has been applied in a variety of different contexts, including schools (Nothhafft 2003), the workplace (Braithwaite 2003b) and community conflicts (McEvoy and Mika 2002), it is within criminal justice that it is fast becoming most influential. Within this arena restorative justice appears to offer little that is different from most conventional definitions of what constitutes a victim. Although restorative justice does acknowledge the dispersal of victimization from a specific person to his or her family and friends (Zehr and Mika 2003), it is essentially a straightforward legal definition of who the victim is – someone who has had a crime committed against him or her. As restorative justice becomes increasingly incorporated into the criminal justice system, its capacity to offer meaningful recourse to a wide range of victims is lessened as its predominant focus becomes the standard range of offences addressed by the courts. Thus, the victims of human rights violations and corporate crimes are still largely sidelined and without access to the potential benefits of restorative processes. More worryingly, as Dignan (2005) reminds us, approximately only 3 per cent of known crime results in a criminal conviction or caution. Hence, for the vast majority of victims whose offenders are either never caught or found guilty restorative justice offers no advantages.

Further, as noted by Christie (1986), victims tend to be thought of in idealized terms. They are either deserving or undeserving. The deserving, or ideal, victim is usually a vulnerable, respectable and blameless individual who has suffered at the hands of an anonymous and comparatively powerful individual (Christie 1986). As Young (2002) has noted, restorative justice tends tacitly to endorse similar stereotypical notions of the victim, or at the very least assumes a uniformity of characteristics among the victim population. Dignan (2005) argues that as a result of such stereotyping some restorative justice advocates have made sweeping and all-encompassing claims about the capacity of restorative justice to benefit all victims. Quite apart from ignoring specific types of victimization or victim–offender relationships that may not be well suited to mediation, this perspective also neglects the structural inequalities that are most closely associated with high levels of both victimization and offending (Sparks et al. 1977; Skogan 1981; Fattah 1994). As such there is no real aetiology of victimization contained within the restorative framework. There is no engagement with the types of social conditions or social groups that are most heavily victimized, or why this is the case. It is then unclear how restorative justice differs from conventional social constructions of the victim and how it can provide a more victim-orientated perspective about how best to provide for different types of crime victims. As a result of this short sightedness, restorative justice has no conceptual space to avoid neoliberal explanations of either victimization or offending. Restorative justice divorces explanations of victimization and offending from wider structural inequalities, leaving intact both a notion of the 'ideal' victim and a presumption of personal responsibility as the primary focus for addressing offending behaviour (O'Malley 2001; Sullivan 2001). Poverty, discrimination, lifestyle and mental illness are therefore not given weight in restorative processes, leaving a massive gap in its understanding of patterns of victimization and the offending that leads to its occurrence.

This suggests yet another form of manipulation; one which is based around the state's interest to shape the meaning and needs of victims for particular purposes. This type of manipulation is discussed by Mawby and Walklate (1994), who have sought to provide a framework for thinking about victims that starts from an analysis of the state's function. For them, the state is not a neutral arbiter of the law or social relations but a self-interested institution that does not always have the best interests of its citizenry at heart. The state therefore constructs the social order around unseen interests. Mawby and Walklate (1994) are concerned with exploring these unseen biases better to understand how victims and victim policy have been constructed. Their particular analysis suggests that since the late 1970s the tensions within state welfare capitalism have become increasingly more evident and unworkable. Hence, the state has sought to commodify its citizenry, turning them into consumer units who access services when they are needed. This promulgates a neutral notion of both the state and crime victims wherein the state provides services and the victim/consumer accesses them. For Mawby and Walklate (1994), this conjures a specific image of the active citizen who is responsible for accessing services. This individualized notion of the victim as consumer of criminal justice services hides the extent to which particular social groups have become economically and socially disadvantaged and they advance a critical victimology concerned to address this issue. A critical victimology aims to 'Understand the mechanisms whereby such collectives are hidden and what might constitute the real policy opportunities, economic circumstances not withstanding, to equip those collectives with "rights"' (Walklate 2003b: 124). Central to this analysis is a concern to locate concepts of victim and victimization within wider historical and cultural conditions. These concepts are not uncomplicated or static, and can only be understood by considering their relationship to the function of the state and the ways in which it has helped generate both a particular construction of the victim and the corresponding policy developments. Mawby and Walklate (1994) are therefore concerned to understand the ways in which the victim has been invoked or manipulated in pursuit of the state's wider interest to maintain the social order.

What this analysis suggests is that restorative justice does not have its own concept of either victim or victimization. It essentially 'buys in' to the established ideological and policy-driven construction of the victim and, as such, has little room to offer an alternative perspective or paradigm from which to advance, or protect, the victim's interests. It lacks its own epistemology. There are no distinctive forms of knowledge that give meaning to how restorative justice understands the victim. Pavlich (2005) makes a similar point, arguing that restorative justice is predicated on the same assumptions or foundations as criminal justice. Hence, there is little basis for believing that restorative justice can, at the moment, defend against external agendas as it becomes increasingly enmeshed within criminal justice systems. The consequences of this for restorative justice are significant. If it is to continue providing a compelling alternative to conventional justice, and if it is serious in its ambition to genuinely represent victim interests, then it needs to find some conceptual space from which to fend off competing notions of how the criminal or victimization process is understood.

Conclusions: the danger to victims and restorative justice

Unlike other types of victim-centred reform, restorative justice is not explicitly a movement that is solely concerned with victims. It is, in fact, an alternative model of justice, and as such is premised on providing a different way in which offending and the consequences of offending are dealt with. While the victim forms a core component in this, it is not the victim that is the focus for such reform but the penal process itself. Measured against the many problems that beset both sentencing and punishment restorative justice has its sights firmly set on providing an alternative that overcomes many of these criticisms, not least of which is its attempt to integrate the victim more fully into penal decision-making. Yet, despite the very clear and very laudable intentions of restorative justice to give the victim a central place within this process, it lacks the necessary language to conceptualize the victim in a way that distinguishes him or her from the types of definition that have allowed the victim to be subordinated to wider ideological or political agendas.

This brings Elias's (1993) quotation at the beginning of the chapter back into sharp focus. Put in context, Elias (1993) is commenting on the failure of the victims' movement to benefit the majority of victims. As we have seen, this same complaint could equally be levelled at restorative justice. Despite its stated aim of promoting the victim to centre-stage, most cannot take advantage of the possible benefits of victim–offender mediation. Elias (1993) also goes on to question whether or not it is accurate even to consider the victims' movement a movement at all. According to both Elias (1993) and Williams (1999), a movement is 'social or political action seeking fundamental change through mostly unconventional means' (Elias 1993: 62). This would seem a reasonably good definition of restorative justice, affirming, rather than denying, its status as a source of radical change. The problem is that as restorative justice becomes more and more embedded in criminal justice it is forced to absorb external priorities that may have little to do with restorative principles. This echoes Elias's (1993) concerns about the political co-option of the victims' movement. While there may be a very different form of co-option going on with restorative justice, the threat is just the same. Without a clear epistemology of the victim (and quite possibly the offender and the community as well) they could easily fall prey to similar types of manipulation that the victims' movement has suffered from. Hints of this happening are already evident. If restorative justice is to take seriously its commitment to the victims of crime, it must find ways of protecting them from rhetoric and policy that has all too often been advanced in the name of the victim without actually being for the victim.

How this is to be achieved given the current direction of restorative practice is hard to imagine. At one level the recent success of restorative justice in becoming more central within penal policy may have unwittingly led it away from victim interests. While there is an element of coercion, or self-interest, prompting offenders to take part in restorative processes, a question mark will understandably remain over offender motives for participating. Perhaps one direction to take restorative justice that would overcome this doubt, as well as make the process more accessible to more victims, would be to divorce it from formal sentencing processes. Instead, separate restorative services for offenders and victims could function in response to the needs of both groups. Of course, they would still engage with each other but would have different referral processes that could be initiated by either victim or offender. Restorative justice could then operate alongside criminal justice, available to all who want it. Schemes could then tailor restorative processes to victims and offenders depending on the availability of other stakeholders. Sentences might include a recommendation that a restorative process is undertaken by an offender, but not make the sentence conditional on the outcome. Victims, on the other hand, could access restorative schemes regardless of whether the offence was reported, or an offender apprehended. This would return restorative practice to a purer voluntary status and allow it more overtly to focus on the wider, arguably extra-legal, goals of restoration such as understanding, tolerance and community cohesion. Others will undoubtedly argue that these goals should be made part of the criminal justice process and that restorative justice is the vehicle for delivering such change. Yet there appears to be a growing amount of evidence that challenges whether this transformation is actually occurring.

The fear is that, as restorative justice becomes increasingly bound to criminal justice, it will succumb to the prevailing ideological, political and practical concerns that affect how justice is delivered. Its reformatory potential would then be stripped bare and replaced with a feeble shadow of its potential, a faint reminder of what might have been. This seems a gloomy prediction but, as we have seen with the victims' movement, one not without precedent. The challenge to restorative justice should not be how much more can it achieve, but how it will define and protect its governing principles. Otherwise, the very real danger is that victims will continue to remain the pawns of other groups' interests.

Selected further reading

Goodey, J. (2005) *Victims and Victimisation: Research, Policy and Practice*. Harlow: Pearson Longman. An excellent up-to-date textbook that deals thoroughly with current knowledge about the victims of crime and the consequences of such victimization.

Dignan, J. (2005) *Understanding Victims and Restorative Justice*. Maidenhead: Open University Press. A new textbook that provides a comparatively rare synthesis of knowledge about victims and restorative justice.

Pavlich, G. (2005) *Governing Paradoxes in Restorative Justice*. London: Glasshouse Press. Chapter 3 is particularly helpful in developing and underpinning some of themes I have raised in this chapter regarding how the victim is understood within the restorative paradigm.

Elias, R. (1993) *Victims Still: The Political Manipulation of Crime Victims*. Newbury Park, CA: Sage. A marvellously thought-provoking and insightful analysis of how crime victims have become the tools of political expediency in the USA.

Christie, N. (1986) 'The ideal victim', in E.A. Fattah (ed.) *From Crime Policy to Victim Policy: Reorientating the Justice System*. Basingstoke: Macmillan. This short but excellent chapter provides a superb discussion of how we continue to construct notions of victimhood that are often wildly out of kilter with complicated social conditions.

References

Achilles, M. and Zehr, H. (2001) 'Restorative justice for crime victims: the promise, the challenge', in G. Bazemore *et al.* (eds) *Restorative Community Justice: Repairing Harm and Transforming Communities*. Cincinatti, OH: Anderson Press.

Baker, N. (1994) 'Mediation, reparation and justice', in J. Burnside and R. Baker (eds) *Relational Justice: Repairing the Breach*. Winchester: Waterside Press.

Blew, C. and Rosenblum, R. (1979) *An Exemplary Project: The Community Arbitration Project, Anne Arundel County*. Washington, DC: US Department of Justice.

Braithwaite, J. (1999) 'Restorative justice: assessing optimistic and pessimistic accounts', *Crime and Justice: A Review of the Research*, 25: 1–127.

Braithwaite, J. (2002) *Restorative Justice and Responsive Regulation*. Oxford: Oxford University Press.

Braithwaite, J. (2003a) 'Restorative justice and a better future', in E. McLaughlin *et al.* (eds) *Restorative Justice: Critical Issues*. London: Sage.

Braithwaite, J. (2003b) 'Restorative justice and corporate regulation', in E.G.M. Weitekamp and H.J. Kerner (eds) *Restorative Justice in Context: International Practices and Directions*. Cullompton: Willan Publishing.

Burnside, J. and Baker, N. (eds) (1994) *Relational Justice: Repairing the Breach*. Winchester: Waterside Press.

Christie, N. (1977) 'Conflicts as property', *British Journal of Criminology*, 17: 1–15.

Christie, N. (1986) 'The ideal victim', in E.A. Fattah (ed.) *From Crime Policy to Victim Policy: Reorienting the Justice System*. Basingstoke: Macmillan.

Coleman, C. and Moynihan, J. (1996) *Understanding Crime Data: Haunted by the Dark Figure*. Buckingham: Open University Press.

Crawford, A. and Newburn, T. (2003) *Youth Offending and Restorative Justice: Implementing Reform in Youth Justice*. Cullompton: Willan Publishing.

Daly, K. (2001) 'Conferencing in Australia and New Zealand: variations, research findings and prospects', in A.M. Morris and G. Maxwell (eds) *Restorative Justice for Juveniles: Conferencing, Mediation and Circles*. Oxford: Hart Publishing.

Daly, K. (2003a) 'Mind the gap: restorative justice in theory and practice', in A. von Hirsch *et al.* (eds) *Restorative Justice and Penal Justice: Competing or Reconcilable Paradigms?* Oxford: Hart Publishing.

Daly, K. (2003b) 'Restorative justice: the real story', in E. McLaughlin *et al.* (eds) *Restorative Justice: Critical Issues*. London: Sage.

Daly, K. and Immarigeon, R. (1998) 'The past, present and future of restorative justice: some critical reflections', *Contemporary Justice Review*, 1: 21–45.

Dignan, J. (2005) *Understanding Victims and Restorative Justice*. Maidenhead: Open University Press.

Elias, R. (1983) *Victims of the System*. New Brunswick, NJ: Transaction Books.

Elias, R. (1986) *The Politics of Victimisation*. Oxford: Oxford University Press.

Elias, R. (1990) 'Which victim movement? The politics of victim policy', in A.J. Lurigio *et al.* (eds) *Victims of Crime: Problems, Policies and Programs*. Newbury Park, CA: Sage.

Elias, R. (1993) *Victims Still: The Political Manipulation of Crime Victims*. London: Sage.

Fattah, E. (1994) *The Interchangeable Roles of the Victim and Victimizer*. Helsinki: European Institute of Crime Prevention and Control.

Flood-Page, C. and Mackie, A. (1998) *Sentencing Practice: An Examination of Decisions in Magistrates' Courts and the Crown Courts in the mid-1990s*. Home Office Research Study 180. London: Home Office.

Garland, D. (1996) 'The limits of the sovereign state: strategies of crime control in contemporary society', *British Journal of Criminology*, 36: 445–71.

Garland, D. (2001) *The Culture of Control*. Oxford: Oxford University Press.

Gill, M.L. and Mawby, R.I. (1990) *Volunteers in the Criminal Justice System*. Milton Keynes: Open University Press.

Goodey, J. (2002) 'Compensating victims of violent crime in the European Union: the case of state restitution', in B. Williams (ed.) *Reparation and Victim-focused Social Work*. London: Jessica Kingsley.

Goodey, J. (2005) *Victims and Victimology: Research, Policy and Practice*. Harlow: Pearson Longman.

Hamilton, J. and Wisniewski, M. (1996) *The Use of the Compensation Order in Scotland*. Edinburgh: Scottish Central Research Unit.

Harding, J. (1982) *Victims and Offenders: Needs and Responsibilities*. London: Bedford Square Press.

Herman, S. (2004) 'Is restorative justice possible without a parallel system for victims?', in H. Zehr and B. Toews (eds) *Critical Issues in Restorative Justice*. Cullompton: Willan Publishing.

Holstrom, L. and Burgess, A. (1978) *The Victim of Rape: Institutional Reactions*. Chichester: Wiley.

Home Office (1990) *Victim's Charter: A Statement of the Rights of the Victims of Crime*. London: Home Office.

Home Office (1996) *The Victim's Charter: A Statement of the Service Standards for the Victims of Crime*. London: Home Office.

Hoyle, C. (2002) 'Securing restorative justice for the "non-participating" victim', in C. Hoyle and R. Young (eds) *New Visions of Crime Victims*. Oxford: Hart Publishing.

Hoyle, C., Young, R. and Hill, R. (2002) *Proceed with Caution: An Evaluation of the Thames Valley Police Initiative in Restorative Cautioning*. York: Joseph Rowntree Foundation.

Johnstone, G. (2002) *Restorative Justice: Ideas, Values, Debates*. Cullompton: Willan Publishing.

Johnstone, G. (2004) 'How and in what terms, should restorative justice be conceived?', in H. Zehr and B. Toew (eds) *Critical Issues in Restorative Justice*. Cullompton: Willan Publishing.

Kelly, D.P. (1990) 'Victim participation in the criminal justice system', in A.J. Lurigio *et al.* (eds) *Victims of Crime: Problems, Policies and Programs*. Newbury Park, CA: Sage.

Kurki, L. (2003) 'Evaluating restorative justice practices', in A. Von Hirsch *et al.* (eds) *Restorative Justice and Criminal Justice: Competing or Reconcilable Paradigms?* Oxford: Hart Publishing.

Maguire, M. and Shapland, J. (1990) 'The victim movement in Europe', in A.J. Lurigio *et al.* (eds) *Victims of Crime: Problems, Policies, and Programs*. Newbury Park, CA: Sage.

Marshall, T. and Walpole, M. (1985) *Bringing People Together: Mediation and Reparation Projects in Great Britain*. London: Home Office.

Mawby, R.I. (2003) 'The provision of victim support and assistance programmes: a cross-national perspective', in P. Davies *et al.* (eds) *Victimisation: Theory, Research and Policy*. Basingstoke: Palgrave Macmillan.

Mawby, R.I. and Gill, M.L. (1987) *Crime Victims: Needs, Services and the Voluntary Sector*. London: Tavistock.

Mawby, R.I. and Walklate, S. (1994) *Critical Victimology*. London: Sage.

Maxwell, G. and Morris, A.M. (1993) *Family, Victims and Culture: Youth Justice in New Zealand*. Wellington: Department of Social Welfare and Institute of Criminology.

McEvoy, K. and Mika, H. (2002) 'Restorative justice and the critique of informalism in Northern Ireland', *British Journal of Criminology*, 42: 534–62.

Mendelsohn, B. (1974) 'The origins of the doctrine of victimology', in I. Drapkin and E. Viano (eds) *Victimology*. Lexington, MA: Lexington Books.

Miers, D. (1989) 'Positivist victimology: a critique', *International Review of Victimology*, 1: 3–22.

Miers, D. (1990) 'Positivist victimology: a critique part 2', *International Review of Victimology*, 1: 219–30.

Miers, D. (2001) *An International Review of Restorative Justice*. Crime Reduction Research Series Paper 10. London: Home Office.

Morris, A.M. and Young, W. (2000) 'Reforming criminal justice: the potential of restorative justice', in H. Strang and J. Braithwaite (eds) *Restoring Justice: Philosophy to Practice*. Dartmouth: Ashgate.

NAVSS (1984) *The Victim and Reparation*. London.

O'Malley, P. (2001) 'Policing crime risks in the neo-liberal era' in K. Stenson and R.R. Sullivan (eds) *Crime, Risk and Justice: The Politics of Crime Control in Liberal Democracies*. Cullompton: Willan Publishing.

Pavlich, G. (2005) *Governing Paradoxes of Restorative Justice*. London: Glasshouse Press.

Phillips, A. (1988) 'Ideologies, political parties, and the victims of crime', in M. Maguire and J. Pointing (eds) *Victims of Crime: A New Deal*. Milton Keynes: Open University Press.

Nothhafft, S. (2003) 'Conflict resolution and peer mediation: a pilot programme in Munich secondary schools', in E.G.M. Weitekamp and H.J. Kerner (eds) *Restorative Justice in Context: International Practices and Directions*. Cullompton: Willan Publishing.

Reeves, H. and Mulley, K. (2000) 'The new status of victims in the UK: opportunities and threats', in A. Crawford and J. Goodey (eds) *Integrating a Victim Perspective within Criminal Justice*. Dartmouth: Ashgate.

Rock, P. (2004) *Constructing Victims Rights: The Home Office, New Labour and Victims.* Oxford: Oxford University Press.

Shapland, J. (1988) 'Fiefs and peasants: accomplishing change for victims in the criminal justice system', in M. Maguire and J. Pointing (eds) *Victims of Crime: A New Deal.* Milton Keynes: Open University Press.

Shapland, J., Willmore, J. and Duff, P. (1985) *Victims of Crime in the Criminal Justice System.* Aldershot: Gower.

Skogan, W. (1981) *Issues in the Measurement of Victimization.* Washington, DC: US Department of Justice, Bureau of Justice Statistics.

South African Truth and Reconciliation Commission (1998) *The Report of the Truth and Reconciliation Commission* (available at: http://www.org.za/truth/report).

Sparks, R.F., Genn, H.G. and Dodd, D.J. (1977) *Surveying Victims: A Study in the Measurement of Criminal Victimisation.* Chichester: Wiley.

Strang, H. (2002) *Repair or Revenge: Victims and Restorative Justice.* Oxford: Clarendon Press.

Strang, H. (2004) 'Is restorative justice imposing its agenda on victims?', in H. Zehr and B. Toews (eds) *Critical Issues in Restorative Justice.* Cullompton: Willan Publishing.

Sullivan, R.R. (2001) 'The schizophrenic state: neo-liberal criminal justice', in K. Stenson and R.R. Sullivan (eds) *Crime, Risk and Justice: The Politics of Crime Control in Liberal Democracies.* Cullompton: Willan Publishing.

Umbreit, M. (1994) *Victim Meets Offender: The Impact of Restorative Justice and Mediation.* Monsey, NY: Criminal Justice Press.

Umbreit, M. (1996) 'Restorative justice through mediation: the impact of programs in four Canadian provinces', in B. Galaway and J. Hudson (eds) *Restorative Justice: International Perspectives.* Monsey, NY: Criminal Justice Press.

Umbreit, M. and Coates, R. (1993) 'Cross-site analysis of victim–offender mediation in four states', *Crime and Delinquency*, 39: 565–85.

Umbreit, M. and Roberts, A. (1996) *Mediation of Criminal Conflict in England: An Assessment of Services in Coventry and Leeds.* St Paul, MN: Center for Restorative Justice and Mediation, University of Minnesota.

United Nations (1985) *Declaration of Basic Principles for Justice for Victims of Crime and Abuse of Power.* UN Doc A/40/53 (1985) Geneva: United Nations.

Van Dijk, J. (1988) 'Ideological trends within the victims movement: an international perspective' in M. Maguire and J. Pointing (eds) *Victims of Crime: A New Deal.* Milton Keynes: Open University Press.

Van Ness, D. (2002) 'The shape of things to come: a framework for thinking about a restorative justice system', in G.M. Weitekamp and H.J. Kerner (eds) *Restorative Justice: Theoretical Foundations.* Cullompton: Willan Publishing.

Von Hentig, H. (1948) *The Criminal and his Victim: Studies in the Sociobiology of Crime.* New Haven, CT: Yale University Press.

Walklate, S. (1989) *Victimology: The Victim and the Criminal Justice Process.* London: Unwin Hyman.

Walklate, S. (1999) 'Can there be a meaningful victimology?', *Criminal Justice Matters*, 39: 5–6.

Walklate, S. (2003a) 'Can there be a feminist victimology?', in P. Davies *et al.* (eds) *Victimisation: Theory, Research and Policy.* Basingstoke: Palgrave Macmillan.

Walklate, S. (2003b) *Understanding Criminology: Current Theoretical Debates.* Maidenhead: Open University Press.

Williams, B. (1999) *Working with Victims of Crime: Policies, Politics and Practice.* London: Jessica Kingsley.

Wright, M. (1996) *Justice for Victims and Offenders.* Winchester: Waterside Press.

Young, R. (2002) 'Testing the limits of restorative justice: the case of corporate victims', in C. Hoyle and R. Young (eds) *New Visions of Crime Victims*. Oxford: Hart Publishing.

Young, M.A. and Stein, J.H. (1983) *The Victim Service System: A Guide to Action*. Washington, DC: NOVA.

Zehr, H. (1990) *Changing Lenses: A New Focus for Crime and Justice*. Scottdale, PA: Herald Press.

Zehr, H. and Mika, H. (2003) 'Fundamental concepts of restorative justice', in E. McLaughlin *et al.* (eds) *Restorative Justice: Critical Issues*. London: Sage.

Chapter 11

Offenders, the making of amends and the state

Linda Radzik

As a moral theorist, my interest has been drawn to restorative theories of criminal justice because they explore and develop a moral concept that is all but absent from the philosophical literature – the making of amends.[1] When philosophers consider the moral issues that arise in the aftermath of wrongdoing – when they ask, that is, what is the best way to respond to wrongdoing – they take the point of view of either an outside observer or a victim, but almost never of the wrongdoer herself.[2] Debates revolve around questions of punishment, and sometimes forgiveness and mercy as well. But it is almost never asked what the *wrongdoer* must do in the aftermath of her wrongful action. The structure of such debates tempts us to regard wrongdoers as 'things to be manipulated', rather than as moral agents who are capable of appropriate and meaningful responses (Adler 1992: 23).

In contrast, restorative justice pays a remarkable amount of attention to the criminal wrongdoer's capacity for positive, constructive action. In paradigm restorative justice practices, such as the sentencing conference, offenders actually help determine what their sentences will be. They are provided the opportunity to suggest ways they might make restitution, to react to the suggestions of others and to agree (or refuse to agree) to a particular resolution. Restorative justice theory is a rich source for reflection on what it might mean for an offender to 'right a wrong' or 'make amends'. It is filled with insights about what requires restoration in the aftermath of wrongdoing, and why the response of the wrongdoer herself is crucial to successful restoration. In short, the literature on restorative justice offers us a more complete and productive view of the moral obligations of wrongdoers than any other literature with which I am familiar.[3] The advantage gained, I believe, is not merely theoretical but ethical. In recognizing that wrongdoers have moral obligations, we recognize their status as agents and not 'things', as subjects and not objects. This is crucial to treating them with the respect that all humans deserve.[4]

However, this very line of praise for restorative justice will suggest to some that it is misguided as a theory of criminal justice. How could the state possibly contribute to the moral goal of criminal wrongdoers making amends? The making of amends requires the sincere repentance and voluntary efforts of the wrongdoer. Sincere and voluntary responses cannot, as a matter of logic, be compelled by the state; and any attempt by the state to use the criminal justice system to persuade offenders to make amends threatens to undermine any credibility that a sincerely repentant offender might otherwise have. So, the making of amends appears to be a moral ideal that the state simply *cannot* pursue. Furthermore, one might argue that the state *should not* pursue this moral ideal. Is it proper for the state to concentrate its efforts on getting offenders to fulfil their moral obligations? Shouldn't the liberal state stay out of the business of morality, and remain neutral among competing notions of the good? Doesn't the blurring of the line between the legal and moral realms actually undermine respect for agency, the very value that I have invoked in defence of restorative justice?

In this chapter, I will explore this tense relation between the making of amends, respect for the agency of the offender and the role of the liberal state. First, I will present a moral theory of the making of amends, which is inspired by the restorative justice literature.[5] This will give us a clearer view of what the ideal in question is. Then I will briefly point out how restorative justice practices in criminal legal systems seem to serve this ideal. In the second half of the chapter, I will develop further the objections already mentioned: that the making of amends is neither a possible nor an appropriate goal for the liberal state. I will also suggest some ways in which restorative justice theorists might attempt to defend themselves against these objections.

The term 'amends' descends from an old French word for 'pecuniary fines' or 'reparation' (*Oxford English Dictionary*, 2005). This might suggest that the making of amends is strictly a matter of material restitution for a wrongful or harmful action. As it has come to be used in moral discussions in both the private and public spheres, though, the term 'making amends' refers to a larger class of responses to wrongdoing than material restitution. For example, estranged family members are described as 'making amends' when an apology is offered and accepted. The apology 'repairs' the wrong, but not by literally compensating the victim. Furthermore, not all cases of material restitution are properly characterized as the making of amends. Restitution payments might be paid to a victim by a third party, such as a family member of the wrongdoer, or restitution payments might be taken from the wrongdoer against his will (Barnett 1977). In neither of these cases does it seem right to say that amends have been made between the wrongdoer and the victim, because the core problem in their relationship has not yet been addressed. Certain harms may have been compensated, but the ill-will or 'bad blood' between victim and wrongdoer is likely to remain. Instead, the making of amends requires a response to wrongdoing that is reparative in a sense that goes beyond mere compensation for harm, that is performed by the wrongdoer himself and that is performed voluntarily.

Another aspect of the concept of making amends is highlighted by expressions such as '*They* have made amends' or 'You should make amends *with* her'. This language suggests that the making of amends is an interaction between the wrongdoer and the person he has wronged. The wrongdoer may *offer* amends, but it is up to the victim to accept that offer and thereby complete the act (Swinburne 1989: 73–92).[6] This interactive aspect of the making of amends shows us, I would argue, that this is a relational concept. The sort of reparation at issue in the making of amends is primarily the reparation of the *relationship* between the wrongdoer and the one he has wronged. Oftentimes, wrongdoing ruptures not only the relationship between the wrongdoer and the victim, but also their relationships with third parties. For example, when one friend betrays another, the people in their social circle often react by taking sides or feeling indignant on behalf of the victim. In such cases, a full making of amends may need to include these parties as well.

The making of amends might then be characterized as a form of reconciliation, or the restoration of relationships. When two friends or family members have succeeded in making amends, they will once again be able to relate to one another on reasonably good terms. While the relationship may never reach the level of ease or intimacy that prevailed before, the parties will stop relating to one another in terms of the roles 'wrongdoer' and 'victim' (cf. Hampton 1988: 36–43). It should be noted that reconciliation could be achieved in other ways. The parties might genuinely forget about the wrong. The victim may simply forgive her friend without having received any apology or other offer of amends. Reconciliation might even be brought about by the forceful imposition of a punishment on the wrongdoer. However, what is distinctive about the ideal of making amends is that the parties reconcile, at least in large part, because the wrongdoer *himself* has provided his victim with good reason to reconcile with him. The wrongdoer will have *merited* reconciliation through his own reactions to his misdeed. He will have given his victim and any involved third parties good grounds for putting aside their feelings of resentment, indignation, fear or distrust and re-establishing a relationship with him.[7] He will also have provided himself with a justification for overcoming negative feelings about himself, such as guilt or sense of worthlessness. In the aftermath of wrongdoing, we need to become reconciled, not only with our fellows, but with ourselves.

While the restoration of relationships could be achieved through something other than the wrongdoer's activity, we can see that there is something of particular moral value in the wrongdoer coming to merit reconciliation through his own efforts. We can say something stronger than this, though. Not only is the wrongdoer's offer of amends morally valuable, it is obligatory. It would be wrong of him to refuse to offer adequate amends. It unfairly would leave the victim and community to bear the costs of his wrongful action. Furthermore, a refusal to offer amends would send the message that he continues to endorse his wrongful action. It would continue to operate as an insult to the victim and even a threat of future wrongdoing (cf. Murphy 1988: 25; Hieronymi 2001: 546).

The overall goal of offering amends, then, is the reconciliation of damaged or threatened relationships among wrongdoers, victims and (at times) communities.[8] But what can the wrongdoer do in order to merit such reconciliation? In order to answer this question, I believe we should identify three subgoals that the wrongdoer must pursue in making particular offers of amends – morally appropriate communication, reparation of harm and personal reformation. In standard cases of moral wrongs committed against others, all these subgoals must be met if the wrongdoer is to count as meriting reconciliation.

First, the wrongdoer must communicate with the victim and (in some cases) the community in an appropriate way. She must withdraw the insult to the dignity of the victim that was expressed by the wrongful act, and retract the threat of future harms that may have been implicit in that act. This communicative task can be pursued by a number of different means – some verbal, some non-verbal. But the main idea is that the wrongdoer must express that she has come to recognize that the victim is a person of equal moral worth to herself, that he should not have been wronged in this way, and that she intends not to repeat this sort of offence in the future. But this is only half the communicative task. The wrongdoer must also listen to what the ones wronged have to say to her. By listening to the victim, the wrongdoer exhibits the sort of respect for the dignity of the victim that was denied by the wrongful action. This sort of dialogue will help provide the victim and the community with reason to trust the wrongdoer again.

Secondly, in order to merit reconciliation, the wrongdoer must repair or compensate for the various sorts of harms she created, where this is possible. The harms that may be created by wrongdoing should be understood to encompass material, physical, psychological and relational harms. It should be kept in mind that these various sorts of harms often come in clusters. For example, physical harm-causing can also create psychological, relational and material harms (say, in the form of medical bills or lost earnings). Almost all cases of wrongdoing committed against another person will involve some form of harm. The payment of material restitution is a clear example of a reparative act, but harms are frequently repaired by subtle, symbolically rich interactions between the wrongdoer and the victim, such as an apology, the giving of a gift or an act of self-sacrifice on the part of the wrongdoer. In cases such as these, the reparative and the communicative tasks become one.

Thirdly, truly to merit reconciliation in the aftermath of wrongdoing, the wrongdoer must reform herself. It is not enough to convince others or herself that she is morally trustworthy, she must actually become trustworthy. She must come to recognize that she was responsible for her past action and that it was wrong. She must also resolve not to repeat such an action in the future.

Communication, reparation and personal reformation are ends that may be achieved by various means, and a single act of amends can serve all three of these ends. For example, the performance of an apology will be valuable as an act of communication with the victim. It might also be just the thing that will restore the victim's self-esteem. At the same time, it may be a humbling experience for the wrongdoer that will help her more fully understand that she acted wrongly and reinforce her intention to behave better in the future. The choice of means to meet the goal of reconciliation allows room for considerable cultural variation and personal creativity, which I take to be an advantage of this conception of the making of amends.

On my understanding of the moral value of making amends, then, it is exactly the value that is highlighted by restorative theories of justice: the restoration of the relationships among the parties affected by wrongdoing (Zehr 1990: 181; Daly and Immarigeon 1999: 22; Braithwaite 2000: 115). The moral theory and the criminal justice theory agree about means as well as ends. As I noted above, the goal of reconciliation might (arguably) be achieved by other methods, such as forgetting, forgiving or punishing. But, restorative justice practices ask offenders to respond actively to their own crimes. Again, this will be most clearly seen in practices such as the sentencing conference (Braithwaite 2000). Here, offenders are placed in direct contact with those people they have harmed. They are asked to communicate with their victims and other affected members of the community. At the least, they are expected to explain why they acted as they did, and to listen to what the other parties have to say to them. Offenders are not required to apologize, express remorse or promise better behaviour. But, not surprisingly, they frequently do (Braithwaite 2000: 123). The discussions in sentencing conferences explore the various effects of crime – not just the cost of damaged property, say, but also the fear, anger and sense of vulnerability that victims and community members experienced. Sentencing conferences explore the causes as well as the effects of crime – such as addiction, gang membership, frustration and broken support networks. The task of the conference is to come to a restitution agreement, and these agreements frequently reflect the broader discussion about the many causes and effects of crime. The agreement may require, not just material repayment, but community service, drug rehabilitation and job training. The interests in compensation for the victim and personal reformation of the offender become intertwined to such a degree that they are not always distinguished. So, communication, restitution and personal reformation, the three parts of a proper offer of amends, are enabled and encouraged by the sentencing conference. When restorative justice procedures work well the relationships among the parties will be restored. Each will be able to live on reasonably good terms with the other.

The link between restorative justice practice and the moral ideal of making amends is strong then. It is worth emphasizing how distinctive this is. Standard, punitive criminal justice systems not only fail to encourage the making of amends, they often actively prevent it (Zehr 1990: 51–2). Communication between wrongdoers and victims is discouraged, and sometimes prohibited. Incarceration severely inhibits most offenders' ability to pay restitution. Personal reformation is also hard to achieve in prison, where violent conflict is the norm (Zehr 1990: 35). Elsewhere I have argued that, if treating someone as a moral agent requires treating them as an agent who has moral obligations then criminal justice systems that prevent offenders from making amends might be guilty of injustice (Radzik 2003).

Restorative justice systems, in providing offenders with the opportunity to make amends, and especially in giving them an active role in helping to determine what form those amends should take, seem to be show great respect for offenders' moral agency. Offenders are treated as people who are capable of both understanding and being motivated by their moral obligations to others. However, in the next two sections, we will consider objections that suggest that restorative justice's apparent respect for offenders' moral agency is *merely* apparent, and that the state neither can nor should pursue the making of amends by offenders.

Let us begin with the objection that the ideal of the making of amends as a resolution of crime is an impossible or self-defeating goal for the state to pursue. As our moral theory has claimed, amends can only be made through the voluntary efforts of the offender. An offer of amends must include sincere communication and an improvement in the offender's character as well as his behaviour. Reparations must not only be offered, they must be offered for the right reasons. Anything short of this simply does not count as a genuine offer of amends (cf. Garvey 1999: 1849–50). Furthermore, the making of amends requires meaningful and voluntary responses from those harmed by crime. According to the moral theory, the making of amends is not merely an action of offenders, it is an *interaction* among offenders, victims and (often) communities. The voluntary reconciliation of victims and communities with the offender, their willingness to normalize relations with the offender, complete the act of amends. How could the state plausibly claim to be pursuing the goal of making amends, if the making of amends is so clearly out of the state's sphere of control? Voluntary actions and sincere, deeply held attitudes simply cannot be compelled by the state.

In response, the defender of restorative justice might point out that *pursuing* a goal is not the same thing as *guaranteeing* that the goal will be met. Even though the state cannot guarantee that offenders will be remorseful and victims will be willing to forgive, it can try to create conditions in which this is more likely to happen. Restorative justice practices seem designed to do just that.

The objector might retort that the state's attempt to encourage the making of amends will backfire so that, instead, it will inhibit the goal of making amends. In most actual systems of restorative justice, restorative sentencing practices are made available as alternatives to punitive sentencing practices. If offenders do not participate in these restorative programmes, or if they fail to negotiate a resolution with their victims, their cases will be turned over to the standard criminal justice system, where they may face jail-time. Given this highly undesirable option, one might charge that the offenders are coerced into offering restitution, which disqualifies this as an offer of amends (Delgado 2000). Even if the offender's experience in a sentencing conference inspires sincere remorse and a desire to right the wrong, one might argue that he is coerced, none the less. Furthermore, the possibility of punishment if restorative justice procedures do not come to a resolution will give offenders good reason to fake a sincerity they do not feel and victims to be suspicious of any expressions of remorse on the part of the offender. In these ways, the use of the criminal justice system to pursue amends might be self-defeating.

There is an element of coercion in any criminal justice system backed by the punitive power of the state. However, voluntariness seems to be something that comes in degrees. If restorative justice programmes allow offenders at least a significant degree of voluntariness, and if victims and community members believe that they can tell when offenders are being sincere, then the making of amends remains a possibility.

Let us now turn to the objection that the making of amends is a goal that the criminal justice system *should not* pursue. In both theory and practice, restorative justice is interested in the reconciliation of the parties affected by crime. Yet, as Timothy Garton Ash has objected, 'taken to the extreme, the reconciliation of all with all is a deeply illiberal idea. As Isaiah Berlin has taught us, liberalism means living with unresolvable conflicts of values and goals' (1997: 37).[9] Amy Gutmann and Dennis Thompson concur, writing: 'Reconciliation of this comprehensive sort is also deeply undemocratic ... a substantial degree of disharmony is not only inevitable but desirable. It can be both a sign and a condition of a healthy democracy' (2000, 33–4). Meaningful liberty requires the freedom of individuals to develop and pursue their own conceptions of the good, at least within reasonable limits (Rawls 1993). To the extent that a criminal justice system tries to enforce a particular, contestable conception of the good on citizens, it is illiberal. It violates the principle of liberal neutrality – i.e. the idea that the liberal state must be neutral among reasonable conceptions of the good (cf. Garvey 1999: 1855–8).

But how, precisely, is restorative justice meant to violate liberal neutrality? The general objection, as I interpret it, can take three more specific forms, each of which will require a different response. First, restorative justice seems to aim at the personal improvement of the criminal. This presupposes some conception of the good. Furthermore, this personal reformation that restorative justice has in mind is not merely outward improvement. The goal is not merely that the offender stops acting in ways that are deemed wrongful by the state. Instead, the emphasis on face-to-face interactions and deep and wide-ranging communication about the causes and effects of crime suggests that the goal is the offender's internal improvement – a change in her point of view, values or motivations, where those are judged to be lacking according to the moral conception in question. The state uses its monopoly on force in order to pursue this goal.

A second way in which restorative justice seems to violate liberal neutrality is in the influence it apparently hopes to have, not just over the moral views of the offender, but also over the moral views of the victim and the community. Restorative justice is aimed at the restoration of the relationships among the victim, the offender and the community. Reconciliation – where this involves a renewal of civil relationships and, perhaps, even forgiveness – is held up to victims and communities as the ideal resolution of crime. Once more, this presupposes particular and controversial moral views: here, about the value and appropriateness of reconciliation or forgiveness as responses to offers of amends.

The third aspect of restorative justice that seems to put it in opposition to liberal neutrality concerns the particular nature of the sentencing agreements that may emerge from restorative justice processes. When individual victims confront individual offenders to discuss what was done, why it was wrong and what should happen next, contestable moral values will come to the fore. The participants in a sentencing conference will give voice to their own conceptions of the good, their views of God and the value of community, and their ideas about class, family and gender. Participants will argue from their particular conceptions of the good to particular demands that will make up part of the negotiated sentencing agreement. This agreement will then be enforced by the state. It might turn out, then, that the state will require offenders to perform certain actions that could only be defended from a particular point of view. For instance, the state might find itself monitoring and enforcing an offender's regular attendance of a particular church service or religious education class, if such attendance was part of the sentencing agreement. More worrying still, the sentencing agreement might be the result of negotiation with one or more conceptions of the good that are not merely contestable but patently *unreasonable*. For example, a sexual offender may receive a lighter than usual sentencing agreement because he, his victim, or the community representatives proceed from the point of view that the victim was partly responsible for her victimization because she wore revealing clothing (Braithwaite and Roche 2001: 74). When the state is put in a position of enforcing such an agreement, is it not also put in the position of endorsing the illiberal moral views that lead to the agreement? Let us consider each of the three versions of the critique from liberal neutrality in turn.

The objection to making personal improvement a goal of the criminal justice system has a precedent in the literature on rehabilitative and moral education theories of punishment (e.g. Murphy 1985). The suggestion that the state could have a legitimate interest in changing, not simply the behaviour of criminals, but their moral views or personalities has, in itself, been taken as a gross overstepping of the legitimate bounds of the state into the realm of private conscience. Even if an offender's character or moral views are unreasonable – as when, for example, the offender views other people as mere means to his own pleasure and convenience – it is not clear that this is any of the state's business. The state has a legitimate interest in curbing the harmful and illegal behaviour that would be likely to follow from such unreasonable states of mind. But, were the state to try to change the offender's character or beliefs, it would violate the offender's freedom of conscience.

The restorative justice theorist may well be able to defend his interest in the moral improvement of the offender against this objection. While it is true that the liberal state is committed to freedom of conscience and the pluralism of reasonable conceptions of the good, there is no point or value in denying that liberalism is committed, at its core, to certain moral values

– specifically the freedom and equality of persons (Hampton 1994).[10] These values undergird the liberal state's commitment to freedom of conscience as well as the other defining aspects of the liberal state, such as democracy and the protection of basic rights. While the liberal state values neutrality among reasonable conceptions of the good, the bounds of the reasonable are proscribed by the values of freedom and equality. If this is the case, then the state can use the criminal justice system to educate the citizenry about the moral importance of following just laws without violating its commitment to neutrality about *reasonable* conceptions of the good.

Of course, there are certainly restrictions on what the liberal state can do in attempting to educate its citizenry. Brainwashing, for instance, is out of bounds since it would itself violate the principle of respecting freedom. Liberal moral education, then, must be education that approaches its subjects as free and equal persons. But does this not suggest that this education may not be based on coercion? Yet, as we have already noticed, the criminal justice system, even one based on restorative justice models, is inherently coercive. How, then, could it be permissible for the liberal state to use the criminal justice system as a means of education?

Here, the restorative justice theorist might appeal to an argument that Jean Hampton makes in her defence of the moral education theory of punishment (1984). She argues that, while there is an element of coercion in the criminal justice system, the educative element itself is not coercive. According to Hampton, the educative work of punishment is performed through the expressive content of the punishing act. The idea is not to punish the offender until he has changed his moral views or character. Instead, the idea is to inflict a punishment on the offender in order to communicate to the offender that the community finds his behaviour wrongful. The punishment is made proportional to the crime in order to communicate the severity of the wrongdoer's guilt in the eyes of the community. The offender may listen to this moral message and reform himself, or he may reject it, protest against it or simply ignore it.

Similarly, the restorative justice theorist hopes that the offender will have learnt a lesson through listening to his victim, having to explain and evaluate his own actions, and making reparations. However, whether this moral improvement actually comes about will be up to the offender himself. He may well refuse to listen to the moral message he is being sent. Furthermore, restorative justice systems allow the offender ample opportunity to reject those messages pointedly. He can disagree with the alleged victim, voice his own interpretation and evaluation of his actions, refuse to agree to a particular sentence and even opt out of the restorative process altogether. In this way, the offender's freedom of conscience is better served by restorative justice than by a moral education theory of punishment.

Following Hampton's lead, then, the restorative justice theorists might argue that the use of a criminal justice system to pursue the personal improvement of criminal wrongdoers is compatible with the nature of the liberal state, as long as the methods of moral education used are compatible with respecting the right of offenders to form their own conceptions of the good. Restorative justice procedures, which make offender participation optional and allow the offender ample opportunity to voice his own views, appear to be consistent with such agency. There is certainly much more to be said on this topic. But we have here at least the beginnings of a defence of restorative justice's interest in the personal reformation and moral education of criminal wrongdoers.

However, criminal offenders are not the only apparent targets of the moral lessons implicit in restorative justice procedures; so are victims and communities. Restorative justice procedures are designed to encourage the restoration of the relationships among victims, communities and offenders. Such restoration includes some idea of reconciliation and arguably even forgiveness. But people differ over the value and appropriateness of forgiveness and reconciliation. Even of those who might think that there is a moral obligation to reconcile with or forgive those who have harmed us, or perhaps only those wrongdoers who have also offered appropriate amends, few would agree to permit the state to enforce such a moral obligation.

This particular version of the objection from liberal neutrality was raised against the restorative efforts of the Truth and Reconciliation Commission (TRC) in South Africa (Ash 1997). In response, it was emphasized that, during the TRC hearings themselves, victims were allowed to express the refusal to forgive and the policy was neither to discourage nor criticize these victims (Kiss 2000: 84). Similarly, although restorative justice theorists and practitioners may value restorative justice for its ability to promote forgiveness, victims are neither pressed nor even asked by the state to forgive their offenders. The general agenda for a sentencing conference includes discussion of the nature of the crimes, its causes and effects, and the making of a plan about what the offender will do next that the parties themselves judge to be appropriate and fair. The state asks, but does not require, that the participants come up with a plan that would make possible the settlement of their dispute. It need not ask them to reconcile as friends or family members, but as fellow citizens.[11] While, for many participants, such a request raises issues of apology, repentance, forgiveness and more personal forms of reconciliation, this is a consequence of their own moral understandings and expectations rather than any state requirements that are inherent to the restorative justice process.

Restorative justice, its advocates emphasize, is what the participants make of it (Braithwaite 1994). Their own judgements of what restoration means, or with what forms of restoration they will be satisfied – whether mere restitution, genuine repentance, or forgiveness – is left to the people who are stakeholders in the conflict itself. When victims are empowered in determining what counts as an appropriate sentence, and when they meet their offenders face to face, they come to see their offenders as individuals rather than simply causes of harm (cf. Zehr 1990: 31–2). Forgiveness under such circumstances should not be a surprising reaction. But to say that the system makes forgiveness a reasonable reaction for a wide range of victims is different from saying that the system enforces forgiveness.

So, in opposition to the objection that the state is forcing a particular, contestable moral conception onto victims, one might rather argue that restorative justice systems better enable victims to live in accordance with their own conceptions of the good than standard, punitive criminal justice systems. While the theory and rhetoric of restorative justice are clearly interested in reconciliation, the victims may voice their own views of what, if anything, could earn reconciliation in the case at hand. They are free to demand that their own standards for the making of amends are met (within limits). If their demands are not met to their own satisfaction, they are free to object, withhold forgiveness, and even to bring the restorative justice proceedings to a halt.

Do restorative justice systems, rather, give *too much* latitude to differing conceptions of the good? Earlier I suggested that we can defend subjecting criminal offenders to the moral lessons of the liberal state, but can we defend subjecting them to the moral lessons of their fellow private citizens? The moral education efforts of the liberal state are permissible in so far as they focus on the core values of liberalism – freedom, equality, human rights and perhaps the obligation of citizens in a just state to obey the law. These values define the limits of reasonable disagreement in the liberal state. But the values that fellow citizens are likely to try to impress upon one another in a sentencing conference are likely to be much more varied and contestable.

To recall the examples raised earlier, we might find victims insisting that their offenders attend a specific form of religious instruction, or it might be that a sexual assault victim is talked into agreeing to a light sentence for her abuser because he and the community representatives insist that she take partial responsibility for her attack because she wore revealing clothing, became intoxicated or frequented a particular bar. Given that the state is put in the place of enforcing negotiated sentencing agreements, it would be put in the place of enforcing the particular values that shape these agreements. In the religious instruction case, the state would be required to enforce a conception of the good that, while reasonable, is also considered outside the scope of the legitimate interest of the state. In the sexual assault case, the state would be put in a position of lending credence to a moral view (that women have at best a limited right to bodily integrity) that stands in opposition to the core values of the liberal state. To these specific worries we might add quite general ones that are sometimes raised with regard to the ideals of proportionality and consistency in sentencing (Brown 1994; Delgado 2000; Ashworth 2002). Will particularly vengeful victims insist upon too much in terms of restitution, while unusually kind and forgiving victims insist upon too little? Will especially repentant offenders agree to too much, while the most hard-hearted offenders will be able to negotiate lighter sentences?

A variety of responses to these objections are open to the restorative justice theorist. The most radical one would be to insist that a just sentencing agreement is whatever is agreed to by the particular parties. If the offender and the victim agree that religious education is desirable and appropriate in this case, then who is the state to disagree? The offender could, after all, opt out of the sentencing conference if he believed that the victim's insistence of religious instruction was an infringement on his freedom of conscience. Similarly, the sexual assault victim could opt out of the process if her offender unjustly tries to make her share the blame for the offence. In both examples, the cases would be turned over to a standard, punitive sentencing procedure.

This response is inadequate, however. For one thing, given the strength of offenders' interests in avoiding imprisonment and victims' interests in receiving some degree of restitution, we may well worry that these parties will agree to the negotiation even if they believe that their rights are not being properly respected. Secondly, especially with regard to the sexual assault example, we may well worry about the advisability of making the parties themselves responsible for defending their own rights. If a woman has been raised in a community that constantly sends her the message that to express sexuality is to 'ask for' male aggression, we should not assume that she will both recognize and have the courage to insist upon her rights.

In response to such worries, restorative justice theorists sometimes insist on the importance of procedural safeguards (Johnstone 2002: 30–1). There are a number of conceivable forms such safeguards could take. For example, well trained mediators should be both willing and able to intervene in a sentencing conference in order to help particular participants defend their own rights. It is even possible to design restorative systems to give either mediators or judges the power to invalidate sentencing agreements. This might be done by setting minimums or maximums on sentences, and placing limits on what sorts of things can be included in sentencing agreements (e.g. disallowing the requirement of the attendance of religious services). In these ways, the state could be given a kind of veto power over restorative justice procedures in order to ensure that unreasonable conceptions of the good are not allowed to rule the day, and to ensure that reasonable conceptions of the good are not applied in ways that interfere with the rights of others. The difficulty of designing and implementing such procedural safeguards, especially in a way that continues to permit the high degree of stakeholder autonomy that restorative justice values, should not be underestimated. However, this line of response to the objection seems promising.

Still, a fundamental question remains to be addressed. Even when reasonable limits are observed and protections of rights are in place, restorative justice systems put offenders in the position of being morally educated *by other private citizens*, under the auspices of the state. In order to come to a sentencing agreement, the offender needs to respond to and, to some degree, satisfy the victim's conception of justice. This feature of restorative justice procedures reflects the claim that crime must be 'given back' to the stakeholders (Christie 1977; Braithwaite 1994). Instead of continuing to conceive of crime as a wrong committed against the state, we should see crime as a conflict among offenders, victims and their communities. We should allow these interested parties, these stakeholders, the power to resolve their conflicts as they deem appropriate. The state should be relegated to a supporting role. Fully to evaluate the third version of the objection from liberal neutrality – the objection that the state should not place offenders at the mercy of their fellow citizens and their private conceptions of the good – we would need to evaluate this reconception of the nature of criminal wrongdoing. Unfortunately, that task takes us beyond the scope of this chapter.

I have suggested that restorative justice is guided by a moral ideal that I have labelled 'the making of amends'. According to this ideal, wrongdoers should themselves work to right the wrongs they have committed. Wrongs will be righted when all the parties to the criminal offence – victims, communities and wrongdoers themselves – have been reconciled with one another. This project of restoration is to be pursued through the communication of the stakeholders, the reparation of the various kinds of harm created by crime and the personal reformation of the offender. As a moral ideal of the resolution of wrongdoing, the making of amends is powerful and persuasive. The difficult question is whether it is appropriate for this moral ideal to play a role in either the design or justification of the criminal justice system of a liberal state. While I have tried to point out some ways in which the restorative justice theorists can defend themselves against this objection, there is surely much more that will need to be said on this topic.

Selected further reading

Garvey, S.P. (1999) 'Punishment as atonement', *UCLA Law Review*, 46: 1801–58. In defending an atonement-based theory of punishment, Garvey addresses the objection from liberal neutrality, arguing that state-sponsored atonement is compatible only with perfectionist versions of liberalism.

Murphy, J.G. (1985) 'Retributivism, moral education, and the liberal state', *Criminal Justice Ethics*, 4: 3–11. Murphy emphasizes that the justification of the state's response to crime must always be understood within the scope of the larger issues concerning the justification of the existence of the state.

Radzik, L. (2004) 'Making amends', *American Philosophical Quarterly*, 41: 141–54. This article rejects accounts of the moral obligations of wrongdoers that focus solely on self-retribution and repentance and argues instead for a theory that centres on the restoration of relationships.

Swinburne, R. (1989) *Responsibility and Atonement*. New York, NY: Oxford University Press. Renowned philosopher of religion, Richard Swinburne argues for his view of theological atonement by first developing a theory of the wrongdoer's moral obligation to atone.

Acknowledgements

I would like to thank Christopher Bennett, Gerry Johnstone, Colleen Murphy, Robert R. Shandley and Daniel Van Ness for their valuable contributions. Thanks are also due to the Alexander von Humboldt Foundation for a research fellowship that supported this work.

Notes

1 The few exceptions include Swinburne 1989, Morris 1976 and Morris 1988.
2 My preferred method of pursuing gender-neutrality in language is to alternate between using "she" and "he".
3 Theology, for instance, has much to say about how sinners might make amends, or atone, to God. However, the human victims of our wrongful actions, and

what we might owe to them, receive little (when any) direct attention. It takes only a bit of reflection, though, to see that what we might owe to an immaterial, eternal, all-knowing and all-powerful God is likely to differ greatly from what we owe to our embodied, mortal, epistemically limited and vulnerable fellow humans.

4   My own understanding of the value of making amends is informed by a broadly Kantian moral theory. However, it is also possible to defend the value of making amends in terms of other moral theories, such as consequentialism or virtue theory. One might also defend restorative justice without any appeal to the moral ideal of making amends at all. My interest in this essay, though, is to suggest that this moral ideal lends powerful support to restorative justice, while at the same time raising certain problems.

5   The restorative justice works that suggest the ideal of making amends to me most strongly include Zehr 1990 and Braithwaite 2000. On the topic of making amends generally, my view has been influenced by Swinburne 1989, Garvey 1999, Morris 1976 and Morris 1988.

6   According to Swinburne, the making of amends (or "atonement," as he puts it) requires the victim's forgiveness (1989: 81). Colleen Murphy points out, however, that some forms of reconciliation are possible without actual forgiveness (2004). Reconciliation, most generally, seems to be the re-establishment of a relationship. Following Bishop Butler, forgiveness is frequently defined as a foregoing of resentment (1726, Sermons VIII and IX). The former is surely possible without the latter, although the richest or "thickest" form of reconciliation (to use Murphy's language) would involve both. In offering amends, the wrongdoer ideally will aim to merit both reconciliation and forgiveness, but we seem to describe two parties as having made amends when they have at least reconciled.

7   There are surely cases where this ideal could never be achieved, where nothing the wrongdoer could do would count as meriting reconciliation. Even in these cases, though, the wrongdoer is obliged to do what she can to reduce the victim's resentment and her own blameworthiness. Reconciliation, the healing of relationship and re-building of trust, are tasks that admit of degrees.

8   Although terms like "reconciliation" and "restoration" imply that a previous, good relationship existed, the terms are also applied in cases where a proper relationship is being established for the first time.

9   In this essay, Ash is specifically addressing the appeal to the values of reconciliation and restorative justice in defence of South Africa's Truth and Reconciliation Commission (TRC), which saw as its charge the reconciliation of the entire South African nation in the aftermath of the apartheid. For more on the debates surrounding the TRC and its vision of restorative justice see Robert I. Rotberg and Dennis Thompson, eds. *Truth v. Justice* (Princeton, NJ: Princeton, 2000).

10 Of course, particular defenders of the liberal state disagree about exactly what freedom and equality involve (Hampton 1994).

11 Colleen Murphy explores different conceptions of reconciliation that have been associated with the restoration of relationships among fellow citizens (2004).

Bibliography

Adler, J. (1992) *The Urgings of Conscience*. Philadelphia, PA, Temple.

Ash, T.G. (1997) 'True confessions', *New York Review of Books*, 17 July: 33–8.

Ashworth, A. (2002) 'Responsibilities, rights and restorative justice', *British Journal of Criminology*, 42: 578–95.

Barnett, R.E. (1977) 'Restitution: a new paradigm of criminal justice', *Ethics*, 87: 279–301.

Braithwaite, J. (1994) 'Thinking harder about democratising social control', in J. Alder and J. Wundersitz (eds) *Family Conferencing and Juvenile Justice: The Way Forward or Misplaced Optimism*. Canberra: Australian Institute of Criminology.

Braithwaite, J. (2000) 'Repentance rituals and restorative justice', *Journal of Political Philosophy*, 8: 115–31.

Braithwaite, J. and Roche, D. (2001) 'Responsibility and restorative justice', in G. Bazemore and M. Schiff (eds) *Restorative Community Justice: Repairing Harm and Transforming Communities*. Cincinnati, OH: Anderson Press.

Brown, J.G. (1994) 'The use of mediation to resolve criminal cases: a critique', *Emory Law Journal*, 43: 1247–309.

Butler, Bishop J. (1726) *Fifteen Sermons Upon Human Nature*. London.

Christie, N. (1977) 'Conflicts as property', *British Journal of Criminology*, 17: 1–26.

Daly, K. and Immarigeon, R. (1999) 'The past, present, and future of restorative justice: some critical reflections', *Contemporary Justice Review*, 1: 21–45.

Delgado, R. (2000) 'Prosecuting violence: a colloquy on race, community, and justice. Goodbye to Hammurabi: analyzing the atavistic appeal of restorative justice', *Stanford Law Review*, 52: 751–75.

Garvey, S.P. (1999) 'Punishment as atonement', *UCLA Law Review*, 46: 1801–58.

Gutmann, A. and Thompson, D. (2000) 'The moral foundations of truth commissions', in R.I. Rotberg and D. Thompson (eds) *Truth v. Justice*. Princeton, NJ: Princeton University Press.

Hampton, J. (1984) 'The moral education theory of punishment', *Philosophy and Public Affairs*, 13: 208–38.

Hampton, J. (1988) 'Forgiveness, resentment and hatred,' in J.G. Murphy and J. Hampton (eds) *Forgiveness and Mercy*. New York, NY: Cambridge University Press.

Hampton, J. (1994) 'The common faith of liberalism', *Pacific Philosophical Quarterly*, 75: 186–216.

Hieronymi, P. (2001) 'Articulating an uncompromising forgiveness', *Philosophy and Phenomenological Research*, 62: 529–55.

Johnstone, G. (2002) *Restorative Justice: Ideas, Values, Debates*. Cullompton and Portland, OR: Willan Publishing.

Johnstone, G. (ed.) (2003) *A Restorative Justice Reader: Texts, Sources, Contexts*. Cullompton and Portland, OR: Willan Publishing.

Kiss, E. (2000) 'Moral ambition within and beyond political constraints: reflections on restorative justice', in R.I. Rotberg and D. Thompson (eds) *Truth v. Justice*. Princeton, NJ: Princeton University Press.

Morris, H. (1976) *On Guilt and Innocence*. Berkeley, CA: University of California Press.

Morris, H. (1988) 'The decline of guilt', *Ethics*, 99: 62–76.

Murphy, C. (2004) 'The nature and importance of political reconciliation'. Dissertation, University of North Carolina.

Murphy, J.G. (1985), 'Retributivism, moral education, and the liberal state', *Criminal Justice Ethics*, 4: 3–11.

Murphy, J.G. (1988) 'Forgiveness and resentment', in J.G. Murphy and J. Hampton (eds) *Forgiveness and Mercy*. New York, NY: Cambridge University Press.

Oxford English Dictionary (2005) 'Amends' (available online at http://dictionary.oed.com/cgi/entry/ 50007114).

Radzik, L. (2003), 'Do wrongdoers have a right to make amends?' *Social Theory and Practice*, vol. 29, no. 2, pp. 325-341.

Radzik, L. (2004) 'Making amends', *American Philosophical Quarterly*, 41: 141–54.

Rawls, J. (1993) *Political Liberalism*. New York, NY: University of Columbia Press.

Rotberg, R.I. and Thompson, D. (eds) (2000) *Truth v. Justice*. Princeton, NJ: Princeton University Press.

Swinburne, R. (1989) *Responsibility and Atonement*. New York, NY: Oxford University Press.

Zehr, H. (1990) *Changing Lenses*. Scottdale, PA: Herald Press.

Part 3

Restorative Processes, Outcomes, Stakeholders

Gerry Johnstone and Daniel W. Van Ness

Part 3 starts from a 'micro' focus upon the key processes of restorative justice, and from that base examines such fundamental questions as: what needs are created by crime and wrongdoing? Who should take part in the process by which these needs are identified and addressed? What sort of process should this be? What roles should various 'stakeholders' play in these processes? What are the responsibilities of these 'stakeholders'?

A bewildering range of processes have emerged under the rubric 'restorative justice'. It is common to group these into three broad types: victim–offender mediation, conferencing and circles. In reality, many actual processes do not fall neatly into one or other of these types and new restorative processes are emerging beyond these three types. Nevertheless, anyone wishing to understand what the practice of restorative justice is about needs to start by grasping the key features of each. Accordingly, in Chapter 12 Barbara Raye and Ann Warner Roberts provide an overview of the three basic types of restorative process and explain for each the stages in the criminal justice process in which it is commonly used; the sorts of cases that it tends to deal with; the role of facilitators; who participates and what their roles are; and the nature of pre-encounter preparation. They go on to suggest that, underneath the diversity, what all three types have in common is their focus on dialogue-guided conflict resolution. What distinguishes restorative processes from non-restorative processes, then, is that in the former those affected by an instance of criminal wrongdoing – be they victims, perpetrators or others deemed to have a significant stake in the case – have an opportunity to tell their stories, to discuss issues and to come to a common understanding or agreement. Accordingly, Raye and Warner Roberts look in detail at the key elements of 'restorative dialogue' and explain why it is so important to the idea of restorative justice.

One of the key claims made on behalf of restorative dialogue is that through it the needs and interest of the different 'stakeholders' in a criminal case – and ways of satisfying these needs and interests – can be fully identified, explored and articulated. In Chapter 13, Mara Schiff reflects on the thinking within the restorative justice movement on what the needs and interests – and the responsibilities – of various stakeholders are. Three crucial themes emerge. One is that the needs and interests of any particular stakeholder are quite individual; they cannot be 'read off' from a list of the needs of any particular category of stakeholder. For example, while it may be possible and useful to speak in general terms of 'victims' needs', the actual needs of any particular victim will be quite unique, and are likely to be influenced by a multitude of factors. The second important theme is that the needs of stakeholders are not static; rather, they have a dynamic and evolving nature. Hence, Schiff points out, stakeholder needs and interests must be considered in their immediate, intermediate and long-term contexts. The third theme is the importance of identifying responsibilities as well as needs, and in particular identifying who has the responsibility for meeting needs recognized within restorative processes. While all stakeholders in restorative justice are deemed to have responsibilities, Schiff's chapter focuses – in particular – upon the responsibilities of the community and the government.

In Chapter 14, Christopher Bennett – like Linda Radzik in Part 2 – provides a perspective on these issues from moral philosophy. This chapter focuses upon two questions which lie at the heart of restorative justice. First, what responsibilities have offenders towards the victims of crime? Bennett combines insights from the work of leading restorative justice proponents, such as Howard Zehr, with that of leading moral philosophers to argue that the primary obligation of offenders is to retract and repudiate the claim, expressed in their criminal actions, that the victims are their inferior and can be used for the offenders' own ends. It is through such 'repentance' that the relationship between offenders and victim can be put right. The second question addressed by Bennett is what responsibilities the state would have towards victims if restorative justice were the dominant form of criminal justice. Victims, he argues, are entitled to vindication from their community, which should declare its intolerance of the offender's action. However, in a society which professes liberal concern for freedom of conscience, it must also be recognized that there are limits which the collective should respect – i.e. while it can demand a formal apology it cannot compel offenders actually to apologize as though they meant it. Just as important as these conclusions are the issues which Bennett tackles to reach them. Along the way he addresses – in accessible style – questions of fundamental importance in the debate about restorative justice, such as what it means to say that crime is a violation, in what sense there can be symbolic reparation for crime, in what sense it is important to restore the relationship between victim and offender, and what is the relationship between private and public concerns within the sphere of restorative justice.

Chapter 12

Restorative processes

Barbara E. Raye and Ann Warner Roberts

Introduction

Since ancient times, forms of dialogue, often with neutral or wise third parties in a facilitator role, have been widely used in both secular and religious traditions to resolve conflicts, including those between victims and offenders. Many tribal cultures and small societies have used conciliatory, co-operative, consensual approaches to maintain social harmony in the community. However, while these approaches are 'well nigh universal in all kinds of societies from the simple to the most complex', legal anthropologists have minimized them as 'informal procedures, private conciliation and the judicial process in one of its pre-nascent forms' (Gulliver 1979). But they are clearly more than that.[1] This chapter will focus on the recovery of dialogue-guided conflict resolution in recent decades and its development as a key part of the burgeoning restorative justice movement.

We have organized the chapter into sections. The first provides an overview of three prototypical models typically associated with restorative justice. Next we note similarities and differences among those models, and suggest that each contains a common focus, which we call restorative dialogue. Viewing these processes in their prototypical forms, however, can be misleading, since in reality many forms of these three models are in use, with more variations emerging all the time. We suggest, therefore, that it might be useful to think in terms of six categories of restorative processes based on the parties present, the decision-making role each party plays and the form their dialogue takes. Finally, as restorative justice has expanded worldwide, questions of quality control have arisen. Our final section discusses two disparate approaches and the values that hold them together.

Prototypical models

Victim–offender mediation (VOM)

Many credit an impromptu experiment, sometimes called the 'Elmira Case', with being the birth of victim–offender mediation (VOM). This was a case of teenage vandalism in 1974 in Ontario, Canada, and the response by a probation officer (Mark Yantzi), a volunteer and a judge who thought that there would be a therapeutic effect if the offenders met face to face with their victims and paid restitution. There were other similar experiments at about this time in North America and England. For example, in 1975 Phillip Priestley produced a documentary entitled 'Just One of Those Things', which followed the case of a man who had repeatedly stabbed another man in an unprovoked attack in a railway station. The documentary shows Priestley facilitating[2] a meeting between the perpetrator and the victim; in retrospect, Priestley regarded the encounter as mediation, albeit not a very good one.[3] At roughly the same time, Nils Christie, a Norwegian criminologist, published an influential journal article, 'Conflicts as property' (1977), setting forth the idea that the parties to a crime themselves own the conflict, and that state-directed criminal prosecution and sentencing represented a theft of that conflict.

However, it was the Elmira case that became the catalyst for what was initially called victim–offender reconciliation programmes in Canada and the USA. The first British VOM scheme began in Exeter and, by the mid-1980s, government-funded pilot schemes were in place across England.

The initial (VOM) was a one-to-one meeting with a third-party facilitator who acted impartially (or equally partially, perhaps). As time went on, programmes departed from this initial model in numerous ways. Many meetings began to include more participants, such as parents and/or supporters and, while solo mediators were portrayed as the norm, the use of co-mediators became common as well.

Until 1989, VOM was essentially the only restorative process and consequently, became an umbrella term for these diverse approaches. As a result, significant variations developed in programmes using the same name. For example, some programmes in the USA and Europe developed a form of mediation that might be called 'shuttle diplomacy'. Rather than the victim and offender meeting directly, opportunities were given for communication through the mediator, who acted as a go-between, passing information back and forth between the parties. Other creative ways to facilitate discussions were developed as well, such as the use of audio-recordings, video-recordings, phone, letters, faxes, Internet discussions and email. Unfortunately, indirect VOM has not been well reported or researched.

Because there are such a variety of approaches calling themselves VOM, it might be useful to contrast the prototypical VOM (a victim, an offender and a facilitator) from its diverse progeny. For example, indirect VOM, although most often process focused, may alternatively be settlement focused. Under the latter scenario, indirect mediation may resemble models of civil mediation used in North America and Europe. Where a civil mediator may be quite willing to offer opinions about a party's position and direction about a possible outcome, most VOM facilitators do not: their role is to ensure that the context is set for meaningful communication between the parties. A further difference is that the prototypical VOM puts an emphasis on the need for in-person preparation meetings, which is not necessarily standard in civil mediation. Techniques such as paraphrasing, reframing and summarizing are not typically part of VOM and, indeed, are not particularly compatible with providing the parties with an uninterrupted narrative, storytelling format. In serious and violent crimes in particular, the typical approaches focus far more on the needs of the parties for healing than on arriving at an agreed solution.

The participation of an identified victim or victims is essential if the prototypical VOM is to take place – there can be no dialogue if there is no victim. Early research on VOM programmemes in the USA, Canada and the UK revealed a strong offender orientation, largely due to the relationship these programmes had to the criminal justice system. Consequently, significant work has been done over the years to identify ways that VOM can be more 'victim friendly' in approach, although this continues to be an issue requiring ongoing commitment and evaluation.Table 12.1 presents the common characteristics of the prototypical VOM.

Table 12.1 Common characteristics of the prototypical VOM

Stage in the criminal justice process	Diversion, pre-court, post-process adjudication,post-sentence
Kinds of cases	Initially minor crimes; increasingly more serious and violent crimes
Role of facilitator(s)	Create safety, guide process
Participants	Initially, one victim, one offender and mediator(s). Now may also be multi-party to include victim(s), offender(s) and possibly family members and supporters
Preparation	In-person strongly recommended

Conferencing

Family group conferencing (FGC) began in 1989 under provisions of the Children, Young Persons and Families Act in New Zealand, which addressed both child welfare and youth justice matters. This reform was intended to empower the extended families of the Maori, the aboriginal peoples who inhabited the country before the arrival of Europeans and whose children were over-represented in the system. The process was designed to bring families of victims and offenders together to find their own solutions to conflicts. This was done with the assistance of a facilitator provided by the government. One of conferencing's significant differences from the prototypical VOM, therefore, was the inclusion of family members and supporters of the victim and offender in the meeting.

FGC migrated to Australia and was initially adapted in several important ways in the town of Wagga Wagga; it was offered by the police service, a formal script was added for the facilitator to use and all participants stayed together in the room throughout the entire meeting, including when options were explored and decisions made.[4] Later, FGC spread to Canada, the USA, the UK and then around the world. As it spread, alternative terms such as 'community conferencing', 'restorative conferencing' and simply 'conferencing' were used for the variety of conferencing processes.

Early VOM proponents were conflicted about conferencing. Some regarded it merely as a variation of the VOM practice they had been developing for over two decades and maintained that there was little difference between a multi-party VOM and conferencing. Others, however, were concerned that the emphasis on family participation might cause offenders or victims, particularly if they were juveniles, to be overshadowed by adult participants. Although conferencing was not originally called a restorative process, the term was soon applied. Over time conferencing, like VOM, has been used in a variety of settings other than criminal justice, such as in schools, families and workplaces.

Because FGC replaced court for a number of juveniles in New Zealand, conferences are used there even when the victim was unable or unwilling to participate. This practice has continued as conferencing has expanded; victim presence is considered valuable but not essential. However, research from New Zealand suggests that the presence of the victim at a conference

Table 12.2 Common characteristics of the prototypical conferencing

Stage in criminal justice process	Diversion, pre-court, post-adjudication, post-sentence
Kinds of cases	Initially child welfare and less serious crimes; increasingly more serious and violent crimes
Role of facilitator	Create safety, guide process; script option possible, but not recommended in some forms of conferences
Participants	Primarily victims, offenders, family members, supporters and some government staff; can take place without victims
Preparation	Phone contact in some; in-person recommended in others

is a factor in reducing recidivism. Table 12.2 presents common characteristics of the prototypical conference.

Circles

Circles are based on the values and traditions of North American aboriginal peoples. Their first use in the criminal justice system came in 1990 as part of a judge's pre-sentence hearing. The meetings are strongly community based, with victims, offenders, their families and supporters, any other interested member of the community (whether or not they have knowledge of the parties or the crime), and criminal justice personnel participating as equal members. A 'talking piece' is part of the tradition, and is used to manage the communication as it is passed clockwise around the circle. Participants are given uninterrupted time, in turn, to say whatever they wish related to the purpose of the circle when they hold the talking piece.

Circles are used for purposes other than sentencing. They may be used to resolve a community problem, to provide support and care for victims or offenders (sometimes to prepare them for a sentencing circle) and to consider how to receive back into the community offenders who have been imprisoned. There can be considerable overlap with the approaches taken by VOM, conferencing and circles.

Circles are a more recent addition to the collection of restorative processes and, as a result, there has been considerably less research into their processes and effectiveness. They are arguably the most inclusive process of the three

Table 12.3 Common characteristics of the circle prototype

Stage in criminal justice process	Diversion, pre-court, post-adjudication, as sentence, post-sentence
Kinds of cases	Initially minor crimes; increasingly more serious and violent crimes; cases needing extensive follow-up
Role of facilitator	Create safety, talking piece to guide process
Participants	Primarily victims, offenders, family members, supporters, criminal justice system personnel, members of the local community
Preparation	In-person recommended; sometimes done through the use of preliminary circles

prototype models because any members of the community who wish to participate may do so, even if they do not know the parties involved. Table 12.3 presents common characteristics of the prototypical circle.

Emerging models

Other approaches have emerged over time to address particular needs or circumstances. For example, when victims or offenders would like to meet, but the other party will not or cannot do so, groups of victims will sometimes meet with unrelated groups of offenders in a surrogate process; that is, the offenders did not commit the crimes against those particular victims. Meetings are structured to allow victims, offenders and sometimes community representatives to talk about the causes and consequences of crime. These may be one-time meetings or take place over a series of meetings (e.g. Walker 1999).

Another example is the use of 'video-letters'. These are being used to facilitate reconciliation in the Balkan states. Originally, film-makers invited individuals and families to record video messages to their former friends and acquaintances. War and conflict have driven even close friends, neighbours and work colleagues into now ethnically-separate states. The success of this has resulted in its adaptation and application in a number of countries, with TV broadcasts, Internet cafés dedicated to sending such messages and a touring show.

In place of suspicion and animosity a new climate of optimism and trust is being built. These are merely two examples of responses to the desire of one or both parties for dialogue in settings in which the prototypes described above are not feasible. Adaptations are also stimulated by an increasing sensitivity to the issues of race, gender, class, power dynamics and cultural bias in how current models are being applied in the Western cultural context and in its judicial and alternative dispute resolution (ADR) systems (see Raye 2004).

In addition, many of the aboriginal processes that have inspired restorative justice practice and theory include features that do not fit easily within the three models. For example, an elder may be more directive than would be expected of facilitators in the prototypical processes. Nevertheless, the parties are able to participate in dialogue about the crime in an effort to identify appropriate responses while respecting kinship or community authority (see Cunneen, Chapter 7, this volume).

Restorative dialogue

Differences and similarities between the models

A useful starting point for a comparison of these processes is a frequently used definition of restorative justice: 'Restorative justice is a process whereby all parties with a stake in an offence come together to resolve collectively how to deal with the aftermath of the offence and its implications for the future' (Marshall 1996: 5). This is a description within which each of the prototypical models fits comfortably.

Furthermore, all agree on the need to incorporate three basic principles of restorative justice: 1) repair of harm; 2) direct involvement of stakeholders; and 3) community as the first responder, with the government occupying a safeguard position (Van Ness and Strong 2006). Additionally, all reflect certain restorative values such as respect, collaboration, empowerment and voluntariness, although each offers flexibility in how those values should be demonstrated in specific settings or communities (Roberts 2004). These basic principles and values express what might be called the 'spirit of restorative justice'. If these are experienced by all the participants, the specific processes or variations used are not particularly important. Restorative processes are 'robust', meaning that they can be changed in multiple ways around the needs of the parties while maintaining restorative goals and achieving restorative outcomes. Without those goals and values, even the most restorative process will be damaging rather than restoring in outcome.

A common characteristic among all restorative processes is the use of narrative, or storytelling, as a means to communicate thoughts and feelings among the group members. In this way, people are encouraged to speak from the heart as well as the head. This type of interaction draws participants into the conversation and increases the likelihood that they will be fully present – physically, emotionally, intellectually and even spiritually.

The goals of the prototypical VOM were to create a 'safe place' for the victim and offender to discuss the crime and its aftermath. This is true as well of all restorative processes although, as noted earlier, the prototypical conference added family members and supporters of the parties, and the prototypical circle included members of the community. Justice officials may also be present in the latter two models.[5]

While the specific mechanisms for dialogue in the three models are somewhat different, all are intended to allow an opportunity for participants to tell their stories, to discuss issues and to come to a common understanding or agreement. Each has its own method of introducing the participants to each other and explaining the process at the outset, and closing when the discussion has ended.

Finally, as discussed earlier, each of the processes has changed from its original prototype. Initially, VOM was a one-to-one meeting – one victim and one offender – typically sitting around a table with one mediator who facilitated their discussion. While that format continues today, early practitioners began to make changes to the 'formula' almost from the outset. Examples of these changes include: 1) adding parents or guardians in juvenile cases; 2) allowing other supporters or relevant parties to participate; 3) using co-mediators; and 4) allowing multiple victims and/or offenders to participate in the same meeting.

There have been similar changes in the conferencing model. The New Zealand FGC included a 'private family planning time'. When it was adapted in Australia, the new model kept everyone together for the entire meeting and required the facilitator to use a prescribed script to guide the discussion.

As originally designed, victims were to be a part of the conference, but they were not required, which means that some conferences include all the parties but others do not.

The first use of circles in restorative justice was to help design a sentence for an offender. The usage has expanded substantially, with circles now used to prepare parties for sentencing circles, to help individual parties heal and to help prisoners re-enter and succeed long term in the community.

Six categories of restorative dialogue

As should be clear by now, one cannot tell what the precise process is by looking at its name. VOM can be run in ways that are quite similar to conferences, for example. While conferences and circles will not typically operate with a single victim, single offender and a single facilitator, they nevertheless reflect a great deal of diversity from programme to programme and even meeting to meeting. While it is useful for purposes of explanation, training, and evaluation to be able to describe distinct approaches and give them names, the names customarily used can be misleading if the listener assumes that the programme will be like the prototype.

Furthermore, the purpose of the programmes is to facilitate restorative dialogue among the participants, not to run particular kinds of meetings regardless of the participants' wishes. As experienced practitioners have adjusted processes to fit the participants and context, many have come to the conclusion that it is more useful to think in terms of a single model with many variations. The key dynamic of this model is restorative dialogue.

Restorative dialogue has three characteristics: 1) it is inclusive, in that it invites all stakeholders to participate, and is willing to adjust its processes to meet their needs and interests; 2) it is grounded in restorative principles and values; and 3) facilitation is conducted in such a way that participants are free to communicate as fully as they wish with each other by sharing experiences, perceptions, emotions and perspectives.

We suggest that it may be useful to think of in terms of six categories, or generic models, of restorative processes designed to facilitate restorative dialogue. These models are distinguished by who attends, who the decision-makers are and how the communication flows in the course of the meeting. The models are not mutually exclusive; a process that begins by using one model may transition to another based on the needs and interests of the parties. Some of the models are similar to the three prototypical models described earlier, but because we adopt descriptive names they are less likely to lead to confusion about what the processes actually entail. Each arguably falls within the Marshall definition we used earlier, although some fit more comfortably than others. All are based on actual programmes operating within the restorative justice field.

Model 1: 'Indirect dialogue'
In the indirect dialogue model, as Figure 12.1 shows, the victim and offender do not come together physically, but instead do so indirectly through a third

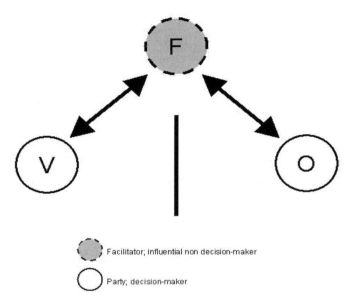

Figure 12.1 Indirect dialogue

party, usually the facilitator. The interaction is done through letters, videos or verbal comments made to the facilitator who passes them along to the other party. This approach is sometimes called shuttle diplomacy. The programmes that use this approach are sometimes more settlement driven than process driven; this is the case for a number of VOM programmes in Europe, for example, in which the communication is largely related to the amount and method of payment of restitution. However, this approach may also be used when there is a serious issue of power imbalance, as when an adult has sexually abused children who are related to the adult. The interaction may be deemed important because of the familial relationship, but direct contact may be too intense for the child.

If decisions are made during indirect dialogue, it is the parties who make them. The facilitator's role is officially to transmit the messages to the other parties, although given that the parties are not communicating directly, the facilitator can knowingly or unknowingly influence the outcome by how the information is presented.

Model 2: 'Facilitated victim–offender dialogue'
The facilitated victim–offender dialogue model (Figure 12.2) is described above in the section on the prototypical VOM. Here the parties interact directly with the assistance of a facilitator who creates an environment conducive to effective communication, prepares the parties ahead of time and is present to help them speak to each other if necessary.

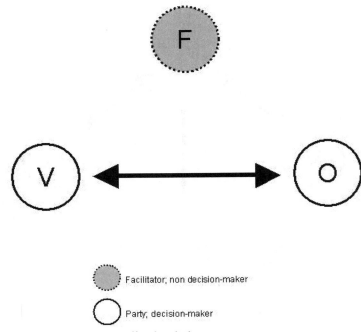

Figure 12.2   Facilitated victim–offender dialogue

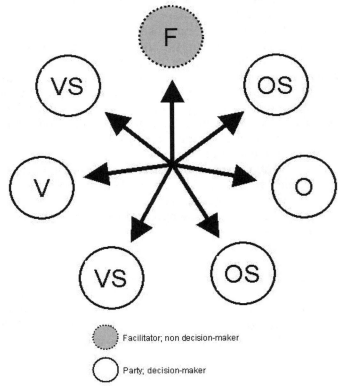

Figure 12.3   Facilitated victim–offender–supporter dialogue

Model 3: 'facilitated victim–offender–supporter dialogue'

The facilitated victim–offender–supporter dialogue model (Figure 12.3) is described above in the section on the prototypical conferencing model. Here supporters (sometimes called the 'community of care') of the victims and the offenders join in a facilitated conversation. The discussion in these processes tends to expand beyond the specific incident to underlying needs and issues related to the victim and offender.

Model 4: 'facilitated all-party dialogue'

The facilitated all-party dialogue model (Figure 12.4) is described above in the section on the prototypical circle model. In this model, government officials and/or community members join the victims, offenders and communities of care in a facilitated conversation. The figure depicts the conversation proceeding around the circle, but it could also take place as is illustrated in models 3, 5 and 6. The discussion in these processes tends to expand beyond the specific incident and the underlying needs and issues related to the victim and offender, to include community issues as well.

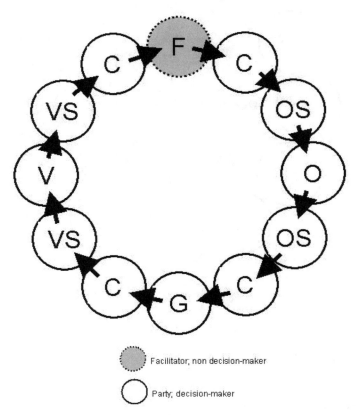

Facilitator; non decision-maker

Party; decision-maker

Figure 12.4 Facilitated all-party dialogue

Model 5: 'guided dialogue'

The guided dialogue model (Figure 12.5) could take place in any of the three models above, either as a substitute for the methods described or as one of several methods used in a particular meeting. The victim and offender, at least, are present; the others may participate as well. The difference between this and the other models is that the facilitator changes from a facilitation role to one that is more active by interjecting questions, comments, summaries and other observations to the parties present. This approach is used in VOM programmes that have features of civil mediation, and is also used in some aboriginal circles in North America. Figure 12.5 shows guided dialogue being inserted into a conferencing form of interaction.

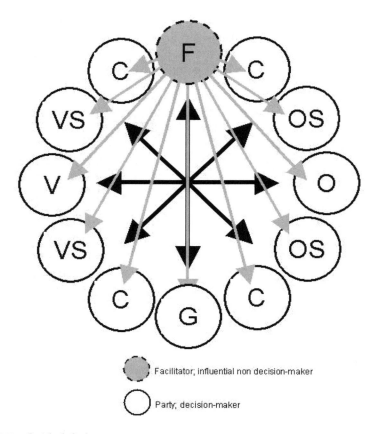

Facilitator; influential non decision-maker

Party; decision-maker

Figure 12.5   Guided dialogue

Model 6: 'directed dialogue'

In the directed dialogue model (Figure 12.6), the facilitator assists the parties in conversation, as with other models, but in the end the facilitator makes or announces the decision. The model is not, however, like a court proceeding in which the parties attempt to persuade an authority figure who imposes a decision on them; instead, the facilitator seeks to help the parties find

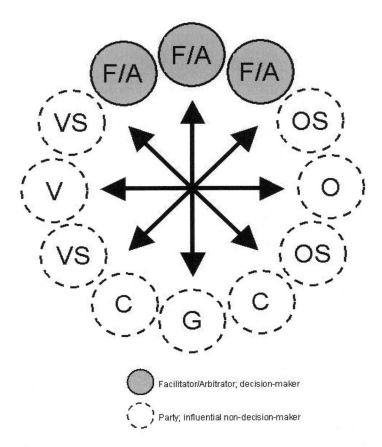

Figure 12.6   Directed dialogue

common ground, and in a sense announces the group's decision as much as makes the decision him or herself. This approach is taken in some traditional or customary dispute resolution mechanisms. Decisions in those cultures are not made democratically, so it is difficult to describe the parties as decision-makers even though they participate fully and have great influence over the final decision. (Examples are the traditional roles of a council of elders or wise tribal chief.)

Models 2, 3, and 4 are universally accepted as restorative. We have included the other three, nevertheless, because they do fit the Marshall definition mentioned earlier: 'the victim and the offender, and, where appropriate, any other individuals or community members affected by a crime, participate together actively in the resolution of matters arising from the crime, generally with the help of a facilitator'. While models 1, 5 and 6 involve significant limitations on the parties' ability to do this directly, those models may be the ones the parties prefer for a variety of reasons – including cultural values/contexts.

These models have arisen out of practice, and others may emerge as well. They help underscore the diversity in practice as well as the commonality within restorative processes. Thinking of the models as *categories* of processes allows for technical differences, such as the number of facilitators, etc., within similar approaches. Distinguishing among those approaches allows for the development of advanced training, particularized evaluation and the design of new approaches. Recognizing that, seen together, the processes are variations on a single theme reminds practitioners that the specific processes are a means to an end, rather than an end in and of itself. It also underscores that restorative dialogue (the spirit of restorative justice described above) must remain at the core of any process or innovation.

Maintaining high quality in practice

Quality is important to practitioners and participants in all restorative processes. Victim-survivor participants take significant risks when they share their experiences and the hurt and emotions connected to them. They are entitled to a safe space, facilitation by someone with the necessary empathy and skills, and a process that will allow them to gain what they seek in participating. Those who have offended become vulnerable as they seek ways to make amends and regain a sense of human connection. They are entitled to facilitation by someone who can protect them from abuse, a process that will help them communicate effectively their compassion, regret and apology, and assistance as they begin to make amends. Referral sources, funders and the public expect high-quality processes because they have invested resources seeking to solve problems, not create more conflict, errors and controversy. Finally, practitioners themselves have an interest in being part of a profession and life work that is admired and in which they can take pride and gain the respect of others. A fundamental principle for all practitioners is to do no additional harm; high quality makes additional harm unlikely.

There have been at least two approaches taken to maintain high quality. The first has been to select practitioners with natural gifts and temperament for facilitation, hone those through training and practice, and provide them with a set of principles and ethical guidelines. The test of this approach is whether the parties believe that the facilitator provided the services they needed. The second approach has been to identify the skills and practices that lead to effective processes, and to develop programmes for training, ongoing supervision, practice standards and certification or accreditation. This approach reflects a sense of professional obligation to protect the public and the parties from bad practice. The test of this approach is whether practice has satisfied standards that are reinforced through training, peer review and/or certification.

The approaches are not mutually exclusive, and neither is without controversy. A 2005 survey co-sponsored by the American Bar Association and the Association for Conflict Resolution regarding a proposed certification programme had over 3,000 responses. A consultant working with the project began the analysis by noting wryly that 'the issue is certainly one about which people in the field both feel strongly about and are willing to express their feelings'.[6] In that particular effort the short-term decision was that opinions were so divergent that the civil conflict resolution field in the USA is not yet able to build consensus on the issue.

Conclusion

The restorative justice field is a profession, a movement, a set of values and a vision of social reform. Its advocates and practitioners come from all walks of life and speak many professional and cultural languages. It is in an entrepreneurial phase where programme creation, practice, research and outreach are carried out both collaboratively and competitively across diverse intersecting groups. Its roots are broad and deep, stemming from a plethora of founding influences and leaders. What it has in common is a set of beliefs related to the dialogue that occurs in restorative processes: 1) the dialogue itself is as important and perhaps more important than the outcome; 2) non-violent and non-adversarial solutions are better than the alternative; 3) facilitation and the witness of others can be useful in exploring human conflict and its resolution; and 4) there is hope for human transformation and connection.

Many who participate with restorative justice find that the values become life commitments, that the processes continue to evolve and that new applications continue to emerge to address human needs and relationships. They differ in personal motivation, personality, ego investment and organizational affiliation. They also differ in psychological approaches, professional education and assumptions about conflict. These differences contribute to diverse preferences for particular processes, quality measures and methods of accountability. The common vision of an alternative to a punitive and adversarial justice system is a profound unifier. Nevertheless, it is clear that disputes over preferred practice models, facilitator style and role, certification, training requirements, professional standards and other issues will continue to add spice to the stew of co-creation and individuality in the field for many years to come.

Selected further reading

Umbreit, M. (2001) *The Handbook of Victim Offender Mediation: An Essential Guide to Practice and Research*. San Francisco, CA: Jossey-Bass. One of the important pioneers and researchers of victim–offender mediation, Mark Umbreit, reviews VOM and other dimensions of practice.

Roberts, A. and Masters, G. (1999) *Group Conferencing: Restorative Justice in Practice*. St Paul, MN: University of Minnesota Press. A useful overview of conferencing.

Pranis, K., Stuart, B. and Wedge, M. (2003) *Peacemaking Circles: From Crime to Community*. St Paul, MN: Living Justice Press. The authors of this book – pioneers in the adaptation of circles from their aboriginal roots into mainstream culture – offer a helpful introduction to peace-making circles.

Raye, B. (2004) 'How do culture, class and gender affect the practice of restorative justice?, in H. Zehr and B. Toews (eds) *Critical Issues in Restorative Justice*. Monsey, NY: Criminal Justice Press. This chapter explores the systematic issues within restorative practice and recommends action to address these issues.

Roberts, A. (2004) 'Is restorative justice tied to specific models of justice?', in H. Zehr and B. Toews (eds) *Critical Issues in Restorative Justice*. Monsey, NY: Criminal Justice Press. As the field of restorative justice has expanded from one practice to multiple models with hybrids, it is importnat to focus on the core: 'dialogue'.

Notes

1 We acknowledge that the tribal cultures also had practices that, by today's standards, would not be considered restorative. Indigenous resolutions to harm have evolved over time in response to social sensitivity to issues such as crimes against women, inter-tribal marriage and public execution in the same way as has the Western justice system.

2 'Mediator' and 'facilitator' and sometimes 'co-ordinator' are terms used for the third party in VOM and conferencing, while 'keeper' is the name usually used in circles. Throughout this chapter we will use 'facilitator' as an umbrella term to refer to all of those roles, unless we are focusing on distinctions in the roles in particular models.

3 Priestley, (personal interview, 25 May 1994).

4 The FGC models used in Australia have changed over time and now are closer to the New Zealand model than the Wagga Wagga model (see the discussion in the Pacific regional review in Chapter 24, this volume).

5 The prototypical VOM, as we have defined it, does not have participants other than the victim, the offender and the facilitator. However, as noted earlier, many actual VOM programmes are more inclusive than the prototype, and will invite police, probation officers and others as well.

6 Quotation from David Hart, Executive Director of the Association for Conflict Resolution during a teleconference with members of the National Coalition of Dispute Resolution Organizations (NCDRO). Author Raye is a member of NCDRO and was present on the call.

References

Christie, N. (1977) 'Conflicts as property', *British Journal of Criminology*, 17: 1–15.

Gulliver, P. (1979) 'On mediators', in I. Hamnet (ed.) *Social Anthropology and Law*. London: Academic Press.

Marshall, T. (1996) *Restorative Justice: An Overview*. London: Home Office.

Pranis, K., Stuart, B. and Wedge, M. (2003) *Peacemaking Circles: From Crime to Community*. St Paul, MN: Living Justice Press.

Raye, B. (2004) ' How do culture, class and gender affect the practice of restorative justice?' in H. Zehr and B. Toews (eds) *Critical Issues in Restorative Justice*. Monsey, NY: Criminal Justice Press, 325–36.

Roberts, A. (2004) 'Is restorative justice tied to specific models of practice?', in H. Zehr and B. Toews (eds) *Critical Issues in Restorative Justice*. Monsey, NY: Criminal Justice Press, 241–52.

Roberts, A. and Masters, G (1999) *Group Conferencing: Restorative Justice in Practice.* St Paul, MN: University of Minnesota Press.

Umbreit, M. (2001) *The Handbook of Victim–Offender Mediation: An Essential Guide to Practice and Research.* San Francisco, CA: Jossey-Bass.

Van Ness, D. and Strong, K. (2006) *Restoring Justice*, (*3rd edn*). Cincinnati, OH: Anderson Publishing.

Walker, P. (1999). 'Saying sorry, acting sorry: the Sycamore Tree Project, a model for restorative justice in prison', *Prison Service Journal*, May: 19–20.

Chapter 13

Satisfying the needs and interests of stakeholders

Mara Schiff

Introduction

This chapter identifies and characterizes the needs, interests and responsibilities of various stakeholders in restorative processes. Restorative processes include stakeholders not traditionally involved in criminal or other adversarial processes (or perhaps only minimally or peripherally included), and do so because it is viewed as central to a fair and just outcome (e.g. Bazemore and Schiff 2004; Van Ness and Strong 1997, 2002, 2006). Restorative processes offer key stakeholders an opportunity to come together to discuss the event, its impact and how the resulting needs, interests and responsibilities should be met. Restorative processes seek to provide a more 'user-friendly' forum for informal decision-making concerning these, and represent a fundamental shift in the community and government roles necessary to accomplish this (Morris and Maxwell 2001). Much has already been written about the needs, interests and responsibilities of stakeholders in restorative justice processes (Umbreit 1998, 1999, 2001; Van Ness and Schiff 2001; Young and Hoyle 2002; Hays and Daly 2003; Strang 2003; Umbreit *et al.* 2003), so my task here is to encapsulate what has already been said, and perhaps to do so in a way that helps organize these needs and interests in a useful and compelling way.

In this chapter I will discuss the importance of restorative principles in identifying and understanding stakeholder needs, interests and responsibilities; I will distinguish between immediate, intermediate and long-term stakeholder needs, interests and responsibilities; I will elaborate on some key stakeholder needs, interests and responsibilities; lastly, I will summarize key points of the chapter. Throughout the chapter, I will consider recent research that compares restorative and traditional approaches in terms of participant satisfaction and other important outcomes. Readers should note that this analysis represents primarily the experience of restorative processes in the USA, especially in terms of the roles of government and community. While some of the concepts discussed here will translate easily to other countries and cultures, differences in government structure, interpretation of 'community' and the relationship between government, community and individual citizens suggest that readers should interpret these comments and their application across cultures and jurisdictions carefully.

Defining and understanding stakeholder needs, interests and responsibilities

Distinguishing stakeholder needs, interests and responsibilities

A standard way of defining an interest is to say that Y is in X's interest if X would benefit from Y. This reason for providing Y can be over-ridden by other considerations. But to say that X *needs* Y is to say something much stronger, and the other considerations must be much more compelling than in the case of an interest. Needs are more fundamental to existence than interests; interests can, in the end, be done without. A need may be essential to survival – something as critical to well-being as food or water. An interest, on the other hand, is important and relevant, but not critical. It is desirable, it is meaningful, it significantly affects well-being, but viability and sustainability do not depend upon it. A *responsibility* is something that must be done, not in order to survive (those are needs) nor necessarily because one desires it (those are interests), but because one is obligated. So, for example, we may speak of an offender's 'need' to be accountable, but that is clearly different from the need the offender may face to find work or kick a drug habit. Reparation is in fact an obligation, or responsibility, that arises from having harmed another.

Each person is different and, while some standard needs, interests and responsibilities can be identified, the degree to which the issues mentioned below represent 'needs' or 'interests' or 'responsibilities' will depend on the individual and the particular circumstances. Thus, this chapter will not focus on characterizing a particular concern as a need, interest or responsibility but, rather, on the underlying issues and the degree to which these concerns are best met through a restorative response to crime. To avoid pointless repetition, I will sometimes use the term 'concerns' to mean the combination of needs, interests and responsibilities involved.

The relevance of restorative principles for contextualizing stakeholder needs, interests and responsibilities

At best, conventional criminal justice processes meet only a small proportion of victims, offenders and community concerns after a criminal offence. This is because the traditional justice system is focused on establishing legal guilt, assessing blameworthiness and then determining the appropriate degree of punishment to impose on the offender or, in Zehr's (2001) words, what laws were broken, who broke them and who needs to be punished. The conventional criminal justice system generally makes victim concerns secondary to the effectiveness and efficiency of the justice process, and community concerns are virtually invisible. Moreover, the justice system assumes it is the government's responsibility to address *all* stakeholder concerns, rather than considering the possibility that some can be better met through other resources. That is, the government assumes responsibility for representing and managing the concerns of stakeholders, leaving the actual players more or less on the sidelines.

In a restorative approach, stakeholders express their own needs, interests and responsibilities in a safe environment where victims and offenders, as well as family and community members, encounter one another with the help and support of trained facilitators. Specifically, restorative dialogue provides a means for victims to speak about the impact of the crime, its effect and how reparation can be accomplished. Offenders can speak about what happened and are held, and hold themselves, *directly* accountable to the victim and the community for the harm they have caused. Victims and especially offenders have the opportunity to develop empathy for the other and understanding of the circumstances that may have contributed to the crime. Community members may participate in the process as peers, mentors, supporters and monitors, as persons who were indirectly affected by the crime and as those who are responsible for establishing and upholding the norms and standards of the community. The government's role in a restorative system is to facilitate reparation for victims and communities, and to assist in the reintegration of both offender and victim. In contrast to the traditional model, government does not operate as a third-party representative whose primary role is to establish culpability and impose punishment.

Restorative justice aims to ensure that as many stakeholder concerns as possible are addressed in the response to the crime; it accomplishes this by ensuring that practices are focused on a specific set of *principles* that ground and inform the justice response and centre on the repair of harm. These principles include:

- repairing the harm caused by crime;
- involving and including key stakeholders to the greatest extent possible; and
- transforming the relationship between governments and communities into one of collaborative problem-solving (Bazemore and Schiff 2005; Van Ness and Strong 2006).

In the restorative model, victim and offender needs, interests and responsibilities are derived primarily from their relationship to the harm caused by the crime and their roles in repairing that harm. The long-term goals of restorative justice also assume greater responsibility by communities for their members along with a shift in the traditional governmental role in the justice process. The restorative model posits that community members offer resources not available to government professionals, such as mentoring, leadership, involvement and relationships not possible among government workers.

Victims and offenders

Immediate needs, interests and responsibilities

Immediate needs, interests and responsibilities are those that occur during and in the immediate aftermath of the crime and during the restorative intervention in which the parties come together to identify what happened, who is responsible and how best to repair the harm (Zehr 2001). These are needs which, having been met, could cause the restorative intervention to have been considered successful immediately following its conclusion. The following victim and offender concerns each address some form of reparation accomplished thorough the interaction of the parties that can be met and measured by the end of the dialogue process.

Information about the process, the victim/offender and the offence

First and foremost, both victims and offenders need to know what will happen and when. For victims, this is central to regaining the sense of control that was taken by the offender at the time of the crime (Achilles and Zehr 2001). A victim needs to know if the offender has been identified and, if so, what is being done with him or her. Victims need to know that they are safe from future harm, and that they are not at risk of a new violation by this perpetrator. Some research has shown that victim satisfaction with the restorative process is directly linked to how well they have been informed about the process (Maxwell and Morris 1993).

For the offender, it is equally important to know what will happen and how. In a restorative intervention, the offender is made aware of the process and the potential consequences of non-participation or non-compliance as fully and as early as possible. Additionally, a restorative encounter can help 'humanize' the victim for the offender (Umbreit 2001).

Reassurance and acknowledgement

Victims need to know that they are not responsible for the crime because they were not 'smarter', 'better prepared', 'more cautious', 'more aware', 'less suggestive', or some other attribute theoretically within their control. In restorative processes, the victim has the opportunity to witness the offender taking responsibility for his or her actions and apologizing for his or her behaviour. For the offender, this means taking responsibility for what happened, but doing so in a context in which he or she is reassured that he or she need not be defined by that action nor ostracized forever by family, friends and community. Traditional processes tend to stigmatize both the act and the actor; in the restorative process, the two are distinguished so that the offender, having acknowledged responsibility and made reparation, can 'earn his or her way back' to acceptance by the community (Bazemore 1998). Empirical evidence suggests that viewing restitution as 'earned redemption' appears to change offender attitudes. It leads to increased completion of reparative orders, and that has been associated with reductions in recidivism through increasing commitment to the common good (Van Voorhis 1985; Schneider 1990).

A fair, satisfying and 'just' process

Both victims and offenders need to feel that they have been treated fairly and respectfully, that their voices have been heard and that they have had an impact on the outcome of the process. Some research shows that the components of a fair and just process for victims include feeling that the mediator is unbiased; that they are compensated for losses; and that the offender is appropriately punished (Umbreit 1989). There is now a considerable body of research showing that most victims (and offenders) who participate in restorative processes feel they were treated fairly and were satisfied with the process (Umbreit 1989; 1995; 1997; Strang *et al.* 1997; McCold and Wachtel 1998; Daly 2001; McGarrel 2001; Karp *et al.* 2002). For offenders, being treated with respect and dignity, participating fully in the development of a reparative agreement and believing that the agreement was created through a fair process improve the likelihood of compliance with the conditions of the agreement and decrease the probability of reoffending (Latimer 2001; Maxwell and Morris 2001; Hayes and Daly 2003).

Support from family, friends, community and the justice process

Victims may feel isolated and alone following a crime. As their sense of safety and security has been violated, so too has their sense of 'belonging'. In traditional processes, victims experience a triple marginalization – first to occur is marginalization by the offender; then relatives and community members may give support early in the immediate aftermath of the crime but not in the weeks and months following the event; and then thirdly, by a justice process interested in them only if and until the offender is convicted. Restorative justice aims to develop ongoing relationships that can sustain care for victims over time.

For the offender, support is equally critical. While offenders may be initially motivated to complete the terms of their agreements in the aftermath of restorative conferences, this commitment may wane over time, and they need mentorship and support to complete their agreements and become productive and valued community members. Research shows the degree to which offenders feel competent and valued by others appears to have a positive effect on compliance with reparative agreements, desistance from criminality and improved self-worth over time (Maxwell and Morris 2001; Wilson and Prinzo 2001; Rodriguez 2005).

Full participation in the process

Both victims and offenders need to be heard. Furthermore, the victim's participation is critical to the success of a restorative process. Van Ness and Strong's (2006) second principle focuses on the importance of victim (and other stakeholder) participation in the process as a means by which to ensure a restorative process and a reparative outcome. Bazemore and Schiff (2005) expand on this by arguing that the extent of such participation is a key means by which to 'recognize a restorative process when we see it' and, moreover, to evaluate the restorativeness of any given intervention.

Apology from the offender

Along with reassurance that this was not their fault, victims may want an apology directly from the offender. This adds to their sense of vindication while also demonstrating that the offender has gained some empathy for the victim's situation. Some research suggests that an apology may be equally or more important to the victim than reparation (Umbreit 1999). When asked what they most want to come out of the process, many victims who participated in restorative processes initially stated restitution, but later revised that to meeting with their offenders face to face and hearing their apologies; it 'humanized the process' (Umbreit 1988, 1989; Dissel 2000; Miers *et al*. 2001), which in the end was equally, if not more, important.

Reaching a reparative agreement

Some argue that the reparative agreement between the victim and the offender is the heart of the restorative mandate. Others, however, contend that the process itself is most important because it enables the healing dialogue through which broken relationships can be repaired (Braithwaite 2001; Stuart 2001; Bazemore and Schiff 2005). Empirical evidence suggests that, for some victims, obtaining a reparative agreement will be the most important part of the process, while for others, hearing the offender apologize and experiencing empathy from and for the offender may be sufficient. For some offenders, an agreement concludes the process and offers a substantive means by which to express regret, repair the harm and earn redemption.

Receiving reparation/compensation for material and nonmaterial damage or loss

In general, most victims are interested in being compensated for losses to the extent possible. While this is obviously not fully possible for some severe offences, the majority of offences can command some type of reparation in the form of repair to damaged property, financial reimbursement or repayment for medical or other living expenses. There is evidence that restitution is more likely to be completed through restorative than traditional justice processes (Schneider 1986; Umbreit and Coates 1992; Evje and Cushman 2000).

Intermediate needs, interests and responsibilities

Intermediate needs, interests and responsibilities are those that may occur in the weeks to months following the restorative intervention and which might be used to measure success several months later. These may not be apparent in the immediate aftermath of the encounter, but may arise over time, once the initial emotions have abated, but when there is still a need for resolution.

Victim and offender reintegration

Crime damages relationships (Van Ness and Strong 2006), not just between the victim and the offender, but also between members of their communities. In restorative dialogue, attention is placed on relationships rather than punishments, so that victims and offenders can (re)gain their sense of identity as people with a rightful place in the community. For victims, this means feeling safe from harm at the hands of this or another offender and a sense of belonging to a family and community. For the offender, desisting from future crime may depend on feeling connected to and supported by a community that, having recognized a genuine attempt at reparation, welcomes the offender back 'into the fold'. This is consistent with Braithwaite's (1989) idea of reintegrative shaming as well as Bazemore's (1998) concept of 'earned redemption'. In addition, offenders may need help in areas such as drug treatment, job training, academic assistance, social adjustment (e.g. anger management), skills training or other social services that may encourage self-control and social acceptance.

Relationship-building

While friends and family are often available in the immediate aftermath of the crime, this support may subside over time as life 'returns to normal'. An important component of restorative dialogue focuses on establishing long-term connections that can support victims until they feel strong and safe again. For offenders, relationships are key to maintaining law-abiding and productive behaviour over time.

Specifically, social relationships with other law-abiding individuals and groups are a primary factor in desistance from crime (Cullen 1994; Bazemore et al. 2000). The degree to which the offender feels responsibile to others is central to belonging; while an offender may be indifferent to the reactions or feelings of strangers, the feeling of shame that may occur when he or she learns of the impact of his or her behaviour on close friends and family can have considerable impact (Bazemore and Schiff 2005).

Completing reparation

Completing the reparative agreement is central to establishing the offender as a trustworthy and productive member of the community. For victims who have been promised such reparation, this is central to a satisfying restorative justice experience. A recent meta-analysis of 35 restorative programmes found that, in general, offenders who participated in restorative justice programmes tended to have substantially higher compliance rates than those processed through other arrangements (Latimer et al. 2001).

The offender will not harm others

As much as victims want to know that they will be free from harm in the future, they are often also concerned about the well-being of others. Van Ness and Strong (2006) contend that one of the important components of the offender's ability genuinely to make amends is his or her ability to demonstrate changed behaviour over time. When compared with traditional court processes, research shows that recidivism is likely to be reduced as a result of restorative conferencing (Nugent and Paddock 1995; Sherman et al. 1999; Bonta et al. 2002; Hayes and Daly 2003; Nugent et al. 2003). Completing restitution has also been associated with reductions in recidivism through increasing commitment to the common good (Schneider 1990).

Long-term needs, interests and responsibilities

Victims and offenders have a variety of needs, interests and responsibilities that may emerge or continue years after the crime was committed. These long-term interests may represent the ultimate goals of restorative justice shifting the justice objective from doing proportionate harm to offenders to repairing the harm done to victims and communities. Addressing long-term concerns indicates that harms broader than those of the individual case and its participants are being addressed. This suggests the importance of developing a collective community capacity to facilitate victim support and offender reintegration, and to prevent and respond to crime. The extent to which restorative dialogue helps build such capacity remains an unanswered empirical question. However, it is clear that traditional justice processes contribute little to this.

There is also insufficient empirical evidence to date clearly to determine clearly whether restorative justice results in significant long-term and sustained change in victims, offenders or communities. However, available evidence shows decreased recidivism rates for offenders, high levels of satisfaction and perceptions of fairness for both victims and offenders and increased community participation in justice decision-making.

Community

What is community and what is its function?

The third key stakeholder in restorative justice, the community, has multiple facets. Community can be considered geographically, such as the neighbourhood in which the event took place (a 'community of place'), or it can be a social definition, such as in a church, work or recreational community (a 'community of interest') . Moreover, it might be a localized 'micro-community' such as a school, prison or housing project (Bazemore and Schiff 2005). A concept often used in the restorative context is that of a 'community of care' (McCold 1996; Pranis 1998; Daly 2001; Braithwaite 2003), which includes anyone who feels connected, either directly or indirectly, to the persons involved in the crime or the event itself. This conceptualization arises because a geographic or social definition may be insufficient to capture the maze of emotions, harms and relationships that the criminal event may have spawned. Thus, the definition typically used in restorative justice includes anyone who feels connected emotionally, physically or in other ways to the victim(s), the offender(s) or the event itself.

It is easier to talk about the responsibilities of community because its fluid boundaries and pluralistic nature make ascribing it with specific needs or interests difficult. Moreover, since community is a collective that includes victims (direct and indirect), offenders and others, it has no needs or interests save those of its individual members. However, the notion of community serves several purposes in the restorative process. First, it represents people who have been indirectly harmed by the offence. As such, they are responsible for communicating that harm, its degree and their expectations for appropriate repair. Secondly, community serves an important normative function by developing, communicating and upholding the standards to which its members are expected to adhere as well as the values that undergird those norms. This includes censuring the behaviour of members who have failed to uphold the standards of collective living.[1] Finally, community is responsible for developing a 'collective ownership' of the problem of crime, such that a collective efficacy for responding to crime – informal control, social support and informal sanctioning (Sampson *et al.* 1997) – can be developed. This requires building the skills of community members to respond to problems without relying exclusively on the 'expertise' of justice professionals who have been trained to take responsibility for preventing and responding to crime and who have, inadvertently, diminished the capacity of the community to handle its own problems. The sections that follow address immediate, intermediate and long-term responsibilities of community in the restorative justice process.

Immediate responsibilities

Provide a forum to talk about the crime and its resolution
The community is responsible for providing a safe relational space for victims, offenders and others to talk about what happened, its impact and what needs to be done about it. While governments can create forums for such dialogue, it is ideally the community that cares for the well-being of its members and therefore can create an environment within which they feel safe and welcomed. Communities are sometimes exclusive, rather than inclusive, but it is possible for restorative programmes to help the community 'own' its process without needing to rely on government facilitators. Examples of this in the USA include neighbourhood accountability boards in San Jose, CA and circles in North Minneapolis, MN (Bazemore and Schiff 2005).

Include community members in determining what happened, who should be held responsible and in what way
In many forms of restorative dialogue, community representatives are empowered to participate. Those representatives closest to the event and its participants may be in the best position to identify the impact of a crime and to assert informal social control as well as support (Cullen *et al.* 1999). In shifting the focus from 'punishment' to 'accountability', restorative justice considers that offenders may be more likely to hold themselves accountable to persons close to them and before whom they feel ashamed (Bazemore 2001; Bazemore and Schiff 2005).

Communicate about the impact of the crime on community members
As part of its normative function, community representatives may speak of the impact of crime on secondary victims (Van Ness and Strong 2006), persons aside from the immediate victim, offender and their respective families, and the extent to which the norms and standards of collective living have been violated. This can lead offenders to realize that their actions have far greater consequences than the harms to direct victims (Clear and Karp 1999).

Be informed about available services and resources for both victims and offenders
Finally, the community is responsible to offer the victim and offender various forms of support (Hook and Seymour 2001). Community members often have access to resources unknown to government professionals which can strengthen and support bonds between members (Clear and Karp 1999). Most importantly, community members can provide mentoring and other forms of informal social support and control that government is intrinsically incapable of providing due to its official monitoring and enforcement roles.

Intermediate responsibilities

Create a safe environment for community members, including victim and offender
As proposed by Van Ness and Strong (2006), the government is responsible for maintaining a just order, but the community is responsible for creating a just peace. In essence this means that community must stay connected to its members and to what is happening within its boundaries. This includes many of the items listed above under immediate responsibilities, but suggests an ongoing focus, rather than attention only in the aftermath of an individual event.

Develop mentorship for offenders and ensure victims are supported: materially, physically and emotionally
Part of establishing peace is demonstrating caring beyond the formal structure of one's professional responsibility. A significant component of the restorative process is to involve and include community members who can serve as personal and professional mentors for both victims and offenders in need.

Follow-up to ensure reparative agreements are met
Finally, the community has an important role to play in monitoring the completion of restorative agreements. In some programmes, this is a formal part of the restorative dialogue process that may fall to parents and other family members and/or to concerned and available community members. In others, it is a more organic process that arises when similar interests or resources between offenders and community members are identified. In the traditional system, follow-up is performed only by professionals; in the restorative process it becomes a means of building trusting and supportive relationships among citizens.

Long-term responsibilities

Develop capacity to resolve problems without government involvement
Over time, the most significant restorative responsibility of the community is to minimize the overall need for government intervention. To the degree that problems can be kept out of the formal system, many persons, especially juveniles, could avoid the stigma and isolation that come from criminal and juvenile justice system involvement. One of the best examples comes from Woodbury, MN, wherein a local tree-house, considered a neighbourhood resource for local children, was severely damaged while the owners were

on vacation. When the police conferencing co-ordinator called to schedule a conference to resolve the incident, he was told 'it's already been taken care of' by community members who had already met, discussed the incident and formulated a reparative agreement (Bazemore and Schiff 2005).

Develop and support reintegrative strategies for victims and offenders

Communities are resource-rich environments with assets that are unavailable to governments. Governments, in turn, have goods and services not always accessible to communities. Both victims and offenders may require a variety of reintegrative services that must be jointly developed and accessed through community and government resources. Restorative justice (and its philosophical sister, community justice) holds that community engagement is key to the reintegration of its members and that minimizing the need for government intervention empowers and enriches the community in recognizing its own native assets. Important community resources for reintegration and support may be systematically undervalued when governments absorbed more and more responsibility for victim and offender service provision.

Government

Government has traditionally devoted the majority of its criminal justice resources to blaming, fixing, treating or punishing offenders. Some resources have been devoted to rehabilitation, though the 'what works' dilemma of the mid-1970s (Martinson 1974), in conjunction with increasingly punitive political ideologies of the last several decades, have resulted in consistently decreasing resources devoted to rehabilitative and reintegrative programmes. Restorative justice shifts the focus from punishing offenders by inflicting proportionate pain to accountability for the purpose of making amends and repairing harm.

In restorative justice philosophy, government encourages community members to take responsibility for and make decisions about their own well-being. Specifically, governmental agencies provide support, education, resources, guidance and oversight that empowers communities to respond effectively to the problems crime causes. What is needed is not simply to devolve responsibility to the community level (Bazemore and Griffiths 1997; Crawford 1997), but, rather, to transform the work of justice professionals from 'expert' service providers to supporters of community and citizen-driven restorative responses (Pranis 1998). As such, the role of the government in a restorative system relates less to time (immediate, intermediate and long term) and more to transforming how stakeholder needs, interests and responsibilities are defined and addressed.

Government responsibilities

Address victims' needs irrespective of their offenders' legal status
Government has a responsibility to respond to the needs of crime victims irrespective of their offenders' legal status – that is, whether or not they have

been caught, convicted and sentenced. This suggests facilitating a system of what Susan Herman (2004) has called 'parallel justice' for crime victims whereby government resources are marshalled to help victims feel safe and in control of their lives again. While offenders may be held accountable for meeting some of their victims' needs (such as remorseful apology, restitution, reassurance of future safety), only the government can deploy the extensive resources needed to address victims' long-term, complicated problems that may require health care, job training or relocation needs. In essence, parallel justice does two things: it underscores the need to create a separate path of response to the concerns of victims apart from, but related to, the criminal justice system; it also highlights the contemporaneous nature of the process – society must provide justice for both victim and offender simultaneously.

Support offenders taking responsibility for their actions

The first goal of the current justice system is to establish culpability through the legal process. While this is an important feature of a rights-based and adversarial system, it also encourages offenders to deny responsibility and be held accountable only in so far as they can be held *legally* responsible for their actions. In contrast, a restorative system encourages offenders to take personal responsibility for their own actions, so that resources can instead be devoted to making amends to the victim and community. A restorative strategy requires government to shift its focus from an individual rights-based, adversarial-oriented justice process, to a reparative one in which justice is defined by the degree to which the victim is redressed (within the bounds of reasonable standards and norms) and relationships are enhanced.

Create resources for offender competency development

According to the Balanced and Restorative Justice project (BARJ 2000), competency is the capacity to do something well that others value. Ultimately offenders, like others, need to be viewed and to view themselves as competent individuals who can contribute to those around them. In a restorative scheme, offenders are held accountable and, with victim and community input, are assisted in determining how to make amends while capitalizing on strengths that can enhance their (re)integration into the community. Both governments and communities would consider a new holistic perspective wherein a person may have done *something* wrong, but is not necessarily a *bad person*.

Recognize community as an integral element in preventing and responding to crime and develop its capacity to do so

Government must recognize the inherent capacities of communities to mobilize resources and provide services to victims and offenders. Faith communities may play an essential role here, as local spiritual leaders can often motivate and engage citizens in ways that governments cannot. Moreover, offenders appreciate when such support is provided by persons not 'paid to care about them' (Pranis 2001). Positive connections with citizens and community groups can provide ongoing guidance and assistance to support healing and adjustment in the aftermath of a crime. The government can provide resources and structure for the community to support victims and offenders by developing access to restorative programming and by refocusing the governmental response to wrongdoing into one that values and includes community involvement and input.

Summary and conclusion

This chapter has suggested that examining the needs, interests and responsibilities of stakeholders in the restorative justice process must be considered within the context of restorative justice principles: repairing the harm, involving and including stakeholders, and transforming the relationship between the government and the community. Moreover, stakeholder needs and interests must be considered in their immediate, intermediate and long-term contexts because of their dynamic and evolving nature. Of central importance in the restorative strategy is the degree to which key stakeholders are included and play a central role in determining what happened, who is responsible and what needs to be done in response (Zehr 2001).

Key concepts raised in this chapter include the degree to which victims, offenders and community members are made active participants in a justice process that allows them to communicate about the harm inflicted and the resulting reparative needs. For victims, immediate concerns include feeling safe following the criminal incident; being kept aware of and included in the process; receiving apology and reparation; feeling that both the process and outcome was fair; and being supported over time by family and friends. Intermediate and long-term concerns include acceptance and integration into the community; having the reparative agreement completed; building supportive relationships that will sustain over time; and knowing that this offender will not commit additional crimes.

For the offender, immediate concerns include being kept aware of and included in the process; learning about and developing empathy for the victim; being respected in a fair and just process; being supported by family and friends; creating an agreement that enables reparation of harm and earned redemption; and identification of a variety of options for making amends. Intermediate and long-term concerns include resources and support for completing the reparative agreement; actually completing the agreement; viable strategies and mechanisms for reintegration and acceptance into the community; and finding long-term supportive relationships with others that encourage law-abiding and productive behaviour.

For communities and government, the focus shifts from needs and interests to responsibilities. Community, which comprises victims, offenders and others, inherently includes the needs and interests of its members but, as a collective, is also responsible for their well-being. Such responsibilities include developing and maintaining forums to discuss crime and its impact; identifying and communicating normative standards of collective living; conveying censure when such norms have been violated; and developing 'collective ownership' of the problems that crime presents in a context of informal social control and support. Moreover, communities must include and engage members in responding to crime; be informed about services and resources for victims and communities; and create a safe environment for citizens. Important long-term responsibilities include developing the collective capacity to resolve problems without government intervention and creating reintegrative strategies for both victims and offenders.

Lastly, governments are responsible for shifting the justice focus away from punishment and isolation of offenders to a more robust process that includes satisfying the needs and interests of a variety of stakeholders. Specific governmental responsibilities under a restorative system require addressing victims' needs irrespective of offender status, perhaps through a system of 'parallel justice', while also making it easy for them to participate in justice processes that affect them. Additionally, governments must support offenders' taking responsibility for their actions, paying attention to and developing resources for competency development, and structuring strong and consistent reintegrative resources for offenders.

Perhaps most importantly, government professionals must shift their organizational roles away from being authoritative problem-solvers to being facilitators who invite and include communities in justice decision-making. Communities must also be encouraged to develop their own capacities to resolve crime and justice dilemmas with minimal government intervention. This requires a significant shift in priorities as well as a willingness to devolve power and responsibility to communities that are willing to accept such terms. As such, a significant component of governments' roles include being willing to move organizational culture towards developing such community capacity.

Ultimately, addressing the needs, interests and responsibilities of stakeholders in the justice process is both an interpretive and an empirical question. It is interpretive because satisfying the concerns of individual stakeholders depends on a great variety of case and participant-specific factors, such as the nature of the event itself; its severity; the persons involved; the jurisdiction and community in which the crime occurred; the cultural context of the participants; and a multitude of other important and not always quantifiable factors. It is empirical because satisfying the concerns of stakeholders ultimately depends on current knowledge of 'what works' and our ability to generate such satisfaction across a wide variety of cultures and contexts. Research in restorative justice has evolved considerably in the last decade and articulation of desired outcomes, as well as our capacity to measure them, has become significantly more sophisticated than the simple offender-based measures of recidivism historically used to measure 'success'. As this chapter suggests, restorative justice must examine multiple outcomes for multiple stakeholders over varying timeframes in order validly and reliably to assess its success in meeting their needs and interests. Correspondingly, the degree to which stakeholder concerns can be identified, met and evaluated requires increasingly sophisticated methodology that research has only begun to examine.

Selected further reading

Bazemore, G. and Schiff, M. (2005) *Juvenile Justice Reform and Restorative Justice: Building Theory and Policy from Practice*. Cullompton: Willan Publishing. A detailed examination of restorative justice conferencing in the USA. Identifies key practical and conceptual issues for repairing harm, stakeholder involvement and community/government partnership in restorative conferencing based on the experiences of practitioners around the USA.

Herman, S. (2004) 'Is restorative justice possible without a parallel system for victims?', in H. Zehr and B. Toews (eds) *Critical Issues in Restorative Justice*. Monsey, NY: Criminal Justice Press. A critical examination of the needs of victims in the context of restorative justice. Concludes that restorative justice offers possibilities but also falls short for victims in a variety of ways. Recommends 'parallel justice for victims' as an alternative approach.

Umbreit, M.S., Coates, R.B. and Vos, B. (2001) *The Impact of Restorative Justice Conferencing: A Review of 63 Empirical Studies in Five Countries*. Minnesota, MN: Center for Restorative Justice and Peacemaking, University of Minnesota School of Social Work. Reviews 63 empirical studies that examine the impact of restorative justice around the world on such outcomes as client satisfaction, perceptions of fairness, recidivism, cost and diversionary impact.

Note

1 This is, of course, particularly difficult when members have never considered them-selves (nor been considered by others) integrated members of any community, and thus feel no obligation to live by its rules and regulations.

References

Achilles, M. and Zehr, H. (2001) 'Restorative justice for crime victims: the promise, the challenge' in G. Bazemore and M. Schiff (eds) *Restorative Community Justice: Repairing Harm and Transforming Communities*. Cincinnati, OH: Anderson Publishing.

Ashworth, A. (2002) 'Responsibilities, rights and restorative justice', *British Journal of Criminology*, 42: 578–95.

Balanced and Restorative Justice (BARJ) (2000) *Curriculum*. Washington, DC: Office of Juvenile Justice and Delinquency Prevention.

Bazemore, G. (1998) 'Restorative justice and earned redemption: communities, victims and offender reintegration', *American Behavioral Scientist*, 41: 768–813.

Bazemore, G. (1999) 'The fork in the road to juvenile court reform', *Annals of the American Academy of Political Social Science*, 564: 81–108.

Bazemore, G. (2001) 'Young people, trouble, and crime: restorative justice as a normative theory of informal social control and social support', *Youth and Society*, 33: 199–226.

Bazemore, G. and Griffiths, C. (1997) 'Conferences, circles, boards, and mediation: the new wave in community justice decisionmaking', *Federal Probation*, 59: 25–37.

Bazemore, G., Nissen, L. and Dooley, M. (2000) 'Mobilizing social support and building relationships: broadening correctional and rehabilitative agendas', *Corrections Management Quarterly*, 4: 10–21.

Bazemore, G. and Schiff, M. (eds) (2001) *Restorative and Community Justice: Repairing Harm and Transforming Communities.* Cincinnati, OH: Anderson Publishing.

Bazemore, G. and Schiff, M. (2004) 'Paradigm muddle or paradigm paralysis? The wide and narrow roads to restorative justice reform (or, a little confusion may be a good thing)', *Contemporary Justice Review,* 7: 37.

Bazemore, G. and Schiff, M. (2005) *Juvenile Justice Reform and Restorative Justice: Building Theory and Policy from Practice.* Cullompton: Willan Publishing.

Bonta, J., Wallace-Capretta, S., Rooney, J. and Mackanoy, K. (2002) 'An outcome evaluation of a restorative justice alternative to incarceration', *Contemporary Justice Review,* 5: 319–38.

Braithwaite, J. (1989) *Crime, Shame, and Reintegration.* New York, NY: Cambridge University Press.

Braithwaite, J. (1998) 'Restorative justice', in M. Tonry (ed.) *The Handbook of Crime and Punishment.* New York, NY: Oxford University Press.

Braithwaite, J. (2001) 'Youth development circles', *Oxford Review of Education,* 27: 239–52.

Braithwaite, J. (2003) 'Principles of restorative justice' in A. Von Hirsch *et al.* (eds) *Restorative Justice and Criminal Justice: Competing or Reconcilable Paradigms.* Oxford: Hart Publishing.

Christie, N. (1977) 'Conflict as property', *British Journal of Criminology,* 17: 1–15.

Clear, T. and Karp, D. (1999) *The Community Justice Ideal: Preventing Crime and Achieving Justice.* Boulder, CO: Westview Press.

Crawford, A. (1997) *The Local Governance of Crime: Appeals to Community and Partnerships.* New York, NY: Oxford University Press.

Crawford, A. (2003) 'The prospects for restorative youth justice in England and Wales: a tale of two acts', in K. McEvoy and T. Newburn (eds) *Criminology, Conflict Resolution, and Restorative Justice.* Basingstoke: Palgrave Macmillan.

Crawford, A. and Clear, T. (2001) 'Community justice: transforming communities through restorative justice?', in G. Bazemore and M. Schiff (eds) *Restorative Community Justice: Repairing Harm and Transforming Communities.* Cincinnati, OH: Anderson Publishing.

Cullen, F.T. (1994) 'Social support as an organizing concept for criminology: Residential Address to the Academy of Criminal Justice Sciences', *Justice Quarterly,* 11: 527–59.

Cullen, F., Wright, J. and Chamlin, M. (1999) 'Social support and social reform: a progressive crime control agenda', *Crime and Delinquency,* 45: 188–207.

Daly, K. (2001) 'Restorative justice in Australia and New Zealand: variations, research findings, and prospects', in A. Morris and G. Maxwell (eds) *Restoring Justice for Juveniles: Conferencing, Mediation and Circles.* Oxford: Hart Publishing.

Dissel, A. (2000) *Restoring the Harmony: Report on a Victim Offender Conferencing Pilot Project.* Johannesburg: Restorative Justice Initiative and Center for the Study of Violence and Reconciliation.

Evje, A. and Cushman, R. (2000) *A Summary of the Evaluations of Six California Victim Offender Rehabilitation Programs.* San Francisco, CA: Judicial Council of California, Administrative Office of the Court.

Hayes, H. and Daly, K. (2003) 'Youth justice conferencing and re-offending', *Justice Quarterly,* 20: 725–64.

Herman, S. (2004) 'Is restorative justice possible without a parallel system for victims?', in H. Zehr and B. Toews (eds) *Critical Issues in Restorative Justice.* Monsey, NY: Criminal Justice Press.

Hook, M. and Seymour, A. (2001) 'Offender reentry requires attention to victim safety', *The Crime Victims Report,* 5: 33–48.

Young, R. and Hoyle, C. (2002) 'New, improved police led restorative justice? Action research and the Thames Valley police initiative', in A. Von Hirsch *et al.* (eds) *Restorative Justice and Criminal Justice: Competing or Reconcilable Paradigms*. Oxford: Hart Publishing.

Karp, D., Bazemore, G. and Chesire, J. (2004) 'The role and attitudes of restorative board members: a case study of volunteers in community justice', *Crime and Delinquency*, 50: 487–515.

Karp, D. and Walther, L. (2001) 'Community reparative boards in Vermont', in G. Bazemore and M. Schiff (eds) *Restorative Community Justice: Repairing Harm and Transforming Communities*. Cincinnati, OH: Anderson Publishing.

Karp, D., Sprayregen, M. and Drakulich, K. (2002) *Vermont Reparative Probation Year 2000 Outcome Evaluation Final Report*. Waterbury, VT: Vermont Department of Corrections.

Latimer, J. (2001) 'A meta-analytic examination of youth delinquency, family treatment, and recidivism', *Canadian Journal of Criminology*, 43: 237–53.

Latimer, J., Dowden, C. and Muise, D. (2001) *The Effectiveness of Restorative Practices: A Meta-analysis. Research and Statistics Division Methodological Series*. Ottawa: Department of Justice.

Martinson, R. (1974) 'What works? Questions and answers about prison reform', *Public Interest*, 35: 22–54.

Maruna, S., LeBel, T. and Lanier, C. (2002) 'Generativity behind bars: some "redemptive truth" about prison society'. Draft paper.

McCold, P. (1996) 'Restorative justice and the role of the community', in B. Galoway and J. Hudson (eds) *Restorative Justice: International Perspectives*. Monsey, NY: Criminal Justice Press.

McCold, P. (2004) 'What is the role of community in restorative justice theory and practice?', in H. Zehr and B. Toews (eds) *Critical Issues in Restorative Justice*. Monsey, NY and Cullompton: Criminal Justice Press and Willan Publishing.

McCold, P. and Wachtel, T. (1998) *Restorative Policing Experiment: The Bethlehem Pennsylvania Police Family Group Conferencing Project*. Pipersville, PA: Community Service Foundation.

McGarrell, E. (2001) *Restorative Justice Conferences as an Early Response to Young Offenders*. Washington, DC: Office of Juvenile Justice and Delinquency Prevention.

McKnight, J. (1996) *The Careless Society*. New York, NY: Basic Books.

Miers, D., Maguire, M., Goldie, S., Sharpe, K., Hale, C., Netten, A., Uglow, S., Doolin, K., Hallam, A., Newburn, T. and Enterkin, J. (2001). *An Exploratory Evaluation of Restorative Justice Schemes*. Home Office Occasional Paper. London: Home Office.

Maxwell, G. and Morris, A. (1993) *Family Participation, Cultural Diversity and Victim Involvement in Youth Justice: A New Zealand Experiment*. Wellington: Victoria University.

Maxwell, G. and Morris, A. (2001) 'Family group conferencing and reoffending', in A. Morris and G. Maxwell (eds) *Restorative Justice for Juveniles: Conferencing, Mediation and Circles*. Oxford: Hart Publishing.

Morris, A. and Maxwell, G. (2001) 'Restoring conferencing', in G. Bazemore and M. Schiff (eds) *Restorative Community Justice: Repairing Harm and Transforming Communities*. Cincinnati, OH: Anderson Publishing.

Nugent, W. and Paddock, J. (1995) 'The effect of victim–offender mediation on severity of reoffense', *Mediation Quarterly*, 12: 353–67.

Pranis, K. (1997) 'From vision to action: church and society', *Presbyterian Church Journal of Just Thoughts*. 87: 32–42.

Pranis, K. (1998) *Restorative Justice: Principles, Practices and Implementation. Section 6. Building Community* (National Institute of Corrections curriculum). Washington, DC: US Department of Justice, Federal Bureau of Prisons, National Institute of Corrections.

Pranis, K. (2001) 'Restorative justice, social justice, and the empowerment of marginalized populations', in G. Bazemore and M. Schiff (eds) *Restorative Community Justice: Repairing Harm and Transforming Communities*. Cincinnati, OH: Anderson Publishing.

Riessman, F. (1962) *The Culturally Deprived Child*. New York, NY: Harper & Brothers.

Rodriguez, N. (2005) 'Restorative justice, communities, and delinquency: whom do we reintegrate?', *Criminology and Public Policy*, 4: 103–31.

Sampson, R., Raudenbush, S. and Earls, F. (1997) 'Neighborhoods and violent crime: a multi-level study of collective efficacy', *Science Magazine*, 277: 918–24.

Schneider, A. (1986) 'Restitution and recidivism rates of juvenile offenders: results from four experimental studies', *Criminology*, 24: 533–52.Schneider, A. (1990) *Deterrence and Juvenile Crime: Results from a National Policy Experiment*. New York, NY: Springer-Verlag.

See, C. (1996) 'Interview with Reverend Charles See', in *Restoring Justice* (video). Louisville, KY: Presbyterian Church (USA).

Seymour, A. (2001) *A Community Response Manual: The Victim's Role in Offender Reentry*. Washington DC: Office for Victims of Crime and American Probation and Parole Association.

Sherman, L., Strang, H. and Woods, D.J. (2000) *Recidivism Patterns in the Canberra Reintegrative Shaming Experiments*. Canberra: Australian National University.

Strang, H. (2003) *Repair or Revenge: Victims and Restorative Justice*. Oxford: Oxford University Press.

Stuart, B. (1996) 'Circle sentencing – turning words into ploughshares', in B. Galaway and J. Hudson (eds) *Restorative Justice: International Perspectives*. Monsey, NY: Criminal Justice Press.

Stuart, B. (2001) 'Guiding principles for designing peacemaking circles', in G. Bazemore and M. Schiff (eds) *Restorative and Community Justice: Repairing Harm and Transforming Communities*. Cincinnati, OH: Anderson Publishing.

Sykes, G. and Matza, D. (1957) 'Techniques of neutralization: a theory of delinquency', *American Sociological Review*, 22: 664–70.

Umbreit, M.S. (1988) 'Mediation of victim offender conflict', *Missouri Journal of Dispute Resolution*, 31: 85–105.

Umbreit, M.S. (1989) 'Crime victims seeking fairness, not revenge', *Federal Probation*, 53: 52–7.

Umbreit, M.S. (1995) 'The effects of victim offender mediation', in M. Tonry and K. Hamilton (eds) *Intermediate Sanctions in Overcrowded Times*. Boston, MA: Northeastern University Press.

Umbreit, M.S. (1997) 'Victim offender mediation in criminal conflict', in E. Kruk (ed.) *Mediation and Conflict Resolution in Social Work*. Chicago, IL: Nelson-Hall.

Umbreit, M. (1998) 'Restorative justice through victim offender mediation: a multi-site assessment', *Western Criminology Review*, 1: 1–29.

Umbreit, M. (1999) 'Avoiding the marginalization and McDonaldization of victim offender mediation: a case study in moving toward the mainstream', in G. Bazemore and L. Walgrave (eds) *Restoring Juvenile Justice: Repairing the Harm of Youth Crime*. Monsey, NY: Criminal Justice Press.

Umbreit, M. (2001) *The Handbook of Victim–Offender Mediation*. San Francisco, CA: Jossey-Bass.

Umbreit, M. and Coates, R. (1992) *Victim Offender Mediation: An Analysis of Programs in Four States of the US*. Minneapolis, MN: Minnesota Citizens Council on Crime and Justice.

Umbreit, M.S., Coates, R.B. and Vos, B. (2003) 'Community justice through peacemaking circles', *Contemporary Justice Review*, 9: 7–21.

Nugent, W., Williams, M. and Umbreit, M.S. (2003) 'Participation in victim–offender mediation and the prevalence of subsequent delinquent behavior: a meta-analysis', *Utah Law Review*, 14: 408–16.

Van Ness, D. and Strong, K.H. (1997) *Restoring Justice*. Cincinnati, OH: Anderson Publishing.

Van Ness, D. and Schiff, M. (2001) 'Satisfaction guaranteed? The meaning of satisfaction in restorative justice', in G. Bazemore and M. Schiff (eds) *Restorative and Community Justice: Repairing Harm and Transforming Communities*. Cincinnati, OH: Anderson Publishing.

Van Ness, D. and Strong, K.H. (2002) *Restoring Justice* (2nd edn). Cincinnati, OH: Anderson Publishing.

Van Ness, D. and Strong, K.H. (2006) *Restoring Justice* (3rd edn). Cincinnati, OH: Anderson Publishing.

Van Voorhis, P. (1985) 'Restitution outcomes and probationers assessment of restitution: the effects of moral development', *Criminal Justice and Behavior*, 12: 259–87.

Von Hirsch, A., Ashworth, A. and Shearing C. (2003) 'Specifying aims and limits for restorative justice', in A. von Hirsch *et al.* (eds) *Restorative Justice and Criminal Justice: Competing or Reconcilable Paradigms?* Oxford: Hart Publishing.

Wilson, R. and Prinzo, M. (2001) 'Circles of support: a restorative justice initiative', in M.H. Miner and E. Coleman (eds) *Sex Offender Treatment: Accomplishments, Challenges, and Future Directions*. Binghamton, NY: Haworth Press.

Zehr, H. (2001) *Transcending: Reflections of Crime Victims*. Intercourse, PA: Good Books.

Chapter 14

Satisfying the needs and interests of victims

Christopher Bennett

This chapter approaches restorative justice from the point of view of moral philosophy. I am interested in the basic principles that underlie the elements of restorative justice (elements such as victim–offender interaction, reparation from offender to victim and collective decision-making about how to address the offence – elements most theorists agree are important parts of the restorative process) and those things which tie these elements into a unified narrative. This chapter is concerned with two questions: first, what responsibilities the offender has towards the victim of crime and, secondly, what responsibilities the state would have towards the victim, should restorative justice be adopted as the major form of criminal justice. I begin with a brief defence of my philosophical approach, arguing that if we look at what is owed to the victim we get a clearer idea of the principles behind restorative justice than if we look at victims' desires or needs. Next I draw on and elaborate Howard Zehr's understanding of crime and its effects, and on his view of what the offender owes to the victim. Finally I look at the possibility of state-sponsored restorative justice and ask what the state – or some other collective like a local community – has a responsibility to the victim to do to the offender.

What is owed to the victim of crime?

What do victims want from criminal justice? This question seems a fundamental one to restorative justice, which has often been thought of as a development of the victims' movement. It promises to move us away from a bureaucratic system of justice that has been designed for an abstract 'public interest' and to make it more democratic. It promises to take criminal justice out of the hands of lawyers, politicians and theorists and to put it back into the hands of the people (Wright 1991; Braithwaite 1998). Thus Heather Strang poses this question of what victims want and gives a list of six answers

(2002: ch. 1) – answers that she presents as coming from empirical research into victims' attitudes rather than her own moral views. Many will take this as a good example of the empowerment of victims and their justified influence over criminal justice theory and practice.

This focus on the victim's perspective and on what can be done to repair harm or wrong suffered is indisputably important. But there is also something to be said for considering the moral basis of restorative justice. Focusing solely on empirical studies of what victims want can suggest that criminal justice is being thought of as a service like any other commercial or public enterprise, with victims as its consumers and where 'the customer is always right'. However, a purely consumerist approach would be problematic, for there are many things that victims *may* want – or may say that they want – that proponents of restorative justice would not wish to endorse. For instance, sometimes victims are vindictive and vengeful: a victim might want something very harsh imposed on the offender. A victim of rape might demand that her offender be castrated. And yet, although some might accept that it is all right for the victim to express this demand in a conference as a cathartic way of communicating her feelings about the crime (cf. Zehr 1990: 191–2), acting out such feelings is not consistent with what many would take to be the aims of restoration.

This suggests that many theorists of restorative justice do not really accept that the customer is always right (Johnstone 2002: 70–1, 83–4). While 'consumers' are often thought of as having relatively fixed preferences they are looking to satisfy, one of the things that characterizes a lot of thinking about restorative justice is the idea that victims should approach the process with a reasonably *open* attitude. Therefore, in practice, restorative justice theorists tend to recognize that the victim's immediate judgement about what should happen is not infallible, and they see restorative justice as having an important role not just in *satisfying* but in *transforming* the victim's attitudes and desires. Therefore, if restorative justice indeed represents a turn to a more democratic model of justice, it is democracy not as the free market but as a process of dialogue that can change and enlighten us.

This suggests that restorative justice operates with a conception of what victims *reasonably* want or expect; that is, a conception of those attitudes that are consistent with the right spirit of participation in the process. This is not just an empirical question but a normative one, for it asks what attitudes and demands it is *appropriate* for victims to bring to the restorative process – in the way that we think vengefulness is *inappropriate*.[1]

I am concerned with what victims can reasonably expect from offenders in restorative justice, and with what victims can reasonably expect from the state if restorative justice were used by the state as part of a criminal justice system. Throughout, in discussing reasonable expectation, I use the sense of 'expectation' that implies a responsibility on someone else's part. Thus if I can reasonably expect the state to provide me with a decent pension on my retirement, then this does not mean – in the sense I am using it – just that it is *probable* that the state will provide me with such a thing. Indeed, that might be quite *improbable*. What I mean is that, whether or not it discharges it, the state *owes* me a decent pension. Therefore what I am asking about in this chapter is what the offender and the state owe to victims in restorative justice.

Now it might seem that this is an unusual approach: perhaps restorative justice theorists are more likely to talk in terms of what victims want than in terms of what is owed to them (though see Dignan 2005). However, at least some theorists recognize that, although it is in some way victim centred, restorative justice ought not to be victim centred in a consumerist way. For instance, in their 'Fundamental principles of restorative justice', Howard Zehr and Harry Mika talk about the *needs* of victims of crime for 'information, validation, vindication, restitution, testimony, safety, and support' (1998). The concept of need differs from the concept of desire because, although there are many things that I may *want* that can be trivial or actually detrimental to me, what I actually *need* is what is really important for me. Talking about needs allows Zehr and Mika to deny that offenders should be locked away for 30 years at a time even if the victim *thinks* that she would be best satisfied by that outcome. Yet they can still insist that restorative justice is victim centred.

Furthermore, there is a close connection between my talk of responsibilities and Zehr and Mika's talk of needs: if someone really needs something, then this is a fairly good reason to think that someone ought to provide him with it. However, talking about needs leaves it unclear exactly *how* and *by whom* that need is going to be catered for. Therefore I believe it is clearer and more illuminating to translate talk about victims' needs into talk about what one party owes to another.[2]

Hence I think that the moral philosophical approach of thinking of restorative justice as a structure of mutual responsibilities is a fruitful one. It is an improvement on the consumerist idea that one should seek to satisfy victims' wants whatever they might be. But it is also clearer than the idea that victims have certain needs. For, in giving an account of who is responsible for meeting which needs, we can get a deeper analysis of how restorative justice processes need to be designed in order to meet their fundamental aims. None of this is to say, of course, that finding out what victims want is unimportant. Rather, they provide the raw material for a moral argument about which such attitudes are reasonable, appropriate and consistent with the aims of restoration. The rise of victimology, in other words, does not make moral philosophy irrelevant; the two have to work together if we are to put forward the most adequate theory we can.

Zehr on crime and its effects

A theory of what victims need, or what is owed to them (and by whom), requires a theory of the damage done by crime. An influential account is provided by Howard Zehr:

crime is in essence a violation: a violation of the self, a desecration of who we are, of what we believe, of our private space. Crime is devastating because it upsets two fundamental assumptions on which we base our lives: our belief that the world is an orderly, meaningful place, and our belief in personal autonomy. Both assumptions are essential for wholeness (1990: 24).[3]

Crime, on Zehr's account, comes out of the blue and destroys our sense of order. We want to know why it happened and we want to know that it will not happen again. Positive answers to these questions are necessary in order to restore our sense that the world is an ordered, meaningful place. In crime, we are subjected to the will of another person: our freedom to decide for ourselves how to act within our private 'space' is taken away and another person decides what we will do without our consent.

This account of the nature of crime and its effects informs Zehr and Mika's view of what victims need from criminal justice. For instance, the victim may have undergone a fairly traumatic experience and she will perhaps fear that it is going to be repeated: she is suddenly alerted to the potential dangers hidden in any situation and it may be hard for her to maintain good judgement about when a situation is or is not a genuinely risky one.[4] Such a victim needs reassurance that she is safe and that the person who wronged her – or another person – will not do so again. She will need support in the sense that she might want someone to look after her in the immediate event of the crime and to lend a sympathetic ear to her distress. Furthermore, Zehr argues, she needs to understand why she became the victim, why the crime occurred and why it happened to her. She also needs to tell her own story about how the offence affected her and to have that story accepted and affirmed as important by other people (Zehr 1990: 27–8).

As we will see below, what we have said so far does not give the full picture of Zehr's profound understanding of crime and its effects. However, it is a good account of the material and psychological harms that crime can cause to victims and the steps that might be taken to address them. As it stands, though, there are two problems with this account – problems that, I will argue below, give us reason to switch our focus from 'repairing harms' to 'righting wrongs' (cf. Duff 2002; Hampton 1992). The first is that it does not explain how the harm caused by crime is different from that caused by illness. If I fall seriously ill, that might similarly disrupt my sense of the order in the world. I may similarly want to find out why it has happened, why it happened to me. And becoming seriously ill might also severely limit my autonomy: it can be like an external force that suddenly restricts my abilities to move and pursue my projects, and perhaps to think. What Zehr's account leaves out is the fundamental fact that, in crime, these harms are visited upon us more or less deliberately by another person; and this makes our feelings about crime and our reactions to it quite different (Johnstone 2002: 79–80).

The second problem is that Zehr's account of the victim's needs does not explain why the *offender* has to have a central role in meeting these needs. It is clearly central to Zehr's view that the victim's needs are met in part through a meeting in which the offender is held to account for his actions, and is given the chance to engage with his victim. But I am not sure that this is fully explained. Let us think briefly about how one might go about meeting these needs. Involving the offender is a risky strategy which may or may not be helpful, depending on the offender's means to give restitution and his willingness to co-operate. Why should the victim open herself up to the risk of further abuse from her offender?

If Zehr's account of crime and its effects is at all right, then victims need some kind of care. They need to be assured that they are safe from a repeat of the crime, perhaps because the threat from the offender has been removed – say because the offender has been incapacitated – or because someone is looking after them and will prevent anything like that happening to them again. They need someone to listen to them expressing their deep feelings about the crime and to have these feelings affirmed as important. They may need restitution. It might seem that the best way for victims to meet these needs would be to gather together into networks of mutual support and protection with people who understand what they have been through and who are strongly motivated to prevent it happening again (see Johnstone 2002: 79 on 'clubbing together'). Furthermore, if there is a need for significant restitution, then this could be funded either by a state compensation fund or else by private insurance as it is with many non-criminal damages (Barnett 1977). It is hard to see why, in meeting *these* needs, the offender has to be involved.

However, as I said above, the account of crime given earlier does not fully represent Zehr's position. Elsewhere he suggests that, as well as safety and security, information and validation and so on, victims need *vindication* (Zehr 1990: 194); and he suggests that victims can want 'restitution, not just for the material recovery involved but for the moral statement implied in the recognition that the act was wrong and in the attempt to make things right' (1990: 28). Furthermore, he returns to his claim that crime is 'at its core a violation of a person by another person' and explains that 'It is a violation of the just relationship that should exist between individuals' (1990: 182). These remarks give us the key, I believe, to what is distinctive about crime. In what follows I will suggest that victims need to be vindicated because the harm they have suffered has been deliberately caused to them by another person. I will argue that apology is an apt way of vindicating the victim, and that this explains why the offender has to be involved in the process and has to be held to account in it.

What does the offender owe to the victim?

Zehr's account of crime as a violation of just relationships is in some ways similar to the account of what we class as moral wrongdoing given by some moral philosophers. The claim made by these philosophers is that what is central to wrongdoing is not so much the material harm that it causes to the victims but rather the *attitude* towards the victim that it expresses (Swinburne 1989: 81–2). For instance, Peter Strawson, in his paper

'Freedom and resentment', points out that, as social beings, we expect, and are concerned that we receive, a certain degree of goodwill or regard from others (1982: 62–3). Strawson understands some of our basic emotional reactions as responses to people either showing us or failing to show us the goodwill we expect. In a telling example, he points out that my reaction to someone standing on my hand is likely to be very different depending on whether I think that he did it by accident or whether I think he meant it, even if the material harm that is caused in the two cases is exactly the same (1982: 63). If I think it was an accident then I do not think he expressed any hostile attitude towards me. However, if I think that a hostile attitude has been expressed then I will think that I have been, not just harmed, but *wronged*; that is, that I have been deliberately treated in violation of the usual standards of respect and goodwill.

This insight into the difference between harming someone and wronging her has been developed by Jeffrie Murphy and Jean Hampton, who both understand the latter as being characterized by the attitude towards the victim that is being expressed (1988). Murphy tries to capture what is central about the attitude expressed in crime or wrongdoing as follows:

> One reason we so deeply resent moral injuries is not simply that they hurt us in some tangible or sensible way; it is because such injuries are also messages – symbolic communications. They are ways a wrongdoer has of saying to us, 'I count but you do not', 'I can use you for my purposes', or 'I am up here high and you are there down below'. Intentional wrongdoing insults us and attempts (sometimes successfully) to degrade us – and thus it involves a kind of injury that is not merely tangible and sensible. It is a moral injury, and we care about such injuries (1988: 25).

What Murphy assumes here is that, really, we take ourselves to be in an important sense equal: equal in rights, equal in the basic respect that we are due. In wronging me, a person effectively denies this equality, treating me as someone whom she can use as she wishes.

What defines crime or wrongdoing, on these accounts, is not so much the material or sensible harm it causes to the victim as the attitude expressed by the wrongdoer: what Murphy calls the moral injury. A moral injury consists in being treated as if you do not really count. Of course, the wrongdoer *may* harm the victim as well. But the reason the harm counts as crime is that, as Zehr himself puts it, it is a *violation* of another person. It is a way of treating the other person as if he does not really count. Crime and wrongdoing, on this view, are a violation of something that is in some way sacred: a human being's right to basic respect.[5]

This account of wrongdoing suggests that one need that victims might have – as well as needs for safety, security and sympathy – is that the moral injury be addressed. If we ask what might address the experience of having been treated as if you do not count, then the answer could be, as Zehr says, vindication:

[victims] need to know that what happened to them was wrong and undeserved and that others recognize this as wrong. They need to know that something has been done to correct the wrong and to reduce the chances of its recurrence. They want to hear others acknowledge their pain and validate their experience (1990: 191).

Thus a victim centred form of justice ought to be concerned, not just with relieving harm but with 'righting wrongs' (Hampton 1992). Victims need to be vindicated in such a way that the fact that they were wronged – and not merely the fact they were harmed – is undone. Now this is a hard thing to think about (Johnstone 2002: 103). If it is material harm that we are talking about then we have a good idea what would count as repairing the harm. Even if in some cases it might be physically impossible to repair a particular harm, we have a conception of what it is materially to break something and what it is to repair it, just like repairing a car. However, we do not always have a clear conception of how a wrong is to be righted, particularly because it seems quite correct to say that wrongs, once done, cannot be undone. This leads many to declare the very idea nonsensical and to concentrate on supposedly clearer, more empirical notions, such as that of repairing material or psychological harm.

However, the Murphy/Strawson account of what bothers us about wrongdoing seems to get at something important. We can explain what this is by looking at the notion of *relationships*. Zehr himself does this, explaining that the Hebrew term *shalom* signifies a sense of living rightly in common with others, in the correct relationship with them (1990: 130–2). What he is talking about is a concern for whether our relationships are *good* relationships, whether they are as such relationships ought to be. Now one way of understanding what it means for relationships to be as they ought is to appeal to ideas we have already discussed. Strawson talks about relationships as being structured by the expectations of goodwill or regard that the parties have of each other. Murphy talks about the responsibilities that we have towards one another to treat others as equals and not to impose ourselves on others as though we were their natural superiors. Both these accounts involve some notion of right relationship, meaning a relationship that goes well because and in so far as the parties treat each other as they ought to be treated. Strawson and Murphy point the way to making secular sense of *shalom*.

If this is plausible, then we could say that what moral injury consists of is damage to a relationship between the offender and victim.[6] This is to say that, when the relationship between two people is a good one, each person respects his responsibility to treat the other in a certain way (as an equal, say, not as a mere resource). However, what exists between victim and offender in the aftermath of crime is a bad, unhealthy or damaged relationship in which one party has attempted to subjugate the other. Note that this is the case even if no relationship existed between the two prior to the crime. For, as a result of the crime, they certainly have a relationship now (1990: 81–2). We have an idea of what a relationship between two such people would be like if it was a good relationship (these two people, after all, even if strangers, share a neighbourhood, are fellow citizens, are fellow human beings – and have certain responsibilities to one another as a result). This allows us to understand what it means to say that the relationship that exists between them is bad or damaged even if there was no prior good relationship that actually *was* damaged. In other words, what exists between them now is, in Murphy's terms, a relationship in which one party is superior and the other inferior, and this is a bad relationship because relations between the two ought to show equality.

We can get some idea of what it is to right a wrong through the notion that the offender has a responsibility to repair the relationship and make it good again. However, this notion of repairing a relationship may seem just as obscure as the notion of restoring a wrong. It may be, for instance, that after the restorative justice process the victim and the offender will not continue to see each other. Or it might be that, no matter what the offender does by way of restoration, his victim will always hate him. In these cases it might seem highly artificial to say that their relationship has been restored.

I think that the best way to understand this point is to distinguish between the *moral* and *empirical* state of a relationship (Duff 2002: 86–7). A relationship's empirical state consists of how the participants actually get on, whether they are on good terms and so on. But the moral state of the relationship depends on whether or to what extent the participants treat each other as they should. Thus a relationship that is based on deception might (empirically) be one in which the parties get on very well: they get on well, however, only because one party is not aware of the bad moral state of their relationship, of how she is being deceived or exploited by the other. If we can make this distinction we can say that what an offender has a responsibility to do is to restore the relationship in the moral sense, even though this might not be enough actually to put him back on good terms with his victim.

So how does one restore a relationship in this moral sense? What has damaged the relationship, on the account being developed here, lies in the attitude of the offender and in the expression of that attitude – the message sent out – in the offender's action against the victim. That attitude and its expression are incompatible with a good relationship, with the relationship being as it ought. In order for the relationship to be restored, the offender's attitude has to change – he has to recognize that he has responsibilities to his victim, responsibilities that he violated in his treatment of her – and he has to 'take back' or retract the message that he sent out in his action. In other words, he has to admit that what he did was wrong. If this happens then the relationship can be considered as restored. Whether or not the parties choose to pursue or further the relationship, the important thing is that it does not continue to exist in its damaged state, with one party claiming to be superior over the other.

It is because the offender's admission of wrongdoing is essential to righting the wrong and restoring the relationship between the offender and victim that writers like Zehr talk about the importance of repentance (cf. Duff 2001: 107–8). When a person *repents* of a wrong she rejects it, in the sense that she accepts that it was wrong and that it came from her;

and she repudiates that aspect of herself – the weakness or failing – that caused it to occur (Swinburne 1989: 82–3). Now repentance may seem to be a strictly theological concept, and those wishing to establish restorative justice in a multicultural society might be wary of it. However, the admission of wrongdoing and the retraction of the offence involved in repentance also characterize our understanding of a sincerely meant *apology*. Erving Goffman describes a full apology as follows:

> in its fullest form, the apology has several elements: expression of embarrassment or chagrin; clarification that one knows what conduct had been expected and sympathizes with the application of negative sanction; verbal rejection, repudiation and disavowal of the wrong way of behaving along with the vilification of the self that so behaved; espousal of the right way and an avowal henceforth to pursue that course; performance of penance and the volunteering of restitution (1971: 113).[7]

For Goffman, apology has several elements – admission of wrongdoing and repudiation of what is bad in oneself; determination not to do wrong in the future; making of amends both symbolically and materially – all of which have something to do with coming to see one's action as something one should not have done. The person who makes a sincere apology has come to see her victim as a person who deserves better treatment; she is pained by the thought that she wronged him, because she now sees him as an important autonomous person who is in important respects the same as her and who needs to be given the same consideration she would wish for herself; furthermore, she is disappointed in herself, that she should have failed to treat him with greater respect; and she is moved to do what she can to make things good.

A sincere apology can right the wrong and restore the relationship. This is because it involves retracting the attitude to the victim that the offence expressed. However, in order for this retracting to take place, the offender has to show that she really understands what was wrong about what she did. She has to repudiate it for the right reasons, showing that she now understands that her victim deserved better. She therefore has to show that she understands the seriousness of what she did. And in order to show that she understands its seriousness not only has she to do what she can to remove the bad effects of what she has done but also offer more symbolic amends for her wrong. To illustrate this claim, consider a mundane case in which I have forgotten my spouse's birthday. In order to make it up for her, I might feel that I have to buy her, not just the present which she should have got anyway, but something further in order to say sorry. I might feel that I have to do something for her that I would not normally have needed to do, just to show that I am sorry. I have to do something that involves some sacrifice on my part in order to put things right. This is what I interpret Goffman to mean by 'performance of penance'.

Furthermore, what I do for her – the sacrifice that I am willing to make – will reveal how sorry I am, or how bad I think it was that I forgot her birthday. For instance, if I offer to do the dishes for her then I am sorry, but I don't think I've done anything very bad; if I buy her a bunch of flowers then I am taking it a bit more seriously; if I offer to do all the housework for a week then maybe I indicate that I think of what I have done as requiring a fairly significant response to put right. Although it is very hard to quantify degrees of seriousness of wrongdoing, I take it that there is an important general point here that seems to underpin our practice of saying sorry. This is that we assume that there is some *proportionality* between the seriousness of what we do in wronging someone and the sacrifice that has to be made to put it right. My spouse might be disappointed if I saw no need for 'penance', or if what I did was not very much: whether or not she would be justified in her judgement, what her disappointment shows is that she takes it that what I am prepared to do reveals how seriously I take what I have done (Duff 2002: 94–5).[8]

It is in these mundane situations of saying sorry, therefore, that we find the intuitive basis of the principle of proportionality that has proved so controversial in the debate between proponents of restorative justice and desert theorists.[9] The thought that the punishment should fit the crime has its basis, if I am right, in the thought that what you have to do to show that you are properly sorry for an offence is proportional to how bad the offence was. However, if I am right to see the practice of saying sorry as essential to the nature of apology, and to see apology as underpinning restorative justice, then there are grounds for thinking that proportionality is something its proponents should welcome rather than reject. Restorative justice, in its concern for restoring relationships, ought to be concerned with righting wrongs and vindicating victims. The way in which this is done – according to our informal practice outside criminal justice – is through apology and proportionate amends. Thus proponents of restorative justice ought to recognize at least some truth in the point of view of those who argue in favour of proportionality.

What I have given in this section is an account of what the offender owes to the victim. I have argued that the fundamental thing that he owes is vindication or repentance: the retraction and repudiation of the claim, expressed in his action, that the victim is his inferior and can be used to his own ends. It is this repentance that allows the relationship between the two to be put to rights: through repentance the offender reaffirms the victim's equality and acknowledges how wrong of him it was to deny it. His repentance is expressed in apology and proportionate reparation. This account explains what it means to say that crime is a violation and in what sense there can be symbolic reparation for such a crime. It also explains in what sense it is important to restore the relationship between victim and offender.

What does the state owe to the victim to do to the offender?

The account I have given so far explains the open-mindedness restorative justice asks of victims but also explains in what sense victims can reasonably expect something from offenders. Restorative justice asks victims to be open to the offender in the sense of engaging with him in a dialogue that aims to get him to understand and accept what was wrong about what he did. The victim has to be prepared to work *with* the offender in some respects in order to get to this point. Vindictive or vengeful responses, on the other hand, lack this openness because they are simply concerned with doing something *to* the wrongdoer – imposing something *on* him. However, if it makes sense to enter into a dialogue with the offender about how what he did was wrong, then it is also reasonable for the victim to expect that, when called to account, he will understand, admit his offence and offer to make proportionate amends.

The focus on saying sorry ties restorative justice to what is a widely shared and intuitive sense of justice: a sense of what offenders owe others as a result of their offence. It explains why restorative justice is often put forward as a more meaningful form of justice for participants than conventional criminal justice. However, we must now think about how restorative justice is to relate to that conventional system. Is it offered as an alternative to that system, which will run alongside it but without interacting with it? Or should restorative justice be thought of, in the end, as a better candidate for dispensing criminal justice than the current model?

Keeping restorative justice separate would allow the restorative ideal to be left uncontaminated by the different needs and purposes that drive state criminal justice. However, I suggest that this purity would be achieved at the cost of failing properly to challenge the supremacy of the conventional system. For, presumably if restorative justice is considered as operating purely outside the state system, then the conventional state system will continue to claim authority over citizens as before. But the restorative ideal of justice, if valid, shows the conventional system to be seriously *un*just: it clearly lacks the transformative, dialogic possibilities of restorative justice and seems to encourage offenders to deny responsibility rather than offering apologies or making meaningful amends. It seems important, then, to think about how the problematic features of the central system might be removed and the restorative model used to replace or at any rate significantly reform the present system. Whatever compromises or separations might be needed in the short term, it is important for restorative justice practitioners to have a model of what restorative justice would look like if it had to cope with the demands placed on the present system (Van Ness 2002: 147).

When this question of restorative justice becoming more mainstream is raised, it is often asked whether criminal justice should remain in centralized state control or whether it ought to be devolved to local communities (cf. Van Ness 2002). However, I want to raise a critical question about formal or centralized restorative justice that arises whether it is the state or some more local community authority that dispenses justice. It asks: why is it the business of the collective whether or not the offender apologizes or makes amends to his victim? Why is this something in which the state (or local community) has a legitimate interest?[10]

This problem is raised because the centralized system of criminal justice in a modern society will almost certainly be coercive. What I want to know is whether coercing offenders to take part in restorative justice is legitimate. If restorative justice is to become a fundamental part of the way a society does justice, we have to know how it will deal with recalcitrant (alleged) offenders who may not be willing to attend a conference or who, even if they do attend, may refuse to admit that they are in the wrong. This class of defendants may range from those who callously do not care; to those who conscientiously believe that what they have done is no crime; to those who are genuinely innocent. How far can it be right to compel such individuals to participate in restorative justice processes against their will?

A common answer to this question is to invoke something like Braithwaite's 'enforcement pyramid', according to which involvement in restorative justice is voluntary but offenders are subject to a harsher alternative if they refuse to take part (1999: 61). Coercion might in the end be necessary, but processes will be preferable and more restorative if participants attend through their own free choice (Van Ness 2002: 134). However, although it might look as though this set-up preserves the offender's freedom of choice, it is not clear that the choice is genuinely free when the offender who refuses to comply with restorative justice will be penalized by being subjected to a harsher alternative (Ashworth 2002). My question is then raised: by what right does the collective penalize an offender for refusing to restore his relationship with the victim? Why is the relationship between offender and victim the business of the collective at all?

The problem of whether the collective has the authority to coerce an offender into a restorative process arises because apologizing could well be regarded as a matter of conscience for the offender.[11] Traditionally, liberal theorists have insisted that there is a limit on the extent to which the collective has a right to intervene in citizens' lives to settle matters of 'private' morality. Appealing to some understanding of J.S. Mill's Harm Principle,[12] such theorists have claimed that citizens ought to be regarded as having a sphere of freedom of conscience and action that can only be invaded when doing so is necessary to prevent significant harm to others.[13] There seems to be a conflict between this liberal stance and the claim that some collective has the right to compel someone to apologize for his wrongs.

Furthermore, this problem is not fixed by saying that it is the local community that will be intervening in the offender's life rather than the state. The local community is not the offender's family: it is not clear why it should have rights over him that differ markedly from those that the state has. Therefore the problem of the authority of the collective over the individual with regard to matters of conscience like apologizing recurs for the local community as it does for the state.

I will look at three sorts of responses to this problem. The first would be to take the anti-liberal position and assert that it *is* the legitimate business of the collective whether or not the offender restores his relationship with the victim. However, for many this assumes too intimate a relation between community (or state) and individual, as though the communal authority had the paternalistic job of making sure individuals met all their moral responsibilities. Many today believe that the state has to leave room for individual autonomy, for individuals to make their own decisions unforced, even if sometimes what they decide to do is wrong. A comparable example might be thinking about whether the collective has any right to enforce marital fidelity: it might be argued that, even on the assumption that such infidelity is morally wrong, it is none of the collective's business to police it.

However, any rejection of the anti-liberal position has implications for what victims can reasonably expect from state-sponsored restorative justice. For, although we have said that victims should expect an apology and proportionate amends from offenders, we have now seen grounds for thinking that there is a limit to the extent to which the state can pursue this goal on the victim's behalf. However, I will suggest below that there is a sense in which the collective can require some sort of apologetic action from the offender.

The second response would be to deny that the collective should ever take a coercive role in restorative justice, and to claim that all it can do is to facilitate an interaction between victim and offender if the two parties are willing. This is to take the view that, because coerced apology is out of the question, there is no legitimate role for coercion in restorative justice. Hence the voluntary nature of the process is to be preserved at all costs in order to encourage the offender to comply spontaneously and sincerely with his responsibility to apologize and make things right.[14]

However, the problem with leaving it up to the offender whether the offence is addressed is that it treats the offence as a private matter between him and the victim. Now, although it is of course true that these two are at the epicentre of the events and have the greatest stake in the process, we should not think that the offence is no concern of the community in general. The community in general – including many people who have never met the victim before – ought, where the offence is a serious one, to express its concern at what she has suffered and to demonstrate its solidarity with her. Indeed, the community in general has a role in vindicating the victim by asserting that what was done to her was unacceptable. This suggests that the offence against the victim is not just a matter for the offender and victim to decide upon and that it is inappropriate to treat the offender's participation as a voluntary matter.

This suggests a third response to the problem. R.A. Duff and other 'censure' theorists of punishment have argued that we ought to subscribe to the notion of crime as a 'public wrong' – a wrongful action in which (unlike the case of marital fidelity) the community as a whole legitimately takes an interest (Duff 2001: 61). It sends out the opposite message – a message of indifference – if the community does not stand up against the abusive treatment of victims, if it treats it as a private matter between victim and offender. Duff might say that through his crime the offender has damaged his relationship, not just with the victim, but with the collective (cf. Morris 1981): this would be the case, for instance, if the collective as a whole is concerned (as it should be) that its members respect one another's basic rights. In demanding that the offender appear at the meeting – in coercing him – the community vindicates the victim by making it clear that the attitude of superiority to the victim expressed in the offence cannot be allowed to stand: it makes it clear that the offender has to retract it. He has to retract it, as we saw above, by apologizing and making proportionate amends.

This position differs, however, from the anti-liberal view that the collective ought to intervene to ensure that the offender restores his relationship with the victim. It answers the question of why the offender's relationship with the victim is any of the collective's business by claiming that the reason the collective condemns is because the offence changes the offender's relationship with the community as a whole – and that is something that is the collective's business. It can therefore demand that the offender restore his relationship with the collective by requiring him to retract the symbolic message expressed in his offence. He can be required – on Duff's view of punishment as secular penance – to make amends proportionate to the seriousness of his public wrong.

However, the question of freedom of conscience is still to be addressed: is it any business of the collective what the offender really thinks about his offence (von Hirsch 1993: 74)? Should not the process respect unrepentant offenders (offenders, after all, who may have been wrongfully accused or conscientiously disagree that what they did was wrong)? The collective, on Duff's view, owes it to the victim to vindicate her by demanding an apology from the offender. But if it is to respect the liberal concern for freedom of conscience, it has to do so in a way that allows the offender to disagree that the apology is necessary. Therefore the collective, though it can vindicate the victim by compelling the offender to listen to the case for an apology and to make sufficient amends, ought not to compel him actually to apologize *as though he meant it*. For this reason Duff has recently talked about the offender being required to undergo an 'apologetic ritual' (2001: 110–11). The idea is that, if the apology is made ritualistic, then the offender can be required to undertake some apologetic action, but which he can perform adequately whether or not he *is* genuinely repentant, thereby preserving his freedom to disagree. On this view, what it takes for the offender to restore his relationship with the collective is that he undergo the ritual, regardless of whether he does so sincerely or not (for further discussion of this idea, see Bennett forthcoming).[15]

In such a case the victim might be in a position in which, though she has been vindicated by the collective, the offender has remained unrepentant. But if the offender has done all that the collective can legitimately require him to do, she might have to accept that, although she is still entitled to an apology from him, the collective can do nothing more to ensure that she gets one. In this case, the victim's relationship with the offender exhibits a sort of schizophrenia. As a member of the collective, she has to regard the offender as having restored his relationship with her; but as the direct victim of his offence, she still, quite rightly, expects more. This is an unfortunate outcome, though a familiar one, stemming from the limitations of what victims can reasonably expect from state-sponsored restorative justice.

Conclusion

What do victims want from restorative justice? In this chapter I have argued that we should talk, not so much about what victims want but about what they rightly feel entitled to in the wake of an offence. I have argued that they rightly feel entitled to vindication from the offender, in which a wrong is retracted by the offender through apology and proportionate amends. However, victims are also entitled to the vindication from their community. The community should also declare its intolerance of the offender's action and the message it conveys. However, while the offender's relationship with the victim can only be restored by a sincere apology, the collective cannot require sincere apology – at least not if we accept the liberal view that such things should be left to the individual's own conscience. Therefore what it takes to restore the offender's relationship with the collective has to be thought of as something less, such as the making of proportionate amends regardless of the spirit in which this is carried out.

Selected further reading

Morris, H. (1981) 'A paternalistic theory of punishment', *American Philosophical Quarterly*, 18: 263–71. By putting forward an account of punishment, Morris makes many points that restorative justice theorists should appreciate about how punishment can reconcile and restore.

Duff, R.A. (2002) 'Restorative punishment and punitive restoration', in L. Walgrave (ed.) *Restorative Justice and the Law*. Cullompton: Willan Publishing. Duff attempts to reconcile punishment and restorative justice by suggesting that punishment, properly carried out, should have a restorative element, and that restoration, properly carried out, should have a punitive element.

Tavuchis, N. (1991) *Mea Culpa: A Sociology of Apology and Reconciliation*. Stanford, CA: Stanford University Press. One of the few in-depth works on apology, this book suggests that saying sorry has an almost magical power to restore relations after wrongdoing.

Ashworth, A. (2002) 'Responsibilities, rights and restorative justice', *British Journal of Criminology*, 42: 578–95. This paper asks tough questions about whether restorative justice can respect some of the important values that (ideally) underpin criminal justice.

Notes

1 In Strang (2002: ch. 1), one suspects that the author has already 'filtered out' those victims' desires that she finds inappropriate or incompatible with restorative justice, rather than giving us an unadulterated picture of what victims say they want. My claim is not that this is a mistake, but simply that it should alert us to the fact that the issues here involve moral as well as empirical questions.

2 I should make it clear that this is not a criticism of Zehr, who often writes as though he shares my approach (see 1990: 196–9; see also Zehr and Mika 1998, whose principle 2.0 states: 'Violations create obligations and liabilities'), so much as an attempt at clarification. My aim is to clarify the relation between

talking about needs and talking about obligations (that a genuine need gives a *prima facie* reason to think *someone* has an obligation, though it does not in itself explain who) and to defend the need for these terms and the moral philosophical approach they entail.

3 Cf. Weisstub (cited in Strang 2002: 2).

4 A note on gendered pronouns. I find it awkward always to use 'they' when discussing cases of people who are really meant to be gender neutral. I have found it easier to use 'him' and 'her', but have tried to do so more or less randomly.

5 Because our concern is with what is owed to victims, we are looking at a rather victim centred account of crime. However, it is clear that not all crimes will fit this account. For instance, not all crimes (such as tax evasion) have individual victims. In response, Murphy might argue that there is still a sense in which the tax evader acts as though he is a superior and is not bound by the rules everyone else has to live by. But it is not the case that the tax evader violates the basic respect due to another individual human being. Thus Zehr's account of crime would need to be extended or revised in order to cover all criminal acts.

6 Cf. crime is 'a violation of the just relationship that should exist between individuals' (Zehr 1990: 182).

7 For more on apology, see Tavuchis (1991) and Bottoms (2003).

8 For more on the view given in the previous three paragraphs, see Bennett (2002).

9 Cf. for instance, Braithwaite and Pettit (1990: ch. 7) and von Hirsch (1993: ch. 3).

10 This is a version of a point made (against his own earlier views) by Jeffrie Murphy (1992).

11 This seems to be the principle behind, for example, von Hirsch's objection to 'compulsory attitudinizing', (see von Hirsch 1993: 83 and, for further discussion, Bennett 2006).

12 'That the only purpose for which power can rightfully be exercised over any member of a civilised community, against his will, is to prevent harm to others … The only part of the conduct of any one, for which he is amenable to society, is that which concerns others. In the part which merely concerns himself his independence is, of right, absolute. Over himself, over his own body and mind, the individual is sovereign' (Mill 1991: 14).

13 For some discussion, see Richards (1989).

14 This seems to be the standard position in the restorative justice literature. See, for instance, the 'Declaration of Leuven' (proposition 4/2): 'The offender cannot be involved in any voluntary restorative process unless he or she freely accepts the accountability for the harm caused by the offence'. However, many theorists would assume that we can understand 'freely accept' as compatible with 'accepts in order to avoid a harsher alternative'. I have raised the question of whether this is really legitimate.

15 It is not clear that this position, though quite different from that typically associated with restorative justice, is really different from that of Howard Zehr: '[P]ersons often will not willingly assume their responsibilities. One of the reasons many offenders get into trouble is a lack of certain kinds of responsibility. One cannot overcome such irresponsibility quickly. What society *can* say to offenders, then, is simple: "You have done wrong by violating someone. You have an obligation to make that wrong right. You may choose to do so willingly, and we will allow you to be involved in figuring out how this should be done. If you do not choose to accept this responsibility, however, we will have to decide for you what needs to be done and will require you to do it"' (1990: 198).

References

Ashworth, A. (2002) 'Responsibilities, rights and restorative justice', *British Journal of Criminology*, 42: 578–95.

Barnett, R. (1977) 'Restitution: a new paradigm of criminal justice', *Ethics*, 87: 279–301.

Bennett, C. (2002) 'The varieties of retributive experience', *Philosophical Quarterly*, 52: 145–63.

Bennett, C. (2006) 'Taking the sincerity out of saying sorry: restorative justice as ritual', *Journal of Applied Philosophy*, 23: 127–43.

Bottoms, A. (2003) 'Some sociological reflections on restorative justice', in A. von Hirsch *et al.* (eds) *Restorative Justice and Criminal Justice: Competing or Reconcilable Paradigms?* Oxford: Hart Publishing.

Braithwaite, J. (1998) 'Restorative justice', in M. Tonry (ed.) *The Handbook of Crime and Punishment*. Oxford: Oxford University Press.

Braithwaite, J. (1999) 'Restorative justice: assessing optimistic and pessimistic accounts', *Crime and Justice: A Review of Research*, 25: 1–110.

Braithwaite, J. and Pettit, P. (1990) *Not Just Deserts: A Republican Theory of Criminal Justice*. Oxford: Clarendon Press.

Dignan, J. (2005) *Understanding Victims and Restorative Justice*. Maidenhead: Open University Press.

Duff, R.A. (2001) *Punishment, Communication and Community*. Oxford: Oxford University Press.

Duff, R.A. (2002) 'Restorative punishment and punitive restoration' in L. Walgrave (ed.) *Restorative Justice and the Law*. Cullompton: Willan Publishing.

Goffman, E. (1971) 'Remedial Interchanges', in *Relations in Public*. London: Allen Lane.

Hampton, J. (1992) 'Correcting harms versus righting wrongs: the goal of retribution', *UCLA Law Review*, 39: 1659–702.

International Network for Research on Restorative Justice for Juveniles (1997) 'Declaration of Leuven on the advisability of promoting the restorative approach to juvenile crime', in G. Johnstone (ed.) (2003) *A Restorative Justice Reader: Texts, Sources, Contexts*. Cullompton: Willan Publishing.

Johnstone, G. (2002) *Restorative Justice: Ideas, Values, Debates*. Cullompton: Willan Publishing.

Mill, J.S. (1991) 'On Liberty', in J. Gray (ed.) *On Liberty and Other Essays*. Oxford: Oxford University Press.

Morris, H. (1981) 'A paternalistic theory of punishment', *American Philosophical Quarterly*, 18: 263–71.

Murphy, J.G. (1988) 'Forgiveness and resentment', in J.G. Murphy and J. Hampton (eds) *Forgiveness and Mercy*. Cambridge: Cambridge University Press.

Murphy, J.G. (1992) 'Retributivism, moral education and the liberal state,' in *Retribution Reconsidered: More Essays in the Philosophy of Law*. London: Kluwer.

Murphy, J.G. and Hampton, J. (eds) (1988) *Forgiveness and Mercy*. Cambridge: Cambridge University Press.

Richards, D.A.J. (1989) 'Autonomy in law', in J. Christman (ed.) *The Inner Citadel: Essays on Individual Autonomy*, Oxford: Oxford University Press.

Strang, H. (2002) *Repair or Revenge: Victims and Restorative Justice*. Oxford: Clarendon Press.

Strawson, P.F. (1982) 'Freedom and resentment', in G. Watson (ed.) *Free Will*. Oxford: Oxford University Press.

Swinburne, R. (1989) *Responsibility and Atonement*. Oxford: Clarendon Press.

Tavuchis, N. (1991) *Mea Culpa: A Sociology of Apology and Reconciliation*. Stanford CA: Stanford University Press.

Van Ness, D. (2002) 'Creating restorative systems', in L. Walgrave (ed.) *Restorative Justice and the Law*. Cullompton: Willan Publishing.

von Hirsch, A. (1993) *Censure and Sanctions*. Oxford: Oxford University Press.

Wright, M. (1991) *Justice for Victims and Offenders*. Milton Keynes: Open University Press.

Zehr, H. (1990) *Changing Lenses*. Scottsdale, PA: Herald Press.

Zehr, H. and Mika, H. (1998) 'Fundamental principles of restorative justice', *Contemporary Justice Review*, 1: 47–55.

Part 4

Restorative Justice in Social Context

Gerry Johnstone and Daniel W. Van Ness

Part 4 explores how restorative justice is being developed in various social contexts. The first three chapters consider its initial setting – in juvenile and adult criminal justice – as well as its use in associated institutions, such as the police and prisons. The next chapter examines another institutional context in which experiments in restorative justice have particularly flourished of late: schools. The final two chapters shift the focus to the role of restorative justice in truth commissions designed to deal with gross violations of human rights in transitional regimes and to the development of restorative justice as a response to terrorism and religious violence. Throughout, the emphasis is not only on how restorative justice has been applied – and adapted to apply – in these various settings, but also on how restorative justice can play a role in transforming the nature of controlling institutions and on how the idea of restorative justice has itself been developed as a result of efforts to address a wider range of problems than juvenile and adult offending.

In Chapter 15, James Dignan – using the UK (which itself contains a number of distinct legal systems) as an illustrative study – explores the various ways in which restorative processes are used in juvenile and adult criminal justice. He distinguishes not only between the different stages of a criminal justice process at which restorative justice might be used, but also the different ways in which it can be brought into play (e.g. as an adjunct to sentencing, as a post-sentencing intervention and so on). A crucial issue addressed by Dignan is that of what factors facilitate or impede the use of restorative justice initiatives within criminal justice. In this context, he points in particular to the major adjustments which criminal justice agencies will need to make in their working cultures and practices if restorative justice is to become part of the mainstream response to crime.

One criminal justice agency in which there has been a lot of interest in restorative justice is the police. In Chapter 16, Carolyn Hoyle explains the nature of this interest through a survey of the development of police-led restorative justice from the now renowned experiments with police-facilitated conferencing in Wagga Wagga, New South Wales through to contemporary schemes in the UK and North America. Hoyle goes on to analyse the debates that have emerged alongside police-led restorative justice, in which forceful critiques of police involvement in conferencing have been countered by equally fervent arguments pointing to the benefits of police facilitation and to evidence that the risks – while real enough – can be managed. While one strand of criticism focuses upon the tensions between 'cop culture' and the values of restorative justice, Hoyle also addresses a question of significant interest: how police involvement in restorative justice is itself related to changes in the occupational culture of policing.

Daniel Van Ness, in Chapter 17, reviews recent attempts to use restorative justice in the context of a prison and a related debate about whether it is possible to conceive of a restorative prison regime. Van Ness shows how, despite a range of practical obstacles, numerous restorative justice initiatives are taking place in prison, instigated by – among others – prisoners themselves, government officials and community groups. These programmes have a range of objectives, some of them fairly modest, others highly ambitious. The most ambitious programmes – which talk of a 'virtuous' or 'restorative' prison – raise important questions about whether incarceration is itself compatible with the key values of restorative justice, such as voluntariness and respect. Van Ness identifies the issues and complexities of this debate and suggests that, in order to think through the issues more clearly, it might be helpful to think of restorative justice as a multi-dimensional concept (as outlined in Chapter 1 of the *Handbook*).

One of the obstacles to the creation of a society in which restorative justice is the routine response to criminal wrongdoing is that, from an early age, children are so familiar with authoritative punishment that they come to think of it as the natural response to any wrongdoing. Hence, for many proponents, if the restorative justice movement is to succeed in its goal, it needs to introduce restorative approaches into the broader field of social control, rather than presenting it only as a response to crime. Experiments with restorative justice in schools – which are the subject of Chapter 18 by Brenda Morrison – therefore have a crucial role to play in the campaign for restorative criminal justice, as well as being important in their own right. Morrison provides a survey of existing initiatives with restorative justice in schools, and describes how they dovetail with other initiatives such as those designed to promote social and emotional intelligence. Her chapter points, in particular, to one of the most interesting features of these initiatives: the progress of restorative justice in schools from early experiments with conferencing as a response to fairly serious incidents of wrongdoing to the development of a continuum of policies and practices resulting in some cases in a 'whole-school approach' in which all aspects of regulation in schools are approached restoratively.

The focus shifts, in Chapter 19, to the role of restorative justice ideas, practices and values in truth commissions designed to respond to collective violence, state-sponsored atrocities and gross human rights abuse. As

Jennifer Llewellyn points out, truth commissions have been regarded by some critics as, at worst, a means of sacrificing justice in order to achieve peace and stability and, at best, as a 'second best' form of justice when the ideal of trials and punishments is not possible or regarded as a threat to future reconciliation. However, the discourse of restorative justice has provided defenders of truth commissions with concepts with which they can defend truth commissions *in justice terms* – i.e. as methods of achieving a richer form of justice than is likely to emerge from reliance on trials and punishments alone. In Llewellyn's account, 'restorative justice' must function as more than a rhetorical device to support the work of truth commissions. Rather, there would be much value in bringing restorative justice theory and practice to bear on the actual design of truth commissions. A more explicit understanding of truth commissions as vehicles of restorative justice would benefit both truth commissions and the development of the theory of restorative justice.

In Chapter 20, Christopher Marshall expands the horizons of thinking about the applications of restorative justice even further by asking what restorative justice might contribute to the search for solutions to the problems of religious violence and terrorism. Marshall makes it clear that religious terrorism is a particularly dangerous and complex phenomenon, which needs to be counteracted by a range of internationally co-ordinated measures. We should resist the temptation, then, to think of restorative justice as a panacea for religious terrorism. It does, however, have specific and important roles to play within a broader set of responses: as a means of addressing the pain of those who have been personally caught up in terrorist atrocities and of promoting reconciliation between estranged communities. For Marshall, although religious terrorism and the reaction it provokes provide an extremely tough environment for collaborative, dialogical mechanisms of restorative justice to operate in, restorative justice approaches do have real potential and there are encouraging stories of restorative encounters making a real difference, especially when used as part of broader ongoing work at reconciliation and structural transformation.

Chapter 15

Juvenile justice, criminal courts and restorative justice

James Dignan

The aim of this chapter is to explore the variety of ways in which restorative justice may be used in connection with juvenile and adult criminal justice processes, but not those that operate independently. Restorative justice is taken to refer to processes that seek to engage victims, offenders and sometimes members of the wider community in deliberations that focus on the impact of a particular offence and the most appropriate ways of responding to it. It thus excludes a number of potentially reparative or restorative measures – including compensation orders, community service orders and victim awareness programmes – on the grounds that they do not attempt to include key protagonists in the decision-making process. Restorative justice processes that *are* inclusive in this sense can nevertheless take a number of different forms, the most important of which in the present context are victim–offender mediation, different forms of conferencing and citizen panels.[1]

Figure 15.1 shows the principal dimensions that need to be taken into account when considering how, and also the extent to which, restorative justice processes might in principle be incorporated within the regular criminal justice system. As can be seen, the various possibilities range beyond the conventional distinction that is often drawn between 'mainstream' and 'marginal' positions.

One important dimension relates to the 'scope' of a given restorative justice procedure, which encompasses the range and type of cases to which it applies: whether they are restricted to juvenile offenders and minor offences, for example, or also take in adult offenders and more serious offences. A second dimension – which also has an important bearing on the scope of restorative justice processes – relates to their 'legal standing', which could be described as 'formal' if the type of intervention is recognized or encouraged by law, or 'informal' if it is merely tolerated and not prohibited by law.[2] A third dimension relates to the 'degree of prescriptiveness' to which the procedure is subject: whether, in other words, it is mandatory or merely

Depth	Dimensions			
	'Scope'	'Legal standing'	Degree of prescriptiveness	'Status'
Degree of incorporation	Juveniles Minor offences ⇕ Adults Serious offences	Informal ⇕ Formal	Permissive Mandatory	Subordinate ⇕ Pre-eminent

Figure 15.1 Restorative justice and criminal justice: forms of incorporation

permissive.[3] Finally, the remaining dimension has to do with the relative 'status' of the restorative justice process *vis-à-vis* conventional criminal justice responses: whether it is subordinate, of equivalent standing or enjoys pre-eminent status. In practice the status of a restorative justice initiative or procedure is likely to be largely determined by its scope, legal standing and degree of prescriptiveness. In the discussion that follows we will come across examples of most of these variants.

Another important issue when examining criminal justice-based restorative justice initiatives concerns the stage in the criminal justice process, or 'intervention points'[4] at which it is possible for them to operate. Four principal intervention points are identified below,[5] and these provide the framework for the rest of this chapter:

• As an *alternative* to prosecution or purely admonitory disposals such as cautions.
• As a *substitute* for the conventional sentencing process.
• Pre-prosecution, as an *adjunct* to the sentencing process.
• Post-sentencing, as a *supplement* to any penalty that may have been imposed.

Having established the various ways in which it is possible for restorative justice to operate with regard to juvenile justice and criminal court settings, most of the examples I will be using to illustrate these variants are drawn from across the UK. It is important to note that, although the countries of England and Wales share the same basic legal system, this is not the case with Scotland and Northern Ireland, both of which have retained their own separate legal systems. It is also important to note that the development of restorative justice processes is still at a fairly formative phase in all three countries, though the extent and nature of its progress has been quite different in each of them.

Summarizing greatly, the restorative justice reform movement has had least impact on the criminal justice system in Scotland, where the degree of incorporation has until recently been very shallow (Bottoms and Dignan 2004: 164ff; Miers 2004: 30). Thus, the only restorative justice initiatives to date operate informally, without any legislative backing, and are mostly restricted to minor offences committed by juvenile as opposed to adult offenders. The impact of the restorative justice reform movement has been somewhat more pronounced in England and Wales, particularly with regard to the juvenile justice system where changes in the law since 1998 have firmly incorporated some elements at least of a restorative justice approach as part of the regular process. Moreover, some restorative justice initiatives are now being introduced for adult offenders. Although the restorative justice reform movement has been slowest to take off in Northern Ireland, the pace and scale of recent developments in the province have in many respects eclipsed those in other parts of the UK. Some of these developments[6] have resulted from a wider review of the Northern Irish criminal justice system that was set in train as part of the peace process.[7]

Although frustrating for its advocates, the variable and uneven progress of restorative justice in the UK makes it a useful showcase for illustrating the diverse contexts in which restorative justice can be deployed within the regular criminal justice and youth justice systems.

Restorative justice as an alternative to prosecution or purely admonitory disposals such as cautions

The first main intervention point for restorative justice approaches within the regular criminal justice process occurs at the pre-prosecution phase, either immediately following an arrest or after an offender has been charged. The impact of any such initiative during this or any other phase depends on its scope (how wide ranging it is) and also its legal standing: whether it is authorized by statute or the criminal code and, if so, on the status of such legal provisions. Unless the legal framework is all-embracing and completely mandatory its impact will also depend on the way the relevant gatekeeping agencies exercise their discretion. In most common law systems the most important of these gatekeepers has typically been the police rather than the prosecutor, whereas in most civil law systems the converse has been true. However, the pattern in the UK is variable and becoming more mixed, as we shall see. One other preliminary remark may also be helpful at this point. It cannot be assumed that restorative justice approaches at this initial intervention point are always intended as a means of diverting cases from prosecution. Often such approaches are introduced as alternatives to other low-level admonitory disposals such as police cautions or even informal warnings. Where this is the case there is a real danger of 'up-tariffing' by increasing the demands placed on the offender, or 'net-widening' by drawing in cases that would not in the past have been met with such a formal response.

In England and Wales the only restorative justice approaches operating at a pre-prosecution phase prior to 1997 relied on the discretionary powers of the police and others[8] to divert offenders to a limited number of voluntary mediation and reparation schemes (for details, see Davis et al. 1987; Marshall and Merry 1990; Davis 1992). Usually, offenders who were dealt with in this way were also cautioned, which gave rise to the term 'caution plus'. Most such schemes were aimed at juvenile offenders, though the Kettering Adult Reparation Bureau showed that a similar approach could also be adopted for adult offenders (see Dignan 1990; 1992). Although the latter ultimately evolved into a county-wide initiative dealing with both adult and juvenile offenders, most such schemes found it difficult to gain recognition and referrals from established criminal justice agencies, and many experienced problems over funding. Consequently, the impact of such informal initiatives remained very limited throughout the 1980s and early 1990s.[9]

Since then there have been three important sets of developments, one of which relates exclusively to juvenile offenders. First, as part of a comprehensive overhaul of the juvenile justice system beginning in 1998, the former non-statutory system of cautioning, which operated on a discretionary basis, has been replaced by a much more structured statutory system of pre-trial interventions. Under this revised régime, young offenders whose offences are not deemed sufficiently serious to warrant an immediate prosecution can normally expect to receive a single reprimand followed, if they offend again, by a final warning that also offers scope for limited reparative initiatives. Those who receive a final warning may also be required to participate in a 'change programme' that is designed to confront and address their offending behaviour, which could result in offenders writing a letter of apology to, or even meeting with, the victim, though in practice this is relatively unusual.[10]

The second development has evolved from a pioneering scheme adopted by Thames Valley police,[11] which set out to replace the old-style police caution for both juvenile and adult offenders with a restorative justice-inspired conferencing model. This involves the use of a partially scripted approach on the part of the police officers who mostly facilitate such conferences, the aim of which is to encourage offenders to acknowledge the impact their offence may have had on others. The process is known as a 'restorative caution' when the only participants are the facilitator, offender and members of the offender's family; as a 'restorative conference' where victims plus supporters, if any, are present; and as a 'community conference' where members of the wider public are also invited to participate. Initially this was just an informal local initiative adopted by a small number of local police forces in England and Wales. However, the Thames Valley approach was thoroughly evaluated (see Hoyle et al. 2002), and has subsequently secured 'soft law' endorsement from the government, in the form of official Home Office guidance issued to all forces (Home Office 2000; Home Office/Youth Justice Board 2002). The effect is to encourage, though not require, local police forces to adopt a Thames Valley-style restorative justice approach in order to make final warnings more meaningful and effective.

The third development represents an attempt to formalize and provide statutory endorsement for the pre-1997 practice known as 'caution plus', but only in respect of adult offenders, who are not affected by the aforementioned reform of the juvenile cautioning system. Following an official review of its restorative justice strategy (Home Office 2003), the government introduced a new scheme of conditional cautions enabling first-time or minor adult offenders[12] who admit their offence to be diverted from prosecution subject to certain conditions (Criminal Justice Act 2003, ss. 22–27). Conditional cautions are only authorized on the recommendation of the prosecutor,[13] who also determines the conditions that may be attached to them. Two types of conditions are authorized: those aimed at rehabilitation (including, for example, treatment for alcohol or drug dependency); and those aimed at reparation, which might include practical tasks (e.g. cleaning graffiti), rendering an apology, paying modest compensation or involvement in a restorative justice process of some kind. Although the new scheme incorporates a system of conditional cautioning on a formal statutory basis, its scope is limited to minor offences and recourse to restorative processes or outcomes is permissive rather than prescriptive. Moreover, no attempt is made to 'privilege' or 'prioritize' restorative over rehabilitative interventions, even in cases involving direct victims. As such, the new scheme typifies the rather tentative, cautious approach towards restorative justice that has characterized pre-prosecution developments in England and Wales, which does little more than facilitate and, in some cases, encourage restorative justice initiatives rather than prescribing them. Not surprisingly, perhaps, most evaluations report a relatively low rate of victim participation and a preference for indirect reparative outcomes involving community reparation.[14]

In Scotland, restorative justice approaches have until very recently made very little impact at the pre-prosecution phase, whether for juvenile or adult offenders.[15] However, the general discretionary powers enjoyed by Procurators Fiscal enable them to divert cases from prosecution where this is thought appropriate.[16] As in England, this has stimulated the development of a few small-scale mediation and reparation schemes operating informally in specific localities, to which such cases may be referred provided both parties consent (Young 1997: 66). In 1997 the Scottish Office funded 18 pilot schemes that allowed minor offenders to be diverted either to mediation and reparation schemes or to social work interventions, and these were evaluated over an 18 month period (Barry and McIvor 1999).[17]

Scotland's relative lack of progress in developing restorative justice approaches for juvenile offenders is somewhat unusual, and may reflect the still rather unique predominantly welfare orientation of its overall juvenile justice system (see Bottoms and Dignan 2004). Since the Scottish Executive was made largely responsible for formulating policy in the spheres of juvenile and criminal justice following 'devolution', however, it has signalled a change of emphasis by calling for victims to be given an appropriate place in the youth justice process, and for restorative justice approaches to be extended across Scotland (see, in particular, Scottish Executive 2002). In June 2004, a new national system of police restorative warnings was introduced, in place of the old-style system of senior police officer warnings.[18] This system differs in several important respects from the somewhat analogous schemes that have been adopted in other parts of the UK.

First, in terms of its 'legal standing', the scheme is not based on any change in the law, but is founded on a new set of police guidelines published in June 2004 (Children's Reporter *et al.* 2004).[19] Secondly, police in Scotland retain the discretion to deal informally (for example, by means of warning letters) with minor offences. Moreover, unlike their English counterparts, they are explicitly authorized to issue a restorative warning in respect of more serious offences or even repeat offenders provided the officer thinks the young person may be amenable and likely to respond positively. Thirdly, the scheme reflects the 'child centred' philosophy underpinning the Scottish juvenile justice system in general inasmuch as the needs of the child offender, and in particular his or her welfare needs, are said to be a primary consideration 'unless the offence is of a particularly serious nature' (Children's Reporter *et al.* 2004: 13). In practice this means that a restorative warning can only be issued after seeking confirmation from the Children's Reporter that there are no welfare concerns in respect of the child which would make it more appropriate for the case to be dealt with under the Scottish children's hearing system (described more fully in Bottoms and Dignan 2004: 47ff).

Fourthly, the scope for victim participation in the scheme is even more limited than in those operating south of the border since the victim will normally not be invited to participate in the process. Instead, the police will generally seek information from the victim concerning the impact of the offence, relay such information to the offender while issuing the warning and, if the victim wishes, inform the victim when the warning has been given and also of any outcome. A restorative warning conference, which may (subject to the consent of the offender) be attended by the victim and possibly others (including supporter, social workers, etc.) is envisaged only in exceptional circumstances where the victim's needs are thought to require it.[20] Fifthly, participation in the scheme is explicitly said to be a voluntary matter for all parties. And, sixthly, a young person should not be *required* to undertake reparation as part of the process, though voluntary acts of reparation are not precluded,[21] whereas young offenders in England may be obliged to undertake certain reparative acts, though they cannot be compelled to meet a victim.

As with its English counterpart, the warning is intended to impress on the young person the impact of the offence on all those affected by it, to encourage the young person to take responsibility for his or her actions and to understand the implications of any future offending. The warning itself has to be carried out by police officers who are trained in restorative justice methods. The emphasis is supposed to be on changing the attitudes and behaviour of the young people concerned rather than humiliating them. As in England, the scheme is permissive rather than mandatory and lacks statutory backing, though the scope for direct victim participation is even more restrictive since it is liable to be over-ridden by welfare or even straightforward diversionary considerations.

Prior to 2000 there were no 'formal' restorative justice initiatives operating at a pre-prosecution phase in Northern Ireland.[22] The police had for many years operated a system of juvenile liaison schemes, but their aim was simply to divert young offenders where possible from prosecution by either cautioning them or dealing with them informally. A major review of the police and criminal justice systems in Northern Ireland in 2000, however, recommended that a restorative justice approach should be formally integrated into Northern Ireland's youth justice system as a 'mainstream' initiative (Criminal Justice Review Commission 2000). Shortly after this the police launched two pilot projects[23] based on the use of a police-led restorative cautioning model – somewhat akin to the Thames Valley model – for juveniles under the age of 17. The pilot schemes were evaluated for six months and found to have been reasonably successful in securing some of the values associated with a restorative justice approach, though concerns were also raised about a degree of net-widening and up-tariffing, and over the relatively low level of victim participation (O'Mahony et al. 2002; see also O'Mahony and Doak 2002). Since February 2001, all juvenile cautions in Northern Ireland have been administered within a restorative framework.

In addition to this informal police-based initiative, the government has also formally integrated a restorative justice approach as part of the mainstream response for young offenders who are facing prosecution in Northern Ireland. Under the Justice (Northern Ireland) Act 2002, a system of youth conferencing has been introduced,[24] which has two main facets. The first type – known as *diversionary youth conferences* – is convened following a referral by the Public Prosecution Service provided the young person consents to the process, admits the offence and the case would otherwise have been dealt with by prosecution.[25] The second type – known as *court-ordered youth conferences* – will be described more fully in the next section. The entire youth conferencing scheme is being evaluated, and preliminary findings, based on the first nine months of operation, have recently been published (Beckett et al. 2005).[26] Although the process is by no means complete, it is clear that the restorative justice reforms being implemented in a pre-prosecution context in Northern Ireland are much broader in scope with regard to the range of offences they embrace, even though they only apply to juvenile offenders. Moreover, they are also being much more fully incorporated as a regular and mainstream part of the overall youth justice system in Northern Ireland than has happened to date elsewhere in the UK.

Restorative justice as a substitute for the conventional sentencing process

The second main intervention point for restorative justice approaches within the regular criminal justice system occurs after an offender has been prosecuted and convicted, at the time when he or she would normally be sentenced. It is generally accepted that restorative justice processes do not provide an acceptable means of determining guilt or innocence since they lack the normal procedural safeguards associated with a conventional contested criminal trial. Consequently, virtually all restorative justice processes require offenders to accept responsibility for any harm they have caused[27] as an essential precondition for accepting a referral.

Allowing restorative justice processes to operate as a substitute forum within which to determine how an offence should be dealt with after conviction represents potentially the most important and radical of all the possible settings in which they might operate within a criminal or juvenile justice context. But even where this possibility exists, much will depend on the degree and manner of its incorporation within the regular criminal justice system.

The UK once again illustrates a variety of approaches, though virtually all the initiatives discussed in this section relate to juvenile rather than adult offenders. In England and Wales most young offenders who are prosecuted for the first time and who plead guilty are now dealt with[28] by means of a 'referral order',[29] instead of being sentenced in the normal way. The substitute forum to which they are referred is known as a 'youth offender panel', comprising two lay members of the community, who are drawn from an approved list, and a member of the local youth offending team. The latter is a multi-agency organization that is responsible for co-ordinating and delivering youth justice services within each local authority area. Technically youth offender panels represent a form of restorative justice process that is often referred to as a community reparation board or citizen panel, though they were inspired in part by the New Zealand family group conferencing model and in part by the Scottish children's hearings system. Consequently, they exhibit an amalgamation of features drawn from both sets of forebears.

Procedurally, the panel's rôle is to provide a forum in which the young offender, his or her parents, panel members and, where appropriate, victims can discuss the offence and its impact and, if possible, reach an agreed outcome that takes the form of a 'contract'. Outcomes mainly take the form of reparative or rehabilitative measures; restrictions on movement are also possible, but not if they entail physical constraints or electronic monitoring.[30] Assuming that a contract is agreed and successfully completed, one distinctive aspect of the referral panel process is that the conviction is considered 'spent' for the purpose of the Rehabilitation of the Offender Act 1974. This 'wiping clean of the slate' is consistent with Braithwaite's (1989) theory of reintegrative shaming which opposes indelible or indefinite shaming on the grounds that it is stigmatic and likely to be counterproductive. Where agreement cannot be reached, or the contract is breached, the young offender is referred back to the court to be re-sentenced.

Somewhat unusually – at least within an English context – the referral order procedure has been incorporated reasonably fully and also fairly prescriptively within the juvenile justice process as a mainstream initiative even though it is restricted in scope to a somewhat limited category of offenders. Thus, in marked contrast to many other restorative justice measures that have been introduced in England and Wales in recent years, the referral order process is a semi-mandatory disposal. Consequently, it applies to all young offenders who plead guilty the first time they are prosecuted in respect of an imprisonable offence,[31] unless the court considers the offence is one that merits a custodial sentence or a hospital order or can be dealt with by means of an absolute discharge.

From a restorative justice perspective, however, one of the biggest concerns arising from the pilot evaluation related to the disappointingly low level of victim participation since victims actually attended a panel meeting in only 13 per cent of relevant cases (Newburn *et al.* 2002: 41). This was partly to do with implementational difficulties of the kind experienced with other victim-oriented reforms rather than reluctance on the part of victims themselves to take part in the process.[32] However, Crawford and Newburn (2003: 241) also point to the tension that undoubtedly exists between the interests of 'the community' and those of 'the victim', which carries the risk that the goal of community involvement may in practice be prioritized at the expense of victim participation.

In Scotland, although the distinctive and internationally renowned children's hearing system shares some features that are associated with restorative justice processes – notably an informal decision-making process involving the child and his or her family – this inclusiveness did not originally extend to victims, who were conspicuous by their absence (Bottoms and Dignan 2004: 164). Nor was there any obligation or expectation that hearings would facilitate 'restorative outcomes'. For many years, therefore, the prospects for restorative justice at this phase of the Scottish criminal justice process looked fairly bleak. The only notable initiative involved a pioneering ad hoc local scheme – known as the Young Offenders' Mediation Project – that was set up by SACRO (Scottish Association for Safeguarding Communities and Reducing Offending) in Fife in 1996.[33] This multi-agency project was aimed at offenders who showed signs of developing a pattern of offending behaviour, and sought to explore the possibility of mediation between child offender and victim following a referral by the reporter to the children's hearing. Following the change of emphasis signalled by the Scottish Executive, however (see above), national protocols have been drafted that seek to incorporate a somewhat similar approach throughout the Scottish youth justice system. Once implemented, the protocols will enable the reporter to a children's hearing to request an assessment of suitability from local Restorative Justice Services. Then, if both victim and offender are willing, the service might be asked to facilitate a restorative justice process[34] and report back to the Children's Reporter, who will make a final decision on any measures that might be required. Compared with other parts of the UK, however, the Scottish approach towards restorative justice remains cautious and tentative, with little attempt to incorporate it formally even within the children's hearings system.

In Northern Ireland, the above-mentioned court-ordered youth conference scheme was heavily influenced by the New Zealand family group conferencing model, which it closely resembles in terms of both its scope and degree of incorporation within the recently reformed youth justice system. Thus, virtually all young offenders are eligible to be dealt with by means of a youth conference, with the sole exception of those facing a charge of murder (Justice (Northern Ireland) Act 2002, s. 59). Moreover, in the vast majority of cases, provided an offender admits guilt or is convicted, and so long as he or she consents,[35] referral to a youth conference is mandatory. The only exceptions relate to those charged with offences that, in the case of adult offenders, are triable only on indictment or those charged with terrorist offences,[36] and even these are eligible for referral at the discretion of the court. This heavily prescriptive aspect of the Northern Irish system underscores the extent to which a restorative justice approach is intended as the mainstream response for the great majority of young offenders. In many respects the conferencing process itself closely resembles the much better-known New Zealand model (see Maxwell and Morris 1993, for details), as does the format. One distinctive feature, however, is that the conference co-ordinator has to be employed as a civil servant within a government department, a stipulation which rules out both the police and community representatives acting as co-ordinators.[37]

Unlike the New Zealand model, victims are not required to withdraw from the conference once the focus turns towards the negotiation of a youth conference plan. As part of the plan, the co-ordinator may propose that a non-custodial sentence be imposed on the offender. It is also possible for the co-ordinator to recommend the imposition of a custodial sentence, but not the form or duration of such a sentence. Once a plan has been agreed it is put to the court, which has three options. It can either accept the plan as the sentence of the court (though this still counts as a conviction). Or it may accept the plan but, on the recommendation of the co-ordinator and, provided the young person consents, may also impose a custodial sentence. Or it may reject the plan and deal with the offence by exercising its own sentencing powers. The involvement of the court in adopting or rejecting the plan is intended to act as a safeguard for the offender to ensure that the outcome is not disproportionate having regard to the seriousness of the offence.

Preliminary findings from the ongoing evaluation of the conferencing initiative indicate a relatively high level of victim participation (62 per cent) (Beckett *et al.* 2005). Just over three quarters of all plans (deriving from both diversionary and court-ordered conferences) included some form of reparation, including an apology; conversely, only 8 per cent of plans contained any punitive element. Finally, of the 22 court-ordered conferencing plans, a majority (59 per cent) were ratified without change; just under one quarter were replaced with an alternative disposal; while the remainder (18 per cent) were amended or granted in alternative form.

Restorative justice as an adjunct to the sentencing process

The third main intervention point for restorative justice approaches within the regular criminal justice system occurs in conjunction with the process of sentencing. For many years the sentencing powers of the courts have in various countries been amended to embrace a variety of potentially restitutive or reparative measures such as compensation orders or community service orders. However, these lack many of the attributes associated with restorative justice processes since they simply involve the imposition of restitutive or reparative outcomes and do not attempt to engage key players such as the victim, offender and other interested parties in the decision-making process itself. Nevertheless, there are a number of conventional sentencing measures that do potentially offer scope for restorative justice processes to operate in conjunction with the sentencing process.

One such measure is the deferred sentence which, as its name suggests, allows a court to postpone the imposition of a penalty for a specified period of time.[38] This power, which is available in a number of common law jurisdictions, enables the court to assess the behaviour of the offender for a while before passing sentence, normally on the basis of a pre-sentence report (PSR). Although the measure is used relatively infrequently within the UK, it did form the basis of some of the earliest restorative justice initiatives in England and Wales (see, e.g., Marshall and Merry 1990: 76). In addition, it is also possible for restorative justice processes to be conducted under the auspices of a probation order,[39] either informally or as one of the conditions imposed by the court as part of the order. This permissive power was also used in some of the early English restorative justice initiatives. More recently, as we shall see, both sets of measures have again been utilized in order to test the scope for restorative justice approaches in conjunction with more serious offences committed, in the main, by adult offenders.

In addition to these conventional sentencing disposals that allowed restorative justice processes – albeit incidentally – to be conducted in conjunction with the sentencing process, a number of new sentencing provisions have been introduced for young offenders that are more directly and explicitly influenced by restorative justice precepts. Unlike the other main intervention points we have been considering, the primary locus for virtually all these more recent initiatives involving the use of restorative justice processes at the sentencing stage has been England and Wales.

The scope for restorative justice processes to be utilized in conjunction with the sentencing of young offenders was initially extended as part of a much broader reform of the entire youth justice system that began taking shape in England and Wales in 1997. Two new sentencing disposals – the reparation order and the action plan order[40] – were introduced in 1998, both of which contained elements of restorative justice thinking. The reparation order was envisaged as a routine low-level penalty for relatively minor young offenders. The action plan order was envisaged as a more intensive and focused intervention for more serious young offenders who might otherwise be dealt with by an intermediate-level community sentence. Here, the aim was to combine reparation with other rehabilitative or punitive elements designed to tackle the offending behaviour and so prevent further crime.

Various kinds of reparative activity are possible for offenders who are dealt with by means of either order. One option is to meet with the victim to discuss the offence and its consequences and to explore the possibility of a reparative outcome. The latter could take form of an apology to the victim or some form of practical activity for the benefit of either the victim or the community at large. This type of reparation is only possible if the victim consents, however, which means that he or she first has to be identified, contacted and consulted, all of which takes time. Many courts are reluctant to grant adjournments to facilitate this because of government pressure to speed up the process of justice (Dignan 2002: 79; see also Holdaway *et al.* 2001). For this and other reasons, the pilot evaluation found that only a minority of reparative outcomes involved a direct meeting between victim and offender (8 per cent), though a further 12 per cent resulted in some other form of direct reparation (usually an apology). Instead, most reparative interventions (80 per cent in the pilot evaluation) actually take the form of indirect reparation. And in 63 per cent of cases the community – rather than the victim – is the main beneficiary (Dignan 2002: 80).

Until recently, the possibility of using restorative justice approaches as an adjunct to sentencing in the case of adult offenders has involved small-scale ad hoc projects receiving relatively low numbers of referrals. Under the auspices of its Crime Reduction Programme, however, the government decided in 2001 to fund a number of pilot projects to test the scope for restorative justice approaches in connection with more serious relatively 'high volume' offences such as robberies, burglaries and grievous bodily harm. An explicit aim of the pilots is that they should involve a substantial proportion of adult offenders instead of focusing primarily on juveniles as so many restorative justice initiatives have done in the past. The three schemes that have been funded in this way are quite distinct in many respects, including the type of restorative justice interventions on offer and also the stage in the criminal justice process at which they are intended to be available. All three schemes are being independently evaluated, a process that will not be completed until the end of 2006, though two interim reports have been produced (Shapland *et al.* 2004, 2006).

The first scheme, CONNECT,[41] is based in inner London and offers a variety of restorative justice interventions including mediation and conferencing in cases involving adult offenders who have committed a wide range of offences. It originally planned to offer restorative justice interventions in one (later two) inner London magistrates' court(s) exclusively in the context of deferred sentences but, when this proved unrealistic, also accepted referrals via probation service recommendations contained in pre-sentence reports.

The second scheme is run by Justice Research Consortium (JRC), which operates in three separate sites: in London, in Northumbria and in the Thames Valley. The scheme offers conferencing on the basis of an experimental model whereby cases are randomly allocated either to conferencing or to a control group.[42] In the London site, the scheme eventually decided to concentrate on adult cases, most of which have been drawn from the Crown Court. Provided the necessary consents have been obtained, conferencing is undertaken after the offender pleads guilty but before sentencing so that the results of the conference can be featured in the pre-sentence report that is prepared for the sentencing judge. In the Northumbria site, restorative justice interventions were used as an adjunct to sentencing in respect of both adult and young offenders. In the Thames Valley site, where JRC has worked almost exclusively with adult offenders, restorative justice interventions have mostly taken place after sentencing. Consequently, they will be dealt with in the next section even though, in some circumstances, the offender's agreement to take part in conferencing forms a binding requirement of the sentence itself.

The third scheme, REMEDI, concentrates on the provision of mediation services (both direct and indirect), in the county of South Yorkshire. Remedi works with both young and adult offenders, but since most of its adult work takes place outside the framework of criminal justice decision-making and after a sentence has been imposed, this scheme will also be discussed more fully in the next section.

Although the evaluation of the above schemes is still ongoing it has already identified a number of emerging issues, two of which will be mentioned at this point. First, it has confirmed how difficult it is, at least in the absence of some form of statutory entrenchment, for restorative justice initiatives to gain a sufficient number of referrals to maintain an adequate case flow (Shapland *et al.* 2004: vii; see also Dignan and Lowey 2000: 48). Secondly, it highlights the extent to which such informal initiatives are likewise dependent in a variety of other respects on an overwhelmingly dominant criminal justice system (Shapland *et al.* 2004: viii). Examples range from the difficulties encountered in seeking to involve victims in the process,[43] to problems over timing. The latter stem in part from the existing cultures and working patterns of criminal justice agencies and in part from new external pressures such as the demand to speed up the criminal justice process.

Restorative justice as a post-sentence intervention

The fourth and final principal intervention point for restorative justice approaches within the regular criminal justice system occurs at the post-sentencing stage. In principle this can happen irrespective of the nature of the sentence – whether it involves imprisonment or a community penalty – though in practice most of the relatively limited experience in the UK relates to the use of restorative justice in custodial settings. Once again, most of the initiatives that have been developed in this context have been located in England and Wales. In Scotland, SACRO does offer a victim–offender mediation service in respect of crimes involving severe violence, including murder and serious assault, but only on a very limited basis. A 1999 survey of restorative justice in custodial settings reported that there were no obvious initiatives of this kind at that time in Northern Ireland (Liebmann and Braithwaite 1999).

In contrast to the use of restorative justice approaches in other criminal justice contexts, most initiatives at the post-sentence stage have mainly involved adult rather than juvenile offenders. Indeed, a 2003 Youth Justice Board survey reported that 'there is little restorative justice intervention of any kind taking place in the juvenile secure estate' (Curry *et al.* 2004: 4), though an earlier survey referred to restorative justice initiatives including direct and indirect mediation at three separate young offender institutions (Liebmann and Braithwaite 1999). And even with regard to adult offenders, as we shall see, most of the English initiatives have to date been informal, small scale, ad hoc and locally based. For the most part they were instigated by individual probation officers, occasionally in response to direct requests by victims, though one or two victim–offender mediation services undertook mediation in a prison setting on a more regular basis.[44]

The absence of any attempts to incorporate restorative justice approaches more systematically within custodial settings is not unusual. Indeed, the Belgian Ministry of Justice is almost unique in seeking to promote the development of restorative justice initiatives throughout the Belgian prison system as a matter of national policy (Aertsen and Peters 1998).[45] The nearest English equivalent is an initiative called the Restorative Prison Project, which was established in 2000 and involves three prisons (one of which is a young offenders institution) in the north east of England. Its aim, like that of its Belgian counterpart, is to promote the concept of restoration in its broadest sense within a prison setting. Thus, it is more concerned with restoring and strengthening the relationships between inmates and their families and communities, and in promoting victim awareness in general than in fostering opportunities for dialogue between offenders and their victims, which is the main focus of this chapter.

More recently, as mentioned in the previous section, the government has since 2001 funded a number of pilot projects that aim to test the use of restorative justice approaches in connection with relatively serious offences. Two of the three pilot schemes – the Justice Research Consortium and REMEDI – set out to examine the use of restorative justice in a post-sentence context, in both custodial and community settings.

The Justice Research Consortium is exploring the use of restorative conferencing in a post-sentence context in just one of its three sites – Thames Valley – where the focus is mainly on adult offenders and their victims. Referrals for this scheme are drawn in the main from offenders[46] who are either serving custodial sentences at Bullingdon prison, near Bicester, or have been given community penalties (mostly community punishment orders or community rehabilitation orders) following conviction in one of the Oxfordshire courts.

Not surprisingly, perhaps, the interim evaluation has disclosed that offences comprising the custodial sentence sample were mostly very serious, with robbery and the more serious forms of assault predominating. Far more surprising, in view of this offence profile, is the relatively high proportion of offenders (35 per cent) who were willing to take part in a conference, and the fact that only about a quarter refused.[47] This relatively high level of enthusiasm on the part of offenders is also remarkable in view of the fact that there were no obvious 'incentives' for them to take part, since it would be most unlikely to have any effect on criminal justice decisions such as release dates. Victims were somewhat more likely to refuse to participate (30 per cent of the total), though a similar proportion of cases fell by the wayside because of difficulty in contacting the victim or, more commonly, obtaining contact details. Nevertheless, between 12 and 15 per cent of potentially eligible cases did proceed to conference, notwithstanding the much more serious nature of the offences involved. Most of the problems encountered appeared to relate to practical and logistical difficulties involved in recruiting facilitators (mainly because of staffing shortages), making contact with victims and setting up the conferences within a reasonable time (Shapland *et al.* 2004: 29).

With regard to the community sentence sample, early attempts to implement restorative justice at the post-sentence stage encountered difficulty in gaining consent from offenders. This is not surprising since they were, in effect, being asked to sign up for additional requirements on top of the conditions that had already been imposed by the court while at the same time increasing their exposure to possible 'breach' procedures in the event of something going wrong. Accordingly, the scheme gradually moved to a position in which offenders are assessed for suitability at the PSR stage and asked if they would be willing for conferencing to be inserted as a binding requirement of any community order that is imposed. Somewhat controversially from a restorative justice standpoint, offenders who agree to this are effectively obliged to participate in conferencing by order of the court instead of being free to withdraw without penalty, as is normally the case.

This strategy appears to have been more successful in recruiting offenders who are willing to participate in conferencing, though the proportion of offenders who were willing to do so during the initial 12 months of the scheme was still only one quarter, compared with one half for the custody sample. Because victims were less likely to refuse if the case got to that stage, however, the overall 'completion rate' of 16 per cent for the community sentence sample was slightly higher than that for the custody sample (13 per cent). Offenders who agreed to take part were similar in age to the custody sample (just under 30), and the offences – though less serious than for the custody sample, as might be expected – were still predominantly violent in nature.

The other Home Office-funded pilot scheme that has attempted to explore the scope for using restorative justice in a post-sentence context is REMEDI, which has for some years provided opportunities for victims and offenders to take part in restorative justice initiatives. With regard to the Home Office pilot scheme, there was an automatic referral process from the probation service in respect of adult offenders who were given community sentences such as community rehabilitation orders and community punishment and rehabilitation orders. They were given a one-to-one victim awareness session as part of the rehabilitation package and, if assessed as being suitable, were informed of the possibility of taking part voluntarily in victim–offender mediation. Despite the automatic referral protocol, the number of referrals obtained via this route was lower than expected, mainly because concerns over data protection issues resulted in the insertion of an additional requirement for probation case managers to obtain consent before referring an offender to REMEDI.

Another source of referral was via leaflets about the service that were included in an information pack supplied by the probation service to adult offenders. This resulted in relatively few cases getting to mediation, however, partly due to offender reluctance but also because of serious difficulties in establishing contact with victims. Here again, one of the biggest problems was caused by the restrictive way in which the data protection legislation has been interpreted (Shapland *et al.* 2004: 43).[48] The problem is that obtaining victim consent is deemed to be the responsibility of the police, for whom, however, this is not considered to be a very high priority.

REMEDI has also sought to work in a variety of ways with young offenders[49] and their victims, though this is something that needs to be negotiated separately with each individual youth offending team (YOT) office. Once again, victim contact has proved to be a major obstacle, though fewer problems were experienced in relation to victim or offender refusal to participate (Shapland *et al.* 2004: 45). Consequently, the proportion of such cases resulting in some form of restorative justice encounter was higher overall than for adult offenders, and in one or two area offices it was considerably higher. In part, this is likely to be because the restorative justice element can often form an integral component of certain disposals such as final warnings, referral orders or reparation orders (Shapland *et al.* 2004: 54). Where restorative justice is offered on a purely voluntary 'opt-in' basis with no set consequences for either party, the take-up rates have been far lower. However, the experience with Thames Valley custody cases suggests that this is by no means inevitable.

Conclusion

Countries constituting the UK provide a useful showcase for illustrating both the range of contexts in which restorative justice may be deployed, and also the varying degrees to which such processes may be incorporated within the regular criminal justice system itself. The fact that most of these restorative justice initiatives have been evaluated means that they also furnish a valuable test bed for assessing the performance of restorative justice in such settings. A number of conclusions can be drawn from this exercise.

First, at least within a common law context, restorative justice interventions are capable of operating reasonably successfully at various stages of the criminal justice process, though in practice the scope is mainly limited to the four principal intervention or entry points that have been examined in this chapter. Secondly, all but one of the intervention points are either directly related to key decision points in the criminal justice process or provide a substitute decision-making forum within which certain outcomes can in principle be discussed and provisionally agreed. The remaining intervention point, at the post-sentencing phase, can often – though not invariably – be the most problematic in engaging victims and offenders. Thirdly, there is a need for close co-operation between those responsible for the interventions and the criminal justice agencies that provide the referrals and, in many cases, deliberate upon the outcomes. Fourthly, this co-operation is most likely to be forthcoming on a routine basis where steps are taken to integrate the restorative justice process as part of the regular criminal justice system – for example, by providing statutory backing of a sufficiently broad and prescriptive nature. Fifthly, the provision of such formal endorsement is not of itself sufficient to guarantee the successful take-up and extensive deployment of restorative justice processes. Much will depend on the 'status' that is accorded to such processes: whether they are intended to function as the primary response for particular categories of cases, or 'just another tool in the toolbox' (Home Office *et al.* 2004). The contrast between the new youth conferencing system in Northern Ireland and the introduction of sentencing disposals such as the reparation order in England and Wales is illuminating in this regard. Much will also depend on the willingness of criminal justice agencies to adapt their working culture and practices to accommodate new responsibilities, especially with regard to victims. And last, but not least, much will depend on the government's willingness to take effective action to deal with well-known impediments such as those associated with the interpretation of data protection legislation that have made it so difficult for English restorative justice initiatives to engage effectively with victims.

Selected further reading

Bottoms, A.E. and Dignan, J. (2004) 'Youth justice in Great Britain', in M. Tonry and A.N. Doob (eds) *Youth Crime and Youth Justice: Comparative and Cross-national Perspectives. Crime and Justice: A Review of Research*. Vol. 31. Chicago, IL and London: University of Chicago Press. Provides a detailed account of the distinctive Scottish children's hearings system, showing how it differs from its English counterpart with regard to a range of issues including (in section VII) some tentative steps in the direction of restorative/reparative justice.

Campbell, C., Devlin, R., O'Mahony, D., Doak, J., Jackson, J., Corrigan, T. and McEvoy, K. (2006) *Evaluation of the Northern Ireland Youth Conference Service*. NIO Research and Statistical Series Report 12 (available online at http://www.nio.gov.uk/evaluation_of_the_northern_ireland_youth_conference_service.pdf). The final report of the Northern Ireland Youth Conferencing evaluation, which appeared after this chapter was completed, provides the most detailed study (apart from those focusing on the long-running New Zealand family group conferencing system) of a statutory restorative justice scheme that is closely integrated with the criminal justice system.

Crawford, A. and Newburn, T. (2003) *Youth Offending and Restorative Justice: Implementing Reform in Youth Justice*. Cullompton: Willan Publishing. Provides a well informed and detailed account of recent attempts to implement a variety of restorative justice reforms (including the introduction of referral orders) in the English youth justice system.

Shapland, J., Atkinson, A., Colledge, E., Dignan, J., Howes, M., Johnstone, J., Pennant, R., Robinson, G. and Sorsby, A. (2004) *Implementing Restorative Justice Schemes (Crime Reduction Programme). A Report on the First Year*. Home Office Online Report 32/04. London: Home Office (available online at http://www.homeoffice.gov.uk/rds/pdfs04/rdsolr3204.pdf). Presents interim findings of the ongoing Home Office-funded evaluation of three restorative justice pilot schemes that seek to provide a variety of restorative justice interventions within a criminal justice context in respect of a range of high-volume and relatively serious offences, many of which involve adult offenders.

Shapland, J., Atkinson, A., Atkinson, H., Chapman, B., Colledge, E., Dignan, J., Howes, M., Johnstone, J., Robinson, G. and Sorsby, A. (2006) *Restorative Justice in Practice: Findings from the Second Phase of the Evaluation of Three Schemes*. Home Office Research Findings 274. London: Home Office (available online at http://

www.homeoffice.gov.uk/rds/rfpubs1.html). A full copy of the report is available online at: http://www.ccr.group.shef.ac.uk/papers/papers.htm. Whereas the first interim evaluation report concentrated on issues relating to the implementation of restorative justice initiatives within a criminal justice context, this second interim report focuses on the process of restorative justice, including the extent of participation and what happened during conferences and direct mediation.

Acknowledgements

I am very grateful to Jonathon Doak, Marie Howes and Gwen Robinson for their helpful comments on an earlier draft of this chapter.

Notes

1 See also Bazemore and Umbreit (2001), Schiff (2003) and Dignan (2005; ch. 4).
2 In many continental countries with a civil law tradition any action generally has to be formally *prescribed* by law, whereas the English common law tradition generally permits any action to be taken that is not specifically *proscribed* by law. Common law systems can thus often appear to those with civil law training to be remarkably 'permissive' in terms of the range of responses that can be adopted by criminal justice agencies (see also Miers and Willemsens 2004: 158; Walgrave 2004: 566).
3 In reality the position may be less clear cut as the degrees of prescriptiveness may depend on how widely drawn the mandatory elements are and the range of any exemptions.
4 Miers (2004: 30) also uses the same term, though in a somewhat more restricted sense.
5 Further subdivisions are possible. See, for example, Auld (2001: 389), who identified six key decision points as a case progresses through the criminal justice process.
6 But not all of them. Northern Ireland has also experienced a number of community-led initiatives that have had an important impact on developments in the 'independent sector', though these fall outside the scope of the present chapter.
7 Following the Belfast Agreement of April 1998, a Criminal Justice Review Group was established as one response to the long-standing 'legitimacy deficit' in Northern Ireland (Dignan and Lowey 2000: 16).
8 For example, multi-agency panels known as juvenile liaison bureaux or cautioning panels (see Cavadino and Dignan 2002: 292 for details).
9 Only 2 per cent of young offenders were given 'caution plus' programmes in 1996 (Audit Commission 1998: 20).
10 A pilot found that victims were contacted in just 15 per cent of cases, and that only 7 per cent of victims were involved in any kind of reparative activity, whether involving direct reparation, including mediation (4 per cent) or indirect (3 per cent) (Holdaway *et al.* 2001).
11 Based on a similar scheme developed in Wagga Wagga, New South Wales, during the early 1990s and subsequently adopted in a number of other common law jurisdictions including Canada and some US states.
12 The Home Office has also commissioned a pilot project investigating the effects of a restorative justice approach as a diversion from court in respect of more

serious adult offenders who would not normally be eligible for a conditional caution. The pilot was launched in 2004, though the complete findings of the evaluation are unlikely to be available until September 2007.

13 This represents a departure from the normal practice of leaving such matters up to the police and, in this limited respect at least, brings England and Wales closer to a continental model in which the public prosecutor has a much more prominent rôle.

14 For example, the final Thames Valley evaluation report disclosed that in only 14 per cent of cautioning sessions that were conducted according to restorative justice principles were victims present (Hoyle *et al*. 2002: 103 and Table 1). See also note 10 above.

15 See the Scottish Restorative Justice Consultancy and Training Service website (managed by SACRO), which gives a good overview of restorative justice developments in Scotland: (http://www.restorativejusticescotland.org.uk/developments.htm).

16 Diversion can take one of two forms: a decision to prosecute can either be waived at the outset (waiver model) or deferred until the outcome of the diversion is known (deferred model). The latter somewhat resembles the English system of conditional cautions.

17 There are currently three such schemes in Scotland: in Aberdeen, Edinburgh and Motherwell.

18 Similar to the 'old-style' system of police cautions in England.

19 Forces are allowed to introduce the new scheme incrementally, with a view to extending it across Scotland by April 2006.

20 The guidelines also refer to the risk of up-tariffing and the additional resources that may be required when a restorative warning conference is convened inappropriately.

21 If, for example, the young person offers to write a letter of apology, the guidelines state that the police should deliver it to the victim if he or she wants to receive it, though that is as far as their responsibilities extend.

22 A number of community-based restorative justice initiatives, such as the Greater Shankill Alternatives and Restorative Justice Ireland, have been operating on an informal basis since 1997/8, however.

23 Based in Ballymena, County Antrim and Mountpottinger, Belfast.

24 The implementation process is a gradual one. The Youth Conferencing Service was introduced on a pilot basis on 18 December 2003, but only applied initially to 10–16-year-olds living in the Greater Belfast area. It is intended to extend its coverage to include 17-year-olds, and also geographically, to include the entire province, but only once the independent evaluation has been concluded.

25 The scheme is not intended for minor or first-time offenders, who are expected to be dealt with by the police by means of a restorative caution or an informal warning, which might also have a restorative theme.

26 The broadly positive findings suggest that the implementation of the reforms is proceeding well. Moreover, the overall direction of the reforms appears to have received broad endorsement from all major stakeholders despite reservations in some quarters that the reforms had been 'imposed' from above, and concerns about the inappropriate use of conferences in some instances for very minor offences. The final report of the evaluation was published in March 2006, after this paper was completed; see Campbell *et al*. (2006).

27 Either by formally pleading guilty or, as in New Zealand, by not denying responsibility for an offence (McElrea 1994: 97).

28 Under the Youth Justice and Criminal Evidence Act 1999, which took effect nationally in April 2002 after an 18-month pilot evaluation (see Newburn *et al.* 2002).

29 The duration of the referral order can be between three and twelve months. The precise period is determined by the court in the light of the seriousness of the offence. The court also specifies the length of any contract (see below).

30 Such restrictions are specifically prohibited by the Powers of Criminal Courts (Sentencing) Act 2000, s. 19.

31 Prior to 2003 the measure was compulsory even in respect of non-imprisonable offences, but its scope was curtailed (SI 2003/1605) following concerns over the exceedingly trivial nature of many of the offences. Such concerns have not been entirely alleviated since a good many very minor offences – for example theft of a Mars bar – are still imprisonable.

32 The new referral order process was introduced at a time when YOTs themselves had only recently been established and were still coping with a radical change of ethos, so had only had limited time in which to develop victim contact procedures.

33 For further details see Bottoms and Dignan (2004: 165) Miers (2004: 28). See also Sawyer (2000) for an evaluation of the project.

34 Four types of restorative processes are envisaged: restorative justice conference, face-to-face meeting, shuttle mediation or victim awareness.

35 In contrast to the referral order, which is the nearest English equivalent.

36 Also excepted are those with whom the court proposes to deal by making an absolute or conditional discharge.

37 The Review Commission had recommended that the conferencing service should be based in a separate arm of a proposed Department of Justice, which would also supply the co-ordinators, but this proposal was not included in the Act.

38 In England and Wales courts are allowed to defer sentencing for up to six months.

39 Under the Criminal Justice Act 2003, the formerly free-standing probation order (or 'community rehabilitation order') has been replaced by a 'supervision requirement' that constitutes one of a number of options available as part of a generic 'community order'. Another such option, known as the 'activity requirement', provides scope for a range of possible reparative or restorative interventions. See Cavadino and Dignan (2007) for details.

40 Neither of these measures is available in Scotland, though the reparation order has been available in Northern Ireland since 2002 (Justice (Northern Ireland) Act 2002, s. 36(a)).

41 CONNECT is run jointly by NACRO and the Inner London Probation Service.

42 A similar approach was also pioneered by the JRC in the Australian Reintegrative Shaming Experiment (RISE) project, based in Canberra (see Strang *et al.* 1999; Sherman *et al.* 2000).

43 See also Holdaway *et al.* (2001), Dignan (2002) and Newburn *et al.* (2003). Notwithstanding the problems encountered in making contact with victims, a substantial proportion of those who were approached agreed to participate. This included victims of both serious and less serious offences and cases at all stages of the criminal justice process (Shapland *et al.*, 2006: 43).

44 The best-known examples are the Leeds Victim Offender Unit and the West Midlands Victim Unit (see Wynne 1996; also Miers *et al.* 2001).

45 A distinctive feature of the Belgian approach involves the appointment of a restorative justice consultant in each prison whose task is to work with the governor to promote the development of a restorative approach within the prison culture.

46 In order to obtain more cases, attempts were also made to recruit some younger offenders with broadly similar offence profiles from Reading Young Offenders Institution. Very few of these resulted in conferences, however, mainly because of offender refusal or unsuitability.

47 A similar proportion of cases (26 per cent) were felt to be unsuitable.

48 Similar problems have been reported by other restorative justice research; see, for example, Holdaway *et al.* (2001: 87) and Dignan (2002: 78).

49 Including those on referral orders, and also the facilitation of community reparation and victim awareness work (though the latter does not meet the definition of restorative justice that has been adopted for the purpose of this chapter), in addition to direct or indirect mediation between victims and offenders.

References

Aertsen, I. and Peters, T. (1998) 'Mediation and restorative justice in Belgium', *European Journal on Criminal Policy and Reseach*, 6: 507–25.

Audit Commission (1998) *Misspent Youth '98: The Challenge for Youth Justice*. London: Audit Commission.

Auld, Lord Justice (2001) *Review of the Criminal Courts of England and Wales*. London: HMSO (available online at http://www.criminal-courts-review.org.uk/auldconts.html).

Barry, M. and McIvor, G. (1999) Diversion from Prosecution to Social Work and other Service Agencies: Evaluation of the 100% Funding Pilot Programmes. *Crime and Criminal Justice Research Findings* 37. Edinburgh: Scottish Executive.

Bazemore, G. and Umbreit, U. (2001) *A Comparison of Four Restorative Conferencing Models* (available online at http://www.ncjrs.org/html/ojjdp/2001).

Beckett, H., Campbell, C., O'Mahony, D., Jackson, J. and Doak, J. (2005) Interim Evaluation of the Northern Ireland Youth Conferencing Scheme. *Research and Statistical Bulletin* 1/2005. Belfast: NIO.

Bottoms, A.E. and Dignan, J. (2004) 'Youth justice in Great Britain', in M. Tonry and A.N. Doob (eds) *Youth Crime and Youth Justice: Comparative and Cross-national Perspectives. Crime and Justice: A Review of Research*. Vol. 31. Chicago, IL and London: University of Chicago Press.

Braithwaite, J. (1989) *Crime, Shame and Reintegration*. Cambridge: Cambridge University Press.

Campbell, C., Devlin, R., O'Mahoney, D., Doak, J., Jackson, J., Corrigan, T. and McEvoy, K. (2006) *Evaluation of the Northern Ireland Youth Conferencing Service. NIO Research and Statistical Series Report* 12 (available online at http://www.nio.gov.uk/evaluation_of_the_northern_ireland_youth_conferencing_service.pdf).

Cavadino, M. and Dignan, J. (2002) *The Penal System: An Introduction* (3rd edn). London: Sage.

Cavadino, M. and Dignan, J. (2007, forthcoming) *The Penal System: An Introduction* (4th edn). London: Sage.

Children's Reporter, Association of Chief Police Officers in Scotland and Scottish Executive (2004) *Restorative Warnings in Scotland: Guidelines for Police* (available online at http://www.scotland.gov.uk/library5/justice/prwsg-00.asp).

Crawford, A. and Newburn, T. (2003) *Youth Offending and Restorative Justice: Implementing Reform in Youth Justice*. Cullompton: Willan Publishing.

Criminal Justice Review Commission (2000) *Review of the Criminal Justice System in Northern Ireland*. Belfast: HMSO.

Curry, D., Knight, V., Owens-Rawle, D., Patel, S., Semenchuk, M. and Williams, B. (2004) *Restorative Justice in the Juvenile Secure Estate*. London: Youth Justice Board (also available online at: http://www.youth-justice-board.gov.uk/Publications/Scripts/prodView.asp?idProduct=184&eP=YJB).

Davis, G. (1992) *Making Amends: Mediation and Reparation in Criminal Justice*. London and New York, NY: Routledge.

Davis, G., Boucherat, J. and Watson, D. (1987) *A Preliminary Study of Victim Offender Mediation and Reparation Schemes in England and Wales*. Home Office Research Study 42. London: HMSO.

Dignan, J. (1990) *Repairing the Damage: An Evaluation of an Experimental Adult Reparation Scheme in Kettering, Northamptonshire*. Sheffield: Centre for Criminological and Legal Research, University of Sheffield.

Dignan, J. (1992) 'Repairing the damage: can reparation be made to work in the service of diversion?', *British Journal of Criminology*, 32: 453–72.

Dignan, J. (2002) 'Reparation orders', in B. Williams (ed.) *Reparation and Victim-focused Social Work. Research Highlights in Social Work*. London and Philadelphia, PA: Jessica Kingsley.

Dignan, J. (2005) *Understanding Victims and Restorative Justice*. Maidenhead: Open University Press.

Dignan, J. with Lowey, K. (2000) Restorative Justice Options for Northern Ireland: A Comparative Review. *Review of the Criminal Justice System in Northern Ireland Research Report* 10. Belfast: Criminal Justice Review Commission/Northern Ireland Office.

Holdaway, S., Davidson, N., Dignan, J., Hammersley, R., Hine, J. and Marsh, P. (2001) *New Strategies to Address Youth Offending: The National Evaluation of the Pilot Youth Offending Teams. RDS Occasional Paper* 69. London: Home Office (also available online at www.homeoffice.gov.uk/rds/index.html).

Home Office (2000) *Circular Introducing the Final Warning Scheme: Revised Guidance*. London: Home Office (available online at http://www.homeoffice.gov.uk/yousys/youth.htm).

Home Office (2003) *Restorative Justice: The Government's Strategy. A Consultation Document on the Government's Strategy on Restorative Justice*. London: Home Office.

Home Office, Crown Prosecution Service, Department for Constitutional Affairs (2004) *Restorative Justice: the Government's Strategy – Responses to the Consultation Document* (available online at http://www.homeoffice.gov.uk/justice/victims/restorative).

Home Office/Youth Justice Board for England and Wales (2002) *The Final Warning Scheme Guidance for the Police and Youth Offending Teams* (issued in November). London: Home Office.

Hoyle, C., Young, R. and Hill, R. (2002) *Proceed with Caution: An Evaluation of the Thames Valley Police Initiative in Restorative Cautioning*. York: Joseph Rowntree Foundation.

Liebmann, M. and Braithwaite, S. (1999) *Restorative Justice in Custodial Settings. Report for the Restorative Justice Working Group in Northern Ireland* (available online atwww.extern.org/restorative/Rjreport.htm).

Marshall, T.F. and Merry, S. (1990) *Crime and Accountability: Victim/Offender Mediation in Practice*. London: HMSO.

Maxwell, G. and Morris, A.M. (1993) *Family, Victims and Culture: Youth Justice in New Zealand*. Wellington: Social Policy Administration and Victoria University of Wellington.

McElrea, F. (1994) 'Justice in the community: the New Zealand experience', in J. Burnside and N. Baker (eds) *Relational Justice: Repairing the Breach*. Winchester: Waterside Press.

Miers, D. (2004) 'Situating and researching restorative justice in Great Britain', *Punishment and Society*, 6: 23–46.

Miers, D., Maguire, M., Goldie, S., Sharpe, K., Hale, C., Netten, A., Uglow, S., Doolin, K., Hallam, A., Enterkin, J. and Newburn, T. (2001) *An Exploratory Evaluation of Restorative Justice Schemes. Research Series Paper 9*. London: Home Office.

Miers, D. and Willemsens, J. (eds) (2004) *Mapping Restorative Justice Developments in 25 European Countries*. Leuven: European Forum for Victim Offender Mediation and Restorative Justice.

Newburn, T., Crawford, A., Earle, R., Goldie, S., Hale, C., Masters, G., Netten, A., Saunders, R., Sharpe, K. and Uglow, S. (2002) *The Introduction of Referral Orders into the Youth Justice System. Home Office Research Study* 242. London: Home Office (available online at http://www.homeoffice.gov.uk/rds/index.html).

O'Mahony, D., Chapman, T. and Doak, J. (2002) *Restorative Cautioning: A Study of Police-based Restorative Cautioning Pilots in Northern Ireland*. Belfast: NISRA.

O'Mahony, D. and Doak, J. (2002) 'Restorative justice – is more better? The experience of police-led restorative cautioning pilots in Northern Ireland', *Howard Journal*, 43: 484–505.

Sawyer, B. (2000) *An Evaluation of the SACRO (Fife) Young Offender Mediation Project. Crime and Criminal Justice Research Findings* 43. Edinburgh: Scottish Executive.

Schiff, M. (2003) 'Models, challenges and the promise of restorative conferencing strategies', in A. von Hirsch *et al.* (eds) *Restorative Justice and Penal Justice: Competing or Reconcilable Paradigms?* Oxford: Hart Publishing.

Scottish Executive (2002) *Scotland's Action Programme to Reduce Youth Crime 2002*. Edinburgh: Scottish Executive.

Shapland, J., Atkinson, A., Atkinson, H., Chapman, B., Colledge, E., Dignan, J., Howes, M., Johnstone, G., Robinson, G. and Sorsby, A. (2006) *Restorative Justice in Practice: Findings from the Second Phase of the Evaluation of Three Schemes. Home Office Research Findings 274*. London: Home Office (available online at http://www.homeoffice.gov.uk/rds/rfpubsl.html).

Shapland, J., Atkinson, A., Colledge, E., Dignan, J., Howes, M., Johnstone, J., Pennant, R., Robinson, G. and Sorsby, A. (2004) *Implementing Restorative Justice Schemes (Crime Reduction Programme). A Report on the First Year. Home Office Online Report 32/04*. London: Home Office (available online at http://www.homeoffice.gov.uk/rds/pdfs04/rdsoir3204.pdf).

Sherman, L.W., Strang, H. and Woods, D.J. (2000) *Recidivism Patterns in the Canberra Reintegrative Shaming Experiments (RISE)*. Canberra: Centre for Restorative Justice, Australian National University.

Strang, H., Barnes, G., Braithwaite, J. and Sherman, L. (1999) *Experiments in Restorative Policing: A Progress Report on the Canberra Reintegrative Shaming Experiments (RISE)*. Canberra: Australian National University.

Walgrave, L. (2004) 'Restoration in youth justice', in M. Tonry and A.N. Doob (eds) *Youth Crime and Youth Justice: Comparative and Cross-national Perspectives. Crime and Justice: A Review of Research*. Vol. 31. Chicago, IL and London: University of Chicago Press.

Wynne, J. (1996) 'Leeds Mediation and Reparation Service: ten years experience of victim–offender mediation', in B. Galaway and J. Hudson (eds) *Restorative Justice: International Perspectives*. Monsey, NY: Criminal Justice Press.

Young, P. (1997) *Crime and Criminal Justice in Scotland*. Edinburgh: HMSO.

Chapter 16

Policing and restorative justice

Carolyn Hoyle

Introduction

This chapter will describe the rise of police-led restorative practices and examine shifting perceptions about police involvement in the process. It will consider the arguments for and against the police acting as restorative conference facilitators, looking critically at generalizations made about the relationship between police values and restorative values based on stereotypical ideas of 'the police', and conclude with a brief consideration of safeguards required if the police are to be involved in restorative justice.

The development of police-led restorative justice

New Zealand, the first country to put family group restorative conferences into a statutory framework, was influential in the establishment of the most famous police-led conferencing scheme at Wagga Wagga in New South Wales, Australia. The New Zealand Children, Young Persons and their Families Act introduced the new youth justice system in 1989, the same year that Braithwaite's seminal book, *Crime, Shame and Reintegration* was published. John MacDonald, adviser to New South Wales police, and his colleague, Steve Ireland, initially made the link between conferencing in New Zealand and Braithwaite's theory, and recommended that the New Zealand model be introduced in Wagga Wagga (Daly 2001). However, they argued successfully that conferencing should not be organized within the welfare department, as with the New Zealand model, because they thought conferences should be co-ordinated by the department responsible for the first contact – the police. Hence in 1991 the renowned 'effective cautioning' scheme began in Wagga Wagga to caution juvenile offenders according to restorative principles (Moore and O'Connell 1994).

Other Australian jurisdictions, including Northern Territory, Tasmania and Queensland, swiftly followed the Wagga model but towards the mid-1990s intense debate about police-led cautioning or conferencing emerged (Daly and Hayes 2001). There was opposition from youth advocacy groups, Juvenile Justice and the Attorney General's office, who all considered that victims and offenders would not see the police as sufficiently independent. Hence, although most Australian jurisdictions took up diversionary conferencing, almost all, either initially or in short time, rejected police facilitation in favour of community mediators.

By 1995, the New South Wales government had funded community justice centres to manage youth conferences and a working party had recommended legislation resulting in the Young Offenders Act 1998, giving responsibility for youth conferencing in New South Wales to the department of Juvenile Justice. Today, only two Australian jurisdictions still use police-led conferencing: the Australian Capital Territory (ACT) and the Northern Territory. Furthermore, new ACT legislation (the Crimes (Restorative Justice) Act 2004) allows for conferences to be conducted at several points in the criminal justice process and by agencies other than the police, so it remains to be seen whether the police will continue their involvement, which has been dwindling since the end of the famous reintegrative shaming (RISE) experiment in Canberra.[1]

Conversely, other jurisdictions that have subsequently adopted restorative conferencing have tended to use the Wagga police-led scripted model rather than the New Zealand conferencing model, now prevalent in Australia. For example, the police-led model was introduced into America by Anoka County Police in Minneapolis (Minnesota) in July 1994. It soon was being experimented with in other police departments within the state, such as St Paul.[2] By the end of 1995 approximately 200 police from a number of state, county and sheriff jurisdictions were trained and had introduced the model in varying degrees (O'Connell 2000).

The Wagga model provided the basis for the protocols underpinning various high-profile schemes, including Bethlehem (PA), Thames Valley (England) and the Royal Canadian Mounted Police.

Terry O'Connell (a senior Wagga police sergeant) brought police-led restorative conferencing to Thames Valley in 1994 and, following training and ad hoc experimentation in the mid-1990s (Young and Goold 1999), the Thames Valley restorative cautioning scheme started formally in 1998. Academic scrutiny of the two most prominent Wagga-based programmes – in Thames Valley (Hoyle *et al.* 2002) and Canberra (Strang 2002) – raised the international profile of police-led restorative justice. But Charles Pollard, the then Chief Constable of Thames Valley Police, and O'Connell himself also did much to publicize it through conference presentations, publications and in discussions with key policy-makers (Young and Hoyle 2003a).

Other forces, most notably Nottinghamshire and Surrey, were soon conducting experimental work of their own, and Northern Ireland has recently set up pilot restorative justice schemes following a major review of criminal justice (see O'Mahony and Doak 2004). Similarly, the Scottish Executive has embraced restorative justice and in 2004 announced the national roll-out of police restorative warnings for young, mainly first-time, offenders arrested for relatively minor offences.[3]

Unlike legislators in New Zealand and in most Australian territories, the UK Labour government strongly endorsed police-led restorative cautioning, as practised in Thames Valley (Young and Goold 1999). It introduced various new youth justice measures, under the Crime and Disorder Act 1998 and the Youth Justice and Criminal Evidence Act 1999, which had the police and other key agencies engaged in restorative justice (Crawford and Newburn 2003). Following the advice of Halliday (2001: 21) and Auld (2001), the government also introduced the conditional caution, in the Criminal Justice Act 2003 (Part 3, ss. 22–7). This new disposal option includes reparative or restorative conditions stipulated by the police and approved by the Crown Prosecution Service.

While the police are responsible for the delivery of restorative justice interventions, whether by giving conditional cautions to adults or warnings with restorative interventions to youths, it is legitimate to examine critically their role in restorative practices.[4]

The role of the police in restorative justice

In my view, restorative justice needs to operate within the criminal justice system, with its attendant due process checks and balances, in order for its processes and outcomes to be restorative. However, this does not necessarily mean that the police should be involved.

The risks of police facilitation

In many places the police have significant control over restorative justice processes. They can decide which offenders are offered a restorative process, which other stakeholders are asked to participate, how the meeting progresses and they can, to some extent, influence decisions about appropriate reparation. It is therefore crucial that they are perceived by all involved to be both fair and professional. In particular, the facilitator should have no personal agenda in deciding who participates or in the questions they ask of participants (Young and Hoyle 2003b). However, some believe that the police are incapable of this kind of detached professionalism required to ensure fair process.

Part of the unease centres on the fear that police facilitation places too much power in their hands (see Blagg 1997; Cunneen 1997; Ashworth 2002; Roche 2003). The danger is that officers will investigate, arrest, judge and punish someone without sufficient legal safeguards against the abuse of these considerable powers. It has also been argued that the police are exploiting the vogue for restorative justice to expand their punitive function, and, given the chance, will abuse it (Sandor 1994).

In Australia, when police facilitation attracted significant protest from community advocacy and legal organizations, researchers were vociferous in their criticisms of the Wagga model of restorative conferencing. Harry Blagg suggested that the police-led model 'led to the supplementation and extension of already significant police powers over young people' (1997: 481), while Polk (1997) criticized the use of police facilitators because of the Wagga focus on shaming. Although Polk recognized that shaming should be reintegrative, he argued that young people were already marginalized and shamed, and that this could be seen as another opportunity for police to stigmatize and shame them with no safeguards to ensure due process and fair penalties (see also Cunneen 1997). He also believed that the police do not understand the needs of young people, do not have the training or skills to manage the power imbalance between a young disadvantaged person and a group of adults, and cannot be neutral.

These and other critics questioned whether it is realistic to expect police, who are steeped in the adversarial and punitive system, to take a key role in what is supposed to be a restorative process. Given that the police are generally called upon to play contradictory roles in their contact with young people (for example, law enforcement, welfare assistance, peace-keeping), it is argued that the resultant conflict between these groups will mean that they will not be considered to be neutral facilitators (White 1994; Roche 2003).

One of the key requirements of a restorative process is that the facilitator remains respectful of all participants and dispassionate in approach. This does not mean that they treat the offender in exactly the same way as the victim. As restorative conferences are not investigatory processes, they necessarily involve someone who has been a victim of an offence and someone who has admitted to committing that offence, barring, of course, 'miscarriages of justice'. Therefore, as Wachtel has pointed out, the parties are not of equal moral standing as one has clearly wronged the other (1997: 111). The restorative process requires facilitators to have different expectations of offenders and victims. Offenders are asked to account for and take responsibility for their offensive behaviour. They are asked questions which might leave them feeling at the very least uncomfortable and are expected to make amends for their behaviour. Victims, conversely, do not have such expectations placed upon them. It is made clear in the questions the facilitator asks that one is the wronged and one the wrongdoer.

Wachtel argues therefore that, while facilitators should be fair, they cannot be neutral (1997: 111). This suggests a misunderstanding of the concept of neutrality. While the restorative process is predicated on the absence of moral equivalence of the main parties and has different expectations of them, the facilitator in delivering the restorative process must be neutral. By neutral it is meant not just dispassionate but impartial and without bias. The process should hold the offender accountable and the other participants might well, legitimately, express condemnatory sentiments, but the facilitator must not allow any personal or professional biases or pre-judgments to influence his or her behaviour during the conference. Fairness means more than just talking to all parties in an equally respectful way. Without impartiality the facilitator cannot be fair as impartiality in the criminal process is one of the most elementary requirements of fair treatment.

Dennis Galligan (1996) explores in some detail the relationship between impartiality and procedural fairness. He explains that the two main ways of ceasing to be impartial are being biased and losing one's independence, the primary concerns of critics of the police involvement with restorative justice. Galligan's definition of bias is uncontroversial:

> To be biased means broadly to have an inclination or predisposition towards one side rather than the other; it might also have the stronger connotation of being prejudiced. The idea of prejudice as pre-judgment brings out well the core idea that to be biased is in some way to have judged the issue beforehand or to have judged it for reasons which are not the right reasons (1996: 438).

While a facilitator might know that an offender has admitted to a criminal offence he or she will not, in most cases, know the context within which the offence was committed or the role of others in that offence, nor will he or she know how the offender feels about his or her behaviour. To prejudge these things due to a bias, whether personal or professional, is to deny all participants the chance of a fair and restorative process. Galligan identifies three main causes of bias: personal, systemic and cognitive. The first two are the most relevant for police facilitation.

Personal bias emphasizes factors personal to the official: 'It includes personal preferences or feelings; a personal interest ... or a personal connection to the matter' (1996: 438). Such personal bias is likely to impact on a conference if the facilitator is known personally to any of the participants or, more likely, has been involved in the criminal process prior to the conference. Even advocates of police facilitation tend to agree that arresting officers, or officers present when the arrest or investigation was taking place, should never facilitate the ensuing conference. However, empirical studies show that this sometimes happens. Of more concern to restorative justice is Galligan's second category of 'systemic bias':

> those inclinations and predispositions which each person has ... as a result of belonging to a social class or coming from a certain kind of background or working within a particular organisational context ... The attitude of the police to certain kinds of offenders or offences ...[is a notable example] of the dangers of systemic bias within organisations (1996: 438–9).

As Galligan argues: 'the absence of impartiality is a fundamental flaw which renders the process illegitimate' (1996: 441).

The risk of police facilitators being impartial and using their power in an unacceptable way was illustrated by a number of cases from the Thames Valley research. For example, in some conferences the process took on the structure and tone of a police interview. In others, police facilitators lapsed into stigmatic or deterrent language, or became defensive when participants raised concerns about how the police had arrested or otherwise dealt with the offender (Young 2001: 205–9). Even though in police-led conferences the officer responsible for investigating the offence should not convene the conference, reducing the risk of personal bias, there is still the very real risk of systemic bias – for example, that they will dismiss any complaints which may arise against the officer. As Roche points out: 'if state accountability is to be nurtured, the convenor must be independent as much as possible' (2003: 137).

Part of the appeal of restorative justice is in dealing fairly with and empowering indigenous and minority populations who have felt themselves unfairly and systematically discriminated against by established criminal justice processes. Restorative justice is held up as the fairer, more accountable alternative: rooted in the local community and taking seriously distinctive cultural norms (Weitekamp 2001: 155). However, as argued below, criminological theory and research tell us that police 'agendas' are highly likely to result in white middle-class participants being treated more fairly and more respectfully than those from ethnic or other minorities and those from less privileged backgrounds (Bowling and Phillips 2003; Sanders and Young 2003: 233–7). This understanding of the culture of policing, and the dangers of systemic bias, has provided the basis for powerful critiques of police-led restorative processes. Central to these critiques is the view that if the police are not seen as legitimate by indigenous people or other marginalized communities they should not play such a central role in restorative processes.

In a potent critique of police involvement in community conferencing in indigenous communities in Australia, Cunneen has argued that 'In most jurisdictions, community conferencing has reinforced the role of state police and done little to ensure greater control over police discretionary decision-making' (1997: 1). He cites research evidence showing that the police presence increases the reluctance of Aboriginal people to attend meetings and contributes to a non-communicative atmosphere for those who do. He makes the point that in New Zealand there were significant reforms to policing practices at the same time as the introduction of family group conferences. These included tighter controls on police powers in relation to young people, whereas 'The Australian variations have simply seen conferencing as expanding the options available to police' (1997: 7).

There are also concerns that the Wagga process could contribute to net-widening (Polk 1997). There was some evidence of this in the Northern Ireland pilot schemes. The profile of those given restorative cautions and conferences was more similar to those given 'advice and warning' than those cautioned previously and was not at all similar to those referred to prosecution: 'It was not uncommon to come across cases where a considerable amount of police time had been invested in arranging a full conference for the theft of a chocolate bar or a can of soft drink' (O'Mahony and Doak 2004: 495).

Alternatives to police facilitation

There is no systematic research on who could do a better job than the police in facilitating restorative cautions (Daly 2001), but few are as critical about social workers as they are about the police, even though they wield a great deal of power and influence over some people's lives. This is partly because there are far fewer sociological studies on the culture of social work. There are, however, data on social workers in restorative processes from New Zealand, where the facilitator is a 'youth justice co-ordinator', normally a social worker.

Morris and Maxwell (2001) have found that many families attending conferences facilitated by social workers have had bad experiences. They argue that social welfare and restorative justice values are not necessarily reconcilable, and that where conferences have met restorative objectives and reflected restorative values this has happened despite being placed in a social welfare setting rather than because of it. In the few cases where social workers acted as co-facilitators in the Thames Valley research there was similarly a pronounced drift away from a focus on restoration for all the stakeholders and towards assessing and responding to the offender's problems and needs (Young and Hoyle 1999).

All statutory bodies are likely to bring their own cultural assumptions and professional agendas to restorative processes. As Galligan makes clear, the police are not the only professionals in the criminal process who can introduce systemic bias, nor are they the only ones the public are cautious of (some people will have had in the past unpleasant experiences with social workers just as others have with the police). However, this should not lead us to assume that a purely communitarian restorative approach is unproblematic. Even lay community members will have their own personal agenda and neutrality might be even more difficult for them if they are closely involved in the very community that the offender has harmed (Crawford and Newburn 2002).

The benefits of police facilitation

Advocates of police facilitation argue that the police lend 'gravitas' to proceedings, are likely to be more successful in ensuring that undertakings are carried out and that police facilitation, indeed, the presence of the police in uniform, helps victims, and others, feel secure.

Only 9 per cent of the 178 participants interviewed for the study of restorative cautioning in the Thames Valley expressed disapproval of the police facilitating restorative cautions. The majority felt that police officers introduced a welcome degree of authority and formality to the meeting, with a few people (not all of them victims) mentioning that the police presence made them feel safer. Police facilitation was seen as giving the process some gravitas, enhanced by officers being in uniform (Hoyle *et al.* 2002; see also Braithwaite 1994).

So what of the critics who focus on communities where the police suffer a pronounced legitimacy deficit? O'Mahony *et al.* suggest that even in Northern Ireland police-led restorative cautioning appears to be quite popular among participants, although the small-scale nature of the published evaluation means that too much weight should not be placed on this finding (2002: 39). However, the authors also reviewed the other data and literature on police-led facilitation and concluded:

both victims and offenders trust police to organise a fair and non-authoritarian conference in which both sides can feel safe in dialogue. Overall, it would seem less important to have in place a neutral facilitator than to have a facilitator in place who is perceived as being fair ... With a lack of empirical data to the contrary, the results of the studies to date would seem to suggest that police-run conferencing is as consistent an idea with restorative justice principles as other mediation programmes (2002: 16–8).

Weitkamp *et al.* go further, arguing that:

It is absolutely necessary to include the police in a model which is supposed to make community safer, reduce fear of crime levels, create and implement successful prevention strategies, improve the quality of life in a given community, restore peace within the community through a restorative justice approach, and improve the relationship between police and citizens in order to achieve higher levels of satisfaction with the police work (2003: 319–20).

They propose a restorative problem-solving police prevention programme structured and implemented by the community, victims, offenders and the police together. But are all police amenable to restorative approaches, or are some likely to be hostile? Both detractors and supporters of police facilitation talk about 'the police' as if they are all the same. Surely it is as ridiculous to suggest that all police officers are incapable of being fair and neutral as it is to suggest that all police officers are restorative in their treatment of different people. In considering the role of the police in restorative processes we need to think more critically about restorative values and police culture and not assume that they are always antithetical.

Police culture and restorative values

Research conducted in Thames Valley showed that 'traditional police culture, and the authoritarian and questionable practices it can generate, presents a significant obstacle to the successful implementation of restorative justice' (Young 2001: 220–1). However, we should not assume that police behaviour is invariably motivated by such traditional culture. Nor should we assume that all officers are entrenched in the same culture.

In our observations of restorative conferences were many examples of fair and neutral facilitation by officers whose approach displayed restorative values (Hoyle *et al.* 2002). Most define restorative values as mutual respect; the empowerment of all parties involved in the process (except the facilitator); neutrality of the facilitator; accountability; consensual, non-coercive participation and decision-making; and the inclusion of all the relevant parties in meaningful dialogue (Hoyle and Young 2002). These are not necessarily the values that come to mind when considering traditional street policing.

The (stereotypical) culture of the police can be described in terms of sexism, conservatism, racism, defensiveness, cynicism, suspiciousness and a tendency to categorize the world into the rough and the respectable, those deserving of help and those deserving of contempt or even brutality (e.g. Reiner 2000). Few would welcome the idea of a cynical, racist brute having even more powers than he already has. We would rather restrict his authority with further procedural safeguards. However, as those who describe this stereotypical culture would argue, it is applicable to some but not all officers, in particular to a certain type of 'street cop'.

The idea of an homogeneous, monolithic police culture has been rejected by many academic police researchers (e.g. Manning and Van Maanen 1978) in favour of recognition of the distinctive cultures of different ranks, different patrols and different forces. Indeed, various sociological studies have developed typologies of different police orientations and styles (Reiner 2000: 101). It is generally recognized that a distinction exists between stereotypical street cops and stereotypical 'management cops', who try to be more professional, less judgemental, more efficient and more accountable to local communities (Reuss-Ianni and Ianni 1983). Further distinctions can be seen between detectives and uniform officers, and between patrol and community police officers (Foster 2003).

Police culture also needs to be understood as a dynamic force. It is dynamic in that, at least to some extent, it structures choices, and it is dynamic in that it is constantly evolving, partly in response to changing socio-political or legal contexts (Hoyle 1998). As Reiner explains, it is 'neither monolithic, universal nor unchanging' (2000: 87). While the criminological literature is replete with empirical examples of police departments apparently resistant to change, there is also evidence of different, less traditional cultures within the police and of changes in culture in response to structural changes in the organizational goals or laws, policies and directives from above.

Janet Chan's work is germane to this subject. For her 'a satisfactory formulation of police culture should allow for the possibility of change as well as resistance to change' (1996: 112). Developing the ideas of the influential French sociologist, Pierre Bourdieu, in particular his concepts of 'field' and 'habitus', she argues that officers working under a given set of structural conditions (the field) develop and maintain certain cultural assumptions (habitus), and make choices about their actions which influence their practice (Chan 1999). They do not all have the same values, and their values adapt to changes in their organization, the criminal justice framework and in the wider society in which they work and live. So how might recent changes to the field have impacted on police values?

Changes to the 'field': restorative policing in the twenty-first century

Restorative justice was introduced into English policing in the last years of the twentieth century amid a plethora of new policies and legislation and within a changing socio-political context. These structural changes focused attention on the role of victims and the wider community in the state's response to crime. The police service was expected to bring victims and communities centre stage, to work closely with them and with other criminal justice and voluntary agencies.

Under the youth justice legislation of the 1990s, which created youth offending teams, the police were expected to share with other agencies, most notably social services, the responsibility for restorative work with young offenders. The approach of these teams, at least in theory, has much in common with the practices and philosophy of 'professional policing' as described by Chan. This type of professional policing is more congruent with restorative justice values than street policing.

The field and habitus of professional policing, as described by Chan (1999: 134), emphasizes problem-solving and service provision as its core business. It is non-judgemental in its approach to people, with an appreciation of diversity in cultures and lifestyles. It aims to involve the community in policing and problem-solving and strives for citizen and personal satisfaction. This philosophy and approach are consistent with certain restorative values such as inclusiveness, accountability and empowerment. While it would be naïve in the extreme to expect the changes to the criminal justice landscape to have brought about complete professionalization of the police organization, it is highly likely that those police officers who apply to work in restorative processes are much more like Chan's 'professional cops' than street cops, and that they become more so the longer they stay in these roles.

As culture develops from an adaptive response to working conditions, 'two separate subcultures can exist when the two groups work in two different subfields and develop different sets of habitus' (Chan 1997: 227). So patrol work, which is by nature unpredictable and can be dangerous, although often isn't, would foster certain cultural norms and values, while facilitating restorative conferences might foster others. As an example, some of the parents in O'Mahony and Doak's (2004) study of restorative cautioning in Northern Ireland commented on the differences between the 'sympathetic' culture of police restorative justice facilitators and the 'bullying' and heavy-handed tactics of patrol officers (2004: 493; see also Stahlkopf 2005).

Police officers who are recruited into restorative justice programmes are trained in restorative theories and practices. Those engaged *exclusively* in restorative work are likely, after only a few months, to adopt restorative values and behave in more inclusive and restorative ways; in Chan's parlance, to become more 'professional' in their policing, although there are exceptions to this norm (Hoyle *et al.* 2002). Hence their culture begins to change, moving further away from the culture of 'street policing', as described in the literature.

Can restorative policing bring about further changes to the field of policing?

If restorative justice can change the attitudes and behaviours of some individual officers, perhaps it can bring about wider cultural change across the police organization. Pollard (2001) was certainly optimistic that this would happen in the Thames Valley police force. And the force has been explicit in its intention that operational restorative initiatives are part of a strategy to promote fundamental cultural change and bring about:

> a long overdue shift from a militaristic, law enforcement police *force* paradigm, to that of a problem-solving, community safety focused police *service*, concentrating on crime prevention, and where this is not possible, diversion from the criminal justice system … Restorative policing … aims to engender a new way of thinking amongst police officers, such that they think and act restoratively, *all* the time and in *all* their dealings, not just with victims and offenders but with work colleagues, community members, even family and friends (Bowes 2002: 10–11, emphasis in original).

Braithwaite (2002b: 162–3) recognizes that locating conferencing within a police service might bring about the transformation of police cautioning and police culture more broadly: 'Not just in formal cautioning but also in daily interaction on the street, the challenge of transforming police culture from a stigmatising to a restorative style is important.' O'Connell (1998) and Moore (1995 cited in McCold 1996) believe this was happening in Wagga Wagga before the police were prohibited from facilitation: 'The few qualitative studies of the Wagga Wagga program … suggest that involvement by the police in conferencing produced a cultural shift from a punitive legalistic approach to a more problem-solving, restorative approach' (Moore 1995: 212 cited in McCold 1996).

Some of the police facilitators in O'Mahony and Doak's study thought that restorative cautioning had the potential to assist community policing and build better relationships with families living in socially deprived areas (2004: 494). They also go beyond this to consider that 'police-led restorative justice could also aid the transitional process in Northern Ireland by helping to foster improvements in strained police/community relations in many areas' (2004: 501).

The conclusions of the research carried out in Thames Valley were less optimistic. Some police involved in restorative cautioning believed their work was encouraging a community-policing ethos, in which crime prevention through restoration of relationships and moral persuasion took priority over a simple deterrence model of policing and punishment. However, this educative effect was largely confined to those regularly acting as facilitators rather than permeating throughout a police service (Hoyle and Young 2003).

Empirical evidence from America similarly suggests that, when restorative activity is limited to relatively few officers, there will be little impact on general policing culture. Police who facilitated conferences in a scheme in Pennsylvania were positive about restorative justice (displaying a shift away from a crime control conception of policing) but officers not involved were generally indifferent (McCold and Wachtel 1998). The inference one might draw from this is that restorative justice has to be embraced throughout a police service if culture change across all ranks and departments is to be achieved (O'Mahony *et al.* 2002). The Thames Valley police tried to achieve this by giving the majority of officers the chance to attend short restorative justice awareness training sessions, leaving the full one to two weeks' training for those given the task of facilitating restorative conferences regularly. However, this had little impact on those not regularly facilitating or even observing conferences.

Bearing in mind the need for ongoing training and time for restorative values to influence practice, and practice to embed values further, it makes sense for certain officers to do only restorative work, rather than combining restorative and street policing, which are to some extent antithetical. However, this would do nothing to inculcate restorative values across the police service.

It is clearly beneficial for street police to be exposed to restorative values and practices, if nothing else to improve their capacity to seek fair resolutions to conflicts on the beat. Making restorative work an isolated police specialism runs the risk of a schism between restorative justice officers and patrol officers which contradicts the aims of those responsible for bringing restorative processes into British policing (Pollard 2001). However, empirical evidence suggests the aim of infusing all policing with restorative values is overly ambitious.

A safer way forward

Research suggests that the police might be better placed to ensure full involvement of all those affected by crime than other available state or community agents but, given the criticisms described above, if they are to continue to facilitate restorative conferences they need to work sensitively, forming constructive relationships between communities and the state to tame the excesses of both (Crawford 2002). While the state is engaged with communities in deliberative justice there will necessarily be concerns about power imbalances and procedural safeguards, especially where the police are the key players. While police facilitation in pre-court justice is clearly on the wane in some jurisdictions, it seems set to continue in the UK, at least for the foreseeable future. Given that there is no alternative that does not bring with it its own unique problems, rather than further debates at the level of principle, we should adopt a pragmatic approach and consider how in practice police facilitation ought to be regulated.

Constraints on police facilitation

It would seem desirable, at a minimum, for police facilitators to have played no part in the investigation of a case. Additional strategies are needed, however, to guard against systemic bias, such as the risk that facilitators may allow a general police agenda, or even the presence of the investigating officer, to dominate the restorative process. Such strategies could include a requirement that police co-facilitate with a volunteer drawn from the local community, with the hope that each will provide a check on the prejudices of the other; the monitoring of practice by other agencies, peers or supervisors; and the use of feedback forms from participants or, preferably, independent research into practice 'on the ground' (Hoyle and Young 2002). All these practical suggestions will increase the chance of police facilitators being fair and restorative in their approach but cannot alone secure fair and proportionate processes and outcomes.

Safeguards for defendants

Perhaps the most controversial means of increasing accountability and fair process in police-facilitated meetings is for legal advice and representation to be provided to the participants. There is some evidence that minors who consider themselves to be innocent will attend conferences in order to avoid any further legal procedure (Dumortier 2003). Furthermore, either the offender or victim might feel pressurized into agreeing to disproportionate reparation. When we consider that restorative justice, broadly defined, can be coercive, have punitive outcomes and can leave defendants still subject to criminal proceedings for failing to carry out reparation or conditions attached to the penalty, as is the case with the new conditional cautions,[5] it is hard to deny the necessity of sound legal advice. That there is no empirical evidence that these 'miscarriages' happen frequently in practice is no assurance of the legitimacy of the process. The risk justifies the inclusion of lawyers in restorative processes and, while there is some opposition to this (Wright 1999), a few restorativists present a persuasive case for their inclusion at various stages (see, in particular, Shapland 2003).

It is argued that deliberative accountability ensures that other participants in a conference can challenge an offender who proposes inadequate reparation or a victim who urges the offender to proffer more than is fair. Furthermore, it is said that these mechanisms allow participants to challenge inappropriate behaviour by police facilitators (Braithwaite 2002a). Observation of conferences conducted by the Thames Valley police provides some empirical support for mechanisms working in both these ways (Hoyle and Young 2002). However, there will always be meetings where the unacceptable is not challenged and, as Roche (2003) points out, we cannot rely on deliberative accountability to protect the rights of more vulnerable participants.

Lawyers should observe, rather than participate in conferences, not with the aim of guiding the discussion or preventing exploration of the issues considered relevant to all participants, but with the sole aim of ensuring procedural justice. Lawyers would not encroach on the main goals of restorative meetings (empowerment of participants and promotion of reparation and reintegration) but limit their interventions to preventing police questioning of offenders aimed at gathering evidence of other crimes or offenders and preventing agreements that are wholly disproportionate. As Roche (2003) argues, there is not a need within restorative processes for strict proportionality, but there should be a requirement to ensure upper limits are imposed in defence of human rights and lower limits based on public safety. A lawyer would not need to stop the meeting and refer it to court but could point out to all participants the problems with the agreement or line of questioning and suggest alternative routes to restorative outcomes. Of course, the criminal law would need to provide a safety net for those cases where a lawyer's advice was ignored. In this way due process protections should not undermine the dialogic and participatory nature of restorative justice or the goal of holding offenders accountable for the harms they have done.

It is not clear, however, that lawyers would accept limitations on their role. The main problem with legal representation in a process where the police are in the driving seat, apart from the costs involved, is that lawyers are currently trained to play a part in an adversarial process which has clear rules and procedures, whereas the restorative process should be more fluid and interactional than the court process. If lawyers were to be involved in restorative conferences they would likely want clear guidelines or even rules on what is admissible, what due process requires and what clearly contravenes it, and they would need to know whose interests they represent. The guidelines would need to make clear what the role of the lawyer should be with regards to hearsay evidence if an offender discusses the criminal activities of someone not present at the conference. There is no reason why we should expect a lawyer to represent the interests of someone not labelled his or her client. For example, if there is more than one offender in the conference, does each offender need a lawyer or can one represent all? And if a reparation agreement is too lenient should they see their role as defending the concept of proportionality, which could be seen as representing the interests of the victim or the wider community, or should they only object to disproportionately harsh agreements which affect adversely 'their' client?

Arguably, guidelines could be established to make clear how lawyers should respond in such circumstances which would make possible a limited role for legal representation, although it is questionable whether or not there would be enough fully qualified lawyers willing to perform these duties, absent adequate remuneration, which is not likely within this process. However, the difficulties raised by consideration of due process protections provide further evidence of the dangers of police facilitation.

Disproportionate reparation agreements might arise from a conference facilitated by professionals or volunteers outside the police force and can be dealt with by way of an appeals or review process, which could be activated by the facilitator or by one or more of the participants after the conference. But the problem of further offences being exposed during the process is particular to those conferences facilitated by the police. While a lay volunteer would certainly go to the police if a participant claimed to have murdered his mother prior to the conference, he would not pursue information suggesting further offences by the offender in the conference or by others outside the process. Such further offences might be crucial to the offender's explanation of his own behaviour. To create an environment where offenders need to be careful about what they say is to constrain the restorative process. When the police facilitate it is inevitable that, even when promised that the conference is a safe and confidential forum, all participants, not just offenders, are likely to feel inhibited in some situations. A non-police facilitator is more likely to persuade participants that what he or she says is confidential.

Conclusion

Sometimes, restorative justice is presented as an alternative to criminal justice. However, the more likely scenario, at least in the UK, is that restorative justice will become firmly entrenched *within* criminal justice, rather than replacing it. Embedding restorative justice within the criminal justice system allows it to flourish without the risks of a purely informal process but it brings with it risks of a different kind, in particular the risks associated with police facilitation. Although constraints upon police facilitation and due process safeguards for defendants can do a great deal to reassure those sceptical of police involvement, principled criticisms of police facilitation are not easy to dismiss. In particular, the argument that there should be a separation of powers between the key stages of the criminal process is persuasive. It is clearly problematic to have one agency having so much power and control over a criminal process, from arrest to punishment, especially when that agency has a strained relationship with certain, often disadvantaged communities.

However, there are similar principled objections to the involvement of other state agencies in the facilitation of restorative processes (social workers, for example, tend to be offender focused rather than balanced in their approach) and entirely community-based schemes offer none of the protections of a state-based system. There are pragmatic reasons for police involvement: they have the political backing, the resources and apparently the support from victims and offenders. There are also benefits to the police of their involvement in restorative justice in terms of transforming police culture, if only for those officers directly involved. However, with restorative justice now firmly embedded in the criminal justice process, the time may have come to acknowledge that these justifications are insufficient; that there needs to be a new and viable alternative.

If the governments in the UK, Australia and New Zealand, as well as many jurisdictions in North America, are committed to using restorative processes within both the youth and adult justice systems, for minor and serious offences, perhaps they should consider the establishment of specialist teams of professional restorative justice facilitators, rather than relying on police, social workers or volunteers. Quasi-judicial facilitators would, like stipendiary magistrates, bring professional independence to the process and have none of the cultural baggage or professional agendas of other state agents. They would, in the UK, serve the youth offending teams, the police and, for serious offences, the courts and the national offender management service and in other countries their equivalents.

Creating this putative new service or department might reasonably be expected to circumvent many of the drawbacks observed by researchers of restorative justice in action. It would rapidly evolve experience and 'best practice', training and guidelines, and simply by virtue of the fact that its practitioners would spend their entire professional lives on restorative justice, they could be expected not to exhibit the departures from the 'script' and inappropriate interventions frequently seen at police-led conferences (Young 2001). By definition independent, they might also be expected to command the authority and respect which some are wary of awarding to existing institutions, such as social workers and the police. This new service would also free up police resources now devoted to restorative justice in the UK and in parts of Australia and America, which managerialist pressures at present leave vulnerable. It might prevent the demise of restorative justice where the police no longer have the motivation or the resources to take the lead, as may be the case in Canberra now. Such a specialist cadre, fully trained, accredited and accountable to, and financed by, all criminal justice agencies, would signal the full maturation of restorative justice and its complete integration with other parts of the criminal process.

Selected further reading

Von Hirsch, A., Roberts, J. and Bottoms, A. (eds) (2003) *Restorative Justice and Criminal Justice: Competing or Reconcilable Paradigms?* Oxford: Hart Publishing. This edited collection situates critiques of restorative justice within criminal justice. Its internationally renowned contributors critically examine its aims, the limits on its application and the extent to which restorative justice can and should replace criminal justice.

Walgrave, L. (ed.) (2002) *Restorative Justice and the Law.* Cullompton: Willan Publishing. This is an admirable edited collection that questions the extent to which restorative justice can become part of the mainstream response to crime. Adam Crawford's chapter in particular is a 'must read' for all scholars of restorative justice.

Morris, A. and Maxwell, G. (eds) (2001) *Restorative Justice for Juveniles.* Cullompton: Willan Publishing. This book brings together key writers in the field from across the globe, and its chapters – from Daly, Dignan and Marsh, Young, Blagg and Maxwell and Morris – are particularly helpful for exploring the issues raised in this chapter.

Crawford, A. and Newburn, T. (2003) *Youth Offending and Restorative Justice.* Cullompton: Willan Publishing. This book provides an empirically grounded, theoretically informed account of the introduction of restorative justice into the youth justice system, looking in particular at the implementation of referral orders and youth offender panels.

Johnstone, G. (2003) *A Restorative Justice Reader: Texts, Sources, Context.* Cullompton: Willan Publishing. This reader brings together a selection of extracts from the most important and influential contributions to the restorative justice literature and its emergent philosophy. Its contributors are both supporters and critics of restorative justice and deal with the range of topics likely to be of interest to scholars in this field.

Acknowledgements

Thanks are due to Andrew Ashworth, Gerry Johnstone, David Rose and Lucia Zedner for their helpful comments on previous drafts of this chapter.

Notes

1 Personal communication with Heather Strang. The RISE experiment has been extensively reported on by Sherman *et al.* at www.aic.gov.au/rjustice.

2 Interview with Paul Schnell on the Real Justice website at www.realjustice.org/library/pschnell.html.

3 Personal communication with Les Davey, Director of Real Justice, UK and Ireland.

4 There is a wider dimension to this debate: the role of the state in restorative justice. This is covered in this volume by Lode Walgrave (see Chapter 26). Some argue that restorative justice programmes should be kept independent of mainstream criminal justice, while others argue that the state has a legitimate role in restorative processes. The critical point is that any process which purports to change behaviour, and to facilitate agreements between people who might ordinarily be assumed to be opposed to one another, needs to be legitimate and accountable, and this is not so easy to guarantee without a statutory framework. Rejecting the due process protections and other checks and balances that accompany state-administered justice entails grave risks.

5 It could be argued that the new conditional cautions should not be referred to as restorative measures as they impose conditions upon offenders and this might be seen as a perversion of restorative values. However, there is not the space here to explore this legitimate concern.

References

Ashworth, A. (2002) 'Responsibilities, rights and restorative justice', *British Journal of Criminology*, 42: 578–95.

Auld, R. (2001) *Review of the Criminal Courts of England and Wales* (summary available at www.criminal-courts-review.org.uk/summary.htm).

Blagg, H. (1997) 'A just measure of shame?: Aboriginal youth and conferencing in Australia', *British Journal of Criminology*, 37: 481–501.

Bowes, D. (2002) 'Restorative policing: beyond "community" to a new philosophy for policing', (unpublished).

Bowling, B. and Phillips, C. with Shah, A. (2003) 'Policing ethnic minority communities', in T. Newburn (ed.) *Handbook of Policing*. Cullompton: Willan Publishing.

Braithwaite, J. (1989) *Crime, Shame and Reintegration*. Cambridge: Cambridge University Press.

Braithwaite, J. (1994) 'Thinking harder about democratising social control', in C. Alder and J. Wundersitz (eds) *Family Conferencing and Juvenile Justice: The Way Forward or Misplaced Optimism?* Canberra: Australian Institute of Criminology.

Braithwaite, J. (2002a) 'Setting standards for restorative justice', *British Journal of Criminology*, 42: 563–77.

Braithwaite, J. (2002b) *Restorative Justice and Responsive Regulation*. New York, NY: Oxford University Press.

Chan, J. (1996) 'Changing police culture', *British Journal of Criminology*, 36: 109–34.

Chan, J. (1997) *Changing Police Culture: Policing in a Multicultural Society*. Cambridge: Cambridge University Press.

Chan, J. (1999) 'Police culture' in D. Dixon (ed.) *A Culture of Corruption: Changing an Australian Police Service*. Sydney: Hawkins Press.

Crawford, A. (2002) 'The state, community and restorative justice: heresy, nostalgia and butterfly collecting', in L. Walgrave (ed.) *Restorative Justice and the Law.* Cullompton: Willan Publishing.

Crawford, A. and Newburn, T. (2002) 'Recent developments in restorative justice for young people in England and Wales', *British Journal of Criminology*, 42: 476–95.

Crawford, A. and Newburn, T. (2003) *Youth Offending and Restorative Justice.* Cullompton: Willan Publishing.

Cunneen, C. (1997) 'Community conferencing and the fiction of indigenous control', *Australian and New Zealand Journal of Criminology*, 30: 1–20.

Daly, K. (2001) 'Conferencing in Australia and New Zealand: variations, research findings, and prospects', in A. Morris and G. Maxwell (eds) *Restorative Justice for Juveniles: Conferencing Mediation and Circles.* Oxford: Hart Publishing.

Daly, K. and Hayes, H. (2001) *Restorative Justice and Conferencing in Australia.* Trends and Issues 186. Canberra: Australian Institute of Criminology.

Dumortier, E. (2003) 'Legal rules and safeguards within Belgian mediation practices for juveniles', in E.G.M. Weitekamp and H.J. Kerner (eds) *Restorative Justice in Context: International Practice and Directions.* Cullompton: Willan Publishing.

Foster, J. (2003) 'Police cultures', in T. Newburn (ed.) *Handbook of Policing.* Cullompton: Willan Publishing.

Galligan, D. (1996) *Due Process and Fair Procedures.* Oxford: Clarendon Press.

Halliday, J. (2001) *Making Punishments Work: Report of the Review of the Sentencing Framework for England and Wales* (available at www.homeoffice.gov.uk/docs/halliday.html).

Hoyle, C. (1998) *Negotiating Domestic Violence: Police, Criminal Justice and Victims.* Oxford: Oxford University Press.

Hoyle, C. and Young, R. (2002) 'Restorative justice: assessing the prospects and pitfalls', in M. McConville and G. Wilson (eds) *The Handbook of the Criminal Justice Process.* Oxford: Oxford University Press.

Hoyle, C. and Young, R. (2003) 'Restorative justice, victims and the police', in T. Newburn (ed.) *Handbook of Policing.* Cullompton: Willan Publishing.

Hoyle, C., Young, R. and Hill, R. (2002) *Proceed with Caution: An Evaluation of the Thames Valley Police Initiative in Restorative Cautioning.* York: Joseph Rowntree Foundation.

Manning, P. and Van Maanen, J. (eds) (1978) *Policing: A View from the Street.* Santa Monica, CA: Goodyear.

McCold, P. (1996) 'Bethlehem Police Family Group Conferencing project.' Paper presented to the American Society of Criminology annual meeting, Chicago, IL, November.

McCold, P. and Wachtel, B. (1998) *Restorative Policing Experiment: The Bethlehem Pennsylvania Police Family Group Conferencing Project* (available at http://www.iirp.org/library/summary.html).

Moore, D.B. and O'Connell, T. (1994) 'Family conferencing in Wagga Wagga: a communitarian model of justice', in C. Alder and J. Wundersitz (eds) *Family Conferencing and Juvenile Justice: The Way Forward or Misplaced Optimism?* Canberra: Australian Institute of Criminology.

Morris, A. and Maxwell, G. (2001) 'Implementing restorative justice: what works?', in A. Morris and G. Maxwell (eds) *Restorative Justice for Juveniles: Conferencing, Mediation and Circles.* Oxford: Hart Publishing.

O'Connell, T. (1998) 'From Wagga Wagga to Minnesota.' Paper presented at the first North American Conference on Conferencing, Minneapolis (available at http://iirp.org/library/nacc/nacc_oco.html).

O'Connell, T. (2000) 'Restorative justice for police foundations for change.' Paper presented at the United Nations Crime Congress Ancillary Meeting on Implementing Restorative Justice in the International Context, Vienna, Austria, 10–17 April.

O'Mahony, D., Chapman, T. and Doak, J. (2002) *Restorative Cautioning: A Study of Police-based Restorative Cautioning Pilots in Northern Ireland. Northern Ireland and Statistical Series Report* 4. Belfast: Statistics and Research Branch of the Northern Ireland Office.

O'Mahony, D. and Doak, J. (2004) 'Restorative justice – is more better? The experience of police-led restorative cautioning pilots in Northern Ireland', *Howard Journal*, 43: 484–505.

Polk, G. (1997) 'Conferencing in New Zealand and Australia', *VOMA Quarterly* 8 (available at http://www.voma.org/docs/vomaqf97/vomaf97.pdf).

Pollard, C. (2001) 'If your only tool is a hammer, all your problems will look like nails', in H. Strang and J. Braithwaite (eds) *Restorative Justice and Civil Society*. Cambridge: Cambridge University Press.

Reiner, R. (2000) *The Politics of the Police* (3rd edn). Oxford: Oxford University Press.

Reuss-Ianni, E. and Ianni, F. (1983) 'Street cops and management cops: the two cultures of policing', in M. Punch (ed.) *Control in the Police Organisation*. Cambridge, MA: MIT Press.

Roche, D. (2002) 'The regulatory state in South African townships', *British Journal of Criminology*, 42: 514–33.

Roche, D. (2003) *Accountability in Restorative Justice*. Oxford: Oxford University Press.

Sanders, A. and Young, R. (2003) 'Police powers', in T. Newburn (ed.) *Handbook of Policing*. Cullompton: Willan Publishing.

Sandor, D. (1994) 'The thickening blue wedge in juvenile justice', in C. Alder and J. Wundersitz (eds) *Family Conferencing and Juvenile Justice: The Way Forward or Misplaced Optimism?* Canberra: Australian Institute of Criminology.

Shapland, J. (2003) 'Restorative justice and criminal justice: just responses to crime?', in A. von Hirsch *et al.* (eds) *Restorative Justice and Criminal Justice: Competing or Reconcilable Paradigms?* Oxford: Hart Publishing.

Stahlkopf, C. (2005) 'The new youth justice system in the United Kingdom: young people's experiences of early intervention and restorative justice.' Unpublished DPhil, Department of Sociology, University of Oxford.

Strang, H. (2002) *Repair or Revenge: Victims and Restorative Justice*. Oxford: Oxford University Press.

Wachtel, T. (1997) *Real Justice*. Pipersville, PA: Piper's Press.

Walgrave, L. (2002) 'Restorative justice and the law: socio-ethical and juridical foundations for a systematic approach', in L. Walgrave (ed.) *Restorative Justice and the Law*. Cullompton: Willan Publishing.

Weitekamp, E. (2001) 'Mediation in Europe: paradoxes, problems and promises', in A. Morris and G. Maxwell (eds) *Restorative Justice for Juveniles: Conferencing Mediation and Circles*. Oxford: Hart Publishing.

Weitekamp, E., Kerner, H.-J. and Meier, U. (2003) 'Community and problem-oriented policing in the context of restorative justice', in E. Weitekamp and H.-J. Kerner (eds) *Restorative Justice in Context: International Practice and Directions*. Cullompton: Willan Publishing.

White, R. (1994) 'Shame and reintegration strategies: individuals, state power and social interests', in C. Alder and J. Wundersitz (eds) *Family Conferencing and Juvenile Justice: The Way Forward or Misplaced Optimism?* Canberra: Australian Institute of Criminology.

Wright, M. (1999) *Restoring Respect for Justice*. Winchester: Waterside Press.

Young, R. (2001) 'Just cops doing "shameful" business? Police-led restorative justice and the lessons of research', in A. Morris and G. Maxwell (eds) *Restorative Justice for Juveniles: Conferencing, Mediation and Circles*. Oxford: Hart Publishing.

Young, R. and Goold, B. (1999) 'Restorative police cautioning in Aylesbury: from degrading to reintegrative shaming ceremonies?', *Criminal Law Review*, 126–38.

Young, R. and Hoyle, C. (1999) *Restorative Cautioning: Strengthening Communities in the Thames Valley. Confidential Interim Study*. Oxford: Centre for Criminology, University of Oxford.

Young, R. and Hoyle, C. (2003a) 'New improved restorative justice? Action-research and the Thames Valley Initiative in restorative cautioning', in A. von Hirsch *et al.* (eds) *Restorative Justice and Criminal Justice: Competing or Complementary Paradigms?* Oxford: Hart Publishing.

Young, R. and Hoyle, C. (2003b) 'Restorative justice and punishment', in S. McConville (ed.) *The Use of Punishment*. Cullompton: Willan Publishing.

Chapter 17

Prisons and restorative justice

Daniel W. Van Ness

Most restorative programmes take place outside prison. There are several reasons for this: it is easier for offenders in the community to make amends, work with victims and offenders is more easily done in the community, and use of restorative justice programmes as a sentencing diversion means matters are handled before the offender is sent to prison. However, there have been efforts in recent years to explore how restorative justice might be used the context of a prison and, further, whether it is possible to conceive of a restorative prison regime – one based fully on restorative principles and values.

This chapter will consider why attention is being given to restorative justice in prisons, categorize these attempts based on their stated objectives and consider issues relating to the implementation of restorative justice programmes in a captive environment.

Why prisons?

For all but summary offences imprisonment seems to be the sentencing currency of contemporary criminal justice; most sentences are expressed in terms of the length of time in prison or in some form of conditional freedom from imprisonment such as probation or suspended sentence. Aside from offering protection in the instances of offenders who pose a serious risk to community members, there seems to be little in restorative justice theory or vision that embraces imprisonment (Van Ness and Strong 2006).

Nevertheless, restorative initiatives are taking place in prison. Some programmes developed because the direct stakeholders themselves, prisoners or victims, requested it; others because government officials responsible for the prison environment introduced it; and still others because of the initiative of community agencies or individuals. An example of a prisoner-initiated programme is the victim/offender workshop, founded by prisoners of Sing Sing Correctional Facility and the Quaker Worship Group at that prison. This programme allows groups of prisoners to talk with surrogate victims in meetings facilitated by volunteer psychologists (Immarigeon 1994: 8). The Victim Offender Mediation/Dialogue programme in Texas prisons, on the other hand, grew out of a crime survivor's request to meet with the man who had killed her daughter to ask questions that only he could answer (White 2001: 59).

These are examples of programmes initiated by the direct parties to the crime. Other programmes have been initiated by government officials or by community-based groups. Examples of government-initiated efforts include the Conflict Resolution and Team Building training programme for prison staff used by the Philadelphia City Prison, and reinforced by annual four-hour refresher courses. The programme teaches staff to develop skills in conflict resolution; the system reports that the number of incidents in which force was required has gone down (Roeger 2003: 5). Another, more ambitious, programme is the Belgian effort to create a restorative prison culture in each of its 32 prisons with a restorative justice co-ordinator assigned to the prison to introduce restorative justice to prison staff and prisoners (Biermans and d'Hoop 2001: 2). An example of a community-based programme is the Sycamore Tree project being used in several countries, notably in England and Wales, and New Zealand. This programme, administered by the national Prison Fellowship organizations in those countries, brings victims into prisons to meet with groups of unrelated offenders for a series of structured conversations about crime and its aftermath (Walker 1999).

Programmes for relatively small groups of victims and prisoners, like those in Sing Sing Prison and Texas, particularly those started at the request of the victims and offenders, are examples of inclusion of the direct parties in the process of addressing crime and its aftermath. Inclusion has been described as one of the cornerpost values of restorative justice (Van Ness and Strong 2006). Because they are voluntary for victims and offenders, they represent what might be called 'restorative incursions' into the largely non-restorative world of prison life, and they are likely to remain relatively small in terms of the numbers of victims and prisoners affected, though they may be important in personal impact. For example, roughly 600 mediations have been initiated in the Texas programme since 1993 and, to date, approximately 80 have been conducted (Szmania 2004: 4).

Programmes initiated by government officials and community-based organizations may also focus on a limited segment of the prisoner population. However, these may also be extremely ambitious in the breadth and extent of the expected prisoner involvement and the desired impact on the overall prison environment. As discussed later in this chapter, the more ambitious the project, the more issues are raised from the perspective of restorative justice.

What are these programmes' objectives?

Restorative programmes in prison may be categorized based on their objectives, and this section will review them in an order based on the increasing ambitiousness of those objectives. Some programmes seek to help prisoners develop awareness of and empathy for victims. Others seek to make it possible for prisoners to make amends to their victims. A third group facilitates meetings between prisoners and their victims, family members or community members. At least one programme has sought to strengthen the ties and inter-relationships between prisons (and their staff and prisoners) and the communities in which they are located. Restorative justice practices are being used for conflict resolution among prisoners, prison officers, and even between prisoners and prison officers. Finally, some prisons offer restorative interventions as an opportunity for personal transformation of their prisoner participants. Let us consider these in turn.

Victim awareness and empathy programmes

Victim awareness and victim empathy programmes are designed to help prisoners come to understand better the impact of crime on victims. Although consistent with restorative justice philosophy, a significant motivation for offering these programmes is rehabilitative and based on the recognition that victim *unawareness* is very high in prisons. The thinking is that a deepened appreciation of the trauma their crimes cause may lead prisoners to change their attitudes towards crime in a way that reduces recidivism (Thompson 1999: 5).

Some victim empathy programmes teach prisoners about the impact of crime on victims, but do not include contact with victims. An example of this approach is the Focus on Victims programme in Hamburg, Germany, which takes place during the prisoners' first three months in the institution. The project helps prisoners think generally about victimization, consider people they know who have been victims, reflect on their own experiences of being victims and then look in more detail at the consequences and aftermath of victimizations they may have caused. It concludes with an introduction to victim–offender mediation (Hagemann 2003: 225–7).

The Victim Offender Reconciliation Group, initiated by state prisoners at the California Medical Facility, operates weekly meetings to which they invite various victims' groups to make presentations and participate in dialogue. For example, representatives of the Bay Area Women against Rape victim support organization have met with them on a number of occasions to discuss the trauma of rape and its aftermath, and to lead discussions about the attitudes of men who rape. This has led to prisoners doing service projects or making products for sale with the proceeds being donated to victims' rights and support groups (Liebmann and Braithwaite 1999: 17–8).

Still other programmes organize conversations between prisoners and unrelated victims – people who have been victims of crimes, but not of those crimes committed by the offenders with whom they meet. The purpose of these programmes is to make the victims' experience real to offenders by allowing prisoners to develop a relationship with victims, hear their stories and reflect with them on how crime affects the lives of victims. An example is the Sycamore Tree project. Two studies using the Crime-Pics II evaluation tool, one conducted in England and Wales and the other in New Zealand, have concluded that offenders' attitudes change during the course of the project, and that as a result the prisoners appear to be less likely to reoffend (Feasey *et al.* 2004; Bakker 2005).

Amends programmes

One way for offenders to make amends is for them to make financial payments to victims to compensate them for their losses. However, prisoners face a number of financial claims (e.g. lawyers' fees, court costs, fines and, sometimes, 'rental payments' to cover their time in jail or prison), and they have very limited means of obtaining funds to satisfy them. In response, Belgium created a redress fund to which prisoners can apply if they want to acknowledge their wrongdoing and take steps to make amends to the victim. A prisoner who is successful in his or her application must perform a certain number of hours of community service before the funds are released to the victim, and it is the prisoner's responsibility to identify an institution that will accept the community service. The intention behind this approach is to treat compensation to victims differently from other civil judgements that can be enforced once the prisoner has a source of income. Requiring prisoners to take affirmative steps to address their responsibilities to the victim means that they have chosen actively to accept responsibility rather than passively treat it as one of a number of debts that must be paid (Robert and Peters 2003: 112–3; also see Braithwaite and Roche 2001).

Other programmes focus on the offenders' obligations, but not to particular victims. This may be done through projects in which prisoners raise funds to give to a victim support organization or public charity, such as that organized by the Victim Offender Reconciliation Group mentioned above. In others the emphasis is on the community as an indirect victim. One such programme is described below in the section 'Prison–community programmes'.

Mediation/Dialogue programmes

The State of Texas developed a programme at the request of victims that facilitates meetings between victims or co-victims of crimes of severe violence and their offenders. Most of the offenders are serving very long sentences; some are on death row. The programme has no formal effect on the prisoners' sentences. The process begins at the victim's request, and involves a thorough and lengthy preparation process designed to ensure that the victims and prisoners are ready for such a meeting. When they do meet, it is with the assistance of a mediator who will have helped in the preparation. The purpose of the meeting for both victims and prisoners is to achieve a degree of healing (White 2001: 84–141; Szmania 2004: 4–13).

Many prisoners have alienated their families because of their involvement in crime, the embarrassment and harm they have caused, and in some cases because of the crimes they have committed against family members. In addition, victims in their communities may have threatened to harm the prisoners when they return to the communities. Consequently, it may be necessary to facilitate interaction between prisoners, their family members and/or members of the community in order to discuss how the offender will be reintegrated into the community. The New South Wales Department of Corrective Services has created what it calls 'protective mediation' to address those situations. This is not 'face to face' mediation, but takes the form of shuttle diplomacy with trained staff acting as 'go-betweens' to help the parties arrive at a practical agreement, when possible. The agreement is sometimes made part of the conditions of parole (NSW Department of Corrective Services 1998).

The National Parole Board of Canada has created specialized hearings for aboriginal prisoners. An 'elder-assisted hearing' is one in which an aboriginal elder participates in the parole hearing in order to inform board members about aboriginal culture, experiences and traditions, and their relevance to the decision facing the board members. The elder also participates in the deliberations. A 'community-assisted hearing' takes place in an aboriginal community, and all parties, including the victim and members of the community, are invited to participate in what is called a 'releasing circle', which will consider the question of release (National Parole Board 2002).

Communities can be fearful and angry at the prospect of a prisoner returning. Restorative justice programmes have emerged to address this problem as well. A remarkable Canadian example, now used in England as well, is called Circles of Support and Accountability. These programmes assist in the reintegration of serious sexual offenders, typically paedophiles whose prognosis is so serious that they have been held in prison for the full length of their sentence, and are being released without parole supervision or support. There is understandable apprehension on the parts of both the released offenders and the communities to which they return. The circles work with the offender, social services representatives, local law enforcement officials and community members to organize a treatment programme and to negotiate conditions related to community safety and security (Correctional Service of Canada 2002; Quaker Peace and Social Witness 2005).

Prison–community programmes

One interesting effort has been made to reduce the isolation of prisons and prisoners from the communities in which their prisons are located. The International Centre for Prison Studies in the UK initiated a 'restorative prison' project in three prisons. One of the four key objectives was to create opportunities for prisoners to perform community service projects, in or outside prisons, for the benefit of the immediate community, such as reclaiming public parkland. These parks had been donated by wealthy landowners over the past hundred years, but local governments did not have sufficient funds to maintain them. Using funds from the national lottery and other sources, the project used prisoners to clean up the parks, repair or replace boats, fences, benches and other park structures, and generally restore the parks as valuable and usable features of the communities (Coyle 2001: 8; Mace 2000: 4, 2004: 1–2).

Conflict resolution programmes

There are a number of ways in which conflict resolution interventions have been introduced into the prison setting. One is to teach prisoners how to address conflict without resorting to violence. An example of this is the Alternatives to Violence Project (AVP) developed by Quakers at the request of prisoners in Attica, New York. AVP is now used throughout the world. It helps prisoners recognize when potentially violent situations are likely to arise, learn communication skills to alleviate the potential for violence and learn to value others (Sloane 2002: 3). This is essentially a rehabilitation programme that, while not directly connected to restorative justice, has significant congruence with some restorative values (Bischoff 2001).

A second kind of programme helps prisoners who come into conflicts with other prisoners find peaceful ways to resolve them. An Ohio programme called Resolution trains prisoners to serve as mediators. They work in pairs to help other prisoners find solutions to their own conflicts (Roeger 2003: 4). Another example is the 'peace table' created by prisoners in Bellevista Prison in Medellin, Colombia, where imprisoned gang leaders meet to resolve disputes between their gangs both in and outside the prison.[1]

A third category of conflict resolution programme addresses workplace conflicts among correctional staff members, including senior management. Programmes like this have been used in Philadelphia City prisons and the State of Ohio. The programme has not only helped staff address their own conflicts, it has also improved their ability to deal with conflict with prisoners (Roeger 2003: 5).

A fourth category of programme addresses prisoner discipline and grievance processes. This is sensitive because of the authoritarian structure of prisons in which staff control is tested by some prisoners (Newell 2002: 7). However, Kattackal (2003: 26) reports that adapted forms of family group conferences have been used to deal with disciplinary hearings at several prisons in the Yukon, Canada, with good results. The Western Australia Department of Justice Annual Report for 2002/3 described its prisoner grievance procedure as focused 'on mediation, restoration and negotiation rather than arbitration and adjudication'. This has allowed the department to develop 'a better understanding of the nature and extent of prisoner grievances', which in turn has helped the department identify prisoner issues (Piper 2003: 40). As a working paper developed by Tim Newell for the Restorative Justice Consortium in England noted, 'complaints where it is the "system" that is at fault rather than individual members of staff, complaints of attitude or oppressive behaviour and complaints of incivility' might be particularly amenable to a restorative process (Newell n.d.).

Transformation programmes

The sixth objective, and by far the most ambitious, is to create an environment in which the prisoner's entire self may be transformed. Cullen has called this a 'virtuous prison', one in which restorative justice and rehabilitation would be combined in an effort:

to foster 'virtue' in inmates, which is usually defined as 'moral goodness' or 'moral excellence' ... Prisons should be considered moral institutions and corrections a moral enterprise. Inmates should be seen as having the obligation to become virtuous people and to manifest moral goodness. This statement announces that there are standards of right and wrong and that offenders must conform to them inside and outside of prisons. The notion of a virtuous prison, however, also suggests that the correctional regime should be organized to fulfil the reciprocal obligation of providing offenders with the means to become virtuous (Cullen *et al.* 2001: 268).

Are restorative justice and imprisonment compatible?

Particular restorative programmes taking place inside prisons will have to address practical issues such as gaining access to prisoners and introducing victims into the prison environment. However, these appear to be pragmatic and not principled problems with the use of restorative justice in prison. This changes, however, when the attempt is made to create a restorative or virtuous prison, because at that point the reality of captivity works against the key values of restorative justice, such as voluntariness, respect and so forth.

Vidoni Guidoni, writing of his experience with an initiative that sought to create a restorative unit within an Italian prison, identifies six obstacles to achieving prison reform through restorative justice (2003).

I Conflict over the reconstruction of self

Unless prisoners are forced to go through restorative motions, which would violate restorative values and principles, significant change needs to take place within prisoners for them to take responsibility for their acts and for the harm that resulted from those acts. This requires a process of reflection and a reconstruction of the prisoners' identities by the prisoners themselves 'so that the person can say what he is compared to what he was' (p. 62). But virtually every aspect of prison life is designed to force prisoners to conform to the culture of the prison, which takes the prisoner through 'a degradation process which weakens him and makes him docile to the prison's administrative and disciplinary machine' (p.62). Guidoni's research found that only prisoners who for some reason had been meditating for a long time on their identity, who had experiences outside the prison or who were close to release were able to reconstruct their lives. Those who were most caught in the grasp of the prison culture had the most difficulty accepting responsibility for being the sort of person who harmed victims.

2 Competing with the prison culture

Guidoni means the culture within prisons that moves prisoners to accept the conditions of prisoner life. In particular, it leads prisoners to view themselves as victims of corrupt or unjust police, prosecutors, defence attorneys, judges, prison officials and prison guards. When they are so conscious of injustices done to them, it is difficult for them to reflect deeply about the kind of persons they themselves are.

There is a second aspect of the prison culture problem, one that Guidoni did not raise. Prison subcultures are typically deviant, making rejection of deviance more difficult for prisoners. Inviting them to participate in a process of restoration and transformation requires tremendous strength on their part to move against the prevailing culture. One of the ironies of prisons is that they were once thought of as a means of removing offenders from the criminogenic influences in which they were immersed outside prison. Penitentiaries, or places of penitence, were to be settings in which they would be protected from such negative moral influences, and would therefore be free to do the kind of reflection of which Guidoni speaks. The attempt to create penitentiaries hospitable to such moral reflection and renewal, of course, failed.

3 Non–violent conflict resolution versus prison disciplinary action

Prisons use or threaten physical and moral violence, making adoption of peaceful conflict resolution difficult. Force is used or threatened to keep prisoners from escaping and to control their movement in the prison. Furthermore, life among prisoners is typically characterized by threatened or actual use of violence (Flanders-Thomas *et al.* 2002: 1). Such realities work against efforts to instil in prisoners a strong value for peaceful conflict resolution. Furthermore, they create the risk that decisions that appear to be restorative might in fact have been coerced because of unrecognized power imbalances among prisoners, between prisoners and staff, and among staff.

4 The difference between stated and perceived goals

Guidoni found that the goals of the restorative justice staff were different from those of the prisoners who participated in the programme. The staff viewed the project as a way of creating a different sort of prison which would improve conditions for prisoners. Prisoners, on the other hand, viewed the programme more instrumentally, as a way of obtaining prison leave for good behaviour. The prisoners viewed the programme as a way of gaining work experience outside prison rather than participating in it because of a deep commitment to the principles and values of the programme.[2] In addition, some prison staff viewed the programme as a way of gaining more control over the prisoners because it was a privilege that they could be required to earn.

5 Autonomy denied

Prisons are authoritarian and hierarchical, controlling virtually all aspects of the lives of prisoners, making it difficult for them to exercise personal responsibility. Yet, responsibility is a key value of restorative justice. Programmes that are required by the prison administration or by parole boards, such as victim empathy training, may be beneficial to prisoners, but are not as restorative as ones that are pursued at the initiative of the prisoners.

But the issue of the control of prison regimes cuts both ways. Just as it may reduce the opportunities for prisoners to take responsibility by requiring particular activities, it may also prevent prisoners from taking responsibility. Barb Toews, who has worked on restorative justice initiatives in Pennsylvania prisons, found that many prisoners would like to have direct or indirect contact with their victims, but are prohibited by law from contacting them. So they wait, hoping that the victim will initiate contact (Toews 2002: 5).

6 The social conditions of a restorative justice prison

Prison conditions are seldom good. Problems can include the mental and physical health risks caused by overcrowding, bad hygiene, racial and ethnic tensions within the prisons and so forth. This reality can become part of a prisoner's incentive for participating in the programme (see subsection 4 above). But it is not likely that the restorative unit will have substantially better conditions than those of the rest of the prison. Given the very difficult physical and social conditions in which prisoners live, is it reasonable to expect them to take part in conversations about how their actions have harmed others?

These are the six 'ambivalences' that Guidoni offered concerning restorative justice in prison. Others might be added to the list.

7 The offender focus of prison

Prisons are necessarily preoccupied with prisoners, making it difficult for restorative justice programmes in the prisons to maintain a focus on the needs of victims. This is a problem confronted in varying degrees by all restorative justice programmes that intersect significantly with the criminal justice system, but it is particularly acute in prisons because it is there that prisoners, not victims, reside. The prison is a unique community with a society made up entirely of people sent there by the criminal justice system and of the people who keep them there.

8 Legitimation of prisons

Robert and Peters speak of the 'hijacking of restorative justice initiatives' as a real and present threat, 'certainly when it concerns a possible new legitimation of imprisonment' (2003: 116). Their concern is that the promise and appeal of restorative justice might distract the public and policy-makers from the bankruptcy of prisons.

Conclusion

To date there has not been a clear restorative justice justification for imprisonment. Early distinctions between restorative justice and retributive justice at least implicitly linked imprisonment with retributive justice, thereby raising questions about its legitimacy. But as Roche (Chapter 5, this volume) and Burnside (Chapter 8, this volume) have shown, a growing number of restorative justice proponents question whether restoration and retribution are in fact polar opposites. Furthermore, prisons cannot fairly be linked exclusively to retributive deterrent justice; their development and expansion were defended as rehabilitative at one time.

This is why conceptions of restorative justice can be helpful (see Johnstone and Van Ness, Chapter 1, this volume). The *encounter* conception does not offer a critique of imprisonment. Many who ascribe to this conception object to the overuse of imprisonment (and perhaps to the use of it at all), but those objections would be on grounds other than restorative justice, for restorative processes can be conducted inside and outside prison. The *reparative* conception might be able to marshal a critique on the grounds that imprisonment causes harm that can be justified only to the extent that it prevents greater harm. That is, the focus on repair means that responses to crime should be assessed based on the amount of harm that has been repaired and on whether that was done in a way that produced the least amount of new harm possible. Imprisonment would be justified if it prevented more harm than it caused, subject to limiting considerations such as proportionality. The *transformative* conception would add reflection on the relational and social impact of imprisonment, and on the structural impediments in society that result in unjust or broken relationships.

However, even if restorative justice adds new dimensions to the long tradition of critiques of prisons, or amplifies criticisms already raised, the reality appears to be that prisons will be with us for some time. This raises a dilemma for those who feel imprisonment is unjust: do restorative proponents refuse opportunities to extend the benefits of restorative justice to prisoners on the grounds that the institutions in which they have been confined are unjust, or do they work to transform the prison experience along restorative lines, running the risk that this creates a new justification for an unjust institution? Of course, such schemes involve contradictions and will meet with disapproval of those who believe that any constructive reform of repressive institutions simply shores up those institutions. But that is inevitable in any attempt actually to reform the world – and in the case of restorative justice this tension can perhaps be managed if advocates and practitioners of restorative justice in prisons keep reminding themselves of the broader values and principles of restorative justice towards which they are working.

On the other hand, if prisons can be justified restoratively, then restorative principles may be able to help identify the people who should be imprisoned and the conditions in which they should live. They may even suggest the kinds of regimes in which the work of restoration can be optimized. The examples in this chapter suggest that there are a number of ways in which prisons can offer restorative programmes, but these are a far cry from amounting to restorative prisons.

Selected further reading

Hagemann, O. (2003) 'Restorative justice in prison?', in L. Walgrave (ed.) *Repositioning Restorative Justice*. Cullompton: Willan Publishing. Hagemann considers whether it is possible to attempt restorative justice inside the walls of prison systems that are coercive and destructive.

Liebmann, M. (2006) 'RJ in prisons – an international perspective.' Paper presented at the 3rd International Winchester Restorative Justice Group Conference, 29–30 March, Winchester. Liebmann offers a thorough, country-by-country survey of restorative justice programmes conducted inside prisons, with helpful information about how they were organized and who manages the programmes.

Mace, A. (2000) *Restorative Principles in the Prison Setting. A Vision for the Future*. London: International Centre for Prison Studies, King's College London (available online at www.kcl.ac.uk/depsta/rel/icps/restorative_prison.doc).

Vidoni Guidoni, O. (2003) 'The ambivalences of restorative justice: some reflections on an Italian prison project', *Contemporary Justice Review*, 6: 55–68. Writing of his experience with an initiative that sought to create a restorative unit within an Italian prison, Vidoni Guidoni identifies six obstacles to achieving prison reform through restorative justice.

Notes

1 The author has visited this prison and met with peace-table participants.
2 This criticism could undoubtedly be raised about any restorative justice programme: prisoners, offenders outside prison, victims, community members and others who participate undoubtedly do for a variety of reasons, and those are not likely to be identical with programme goals. However, if the programme participants do not over time begin to share some of the objectives of staff as a result of their experiences in the programme, one may wish to question the extent to which the programme is achieving its objectives. In other words, the issue of the lack of congruence between the goals of prisoner participants and programme staff is quite different from that between programme staff and prison staff, since the prison staff are less likely to adjust their objectives over time.

References

Bakker, L. (2005) 'Sycamore Tree Project impact evaluation for Prison Fellowship New Zealand.' Unpublished study (available online at http://www.pficjr.org/programs/stp/report/bakker).

Biermans, N. and d'Hoop, M.-N. (2001) 'Development of Belgian prisons into a restorative perspective.' Paper presented at the Positioning Restorative Justice fifth international conference, International Network for Research on Restorative Justice for Juveniles, Leuven 16–19 September.

Bischoff, M. (2001) 'How restorative is AVP? Evaluating the Alternatives to Violence Project (AVP) according to a restorative justice yardstick.' Unpublished paper available online at mediate.quaker.org/papers/rj.htm.

Braithwaite, J. and Roche, D. (2001) 'Responsibility and restorative justice,' in G. Bazemore and M. Schiff (eds), *Restorative Community Justice. Repairing Harm and Transforming Communities*. Cincinnati, OH: Anderson Publishing.

Correctional Service of Canada (2002) *Circles of Support and Accountability: A Guide to Training Potential Volunteers.* Ottawa: Correctional Service of Canada.

Coyle, A. (2001) 'Restorative justice in the prison setting.' Paper presented at the International Prison Chaplains' Association conference, Driebergen, Holland, May.

Cullen, F. Wozniak, J. and Sundt, J. (2001) 'Virtuous prison: toward a restorative rehabilitation', in H. Pontell and D. Shichor (eds) *Contemporary Issues in Crime and Criminal Justice: Essays in Honor of Gilbert Geis.* Upper Saddle River, NJ: Prentice Hall.

Feasey, S., Williams, P. and Clarke, R. (2004) 'Evaluation of the Sycamore Tree programme.' Unpublished report issued by the Research Centre for Community Justice at Sheffield Hallam University.

Flanders-Thomas, J., Giffard, C. and Nair, R. (2002) *Advancing a Human Rights Culture in our Prisons: The Usefulness of a Conflict Resolution Approach.* Centre for Conflict Resolution (available online at ccrweb.ccr.uct.ac.za/two/11_2/humanrights.html).

Guidoni, V.O. (2003) 'The ambivalences of restorative justice: some reflections on an Italian prison project', *Contemporary Justice Review*, 6: 55–68.

Hagemann, O. (2003) 'Restorative justice in prison?' in, L. Walgrave (ed.) *Repositioning Restorative Justice.* Cullompton: Willan Publishing.

Immarigeon, R. (1994) *Reconciliation between Victims and Imprisoned Offenders: Program Models and Issues.* Akron, PA: Mennonite Central Committee US Office on Crime and Justice.

Kattackal, R. (2003) *Research Framework for a Review of Community Justice in Yukon.* Whitehorse, AK: Government of Yukon.

Liebmann, M. and Braithwaite, S. (1999) *Restorative Justice in Custodial Settings: Report for the Restorative Justice Working Group in Northern Ireland.* Restorative Justice Ireland Network.

Mace, A. (2000) *Restorative Principles in the Prison Setting. A Vision for the Future.* London International Centre for Prison Studies, King's College (available online at www.kcl.ac.uk/depsta/rel/icps/restorative_prison.doc.

Mace, A. (2004) 'The restorative prison project', (Newsletter), February/March.

National Parole Board (2002) *Facts: Hearings for Aboriginal Offenders* (available online at http://www.npb-cnlc.gc.ca/infocntr/factsh/hearings_e.htm).

Newell, T. (2002) *Restorative Justice in Prisons: The Possibility of Change.* Cambridge: Cropwood Fellowship Programme, Institute of Criminology, University of Cambridge. (available online at http://www.crim.cam.ac.uk/research/cropwood/documents/RestorativeJusticeinPrisons.doc).

Newell, T. n.d. *How to Make Prisons more Restorative.* London: Restorative Justice Consortium (available online at http://www.restorativejustice.org.uk/Resources/pdf/How2makeprismorerest.pdf).

NSW Department of Corrective Services (1998) *Protective Mediation* (available online at http://www.dcs.nsw.gov.au/res_just/protmed.htm).

Piper, A. (2003) *Department of Justice Annual Report 2002/2003.* Perth: Department of Justice (available online at http://www.sat.justice.wa.gov.au/portal/server.pt/gateway/PTARGS_0_2_323_201_0_43/http%3B/justicecontent.extranet.justice.wa.gov.au/content/files/DOJ_Annual_Report_2002-03.pdf).

Quaker Peace and Social Witness (2005) *Circles of Support and Accountability in the Thames Valley: The First Three Years April 2002 to March 2005.* London: Quaker Communications for Quaker Peace and Social Witness.

Robert, L. and Peters, T. (2003) 'How restorative justice is able to transcend the prison walls: a discussion of the "restorative detention" project', in E. Weitekamp and H.-J. Kerner (eds) *Restorative Justice in Context: International Practice and Directions.* Cullompton and Portland, OR: Willan Publishing.

Roeger, D. (2003) 'Resolving conflicts in prison', *Relational Justice Bulletin*, 19: 4–5.

Sloane, S. (2002) *A Study of the Effectiveness of Alternatives to Violence Workshops in a Prison System*. Simon Fraser University Center for Restorative Justice (available online at www.sfu.ca/cfrj/fulltext/sloane.pdf).

Szmania, S.J. (2004) 'Beginning difficult conversations: an analysis of opening statements in victim offender mediation/dialogue.' PhD dissertation, Faculty of the Graduate School, University of Texas at Austin.

Thompson, D. (1999) 'Towards restoration (victim awareness programmes for adult offenders in South Australia).' Paper presented at the Restoration for Victims of Crime Conference, Australian Institute of Criminology in conjunction with Victims Referral and Assistance Service, Melbourne, 9–10 September (available online at http://www.aic.gov.au/conferences/rvc/thompson.pdf).

Toews, B. (2002) 'Listening to prisoners raises issues about prison-based restorative justice', *VOMA Connections*, Summer: 1–6.

Van Ness, D.W. and Strong, K.H. (2006) *Restoring Justice* (3rd edn). Cincinnati, OH: Anderson Publishing.

Walker, P. (1999) 'Saying sorry, acting sorry: the Sycamore Tree Project, a model for restorative justice in prison', *Prison Service Journal*, May: 19–20.

White, L.L. (2001) 'Hope in process: a qualitative study of victim offender mediation/dialogue in Texas.' Unpublished doctoral dissertation, Texas A&M University.

Chapter 18

Schools and restorative justice

Brenda Morrison

The emergence of restorative justice in schools

As the field of restorative justice began to define itself in the 1990s, the role of schools in promoting restorative justice was seen as central to developing a more restorative society as a whole:

> Even more crucial [than the work in juvenile and criminal justice] is the work just beginning in schools – anti-bullying systems, the prevention of truancy and exclusions, class circles, conflict resolution training, peer mediation. In schools we have society in miniature and persons in the process of learning to become citizens. It is not simply a milieu for job-training. How well we manage our schools will determine how well our society works a generation later (Marshall 1997: n.p.).

One could make a strong case that many different education leaders have long mounted similar arguments (see, for example, Dewey 1990, 1916) being a notable example, and have, in different ways, practiced being 'restorative' within the school community. Within this milieu of theory and practice, the use of restorative justice in schools, per se, made the leap from courts to schools in the mid-1900s. In Australia, for example, Margaret Thorsborne, a school-based guidance officer (school counselor) in a large high school in Queensland, had heard about community conferencing, an approach that police in New South Wales were trialling to divert young offenders from court. She used the same approach to facilitate a school-based conference to address the issues raised by a serious assault at a school dance. The success of this first, and subsequent, face-to-face restorative conference abated her

> search for a non-punitive intervention for serious misconduct … In particular, an intervention for serious cases of bullying which did not put the victim at further risk and also involved parents of both the offender and the victim … [C]onferencing seemed to fit the bill of the ultimate intervention which increased empathy and lowered impulsivity on the part of the bully (Cameron and Thorsborne 2001: 181).

Since these early days, there have been many developments in the practice of restorative justice in schools. One of these developments has been adapting the judicial language of restorative justice for use in schools. For example, many schools struggled with the word 'justice' in a school context, preferring terms such as restorative practices, restorative approaches, restorative measures, restorative discipline and restorative action. Schools also struggled with the terms 'victim' and 'offender', preferring phrases like 'students who have caused harm' and 'students who have been harmed' or 'students who bully' and 'students who have been bullied'. Likewise, a face-to-face restorative justice conference has also been referred to by a number of other names, community accountability conferences (Education Queensland); school community forums (New South Wales Department of Education and Training); community group conferencing (Colorado School Mediation Center); community conferencing (Calgary Community Conferencing); and restorative conferencing (Home Office, England). Beyond these preferences, schools have also drawn on other large circle processes, each having unique features. For example, peace-making or healing circles use rituals associated with the First Nations of North America, such as a talking piece (see Pranis *et al.* 2003); other schools used concentric circles (or circles within circles) to address classroom concerns, where the inner circle includes those most affected by an incident, and the outer circle, the remaining classroom members (see Morrison and Martinez 2001); schools also use the New Zealand family group conferencing model, where private family time is provided (see Marsh 2004).

Restorative justice conferencing, in the contexts of schools, has now been used to address a range of harmful behaviour, including bullying, assaults, drugs, property damage and theft, bomb threats, as well as guns at school. The process has also been used to address defiant and disrespectful behaviour. Harmful behaviour happens every day in schools. The aim of restorative justice in schools, as with other jurisdictions, is to repair the harm done; at the same time, the practice of restorative justice in schools goes a step further. Many schools today practise proactive, as well as reactive, restorative measures. The broad aim is to build the social and emotional intelligence and skills within the school community such that a normative capacity for safe and just schools can be realized. It is in this latter capacity that the development of restorative justice in schools has augmented other movements driving school safety reforms.

Paralleling the rise of restorative justice, that initially grew out of concerns within criminal and juvenile justice, was the rise of Peace Education or Conflict Resolution Education (CRE) in schools, largely responding to social justice concerns. Some of these early programmes, such as Discipline that Restores (Claassen 1993) and Restitution: Making it Right (Gossen 1992), were also offering clear alternatives to punitive forms of discipline in schools; as such, the philosophical base of these programmes shows strong parallels with the philosophical base of restorative justice. The Association for Conflict Resolution's understanding of CRE demonstrates clear parallels with restorative justice:

[CRE] models and teaches, in culturally meaningful ways, a variety of processes, practices and skills that help address individual, interpersonal, and institutional conflicts, and create safe and welcoming communities. These processes, practices and skills help individuals understand conflict processes and empower them to use communication and creative thinking to build relationships and manage and resolve conflicts fairly and peacefully (Jones and Compton 2003: 19).

There are now numerous programmes and practices that aim to build children's skills in conflict resolution and create safe and welcoming school communities (see Jones and Compton 2003). More recently, within this same movement, has been the rise of programmes in schools aimed at building social and emotional intelligence, based on Daniel Goleman's (1995) work. As the term gained currency, the definition of emotional intelligence evolved, with current views suggesting:

Emotional intelligence refers to an ability to recognize the meanings of emotions and their relationships, and to reason and problem-solve on the basis of them. Emotional intelligence is involved in the capacity to perceive emotions, assimilate emotion-related feelings, understand the information of those emotions, and manage them (Mayer et al. 1999: 267).

This definition embraces Goleman's (1995) five domains of emotional intelligence: knowing one's emotions, managing emotions, motivating oneself, recognizing emotions in others and handling relationships. In recognizing that social and emotional learning was an essential aspect of education (preschool through high school), Goleman co-founded the Collaborative for Academic Social and Emotional Learning (CASEL) in 1994. Goleman (1995: 279) believes that schools are 'the one place communities can turn to for correctives to children's deficiencies in emotional and social competence.' Expanding the notion of emotional intelligence to what it means to be educated, Elias et al. (2001: 133) suggest:

The current view is that to be educated involves being knowledgeable, responsible, and caring, and many would add, nonviolent. It means that the traditional focus on intellectual skills – IQ – must be supplemented by a strong concern with social and emotional skills – 'EQ', the skills of emotional intelligence (EI). The reasons for this are many, but none are more compelling than what we have learnt about brain functioning, human memory, and the difference between learning for test performance and learning for the purpose of living one's everyday life. For the latter, social and emotional factors are paramount.

Internationally, there are now hundreds of programmes that focus on developing social and emotional intelligence in schools. This development dovetails with Sherman's (2003) conceptualization of restorative justice as emotionally intelligent justice. Likewise, Cameron and Thorsborne

327

(2001: 208), reflecting on the early trials of restorative justice, make a clear link between restorative justice and emotional intelligence:

> The lesson for our education system is to introduce restorative measures as early as preschool, and build on creating a climate where relational values are translated into prosocial behaviour by all members of the school community. The teaching and modelling of emotional intelligence and relationship skills becomes part of the daily business in classrooms. Children are taught to understand what they are feeling and how to deal with difficult situations. Situations and their consequent emotions, which, when unacknowledged, feed the need for interpersonal violence, are dealt with openly.

Besides restorative justice conferencing, conflict resolution and peace education, as well as the development of social and emotional learning, there are many other restorative elements that schools practise but that are beyond the scope of this chapter. For example, many people have long argued against the use of rewards and punishment within education and child development (see Kohn 1999; Porter 2001). Thus, there is a rich tapestry of what could be called restorative practices, when contrasted with traditional punitive practices, within schools.

Given this rich tapestry of non-punitive approaches, the question that follows: what defines the practice of restorative justice in schools? In addressing these concerns, the Restorative Justice Consortium (2005) developed set of principles that underpin the practice of restorative justice in schools. These principles are guided by a set of values: empowerment, honesty, respect, engagement, voluntarism, healing, restoration, personal accountability, inclusiveness, collaboration, and problem-solving. A set of 24 principles are outlined that relate to: processes; equalities, diversity and non-discrimination; information, choice and safety; agreements and outcomes; organization and policies.The Restorative Justice Consortium (2005) establishes these principles along side an assessment model that aims to gauge the extent to which any particular school, program or case could be 'fully' restorative (Van Ness and Strong 2002). The model identifies four value tables to gauge the restorative character of a system. These value tables relate to four related aspects of restorative processes: 1) the encounter, where those affected have the opportunity to meet, participate in a dialogue and reach an agreement; 2) the making of amends, where an opportunity is created for reparation, apology and change; 3) maximizing reintegration, through a system that provides mechanisms to support behavioural change, while showing respect to the person; 4) maximizing involvement, through opportunities for the whole school community to learn about restorative process. Based on a continuum of possible responses across these four areas, the school, programme or case can be ranked as fully restorative, moderately restorative and minimally restorative. It should be noted that, because of the voluntary basis of restorative justice, a school can hold a fully restorative policy, while a particular case can rank as moderately or minimally restorative; thus, as Van Ness and Strong (2002) explain, 'When evaluating the handling of a particular case or of a programme the question will be whether the response was as restorative as possible under the circumstances' (Restorative Justice Consortium 2005: 14). Given this framework, it is possible to define when schools, in theory and practice, are being restorative to members of the school community, and when they are not.

Extending the practice of restorative justice in schools

Within this broad and eclectic context, the practice of restorative justice in schools has evolved as the practice defined itself within the institutional framework of education. A significant development within the field was to move beyond the conferencing model, as adopted from criminal and juvenile justice and initially used to address serious incidents of harm in school. What emerged, from a range of practitioners, was an array of continuums of restorative approaches. Wachtel and McCold (2001) defined a continuum of restorative practices, which range from informal to formal. Movements along the continuum 'involve more people, more planning, more time, are more complex in dealing with the offence, more structured and, due to all those factors, may have more impact on the offender' (Wachtel and McCold 2001: 125). These practices move from affective statements, to affective questions, to small impromptu conferences and on to large group circles and formal conferences.

Hopkins (2004) defines a whole-school approach to restorative justice in terms of a framework that pieces together the jigsaw of life at school. The continuum ranges from restorative enquiry, to restorative discussion in challenging situations, to mediation, to community conferences and problem-solving circles, to restorative conferences and family group conferences. Hopkins (2004) explicitly grounds these processes in a range of values and skills. The values that ground the skills include 'respect, openness, empowerment, inclusion, tolerance, integrity and congruence' (Hopkins 2004: 38). The skills that build from these include: 'remaining impartial and non-judgemental; respecting the perspective of all involved; actively and empathically listening; developing rapport amongst participants; empowering participants to come up with solutions rather than suggesting or imposing ideas; creative questioning; warmth; compassion; patience' (Hopkins 2004: 37–8). Together these processes, skills and values seek to involve the school community in decision-making processes that inform the community life of the school, with congruence of values and philosophy being the key to bringing the jigsaw of school life together.

Thorsborne and Vinegrad (2003) extend the continuum of practices to include both proactive, as well as reactive, practices. They differentiate between two types of conferencing processes: 1) proactive processes which enhance teaching and learning; and 2) reactive processes for responding to harm and wrongdoing. The proactive classroom conference provides a robust process to enhance teaching and learning outcomes while being explicit about limits and boundaries and emphasizing the importance of relationships. They aim to provide a process that links curriculum, pedagogy, and behaviour management, which can be used for establishing class rules, curriculum topics, teaching strategies, peer tutoring and support, working styles, learning tasks, project and assignment work as well as providing a forum for experiential and research-based learning, co-operative learning and independent study, student and teacher feedback. Reactive classroom conferences range from individual conferences, involving a teacher and a student; small-group conferences, involving a teacher and several students; whole-class conferences, involving a teacher and a class of students; and large-group conferences, involving a teacher and an entire level/grade/year of students. Together these restorative practices provide:

> the interpersonal and disciplinary link between proactive student management policies and the life of the classroom and the playground. The benefit for schools in the long term is that the staff and student population undergo fundamental behaviour and cultural change. The focus on a more open and transformative dialogue impacts positively on the daily operations of the school (Thorsborne and Vinegrad 2003: 56).

Blood (2004) has defined her approach to restorative practices in schools within Braithwaite's regulatory pyramid (see Ayres and Braithwaite 1992; Braithwaite 2002), which emphasizes building a continuum of responsive practices at three levels: 1) developing the social and emotional capacity of the school as a whole, through a range of proactive practices; 2) managing difficulties and disruptions within the everyday life of the school, through informal conferencing; and 3) restoring relationships when significant harm occurs, through formal conferencing. Within the pyramid structure, whole-school relational practices are heavily emphasized at the preventative level, with particular emphasis on developing the social and emotional capacity within the school to prevent incidents from escalating and to strengthen relationships. At the preventative level, Blood (2004) also draws on the work of Porter (2001), who argues that consideration is the most important skill children need to develop through accountability, responsibility for self and others, working together and personal potency. Thus, Blood (2004) makes the link with the development of social and emotional learning explicit, as well as the link with child development.

Each of these continuums of practice fits into a regulatory framework that Braithwaite has broadly conceived of as responsive regulation, which he has more recently matched with his work on restorative justice (Braithwaite 2002). Building on this regulatory framework, Morrison (2003, 2005, 2006a) has developed the ideas of restorative justice and responsive regulation within the context of schools, particularly in regard to concerns about school safety.

Responsive regulation and restorative justice

As the name implies, responsive regulation seeks to be responsive to the needs of those it regulates, scaling up or scaling down regulatory interventions, depending on the concerns of the agents involved and the extent to which the harmful behaviour has affected other members of the community (see Ayres and Braithwaite 1992; Braithwaite 2002). In other words, responsive regulation advocates a continuum of responses, recognizing that individuals may fall within a range of motivational postures as they move out of compliance with a social institution (Braithwaite *et al.* 1994). This approach can be contrasted with regulatory formalism, where the problem and the response are predetermined, and mandated through codes of conduct, laws and other rules of engagement. Typically a formalized response involves moral judgement about how evil the action is and a legal judgement about the appropriate punishment (Gilligan 2001). In the context of schools, behaviour is often regulated through the rules specified in the student code of conduct. Zero tolerance policies, which mandate suspensions for certain rule violations, however large or small, are an example of regulatory formalism within school communities. While the aim is to maximize consistency, regulatory formalism often targets those most at risk, through an approach that is high on accountability but low on support (see also Skiba and Noam 2001):

> Zero tolerance is, intuitively, a reasonable policy – until you look under the veil. Ideologically it is part of a larger political project of 'accountability', in which youth of color, typically, but not only, the poor and working class, are held 'accountable' for a nation that has placed them 'at risk'. Systematically denied equal developmental opportunities, they are pathologized, placed under surveillance, and increasingly criminalized (Fine and Smith 2001: 257).

Braithwaite's (2002) ideas of responsive regulation and restorative justice, conceptualized as a regulatory pyramid of responses, offer an alternative to zero tolerance and other formalized approaches. The pyramid model aims to address the issue of when to step up and when to step down intervention. The idea is to establish a strong normative base of informal restorative practices but, when that level of intervention fails, the recommendation is to step up intervention to a more demanding level. This multi-level approach to behaviour management and safety is consistent with recommendations from a number of different sources: the National Research Council's report, *Deadly Lessons: Understanding Lethal School Violence* (Moore *et al.* 2002), following the school rampage shootings of the 1990s; Gilligan's (2001) model of violence prevention, based on a health-care model; and a growing number of approaches reacting to the rise of zero tolerance policies in the USA (see Skiba and Noam 2001). As Skiba and Noam (2001: 4) conclude:

> our best knowledge suggests that there is no single answer to the complex problems of school violence and school discipline. Rather, our efforts must address a variety of levels and include universal interventions that teach all students alternatives to violence, procedures to identify and reintegrate students who may be at risk for violence, and interventions specifically designed for students already exhibiting disruptive or aggressive behaviour.

They suggest that the most effective strategies are to 1) provide instruction on resolving conflict and problems, without resorting to violence; and 2) to aim to be inclusive not exclusive. This is consistent with responsive regulation based on restorative justice.

Thus, the growing consensus is that school safety should be regulated in line with public health regulation; that is, along three different levels of preventative efforts that form a continuum of responses, based on common principles, at primary, secondary and tertiary levels. By way of analogy to the health-care model, the primary level of intervention targets all members of the school community through an 'immunization' strategy whereby the community develops defence mechanisms, such that conflict does not escalate into violence when differences first arise. All members of the school community are trained and supported in the development of social and emotional competencies, particularly in the area of conflict resolution, such that members of the school community are enabled to resolve differences in respectful and caring ways, which maximize inclusion. The Responsible Citizenships Programme (Morrison 2001, 2006a) and Help Increase the Peace Programme (Anderson 1999) are examples of two programmes used explicitly within the context of restorative practices. The aim of these programmes is to shift the social and emotional culture of the school. The skills and practices developed through these programmes aim to enhance, normalize and legitimize the higher-level restorative responses.

The secondary and tertiary levels target specific individuals and groups within the school community, drawing on and involving other members of the school community. It is through drawing on other key members of the school community that the intensity of the intervention at the secondary level increases. Typically, at this level of intervention, the conflict has become more protracted or involves (and affects) a larger number of people, with a facilitator being required. Peer mediation and problem-solving circles are examples of this level of intervention. The tertiary level involves the participation of an even wider cross-section of the school community, including parents, guardians, social workers and others who have been affected or need to be involved when serious offences occur within the school. A face-to-face restorative justice conference is a typical example of this level of response.

Taken together, these practices move from proactive to reactive, along a continuum of responses. Movement from one end of the continuum to the other involves widening the circle of care around participants. The emphasis is on early intervention through building a strong base at the primary level, which grounds a normative continuum of responsive regulation across the school community. Across all levels, restorative practices aim to develop inclusive and respectful dialogue that focuses on the health and safety of the whole school community. This is consistent with the conclusion of the National Research Council's (Moore *et al.* 2002: 8) report which states: 'Specifically, there is a need to develop a strategy for drawing adults and youth closer together in constructing a normative social climate that is committed to keeping the schools safe from lethal incidents'.

This tri-level approach has been described in different ways: the primary, or universal, level targets all members of the school community, with an aim to develop a strong normative climate of respect, a sense of belongingness within the school community and procedural fairness; the secondary, or targeted, level targets a certain percentage of the school community who are becoming at risk of the development of chronic behaviour problems; and the tertiary, or intensive, level targets students who have already developed chronic and intense behaviour problems. Within this conceptual model, the students who receive intensive intervention, typically have also been involved in targeted intervention, and all students, including those at the targeted and intensive levels, are involved in the universal, or primary, intervention.

It also needs to be made clear that, while the recommendation is to model violence prevention on a health-care model, the model proposed is much more dynamic. Instead of a one-shot inoculation at the primary level, the intervention must be reaffirmed in the everyday practice of life at school. At the secondary and tertiary level, while particular students or groups of students are targeted, the inclusive practice of restorative justice necessarily involves students not a risk. Targeted strategies are about reconnecting students at risk with the school community; thus, they necessarily involve students not at risk. The behaviour of some students may keep them at this targeted level for an ongoing period of time, others may drift to this level only a few times and others not at all. At the tertiary level, these students will have experienced all levels of intervention; however, relationship patterns have faltered to the extent that relationships need to be repaired or rebuilt. In summary, the focus of primary interventions is re-affirming relationships, the focus of secondary interventions is re-pairing relationships and the focus of tertiary interventions is re-building relationships (see Figure 18.1).

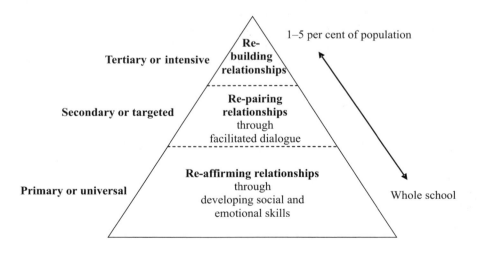

Figure 18.1 A regulatory pyramid for schools based on restorative justice and responsive regulation

Evaluation of restorative justice in schools

This evaluation review does not aim to be definitive but to draw upon the best evidence we have to date, while acknowledging that 1) many individual schools are carrying out research as part of their own learning and development process (unfortunately there are too many to include in this chapter); and 2) a good number of larger research projects in many countries are currently underway. Drawing on the structure of responsive regulation developed, current practice and evidence are presented for intensive (tertiary), targeted (secondary) and universal (primary) practices. The decision to review the evidence in this particular order is intentional, as the practice of restorative justice in schools, *per se*, began with restorative justice conferencing at the intensive level; however, as shown above, the importance of developing a strong base of restorative practices at the universal level is now well recognized. With this evolution, restorative justice is now practised at all levels of the pyramid, with the broad aim being to develop a climate of fairness, dignity and safety for all members of the school community, whereby those affected by harmful behaviour have the opportunity to participate in learning processes that aims to re-affirm, re-pair and re-build relationships.

Intensive restorative interventions

Formal large-group conferences are used at the intensive level of restorative interventions. By far the most predominant model used in schools is a face-to-face conference, as initially trialled in Queensland schools; however, there are now many variations to this model. For example, the use of scripted/non-scripted models, the number of facilitators (and their role), and the use and timing of refreshment breaks are important distinguishing features (see Sharpe 2003; Hopkins 2004; Thorsborne and Vinegrad 2002, 2004). A smaller number of schools are using the family group conferencing model, developed in New Zealand, and the peace and healing circles, developed in North America.

Community conferencing

The introduction of the community accountability conferencing model into the Queensland, Australia, school system in 1994 quickly led, in 1995 and 1997, to the first evaluations of restorative justice in schools (Education Queensland 1996, 1998). The aim of a community conference is to weave a circle of support and accountability around the 'victim(s)' and 'offender(s)', such that an open, honest and respectful dialogue can develop, wherein individuals can build a collective story of what happened, acknowledge how the incident has affected them and allow each participant the opportunity to take responsibility for how best to repair the harm done and keep the community safe. This circle of people includes those who care most about the 'victim(s)' and 'offender(s)', and support them in different aspects of their life. Typically these people include parents, other care givers, brothers and sisters, coaches, teachers, professionals and peers. Importantly they are people whom the victim and offender respect.

Only a handful of evaluations have currently been conducted, with none carried out at a rigorous level (largely due to lack of funding and political will for such activities). The majority of evaluations have been carried out through post-conference interviews and questionnaires, with no comparison group. To date, across a range of countries, Australia, Canada, England and the USA (see Calhoun 2000; Hudson and Pring 2000; Ierley and Ivker 2002; Shaw and Wierenga 2002), results generally replicate those of the initial evaluation of community accountability conferences in Queensland, which remains important in term of outcomes and lessons learnt (Cameron and Thorsborne 2001).

Two pilot studies were conducted in Queensland, wherein a total of 89 (56 and 33 respectively) school-based conferences were convened, in response to serious assaults (43), serious victimization (25), truanting, class disruption, damage to school reputation, and bullying (18), property damage and theft (12), drugs (2) and a bomb threat (1). Overall, positive outcomes were reported by participants, indicating they had a say in the process (96 per cent); were satisfied with the way the agreement was reached (87 per cent); were treated with respect (95 per cent); felt understood by others (99 per cent); and felt agreement terms were fair (91 per cent). Specific to victims, results were also positive, indicating they got what they needed out of the conference (89 per cent); and felt safer (94 per cent). Offenders reported they felt cared about during conference (98 per cent); loved by those closest to them (95 per cent); able to make a fresh start (80 per cent); forgiven (70 per cent); and closer to those involved (87 per cent). Further, offenders complied with most or all of the agreement (84 per cent) and did not reoffend within the trial period (83 per cent). School personnel reported they felt the process reinforced school values (100 per cent) and felt they had changed their thinking about managing behaviour from a punitive to a more restorative approach (92 per cent). As for family members who participated, they expressed positive perceptions of the school and comfort in approaching the school on other matters (94 per cent).

While these early results were encouraging, the evaluation of these trials highlighted tensions between the existing philosophies and practices in managing behaviour in schools, typically characterized by punitive measures emphasizing accountability over support. This was particularly problematic when restorative conferencing was implemented as a 'one-off' intervention for serious incidents, in isolation of other implementation, development and support mechanisms. By way of illustration, 227 school personnel, from 75 schools, were trained for the first Queensland trial, but only 56 conferences were conducted within 12 months of the trial (Education Queensland 1996). The over-riding lesson: broader institutional professional development and support are required to implement, develop and sustain the practice of restorative justice within schools.

Based on the lessons of the two Queensland studies, the State of Victoria conducted a smaller pilot study of restorative justice conferencing, involving 69 school personnel, from 23 schools within four regional clusters, which met 3–4 times during the year through the support of regional staff (Shaw and Wierenga 2002). Over the nine months' trial, 14 conferences and 23 mini-conferences were recorded in eight (of the 23) schools. The key recommendations were from the pilot concluded that 1) a whole-school approach is needed, given ongoing tensions with traditional methods of discipline; 2) involvement of school leadership is essential (in particular, principals and their deputies must be committed to the process of implementation); 3) collegiate support is necessary to sustain and develop practice; and 4) time needs to be made available for training and implementation of restorative justice, as well as the facilitation of conferences. This evaluation concludes that the process of conferencing:

> extended school staff beyond their 'comfort zones', and they have needed the support of regional staff and networks. The information collected through this evaluation affirms that if a conference is selected well, approached thoroughly by a team who are prepared to do the groundwork, and carried out within the spirit of Restorative Practices, it can be a powerful tool for exploring and managing school discipline issues (Shaw and Wierenga 2002: n.p.).

While these results are encouraging, the review of these trials also highlights the tensions between the existing philosophies and practices in managing behaviour and restorative interventions, such as conferencing, illustrating the need for wider institutional reform (see Cameron and Thorsborne 2001; Morrison 2001; Ritchie and O'Connell 2001).

Family group conferencing

Hampshire County Council has been supporting pupils, schools and families since early 1999 through the use of family group conferences (FGC), designed to help young people aged 5–15 with significant problems of behaviour and attendance in schools. The University of Sheffield studied 50 (of over 400) referrals in 1999 and 2000 (Marsh 2004). Referrals came from primary, secondary and alternative schools. Interviews were conducted with young people, their families and professionals. While young people were often unsure of the FGC beforehand, worried that they would be asked difficult questions or be 'got at', 81 per cent said the meeting 'felt good'. All, bar one, thought the meeting was a productive way to address school problems. At the same time, 25 per cent felt unable to say what they wanted to, as adults did not allow them the opportunity to do so. Likewise, while family members felt happy about the way the meeting went, 21 per cent felt they had not been able to participate fully. Some family members felt a lack or support or respect from some professionals, and some family group members. The majority of professionals thought the model was good, or worth a try, while 10 per cent wanted to reserved judgement until the results were out.

The plans were effective in improving home/school links, as well as links with other agencies. When schools were not included in the development of the plan, this appeared to impact negatively on the outcomes achieved. Overall, the outcomes, at least within the six months' follow-up, appeared positive. Attendance and behaviour improved for approximately half of the young people at one month, with most maintaining good records at six months. The conference had the strongest effect on children under the age of 11, with older children more likely to improve their attendance than their behaviour. Girls were more likely to be referred for attendance, while boys were more likely to be referred for behaviour.

Targeted restorative interventions

As conferencing began to be established in schools, schools recognized that a full conference process was not needed for all behaviour concerns. Some schools paired peer mediation with conferencing, others added impromptu (or informal) conferencing, while others developed restorative circle processes as part of normal classroom activities, to address problems and concerns at a classroom level. What is common across each of these practices is that, while harmful behaviour has not reached a level that requires intensive resources, it has reached a point where a third person is needed to help shift the level of dialogue between those affected by the harmful behaviour. Sometimes this person is a fellow student, sometimes a teacher, administrator or other member of the school community. Other than peer mediation, there is little evaluative information on the effectiveness of these practices (a small cross-section is included below).

Problem-solving circles

Problem-solving circles can be developed and run in many different ways. The programme developed here aimed to build students' capacity for collective problem-solving through a process that addressed everyday concerns within the classroom and school. This classroom practice built from initial workshops that develop a normative climate of healthy social and emotional skills, but then took the process one step further through introducing the students to the process of a restorative face-to-face conference, using role play and discussion. Once the students felt confident with the process, they were encouraged to bring problems and concerns within the classroom to the circle. Circles then became a regular feature of the classroom, often using concentric circles.

This programme was evaluated in an Australian elementary school (Morrison and Martinez 2001). All students in three mixed classes (Grades 4, 5 and 6) took part in the study. The intervention was tested in one classroom (n = 12), while the other two classrooms acted as quasi-control groups. Problems brought to the circle included annoying behaviour, teasing, feeling

337

left out, aggressive behaviour and stealing. The teacher reported a number of benefits to the classroom, including: 'Gave us a safe place to share problems face-to-face; modeled effective conflict resolution; encouraged the open expression of emotion; allowed us to move beyond niggling behaviours; contributed to a 'way of being' based on respect, communication and support.' She also reported a number of significant breakthroughs: a boy who would shut down during conflict at the start of the year was asking for open communication by the end of the year; another boy evolved naturally from the role of aggressor to supporter; yet another boy, with extreme learning difficulties, found a voice for his strength in providing positive solutions; another boy's modelling of open expression broke the taboo on shedding tears; a girl, a strong learner, convened two of the circles independently; and a boy integrated from the behaviour support unit willingly contributed and found another tool for managing his relationships.

This programme was also evaluated using an adaptation of the Life at School Survey (see Ahmed *et al.* 2001). Compared with the control group, a number of significant differences were found: students in the intervention class showed higher levels of emotional intelligence; reported greater use of productive conflict resolution techniques; felt that the teacher was more interested in stopping bullying; felt that the teacher held bullies and victims more accountable for behaviour; reported less use of maladaptive shame management strategies; and reported less involvement in bullying (Morrison and Martinez 2001).

Peer mediation

Mediation has been defined as a 'structured method of conflict resolution in which trained individuals (the mediators) assist people in dispute (the parties) by listening to their concerns and helping them negotiate' (Cohen 2003: 111). After the mediator clarifies the structure of the process and allows the parties to explain their thoughts and feelings, participants are encouraged to talk directly, develop options and reach a consensual settlement that will accommodate their needs. In the context of peer mediation, the neutral person is a fellow student (or students), who has been trained in mediation. These students support other students to take responsibility for decisions that affect their lives and the lives of their fellow students. The broader aim is for this self-regulating process to become part of the ethos of the school. The emphasis is on developing students' skills in conflict resolution.

Peer mediation programmes are now an extremely popular means of resolving conflict in schools, with literally thousands of programmes in existence, in many different countries, and grounded in different mediation models (see Cohen 2003). However, while some programmes have been found to be effective, systematic reviews of peer mediation programmes show non-significant or weak effects (Gottfredson 1997). One reason this could be the case is that peer mediation alone is not a strong enough intervention to address chronic offenders, or shift the normative climate.

Indeed, this was the experience of the New South Wales Department of School Education, who launched a School Community Forum Programme

(1997), using restorative justice conferencing, to complement their peer mediation programme. The aim was to reduce the number and length of suspensions in schools through engaging students at risk in a supportive network where they could learn from their experiences in school. Of the 20 conferences carried out in the initial trial, a range of incidents were addressed: bullying and harassment (12); disruptive and aggressive behaviour (6); money (1); and an ongoing dispute between a student, teacher and family (1). Of these, 16 had a successful outcome, in that there was a significant reduction in the target behaviour and no further suspensions. The results were particularly strong for bullying, where 11 of the 12 were successful. The conclusion was that 'school community forums work best when used as an anti-bullying and harassment intervention …' The forum process confronts the bully with the consequences of their anti-social behaviour more powerfully than do many other forms of intervention' (McKenzie 1999: 8). In line with Olweus (1993), who argues that empathy raising is an important element of anti-bullying programmes, the forum process was found to be a powerful empathy builder. Further, through inviting the offending subjects' peer group and friends, these became an important link in sustaining the behavioural change that was hoped for. The process was also found to be satisfying for the victims, in particular because it gave them the opportunity to express their feelings and have some say in the negotiations and outcomes. Moreover, forums were found to address the power imbalances inherent to bullying better than peer mediation. Braithwaite (2002: 60) concurs but goes another step:

> It appears a whole-school approach is needed that not just tackles individual incidents but also links incidents to a change programme for the culture of the school, in particular to how seriously members of the school community take rules about bullying. Put another way, the school not only must resolve the bullying incident; but also must use it as a resource to affirm the disapproval of bullying in the culture of the school.

As such a whole-school approach to restorative justice must not only include intensive and targeted interventions, but must also include universal interventions that ground a normative climate of restorative justice in schools.

Primary restorative interventions

Today, it is widely recognized that the practice of restorative justice must ground a whole-school framework for thinking about how behaviour and relationships are managed in schools. This begins with how behavioural expectations are introduced into the schools, as well as how skills for managing relationships within the school are taught and modelled. A number of different programmes have been used as primary (or universal) restorative intervention programmes. The Collaboration for Academic Social and Emotional Learning maintains an excellent review of many of these programmes (see www.casel.org). As well as these programmes, a number of other programmes have been used to complement higher-level restorative interventions. These include the Help Increase the Peace Project (Anderson 1999) and the Responsible Citizenship Programme (Morrison 2002, 2005, 2006a). Each aims to create a diverse culture of social relationships, which affirms and regulates healthy and responsible behaviour.

Whole-school restorative interventions

More recent evaluations have been conducted in the context of whole-school approaches, incorporating a range of restorative practices, including primary, secondary and tertiary interventions. The Minnesota Department of Children, Family and Learning (MNDCFL 2002; from 2005 the Department of Education) has supported the largest evaluations of restorative justice in schools in the USA. This whole-school initiative was a response to a three-fold rise in expulsions over a two-year period, following the introduction of zero tolerance policies. The aim was to introduce a holistic approach to harmful behaviour that:

> emphasizes problem-solving approaches to discipline, attends to the social/emotional as well as the physical/intellectual needs of students, recognizes the importance of the group to establish and practice agreed-upon norms and rules, and emphasizes prevention and early restorative intervention to create safe learning environments (MNDCFL 2002: n.p.).

Their evaluations have shown that the use of restorative measures, across a range of levels, is an effective alternative to the use of suspensions and expulsions.

The Minnesota legislature, using federal Safe and Drug Free School Funding, supported two rounds of grants. In the first round (1998–2001), four districts were selected, with some applying all the funds to one school (elementary or high school) and some distributing the money over three schools (elementary and high schools). Five grants were awarded in the second round, again varying in geography, number and type of schools, and plan. The Minnesota Department of Education supported the school communities through a range of outreach activities: technical assistance, referrals to community or law enforcement restorative justice programmes, workshops and week-long seminars. Schools developed their own training, development and evaluation package. The only criterion was that the programmes and practices to be developed were grounded in restorative philosophy. Schools generally implemented a continuum of practices, including universal interventions: (Restitution or Judicious Discipline; Second Step, anti-bullying programmes, and community circles); targeted interventions (peer mediation and conflict management programmes); and intensive interventions (victim–offender dialogues, group conferencing and circles to repair harm).

The evaluation aim was to track suspensions, expulsions, attendance, academics and school climate; however, obtaining consistent baseline data proved difficult, and the evaluation focused on only a few measures – suspensions, referrals and attendance – within each school. While outcomes varied from school to school in the three-year period of the first grant, there was an overall decrease in suspensions and referrals. Of particular note, out-of-school suspensions dropped in one junior high school from 110 to 55, and in a senior high school from 132 to 95. Further, office referrals for acts of physical aggression in one elementary school dropped from 773 to 153. From these first rounds of grants, Riestenberg (2000) noted three key learning outcomes: 1) restorative practices, such as circles to repair harm, are viable alternatives to suspensions; 2) restorative philosophy and practices had classroom management and teaching applications; and 3) staff hired on grant money inevitably leave a district when the grant money is spent. It was found that, while schools who hired specialists in restorative practices got up and running quicker, the model was less sustainable, as schools tended to defer to the specialist. On the other hand, it was found that schools who invested in staff training and development were investing in sustaining outcomes; thus, the second round of grants (2002–3) adopted this model. As Riestenburg (2003: n.p.) states:

> Given the uncertainty of grant awards and general funding for education, as well as the natural mobility of teaching staff, it seemed to be more cost effective to teach a lot of people 'how to fish', rather than have them depend on a guide with a good boat for a limited amount of time.

Many schools receiving the second round of grants also reported overall decreases in referrals, suspensions and expulsions; unfortunately, the evaluation reports are variable in their style and content; as such, more specific overall results are difficult to report. While the state can no longer afford to fund the grants, the Minnesota Department of Education continues to support schools with ongoing training opportunities. The onus is on the schools but, when schools take the learning onboard, they continue to develop innovative ideas. For example, one administrator organizes re-entry meetings following a suspension. The meetings focus on four important aspects of a student's life at school: physical safety, academics, and social and emotional well-being. At the re-entry conference, the young person, and typically parents and guardians, is asked to respond to a set of questions, with the young person speaking first. This circle process allows:

> for adults and students to be connected to each other through that profound invisible web woven of talking and listening to words and to silence. The restorative idea of doing things with students rather than to them or for them or simply ignoring them, can be squeezed into the regular order of the day (Riestenberg 2005: 2).

The ideas and innovation of working with students are now broaching many areas of school life, with the ideas of restorative justice now becoming that of youth development (see Braithwaite 2001).

The most comprehensive study of whole-school practices of restorative justice to date was carried out by the Youth Justice Board for England and Wales (YJB 2004). They conducted a national evaluation of the 'Restorative Justice in Schools Programme', involving 26 schools (20 secondary and 6 primary) in nine boroughs across England and Wales. Only three schools were involved in the study for the full three years; the remaining schools were only involved for 18 months. What makes the YJB evaluation distinctive is the use of comparison schools. Specifically, besides the 'programme schools', one 'non-programme' school in each borough was used as a comparison school. Like the Minnesota evaluation, the practice of restorative justice in the programme schools varied widely; however, the continuum of practices was more process oriented (and less programme oriented) and included the practices of active listening, restorative inquiry, circle time, peer mediation, mediation and restorative justice conferences.

In terms of outcomes from restorative justice conferences, the results largely replicate the findings of previous studies in that, if a conference was convened, the results were largely successful. Data were collected from 525 conferences (84 per cent of the official conferences run in the evaluation period). The most common reasons for convening a conference were (in declining rank order): bullying; assault/violent behaviour; name-calling; verbal abuse; family feuds; friendship/relationship breakdowns; incidents involving teachers; gossip; incidents outside school; and theft. Almost a quarter (24 per cent) of the conferences were used to resolve long-term disputes, with boys being twice as likely as girls to be involved in physical violence and girls being three times as likely to be involved in social and emotional violence, such as name-calling and gossip. The conferences were most likely to be facilitated by a school staff member (49 per cent) or by a member of the youth offending team (37 per cent), followed by police officers (8 per cent), staff from the local mediation service (3 per cent) and trained volunteers (3 per cent). Interestingly, less than a fifth of the conferences involved a parent (19 per cent), reflecting the wide variety of processes defined as a conference. Different schools coded for conferences using different criteria. Some included short informal conferences, others did not; further, some a scripted conference model, others used a more open-ended model; other coding schisms were noted as well. In secondary schools (Years 7–10), participation in conferencing peaked in Year 7, then declined. In primary schools participation in a conference peaked in Year 6 and began in Year 3. Agreements were reached in 92 per cent of the conferences, with only 4 per cent of agreements being broken within the three-month follow-up time. Students reported satisfaction with the process (89 per cent) and that the process was fair (93 per cent).

Programme and non-programme schools were also surveyed for levels of bullying and overall safety, using student self-report questionnaires (n = 5,986). Significant differences were only found for the three schools that had been using restorative practices for the full three years of the evaluation.

For these schools, students reported significant differences between programme and non-programme schools across a number of measures, indicating a reduction in being called racist names (11 per cent lower in programme schools); their school was doing 'a good job' at stopping bullying (10 per cent higher in programme schools); and bullying was a serious problem at their school (23 per cent lower in programme schools). There were a number of other significant effects that indicated that individual schools were making a positive impact on the level of bullying and other harmful behaviour, but none of these effects was systematic across all programme schools. This is not surprising given the range of restorative justice practices that were used across the schools included in the study.

The teacher questionnaires ($n = 949$) also indicated significant differences between programme and non-programme schools, with teachers and other school staff reporting that behaviour had improved since the introduction of restorative approaches. However, the introduction of restorative practices did not appear significantly to shift the staff's view that exclusion is an effective approach to dealing with behaviour problems. There was no significant difference between programme and non-programme schools, nor a difference between pre-post measures. While some schools did reduce expulsions, the study was not able to conclude whether the introduction of restorative approaches had an impact on the level of exclusion within the schools. This was largely due to a range of coding and reporting inconsistencies across schools. Teachers in the programme schools reported that they lost less teaching time to dealing with behaviour problems since the introduction of restorative practices; however, a large proportion of staff (43 per cent) in the programme schools reported that they either knew nothing or not very much about restorative justice at the end of the evaluation period. Further, staff who indicated that they knew quite a bit about restorative justice often held misconceptions about the key elements of restorative justice, as evident in the qualitative data ($n = 85$).

The study concludes: 'Restorative justice is not a panacea for problems in schools but, if implemented correctly, it can improve the school environment, enhance learning and encourage young people to become more responsible and empathetic' (YJB 2004: 65). However, the study did highlight a number of issues: 1) given that the intervention was initiated by the YJB and not the Department for Education and Skills (DfES), there was consensus that the latter needed to be involved in the sponsorship of the initiative to make it more relevant to the agenda of schools and education; 2) successful implementation was characterized by leadership and vision, integration into the school behaviour policy and adequate staff training; 3) follow-up is needed to monitor that conference participants are adhering to agreements made in a conference; 4) there was lack of consensus, and definition of, what defines a restorative justice conference; and 5) the language of restorative justice (e.g. 'victim', 'offender') did not transfer easily to the school setting, in particular the term 'justice' itself. The recommendations mirror these concerns with the addition of one further point: 6) implementation of restorative practices is an excellent vehicle for improving interagency partnerships.

The Youth Justice Board's report sets a number of guidelines for implementing restorative justice in schools, which are largely consistent with past reviews. Broadly, these recommendations can be collapsed into two points: 1) restorative practices need to be institutionally relevant to schools; and 2) the implementation of restorative practices must be framed within a broad agenda of institutional reform. Tensions are inevitable when practices defined in one institution (the justice system in the context of restorative justice) are adopted by another institution, in this case the education system. The justice system and the education system have two different mandates. The former embraces the mandate of human and social order, while the latter embraces the mandate of human and social development. At the same time, justice demands development and education demands a social order. Schools, while microcosm of society, are more intense, socially and developmentally, than the latter. It is in this social milieu that the potential of restorative justice becomes broader, while remaining institutionally distinct.

In the context of juvenile and criminal justice, the 'victim' and the 'offender' often do not know each other and are often unlikely to meet each other again. In the context of schools, these people are very likely to meet or see each other again. In the context of juvenile and criminal justice, defining the status of 'victim' and 'offender' is often straightforward; in the context of schools, the status of 'victim' and 'offender' is often unclear, not to forget the semantic appropriateness of these labels within a developmental institution. Schools are tightly woven, face-to-face communities where social influence patterns change with every new day, every new person. Where one sits in the social hierarchy is never secure. Affirming one's status is a constant pursuit during these important developmental years. In the context of the rampage shooting of the 1990s, the National Research Council conclude that concerns over social status are central to understanding, and preventing, deadly school violence:

> One message that come through loud and clear in the [deadly school rampage] cases is that adolescents are intensely concerned about their social standing in their school and among their peers. For some, their concern is so great that threats to their status are treated as threats to their very lives and their status as something to be defended at all costs (Moore *et al.* 2002: 336).

In this context, social and emotional skills are the core element for the health, well-being and safety of the school community. When a member of the school community is harmed, or has harmed, the intensity and collateral effect can be deeper and more extensive in these tightly woven, face-to-face communities. In other words, the snowball effect of harmful behaviour begetting harmful behaviour can be very intense in a school context. There is often a long history of tensions rising through this snowball effect before an incident is brought forward to the school administration. As the National Research Council (Moore *et al.* 2002) conclude, there is often a trail of evidence within the hidden social and emotional curriculum of school life (see also Webber 2003; Newman 2004; Morrison 2006a). For all these reasons, and more, educational systems must think carefully and thoughtfully not only about the importance of restorative justice in schools, but also about the implementation, sustainability and development of restorative justice in schools. While the potential is vast, the field is still in the very early days of implementation. Much more research and development must be carried out across a range of important questions that are specific to schools and education systems. In these early days, it is important for individual schools to monitor their own progress, but the field also needs large-scale systematic evaluations to take place, with significant resources committed. The evaluations highlighted here are a start, but much more is needed, not only in terms of outcomes achieved, but also in terms of implementation, development and sustainability.

Responsive implementation, development and sustainability

Morrison (2006a) has defined a regulatory framework for the implementation, sustainability and development of restorative practices in schools, based on Braithwaite's (2002) ideas on restorative justice and responsive regulation. A four-sided regulatory pyramid is proposed that regulates development within an ongoing action learning and research paradigm. The four sides of the pyramid aim to empower development in many arenas of school life, at many levels of responsive regulation. These are 1) institutional vision to empower responsive policy development; 2) relational practices to empower individual change and development; 3) behavioural evidence to empower responsive decision-making; and 4) professional bridging to empower institutional change and development. Together, responsive regulation and restorative justice are about responding to behaviour and restoring relationships. The regulatory idea is to broaden the vision from a range of responsive practices that restore relationships, to a responsive framework that regulates the implementation, development and sustainability of restorative practices in schools. More to the point, building safe and healthy school communities goes hand and hand with how safe and healthy schools are regulated. This regulatory framework capitalizes on Braithwaite's (1989) notion of separating the behaviour from the person, for too many policies and practices that seek to regulate safe school communities focus too much on the behaviour, emphasizing the rules of behaviour, while failing to address the relational needs of the school community and the web of relationships that sustain the school community's health and safety.

The framework outlines a recursive process of ongoing monitoring and development that must constantly be in place in schools, responding to concerns as they arise. For new problems will always arise, new actors and new behaviours will always be bubbling up from within the foundations of the school system. Schools will always have deviance from the status quo – some of this deviance will breed new life into the school community, some will eat away at the foundation of school life. The school community needs to respond to both, for deviance has the capacity to shut us down or to provide opportunities for growth, as individuals and as institutions.

Within the context of courts, Nils Christie (1977) described the system as stealing conflict and, with this, the voices of those affected. Within the context of schools, conflicts are also stolen, limiting opportunities for growth and development; moreover, the system potentially steals more than conflicts – it steals the hopes, dreams and potential of the next generation. And with that, we do ourselves as individuals, and a society, a great disservice. Children are society's mirror; we know how well we are doing as a democracy when we take the time to reflect on and respond to how well the children of the next generation are doing, individually and collectively. When our children are hurting themselves and each other they are sending us a strong and powerful message, one that should not be dismissed.

Building the vision, practice, evidence and institutional development of restorative justice in schools is aligned to the question: what restores, for whom, under what conditions in schools? This review has revealed both the growth and development of the practice of restorative justice in school, as well as a dearth of evidence on short and long-term outcomes of restorative justice in schools. Further, there is a range of implementation, development and sustainability issues that need to be addressed as restorative justice develops within the institutional context of schools. Theoretical work needs to complement this practical work too, for studies are limited in this area (see Ahmed *et al.* 2001; Morrison 2006b). Schools are our most important developmental institution; they carry young people through their journey from childhood to adulthood. Restorative justice is about creating safe spaces where the pathway that defines a young person's life can be strengthened, through re-affirming, re-pairing and re-building relationships. Creating safe spaces that open pathways is particularly important in the aftermath of harmful behaviours, such as bullying and other acts of violence, which alienate young people from this important developmental institution. Building on Howard Zehr's (2002) analysis of restorative justice as a journey to belonging, restorative justice in schools becomes a journey that enriches that life potential of young people and civil society as a whole.

Selected further reading

Amstutz, L.S. and Mullet, J.H. (2005) *The Little Book of Restorative Discipline for Schools.* Intercourse, PA: Good Books. In keeping with the engaging style of the *Little Books of Justice and Peacekeeping*, this book provides a concise and accessible introduction to the practice of restorative justice in schools.

Armstrong, M. and Thorsborne, M. (2006) 'Restorative responses to bullying', in H. McGrath and T. Noble (eds) *Bullying Solutions: Evidence-based Approaches to Bullying in Australian Schools.* Frenchs Forest, NSW: Pearson Education. This chapter provides a good overview of the use of restorative justice in Australian schools, with other chapters in this volume highlighting the varying efforts to define restorative justice in comparison with other approaches to school bullying.

Morrison, B.E. (2006) 'School bullying and restorative justice: towards a theoretical understanding of the role of respect, pride and shame', *Journal of Social Issues,* 62:371–92. This paper integrates three theories that build the understanding of the practice of restorative justice in schools, and presents empirical evidence that supports the practice and the need for continued research and development.

Morrison, B.E. (in press) *Restoring Safe School Communities: A Whole School Response to Bullying, Violence and Alienation*. Sydney: Federation Press. This book examines the growing concern about bullying, violence and alienation in schools, highlighting the social and emotional issues at stake and pointing a way forward through the use of restorative justice and responsive regulation.

Stinchcomb, J.B., Bazemore, G. and Riestenberg, N. (2006) 'Beyond zero tolerance: restoring justice in secondary schools', *Youth Violence and Juvenile Justice*, 4: 123–47. In the context of school disciplinary policies, this paper compares zero tolerance and restorative justice, and presents empirical evidence supporting the use of restorative justice in schools that, at times, can complement more traditional responses.

Acknowledgements

I would like to acknowledge the supportive environment of the Regulatory Institutions Network within the Research School of Social Sciences at the Australian National University, Canberra, Australia. In particular, the influence and support of Valerie Braithwaite and John Braithwaite. At the University of Pennsylvania, I would like to acknowledge the support of Lawrence Sherman, Director of the Jerry Lee Center of Criminology.

References

Aber, J.L., Brown, J.L. and Henrich, C.C. (1999) *Teaching Conflict Resolution: An Effective School-based Approach to Violence Prevention*. New York: National Center for Children in Poverty.

Ahmed, E., Harris, N., Braithwaite, J. and Braithwaite, V. (2001) *Shame Management through Reintegration*. Cambridge: Cambridge University Press.

Anderson, M. (1999) *Help Increase the Peace Programme Manual*. Baltimore, MD: American Friends Service Committee.

Ayres, I. and Braithwaite, J. (1992) *Responsive Regulation: Transcending the Deregulation Debate*. New York: Oxford University Press.

Blood, P. (2004) 'Restorative practices: a whole school approach to building social capital.' Unpublished manuscript held by Circle Speak, Sydney, Australia, NY.

Braithwaite, J.B. (1989) *Crime, Shame and Reintegration*. Cambridge: Cambridge University Press.

Braithwaite, J.B. (2001). 'Youth development circles', *Oxford Review of Education*, 27: 239–52.

Braithwaite, J.B. (2002) *Restorative Justice and Responsive Regulation*. Oxford: Oxford University Press.

Braithwaite, V., Braithwaite, J.B., Gibson, D. and Makkai, T. (1994) 'Regulatory styles, motivational postures and nursing home compliance', *Law and Policy*, 15: 327–54.

Calhoun, A. (2000). *Calgary Community Conferencing School Component 1999–2000: A Year in Review* (available online at http://www.calgarycommunityconferencing. com/r_and _e/ september_report.html).

Cameron, L. and Thorsborne, M. (2001) 'Restorative justice and school discipline: mutually exclusive?', in H. Strang and J. Braithwaite (eds) *Restorative Justice and Civil Society*. Cambridge: Cambridge University Press.

Christie, N. (1977) 'Conflicts as property', *British Journal of Criminology*, 17: 1–26.

Claassen, R. (1993) 'Discipline that restores', *Conciliation Quarterly Newsletter*, 12: 2.

Cohen, R. (2003) 'Students helping students', in T. Jones and R. Compton (eds) *Kids Working it Out*. San Francisco, CA: Jossey-Bass.

Dewey, J. (1900) *The School and Society*. Chicago, IL: University of Chicago Press.

Dewey, J. (1916) *Democracy and Education*. New York, NY: Free Press.

Education Queensland (1996) 'Community accountability conferencing: trial report.' Unpublished manuscript held by Education Queensland.

Education Queensland (1998) 'Community accountability conferencing: 1997 pilot report.' Unpublished manuscript held by Education Queensland.

Elias, M., Hunter, L. and Kress, J. (2001) 'Emotional intelligence in education', in J. Ciarrochi *et al.* (eds) *Emotional Intelligence in Everyday Life: A Scientific Inquiry*. Philadelphia, PA: Psychology Press.

Fine, M. and Smith, K. (2001) 'Zero tolerance: reflections on a failed policy that won't die', in W. Ayers *et al.* (eds) *Zero Tolerance: Resisting the Drive for Punishment in Our Schools*. New York, NY: New Press.

Gilligan, J. (2001) *Preventing Violence*. New York: Thames & Hudson.

Goleman, D. (1995) *Emotional Intelligence: Why it Can Matter More Than IQ*. New York, NY: Bantam Books.

Gossen, D. (1992). *Restitution: Restructuring School Discipline*. Chapel Hill, NC: New View Publications.

Gottfredson, D. (1997) 'School-based crime prevention', in L. Sherman *et al.* (eds) *Preventing Crime: What Works, What Doesn't, What's Promising. A Report to the United States Congress*. Washington, D.C.: National Institute of Justice.

Hopkins, B. (2004) *Just Schools: A Whole School Approach to Restorative Justice*. London and New York, NY: Jessica Kingsley.

Hudson, C. and Pring, R. (2000) 'Banbury Police Schools Project: report of the evaluation.' Manuscript held by the Thames Valley Police.

Ierley, A. and Ivker, C. (2002) 'Restoring school communities.' *Restorative Justice in Schools Program: Spring 2002 Report Card*. Unpublished manuscript held by the School Mediation Center, Boulder, CO.

Jones, T. and Compton, R. (eds) (2003) *Kids Working it Out: Stories and Strategies for Making Peace in our Schools*. San Francisco, CA: Jossey-Bass.

Kohn, A. (1999) *Punished by Rewards: The Trouble with Gold Stars, Incentive Plans, A's, Praise, and Other Bribes*. Boston, MA: Houghton Mifflin.

Marsh, P. (2004). 'Supporting pupils, schools and families: an evaluation of the Hampshire Family Group Conferences in Education Project.' Unpublished manuscript held by the University of Sheffield.

Marshall, T. (1997) 'Seeking the whole justice', in S. Hayma (ed.) *Repairing the Damage: Restorative Justice in Action*. London: ISTD.

Mayer, J.D., Caruso, D.R. and Salovey, P. (1999) 'Emotional intelligence meets traditional standards for an intelligence', *Intelligence*, 27: 267–98.

McKenzie, A. (1999) 'An evaluation of school community forums in New South Wales schools.' Paper presented at the Restorative Justice and Civil Society Conference, Australian National University, Canberra, ACT, February.

Minnesota Department of Children, Family and Learning (2002) 'In-school behaviour intervention grants: A three-year evaluation of alternative approaches to suspensions and expulsions.' Report to the Minnesota Legislature.

Moore, M.H., Petrie, C.V., Braga, A.A. and McLaughlin, B.L. (2002) *Deadly Lessons: Understanding Lethal School Violence*. Washington, DC: National Research Council.

Morrison, B.E. (2001) 'Developing the schools capacity in the regulation of civil society', in H. Strang and J. Braithwaite (eds) *Restorative Justice and Civil Society*. Cambridge: Cambridge University Press.

Morrison, B.E. (2002) *Bullying and Victimisation in Schools: A Restorative Justice Approach. Trends and Issues in Crime and Criminal Justice*, 219. Canberra: Australian Institute of Criminology.

Morrison, B.E. (2003) 'Regulating safe school communities: being responsive and restorative,' *Journal of Educational Administration*, 41: 689–704.

Morrison, B.E. (2005) *Restorative Justice: Emerging Issues in Practice and Evaluation.* Cullompton: Willan Publishing.

Morrison, B.E. (2006a) *Restoring Safe School Communities: A Whole School Response to Bullying, Violence and Alienation.* Sydney: Federation Press.

Morrison, B.E. (2006b) 'School bullying and restorative justice: towards a theoretical understanding of the role of respect, pride and shame', *Journal of Social Issues,* special edition: restorative justice and civil society.

Morrison, B.E. and Martinez, M. (2001) 'Restorative justice through social and emotional skills training: an evaluation of primary school students.' Unpublished manuscript held at the Australian National University.

Newman, K.S. (2004) *Rampage: The Social Roots of School Shootings.* New York, NY: Basic Books.

Olweus, D. (1993) *Bullying at School: What we Know and What we Can Do.* Cambridge, MA: Blackwell.

Porter, L. (2001) *Children are People Too: A Parent's Guide to Young Children's Behavior.* Adelaide: Small Poppies Press.

Pranis, K., Stuart, B. and Wedge, M. (2005) *Peacemaking Circles: From Crime to Community.* St. Paul, MN: Living Justice Press.

Restorative Justice Consortium (2003) *Statement of Restorative Justice Principles: As Applied in a School Setting* (available online at http://www.restorativejustice. org.uk).

Riestenberg, N. (2000) 'Aides, administrators and all the teachers you can get: a restorative training guide for schools.' Manuscript held by the Minnesota Department of Children, Family and Learning.

Riestenberg, N. (2003) 'Restorative schools grants final report (January 2002–June 2003): a summary of the grantees' evaluation.' Manuscript held by the Minnesota Department of Children, Family and Learning.

Riestenberg, N. (2005) 'Classroom meeting and re-entry meetings: circle visible and invisible.' Manuscript held by the Minnesota Department of Children, Family and Learning.

Ritchie, J. and O'Connell, T. (2001) 'Restorative justice and the need for restorative environments in bureaucracies and corporations', in H. Strang and J. Braithwaite (eds) *Restorative Justice and Civil Society.* Cambridge: Cambridge University Press.

Sharpe, S. (2003) *Beyond the Comfort Zone: A Guide to the Practice of Community Conferencing.* Calgary, AB: Calgary Community Conferencing.

Shaw, G. and Wierenga, A. (2002) 'Restorative practices: community conferencing pilot.' Manuscript held at the Faculty of Education, University of Melbourne.

Sherman, L.W. (2003) 'Reason for emotion: reinventing justice with theories, innovation, and research', *Criminology*, 41: 1–37.

Skiba, R.J. and Noam, G.G. (eds) (2001) *Zero Tolerance: Can Suspension and Expulsion Keep Schools Safe? New Directions for Youth Development: Theory Practice Research.* San Francisco, CA: Jossey-Bass.

Thorsborne, M. and Vinegrad, D. (2002) 'Restorative practices in schools: rethinking behavior management.' Manuscript held by Margaret Thorsborne and Associates, Buderim, Queensland, Australia.

Thorsborne, M. and Vinegrad, D. (2004) 'Restorative practices in classrooms: rethinking behavior management.' Manuscript held by Margaret Thorsborne and Associates, Buderim, Queensland, Australia.

Van Ness, D. and Strong, K. (2002) *Restoring Justice*. Cincinnati, OH: Anderson Publishing.

Wachtel, T. and McCold, T. (2001) 'Restorative justice in everyday life: beyond the formal ritual', in H. Strang and J. Braithwaite (eds) *Restorative Justice and Civil Society*. Cambridge: Cambridge University Press.

Webber, J. (2003) *Failure to Hold: The Politics of School Violence*. Lanham, MD: Rowman & Littlefield.

Woehrle, L.M. (2000) *Summary Evaluation Report: A Study of the Impact of the Help Increase the Peace Project in the Chambersburg Area School District*. Baltimore, MD: American Friends Service Committee.

Youth Justice Board for England and Wales (2004) *National Evaluation of the Restorative Justice in Schools Programme* (available online at www.youth-justice-board.gov.uk).

Zehr, H. (2002) 'Journey to belonging', in E. Weitekamp and H. Kerner (eds) *Restorative Justice: Theoretical Foundations*. Cullompton: Willan Publishing.

Chapter 19

Truth commissions and restorative justice

Jennifer Llewellyn

Introduction

Truth commissions are increasingly commonplace in the toolbox for transition and recovery from repressive rule and internal conflict. The challenges faced in these contexts often include dealing with past, serious and widespread human rights abuse and violence. Abuses range from systematic denial of basic human rights to the more extreme cases of mass violence and even genocide. For the purposes of this discussion, this range of abuse is captured by the term 'gross human rights abuse', signalling its seriousness both in terms of its nature and scope. Since early experiments in the 1970s, truth commissions have undergone significant development and have come to be viewed as a real and legitimate option for states seeking to respond to past wrongs (Hayner 2000; Bronkhorst 1995, 2003).

Depending upon how their purpose and function are viewed, the development and increasing prominence of truth commissions have been both heralded and lamented. Truth commissions are viewed variously as a sacrifice of justice, as able to provide some partial measure of justice or as an institution of justice. Critics are particularly worried about the extent to which truth commissions are being chosen as alternatives to prosecution. In such cases, they argue, the choice to have a truth commission represents a sacrifice of justice – a choice for truth over justice for the sake of peace, stability or some other value (Minow 1998: 9; Allen 1999: 318; Andrews 2000; Rotberg and Thompson 2000). On this view, truth commissions represent a threat to justice and not a legitimate option for dealing with the past. At most, in the view of such critics, truth commissions ought to complement the work of courts or international tribunals either through investigating and providing evidence, or by offering some measure of comfort to victims after prosecutions are complete (Llewellyn and Raponi 1999: 94; Wierda *et al*. 2002; Llewellyn 2003). In the face of such critiques, supporters have sought to defend truth commissions in justice terms. They argue these institutions, far from sacrificing justice, are focused on ensuring justice or at least some measure of it. Restorative justice is often employed in efforts to defend truth commissions as justice institutions, as either the measure or type of justice truth commissions offer. The identification of truth commissions as restorative justice institutions is not, however, merely a strategy to deflect criticism but has, as Elisabeth Kiss notes, developed out of the lived experience of those involved in transitional contexts: 'When truth commissions were first established two decades ago [restorative justice] was not envisaged as an important, or even necessarily relevant, aspect of their purpose. Instead, it has emerged out of reflection on the actual experiences of truth commissions' (2000; 71–72).

This chapter examines the claim that truth commissions can serve as institutions of restorative justice. This potential application of restorative justice has received surprisingly little attention from restorative justice scholars and advocates, an unfortunate oversight given the significant contribution restorative justice stands able to make in these contexts. Omitting consideration of this application from the scholarship is also disappointing for restorative justice advocates as these contexts can reveal, in a poignant fashion, significant truths about the nature and demands of justice that might support and enhance restorative justice theory and practice. This chapter aims to bring the application of restorative justice in response to gross human rights abuse into the main of restorative justice thinking in order that these insights can be more fully recognized and explored.

The chapter first reviews the ways in which restorative justice is associated with truth commissions. What do advocates mean when they claim truth commissions are restorative institutions? The chapter then explores the appropriateness and potential of restorative justice as a response to gross human rights abuse. It concludes with a consideration of the implications a restorative justice approach would have for the design, structure and practice of truth commissions. In doing so attention is paid to the example offered by the South African Truth and Reconciliation Commission.

This examination of the possibility and potential of restorative justice to inform the development and practice of truth commissions is significant for those faced with the task of responding to gross human rights abuse and violence. This is a task most familiar in the process of transition and recovery from repressive rule or internal conflict. It is not, however, the preserve of transitional contexts. Many established and stable democracies face similar challenges.[1] This consideration of the potential of truth commissions to be restorative institutions is thus of great importance for a range of contexts faced with the challenge of dealing with abusive and violent pasts.

The justice of truth commissions

Restorative justice has been invoked with increasing regularity in descriptions and justifications of the work of truth commissions. Advocates have used restorative justice in various ways to explain the contribution of truth commissions to achieving justice in the midst of transition or recovery from internal conflict or repressive rule. Underlying these different invocations are different conceptions of restorative justice. Understanding the ways in which restorative justice is employed in the discourse surrounding truth commissions is important in order to grasp the sorts of claims that are made on behalf of truth commissions and to assess whether the potential of restorative justice in such contexts is being realized.

Justice-based defences of truth commissions typically take one of two forms. The first argues that truth commissions are able to offer some measure of justice in transitional contexts when the full justice of prosecution and punishment is not possible or probable for a variety of reasons. This justification of truth commissions is captured by the familiar phrase 'justice to the extent possible' coined during the Chilean transition (Zalaquette 1993: xxxi).[2] Restorative justice is invoked to denote the measure or part of justice that truth commissions can offer in these circumstances. As such, restorative justice is conceived of as one aspect of justice, which, while normally served by prosecutions, can in their absence be provided by truth commission processes. Specifically, restorative justice can ensure some justice for victims by investigating and acknowledging the truth of what happened and providing a forum through which their stories might be heard. It is notable that those who defend the work of truth commissions in these terms do not generally promote them as a means of ensuring accountability for perpetrators or reparations for victims.[3] They clearly do not contemplate truth commissions as able fully to deliver justice.

The other defence of truth commissions posits that they offer more than simply partial justice but, rather, provide a different type or kind of justice than that of prosecutions and punishment (Villa-Vicencio 1998; Gutmann and Thompson 2000: 32; Kiss 2000: 80; Daly, E. 2002: n. 35). These advocates, in contrast to those who defend truth commissions as 'justice to the extent possible', do not lament the failure to prosecute as a failure of full justice. Instead, they view truth commissions as the preferred means of doing justice in transitional contexts because of the different requirements of justice in response to gross human rights abuse and violence. The sort of justice required according to these advocates is restorative justice.

Justice through a transitional lens

These defences of truth commissions, then, differ in terms of their understanding of restorative justice and what it has to offer in transitional contexts. On the first account, restorative justice is partial justice and can serve as some measure of justice in the absence of the full justice of prosecution. On the second account, restorative justice is viewed as a type or kind of justice particularly appropriate for transitional contexts. Both approaches, however, share a common starting point with respect to the meaning of justice in 'normal' (or non-transitional) times. Underlying both is a clear commitment to the idea of justice as requiring retribution. This conception of justice is not disputed or challenged by either account of the work of truth commissions. Instead, each makes a case for modifying the requirements of justice under the extreme and unusual circumstances faced by transitional contexts.

Restorative justice as it is used in these accounts does not have anything to say about the meaning or requirements of justice generally. It is invoked only to describe the doing of justice in exceptional circumstances. Clearly on these accounts, restorative justice has something to offer transitional contexts. However, the narrow and limited conceptions of restorative justice at work in these accounts have prevented an appreciation of the full potential of restorative justice in transitional contexts.

Thus far, scholars have argued that we must revise our expectations and understanding of the demands of justice for transitional contexts. This fact misses, however, significant insights that are to be gained in dealing with gross human rights abuse and violence in transitions. The importance of these insights concerning the meaning and requirements of justice is not limited to transitional contexts. The context of dealing with gross human rights abuse and violence brings into focus the nature of justice and its demands in a most powerful and poignant way. Perhaps this is why scholars otherwise committed to traditional conceptions of justice – who have not come to question the meaning of justice in its normal day-to-day operation in established democracies – have been forced to rethink their assumptions about justice in the context of transitions. It is disappointing, however, that this reassessment has been limited to these contexts and has not caused a similar reassessment of justice beyond transitional times. Transitional times are not special situations for justice as much as they offer a unique window on the meaning of justice. Specifically, these circumstances make clear the truth restorative justice speaks about the relational nature of justice. The need to focus on restoration of relationships in response to wrongdoing is revealed through these situations in a most compelling and urgent way.

Fully appreciated, these insights make clear the potential application of restorative justice in transitional contexts and the importance of bringing restorative justice theory and practice to bear on the work of truth commissions. The limited view of restorative justice promoted by the prevailing defences of truth commissions tracks some of the existing literature on restorative justice that similarly limits its visions of restorative justice. This literature pays little attention to restorative justice as a conception of justice, viewing it either as an alternative practice option (a form of alternative dispute resolution) or as limited to a theory of criminal justice.

One can see these approaches reflected in conceptions of restorative justice at work in the justice defences of truth commissions. The first, the 'justice to the extent possible' defence, employs restorative justice as an alternative process option to achieve partial justice when other processes (prosecutions) are impossible or impracticable. The other approach invokes restorative justice as a kind or type of justice appropriate for certain circumstances similar to those who view restorative justice only as an approach to criminal justice. Recognizing the ways in which these limited conceptions of restorative justice fail fully to realize its potential in transitional contexts ought to cause advocates of restorative justice to assess the limits of the literature more generally. A conception of restorative justice as a theory of justice generally and not simply as a theory of criminal justice or as a form of practice offers a more comprehensive picture of the potential of truth commissions to do justice during transitions and beyond. A brief sketch of restorative justice as a theory of justice is offered below. From this foundation, the possibility and potential of restorative justice to respond to gross human rights abuse can be fully assessed.

Restorative justice as a theory of justice

Since the term restorative justice has come into vogue, particularly with respect to domestic criminal justice practice, it is sometimes used as a catch-all phrase to refer to any alternative practice that does not look like mainstream justice practices. It is this use of the term that has led to the conception of restorative justice as merely special practice and obscured its significance as a theory of justice. The understanding of restorative justice as a theory of justice is distinct from the claims considered above. Restorative justice is, I suggest, best understood as a theory about the meaning of justice (Llewellyn and Howse 1998; see also Johnstone and Van Ness, Chapter 1, this volume).

Justice understood restoratively is fundamentally concerned with restoring the harm caused to relationships by wrongdoing. It takes as its aim the restoration of relationships to ones of social equality – that is, relationships in which all parties enjoy, and accord one another, equal dignity, concern and respect. Wrongdoing for restorative justice is understood in terms of the resulting harms. In order to restore relationships, the harms experienced by all the parties involved must be addressed. Restorative justice conceives of the harms concerned as primarily to the relationships between and among the parties involved. Thus it is not limited in its focus to the harms caused to the relationship between the wrongdoer and the direct victim. Restorative justice recognizes and seeks to address the harms to all the relationships involved. Determining which relationships were harmed requires careful attention to the specific context. Generally, though, these will include (but are not limited to) the relationship between the victim and wrongdoer, between the victim, wrongdoer and their communities, and between the different communities involved.

Some are led by this focus on relationships to assume that the aim of restorative justice is the restoration of personal or intimate relationships[4]. While this is not precluded by the idea of restorative justice, it is not its goal. Rather, it is concerned with ensuring equality in social relationships between individuals. Social relationships are those relationships that result from the fact that we all exist in networks of relationships – some personal and intimate but the great majority of which result from the fact that we share the same physical or political space. The basic requirement for equality in these relationships is the satisfaction of each party's rights to equal concern, respect and dignity (Llewellyn and Howse 1998).

Restorative justice's focus on the harm to relationships does not mean, however, that the harm experienced by victims and other individuals involved in the wrongdoing is irrelevant. Indeed, harm caused to relationships cannot be understood or repaired without attention to the nature of the particular harms suffered by the parties involved. It is thus important to attend to the harm experienced by the victim; however, such harm is broader than physical or material harms. It also results from the harm to his or her relationship with others – including the wrongdoer, and, in some cases, his or her own community. The familiar claim that restorative justice is 'victim centred' is unhelpful in so far as it obscures this point. While it is true that the victim is a central part of a restorative response to wrongdoing (in contrast to the traditional retributive justice-based systems which have excluded the victim in favour of giving the state the central role), it is not accurate to describe restorative justice as victim centred if what is intended by this description is a flipping of the tables whereby the victim's needs become central at the expense of the wrongdoer's or the communities'. Rather, it is more appropriate to say that restorative justice is 'relationship centred', as the focus of restorative justice is always broader than any individual party because of its goal of restoring relationships (Llewellyn and Howse 1998: 69).

Another common limit unduly placed on restorative justice, as discussed above, is to view it purely as an approach to crime. This limit mirrors the move by transitional scholars to see restorative justice as a special kind or type of justice. Restorative justice does actually offer a different way to view and understand crime and a new perspective from which to design appropriate responses. However, restorative justice is more comprehensive than this. Understood in its full sense, restorative justice as a theory of justice focused on the harms resulting from wrongdoing issues a challenge to the private/public dichotomy existing in traditional Western legal systems. Restorative justice's focus on the harm caused to relationships reveals the extent to which the distinction between tort and crime is illusory. To the extent these labels reflect any relevant difference for the purposes of restorative justice, it is a difference in the scope of the process required to address the harm. For example, wrongdoing classified as crime may have further-reaching effects in terms of the harm caused, and require restorative processes that involve a greater number of parties with a stake in the outcome of the process. For the most part, however, if wrongdoing causes harm to relationships, it does not matter from the perspective of restorative justice whether that harm is called a tort or a crime. Similarly, restorative justice-based truth commissions should not be restricted in terms of the kinds of wrongdoing with which they deal. What is key is the harm caused to relationships, not the label traditionally given to such acts.

Restorative justice, then, offers a new lens through which to see the world – it invites one to see the world relationally. Viewed in this way, it becomes clear that response to wrongdoing requires appreciation of, and redress for, the harm caused to relationships. This truth is perhaps nowhere as evident as in times of transition from conflict. Indeed, it is because the harm from wrongdoing extends beyond the individual victim that the necessity of dealing with the past is felt so strongly even by those not directly injured by wrongdoing. So the fact that justice requires restoration of relationships is readily apparent in transitional contexts, but it is no less true in established societies.

Truth commissions through a restorative lens

Approaching restorative justice as a theory of justice, and not partial justice or a special kind of justice, offers a different view of truth commissions, and their potential and significance for transitional contexts. First and foremost, this understanding of restorative justice as full justice means that truth commissions, in so far as they are restorative justice institutions, ought to be the first and best choice for transitional contexts even where prosecutions (domestic or international) are possible. Indeed, this view of truth commissions turns the 'justice to the extent possible' defence on its head. If justice is understood as fundamentally restorative – that is, requiring the restoration of relationships as the response to wrongdoing – then full justice could not be achieved through retributive-focused prosecutions. There are, of course, some circumstances in which restorative justice might not be possible. For example, continuing hostilities or violence might be a constructive bar to beginning the work of restoration.[5] In such circumstances when the full justice of restoration is impossible, the partial justice of prosecutions might be an alternative. Indeed, it might pave the way for restorative justice by incapacitating those who continue to cause harm to relationships. This would reverse the relationship between prosecution and truth commissions from that currently assumed so that prosecution would represent 'justice to the extent possible' and thus be the second-best option to truth commissions (Llewellyn 2003).

Justice re-envisioned as restorative supports the use of truth commissions as the mechanisms best able to respond to past abuse and violence with a view to building a just future. It makes clear the role truth commissions might play in doing justice in times of transition. But it also points to the potential for such institutions to be of broader significance beyond transition and recovery. The conception of restorative justice as a theory of justice, apt for so-called normal times just as for transitions, points to another way in which truth commissions might play a fundamental role for transitional contexts. As transitional contexts struggle to imagine and construct a future different from their repressive pasts, truth commissions might serve as an example of what justice means and how just institutions might function in the future. Truth commissions, in their design and operation, offer an experience of how to do justice post-transition. They might thus serve as a training ground, building capacity for citizens to do justice in the future (Llewellyn 2005).

Restorative justice fully understood as a theory of justice suggests that truth commissions ought to be favoured over prosecutions for doing justice in response to gross human rights abuse and violence because they are capable of being restorative. This is not to say that they are necessarily nor automatically so. Indeed, there are many truth commissions that, while making some contribution to restoration (through discerning the truth of what happened or providing a forum for victims to tell their story and feel heard, etc.), are not in their design or orientation fully restorative. A helpful distinction is to be made here between processes that are restoratively oriented, in the sense that they are less retributive or serve to pave the way for the restoration of relationships, and those that take restoration as their goal or orienting principle. Some models of truth commissions might serve restorative interests, but yet not be fully restorative. It is important to consider what implications a fully restorative approach to truth commissions would have for the design, implementation and operation of these institutions.

Objections to restorative responses

Before considering the implications of a restorative approach for the design and operation of truth commissions, it is worth considering some of the most common objections or concerns with the application of restorative justice in these contexts. Some objections result from a clash of beliefs about the meaning and requirements of justice. This is the case with those who claim restorative justice mechanisms are unjust because they do not ensure punishment of the guilty. These critics adhere to a fundamental commitment that justice requires punishment. In so far as the restoration of relationships is the goal of restorative justice, it is concerned with what is required to achieve this aim rather than identifying justice with a single mechanism – punishment. There is a general lack of clarity within the restorative justice literature as to whether such processes constitute or involve punishment (Llewellyn and Howse 1998: 70; Daly, 2001; Llewellyn 2001; Braithwaite 2002: 69–70; Roche, Chapter 5, this volume). I do not attempt to resolve this issue here, but only note that, whatever position one takes, it is clear that the primary focus of such processes is not punishment, and that if punishment results it cannot cause the isolation of one party from the relationship so as to make restoration impossible. In so far as retributivists name isolating punishment as necessary for justice, they will view restorative justice mechanisms as inadequate and unjust. It seems unlikely that there will be any way to answer objections of this sort except to challenge the definition of justice underlying the critique and be clear that restorative justice offers a different theory of justice.

There are other objections that are not the product of conflicting conceptions of justice. These objections, however, generally reflect underlying misconceptions of restorative justice. They nevertheless beg response because they ring out as common refrains in contexts contemplating restorative responses to gross human rights abuse and violence. Two objections frequently made are that restorative justice is inappropriate in situations where there was no pre-existing peace or equality, and that previous experience suggests restorative justice simply does not work in transitional contexts.

In regards to the first objection – that restorative justice is inappropriate in circumstances where there exists no prior state of social equality to be restored – critics point out that this is almost always the case in transitional contexts, and elsewhere, where gross human rights abuse and violence have occurred. Such serious wrongdoing is typically the result of longstanding inequalities and conflict. Where this is the case, critics charge, there is no prior state to which to restore things, and thus processes that take restoration as their goal are inappropriate and unworkable (see, for example, Dyzenhaus 2000: 481; Teitel 2000: 216; Daly, 2002: n. 35)[6] A common misunderstanding flowing from the term 'restoration' underlies this objection. Responding to this critique entails a clarification of the sense in which restorative justice aims at restoration. This requires one looks beyond the 'common sense' notion of *restore* to the origins and aspirations of restorative justice theory. Restorative justice does not aim at a return to the *status quo ante* (Llewellyn and Howse 1998: 2, 1999: 375). It is not focused on discovering some prior state of equality to which to return. If this were its aim, critics would be right to suspect it inappropriate for transitional contexts where typically the history of the society is one of significant inequality and intergroup conflict. Instead, however, the term restore is apt because it is premised on the fact that human beings live in relationship with one another. Indeed, the ability of human beings to flourish requires relationship with others. Further, it matters what sort of relationships we live in – some will detract and others contribute to our ability to realize our full potential. A basic requirement for human beings to flourish is that they are in relationships of dignity, respect and mutual concern.[7] Restorative justice seeks to restore relationships to this ideal of relationship – an ideal that is derived from the nature of the human self. Thus it is not necessary for such relationships to have existed previously in order to make sense of the idea of restoration. The possibility of relationships of social equality is latent in our humanity.

Another version of this first objection claims that restorative justice cannot work in these circumstances because there is no existing community capable of generating or participating in the process (Leebaw 2001: 273). This objection is built on the assumption that restorative justice only works where there is a strong and functioning community. This assumption misses the role that restorative justice processes can play in the creation, repair and strengthening of community. Just as restorative justice processes do not rely on a pre-existing state of equality, they do not require an existing strong and functioning community.

The other significant objection raised against the use of restorative justice in response to gross human rights abuse and violence is that such processes simply do not work. This objection typically uses as a measure of the success of restorative processes the extent to which individuals involved, or society itself, are reconciled after the work of the process is completed. The South African Truth and Reconciliation Commission was subjected to this sort of critique. Critics point to two significant facts as proof of its failure. First, they note the number of individual victims who do not forgive or feel reconciled with their perpetrators. Secondly, they point to public surveys and ongoing tensions in the country as evidence that the nation is not reconciled and thus the commission has failed in its efforts (Murphy 1998; Tepperman 2002: 135). Both these critiques are premised on the misperception that restorative encounters are the totality of the restorative process and thus measure the success of restorative justice by the results of the encounter. While it is certainly the case that encounters make a significant contribution to the restoration of relationships, the purpose of these encounters is to make a plan for the future work that needs to be done to address the harms resulting from wrongdoing and to contribute to restored relationships. This objection to restorative justice is perhaps the most difficult to respond to because it reveals the extent to which restorative justice requires a new way of thinking about justice. On a restorative conception, justice is more akin to a process than to an end state. There is an ideal just state envisioned by restorative justice which, when existing, would allow one to say that things are just – namely, the existence of relationships of social equality. The restoration of relationships, though, often involves a lengthy process and ongoing work to maintain such relationships. In this way, restorative justice is significantly different from retributive justice, which is done or 'achieved' when punishment is meted out. Restorative justice maintains what justice requires depends upon the particular relationships at issue and what is necessary to restore them.[8] It is this contextual and complex nature of restorative responses that enables them to be tailored to the particular context. Restorative justice is not, however, as we are used to thinking about justice, something done; rather it is something we do. It involves a commitment continually to strive for just relationships.

Encounter is thus part of the process of doing restorative justice, but it is not the only step. One cannot judge a restorative encounter process (like a truth commission) by the extent to which it results in immediate restoration or reconciliation. Properly understood, a restorative justice process involves significant work before and after the encounter and both are fundamentally important to restoration. This clarity about the role truth commissions can play in restoring relationships is important to avoid inappropriate expectations of these processes. Restorative justice-based truth commissions, then, are important to the restoration of relationships – one cannot diminish the significance of a process through which all the parties involved in a situation come together to understand one another and work together to design a plan for the future. After this process, however, the work of restoring relationships remains to be carried out. This work aims to address the harms resulting from wrongdoing and create the conditions in which relationships of mutual concern, respect and dignity can emerge and be sustained.

This is not to suggest that assessment of the success of restorative encounter processes is impossible. Rather, such processes ought to be assessed in terms of the extent to which they reflect restorative principles and contribute through the resulting plan for the future to establishing restored relationships. Determining the ultimate success of restorative processes may thus require a significant amount of time after the encounter process. The work of restoring relationships requires a sustained commitment to a different way of being in relationship. Nowhere is this more true than when dealing with gross human rights abuse and violence which are so often rooted in deep and longstanding inequalities.

Instituting restorative justice: lessons from South Africa

The South African Truth and Reconciliation Commission (TRC) is instructive as an example of how truth commissions might be restorative institutions. The South African TRC represents a significant development in truth commissions as institutional models of restorative justice. The South African commission self-identified as concerned with restorative justice (Truth and Reconciliation Commission 1998: vol. 1, ch. 5, para. 80 (hereafter TRC report); Tutu 1999: 54–5). In using the South African Commission as a basis for considering how truth commissions might be restorative institutions, I do not hold it out as a perfect or ideal example. The South African TRC is nevertheless worthy of careful attention because it represents the most advanced model thus far of a truth commission oriented towards restorative justice. It is instructive to examine the ways in which the South African commission attempted to embody the principles of restorative justice in its response to gross human rights abuse and violence. However, in looking to the commission for what it has to teach about creating institutions for restorative justice, it is important to attend to both its successes and failures in this respect.

A note of caution is warranted before undertaking this examination. In recognizing the weaknesses of the South African commission there is a danger of falling into retrospective critique. It is easy to find fault from a distance and with the luxury of time. This is not my intent. Rather, the model developed by the TRC is so significant an advance in the potential of truth commissions as institutions of justice that it deserves attention to ensure the insights of this experience are preserved for others who will face similar tasks in future. While in retrospect we can and must identify aspects of the commission process that could be improved, at the same time we must acknowledge how remarkable it is that the South African commission achieved the innovations and successes it did. The commission did not have time in advance of its work to contemplate and delineate a theoretical framework to inform its work. The commission came to restorative justice as it sought to explain the convictions of those working within the commission – far from sacrificing justice, as its critics charged, the commission was in fact doing justice. In some sense this makes the South African commission an even more powerful example of the potential of restorative justice in response to gross human rights abuse because its identification with restorative justice was not the result of an experiment aimed at proving the truth of restorative dogma, but rather flowed from the reality and demands of justice in that context.

Finally, it is important to be clear that this consideration of the South African commission should not be taken as a blueprint for restorative justice-based truth commission processes. Restorative justice is fundamentally committed to restoring relationships and doing this requires careful attention to the specific details and the context of those relationships. Restorative processes must thus be designed after consideration of the needs of particular parties and the issues involved. It is not possible or desirable, then, to provide a model of a restorative process absent knowledge or experience of the specific context. To be restorative, such processes must emerge from the context in which they will operate. If they are to comprehend the nature of the harms to relationships and how to address them, restorative justice-based truth commissions should be homegrown – developed through a process that includes all the parties concerned.

The struggle to do justice in transitional contexts has been the subject of a great deal of international attention over the last two decades. In response to contexts lacking the resources, skills and/or the will to ensure justice is done, the international community has come to the rescue with money, expertise and sometimes even ready-made institutions (tribunals or truth commissions). If restorative justice is taken as the goal in transitional contexts, this will have implications for international assistance. Ready-made international models will not achieve the restoration of relationships absent attention to context and without involvement and commitment of the parties concerned. Thus, while outsiders might assist in developing the skills and capacity needed for participation in such processes, they cannot create or run such institutions. The South African model, therefore, ought not to be taken as one simply to replicate. It is significant not for its institutional detail, but as an example of how restorative justice might inform an institutional model designed to deal with gross human rights abuse and violence.

What insights, then, might we draw from the South African TRC as a model of a restorative process? Arguably the most significant innovation of the South African commission was the inclusion of perpetrators in the process through the provision of amnesty. Restorative justice processes aim to bring all those affected by wrongdoing together to make a plan to address the resulting harm with a view to restoring relationships. Inclusion of perpetrators is thus vital to a restorative process. Other restoratively oriented processes aimed primarily at the needs of victims and communities might be possible without the participation of the perpetrator, but would leave a significant aspect of the work of restoration undone. Until the South African TRC, truth commissions were typically preceded or followed by a general amnesty. These previous models thus offered little incentive (and in many cases made no attempt) to involve those responsible for the abuse or violence in the process. While the South African commission was also created in the shadow of an amnesty provision agreed to at the last minute of the political negotiations for the transfer of power (Constitution of the Republic of South Africa No. 200 1993),[9] the South African Parliament chose to build this amnesty grant into the truth commission process. Amnesty was not a blanket provision applying across the board, but rather was granted to individuals who applied for it, offered full disclosure of their acts, demonstrated a political motive and showed proportionality between their motive and the means (Promotion of National Unity and Reconciliation Act No. 34 1995, s. 20, as amended by the Promotion of National Unity and Reconciliation Amendment Act No. 87 1995; hereafter TRC Act). Amnesty thus became part of the truth commission process as it was offered in exchange for truth (for further discussion, see Slye 2000a, 2000b). The significance of this development of including perpetrators was not simply that it allowed greater access to information. It was also significant from the perspective of restorative justice, for bringing perpetrators into the process created an opportunity for accountability and reintegration.

In addition to the participation of perpetrators, another significant aspect of the South African TRC as a restorative justice-based truth commission was its definition, inclusion and treatment of victims. The TRC encompassed relatives and dependants within its definition of victims, thereby recognizing that the harm resulting from wrongdoing extended beyond direct victims to those connected to the victim (TRC Act, s. 1(xix)). The TRC reflected restorative principles in providing opportunities for victims to tell their stories and identify their needs for reparations. The commission was committed to ensuring respect for victims and their experiences in all their dealings (TRC Act, s. 11),[10] corresponding to the victim-centred approach of restorative justice (Llewellyn and Howse 1998: 69). The commission did not, however, attend to the needs of victims at the expense of fair and respectful treatment of perpetrators.

The TRC also embodied the principles of restorative justice through the public's involvement in the process. This is consistent with the understanding at the core of restorative justice that communities play a fundamental role in the creation and resolution of conflict and that wrongdoing affects communities. The importance of public participation is most obvious perhaps in transitional contexts recovering from gross human rights abuse and violence. In such contexts, communities face the challenge of rebuilding and healing from the harmful effects of past conflict. Bringing community into the process to play a role in understanding and developing a response to the harmful effects of past abuse and violence restores a sense of community and reinforces the values of a healthy community.

The South African TRC included community as both witnesses of, and participants in, the process. The commission's hearings were public unless cause was shown to hold a closed hearing (TRC Act, s. 33).[11] These hearings were also broadcast on public radio and television ensuring access to the widest possible number of citizens. Community members were involved in some of the hearings thereby offering an opportunity for them to bring context to the events and highlight the wide-ranging effects of abuse and violence. Communities were also consulted broadly on the issue of reparations. In addition, the appointed commissioners brought the public into the process. Typically in a restorative justice process it is not ideal or advisable to rely upon the facilitator to bring community perspectives. In the case of the South African TRC, however, members of the commission were not charged with the central role of facilitating the process (though occasionally some members did act in this capacity). Generally, commission staff fulfilled this function. The commissioners were thus freed to represent community views and concerns. Indeed, commissioners were selected from civil society groups through a public process (Truth and Reconciliation Commission 1998, vol. 1, ch. 1, para. 37, hereafter TRC Report).[12]

Finally, the TRC stands as an example of a restorative justice process in its forward-looking orientation. The commission was tasked with making recommendations to ensure a better future. It was not focused purely on affixing blame for past crimes. The goal of the South African TRC was thus a restorative one – to make a plan for the future aimed at restoring relationships to ones of equal respect, concern and dignity. The words of the mandate of the commission reflect this ambition to 'promote unity and reconciliation in a spirit of understanding which transcends the conflicts and divisions of the past' (TRC Act, s. 3(1)).

The South African commission is significant for what its developments reveal about the potential of truth commissions to be institutions of restorative justice. It was not, however, without flaws or weaknesses when viewed from the perspective of restorative justice. The design and operation of the South African commission raise some concerns and cautions for those who might follow in its footsteps in attempting to develop a restorative truth commission.

The most significant weakness of the commission, from a restorative point of view, was structural. The commission separated the processes designed to deal with victims and perpetrators. Perpetrators were dealt with through the Amnesty Committee and victims through the Human Rights Violation Committee (TRC Act, ss. 17 and 14, respectively). This separation caused a number of problems for the commission as a restorative justice process. It reduced the opportunities for face-to-face encounters between the parties involved (victims, perpetrators and community). These encounters are fundamental to restorative justice as they provide an opportunity for dialogue about the nature of the harms and how to address them. Such encounters were not wholly absent, however. They occurred during victim appearances at amnesty hearings and informally when the commission arranged and facilitated meetings between victims and perpetrators outside the formal amnesty and victims' hearings (TRC report, vol. 5, ch. 9, para. 62 et seq.).[13] In addition to the standard victims' hearing held by the Human Rights Violation Committee, there were special hearings into events of particular significance. These special event hearings offer some guidance as to how such encounters might become more central to truth commission processes. All the parties involved in a major event during the conflict were brought together in these hearings. They 'allowed [the Commission] to explore the motives and perspectives of the different role players' (TRC report, vol. 5, ch. 1, para. 33). While these hearings still did not fully conform to the principles of restorative justice in that victims, perpetrators and the community were dealt with at separate times, the hearings did bring all three groups into the same process so that they might hear one another and understand one anothers' perspectives on the events.[14]

These processes were, however, the exception rather than the norm in the South African process. When they happened they provided an opportunity for communities to address collective experiences and harms. These experiences teach how important it is for restorative processes to create space in which those involved can encounter one another and engage in dialogue aimed at making a plan to restore relationships in the future.

The separation of the amnesty and victim processes was also problematic for the South African TRC as a restorative process because it resulted in the exclusion of perpetrators from the process of repairing harm. Perpetrators were not required under the amnesty provision to make any reparations to their victims or to the community. In fact, no formal option existed within the process whereby perpetrators could voluntarily participate in making reparation to their victims and to the community.[15] Restorative justice requires that the perpetrator take an active role in repairing the harm caused by wrongdoing because it is crucial for reintegration and, ultimately, for the restoration of relationships. An institutional model of restorative justice, then, should ensure all parties are actively engaged in the process of reparation.

The commission suffered another related problem in realizing its potential as a restorative process as a result of its limited power over reparations. Not only were the perpetrators not required or given the opportunity to participate in reparations, the commission itself had only recommending power with respect to reparations (TRC Act, ss. 3(1)(c), 3(1)(d), 4(b), 4(f), 4(h)). This meant that, while the commission could grant amnesty to perpetrators, thereby offering them an immediate benefit, it was not similarly empowered to respond to victims' needs. The South African government retained the right to determine reparations, including when and whether they would be granted. In the South African context, this was possibly the greatest threat to the restorative potential of the commission (Llewellyn 2004: 178–9). The government recently acted upon some of the recommendations of the commission and provided a measure of reparation for victims. However, they waited over five years after the commission submitted its reparation recommendations (Terreblanche 2003a). The delay cast serious doubt on their intentions to make good on reparations in any significant way and threatens the foundation laid for restoration laid by the Commission (Llewellyn 2004). Without reparations a significant aspect of the work of restoration remains undone. Perhaps even more worrisome is that failure to make good on reparations could cast doubt on the legitimacy and sincerity of the process as a whole, given that victims participated on the basis of a commitment to address their harm. The struggle over reparations in South Africa makes clear the importance of a sufficient commitment to follow through on the outcomes of the restorative process.

Another lesson can be learnt from the South African experience about the relationship between truth commissions and trials. Amnesty in the South African commission was used as a means to bring perpetrators into the process. For their participation and willingness to contribute to restoration (at the very least in the form of truth-telling and public accountability for their actions), perpetrators were granted amnesty so that they might be reintegrated into society. If amnesty is to be meaningful, however, the failure to apply or be granted amnesty must be met with some consequence. From the perspective of restorative justice, the problem here is not simply that of the free-rider, it is also that those who have not chosen to participate in the restorative process may continue to cause harm either directly through their actions or resulting from their lack of accountability. It is thus important that a restorative justice truth commission be backed by mechanisms aimed at ensuring accountability for those who do not participate. Prosecution is typically the mechanism used for such purposes. Failure to pursue prosecutions against those who were refused or failed to apply for amnesty may thus be problematic for the prospects of restorative justice (Llewellyn 2003). South Africa has not as yet pursued a significant number of prosecutions related to crimes committed in the past.[16] Additionally, the failure to enforce the threat of prosecutions in one context might jeopardize the success of restorative-based truth commissions in the future as perpetrators may refuse to participate, instead counting on there being no future consequences. Unfortunately, the failure to pursue further prosecutions following a truth commission process is not always a matter of will on the part of governments. It is often a consequence of scarce resources and the many demands for urgent and basic needs faced by transitional contexts (Llewellyn 2005).[17]

Finally, the experience of the South African Commission offers insights into the importance of preparation for the participants – particularly for the victim and perpetrator – so that they can understand the nature of the process and its goals. The South African commission had support personnel available for victims who testified before public hearings but significantly less support was available to the thousands of victims who spoke to statement-takers about their experiences. Less support still was provided to offenders; typically legal counsel was their primary support. Follow-up is equally, if not more, important than preparation to the restoration of relationships. It is important to support victims after the process and to ensure that reparation recommendations are carried out. For the perpetrator, it is important to provide support for reintegration if restoration is to become a reality. The South African commission's follow-up was weak. There were no formal provisions made with respect to reintegration of perpetrators or follow through on reparations. Additionally, whatever limited psychological support existed for victims was one of the first services to be eliminated towards the end of the commission's work.

Conclusion

Restorative justice is being invoked with increased frequency as an approach to dealing with gross human rights abuse and mass violence, yet the full promise and potential of restorative justice to address these circumstances have not been realized. The developments brought by the South African TRC show the possibility of truth commissions to be restorative justice processes. The time is ripe for careful attention to the application of restorative justice principles and practices in response to large-scale, systemic abuse and violence, both in transitional contexts and established democracies. Such attention will be fruitful for these contexts, and for the development and understanding of restorative justice, as it reveals that justice can only be realized if relationships are restored to ones of equal dignity, concern and respect.

Selected further reading

Borer, T. (ed.) (2005) *Telling the Truths: Truth Telling and Peacebuilding in Post-conflict Societies*. Notre Dame, IN: University of Notre Dame Press. This book is part of a three-volume series that explores the complex relationship between truth telling and establishing sustainable peace in post-conflict societies.

Hayner, P.B. (2000) *Unspeakable Truths: Confronting State Terror and Atrocity*. New York, NY: Routledge. A helpful introduction to the different models of truth commissions and the experiences of transitional countries employing such institutions.

Llewellyn, J. and Howse, R. (1999) 'Institutions for restorative justice: the South African Truth and Reconciliation Commission', *University of Toronto Law Journal*, 49: 355–88. This article offers an introduction to, and defence of, the South African Truth and Reconciliation Commission as an institutional model of restorative justice principles and practice.

Tutu, D.M. (1999) *No Future without Forgiveness*. New York, NY: Doubleday. Archbishop Desmond Tutu, Chairperson of the South African Truth and Reconciliation Commission, reflects on the aspirations, work and challenges the commission faced in examining past atrocities with a view to reconciliation.

Notes

1 For example, Canada and Australia face the challenge of dealing with past treatment of their aboriginal peoples. Germany continues to struggle with the holocaust. In the USA the human rights abuses committed during the civil rights struggle beg attention and redress as demonstrated by the current Greensboro Truth Commission (see www.ictj.org).

2 This idea was articulated during the Chilean transition in which the Aylwin government promised 'the whole truth, and justice to the extent possible'. In the introduction to the English edition of the *Report of the Chilean National Commission on Truth and Reconciliation*, Jose Zalaquette noted in explaining the decision to pursue 'justice to the extent possible' that '[r]esponsibility dictated that during the transition this was the most that could be aimed for. In fact, if the government had made an attempt (however futile, given Chile's existing legality) to expand the possibilities for prosecution, most likely it would have provoked tensions and reactions resulting in that neither truth nor justice could have been achieved' (Zalaquette 1993: xxxi).

3 This may be a reflection of the fact that before the South African commission perpetrators were not generally included within the process. Truth commissions have more commonly focused on victims and taken up the cause of understanding the truth of what happened in order to create public pressure for prosecutions or to offer some response in the wake of an amnesty grant.

4 Among the most notable examples of this misunderstanding is Dyzenhaus (2000) who moves from this mistaken conception to assume that restorative justice demands or relies upon personal catharsis, repentance and forgiveness. While some of the literature describing the experience of restorative practices does focus upon these elements they are not central to or dictated by restorative justice understood fully as a theory of justice. Indeed, this interpretation is premised on a clear misunderstanding of aim and focus of restorative justice.

5 This does not mean that there can be no violence ongoing. Many transitions from conflict and repression are marked by so-called 'spoiler violence' or isolated acts of violence aimed at disrupting the transition undermining the peace. A general

end to hostilities and a commitment by the major parties to move beyond the abuses and violence of the past are necessary in order to create a safe space for the work of a truth commission to begin.

6   Erin Daly maintains that restorative justice is 'useful only to the extent that relationships had previously been healthy and that trust and friendship had previously existed' (2002: n. 35). Ruti Teitel similarly misconceives restorative justice, as she claims it 'draws normative force from a return to the state's prior legacies' (2000: 216). Dyzenhaus also displays this misunderstanding of the term restore insisting that restorative justice aims at the restoration 'of some good that has been lost when the problem in a transition is one about how to bootstrap that good into existence' (2000: 481).

7   This idea of the human self as relational is familiar from relational theory (see generally Harris 1987; Koggel 1998; Nedelsky 1993).

8   It is perhaps not entirely correct to say 'it depends' for there are some responses that cannot be accepted if justice means the restoration of relationships. Specifically, justice cannot be served on a restorative account by any response that isolates and removes a party from the relationship altogether. For a relationship to be restored, both parties must remain in the relationship. Most obviously this would preclude the death penalty as a possible requirement of justice. Notice that this is a point often missed by those who maintain restorative justice as victim centred. On a victim centred account, the aim of restorative justice is understood as restoring the victim. This conception of restorative justice would place the victim in a privileged position since he or she would know better than others what would restore his or her harm and make him or her whole. A victim could, for example, assert that only the death of the perpetrator would suffice (Llewellyn and Howse 1998; Llewellyn 2005).

9   It was contained in the 'postamble' to the interim constitution. The interim constitution was drafted by a multi-party negotiating council and set out principles for the transition period and the development of the final constitution. The interim constitution was in force from 1993 to December 1996 when the new constitution was promulgated. The provisions contained in the postamble were incorporated into the final constitution tabled 8 May 1996 under s. 22 of Schedule 6 on Transitional Arrangements (*Constitution of the Republic of South Africa* No. 200 1993).

10 The Promotion of National Unity and Reconciliation Act identified seven principles to guide the treatment of victims in all aspects of the commission's work. Victims were to 1) be treated with compassion and respect for their dignity; 2) be treated equally and without discrimination of any kind; 3) encounter expeditious, fair, inexpensive and accessible procedures when making application to the commission; 4) be informed through the press and other media of their rights in seeking redress through the commission; 5) have their inconvenience minimized and when necessary measures taken to protect their safety and that of their family, and to protect their privacy; 6) be able to communicate in their chosen language; and 7) be able to access informal mechanisms for the resolution of disputes, including mediation, arbitration and any procedure provided for by customary law and practice, where appropriate (TRC Act, s. 11*)*.

11 The presumption of transparency can also be found elsewhere in the Act (See ss. 29 and 30)

12 The commissioners were Archbishop Desmond Tutu (chairperson), Dr Alex Boraine (vice-chairperson), Mary Burton (former Black Sash President), Advocate Chris de Jager (lawyer, former Member of Parliament and human rights commissioner), Rev. Bongani Finca (Minster in the Reformed Presbyterian Church), Ms Sisi

Kamphephe (lawyer and vice-chairperson of Mediation and Conciliation Centre), Mr Richard Lyster (Director, Legal Resources Centre, Durban), Mr Wynand Malan (lawyer and former Member of Parliament), Ms Hlengiwe Mkhize (Director, Mental Health and Substance Abuse, Department of Health), Mr Dumisa Ntsebeza (lawyer), Dr Wendy Orr (medical doctor), Dr Mapule Ramashala (clinical psychologist), Dr Fazel Randera (medical doctor and deputy chairperson, Human Rights Committee), Dr Yasmin Sooka (lawyer and President, World Conference on Religion and Peace, South Africa Chapter), Ms Glenda Wildschut (chairperson, Trauma Centre for Victims of Violence and Torture), Rev. K.M. Mqojo (Methodist minister) and Advocate Denzil Potgieter (lawyer).

13 The inclusion of amnesty into the overall work of the commission was important from the perspective of restorative justice as it brought perpetrators into the process and kept open the possibility of reintegration and thus restoration of relationships. However, the amnesty process itself was not, for the most part, a restorative one. In fact, the amnesty hearings more closely resembled adversarial court processes than the other hearings of the commission. The structure of this process limited the participation of the victims and community and the opportunities for restorative encounters. This is one of the weaknesses of the commission if viewed as a restorative process.

14 An example of such a hearing was that concerning the 'Trojan Horse' incident which occurred in Athlone, Cape Town in October 1985. The hearing was held in Athlone in the presence of community members and heard testimony from the community, victims and perpetrators. These hearings are addressed in the TRC report (vol. 5, ch. 1 paras 33–7).

15 The case of Brian Victor Mitchell, who was granted amnesty with respect to the Trust Feeds Massacre, serves as a well publicized example of a perpetrator who sought a way to make amends for his actions. There was no official mechanism within the commission to do this so he struggled to find some means of doing it on his own (see Amnesty Application No. 2586/96). The commission did, however, informally assist Mitchell in making contact with the community. The commission discusses this example in its report as one in which some important steps towards reconciliation were ultimately made (TRC report 1998: vol. 5, ch. 9, paras. 70–82).

16 The current government even floated the prospect of a general amnesty for acts committed during apartheid, although it has recently announced that no such amnesty will be granted. However, as part of a new prosecution policy some indemnity may be granted in connection with apartheid-related crimes. Details of the policy have yet to be released, but it would not offer immunity from civil claims (Terreblanche 2003b; Naidu 2005).

17 The experience of South Africa with two early attempts to prosecute apartheid crimes demonstrates how difficult and costly these prosecutions can be. The trials of General Magnus Malan and Eugene de Kock, two of apartheid's most notorious perpetrators, were long, expensive (costing a combined R17 million) and ultimately unsuccessful (Katz 1996; Leebaw 2001: 276; Tepperman 2002: 143–4).

References

Allen, J. (1999) 'Balancing justice and social unity: political theory and the idea of a truth and reconciliation commission', *University of Toronto Law Journal*, 49: 315–53.

Andrews, P. (2000) '*Judging the Judges, Judging Ourselves: Truth, Reconciliation and the Apartheid Legal Order*, by D. Dyzenhaus (review)' *Melbourne University Law Review*, 24: 236–47.

Braithwaite, J. (2002) *Restorative Justice and Responsive Regulation.* Oxford: Oxford University Press.

Bronkhorst, D. (1995) *Truth and Reconciliation: Obstacles and Opportunities for Human Rights.* Amsterdam: Amnesty International.

Bronkhorst, D. (2003) *Truth Commissions and Transitional Justice: A Short Guide* (available online at http://www.amnesty.nl/downloads/truthcommission_guide.doc).

Daly, E. (2002) 'Transformative justice: charting a path to reconciliation', *International Legal Perspective*, 12: 73–184.

Daly, K. (2001) 'Revisiting the relationship between retributive justice and restorative justice', in H. Strang and J. Braithwaite (eds) *Restorative Justice: Philosophy to Practice.* Aldershot: Ashgate.

Dyzenhaus, D. (2000) Survey Article: Justifying the Truth and Reconciliation Commission. *The Journal of Political Philosophy*, 8: 470–96.

Gutmann, A. and Thompson, D. (2000) 'The moral foundations of truth commissions', in R.I. Rotberg and D. Thompson (eds) *Truth v. Justice: The Morality of Truth Commissions.* Princeton, NJ: Princeton University Press.

Harris, M.K. (1987) 'Moving into the new millennium: towards a feminist vision of justice', *Prison Journal*, 62: 27–38.

Hayner, P.B. (2000) *Unspeakable Truths: Confronting State Terror and Attrocity.* New York, NY: Routledge.

Katz, M.L. (1996) 'Apartheid era unveiled: South African commission may reopen massacre case', *USA Today*, 14 October: 4A.

Kiss, E. (2000) 'Moral ambition within and beyond political constraints', in R.I. Rotberg and D. Thompson (eds) *Truth v. Justice: The Morality of Truth Commissions.* Princeton, NJ: Princeton University Press.

Koggel, C. (1998) *Perspectives on Equality: Constructing a Relational Theory.* Lanham, MD: Rowman & Littlefield.

Leebaw, B. (2001) 'Restorative hustice for political transitions: lessons from the South African Truth and Reconciliation Commission', *Contemporary Justice Review*, 4: 267–89.

Llewellyn, J. (2001) 'Punishment and restorative justice.' LLM thesis, Harvard University.

Llewellyn, J. (2003) 'Justice to the extent possible: the relationship between the International Criminal Court and domestic truth commissions', in H. Dumont and A. Boisvert (eds) *The Highway to the International Criminal Court: All Roads Lead to Rome.* Montreal: Journées Maximilien-Caron.

Llewellyn, J. (2004) 'Doing justice in South Africa: restorative justice and reparation', in E. Doxtader and C. Villa-Vicencio (eds) *To Repair the Irreparable: Reparation and Reconstruction in South Africa.* Cape Town: David Philip.

Llewellyn, J. (2005) 'Restorative justice in transitions and beyond: the justice potential of truth telling mechanisms for post-peace accord societies', in T. Borer (ed.) *Telling the Truths: Truth Telling and Peacebuilding in Post-conflict Societies.* Notre Dame, IN: University of Notre Dame Press.

Llewellyn, J. and Howse, R. (1998) *Restorative Justice – A Conceptual Framework.* Ottawa: Law Commission of Canada.

Llewellyn, J. and Howse, R. (1999) 'Institutions for restorative justice: the South African Truth and Reconciliation Commission', *University of Toronto Law Journal*, 49: 355–88.

Llewellyn, J. and Raponi, S. (1999) 'The protection of human rights through international criminal law: interview with Madam Justice Louise Arbour', *University of Toronto Faculty of Law Review*, 57: 83–100.

Minow, M. (1998) *Between Vengeance and Forgiveness: Facing History after Genocides and Mass Violence*. Boston, MA: Beacon Press.

Murphy, D.E. (1998) 'South Africa braces for findings on apartheid years', *Los Angeles Times*, 23 October: A5.

Naidu, E. (2005) 'No general amnesty for apartheid crimes: the government is still looking for a way to deal with issues that will promote reconciliation and national unity', *Sunday Independent*, 3 July.

Nedelsky, J. (1993) 'Reconceiving rights as relationship', *Review of Constitutional Studies*, 1: 1–26.

Rotberg, R.I. and Thompson, D. (eds) (2000) *Truth v. Justice: The Morality of Truth Commissions*. Princeton, NJ: Princeton University Press.

Slye, R.C. (2000a) 'Amnesty, truth and reconciliation: reflections on the South African amnesty process', in R.I. Rotberg and D. Thompson (eds) *Truth v. Justice: The Morality of Truth Commissions*. Princeton, NJ: Princeton University Press.

Slye, R.C. (2000b) 'Justice and amnesty', in C. Villa-Vicencio and W. Verwoerd (eds) *Looking Back Reaching Forward: Reflections on the Truth and Reconciliation Commission of South Africa*. Cape Town: University of Cape Town Press.

Tepperman, J.D. (2002) 'Truth and consequences', *Foreign Affairs*, 81: 129–45.

Teitel, R.G. (2000) *Transitional Justice*. Oxford: Oxford University Press.

Terreblanche, C. (2003a) 'Government ready to pay apartheid reparations', *Independent Online*, 16 November (available online at http://www.iol.co.za/index.php?set_id=1andclick_id=13andart_id=ct20031116122722653P000972).

Terreblanche, C. (2003b) 'New deal 'stops short of general amnesty'', *Independent Online*, 18 May (available online at http://www.iol.co.za/index.php?set_id=1andclick_id=13andart_id=ct20030518102634757A523488).

Truth and Reconciliation Commission (1998) *Truth and Reconciliation Commission of South Africa Report* (vols 1 and 5). Cape Town: Truth and Reconciliation Commission.

Tutu, D.M. (1999) *No Future without Forgiveness*. New York, NY: Doubleday.

Villa-Vicencio, C. (1998) 'A different kind of justice: the South African Truth and Reconciliation Commission', *Contemporary Justice Review*, 1: 407–28.

Wierda, M., Hayner, P. and van Zyl, P. (2002) 'Exploring the relationship between the Special Court and the Truth and Reconciliation Commission of Sierra Leone.' Paper presented at the International Center for Transitional Justice, New York, 24 June (available online at http://www.ictj.org/downloads/TRCSpecialCourt.pdf).

Zalaquette, J. (1993) 'Introduction to the English edition', in *Report of the Chilean National Commission on Truth and Reconciliation* (trans. P.E. Berryman). Notre Dame, IN: University of Notre Dame Press.

Zehr, H. (1990) *Changing Lenses: A New Focus on Crime and Justice*. Scottdale, PA: Herald Press.

Chapter 20

Terrorism, religious violence and restorative justice

Christopher D. Marshall

Over the past 25 years there has been a dramatic upsurge in terrorist violence in many parts of the world. There is nothing new about terrorism of course; it has been around for a very long time. In the past, terrorist activity was largely local in its impact and intention; it was aimed at a defined audience and witnessed only by those who were physically present. But modern terrorism is performed on a global stage for a global audience. It is global in three senses: its targets are spread throughout the world; its instigators are increasingly linked together in elaborate international networks; and its audience includes the worldwide television viewing public which, at times, as in the case of the Beslan school massacre, watches events as they unfold.

It is not surprising, then, that terrorism today is often deemed to be the gravest threat to world peace and security. Its gravity far exceeds the small number of people involved in terror organizations or the limited strategic gains they make. Modern terrorism is considered such a serious risk because it scorns international borders and treaties, exposes the impotence of conventional military might to control it and has the potential to unleash weapons of enormous destructive power on civilian populations anywhere on earth. It may be only a matter of time before we experience nuclear or biological terrorism. As terrorism expert Michael McKinley observes: 'The rule of thumb used to be that terrorists did not want millions of people dead, they wanted millions watching. That's changed. They are now quite happy for both to take place' (cited in Masters 2004: B3–B4).

As well as its epic proportions, another striking feature of much modern terrorism is its *religious* character. Only a generation ago, many Western academics were confidently predicting that secularization would soon see an end of religion and the final death of God – or at least God's belated retirement from public life. With religion banished to the benign fringes of privatized devotion, no need would remain to slaughter opponents on God's behalf. How wrong such predictions have been (Boulton 2004; see also

Berger 1999; Ward 2004)! The proportion of known terrorist organizations claiming a religious identity has increased sharply in the last two decades, and the use of religious language to describe their deeds is commonplace. After the destruction of the Twin Towers, Osama bin Laden declared: 'Here is America, struck by God in one of its vital organs, so that its greatest buildings are destroyed' (Juergensmeyer 2003: 149). Following the attack on the Australian Embassy in Jakarta in September 2004, Jemaah Islamiyah posted an Internet statement saying: 'We decided to call Australia to account, which we consider one of the worst enemies of God and of God's religion Islam' (*New Zealand Herald* 2004: B12). Not to be out-theologized, George W. Bush once told a Christian gathering in the USA: 'God told me to strike at al-Qaeda and I struck them, and then he instructed me to strike at Saddam, which I did' (Austin *et al.* 2004: 9).[1] Religion has resurfaced in the public square of international affairs with, literally, a bang!

This does not mean, of course, that all terrorism is religiously motivated, nor that all religious violence takes the form of terrorism. But so much terror today is inflicted in the name of God that it revives for our generation the centuries-old debate about the connection between religion and violence. Why do religious devotees engage in so much conflict and war? Does religion inescapably generate violence? Or is religion itself a casualty of violence, a violence that originates elsewhere and co-opts religious conviction for its own ends? Could religion even be a *cure* for human violence and, if so, how? These are profound and complex questions that cannot be considered in this chapter. But when passenger planes are flown into skyscrapers, ritual decapitations are displayed on the Internet and schoolchildren are blown to pieces by suicide bombers, all ostensibly at God's behest, the question about religion and violence is far from academic. It demands serious reflection by all people of good will, not least by those who are practising religious believers.

In this chapter I want to focus specifically on whether restorative justice has anything to contribute in the search for solutions to the scourge of religious violence and terrorism. This, we will see, is a very difficult question to answer. Before venturing to do so, we need to be clear on what we mean by 'religious terrorism' and on why it is such a difficult phenomenon to combat.

What is religious terrorism?

The term 'terrorism' comes from the Latin *terrere*, meaning 'to cause to tremble'. At its most general level, terrorism designates 'the intentional effort to generate fear through violence or the threat of violence and the further effort to harness these fears in pursuit of some goal' (Griffith 2002: 6). This definition captures the three key components of terrorism: its reliance on violence, its strategy of fostering fear and its teleological intent. Yet there is a real sense in which *all* violence generates fear and serves some ancillary purpose, not least the violence associated with conventional warfare. Recall the name given to the American invasion of Iraq – 'Operation Shock and Awe' – a clear indication that premeditated violence was being employed to heighten fear and demoralize the opposition. So the question of what distinguishes terrorism from other forms of violence is politically and ideologically highly loaded. Often it is only a matter of political expediency that deems some episodes of violence as terrorism and others as foreign policy.

Within this broad category, *religious* terrorism designates those 'public acts of violence ... for which religion has provided the motivation, the justification, the organisation, and the world view' (Juergensmeyer 2003: 7; see also Griffith 2002: 179). It shares many common features with political terrorism, such as its use of 'performative' violence; that is, violence that serves a theatrical as well as a practical purpose.[2] But arguably religious violence has its own shape or gestalt which is distinguishable from more secular forms of terrorism. Of course every militant group has unique characteristics, and the mix of religious and non-religious motivations varies from case to case. But in so far as it depends upon a religious worldview, faith-based terrorism is marked out by four things in particular: the absolutism of its categories, its tendency to spread contagiously, its heightened symbolism and its relative unconcern for measurable success. It is precisely these features that make religious violence such a formidable challenge to restorative justice theory and practice, so each deserves a brief comment.

Absolutism

Religious militancy is characterized, first, by strong claims to moral justification and by a thoroughgoing dualism that divides the world into 'us' and 'them', truth and falsehood, innocent and guilty, good and bad, with the fault line dividing the categories being absolute. After interviewing many violent activists, Jessica Stern of the Kennedy School of Government at Harvard University writes: 'I've noticed that one thing that distinguishes religious terrorists from other people is that they know with absolute certainty that they're doing good. They seem more confident and less susceptible to self-doubt than most other people' (Stern 2003: 26).

Such people see themselves as caught up in a transcendent battle between good and evil, and consider it their religious duty to purify the world of corruption by force. This results in an unwillingness to make concessions, for how can one compromise with the devil or tolerate impiety? Accordingly, religious zealots are willing to do virtually anything necessary to overcome the enemy, for evil cannot be transformed or accommodated, it must be utterly destroyed. 'Religious terrorists groups are more violent than their secular counterparts', Stern observes, 'and probably are more likely to use weapons of mass destruction' (2003: xxii; see also McTernan 2003: 42, 127). Holy wars historically have been notable for their savagery, and religious terrorism is really a contemporary form of unauthorized holy war.[3] And one of the most troubling features of holy war is its contagiousness.

Contagiousness

There is an important sense in which all violence is contagious, but arguably religious violence is more infectious than any other kind, and more addictive. Faith-inspired terrorism is contagious in two ways. First, its use of religious language expands the pool of potential sympathizers and recruits beyond the immediate battle zone to co-religionists all around the world. Once a holy war has been declared, religious hardliners from far and wide flock to join the contest, creating a multinational armed struggle, or what has been famously called a 'Jihad International Incorporated' (Stern 2003).[4] Secondly, once holy-war organizations are formed and achieve initial success, they seek additional missions elsewhere. This is something the USA did not reckon on sufficiently when it sponsored pan-Islamic terrorist organizations in Afghanistan to oppose the Soviet occupation (Eakin 2004). After the Soviet withdrawal, the *mujahideen* turned their sights on new targets, including America itself. Returning jihadis in Pakistan posed such a law-and-order problem that the government there sent them to fight in Kashmir, deliberately stirring up religious passions to intensify the conflict (Stern 2003). Once unleashed, holy wars acquire a momentum of their own. They have no masters. Holy war excites more holy war (Griffith 2002: 107, 110). Fighting for God becomes addictive.

Any consistent recourse to violence can become physiologically addictive for some individuals. But religious violence is addictive in a psychic and spiritual sense as well. Participation in holy war ranks among the most intense of all religious experiences (Selegnut 2003: 21). Jessica Stern found that only a few of the terrorists she interviewed claimed to be in personal communication with God, but they all described themselves as responding to a spiritual calling and many reported themselves as being addicted to its fulfilment.[5] They were 'spiritually intoxicated' by their cause, Stern observes (2003: 281–2), and experienced 'a kind of bliss' (p.xxvii): 'the bottom line, I now understood, is that purifying the world through holy war is addictive. Holy war intensifies the boundaries between Us and Them, satisfying the inherently human longing for a clear identity and a definite purpose in life, creating a seductive state of bliss' (p.137). Such bliss is its own reward, which leads to the third distinctive feature of religious combat.

Heightened symbolism

All terrorist acts are symbolic events to some degree, in that they are staged events calculated to attract public attention to some cause, but religious violence is almost exclusively symbolic (Juergensmeyer 2003: 125). That is to say, its creations of terror are done not primarily to achieve a strategic goal but to make a symbolic statement. It is a statement about the real condition of the world and about who possesses true power in the universe. The presupposition of religious terrorism is that the world is already at war, an apocalyptic war between good and evil. This war is being played out on the worldly stage of power politics, though few are aware of it. Terrorist acts dramatize or materialize the spiritual struggle that is invisibly underway behind the scenes. Victims are chosen not because they are a threat to the perpetrators but because they serve as symbols of this larger spiritual confrontation.

The symbolic character of current Islamist terrorism is highlighted well in a recent article by Jason Burke on Abu Musab al-Zarqawi, believed to have been personally responsible for the beheading of three Western hostages in Iraq in September–October 2004. These videotaped executions, Burke explains, were carefully scripted dramas intended for the world's 1.3 billion Muslims. They were laden with symbolic meanings missed almost entirely by Westerners. Zarqawi justifies his actions by appealing to 'one of the single most emotive issues in the Islamic world: the supposed imprisonment, and abuse, of Muslim women by non-Muslim men', even though, in reality, very few such prisoners existed. After evoking other sources of Muslim resentment, the videotape climaxes with an act of ritualized slaughter, re-enacting myths about how the first warriors of Islam killed the enemies of God. 'Islamic militant terrorism', Burke explains, 'is primarily propaganda and not usually tied to a specific political objective. Though frightening vital Western contractors out of Iraq and thus generating destabalizing discontent by slowing reconstruction is useful, Zarqawi's primary goal is to communicate' (Burke 2004: B3).

Assessment of success

Secular terrorists assess the utility of their acts to ensure that their violence will advance their political or nationalist goals. Sacred terrorists, by contrast, do not measure success in such worldly or human terms. Their aim is to not to gain strategic advantage in a tactical campaign but to champion God's will, oppose God's enemies and galvanize God's people (Selengut 2003: B1). In fact, Mark Juergensmeyer finds that its perpetrators have often turned to holy war precisely because there was no hope of human success. Their violent acts, he suggests, are 'devices for symbolic empowerment in wars that cannot be won and for goals that cannot be achieved' (2003: 218). For their campaign is not ultimately about politics or economics or even territory, though such concerns may also be involved. It is about the vindication of their theological vision of the world and the fulfilment of their eschatological hopes. Their sense of achievement comes simply from being involved in the struggle, confident that God is on their side and buoyed by contemplation of spiritual or heavenly rewards.

Such, then, is the distinctive shape of sacred terrorism. Why such a style of terrorism has exploded in recent decades is still debated by the experts. Is it the result of *need*, or of *greed*, or of *creed*, or of the *speed* of global change? My own proposal is that religious terrorism emerges where four elements come together: 1) an external situation of real or perceived human suffering; 2) a set of psychological and emotional responses to this situation on the part of certain individuals within larger cultures of resentment; 3) the availability of religious resources to explain present experience and justify violent remedies; and 4) the influence of charismatic religious leaders who exploit feelings of alienation to issue a call to holy war. No single ingredient is sufficient to spawn holy terror; it is the combination that is critical. Yet any attempt to combat religious terrorism must take all four elements individually into account, as well as the circumstances of their combination.

Responding to holy terror

Enough has been said already to indicate that religious terrorism is a particularly complex and dangerous reality to deal with. It is vital that internationally co-ordinated efforts are made to counteract it. A coherent strategy is required that balances short-term and long-term remedies.

The short-term need is to shut down or contain terror groups and networks and bring known perpetrators of murder to justice. The long-term need is to ensure that terrorist ideology loses its appeal among populations made vulnerable to it by perceived humiliation, human rights abuses, economic deprivation, indebtedness, unemployment, military occupation and other forms of collective distress. The challenge is to achieve the goal of containment without making the goal of prevention more difficult. There is also need for a third kind of response, a *therapeutic* response that addresses the pain of those who have been personally caught up in terrorist atrocities and that promotes reconciliation between estranged communities. It is here that restorative justice could have a role to play. Each of these responses needs teasing out in more detail.

The task of containment

Since 9/11, the international response to terrorism has focused primarily on the job of containment. Huge efforts have been made to hunt down known terrorist leaders, to destroy the material and financial bases of their operations, and to enhance domestic security. The predominant means of containment has been by the use of raw military power. Billions of dollars have been spent and tens of thousands of lives sacrificed in the so-called 'war on global terrorism'.

War is always a blunt and bloody instrument for resolving conflict. But the strategy of warring against holy war is a particularly unsophisticated and fruitless way to respond to religious violence (Utley 2004). The problem is not only that large-scale military assaults compound the suffering and the humiliation felt by the constituency from which terrorists emerge in the first place, making future recruitment much easier. The main pitfall of waging war on religious terrorism is that the religious zealots' underlying ideology of holy war is actually strengthened every time military power is directed against them. Military reprisals prove that their diagnosis of the world is correct: a great battle for religious truth truly is underway, the enemy really is a satanic monster and believers must now rally to defend true religion. Displays of massive counter-violence may even be welcomed by terrorist leaders, for it helps to spread the seeds of burning rage and religious zeal that guarantee 'the enlistment of a whole new generation of faith-based terrorists, ready and willing to wage a life and death struggle for the global soul' (McTernan 2003: 155). [6]

Making war on terrorism also validates something even more fundamental – the terrorist conviction that violence is ultimately a *redemptive* medium. Religious warriors believe in the saving efficacy of righteous violence. But so too, apparently, does their opponent.[7] When President Bush initially referred to the attack on Afghanistan as a 'crusade', he was saying more than he realized.[8] The term was quickly abandoned because of its sensitivity to Muslims. But changing the label does not change the product. The war on terrorism retains many of the hallmarks of a crusade – which is the Christian word for 'jihad' or holy war. The campaign is strongly dualistic, with an overt demonizing of the opponent (Marshall 2003: 6–7);[9] it sees total annihilation of the enemy as the only way to lasting peace;[10] it refuses any thought of compromise or negotiation with evil-doers;[11] it expresses suspicion towards those who inquire into the causes of terrorism or who call for moderation;[12] it claims to be fulfilling a sacred duty;[13] it is bolstered by claims of moral purity and certainty;[14] and, most revealing of all, it favours pre-emption over prevention or deterrence. In the judgement of ethicist Edward Leroy Long, the Bush administration's adoption of the doctrine of pre-emptive strike 'clearly illustrates how deeply the model of crusade has taken over as the controlling paradigm since the attacks on the World Trade Centre and the Pentagon' (Long 2004: 90; see further 44–50, 85–6).[15] Holy war, it appears, has elicited holy war, a holy war fought on behalf of American civil religion.[16]

Yet imitation is the greatest compliment that can be paid to terrorism. Not only do both parties compete to instil the greater fear and exact the higher price, but both insist that purity of motive justifies immense cruelty of action. Both conceive of the problem as a battle to be won rather than an injustice to be resolved. But if terror is to be reduced, rather than ratcheted up ever higher, the issue must be conceptualized in different terms. How we speak of a problem is surprisingly important, for it determines how we conceive of solutions. Lee Griffith (2002: 76) bemoans:

> the growing American incapacity to address any problem without resorting to war. This is more than a matter of semantics. Behind the linguistic style that speaks of a war on crime, a war on poverty, a war on drugs, and a war on terrorism lies a style of being and acting. The enemies must be identified, not merely as abstract social problems to be solved, but as real flesh-and-blood enemies to be vilified (which is why the 'war on poverty' so quickly turned into a war on the poor). The enemies must be defeated rather than being transformed, much less loved (which is why there is profligate spending for prisons and executions but scant resources for drug treatment). When there is a problem, America goes to war because the world is viewed as ripe for conquest rather than ripe for redemption.[17]

Instead of conceptualizing the issue in terms of fighting a war, it is more helpful to think of it in a criminal justice terms, or within a law enforcement framework (Cuzzo 2001). Global terrorism, notwithstanding its ideological agenda, may be classified as a type of organized criminal activity in which the whole global community has a stake. Attempts to track down its perpetrators should therefore take the form of international police action, with intelligence-gathering serving as the equivalent of sound detective work.

This is not merely tinkering with words. Police action differs from military action in terms of its normative character. Police work is subject to judicial restraint; it is guided by the requirements of procedural fairness; it has strictly limited aims (*viz.* to control wrongdoing, not to kill all wrongdoers); it does not exercise judgement or administer punishment; its coercive power is applied to the offending party alone; and it is expected to employ minimal force in performing its duties. It is also usually successful in achieving its purpose, and is compatible with longer-term restorative objectives. In all these ways, policing differs from soldiering. Police action against terror cells could still employ military personnel. But their methods and goals need to conform to the normative character of police work, rather than the normal practices of war-making.[18] Even so, as the analogy of domestic justice shows, police action by itself is never sufficient to reduce crime significantly. Efforts at prosecution must be matched by efforts at prevention. The same is true of terrorism. The long-term task of prevention is ultimately more important than the immediate goal of containment.

The task of prevention

Religious terrorism is often likened to a deadly virus that spreads contagiously in deprived, oppressed and traumatized communities where traditional forms of religious adherence are high. This being the case, the most promising remedy is one that boosts the collective immune system so that it does not succumb to the infection.[19] This requires treating the environmental risk factors that predispose communities to violence, such as poverty, joblessness, human rights abuses, indebtedness, ready access to weapons, state failure, political or military repression and other perceived injustices and humiliations, many of which stem from US foreign and economic policy.[20] In this connection, advocates of the new paradigm of 'just peace-making'[21] have several specific proposals to make for helping to prevent or reduce terrorism, such as working to advance human rights, democracy and religious liberty; developing the institutions of civil society; promoting co-operative methods of conflict resolution; strengthening the rule of law; identifying common security interests between adversaries; and, perhaps most crucially of all, making concerted efforts to resolve the Palestinian–Israeli conflict (New 2002). Counter-terrorism hawks sometimes warn against too much emphasis on social justice initiatives lest they be seen as a form of rewarding terrorism. But as Glenn Stassen (2004) observes:

> Terrorists thrive by identifying themselves with just demands of the people. A policy that fears rewarding terrorists easily becomes a policy that avoids doing justice for people. If a region is being oppressed, and the terrorists identify with that oppression, doing justice for the people is not rewarding terrorists, it is doing justice.[22]

Yet religious terrorism is more than a simple response to poverty and oppression; it is also a way of acting out a violent theological worldview that claims absolute divine sanction. This means that prevention must also involve conscious attempts to counter theologies of sacred violence and to forge theologies of peace-making and toleration in their place.[23] Such theological work must be undertaken within (and between) every religious tradition. Fresh thought must also be given to how religion can inform and shape public life in a non-coercive, life-affirming way. Western modernity has sought to banish religion from the public square and to ground civil society on secularist assumptions. Religious terrorism is a violent protest at this model of marginalization and especially at the global export of that model. 'A militant, unthinking secularity', Selengut explains, '… encourages a militant response on the part of traditionalists who see themselves cut off from the central power positions of state and society' (2003: 236). While terrorist ideologues strive for a totalitarian theocracy, what the majority of their co-religionists want is a religious civil society, one in which religion continues to provide a moral and spiritual beacon for collective life but which does not impose its will by force and which respects basic human rights (Etzioni 2003).[24] Nurturing such a form of civil society is a critical factor in combating religious militancy (even in secular pluralist societies there is need for greater recognition of religious contributions to public life and decision-making) (Juergensmeyer 2003: 242–49; Selengut 2003: 236, 135).[25]

It cannot be stressed too strongly that sociopolitical and theological reform are equally important as preventative measures. Religious violence draws its energy from resentment and its conviction from religion in a mutually reinforcing dialectic, so that terrorist ideology can only be disempowered when both its sociological and its sacred roots are severed.

Prevention and prosecution, therefore, belong inseparably together in the campaign to reduce terrorist violence. But a third kind of response is also needed, one that seeks to meet the therapeutic needs of individuals and communities whose lives have been blighted by deeds of terror and counter-terror. Every bomb that explodes leaves victims battered and bereaved in its wake, and every perpetrator of violence who callously extinguishes human life is left morally and spiritually diminished by their actions, and more able to do it again. The wall of hostility between embittered communities also grows higher as mutual recriminations go unanswered and stereotypes get more pronounced. These human realities need attention if strategies of prevention and containment are to be successful.

The therapeutic task: can restorative justice help?

As frequently happens when new terms are coined, 'restorative justice' has acquired both a generic meaning and a technical meaning. The term is used generically to embrace all co-operative approaches to conflict settlement that seek to achieve mutually beneficial outcomes. Emphasis here falls on the adjective 'restorative'; any conflict resolution strategy with a restorative intent qualifies. In the narrower use of the term, however, the noun 'justice' is more critical. Restorative justice refers specifically to situations of legal or moral wrongdoing – offences against justice – where processes are used to bring together affected parties for respectful dialogue and mutual agreement on how to repair the harm. There are merits in both the generic and technical uses of the term and they often shade into each other, but for the sake of clarity it is helpful to distinguish them. In what follows, I will employ restorative justice in the narrow sense to designate restorative responses to specific episodes of interpersonal wrongdoing, and use the term 'conflict transformation' or 'reconciliation' for peace-making initiatives that seek to bring about more comprehensive systemic changes in conflict settings.

There is a temptation for those who believe in the power of restorative justice to view it as a panacea for the world's ills, to seek new frontiers where its magic can be applied. But caution is advisable. Experience teaches that even in the most promising of circumstances, restorative methods do not always achieve restorative outcomes. Practice does not always validate theory. If this is true in relatively straightforward cases of interpersonal offending, how much more will it be true in situations of such enormous complexity, as religious terrorism? Indeed, at first sight, the characteristic features of religious terrorism seem so antithetical to restorative justice values, processes and principles that it is hard to imagine any convergence between the two whatsoever.

Take *values* to begin with. According to restorative justice philosophy, 'justice processes may be considered restorative only inasmuch as they give expression to key restorative values, such as respect, honesty, humility, mutual care, accountability, and trust' (Marshall *et al.* 2004: 268). But many of these values are alien to the psychology of religious killers. They do not respect their victims. On the contrary, they explicitly repudiate the equal dignity of their opponents, whom they view as ontologically and spiritually inferior beings. They do not accept any duty of care towards them, or the existence of any communal bonds that unite them. To admit to social kinship with their foes would be to repudiate their entire dualistic worldview.

Again, restorative justice values restoration over retribution. Religious killers, however, extol vengeance as a moral duty. 'Islam says an eye for an eye', says Abu Shanab, a Hamas leader. 'We believe in retaliation' (Stern 2003: 40). Yitzhak Ginzburg, a militant Jewish rabbi, describes revenge as a purifying experience, something that accords with the essence of one's being. 'It is like a law of nature', he says. 'He who takes revenge joins the "ecological currents of reality" … Revenge is the return of the individual and the nation to believe in themselves, in their power and in the fact that they have a place under the sun and are no longer stepped on by everybody' (Stern 2003: 91). A former Mossad official expresses the same sentiment even more memorably: 'An eye for an eye gives you nothing. You have to go after the head!' (Blumenfeld 2002: 219).

Yet again, restorative justice values the opponent's right to life, and rejects the death penalty. But dealing out death is the stock in trade of terrorism. A document captured in Afghanistan in 2002 included a written oath by an al Qaeda operative which states: 'I Abdul Maawia Siddiqi, son of Abdul

Rahmen Siddiqi, state in the presence of God that I will slaughter infidels all the days of my life' (Selengut 2003: 43). Clearly, then, a vast gulf separates the values of restorative justice and the values of religious terrorism.

A similar incongruity exists with respect to *process*. Restorative justice is a dialogical process where people come together to share their thoughts and feelings. Genuine dialogue can only happen when there is a willingness to shift ground and to compromise. But religious violence represents a radical rejection of dialogue and compromise. The tactic of suicide bombing in particular is proof that establishing dialogue is not the aim of religious terrorists. Yet without a preparedness to dialogue – without give and take, without a willingness to accept differences, without some degree of humility – restorative justice processes simply cannot work.

Similar problems exist over *practice*. The primary participants in restorative justice conferences occupy the roles of victim and offender, and the main goal is to identify the needs of the victim and hold the offender accountable for taking steps to meet them. If an offender denies responsibility for the harm inflicted, or refuses to see it as morally wrong, restorative justice conferences cannot proceed. But a distinctive attribute of religious killers is a refusal to see themselves as culpable offenders. They are not murderers; they are soldiers fighting in a just cause, defending the rights of their own victimized communities against the assaults of an inhuman enemy. As one former Irish paramilitary puts it: 'Within every terrorist is the conviction that he is a victim' (Juergensmeyer 2003: 170; see also McTernan 2003: 84). One of the Chechen fighters at Beslan reportedly told one of the hostages: 'Russian soldiers are killing our children in Chechnya, so we are here to kill yours' (Alibhai-Brown 2004: A19). It is difficult to see how roles could be assigned at a meeting between the perpetrators and recipients of terror when only 'victims' are available!

So initial indications are not encouraging. The attitudes and beliefs that induce people to take up terror are precisely the attitudes and beliefs that make restorative encounters difficult to achieve – such as self-righteousness, disavowal of guilt, refusal of dialogue, unwillingness to compromise, lack of respect for the dignity of the other. The victims of terror, as well, frequently exhibit a parallel set of attitudes and emotions. They view the perpetrators of terror as unnatural monsters bereft of all human feeling and value, incapable of remorse and deserving only of extermination. Political pronouncements constantly reinforce this judgement, stereotyping terrorists as irremediably evil and ruling out any kind of dialogue with them or their supporters as a form of appeasement.[26] Just prior to an American assault on Fallujah in late 2004, US Colonel Gary Brandl told his troops: 'The enemy has got a face. He's called Satan. He's in Fallujah and we're going to destroy him' (*Observer* 2004: A1).

For all these reasons, then, religious terrorism is an extraordinarily difficult environment for collaborative, dialogical mechanisms to operate in. Is the situation therefore hopeless? Is restorative justice dead in the water as a viable response to terrorism? Not necessarily. With due modesty, with stubborn faith in the capacity of the human spirit and with flexibility of practice, restorative justice *does* have something special to offer.

Modesty

This is needed because restorative justice cannot do it all by itself. It is not a cure-all. It is not some miraculous formula that will cause people long indoctrinated in hatred to fall into each other's arms like long-lost relatives. It can only ever be one small fallible tool among many needed to redress terrorism. Yet one of the great virtues of restorative justice is that it is a community-centred process. Most discussions of counter-terrorism focus almost exclusively on what governments, armies and political institutions must do. But non-governmental organizations and informal community groups also have a vital role to play. Terror groups themselves are kinds of community association gone bad, whose members are bound together by extremely strong relational bonds. The groups are so attractive to young men because they offer a sense of identity, power and self-respect to those who feel disempowered by their circumstances and disconnected from others. Restorative justice offers an alternative, non-violent form of community empowerment that can help promote reconciliation between mutually hostile communities.

Peter Shirlow of the University of Ulster has said that 'one of the main problems facing Northern Ireland is that everyone sees him or herself as a victim of the other side and is unable to recognize that self as a perpetrator of violence and intimidation' (McTernan 2003: 84). The challenge, he believes, is to help people on both sides to see that they are *both* victims *and* perpetrators in the current conflict. Restorative justice as a community-based mechanism is perfectly placed to assist this to happen. Typically in restorative justice meetings, the roles of victim and offender are discrete. One party has suffered unjustly at the hands of the other, and the duty of repair runs only one way. But sometimes the roles are not so neatly distinguished. Sometimes both parties have injured each other; both are victims and both are offenders. In these cases, it is helpful for both parties to have the chance to speak as victims, and for both to accept their role as offenders. This allows for the victimized status of each side to be validated and for the duty of repair to run both ways.

Such an approach has real potential in settings where rival communities are victims of mutual terror attacks. Even if individual perpetrators and their victims cannot or will not meet, the communities to which both belong, and which usually harbour bitter antagonism towards each other, can do so in their stead. If members of mutually hostile communities can meet to express the bitterness of victimization they have personally experienced, and to accept some measure of collective responsibility for deeds of violence done on their behalf, the groundwork for peace has been laid. And peaceful co-existence is *always* possible between human beings.

Faith in shared humanity

Among other things, religious terrorism is a sign that we live in a world where people's controlling belief systems differ radically from one another. Some source modern terrorism in a putative 'clash of civilizations' that has ensued in the trail of globalization and express pessimism about the capacity for peaceful co-existence, especially between fundamentalist Islam and the West.[27] Without denying there are civilizational factors involved (Selengut 2003: 141–81), a restorative justice response to terror rests on a fundamental faith in our common humanity. It makes the bold assumption that, whatever divides us, people are always capable of living together peacefully, that there is no difference that cannot be resolved with dialogue. It rejects the view widespread today that there are some people so evil that annihilation is the only option for dealing with them.

Ultimately this confidence in shared humanity is a matter of faith or belief (just as trust in the saving power of violence is also a matter of belief). But it is not blind faith. There *are* examples of terrorists changing. One Christian terrorist in America abandoned his plans to blow up an abortion clinic when he was unexpectedly overcome with an awareness of the humanity of his potential victims, one of whom reminded him of his grandmother. A Kashmiri militant gave up his violent path after becoming aware of how crippling hatred is. 'To hate is venom', he explains. 'When you hate, you poison yourself ... Hate begets hate. You cannot create freedom out of hatred' (Stern 2003: 137).

Even more telling is the example of Patrick Magee, the so-called 'Brighton bomber', who killed five people and injured 30 in a failed attempt 20 years ago to annihilate the British Cabinet staying at the Grand Hotel in Brighton. In sentencing Magee, the judge described him as 'a man of exceptional cruelty and inhumanity', and to this day Magee stands by his actions as a justifiable act of war. But, now out of prison, Magee has become a strong supporter of the peace process. What precipitated this change was a series of meetings with Jo Tuffnell, the daughter of one of his murder victims. The meetings began after Tuffnell was overcome by 'an incredible feeling' as she prayed in a church one day 'for the strength to understand those who had done this and not to stay a victim'. She arranged to meet Magee, who says of their first meeting:

'I had an overwhelming urge to talk to Jo alone. It felt like the presence of anyone else was intrusive and would stop me opening up and being as frank as I needed.' He added however, 'I wasn't prepared, and I felt totally inadequate with someone sitting there with all that pain, telling it to me, while at the same time trying to understand me. There was certainly guilt there, that I'd caused this woman's father's death. But that feeling only came to the forefront when we were coming out of the [IRA] struggle, because during the struggle there wasn't time and you couldn't have engaged in it if you'd had that mind.' (McKittrick 2004: B3).

Jo Tuffnell says of that meeting:

'Only Pat could understand how I felt – he was the only person who actually wanted to hear how I felt. When we first met, he said, "I want to hear your anger and feel your pain". No one else had ever said that to me.' She added: 'I'm no longer scared of my darkest feelings, because I know however negative and awful they are, I can transform them into a passion for change' (McKittrick 2004).

This remarkable story is not unique. Similar initiatives have been taken by other Republican and Loyalist ex-prisoners and dozens of victims groups have been formed, some of which have sought meetings with former terrorist perpetrators (McKittrick 2004).

Flexibility of practice

The moving story of Patrick Magee and Jo Tufnell is also significant from a practice perspective. The meetings between the two appear to have been unfacilitated, were spread over several years and entailed 'long and searching conversations dissecting their roles as victim and perpetrator'. Most standard restorative justice conferences, by comparison, are facilitated by a neutral party, take a couple of hours at most to complete and do not permit disputes about roles. In the Magee case, a preparedness to hear the victim's pain was evidently more important to the victim than the offender's full acceptance of culpability. Magee concedes that his unwillingness to call his actions wrong was hard for Tufnell to hear, and it has been 'an impediment' in their relationship. But that did not preclude them continuing to meet for dialogue. This underscores how pliable and open-ended practice needs to be to accommodate the exigencies of particular situations. No one model of practice is sacrosanct, as long as restorative values and principles remain operative.

Of course, given the complexities surrounding religious violence and the degree of trauma involved, it stands to reason that any restorative intervention needs to be skilfully managed and thoroughly prepared. Victims, in particular, would need careful preparation. They must be at an appropriate stage in their recovery process before venturing to meet those responsible for their suffering. As conflict specialist Vernon Redekop explains:

> It is difficult, if not impossible, to start a process of reconciliation when the pain of violence is visceral, recent and overwhelming. When people are traumatised through the loss of loved ones, through having observed many deaths, or having been terrified to the core of their beings, they are not ready to start a discourse or any process that involves their relationship with an enemy (2002: 290).

Professional counselling and other forms of therapy may be required before any restorative justice meeting occurs, and peer support throughout the process will be critical.

Perpetrators also need preparation. The minimal requirement is a willingness to listen and an agreement to speak truthfully about their own motivations and actions. Skilful management of their encounter is imperative. Because both sides will be hyper-sensitive to threatening signals from the other and will amplify the smallest hint of antagonism into a full-blown physiological 'fight or flight' reaction, extraordinary effort must be taken to provide a safe place and safe process. This could include, as in the Magee case, a readiness to meet many times over an extended period. Given that terrorists commonly view themselves as victims rather than victimizers, it would be important that some of these meetings focus the perpetrator's own prior experience of suffering and betrayal. This is not to excuse their later crimes. On the contrary, it is only when an offender's pain is acknowledged that his or her last refuge from responsibility is removed. If it is flatly denied, he or she will continue to feel justified in his or her actions.

In October 2004, an Australian journalist, John Martinkus, was kidnapped by Sunni militants in Iraq. He was interrogated throughout the night, while a large screen TV tuned into al-Jazeera Television played in the background. The mood of his interrogators darkened every time stories of fighting in Iraq appeared. Martinkus spent much of the night contemplating the possibility of execution in the morning. He had seen the videotaped beheadings of other hostages, which he describes as 'sickening'. He knew the 'old trick of humanising yourself to your captors', and showed some of them a photograph of his girl-friend which he carried in his wallet. One of his captors reciprocated, pulling out a picture of his three-year-old daughter in Fallujah. 'I held it and said "she looks beautiful". He replied, "she is dead now in an American air strike" and his face became hard. My effort had backfired' (Martinkus 2004: B14–15). Such is the kind of anguish hidden driving much terrorist brutality. It does not justify their brutality, but it cannot be ignored in any attempt to bring change.

One further lesson from the Magee story is that, while terrorists may initially lack the values and attitudes essential for involvement in restorative processes, the very act of meeting with their victims has the potential, over time, to evoke them. It is easy to vilify and dehumanize enemies in the abstract; it is much harder to do it to those whose individual identity one has now come face to face with. It is easy to rationalize one's violence at a distance; it is much harder to do so when one hears of its impact on actual human bodies and beings.[28] Perhaps the most powerful contribution restorative justice can make is in the rehumanization of the parties. Demons are expelled when human beings meet together in a state of common weakness to confront the truth about one another and about themselves.

Face-to-face encounters are, of course, the ideal way for this to happen. But given the extraordinary security concerns surrounding detained terrorists, such meetings may be difficult, sometimes impossible, to arrange. Here again flexibility of practice is important; other ways may exist to promote restorative outcomes. In her compelling book *Revenge: A Story of Hope,* Laura Blumenfeld (2002) tells of how she tracked down the individual responsible for the attempted assassination of her father David, a Jewish American tourist, in Jerusalem in 1986. Her father was the target of a random political shooting by a Palestinian terror group. He survived the attack and had no particular desire for retribution, but Laura was consumed with feelings of revenge, and developed an overwhelming desire to understand this most primal and universal of emotions. She set about to 'master revenge', to break it down and to study it (p. 17). She also developed an urge to meet the man responsible for the shooting: 'Confronting him was inevitable. Not with an act of violence – the revenge I wanted was of a different kind, one that responded to the heart of the crime … I wanted him to realize he was wrong' (p. 18). When she eventually located the assassin, a young man called Omar al Khatib, he was half way through serving a 25-year prison term for the crime. Posing as a journalist researching a book, Laura contacted the gunman's family, visiting them in their home frequently over the space of a year without ever disclosing her relationship to Omar's victim. Strong bonds of friendship developed between them, despite the fact that the family often expressed admiration for Omar's heroic and honourable deed. Using his brother to smuggle letters in and out of prison, Laura also began corresponding with Omar himself, again without ever letting on that she was his target's daughter. She probed him about how he felt about his actions, both at the time of the shooting and subsequently, what he would want to say to his victim if he ever had the opportunity to meet him and whether he regretted what he had done.

Through the course of their correspondence both parties were changed. Laura came to recognize how important it was for her that Omar acknowledged his sorrow for shooting an innocent man, and that he came to understand that 'this conflict is between human beings, and not disembodied Arabs and Jews. And we're people, not "military targets". We're people with families. And you can't just kill us' (p. 344). More profoundly, she came to understand that the revenge she craved was not for retaliation – an eye for an eye – but for *transformation*. 'Revenge does not have to be about destroying your enemy; it can mean transforming him, or yourself' (p. 348). Omar was also affected by the correspondence. He later wrote to his victim, David Blumenfeld, that through her letters and actions Laura had been 'the mirror that made me see your face as a human person to be admired and respected' (p. 280).

After a year of writing, Laura and Omar did eventually meet in person, not in a restorative justice conference but at a court hearing where Omar was applying for early parole on health grounds. Laura seized the opportunity to address the bench of judges, declaring for the first time that she was the daughter of the man who had been shot, a confession which stunned Omar and his family. Laura argued passionately, though unsuccessfully, for Omar's early release on the grounds that he was truly sorry for his crime and that he had promised never again to harm anyone in pursuit of his political beliefs. Laura's mother even leapt to her feet saying that the Blumenfeld family had forgiven Omar, and so now should the state of Israel!

Throughout the period of his written exchanges with Laura, Omar repeatedly insisted that his shooting of the innocent American tourist was 'not personal'; it was a justifiable act in the struggle for freedom for his people. It was clear that Omar, like most violent activists, saw the world in terms of collective rather than individual identities. But at one point in his correspondence, he indicated to Laura that he was coming to respect what he called the 'holiness' of other people's lives and the need for people to live in peace. 'People are so different when you get to know them from near', he once observed (p. 280). This, of course, is precisely what restorative justice is all about. It seeks to achieve this recognition by bringing hostile parties into face-to-face contact. But Omar's experience shows that, even where such direct encounters are not achievable, sustained personal contact by letter or through intermediaries can sometimes have the same effect, or at very least can play a powerful role in preparing the ground for direct interaction at some future point.

Conclusion

In his informative book *Violence in God's Name,* Oliver McTernan (2003: xviii) states that 'New initiatives promoting confidence building and understanding among peoples of different political cultures and faiths, and especially between Islam and the West, are urgently needed to lessen the risk of religiously motivated violence'. Restorative justice, with its special concern to confront experiences of victimization and to overturn dehumanizing stereotypes, is one such initiative. In the criminal justice, family and education fields, restorative justice has proved its capacity for bringing together injured parties to promote healing and accountability. Terrorism and religious violence represent a challenging new arena for the adaptation and application of its methods.

Again it needs to be emphasized that restorative justice meetings between the victims and perpetrators of terror cannot, on their own, redress all the effects of terrorism. Without ongoing work at reconciliation and structural transformation, restorative encounters, however powerful in themselves, are inadequate to bring lasting peace. But even if it is only one tool in the box, restorative justice still has a contribution to make. It can help those caught up in terrorist atrocities to address the inner realities bequeathed by the outer reality of violent acts – the profound emotional pain, the ongoing effects of traumatization and the deep-seated feelings of hatred, anger and revenge.[29] It may also help those who have inflicted terror to begin to rethink their own identities, to break free from the structures of violence that hitherto have dictated their worldview, and to learn to see reality differently, a world that is populated by the human children of God, not stalked by demons in disguise.

It is important not to shrink back from the challenge at this point in history. In a world racked with anxiety over security, in a world where we are daily commanded to 'be afraid, very afraid,' in a world where inflicting terror is commended as the only way to end terror, in a world of demonization and counter-demonization, restorative justice is a still, small voice of protest. As trivial as it may seem, terror is renounced not just in the refusal to endorse war, but in every act of human kindness and decency. Promoting peaceful modes of human engagement is the greatest antidote there is to religiously inspired violence, and restorative justice is all about peaceful forms of human engagement. 'Blessed are the peacemakers', one great religious founder said, 'for *they* shall be called the children of God.'

Selected further reading

Griffith, L. (2002) *The War on Terrorism and the Terror of God*. Grand Rapids, MI: Eerdmans. A fine study of terrorism from a Christian pacifist perspective.

Stern, J. (2003) *Terror in the Name of God: Why Religious Militants Kill*. New York, NY: HarperCollins. One of many studies on religious violence based on interviews with terrorist leaders around the world.

Juergensmeyer, M. (2003) *Terror in the Mind of God: The Global Rise of Religious Violence*. Berkeley, CA and Los Angeles, CA: University of California Press. An award-winning study of the anatomy of religious violence, and what psychological needs it satisfies in its advocates.

Jewett, R. and Lawrence, J.S. (2003) *Captain America and the Crusade against Evil: The Dilemma of Zealous Nationalism*. Grand Rapids, MI: Eerdmans. A truly fascinating study of America's proclivity to religiously sanctioned nationalist violence.

Marshall, C.D., Boyack, J. and Bowen, H. (2004) 'How does restorative justice ensure good practice? A values-based approach', in H. Zehr and B. Toews (eds) *Critical Issues in Restorative Justice*. Palisades, NY: Criminal Justice Press. Presents a values-based approach to defining standards of good practice.

Notes

1 See also the claims made at http://www.buzzflash.com/interviews/04/05/int04024.html. Bruce Bartlett, a past Republican presidential policy adviser, says of George Bush: 'this instinct he's always talking about is this sort of weird, messianic idea of what he thinks God has told him to do ... This is why George W. Bush is so clear-eyed about Al Qaeda and the Islamic fundamentalist enemy. He believes you have to kill them all. They can't be persuaded, that they're extremists driven by a dark vision. He understands them, because he's just like them. He truly believes he's on a mission from God. Absolute faith like that overwhelms a need for analysis' (cited by Ron Suskind (2004), who tracks the evolution of what he calls Bush's 'faith-based presidency') (see also John D. Goldhammer (2005).

2 This is Juergensmeyer's (2003: 126) term, which he borrows from linguistics.

3 On the phenomenology of holy war, see Selengut (2003). See also Bainton (1960).

4 The label 'Jihadi International Inc.' was coined by Eqbal Ahmad.

5 One terrorist operative told Stern: 'I am spiritually addicted to jihad' (2003: 200; cf. pp. 217, 221).

6 As John Paul Lederach (2001) observes: 'Military action to destroy terror ... will be like hitting a fully mature dandelion with a golf club. We will participate in making sure the myth of why we are evil is sustained and we will assure yet another generation of recruits.'

7 On the universal appeal of the myth of redemptive violence, see Wink (1998: esp. 42–62). Wink calls the myth 'the simplest, laziest, most exciting, uncomplicated, irrational, and primitive depiction of evil the world has ever known' (p.55), and deems it to be 'the dominant religion in our society today' (p.42). See also the telling analysis by Jewett and Lawrence (2003: 245–72 & *passim*).

8 In a speech given on 16 September, 2001, Bush said: 'This is a new kind of thing – a new kind of evil – and we understand. And the American people are beginning to understand. This crusade, this war on terrorism, is going to take a

while.' Bush used the term again in a speech given in Alaska mid-February 2002. See the insightful discussion by Suskind (2004).

9 Bush has frequently called Osama bin Laden 'the evil one', which to a conservative Christian constituency clearly identifies with Satan. See Achcar (2002).

10 In an insightful discussion, Jewett and Lawrence (2003: 250–61) suggest that the crusading ideal of redemptive violence, which has imparted a unique mystique to American wars, leads to a tendency to use unrestrained violence to obliterate the evil foe. If violence is universally redemptive, then why not use it universally against the enemy, including women and children?

11 For a helpful discussion of evil from a conflict resolution perspective, see Cloke (2004).

12 Richard Perle, a Bush adviser, has argued that we must 'decontextualize terror', which means refusing to ask about the context in which it emerges. 'Any attempt to discuss the roots of terrorism is an attempt to justify it ... It simply needs to be fought and destroyed.' Johann Hari rightly dismisses this as absurd, something that 'invites us all to participate in a strange, wilful ignorance of cause and effect. How can this be a serious response to our problems?' Hari (2004) argues that 'Islamo-fascism' or 'jihadism' is a better term for the current problem than 'terrorism'.

13 An analogy can be drawn between the way terrorists co-opt religion to justify violence and the way that state does. Wink observes that, in the myth of redemptive violence, the welfare of the nation becomes the supreme good. People are expendable; the state is not: 'Not only does this myth establish a patriotic religion at the heart of the state, it gives divine sanction to that nation's imperialism. The myth of redemptive violence thus serves as the spirituality of militarism. By divine right the state has the power to demand that its citizens sacrifice their lives to maintain the privileges enjoyed by the few. By divine decree it utilizes violence to cleanse the world of enemies of the state. Wealth and prosperity are the right of those who rule in such a state. And the name of God – any god, the Christian God included – can be invoked as having specially blessed and favoured the supremacy of the chosen nation and its ruling caste' (Wink 1998: 56–7).

14 In his perceptive account of George Bush's evangelical faith, Jo Klein (2003: 14) suggests that the real problem with it is not dogmatism but its easy certitude. His faith 'does not discomfort him enough; it does not impel him to have second thoughts, to explore other intellectual possibilities or question the consequences of his actions'. Accordingly, his faith 'offers no speed bumps on the road to Baghdad; it does not give him pause or force him to reflect. It is a source of comfort and strength but not of wisdom.' A similar conclusion is reached by Suskind (2004), who describes Bush as 'one of history's great confidence men ... in the sense that he's a believer in the power of confidence'. On the influence of the Christian right on US unilateralism, see Oldfield (2004: 1–6). For an evangelical critique of Bush's theology of war, see Anonymous (2004).

15 In point of fact, the American tendency to turn wars into holy crusades has been present since the beginning of the nation, while crusading idealism has been dominant in American civil religion over the past 60 years, as Jewett and Lawrence (2003) document. In an interview, Tony Blair defended the pre-emptive strike on Iraq, saying: 'What changed for me is, post September 11, you no longer wait for the thing to happen. You go out actively and try to stop it. That's the thing that has changed now' (Rawnsley and Hinsliff 2004: B3.)

16 The contagiousness of the war on terrorism is also worth noting. Stassen (2004) points out that 'as the United States declared its military war against terrorism, Indonesia canceled peace talks with the rebels in Aceh and instead made war against them; Israel increased its military attacks against Palestinian leaders; and Russia pursued its destructive war against Chechnya free of U.S. government criticism'.

17 See also Stern (2003: 238).

18 Gerald Schlabach (2004) rightly observes that 'The just war theory has gained much of its credibility by imagining war to be like police action without facing up to how different the dynamics of warfare can be from policing. But if war is justified through an appeal to the virtually irrefutable need for policing, it consistently becomes something quite different from policing, and just war reasoning itself all too often devolves into propaganda. It becomes permissive rather than stringent – and it sometimes becomes permissive precisely through the reassuring guise of having been stringent.'

19 I am indebted to Lederach (2001) for this analogy.

20 See, for example, Achcar (2002). Achcar notes, for example, that the 'sanctions of mass destruction' used against Iraq caused more deaths than have all the casualties from use of weapons of mass destruction combined (est. at 400,000). The USA has bombed over two dozen countries since the end of the Second World War, and has been involved in direct or indirect support for revolts, coups and invasions in over 70 different nations (see Griffith 2002: 90–1).

21 Just peace-making is a new third paradigm for considering the ethics of war and peace, alongside pacifism and just war theory. It addresses not the 'permission' question (Is it morally permissible to make war in this situation?) but the 'prevention' question (What strategies should be used to prevent war?). It identifies 10 principles that are normative for adherents of both just war and pacifist streams. It is not a narrowly Christian paradigm, although one of its architects, Glen Stassen (2003: 135–55), shows how it coheres with the teaching of Jesus in the Sermon on the Mount. For a large-scale treatment of Jesus' teaching from this perspective, see Stassen and Gushee (2003). More fully on just peace-making, see Stassen (1992).

22 Another advocate of this kind of response to terrorism is Leroy Long (2004: 55–59, 77-81).

23 One powerful example of this process working is the case of Hamoud al-Hitar and four other Islamic scholars in Yemen who challenged five Al Qaeda members in prison to a theological contest over whether terrorist violence could be justified by the Koran. The agreement was that, if the prisoners could convince the scholars of their case, they would join their campaign. Conversely if the scholars won the debate, the prisoners would agree to renounce violence. The results of this unconventional counter-terrorism methodology have been spectacular, with a dramatic decline in terror attacks in the country over recent years. See further Brandon (2005).

24 See also the important piece by Michael Hirsch (2004). Hirsch cites a poll in Iraq in May 2004 that showed that 58 per cent of Iraqis want their religious communities to have a 'great deal of influence' in selecting members of a new election commission. Hirsch contests the current Washington orthodoxy that secular-style democracy in the Arab world is the answer to terrorism, a view which he traces to the work of historian Bernard Lewis (who first coined the phrase 'clash of civilizations'). Hirsch points out that the US invasion of Iraq effectively toppled a secular state and heightened the appeal and influence of Islamic radicalism. Progress in the Arab world will come, Hirsch insists, not by

secularizing it from above but by rediscovering a more tolerant form of Islam, which actually predates modern radicalism. This may be a long, long time in coming, and the West may need to allow Arab states to experience the failures of fundamentalism first.

25 For a very different solution that depends on global acceptance of a non-realist God and an earth-centred spirituality, see Lloyd Geering (1999: esp. 109–21, 135–49).

26 Dr Garret Fitzgerald, former Irish Prime Minister, reflecting on the experience of dealing with the IRA, insists that negotiations with terrorists should only occur when they want a final settlement of the conflict. But they should not be treated in any way that further alienates people who share their grievances. British negotiation with the IRA in 1970s made matters worse because it made the IRA believe that by murdering more people they would get more concessions. A better approach is to negotiate with moderates, and thus try to separate extremists from their wider base of support. See McCurdy (2004: B5).

27 For a discussion and critique of Huntington's well-known thesis, see McTernan (2003: 1–10). See also the valuable observations by Michael Hirsch (2004).

28 This is one of the lessons of the various truth and reconciliation commissions that have been formed. See the excellent analysis by Spencer Zifcak (2003). See also Marshall (2001: 280–4), Wilson (2001), Kerber (2003) and Steinmann (2004).

29 On the trauma associated with suffering terror attacks, see Office for Victims of Crime (2001); also Nath (2004).

References

Achcar, G. (2002) 'The clash of barbarisms: September 11 and the making of the new world disorder', *Monthly Review,* 22 November (available online at http://www.monthlyreview.org/0902achcar.htm).

Alibhai-Brown, Y. (2004) 'Sons of Islam bring shame on religion', *Independent,* reprinted in *New Zealand Herald,* 8 September: A19.

Anonymous (2004) *Evangelicals Slam Bush for his 'Theology of War'.* Ekklesia (available online at http://www.ekklesia.co.uk/content/news_syndication/article_041012bsh.shtml.

Austin, G., Kranock T. and Oommen, T. (2004) *God and War: An Audit and Exploration.* Department of Peace Studies, University of Bradford.

Bainton, R.H. (1960) *Christian Attitudes toward War and Peace: A Historical Survey and Critical Re-evaluation.* Nashville, TN: Abingdon.

Berger, P. (ed.) (1999) *The Desecularisation of the World.* Grand Rapids, MI: Eerdmans.

Blumenfeld, L. (2002) *Revenge: A Story of Hope.* New York, NY: Washington Square Press.

Boulton, D. (2004) 'Who needs religion?', *New Internationalist,* August: 14–16.

Brandon, J. (2005) 'Koranic duels ease terror', *Christian Science Monitor,* 4 February (available online at http://www.csmonitor.com/2005/0204/p01s04-wome.html).

Burke, J. (2004) 'Zarqawi: man behind the mask', *New Zealand Herald,* 17 September: B3.

Cloke, K. (2004) *Mediating Evil, War, and Terrorism: The Politics of Conflict.* Mediate.com (available online at www.mediate.com/articles/cloke4.cfm).

Cuzzo, M.S.W. (2001) *The Code of the Peaceful Warrior: A Restorative Justice Response to Recent Events.* Restorative Justice Online (available online at http://www.restorativejustice.org/rj3/Feature/Cuzzo%20statement.html).

Eakin, H. (2004) 'When U.S. aided insurgents, did it breed future terrorists?', *New York Times* (available online at http://www.nytimes.com/2004/04/10/arts/10MAMD.html?ex=1082612982&ei=1&en=10f192e8a9d399ac).

Etzioni, A. (2003) 'US to support a religious civil society', *The Responsive Community*, 13: 9–11.

Geering, L. (1999) *The World to Come: From Christian Past to Global Future*. Wellington: Bridget Williams Books.

Goldhammer, J.D. (2005) *Dr. Bush and Mr. Hyde: The Fundamentalist Shadow of George W. Bush*. Scoop Independent News (available online at http://www.scoop.co.nz/stories/HL0509/S00292.htm).

Griffith, L. (2002) *The War on Terrorism and the Terror of God*. Grand Rapids, MI: Eerdmans.

Hari, J. (2004) 'Jihadism: the real terror of our age', *Independent*, reprinted *New Zealand Herald*, 27 September: A17.

Hirsch, M. (2004) 'Misreading Islam', *Washington Monthly*, 12 November: 1–9.

Jewett, R. and Lawrence, J.S. (2003) *Captain America and the Crusade against Evil: The Dilemma of Zealous Nationalism*. Grand Rapids, MI: Eerdmans.

Juergensmeyer, M. (2003) *Terror in the Mind of God: The Global Rise of Religious Violence*. Berkeley, CA and Los Angeles, CA: University of California Press.

Kerber, G. (2003) 'Overcoming violence and pursuing justice: an introduction to restorative justice procedures', *Ecumenical Review*, 55 151–7.

Klein, J. (2003) 'The blinding glare of his certainty', *Time*, 24 February: 14.

Lederach, J.P. (2001) *The Challenge of Terror: A Traveling Essay*. Mediate.com (available online at www.mediate.com/articles/terror911.cfm).

Long, E.L. (2004) *Facing Terrorism: Responding as Christians*. Louisville, KY and London, Westminster/John Knox.

Marshall, C.D. (2001) *Beyond Retribution: A New Testament Vision for Justice, Crime, and Punishment*. Grand Rapids, MI: Eerdmans.

Marshall, C.D. (2003) '"But deliver us from evil": George Bush and the rhetoric of evil', *Urban Seed*, 5: 6–7.

Marshall, C.D., Boyack, J. and Bowen, H. (2004) 'How does restorative justice ensure good practice? A values-based approach', in H. Zehr and B. Toews (eds) *Critical Issues in Restorative Justice*. Monsey, NY: Criminal Justice Press.

Martinkus, J. (2004) 'Hostage in death's shadow', *New Zealand Herald*, 30 October: A1, B14–15.

Masters, C. (2004) 'Terror on our minds', *New Zealand Herald*, 11–12 September: B3–B4.

McCurdy, D. (2004) 'Lessons from violence', *New Zealand Herald*, 11–12 September, B5.

McKittrick, D. (2004) '"Brighton Bomber" revisits his paramilitary past with some sorrow', *Independent*, reprinted in *New Zealand Herald*, 7 October: B3.

McTernan, O. (2003) *Violence in God's Name: Religion in an Age of Conflict*. London and Maryknoll, NY: Darton Longman & Todd/Orbis Books.

Nath, P.S. (2004) 'Consider the lilies: teaching the value of vulnerability.' Paper presented to the Seeking the Welfare of the City: Public Peace, Justice and Order conference, Akron, PA, 1–4 August (available online at http://www.mcc.org/peacetheology/Nath.pdf).

New, D.S. (2002) *Holy War: The Rise of Militant Christian, Jewish and Islamic Fundamentalism*. Jefferson, N.C. and London: McFarland.

Office for Victims of Crime (2001) *Handbook for Coping after Terrorism: A Guide for Healing and Recovery*. Washington DC: US Department of Justice, Office of Justice Programs.

Oldfield, D. (2004) 'The evangelical roots of American unilateralism: the Christian right's influence and how to counter it', *Foreign Policy in Focus*, March: 1–6.

Rawnsley, A. and Hinsliff, G. (2004) 'Blair battling with shadow of war', *Observer*, reprinted in *New Zealand Herald*, 28 September: B3.

Redekop, V.N. (2002) *From Violence to Blessing: How an Understanding of Deep-rooted Conflict can Open Paths to Reconciliation*. Ottawa: Novalis.

Schlabach, G. (2004) 'Just policing and the Christian call to nonviolence.' Paper presented to the Seeking the Welfare of the City: Public Peace, Justice and Order conference, Akron, PA, 1–4 August (available online at http://www.mcc.org/peacetheology/Just_Policing_Schlabach.pdf).

Selengut, C. (2003) *Sacred Fury: Understanding Religious Violence*. Walnut Creek, CA: Alta Mira Press, Rowman & Littlefield.

Stassen, G.H. (1992) *Just Peacemaking: Transforming Initiatives for Justice and Peace*. Louisville, KY: Westminster/John Knox.

Stassen, G. (2003) 'Jesus and just peacemaking theory', in K.R. Chase and A. Jacobs (eds) *Must Christianity Be Violent? Reflections on History, Practice and Theology*. Grand Rapids, MI: Brazos Press.

Stassen, G.H. (2004) Fuller theological seminary (available online at http://www.fullerseminary.net/sot/faculty/stassen/Just_Peacemaking/july272004uploadfiles/04%20SCE%20JPTaddress.htm).

Stassen, G.H. and Gushee, D.P. (2003) *Kingdom Ethics: Following Jesus in Contemporary Context*. Downers Grove, IL: IVP.

Steinmann, R. (2004) 'Spiritual elements in the political processes of South Africa's Truth and Reconciliation Commission'. Paper presented to the Seeking the Welfare of the City: Public Peace, Justice and Order conference, Akron, PA, 1–4 August (available online at http://www.mcc.org/peacetheology/rsteinmann.pdf).

Stern, J. (2003) *Terror in the Name of God: Why Religious Militants Kill*. New York, NY: HarperCollins.

Suskind, R. (2004) 'Without a doubt', *New York Times*, 17 October (available online at http://www.truthout.org/docs_04/printer_101704A.shtml).

Utley, J.B. (2004) *Thirty-Six Ways the U.S. is Losing the War on Terror*. Antiwar.com (available online at http://www.antiwar.com/utley/?articleid=3234).

Ward, K. (2004) 'A churchless future?', *Stimulus*, 12: 2–12.

Wilson, R.A. (2001) *The Politics of Truth and Reconciliation in South Africa: Legitimizing the Post-apartheid State*. Cambridge: Cambridge University Press.

Wink, W. (1998) *The Powers That Be: Theology for a New Millennium*. New York, NY: Doubleday.

Zifcak, S. (2003) 'Restorative justice in East Timor: a case study of the nation's truth and reconciliation commission.' Unpublished paper, Australian National University.

Part 5

Evaluation and Restorative Justice

Gerry Johnstone and Daniel W. Van Ness

The first question that occurs to many people on hearing about restorative justice is 'does it work?'. In order to answer this question, restorative justice schemes have been subjected to extensive 'scientific evaluation'. Evaluating restorative justice is, however, anything but a straightforward task. Evaluators are confronted by numerous highly complex conceptual, methodological, practical, ethical and interpretive problems. The two chapters in this part discuss these problems, assess how successful existing approaches to evaluation are in overcoming them, set out ideas for more appropriate approaches to evaluation and look at what we have learnt from existing evaluations – especially about the impact of restorative justice on the future conduct of offenders.

In Chapter 21, Gordon Bazemore and Lori Elis describe the important advances made in restorative justice research in recent years, which now demonstrates the positive impact restorative interventions tend to have upon outcomes such as reoffending, victim satisfaction and other indicators. Less is known, though, about why and how restorative interventions achieve these outcomes. That requires, among other things, a more precise identification of what is distinctively 'restorative' within a particular scheme, the strength and integrity of a 'restorative' scheme, and the development of measures which test the effectiveness of those specifically restorative elements. In the process of developing and explaining such an approach – which they call a principle-based approach to evaluation of restorative interventions – Bazemore and Elis provide a highly sophisticated guide to the issues confronting those who wish to conduct or use research into the effectiveness of restorative justice.

In Chapter 22, Hennessey Hayes looks in close detail at what the research tells us about restorative justice and reoffending. He starts by asking why the question of the impact of restorative justice on reoffending continues to be asked, despite efforts to downplay assertions of some early enthusiasts – who tended to make some extravagant claims about the power of restorative justice to prevent recidivism – and to draw attention to other important advantages of restorative responses to crime. He then goes on to look at how the reoffending question has been posed and answered, looking at the questions of definition and measurement encountered in research, and at the strategies used to produce reliable data. On the basis of a thorough survey of existing research, Hayes cautiously maintains that restorative justice does have significant crime reduction potential – that on balance restorative justice 'works' in reducing reoffending. His careful explanation of how this conclusion is reached will enable others to make their own judgements and, crucially, to embark on further research (which need not be large scale; small case studies have a vital role to play) to address the many limitations and gaps in existing knowledge. Just as importantly, Hayes urges researchers not to confine themselves to the reoffending question, although its importance should not be underestimated either.

Chapter 21

Evaluation of restorative justice

Gordon Bazemore and Lori Elis

Introduction

Little more than a decade ago when asked about the effectiveness of restorative justice, supportive researchers would have to say something like, 'this looks promising or makes sense theoretically'. Today, many studies show the positive impact of restorative practices at multiple levels, with case types ranging from first-time offenders and misdemeanants to more serious chronic and violent offenders (for summaries see, Bonta *et al.* 2002; Braithwaite 2002; Sherman 2003; Hayes, Chapter 22, this volume).

This growing but still relatively recent body of research is not as compelling as some traditions in the programme evaluation literature, including the three to four decades of impact studies that make up the 'effective correctional treatment' or 'what works' research (Lipsey 1992; Andrews and Bonta 1994). However, these experimental and quasi-experimental studies of conferencing provide a basis for ruling out the hypothesis that restorative justice processes have negative impacts on juvenile justice outcomes. Findings of neutral, but not harmful, impacts on recidivism and other offender outcomes are insufficient to diminish support among advocates who provide normative justification for the benefits of restorative justice, such as crime victim satisfaction and input. Moreover, unlike treatment studies that find mixed impacts on recidivism, most studies of restorative programmes, including recent meta-analyses (Bonta *et al.* 2000; Nugent *et al.* 2003), indicate some positive impact (Braithwaite 1999; Schiff 1999; Umbreit 1999; Bazemore *et al.* 2000), and some suggest that restorative programmes may have equal or stronger impacts than many treatment programmes (Umbreit 1999; Sherman 2000). Increasingly, researchers have begun to document positive impacts on crime victims (Strang 2003), and there is a growing commitment to assess community and skill building aspects of restorative justice intervention (Bazemore and Schiff, 2004).

While it would seem that there is little to complain about, there is a great deal of confusion about the meaning and significance of positive research findings. Specifically, research findings that indicate better outcomes for restorative programmes relative to court and similar alternatives do not provide much insight into *why* these programmes produce this impact. On the one hand, there are doubts about whether it is the 'restorative' aspects of the encounter, or some other feature of the process such as procedural justice (Tyler 1999), that explain positive findings. On the other hand, in the relatively few cases in which apparently restorative interventions have *failed* to produce positive impacts – e.g. the drunk-driving component of the Re-Integrative Shaming (RISE) experiments in Australia (Sherman *et al.* 2000; Braithwaite 2001) – there is some uncertainty about whether a restorative justice process, or some other set of intervention characteristics, accounted for this failure. In other words, the field as a whole seems to be less than certain about the 'independent variable' that has most likely produced either negative or positive results.

While there has been some discussion among researchers about theories that might explain success in restorative encounters (Bazemore 1998; Braithwaite 2002; Hayes and Daly 2003; Morris and Maxwell 2003; Bazemore and Schiff 2004), this should not be viewed simply as an issue for academic debate. To advance policy and practice, it is important to identify dimensions of 'restorativeness' and methods of using these dimensions effectively to gauge the strength and integrity of intervention in restorative programmes. These dimensions should help to specify what *aspects* of practice are most responsible for the positive outcomes observed in research. In addition, because restorative programmes have become far too reliant upon what Brooks (2000) calls 'service delivery criteria' (e.g., number of agreements completed, amount of restitution collected) as indicators of intermediate success, it is difficult to determine how these processes are linked to short-term and intermediate outcomes that lead to longer term healing and reintegrative outcomes. Finally, at the most 'hands on' practice level, restorative practitioners seem committed to procedural guidelines that they believe are essential to programme success (e.g. having the victim or offender speak first in the process, providing or not providing face-to-face pre-conference preparation, using or not using a script) and that have yet to be subjected to empirical test.

The purpose of this chapter is to propose principle-based standards for determining the strength and integrity of practice that purports to be restorative. While our hope is to develop standards that have broad application to a wide range of restorative practices, policies and even movements, we focus primarily on restorative group conferencing programmes – i.e. non-adversarial decision-making processes that generally fit one of four generic types (Bazemore and Umbreit 2001; Bazemore and Schiff 2004): victim–offender dialogue/mediation, family group conferencing, neighbourhood boards and peace-making circles. We use examples based on qualitative observation as part of a national case study of restorative group conferencing in the USA (Schiff and Bazemore 2002) to illustrate relative adherence to core restorative principles in practitioner decisions about how to structure and facilitate these encounters.

This study was based on a general proposition, further confirmed through this qualitative research, that restorative practitioners often conceptualize goals and intervention outcomes for conference encounters and that these goals vary based on 'grounded theories' of practice. These theories are in turn linked to core principles and help to connect these intermediate outcomes with longer-term outcomes. First, several conceptualizations have played an important role in defining restorative justice and gauging the strength and integrity of practice.

Current standards for restorativeness

Judgements about what constitutes the strength and integrity of a restorative response are often highly subjective. For some practitioners and advocates, 'restorative' is a term that seems best understood in contrast to what is viewed as its opposite – being punitive, authoritarian or simply mean-spirited. This kind of subjectivity has been partly responsible for judgements that proponents lack rigour in distinguishing restorative justice from other models (von Hirsch *et al.* 2003), while also failing to recognize important parallels between restorative presumptions and those of other models (Bazemore 2001; Toews-Shenk and Zehr 2001).

Beyond this kind of biased assessment, there are several defensible standards for gauging the extent to which a process is restorative. While some who once held these positions may no longer do so, each approach has some apparent value, especially when viewed in historical context, and each continues to enjoy some currency in discussions of the integrity of practice and measurement.

Process standards

Process standards begin with a definition of restorative justice as essentially *that which occurs in a restorative encounter*, usually understood to be a face-to-face meeting between victim, offender and other stakeholders in a crime (Marshall 1996). For Marshall (1996: 37), restorative justice is a 'process whereby the parties with a stake in a particular offense come together to resolve collectively how to deal with the aftermath of the offense and its implications for the future'.

Such definitions have the advantage of positioning restorative justice as a *process* whose integrity is to be judged by participants, not some third party. Yet, while providing greater specificity and clarity than the 'good *v.* evil' distinctions noted earlier, process-only definitions do not provide standards for gauging the relative strength and quality of interventions. Indeed, when the process *is the goal*, they become tautological. For example, while the assertion that 'restorative justice is any outcome reached by participants in a restorative process' gives appropriate emphasis to the value of the restorative encounter as a core centre of action in restorative justice, it does not specify any means of distinguishing a restorative process from one that seeks or leads to outcomes such as punishment, offender treatment, incapacitation or deterrence. Nor does such a definition provide a basis for assessing how the strength and integrity of a restorative process might vary along several continua.

Stakeholder involvement standards

Moving beyond this either/or process-focused distinction, Umbreit (1998) and his colleagues have given priority to a key stakeholder's participation by developing indices for gauging the relative intensity of victim involvement. They do so by ranking victim participation and input into the process on a continuum from indirect or very limited (e.g. in the case of written input into the case) to more intensive (e.g. through surrogate input or a victim impact panel) to face-to-face encounters in an open dialogue.

Given the central role of the victim in restorative justice, this standard should be considered vital for establishing a baseline indicator of restorativeness as a function of victim participation. Others have devoted equal attention to the role played by the offender – especially his or her willingness to acknowledge responsibility and ultimately demonstrate remorse – or the role of family members and intimates believed to have primary impact on the offender (Braithwaite and Mugford 1994; McDonald *et al.* 1995). An improved stakeholder involvement approach, offered by McCold and Wachtel (2003), defines interventions as more or less restorative based on their intent and presumed capacity to engage *all three stakeholders* – victim, offender and community – in restorative justice. This focus is promising in that it defines restorative justice with reference to the extent of participation of each primary stakeholder in a face-to-face decision-making process and gives preference to the core dimension of involvement in the process.

Programmatic standards

The application of this three stakeholder model seems limited by the use of these dimensions to rate programme models and develop a hierarchy of programmes ranked as 1) 'fully restorative' (potential to engage all three stakeholders); 2) 'mostly restorative'; 3) 'partly restorative', and 4) by default, 'not restorative' (see Figure 21.1) (McCold and Wachtel 2003). This ranking seems to have become a programmatic continuum, with three points on a scale of restorativeness depending on the programmatic approach adopted. That is, some programmes (e.g. those in the inner circle of Figure 21.1) rank as a '1' on this scale because they are always presumed to include victims, offenders and communities as participants. Therefore, the model does not provide a way to assess the strength and integrity of individual conferences based upon the actual extent and nature of each stakeholder's participation in a given case, regardless of the model adopted.[1]

Another limitation of this approach is that it does not allow for the possibility that informal encounters *outside the context of formal programmes* might fully engage all three stakeholders without following any particular practice model. For that matter, maximum engagement might be achieved by mixing multiple models: reparative boards using a circle format or community service that give victims and community members input in a

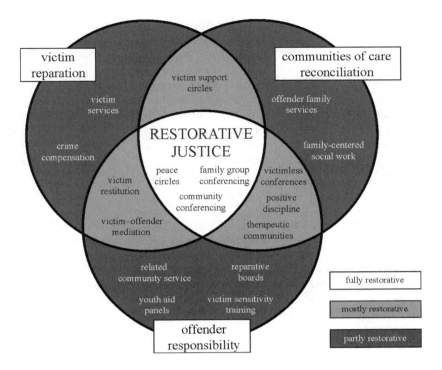

Figure 21.1 McCold and Wachtel's restorative practices typology
Source: McCold and Wachtel (2003)

conference format come to mind. While there is value in distinguishing *between* programmes by systematic measurement of their capacity over time to engage stakeholders, this approach does not seem to emphasize the importance of ongoing comparison of the presence and strength of a restorative process intervention *within* a given programme model or a specific implementation of a restorative process (see Hayes and Daly 2003). It is indeed possible that even the best programmes and programme models may fail in some cases effectively to engage stakeholders (or a key stakeholder), and that some apparently weakly structured programmes may do a very good job in engaging stakeholders in some cases.[2]

Goal-focused standards and beyond

As important as victim, offender and community involvement are to the integrity of a restorative process, the focus on stakeholder participation alone is a one-dimensional approach that seems to be out of touch with most practice standards. Indeed, however implicit, all restorative encounters pursue common healing goals and multiple intermediate objectives. Thus, despite the importance of gauging the extent of stakeholder involvement for its own sake, most group conferencing practitioners, participants, professionals and community members would like to know the extent to which a 'restorative process' achieves or at least pursues a restorative outcome (e.g. see McCold and Wachtel 2003, wherein programme models are compared empirically on their relative ability to accomplish certain outcomes). Ultimately, some goal-focused approach would appear to be essential in distinguishing between encounters that may use a stakeholder-driven process to pursue objectives other than restorative outcomes (e.g. retribution, offender treatment).

Umbreit (2001) and others (see Seymour and Bazemore 1998; Lehman *et al*. 2003), for example, and have proposed *goal-focused* standards that emphasize the degree to which victim needs are met, and have suggested measures of the extent to which interventions address multiple victim needs. Putting needs and involvement together, and assessing the strength of victim and offender input, as is done in a number of satisfaction surveys used at the conclusion of conferences, may be part of the answer. Stakeholder satisfaction alone, however, may be accomplished by features of the process that have more to do with procedural justice or other factors than with purely restorative factors (see Van Ness and Schiff 2001).

Another basis for a goal-focused approach is illustrated in Bazemore and Walgrave's (1999: 48) provisional definition of restorative justice as 'every action that is primarily oriented toward doing justice by repairing the harm that has been caused by a crime'. This general definition has the advantage of not limiting the restorative justice framework to one form of intervention and, indeed, views restorative group conferencing as part of a larger category of practices and actions that seek to repair the harm caused by crime in multiple circumstances (Van Ness and Strong 1997; Bazemore and Walgrave 1999). Yet, while this definition may allow us to assess the strength of intervention as reparative *intent* or the effort to 'make things right' with victims and the community, it may not allow us to assess the integrity of a restorative *process*. We are thereby left with measures of the amount of harm repaired, and may minimize the linkage between the process used to design a reparation agreement and those intervening processes that directly affect the intermediate impact of the restorative encounter. The focus on reparation as the ultimate outcome (or perhaps the intermediate link between a restorative encounter and reduction in reoffending or long-term victim healing) has allowed some tentatively to conclude that a restorative obligation arrived at through an adversarial process is 'more restorative' than a punitive sanction or other outcome, while also maintaining that a restorative process is much *more likely to achieve* a restorative outcome (Bazemore and Walgrave 1999).[3]

Given the choice between process, stakeholder participation, stakeholder needs and outcome-focused approaches to evaluation, Dignan and Marsh's (2001) definition seems to contain the fundamental components that link a core understanding of a restorative process with outcomes that may ultimately lead to a measurement solution. For them, restorative justice is, first, not restricted to a particular approach or programme, but is applicable to *any intervention or process* with certain characteristics. The degree of restorativeness in a given encounter could thus be ranked along a continuum according to the degree to which there is:

- an emphasis on the offender's personal accountability by key participants;
- an inclusive decision-making process that encourages participation by key stakeholders; and
- (pursuit of) the *goal* of putting right the harm that is caused by an offence (emphasis added).

These criteria – in their inclusion of process, stakeholders, personal accountability *and* desired outcome – elaborate on the Bazemore and Walgrave (1999) definition in a way that allows us to move to a more sophisticated measurement approach. Such an approach could be used to determine the strength and integrity of a restorative process by offering a multidimensional alternative to singularly focused standards that could be generalized to multiple contexts. To do so, we need to elaborate on these dimensions to develop indices to gauge restorativeness. In the remainder of this chapter, we identify multiple dimensions that can be deduced from core principles of restorative justice. While consistent with Dignan and Marsh's definition, this principle-based approach to multi-dimensional measurement allows for a clear normative distinction between 'restorative' and other ways of responding to crime and harm and provides the basis for indices that can be used to make internal empirical distinctions between practice priorities, both in strength and integrity.

Normative theory, restorative justice and 'yardsticks'

Principles are generic commitments that reflect core values and ideal standards that are unlikely to be fully achieved. Because no practice or process is inherently restorative, principles provide general guidelines that differentiate restorative justice from other perspectives and prevent co-optation of the model, while allowing for continuous evolution. Unlike programmatic, process, stakeholder and outcome standards, principles appear to help practitioners keep practice consistent with restorative values and outcome standards and, perhaps most importantly, *adapt* restorative justice to different structural and cultural contexts. For researchers, principles suggest *process and impact measures for evaluation* and may ultimately help link practice to theories of intervention that can be tested in the field.

We suggest that principles are best derived from the most general normative theory that reflects values which distinguish restorative practice from other approaches to doing justice. Braithwaite's 'republican theory,' for example, defines justice as dominion, which is essentially the relative absence of domination (Braithwaite and Pettit 1990; Braithwaite 2002). Consistent with this global theory of societies, but more specific to the process of 'doing justice' in response to crime and harm, Van Ness and Strong (1997) provide a direct link to the response to crime and harm in their articulation of three broad principles, which we designate below as the principles of *repair, stakeholder participation* and *community/government role transformation*.

Restorative practices are therefore guided by a priority to repair the harm caused by crime, involve stakeholders in a decision-making process to determine how to repair this harm and transform the relationship between communities and justice systems while empowering the former in response to crime (Bazemore and Walgrave 1999; Van Ness and Strong 2001). Adherence to these principles provides the first general standard for differentiating restorative justice practices from other forms of intervention and allows for determining the relative strength of a restorative justice intervention.

Restorative principles, goals, and objectives

How do principles guide research? Each of the three core principles has outcome and process dimensions that should drive evaluation aimed at understanding whether or not, and *why*, restorative decision-making practices work. Although restorative group conferencing is fundamentally about process, we suggest that, like all restorative practices, these encounters have both process and outcome dimensions.

1 *The principle of repair*: justice requires that we work to heal victims, offenders and communities that have been injured by crime.

The primary goal for any restorative intervention is to repair, to the greatest extent possible, the harm caused to victims, offenders and communities who have been injured by crime. This goal is achieved by focusing attention on the dialogue process in a restorative encounter *and* on the extent to which the offender (often with the help of others) takes action to make things right (Umbreit 2001). Restorative justice responses to intervention therefore begin with a focus on identifying the damage to victims and communities that has resulted from the actions of the offender.

2 *The principle of stakeholder involvement*: victims, offenders and communities should have the opportunity for active involvement in the justice process as early and as fully as possible.

The principle of stakeholder involvement is focused on the goal of maximizing victim, offender and community participation in decision-making related to the response to crime. Although stakeholder involvement is primarily about the process of a restorative encounter, the larger, overall objective associated with this principle is to ensure to the greatest extent possible quality inclusion of victim, offender and community by paying attention to stakeholder interests, the nature of communication, choices for participants, responsibility/ownership and roles in the process of addressing problems presented by crime and harm (Van Ness and Strong 1997, 2001; Bazemore and Schiff 2004).[4]

3 *The principle of transformation in community and government roles and relationships*: we must rethink the relative roles and responsibilities of government and community. In promoting justice, government is responsible for preserving a just order, and community for establishing a just peace.

For this macro-level principle, there are two related primary goals. The first presumes an attempt to move forward with systemic change in criminal justice agencies and systems in order to empower community decision-making and responsibility in the response to crime and harm. Secondly, many communities and community members have been denied opportunities to exercise the skills of informal social control and mutual support and have lost their capacity to respond effectively to crime and harm as justice systems have assumed more of this responsibility. Therefore, part of transforming roles and relationships requires an intentional focus on building, or rebuilding, the community capacity needed for an effective informal response to youth crime. We focus in this chapter only on the community-building goal (for systemic change discussion in the context of restorative group conferencing, see Bazemore and Schiff 2004).

Dimensions of process and outcome

Each of the three core principles provides the basis for multiple, independent, yet mutually reinforcing, dimensions of measurement. We consider several dimensions derived from each principle that can be linked to intervention theories that suggest process, immediate, intermediate and long-term outcomes that can be tested empirically.[5] While our concern with the 'independent variable' in a restorative group conference (RGC) is focused on rating the process, we argue that much of the variation between and within conferencing programmes (and programme models) *in process* is based on the priority given to pursuit of different *intermediate outcomes*. Specifically, all restorative practices may be said to focus generally on the long-term goal of healing/repair and reintegration. Group conferencing practices vary, however, in commitment to pursuit of different conference objectives (i.e. the intermediate outcomes we refer to below as outcome 'dimensions').

A real conference is rarely focused on one intermediate outcome, and the best conference *may* be one that ranks high on all these dimensions. There are, however, no empirical data to suggest that high scores on all dimensions guarantee better short or long-term outcomes (e.g. healing, reintegration, relationship building). With the possible exception of increases in remorse and empathy (see Maxwell and Morris 1999; Hayes and Daly 2003), there are few data to suggest that success in achieving any specific short-term or intermediate outcomes increases the likelihood of achieving long-term outcomes. Because practitioners set priorities among outcomes they hope to achieve based on different 'grounded theories,' we envision evaluations in which measures of multiple independent variables gauge the extent to which a conference is focused on one or more possible outcomes.[6] In doing so, we can measure internal variation in a restorative group conference (Hayes and Daly 2003). Where each of these 'tendencies' is linked to a theory of intervention, we also have an opportunity to test the linkage between process and initial, as well as intermediate, outcomes that can be connected to longer-term outcomes (e.g. reoffending, longer-term victim well-being) between programmes, and allow for objective tests of intervention theories.

In the remainder of this chapter, we consider restorative dimensions that have been identified as common initial objectives or intermediate outcomes pursued in RGCs and are in turn linked conceptually to long-term goals. Based on a national case study of restorative group conferencing practitioners in eight states, involving interviews and observation of conferences in several communities in two jurisdictions (Schiff and Bazemore 2002; Bazemore and Schiff 2004), we also suggest that these dimensions define distinctive priorities for the restorative process. There is some tension between the importance attached to each priority and conferencing outcomes between programmes, as well as variations between practitioners in the same programme. These differences may account for variation in the strength of the restorative process when it is measured along a continuum within each of these core dimensions.

Table 21.1 lists the dimensions presented in the remainder of this chapter. Because these are elaborated with examples and theoretical discussion elsewhere (Bazemore and Schiff 2004), we provide only a few brief illustrations in this chapter. Rather than listing specific measures, we propose questions that provide the basis for measurement indices that can be used to gauge the extent of commitment to each intermediate outcome in a conference. Furthermore, we suggest that indices can be developed to monitor variation both within and between conferences.

Table 21.1 Restorative justice: core principles and dimensions

	Core principles	
Repairing harm	Stakeholder involvement	Community/government role transformation
• Making amends • Relationship building	• Victim–offender exchange • Mutual transformation • Respectful disapproval	• Norm affirmation/values clarification • Collective ownership • Skill building

Measuring healing and repair: dimensions and intermediate objectives for assessing process

Meaning and dimensions of repair

Bazemore and Schiff (2004) identify two core dimensions as RGC practice priorities associated with the principle of repairing harm. Harm to individual victims and communities is commonly addressed by a broad dimension of reparative activity best described as *making amends*. Harm to relationships is addressed in conferences by a dimension labelled *relationship building/rebuilding*.

Amends and relationship building: priorities and theoretical assumptions

Because crime creates an imbalance and inequity in relationships, reciprocity requires an effort of the part of the offender to make up for what he or she has done. Theories of social exchange (Gouldner 1960; Molm and Cook 1995) assume that the failure to make amends results in a sense of imbalance and lack of reciprocity on the part of the offender. Repairing the harm done by making things right is therefore a necessary first step in meeting the material and emotional needs of victims and communities, as well as changing the image of the offender in the eyes of both. The goal of relationship building is based on the assumption in social support theory (Cullen 1994) that offenders in ongoing relationships of informal support who have access to roles that create a legitimate identity and help them build new relationships that commit them to conforming behaviour will be less likely to reoffend (Maruna 2000; Bazemore 2001). Victims in ongoing relationships of informal support will also be more likely than those without such relationships to move forward with a healing process. Specifically, relationship building may increase the resiliency of both offender and victim; informal relationships built in the conference may carry over and provide both instrumental and affective/emotional assistance to offender and victim.

However, these dimensions may be in conflict when there is an emphasis on the *obligation* to repair *v.* supporting the need of offender and victim to reconnect with each other or with their supporters. Current training in victim–offender mediation and dialogue, for example, has stressed attempts to avoid what Umbreit (1999) has called 'settlement-driven' mediation. As a result, victim-offender exchange advocates would agree with the view of a focus group participant that 'we follow a basic prescription *not* to discuss the agreement in the preparation stage'. Instead, volunteer mediators seek to reassure victim and offender, and answer basic questions in hopes of making relationship building possible. Advocates of this position believe that just having the dialogue – regardless of the outcome (including whether or not the agreement was completed) – is a successful result, and as one mediator observed: 'We tell the mediators ... we don't *care* if you get an agreement ... we just don't want them to be pushing for a piece of paper to come out of it – even though we get our funding by producing the paper.'

Alternatively, those who place greater emphasis on ensuring agreements to make amends, on the other hand, such as this police officer director of a family group conference (FGC), may support prompting conferencing participants to think about the final contract:

> a good agreement starts in the preparation phase – we hand out a written 'cheat sheet' with ideas about the kinds of things [restitution, community service] participants have proposed in the past ... I tell them to start thinking about the agreement, directed to repair and prevention ... [this] homework process allows for contemplation ... People in our society have a hard time believing they can make these decisions themselves.

One may question whether ideas for making amends can be effectively proposed without first hearing about the harm itself and in isolation from victim and community. Yet, because the conference itself may be a complex undertaking, specific preparation is needed if a creative and practical contract to achieve reparative goals is to be developed; as suggested in the last comment, an overemphasis on avoiding discussion of the agreement may result in a missed opportunity to practise the skills of making a commitment and then following through with it.

Research questions and sample measures

The relative strength of focus on amends *v.* relationship-building outcome orientations could be addressed by using measures designed to answer key empirical questions. Several examples are included below.

Amends

To gauge the extent to which participants in a restorative process are likely to achieve the intermediate goals of amends to victim and community in the form of reparation as service, restitution, and/or apology, researchers would need to address the extent to which the RGC has achieved the following *immediate* outcomes:

- The offender accepted responsibility for the crime in the conference.
- Offenders, victim and other community stakeholders had meaningful and maximum direct input, played roles in developing, and took ownership of, the reparative agreement.

To document the strength and integrity of intervention to achieve these *immediate* objectives, researchers will need to measure the extent to which the conference *process* has:

- clearly presented the purpose of the conference as repairing harm (*v.* open dialogue or discussion of other issues);
- allowed conference participants the opportunity to hear the story of the harm from offender and victim and devoted a significant proportion of the conference to discussion of this harm;
- assessed the nature and quantity of harm to victims and community; and
- defined clear roles for conference participants in repairing the harm.

Relationship building

To assess the extent to which participants in a restorative conference are likely to achieve the intermediate goals of building relationships of support, assistance and guardianship, researchers would need to address the extent to which the conference has achieved the following social support theory-based, *immediate* outcome:

- Established connections towards new relationships or strengthened existing relationships between victim and offender, offender and community, or victim and community.

To achieve this *immediate* objective, researchers will need to measure the extent to which the conference *process* has:

- included participants who are important in the lives of the offender and victim, bring special resources to the agenda or are willing and able to provide affective or instrumental social support;
- encouraged and built upon supportive comments about the offender or victim; and
- assigned participants a specific role to work with and support the offender and others in carrying out and monitoring the reparative agreement (e.g. participate with him or her in service projects) and victim subsequent to the conference.

Measuring stakeholder involvement: dimensions and intermediate objectives for assessing process

Meaning and dimensions of involvement

Three primary dimensions of the principle of stakeholder involvement suggest immediate process-related outcome priorities for the restorative conference. These priorities can be logically linked to intermediate objectives, and in turn to long-term goals associated with the behaviour and well-being of victim, offender and community, based upon grounded theories that have emerged over the past several years in restorative group conferencing. Two of these dimensions, victim–offender exchange and mutual transformation, have emerged from evolving practice and priorities in restorative conferencing in the past three decades. The third, respectful disapproval, is a core feature of reintegrative shaming theory that has shaped practice associated with family group conferencing and has now had influence on other models (Braithwaite and Mugford 1994; Bazemore and Schiff 2004).

Victim–offender exchange, respectful disapproval and mutual transformation: priorities and theoretical assumptions

Priorities associated with the *victim–offender exchange* orientation are illustrated to some degree in the previous discussion about the relative preference given to the reparative agreement *v.* the need for open expression and dialogue. Following what some have referred to as a theory of 'healing dialogue' (Bazemore and Schiff 2004; see Umbreit 2001), the focus on victim–offender exchange as a primary priority, however, errs on the side of open discourse, whether or not such dialogue is related to an agreement, building relationships or any other apparent goal. Although outcomes related to victim impact, overall participant satisfaction, reduced fear and a variety of procedural justice objectives (see Umbreit 2001) are often implicitly pursued, a focus group participant's comment that 'just having the victim/offender meeting is a success, regardless of the outcome' (Schiff and Bazemore 2002) is illustrative of this tendency. Grounded heavily in victim–offender mediation practice, an essential focus on addressing the needs and involvement of these two primary stakeholders, this difference is seen in part in the selection of conference participants. While victim–offender mediation (VOM) practice in the USA once often restricted the dialogue process to victim and offender, current practice leaves the decision about whether and which other participants should be included up to the victim and the offender.

Proponents of *respectful disapproval* of the offence as a primary conference objective, on the other hand, will generally insist that a family member or other adult emotionally connected to the offender participate in the conference, because of the importance attached to the family group and/or those who matter most to the offender in the encounter. This goal, based on reintegrative shaming theory, is more directive to facilitators than is true in the victim–offender exchange orientation, where neutrality and openness have traditionally been emphasized. As one proponent of this emphasis in reintegrative shaming theory puts it: 'Conferences begin with the assumption that a wrong has been done and that the offender has an obligation to repair that wrong as much as possible (hardly a neutral position)' (McCold 2000: 90).

Based on a theory of 'common ground' (Bazemore and Schiff 2004), advocates of a *mutual transformation* outcome for RGCs seem even more likely to allow facilitators the discretion to make strategic decisions about participants (and advocate for larger group conferences depending on the environment in which the harm or conflict has occurred) (Moore and McDonald 2000). Like the focus on respectful disapproval, advocates of mutual transformation distinguish carefully between harmful behaviour and the public and self-image of the offender and rely heavily on attention to emotions in the conference and the strategic management of dialogue (Moore and McDonald 2000; cf. Braithwaite and Mugford 1994). In addition, in hopes of finding and building on shared understandings between victim, offender, their supporters and other participants, they devote more attention to discovering overlapping or collective interests to build towards a more holistic and possibly complex, yet sustainable, skill building to enhance resolution of conflict and harm.

Structure and strategy in the process itself vary, with victim–offender exchange advocates the least inclined to intervene in a free-flowing dialogue, FGC practitioners pursuing a goal of respectful disapproval and reintegration using a script to structure dialogue, and proponents of mutual transformation employing the most directive methods in efforts to find and build upon common ground among participants as a basis for setting the stage for developing a useful agreement. The latter also share the FGC focus on strategic attention to ensuring movement through conference phases but may also go beyond this focus to ensure that mutual acknowledgement between victim and offender has occurred before moving to the agreement phase. As the following explanation from a programme director using a modified family group conferencing model as a re-entry strategy illustrates, this mutual acknowledgement phase may be subtle and quite brief:

I look for some acknowledgement from the victim [and] the offender that they have humanized the other person, that they have gotten the essential idea that this is not somebody I need to be afraid of, that this is not somebody who's going to do me harm, *on either side* ... I have to see that 'personal' part happen.

While the parties may remain far apart and certainly need not 'bond' for the conference to be considered a success, victim, offender, their supporters and community, at a minimum, should increase their understanding of the other's position and feelings before attempting to complete a reparative agreement.

Research questions and sample measures

The relative strength of focus on victim–offender exchange, respectful disapproval and mutual transformation conference outcome orientations could be addressed using measures designed to answer key empirical questions. Though not exhaustive, or limited to one dimension or outcome orientation, several examples are included below.

Victim–offender exchange

To assess the extent to which participants in a restorative encounter are likely to achieve the intermediate goals of victim–offender exchange, such as general sense of fairness, initial feelings of well-being, reductions in fear and general satisfaction with the process, researchers would need to address the extent to which the conference has achieved the following *immediate* outcomes:

- Victim vindication.
- Offender and victim input and sense of being heard.
- Offender and victim gaining information about the other.

To document the strength and integrity of intervention to achieve these *immediate* objectives, researchers will need to measure the extent to which the conference *process* has:

- ensured a free flow victim–offender communication and open expression;
- positioned the facilitator/mediator in a relatively neutral role with minimal interruption;
- effectively used silence; and
- avoided manipulation of dialogue and rush to agreement.

Respectful disapproval

To assess the extent to which participants in a restorative process are likely to achieve the intermediate goals of reintegrative shame, offender commitment to behaviour change to avoid future disapproval, and support for reintegration of offender and victim, researchers would need to address the extent to which the conference has achieved the following *immediate* outcomes:

- The offender experiences clear sense of disapproval of the behaviour from those whose opinions matter to him or her.
- The offender experiences support from this group along with disappointment in his or her behaviour.

To document the strength and integrity of intervention to achieve these *immediate* objectives, researchers will need to measure the extent to which the conference *process* has:

- included those whose opinions are important to the offender;
- encouraged and built upon disapproving comments about the behaviour combined with positive comments about supporting the offender and victim; and
- encouraged or shown openness to emotional expression from all parties and built upon these as transition points in the conference.

Mutual transformation

To assess the extent to which participants in a restorative process are likely to achieve the intermediate goals of skills gained in conflict resolution, agreement making and maintaining peaceful relationships, researchers would need to address the extent to which the conference has achieved the following *immediate* outcomes:

- The parties (e.g. victims, offenders, supporters, affected community members) gain a shared understanding of the problem.
- There is an increase in empathy between participants and understanding of the position of other parties.
- There is an increase in skills and insight to resolve conflict in the future and a plan to do so.

To document the strength and integrity of intervention to achieve these *immediate* objectives, researchers will need to measure the extent to which the conference *process* has:

- built upon bridging statements, emotional expression and points of common agreement;
- gained increased understanding of the victim and offender perspective;
- given attention to stakeholder mutual acknowledgement as a sign to move to the next phase of the conference;
- reframed and clarified issues as necessary; and
- moved towards the agreement only when there are signs from the group of some shared ownership of the conflict.

Community/government role transformation: dimensions and intermediate objectives for assessing processes

Meaning and dimensions of community building/role transformation

Three primary dimensions are associated with the community-building goal as part of the principle of community/government role transformation (Bazemore and Schiff 2004). These we refer to as *norm affirmation/values clarification, collective ownership* and *skill building*. Linked broadly to social disorganization theory in criminology (Kornhauser 1978; Bursik and Grasmick 1993), in an intervention context, these dimensions specifically address active efforts to 1) develop social capital (Coleman 1988; Putnam 2000) as a structural and cultural basis of support for community action in response to crime; 2) establish collective ownership through civic engagement in the process of involvement in the restorative response to crime (Uggen and Janikula 1999; Bazemore and Stinchcomb 2004); and 3) build the capacity to take such action, or 'collective efficacy' (Sampson *et al.* 1997).

Norm affirmation and values clarification, as conferencing outcomes, allow participants to discover shared values and interests in upholding group behaviour standards (e.g. neighbourhood, school, workplace). In response to youth crime, this implies developing a collective understanding of both consensus and divergent views about what behaviours are 'off limits' (see Pranis 2001). Clarification of the shared values underlying the response to harms should also reinforce the validity of conference agreements and the process itself. Through participation in a process in which community members denounce the behaviour while supporting the offender, proponents of theories of social capital (Putnam 2000) might suggest that participants build relationships of trust and sense of reciprocity and skills in informal social control and conflict resolution. Ideally, these values and skills will then spill over to other decision-making and conflict resolution contexts.

While active participation in decision-making is a normative premise of democratic citizenship, and volunteer initiative and citizen participation have been celebrated at many levels (Toqueville 1956/1835), US and other Western justice systems in the past half century have been at the forefront in the centralization and professionalization of justice functions. A theory of civic engagement would suggest, however, that involvement in public decision-making processes, including those involving crime and justice, is an important threshold for support of these processes. Practical reasons behind the desire to increase citizen ownership in justice decision-making include the belief that the absence of involvement may lead to apathy and a cycle of distrust, withdrawal and opposition: 'Apathy breeds suspicion. Suspicion breeds cynicism. Cynicism prevails. Conversely, participation builds a sense of ownership and a sense of ownership builds personal responsibility. A sense of personal responsibility for the well-being of the community prevails' (Maloney 1998: 1 cited in Bazemore and Schiff 2004).

It may also be argued that those who share a strong sense of responsibility will go to great lengths and effort to see their ideas succeed and will share a strong sense of investment in the outcome of those efforts. Hence, meaningful involvement in decision-making may promote *collective ownership*. Outcomes anticipated for this dimension are that participants in restorative processes play active, leadership roles in all phases of the conference and, in doing so, become resources to meeting the objectives of the conference, as well as catalysts for energizing others.

In the conference setting, the concept of 'shared leadership' (Pranis 2001; Pranis *et al.* 2003) allows participants, indeed asks/requires them, to take on responsibilities for meeting their own needs and those of others. In contrast to victim–offender exchange, or even respectful disapproval and mutual transformation dimensions, this orientation is more explicit about the larger community role and responsibility in the restorative process. Within the restorative group conference setting, this means a transfer of responsibility from professional to participants as suggested by this facilitator:

> If I sit in the conference and I need to re-direct or remind people because they are always looking to me for the final answer, then I'm not doing so well. But if they are treating me like I'm another community person then that is really good. Everyone has a direct role in the process. It is *really happening* when the offender acts as another community member.

Outside the conference, collective ownership in its most advanced form may even result in community members organizing their own conferences without waiting to involve criminal or juvenile justice officials (Bazemore and Schiff 2004). In addition, as suggested by the following comment in response to a question about how to define community building, an important shift in roles and responsibilities may occur:

> When you see community-building happening – when I've seen [it] – there is a *blurring of boundaries* [and a move away] from 'that's not a part of my job description' … the janitor doing conflict resolution in the hall – drawing people toward the larger role. Specialization is shaping our culture – restorative justice helps people see the broader role. Above and beyond what [they're] getting paid for. Count the number of service providers. If [there's] more there who are not being paid – it's a good sign (emphasis added).

Skill building aimed at gaining competencies in the exercise of informal social control and mutual support may occur through several strategies in the conferencing setting. For example, some facilitators rely heavily on participants to ensure that the victim feels comfortable telling his or her story, and/or that the offender is acknowledging responsibility and will be supported during and after the conference (Bazemore and Schiff 2004); participants may also restate points of agreement or common ground, checking with the family for additional input or disagreement with proposed sanctions, eliciting input from the victim.

While typically an unanticipated benefit of conferencing, some practitioners have argued that building competencies and transferring responsibilities for decision-making should become a strategic goal of restorative group conferencing programmes. The rationale for this, according to David Moore (1994: 5, emphasis added), is that formal justice systems have essentially 'deprived people of the opportunity to *practice* skills of apology and forgiveness, or reconciliation, restitution, and reparation'. The skill development task for community building in restorative justice practice is aimed in part at revitalizing these and other capacities related to the responsible exercise of internal social control in democratic societies, both inside and outside the context of any organized response to crime and harm.

Ideally, conferences create a space in which community members feel more comfortable in expressing disapproval of harmful behaviour in a respectful way, while also commending prosocial behaviour and providing support. Over time, the sequence of norm affirmation, collective ownership and skill building may spark collective action. For example, when practitioners and volunteers in Colorado and Wisconsin programmes began to take note of dramatic increases in referrals related to truancy and other school disciplinary problems linked to zero-tolerance policies, they decided their job was not simply to hold conferences with these youths as an alternative to court. Rather, they hoped to 'get beyond the cases to recognize some broader patterns going on' in the way their community's public agencies were dealing with their young people (cited in Bazemore and Schiff 2004: 295).

Arguing that restorative practices should be targeted towards the community where the harm and conflict occurred (i.e. the school community) rather than juvenile justice programmes which address these as individual problems, these practitioners began to assist school personnel in developing *internal* school-based restorative programmes to resolve problems. In doing so, they began to transform what Putnam (2000) calls 'bonding social capital' needed to enable the collective to affirm and enforce its norms and values into 'bridging social capital' that could then be used to leverage government resources to support community members. Participants in these restorative processes also began to link families, their neighbourhood institutions and public controls and supports (Hunter 1985) in a way that may at least indirectly engage social justice issues (Braithwaite and Parker 1999; Pranis 2001).

While the transition from case processing, even in its more collective and three-dimensional stakeholder restorative justice form, to community building may not be straightforward, and has thus far often been serendipitous, it does appear to follow the theoretical sequence of norm affirmation as a means of building relationships of trust, ownership and skill building that leads to, and is then strengthened through, collective action. Community building may also grow naturally from the historical expansion in the range of conference participants from victim and offender to family and extended family, and more recently to community members that may not be directly connected to either victim or offender. The goal of community building will continue to change the make-up of conferences, and pursuit of this goal, in turn, will likely be advanced as conferences include voices beyond those of victim, offender and their immediate supporters. The justification for this wider participation is stated by one programme co-ordinator that acknowledges the potential for both community building *and* a different kind of impact on stakeholders, in this case, the offender:

We are hoping for one outcome – the offender will recognize them [community member participants] as offering a broader connection to the community ... they get a certain kind of feedback from this: *'Look how many people care about me'* [italics added]. In the beginning, [in choosing participants] we stuck to who was impacted directly, but learned how valuable it was to have [broader] community – who have some distance from the offender – bring a different perspective ... I found that in bringing people in that the juvenile *cannot* relate to [directly], yes, they ask, 'Who are these people?' [But we want to] *get more community buy-in* and participation. We are looking for a *bridge to the larger community* (emphasis added).

Research questions and sample measures

The relative strength of focus on norm affirmation/values clarification to build relationships of trust and reciprocity, collective ownership and skill-building conference outcome orientations could be addressed using measures designed to answer key empirical questions. Several examples are included below.

Norm affirmation/Values clarification

To assess the extent to which participants in a restorative process, based on a theory of social capital, achieve the intermediate goals of building relationships and networks of trust and reciprocity based on shared values related to youth crime and trouble, researchers would need to address the extent to which the conference has achieved the following *immediate* outcomes:

- Conference participants discuss broader community values and behavioural norms.
- Participants experience some relief and vindication from other participants for their own beliefs about tolerance limits and norms (while also finding points of disagreement).
- New relationships are developed between conference participants.

To document the strength and integrity of intervention to achieve these immediate objectives, researchers will need to measure the extent to which the conference *process* has:

- invited discussion of values and encouraged respectful debate about tolerance limits;
- a neighbourhood base and has made maximum use of neighbourhood volunteers in the conferencing process;
- linked dialogue on norms and values to conferencing tasks and programme mission;
- allowed for non-threatening dialogue about shared values; and
- encouraged network building and future meetings.

Collective ownership

To assess the extent to which participants in a restorative process, based on a theory of civic engagement, are likely to achieve the intermediate goals of a sense of ownership of the conflict/problem at hand and the exercise of leadership in its solution, researchers would need to address the extent to which the conference has achieved the following *immediate* outcomes:

- Defined leadership roles for participants in managing the conference as well as decision-making and ensured that professionals play support, rather than directive, roles in the process.
- Discussed active roles for participants in monitoring and carrying out, as well as developing, the conference agreement.
- Created new roles for offenders in the requirements and obligations of the agreement that encourage a prosocial identity and change the public's image of these persons.

To document the strength and integrity of intervention to achieve these immediate objectives, researchers will need to measure the extent to which the conference *process* has:

- actively included stakeholder input into resolution and agreement;
- included conference participants who provide alternative perspectives on the problem and are resources to offenders and victims;
- given community members direct input into conference agreements and responsibility for follow-up; and
- promoted shared leadership.

Skill building

To assess the extent to which participants in a restorative process, based on a theory of collective efficacy, are likely to achieve the intermediate goals of increased willingness of participants and other community members to intervene with young people and provide support, researchers would need to address the extent to which the conference has achieved the following *immediate* outcomes:

- Participants identify and express harm caused by the behaviour to community life.
- Youths and adults become more comfortable in expressing disapproval of harmful behaviour in a respectful way.
- Participants gain skills in conflict resolution and peace-making.
- Participants contribute to the agreement and accept responsibilities in follow-up.

To document the strength and integrity of intervention to achieve these immediate objectives, researchers will need to measure the extent to which the conference *process* has:

- allowed for discussion of social justice issues beyond the needs of individual participants;
- identified community-building tasks and/or collective action remedies for these problems;
- encouraged skill-building efforts in other neighbourhood entities and included a broader range of participants (e.g. resource persons) beyond the immediate victim and offender support group; and

- initiated an ongoing focus on one or more neighbourhood or smaller community entities with clear boundaries to maximize skill building impact.

Summary and conclusions

In the past decade, research in restorative justice has made important advances by demonstrating positive impact on outcomes such as reoffending, victim satisfaction and other indicators. Understanding why and how restorative programmes work in achieving these outcomes – when they do – is the next challenge. We have argued that meeting this challenge requires clarity about practice dimensions derived from general normative principles that in turn link different practitioner priorities to desired outcomes at the conclusion of a restorative encounter. Using qualitative findings from a national US study of restorative group conferencing, we conclude that the strength and 'restorativeness' of the independent variable/intervention in restorative conferencing could be best assessed by examining measures which reflect relative focus on several key principle-based practice dimensions.

We suggest that the principle-based approach anchors practice in core restorative values. Though based on ethical value commitments (rather than empirically verified criteria), principle-based process evaluation is like other efforts to establish 'programme integrity,' or consistency between programme intervention and guiding principles (e.g. Andrews and Bonta 1994), in one important sense. That is, to the extent that an intervention is *inconsistent* with restorative principles, impact evaluators can avoid the mistake of claiming that they are testing the effectiveness of 'restorative justice' when they are not, regardless of the name of the programme or initiative being studied. Rather, they are inadvertently testing some *other* normative theory of intervention based on philosophies grounded in other values (e.g. crime control, social welfare/treatment), or some unspecified combination of approaches. When this is the case, neither the failure nor success of the intervention in question can be attributed to restorative justice. To the extent that a programme or practice is implemented in a manner *consistent* with restorative principles, however, evaluators can examine the impact of restorative justice practices, both in comparison with each other, and with alternative interventions informed by other theories and justice philosophies.

The most general basis for comparison of the practice focus of restorative group conferences may well be based upon the relative commitment to one core principle *v.* another. While not mutually exclusive, there are times when two or more principles emphasize different process priorities, as well as push the conference towards some intermediate outcomes rather than others. We provided illustrations which could be interpreted as conflicts between the principle of stakeholder involvement and the principle of repairing harm, when the mandate to maximize time for dialogue and stakeholder expression of emotion appeared to compete with the need to develop a follow-up plan to make amends or rebuild relationships. Similarly, the principle of repairing harm may appear to be in conflict with the desire to support community involvement in decision-making when the participation necessary for community skill building seems to be more focused on punishment than reparation (e.g. Bazemore and Earle 2002). Rather than simply describe this conflict, however, it is more important to measure variation in commitment to each principle in a given conference.

The more complex focus on differences in outcome priorities among practitioners illustrates different tendencies *within the domain of each core principle* and, we suggest, provides the opportunity to test specific assumptions about the effectiveness of various practice approaches. We have suggested that these differences often drive restorative conferences towards different priorities for intermediate outcomes. Though only briefly discussed in this chapter, the next step is explicitly to connect the intermediate outcomes discussed here with long-term outcomes.

Like researchers in other areas of evaluation, some who study restorative justice are also known to be advocates, and few evaluators in any field today make claims to be completely 'value-free'. While there should be no problem with having value-based opinions about what approaches align more closely with restorative values and about what overall strategies for implementation and sustainability seem more likely to succeed, we can be objective in our research if we are willing to state these preferences rather than present them as data-based truths. Because almost all prior research has compared restorative practices with mainstream approaches (e.g. courts), there are few evaluations that help to identify best practices *within* categories of restorative programmes. Yet, there are many claims about the superiority of certain programme models, as well as some rather orthodox commitment to internal practice specifications (e.g. having victims speak first in a conference, insisting on face-to-face preparation) that have not been verified empirically (we recognize that some of these commitments are, appropriately perhaps, value based).

In this context, viewing the theories-in-use and dimensions discussed in this chapter simply as 'tendencies,' rather than monolithic practice and theoretical models, seems to be the best strategy for encouraging objective research. Indeed, a more open-minded attitude regarding the scientifically demonstrated effectiveness of these strategies seems to allow for a less biased method of determining the best strategies for accomplishing immediate and intermediate objectives likely to produce long-term healing results. We need to begin with the simple acknowledgement that an intervention may be very high in 'restorativeness' on one principle domain, yet weak in another; most importantly, we should be willing to see how a strength on one dimension along with a weakness on another effects specific outcomes. Finally, we suggest that the principle-based approach to evaluation of restorative interventions allows for the broadest possible generalization to theory, and provides the best opportunity for replication of effective practice and policy in multiple contexts.

Selected further reading

Bazemore, G. and Stinchcomb, J. (2004) 'Civic engagement and reintegration: toward a community-focused theory and practice', *Columbia Human Rights Law Review*, 36: 241–86. This article discusses theory and research supportive of a restorative model for offender re-entry based on a civic engagement model of community (that argues for felon enfranchisement) built around restorative practice and democratic participation.

Bazemore, G. (2001) 'Young people, trouble, and crime: restorative justice as a normative theory of informal social control and social support', *Youth and Society*, 33: 199–226. Elaborates on a theory of informal social control and social support based on the normative theory of restorative justice.

Hayes, H. and Daly, K. (2003) 'Youth justice conferencing and re-offending', *Justice Quarterly*, 20: 725–64. Discusses empirical research on delinquent youths who participated in restorative conferences in South Australia. Using quantitative empirical data based on measurement of multiple stakeholder perspectives of the quality of restorative conferences, the authors test various explanations for why restorative justice works and find empathy a strong predictor of reduced recidivism.

Walgrave, L. (2004) 'Youth crime and youth justice: comparative and cross-national perspectives', in M. Tonry (ed.) *Crime and Justice: A Review of Research. Vol. 31*. Chicago, IL: University of Chicago Press. Examines several bodies of research and emerging theory of restorative practices in a comprehensive international examination of research literatures.

Bazemore, G. and Schiff, M. (2004) *Juvenile Justice Reform and Restorative Justice: Building Theory and Policy from Practice*. Cullompton: Willan Publishing. Develops a series of theoretical and evaluation models, including intermediate outcomes based on a qualitative examination of restorative practices in several US states. Each model is grounded in a core restorative justice principle.

Braithwaite, J. (2002) *Restorative Justice and Responsive Regulation*. New York, NY: Oxford University Press. A comprehensive examination of restorative practices in a broad theoretical context of effective regulation. Multiple theoretical explanations are explored in a lengthy chapter that examines evidence suggesting why restorative justice 'works' when it does.

Notes

1 In fairness, Figure 21.1 seems intended more as a policy and practice guide to encourage policy-makers and practitioners to give priority to certain programme models than as a tool for guiding measurement. Hayes and Daly (2003) offer another stakeholder process dimension based on the extent of movement of victim and offender towards each other's position. We consider this dimension later in this chapter based on our presentation of the effort of participants in a restorative process to find 'common ground'.

2 Some are also open to the possibility that if we are conceptually clear about the essence of a restorative process as something *independent of* a specific practice model, we could also assess the degree to which these processes are incorporated into court and other structurally adversarial procedures. For example, how should we assess the case in which judges choose essentially to alter the typical court dynamic by suspending court protocol to convene a restorative process – for

example, Canadian Judge Barry Stuart's common practice of routinely moving down from the bench and reconvening all parties in a peace-making circle inside his courtroom, or Austin District Attorney Ronnie Earle's practice of 'plea bargaining' by inviting victims and offenders to participate in a community circle to determine the terms of a court agreement? While many might welcome such adaptations for their potential to influence adversarial protocols, critics can rightly conclude that in focusing on the 'restorativeness' of a sentence or other agreement achieved through non-restorative procedures, we artificially separate outcome from process in the same way that advocates of the 'process-only' definition detach process from a concern with the goal of intervention. In doing so, we must also live with the fact that restorative obligations arrived at by non-restorative means may hinder the movement towards more use of restorative processes.

3 Bazemore and Walgrave's broader, goal-focused definition actually is used by these authors to argue for the principle-based approach to determining the restorativeness of an intervention discussed in the next section of this chapter, though they do not articulate this in the research context. Hayes and Daly (2003) also provide what could be viewed as a goal-focused or multidimensional stakeholder-focused definition in their measure of restorative justice as the extent to which victim and offender move closer to each other's position during the conferencing process.

4 Van Ness and Strong (2001) suggest important generic process dimensions that are essentially about the nature and quality of inclusion in the restorative process. These include *the nature of the invitation* offered, the extent of *acknowledgement of stakeholder (v. system) interests* in the conferencing process, *the acceptance of alternative approaches* – essentially the flexibility and provision of a range of choices and options for participation, and *communication* – essentially the quality, completeness and validity of the narrative presented, especially by victim and offender. Inclusion is also concerned with the extent to which the process allows for the safe expression of emotion, as well as with the extent of understanding achieved from the dialogue between participants (Van Ness and Strong 2001). Bazemore and Schiff (2004) also suggest that the *role* played by victim, offender, supporters and community members in defining the nature of harm is an important dimension of variation in conferences that may impact both the nature and quality of the process and the resulting agreement.

5 The general idea of multiple dimensions of restorative justice is not new. Zehr (1990), in his classic work on restorative justice, for example, provides several 'yardsticks' for practitioners to judge the extent to which their practice reflects restorative justice values. Regarding criminological and other social science theories, we note that reintegrative shaming has probably been the theory most often applied in scholarly research on restorative justice. Although reintegrative shaming has become one of the leading theories in criminology and the sociology of deviance – independent of its restorative justice association – Hayes and Daly (2003) argue that this theory is not strictly speaking a restorative justice theory. In their South Australia studies of restorative conferencing, Daly and her colleagues develop multiple measures of a number of theoretical dimensions, both restorative and non-restorative. There are, moreover, numerous theories other than reintegrative shaming applicable in restorative justice research (Braithwaite 2002), and a number more directly linked to restorative justice principles. While we do not elaborate on these theories in this chapter (see Bazemore and Schiff 2004), they include social support theory (Cullen 1994), exchange theory (Molm and Cook, 1995), social disorganization theory and recent advances focused on social capital and collective efficacy (Sampson *et al.* 1997; Putnam 2000).

6 Intervention outcomes pursued in conferencing and discussed in the remainder of this chapter include, for example, the extent to which participants in a given conference are primarily focused on allowing victim and offender to have a generally uninterrupted dialogue, ensuring that the offender's behaviour is disapproved of in a respectful way while supporting him or her as a person, developing an agreement that allows the offender to make amends in a way that changes the community's image of him or her and ensuring that offenders and victims make connections with prosocial community members who can provide assistance and/or guidance and guardianship.

References

Andrews, D. and Bonta, J. (1994) *The Psychology of Criminal Conduct*. Cincinnati, OH: Anderson Publishing.

Barton, C. (2000) 'Empowerment and retribution in criminal justice', In H. Strang and J. Braithwaite (eds) *Restorative Justice: Philosophy to Practice*. Aldershot: Ashgate.

Bazemore, G. (1998) 'Restorative justice and earned redemption: communities, victims and offender reintegration', *American Behavioral Scientist*, 41: 768–813.

Bazemore, G. (2000) 'Community justice and a vision of collective efficacy: the case of restorative conferencing', in *Criminal Justice 2000. Vol. 3*. Washington, DC: National Institute of Justice, US Department of Justice.

Bazemore, G. (2001) 'Young people, trouble, and crime: restorative justice as a normative theory of informal social control and social support', *Youth and Society*, 33: 199–226.

Bazemore, G. (2002) 'Balance in the response to family violence: challenging restorative principles', (with Earle, T.) in J. Braithwaite and H. Strang (eds) *Restorative Justice and Family Violence*. London: Cambridge University Press.

Bazemore, G. and Earle, T. (2002) 'Balance in the response to family violence: challenging restorative principles', in J. Braithwaite and K.H. Strang (eds) *Restorative Justice and Family Violence*. London: Cambridge University Press.

Bazemore, G., Nissen, L. and Dooley, M. (2000) 'Mobilizing social support and building relationships: broadening correctional and rehabilitative agendas', *Corrections Management Quarterly*, 4: 10–21.

Bazemore, G. and Schiff, M. (2004) *Juvenile Justice Reform and Restorative Justice: Building Theory and Policy from Practice*. Cullompton: Willan Publishing.

Bazemore, G. and Stinchcomb, J. (2004) 'Civic engagement and reintegration: toward a community-focused theory and practice', *Columbia Human Rights Law Review*, 36: 241–86.

Bazemore, G. and Umbreit M. (2001) *A Comparison of Four Restorative Conferencing Models. Juvenile Justice Bulletin*. Office of Juvenile Justice and Delinquency Prevention, Office of Justice Programs, Washington, DC: US Department of Justice.

Bazemore, G. and Walgrave, L. (1999) 'Restorative juvenile justice: in search of fundamentals and an outline for systemic reform', in G. Bazemore and L. Walgrave (eds) *Restorative Juvenile Justice: Repairing the Harm of Youth Crime*. Monsey, NY: Criminal Justice Press.

Bonta, J., Wallace-Capretta, S. and Rooney, J. (2000) 'Quasi-experimental evaluation of an intensive rehabilitation supervision program', *Criminal Justice and Behavior*, 27: 312–29.

Bonta, J., Wallace-Capretta, S., Rooney, J. and Mackanoy, K. (2002) 'An outcome evaluation of a restorative justice alternative to incarceration', *Contemporary Justice Review*, 5: 319–38.

Boyes-Watson, C. (2004) 'What are the implications of growing state involvement in restorative justice?', in H. Zehr and B. Toews-Shenk (eds) *Critical Issues in Restorative Justice*. Monsey, NY: Criminal Justice Press.

Braithwaite, J. (1989) *Crime, Shame, and Reintegration*. New York, NY: Cambridge University Press.

Braithwaite, J. (1999) 'Restorative justice: assessing optimistic and pessimistic accounts', in M. Tonry (ed.) *Crime and Justice: A Review of Research*. Chicago: University of Chicago Press.

Braithwaite, J. (2001) 'Youth development circles', *Oxford Review of Education*, 27: 239–52.

Braithwaite, J. (2002) *Restorative Justice and Responsive Regulation*. New York, NY: Oxford University Press.

Braithwaite, J. and Mugford, S. (1994) 'Conditions of successful reintegration ceremonies: dealing with juvenile offenders', *British Journal of Criminology*, 34: 139–71.

Braithwaite, J. and Parker, C. (1999) 'Restorative justice is republican justice', in G. Bazemore and L. Walgrave (eds) *Restorative Juvenile Justice: Repairing the Harm of Youth Crime*. Monsey, NY: Criminal Justice Press.

Braithwaite, J. and Pettit, P. (1990) *Not Just Deserts: A Republican Theory of Criminal Justice*. New York: Oxford University Press.

Brooks, D. (2000) 'Evaluating restorative justice programs.' Paper presented at the United Nations Crime Congress, ancillary meeting, Vienna, Austria.

Bursik, R.J. and Grasmick, G. (1993) *Neighborhoods and Crime: The Dimension of Effective Community Control*. New York, NY: Lexington Books.

Coleman, J. (1988) 'Social capital in the creation of human capital', *American Journal of Sociology*, 94: S95–S120.

Cullen, F. (1994) 'Social support as an organizing concept for criminology: residential address to the Academy of Criminal Justice Sciences', *Justice Quarterly*, 11: 527–59.

Dignan, J. and Marsh, P. (2001) 'Restorative justice and family group conferences in England: current state and future prospects', in G. Maxwell and A. Morris (eds) *Restoring Justice for Juveniles: Conferences, Mediation and Circles*. Oxford: Hart Publications.

Duff, A. (2003) 'Restoration and retribution', in A. von Hirsch *et al.* (eds) *Restorative Justice and Criminal Justice: Competing or Reconcilable Paradigms?* Oxford: Hart Publishing.

Gouldner, A. (1960) 'The norm of reciprocity: a preliminary statement', *American Sociological Review*, 25: 161–78.

Hayes, H. and Daly, K. (2003) 'Youth justice conferencing and reoffending', *Justice Quarterly*, 20: 725–64.

Hunter, A. (1985) 'Private, parochial and public social orders: the problem of crime and incivility in urban communities', in G.D. Suttles and M.N. Zald (eds) *The Challenge of Social Control: Citizenship and Institution Building in Modern Society*. Norwood, NJ: Aldex.

Kornhauser, R. (1978) *Social Sources of Delinquency: An Appraisal of Analytic Models*. Chicago, IL: University of Chicago Press.

Lehman, J., Maloney, D., Seymour, A., Gregorie, T., Russell, S. and Shapiro, C. (2003) *The Three R's of Reentry* (monograph). Washington, DC: Justice Solutions.

Lipsey, M.W. (1992) 'Juvenile delinquency treatment: a meta-analytical inquiry into the variability of effects', in T.D. Cook *et al.* (eds) *Meta-Analysis for Explanation: A Casebook.* New York, NY: Russell Sage Foundation.

Marshall, T. (1996) 'The evolution of restorative justice in Britain', *European Journal on Criminal Policy and Research,* 4: 21–43.

Maruna, S. (2000) *Making Good: How Ex-convicts Reform and Rebuild their Lives.* Washington, DC: American Psychological Association.

Maxwell, G. and Morris, A. (1999) *Understanding Re-offending.* Wellington: Institute of Criminology, Victoria University of Wellington.

McCold, P. (2000) 'Toward a holistic vision of restorative juvenile justice: a reply to the maximalist model', *Contemporary Justice Review,* 3: 357–72.

McCold, P. and Wachtel, T. (2003) 'A theory of restorative justice.' Paper presented at the XIII World Congress of Criminology, 10–15 August, Rio de Janeiro.

McDonald, J., Moore, D., O'Connell, D. and Thorsborne, M. (1995) *Real Justice Training Manual: Coordinating Family Group Conferences.* Pipersville, PA: Piper's Press.

Molm, L. and Cook, K. (1995) 'Social exchange and exchange networks', In K. Cook *et al.* (eds) *Sociological Perspectives on Social Psychology.* Boston, MA: Allyn and Bacon.

Moore, D. (1994) 'Illegal action – official reaction.' Paper prepared for the Australian Institute of Criminology.

Moore, D. and McDonald, J. (2000) *Transforming Conflict in Workplaces and Other Communities.* Sydney: Transformative Justice Australia.

Morris, A. and Maxwell, G. (2003) 'Restorative justice in New Zealand', in A. von Hirsch *et al.* (eds) *Restorative Justice and Criminal Justice.* Oxford: Hart Publishing.

Nugent, W., Williams, M. and Umbreit, M.S. (2003) 'Participation in victim–offender mediation and the prevalence of subsequent delinquent behavior: a meta-analysis', *Utah Law Review,* 137–66.

Pranis, K. (2001) 'Restorative justice, social justice, and the empowerment of marginalized populations', in G. Bazemore and M. Schiff (eds) *Restorative Community Justice: Repairing Harm and Transforming Communities.* Cincinnati, OH: Anderson Publishing.

Pranis, K., Stuart, B. and Wedge, M. (2003) *Peacemaking Circles: From Crime to Community.* St Paul, MN: Living Justice Press.

Putnam, R. (2000) *Bowling Alone: The Collapse and Revival of American Community.* New York, NY: Simon & Schuster.

Sampson, R., Raudenbush, S. and Earls, F. (1997) 'Neighborhoods and violent crime: a multi-level study of collective efficacy', *Science Magazine,* 277: 918–24.

Schiff, M. (1999) 'The impact of restorative interventions on juvenile offenders', in G. Bazemore and L. Walgrave (eds) *Restorative Juvenile Justice: Repairing the Harm of Youth Crimes.* Monsey, NY: Criminal Justice Press.

Schiff, M. and Bazemore, G. (2002) *Final Report on Understanding the Community Role in Restorative Conferencing for Youthful Offenders.* Princeton, NJ: Robert Wood Johnson Foundation.

Seymour, A. and Bazemore, G. (1998) *Victims, Judges and Parnerships for Juvenile Court Reform Project. Office for Victims of Crime Final Report.* Washington, DC: Offices for Victims of Crime, US Department of Justice.

Sherman, L. (2000) 'Repeat offending in the Canberra RISE Project: an overview.' Paper presented at the Annual Meeting of the American Society of Criminology, November, San Francisco.

Sherman, L. (2003). 'Reason for emotion: reinventing justice with theories, innovations, and research: the American Society of Criminology Presidential Address', *Criminology,* 41: 1–38.

Sherman, L., Strang, H. and Woods, D.J. (2000) *Recidivism Patterns in the Canberra Reintegrative Shaming Experiments*. Canberra: Australian National University.

Strang, H. (2003) *Repair or Revenge: Victims and Restorative Justice*. Oxford: Oxford University Press.

Tocqueville, A. (1956) *Democracy in America*. New York, NY: Mentor (original work published in 1835).

Toews-Shenk, B. and Zehr, H. (2001) 'Restorative justice and substance abuse: the path ahead', *Youth and Society*, 33: 314–28.

Tyler, T. (1999) *Why People Obey the Law*. London, Yale University Press.

Uggen, C. and Janikula, J. (1999) 'Volunteerism and arrest in the transition to adulthood', *Social Forces*, 78: 331–62.

Umbreit, M. (1998) *Victim Offender Mediation Continuum: From Least to Most Restorative Impact*. St. Paul, MN: Center for Restorative Justice and Peacemaking, University of Minnesota.

Umbreit, M. (1999) 'Avoiding the marginalization and McDonaldization of victim offender mediation: a case study in moving toward the mainstream', in G. Bazemore and L. Walgrave (eds) *Restoring Juvenile Justice: Repairing the Harm of Youth Crime*. Monsey, NY: Criminal Justice Press.

Umbreit, M. (2001) *The Handbook of Victim-Offender Mediation*. San Francisco, CA: Jossey-Bass.

Van Ness, D. and Schiff, M. (2001) 'Satistfaction guaranteed? The meaning of satisfaction in restorative justice', in G. Bazemore and M. Schiff (eds) *Restorative and Community Justice: Repairing Harm and Transforming Communities*. Cincinnati, OH: Anderson Publishing.

Van Ness, D. and Strong, K. (1997) *Restoring Justice*. Cincinnati OH: Anderson Publishing.

Van Ness, D. and Strong, K. (2001) *Restoring Justice* (2nd edn). Cincinnati OH: Anderson Publishing.

von Hirsch, A. (1976) *Doing Justice: The Choice of Punishments*. New York, NY: Hill & Wang.

von Hirsch, A. *et al.* (2003) 'The future of the proportionate sentence', in T. Bloomberg and S. Cohen (eds) *Punishment and Social Control* (2nd edn) New York, NY: Aldine de Gruyter.

Walgrave, L. (1999) 'Community service as a cornerstone of a systemic restorative response to (juvenile) crime', in G. Bazemore and L. Walgrave (eds) *Restorative Juvenile Justice: Repairing the Harm of Youth Crime*. Monsey, NY: Criminal Justice Press.

Walgrave, L. (2004) 'Youth crime and youth justice: comparative and cross-national perspectives', in M. Tonry (ed.) *Crime and Justice: A Review of Research*. Chicago, IL: University of Chicago Press.

Zehr, H. (1990) *Changing Lenses: A New Focus for Crime and Justice*. Scottdale, PA: Herald Press.

Chapter 22

Reoffending and restorative justice

Hennessey Hayes

Introduction

It seems clear that restorative justice processes have many benefits for victims, offenders and their communities. Victims benefit from active participation in a justice process. Offenders benefit from the opportunity to repair harms and make amends. Communities (of care) benefit from the negotiation of restorative resolutions to conflict (Braithwaite 2002). In this sense, restorative justice has achieved many of its aims (i.e. holding offenders accountable and affording them opportunities to make amends in symbolic and material ways; encouraging reconciliation between offenders, victims and their communities of care). When these aims are achieved, advocates claim that '… we might … expect … restorative processes … to impact [positively] on reoffending' (Morris 2002: 600).

In contrast to conventional justice, restorative justice seems to offer more to offenders, victims and other participants (Morris and Young 2000). However, satisfying offenders and victims and offering them a fairer justice experience are not in themselves likely to persuade governments to support restorative justice. Because advocates make the claim that restorative justice has the potential to reduce crime, even when acknowledging that crime prevention is not a primary aim of restorative justice processes, governments and criminal justice agencies continue to scrutinize restorative justice on its ability to control crime. In this chapter I review what currently is known about restorative justice and its crime reduction potential.

I begin first by considering why the 'reoffending question' persists. Next, I summarize and critically assess the limited but growing body of empirical research on restorative justice and reoffending. [1] This summary is organized around two key questions posed by researchers: 1) How does restorative justice *compare* with traditional interventions in reducing crime? 2) How are the *variable features* of restorative interventions related to future offending? Finally, I conclude with some reflections on the restorative justice–reoffending relationship.

The dogged nature of the 'reoffending question'

Traditional responses to offending behaviour (ranging from police warnings and formal cautions through to court trials and various forms of state punishment, such as fines, community sentences and imprisonment) are mainly offender centred and punitive. Key aims are to punish offenders and to deter future offending, although offenders are increasingly ordered to compensate their victims. Restorative interventions, on the other hand, make justice to victims a central goal of the criminal justice process and are reparative. Restorative interventions balance the needs of offenders and victims, engage offenders and encourage them to accept responsibility, and provide victims with an active role in the official criminal justice process (Johnstone 2002). Restorative interventions respond equitably to offending behaviour and to the needs of victims by treating offenders and victims respectfully and fairly. Common outcomes of restorative processes include apologies to victims, work performed for victims or communities, monetary restitution and, where appropriate, rehabilitation.

Thus, the primary goal of restorative justice is not to deter future offending but, rather, to provide reparative or healing ways of responding to crime (e.g. to restore offenders, victims and communities from the harmful effects of crime) (Morris and Young 2000). However, if restorative justice 'restores and satisfies [offenders, victims and communities] better than existing criminal justice practices' (Braithwaite 2002: 45), then future offending behaviour should be less likely. While advocates are quick to point out that crime reduction is not the primary goal of restorative justice, they nevertheless claim that restorative justice is likely more effective than traditional justice in preventing crime (Braithwaite 2002). It is this claim about restorative justice's ability to prevent future offending that drives 'the pervasive tendency to think of restorative justice simply as a new technique for controlling crime' (Johnstone 2002: 5).

Despite advocates' views that restorative justice offers more to offenders, victims and the community than simply a new way of controlling crime (Morris 2002), the reoffending question continues to preoccupy observers. In the past decade, we have witnessed an explosion of empirical research designed to test the claims made about restorative justice's ability to restore and satisfy participants and prevent crime. Much of the research to date on the restoration and satisfaction claims is generally consistent and suggests that restorative justice can restore offenders and victims and offer a more satisfying justice experience. In addition, we have seen a growing number of empirical studies designed to test the reoffending question. However, results from this body of research have not provided a straightforward answer.

What seems unclear about the reoffending question is what any answer might imply. Evaluations of restorative initiatives that suggest they have no effect on future offending may demonstrate restorative justice's limited crime reduction ability. On the other hand, evaluations that show restorative justice is meeting its key aims of victim restoration and offender accountability, even if not effecting reductions in future offending, may be regarded by some as illustrative of restorative justice's 'success'. Advocates may remain uncomfortable with the persistent empirical focus on the reoffending question. However, as long as claims continue to be made about restorative justice's crime reduction potential, interest in the reoffending question will likely endure.

Answering the reoffending question

During the past decade, a number of studies have emerged to test restorative justice's ability to reduce crime. Much of this research has been designed to answer two questions about restorative justice and reoffending: 1) How does restorative justice *compare* with traditional justice in preventing future offending? 2) How are the *variable effects* of restorative justice related to post-intervention offending? Answers to the first question tell us *if* restorative justice effects reductions in crime, compared with traditional justice. Answers to the second question tell us *how* restorative justice is associated with reductions in crime.

Before researchers can set out to assess the restorative justice–reoffending relationship, they must first resolve two methodological issues: 1) How should restorative justice be defined and measured? 2) How should reoffending be defined and measured? Defining restorative justice seems anything but straightforward. However, Marshall (1999) provides a useful starting point. He defines restorative justice as: 'a *process* whereby parties with a stake in a specific offence collectively resolve how to deal with the aftermath of the offence and its implications for the future' (1999: 5, emphasis added). Under this working definition, examples of restorative processes include victim–offender mediation and restitution, victim–offender reparation programmes, circles and group conferencing.

While Marshall's definition may help us to recognize restorative justice when we see it, there seems to be less agreement over how reoffending should be conceptualized and measured. Indeed, scanning across studies of restorative justice conferencing and recidivism, one sees a large degree of variation in how reoffending is conceptualized and measured. For example, a recent review of conferencing and reoffending studies (Luke and Lind 2002) showed that measures of reoffending varied from post-intervention arrest to reconviction.

In addition to debate over what qualifies as reoffending, there is disagreement over how recidivist events should be counted. Some studies have conducted *prevalence* analyses, in which any post-intervention criminal incident qualifies as a recidivist event (McCold and Wachtel 1998; McGarrell *et al.* 2000; McGarrell 2001; Hayes and Daly 2003, 2004). Other studies have conducted *incidence* analyses, which include a count of all post-intervention criminal events per offender (Sherman *et al.* 2000; Maxwell and Morris 2001; Luke and Lind 2002). Prevalence analyses provide information about the number of recidivist offenders in the community, while incidence analyses provide information about the number of crimes in the community (Sherman *et al.* 2000).

For some analyses, incidence may be the more appropriate measure of recidivism. For example, in field experimental designs, in which researchers examine how a restorative intervention compares with some other intervention in reducing *levels* of offending in the community, incidence seems the better measure (Sherman *et al.* 2000). On the other hand, in studies that examine how restorative interventions effect *any* change in future offending, prevalence or participation is the more appropriate measure (McCold and Wachtel 1998; McGarrell *et al.* 2000; Hayes and Daly 2003, 2004).

There is also some debate over when follow-up periods should begin and end. In the RISE research (summarized below), the incidence of reoffending was measured for 12 months following random assignment to an intervention (i.e. police-run conference or court), rather than the intervention itself. Because there were sometimes substantial delays from assignment to intervention, following offenders from date of assignment rather than date of the intervention equalized the follow-up periods for all offenders. In the Indianapolis Juvenile Restorative Justice Experiment (discussed below), the decision was to measure the prevalence of reoffending for the 12 months following the initial arrest, rather than assignment to an intervention or the intervention itself (McGarrell 2001). In other research, follow-up begins after the intervention (Maxwell and Morris 2001; Hayes and Daly 2003, 2004).

Deciding when follow-up periods should begin is important because this can influence how study findings should be interpreted. If follow-up begins at initial arrest or assignment, study results demonstrate the effects of initial arrest or assignment on recidivism, rather than the effects of a legal intervention. Even if offenders' awareness of an intervention has an effect on reoffending behaviour (Sherman *et al.* 2000: 10), such effects are likely not the same as the effects of the intervention itself. Nevertheless, how the anticipation of an intervention affects reoffending is itself an important research question.

A related question about appropriate follow-up periods is whether offenders should be followed for equal or unequal periods of time. In studies where data on a legal intervention are gathered over a period of time (e.g. observing a number of restorative encounters during a six-month period) and reoffending data are gathered at some time several months or years later, follow-up periods for offenders will be unequal. Reoffending data in such studies are said to be 'censored'. This is problematic because offenders will not have had the same opportunities (in terms of time) to commit new offences. One option is to standardize the follow-up period for all offenders so they have the same opportunities to reoffend. Another option is to retain unequal follow-up periods and analyse reoffending data in ways that are appropriate for censored data.

All these considerations illustrate that answering the reoffending question is by no means straightforward. Even when researchers are able to settle on what they believe is the best measure of reoffending, an equally important concern is determining the best method of assessing the relationship between restorative justice and reoffending. The most common approach is field experimental, which attempts to show how restorative justice compares with traditional interventions. However, some studies have emerged that attempt to gauge the ways that variation in restorative justice processes bears on future offending.

How does restorative justice compare with traditional justice in preventing crime?

The most common and rigorous research design among comparison studies is field experimental, in which *eligible* offenders are randomly assigned to a restorative intervention (experimental or treatment group) or a traditional intervention such as court or probation (control group). This design (or some variation) has been used in several studies in North America (McCold and Wachtel 1998; McGarrell *et al.* 2000; Latimer *et al.* 2001; McGarrell 2001) and in only one study in Australia – the RISE (ReIntegrative Shaming Experiments) study (Sherman *et al.* 2000).[2] Eligibility usually refers to the type of offence, the age and/or sex of the offender and prior offending history. These offender and offence characteristics are known predictors of recidivism (Gendreau *et al.* 1996) and researchers adopting the comparative approach attempt to control for these potential 'causes' of recidivism.

There is a sound rationale underpinning the field experimental research design chosen to assess the impact of restorative justice on offenders, victims and future offending behaviour. Equalizing the treatment (e.g. diversionary conference) and control (e.g. court or other diversionary programme) groups on key variables known to be associated with reoffending means that any differences observed between the two groups may be attributed to the effects of the treatment. This design has little susceptibility to many 'threats' to internal validity (e.g. history, maturation and selection bias). Because young offenders are randomly assigned to either a treatment or control group, there should be no selection effects to bias study outcomes. Also, because anything occurring outside the experiment should affect the treatment and control groups equally, and because offenders are randomly assigned to treatment and control conditions, this design guards against potential problems of history and maturation (Maxfield and Babbie 1998).

Field experimental designs do face some problems with external validity (i.e. generalizability). The random assignment of young offenders to treatment and control conditions ensures that no selection bias enters into the experiment. In practice, however, juvenile justice system officials normally do not assign young offenders to restorative justice programmes on a random basis. Police officers and court officials consider young offenders' prior offending history and the nature of the offence when determining whether referral to restorative justice is appropriate. Nevertheless, field experimental designs go a long way in examining restorative justice in 'natural' settings.

Limitations of the comparative approach
Proponents of the comparative/experimental approach argue that 'true' experiments are 'valued because the random assignment produces treatment and control groups that are equivalent in all respects other than the programme intervention itself' (McGarrell *et al.* 2000). However, true equalization or equivalence has been difficult to achieve for researchers

adopting this approach. This is because field experimentation in restorative justice and reoffending research cannot fully eliminate the problem of self-selection bias. In studies where field experimentation has been used, not all young offenders assigned to treatment conditions (e.g. restorative justice conferences) experienced the treatment. For example, in the RISE study, some offenders who were randomly assigned to a restorative justice conference may not have received this intervention because the offender may not have attended. For this reason, comparisons in RISE are of 'assigned' interventions rather than 'delivered' interventions (Sherman *et al.* 2000). As the RISE researchers note: 'using "assigned" treatments preserves the level playing field between the two treatments [conference or court], rather than letting other circumstances stack the deck against one or the other of the two approaches' (Sherman *et al.* 2000: 9–10).

Another concern with field experimental designs is associated with some eligibility criteria. Returning to the RISE research for illustration, offenders had to admit to an offence to enter the experiment. Admitted offenders were then randomly assigned to conference or court interventions. Requiring offenders to admit to the offence may impede generalization of study findings to offenders in the control condition. This is because admitted offenders randomly assigned to court in the RISE study are likely different from offenders who would normally proceed to court in several important ways. For example, we might assume that admitted offenders assigned to court have moved further towards taking responsibility for their behaviour than other offenders in court. In this way, they are similar to offenders in conferences in ways theoretically related to reoffending (Hayes and Daly 2003). While requiring admission maintained equalization across the treatment and control groups, this also may partly explain why little or no differences in reoffending for conference and court offenders were observed in the RISE study (Sherman *et al.* 2000), as well as several other comparison studies (Marshall 1999; Kurki 2003).

When problems of equivalence and self-selection bias can be effectively addressed, field experimental designs provide needed information about whether restorative justice interventions affect recidivism. When researchers are able to control key variables known to be associated with reoffending (e.g. prior offending, age, gender, race), they may be more confident in concluding that observed differences in reoffending for treatment and control offenders are, in fact, due to treatments. Learning that a new justice intervention has a positive impact on offenders and offending is important for criminal justice policy. Equally important is learning what features of new justice interventions effect change in future offending behaviour. While field experimental studies tell us *if* restorative interventions are effective, a focus on the variable nature of restorative interventions may tell us something about *how* restorative interventions 'work'.

How are the variable effects of restorative justice related to post-intervention offending?

Another approach, which has been adopted in only a very small number of studies, is to examine variation *within* restorative justice programmes

(Maxwell and Morris 2001; Hayes and Daly 2003, 2004). Variation analyses, unlike comparison studies, do not assume that all restorative events are equal. The focus is on the highly variable nature of restorative events and how this relates to further offending. Rather than randomly assigning offenders to a restorative justice intervention or to court, researchers examine how restorative justice interventions affect reoffending behaviour beyond those things known to be associated with recidivism, such as offender characteristics (age, gender, offending history) and nature of the offending behaviour (property/violent). Researchers studying variation ask whether things that happen in restorative justice predict future offending, beyond those things already known to be associated with recidivism, such as age, gender and prior offending (Hayes and Daly 2003).

Limitations associated with studying variation
Some may assert that, because variation analyses offer no information about how restorative justice affects recidivism compared with other interventions, any information yielded is of diminished value. However, a key point to make is that variation analyses answer other important research questions. The primary concern about examining variation in restorative justice is that any observed 'effects' on reoffending may be due to things other than what happened in the conference. Prior offending, age and gender, for example, bear heavily on one's future offending propensity. This is why offenders are often matched on such 'static predictors' (i.e. things that cannot be changed) (Gendreau *et al.* 1996) in randomized field experiments. When equivalence on static predictors is maintained across treatment and control groups in field experiments, observed differences in reoffending can be attributed to the treatment.

While the lack of a control group may be viewed as a 'weakness' among researchers who have a penchant for field experimentation, it is important to note that isolation of treatment effects is not the focus of variation analyses. In addition to measuring the differential impact of new and traditional interventions of reoffending, variation studies may tell us *what it is* about restorative justice that effects reductions in future offending.

Answers to the reoffending question

Opportunities to study the impact of restorative justice on reoffending have been limited, as restorative justice is relatively a 'new' justice phenomenon.[3] There is now an established literature on the restorative justice process and its effect on offenders and victims. This literature has produced remarkably consistent outcomes, and results suggest that offenders and their victims have better justice experiences compared with offenders and victims in traditional justice (e.g. Maxwell and Morris 1996; Hayes *et al.* 1998; Umbreit 1994, 1996, 1998; Strang *et al.* 1999; Miers *et al.* 2001). When the empirical focus shifts to reoffending, the number of studies available is smaller and the results are more varied.

How does restorative justice compare with traditional justice in preventing crime?

Much of the empirical work on restorative justice and reoffending is comparative. Several field experimental studies have been conducted in North America, the UK and Australia.

In Australia, researchers working on the RISE (Re-integrative Shaming Experiments) study in the Australian Capital Territory (Canberra) followed four types of offenders[4] randomly assigned to a police-run conference or court for 12 months following assignment and compared reoffending outcomes. Results suggest that conferences may be more effective in reducing further offending for young violent offenders, but not for young property offenders or drink drivers. Findings from RISE showed that violent offenders (up to the age of 29) randomly assigned to conference had a significantly lower rate of post-assignment reoffending compared with violent offenders assigned to court.[5] That is, violent offenders assigned to conference committed 38 fewer post-conference offences per 100 offenders per year, compared with similar offenders assigned to court (Sherman *et al.* 2000). No significant differences were observed in post-assignment offending rates for property offenders, and drink drivers assigned to conference had a slightly (albeit insignificantly) higher rate of post-conference offending compared with drink drivers assigned to court.

In New South Wales, Luke and Lind (2002) conducted a retrospective analysis of several thousand first offenders (i.e. those with no prior proven court appearance) who went to conference or court from 6 April 1997 to 5 April 1999. They compared post-intervention offending for three groups of offenders: 5,516 offenders in court during the 12 months before the introduction of conferencing; 3,830 offenders in court during the first 12 months of conferencing; and 590 offenders in conference during the first 12 months of operation. Records for first offenders were chosen to control for the effects of prior offending. After making several comparisons between the conference and court groups, Luke and Lind (2002) concluded that conferencing rendered a 15–20 per cent reduction in predicted risk of reoffending.

In the USA, comparisons of restorative justice conferences with other interventions, such as court or other court diversion, have produced mixed results. McCold and Wachtel compared reoffending among young offenders randomly assigned to a police-run restorative justice conference or to the youth court in the Bethlehem, Pennsylvania Restorative Policing Experiment (McCold and Wachtel 1998). Key findings suggest that reoffending was significantly less likely for certain types of offenders attending conference (e.g. violent offenders) compared with offenders who went to court. However, researchers were not able to conclude that the effects of the conference led to reductions in reoffending. Because some offenders who were assigned to a conference declined to participate and instead went to court, the authors noted the following: 'It appears that any reductions in recidivism are the result of the voluntary programme diverting from formal processing those juveniles who are least likely to reoffend in the first place' (1998: 107).

In another experiment, McGarrell *et al.* (2000) compared rearrest rates for very young (14 years of age or younger) first-time offenders randomly assigned to restorative justice conferences or other court diversion programme. Their results suggest that restorative justice conferences significantly reduced rates of rearrest, compared with other court diversion programmes (which included victim–offender mediation). At six months following initial arrest, there were nearly 14 per cent fewer recidivists among the restorative justice conferencing group than among the control offenders. This difference was statistically significant and represented a 40 per cent reduction in reoffending. Differences in rearrest between the restorative justice conferencing offenders and control offenders diminished after 12 months of follow-up. While there were more recidivists among the control offenders 12 months following their initial arrest (cf. 29 per cent for the control group and 23 per cent for the restorative justice group), differences in rearrest were not statistically significant.

In Canada, researchers compared reoffending for matched groups of offenders referred to restorative justice or receiving a traditional justice sanction (Bonta *et al.* 1998). In this study, the restorative justice initiative was implemented as a diversion from court. The Restorative Resolutions (RR) programme (run through the John Howard Society in Manitoba) was designed for offenders who would likely receive a custodial sentence in court. Offenders (who pleaded guilty) referred to the programme co-operated with programme staff in developing a 'community management' plan. Where victims were willing, they were able to meet offenders and assist in the development of plans.[6]

Because the average RR programme duration was 28.5 months, the researchers chose to assess in-programme rather than post-programme offending. Offenders in RR were matched on age, race, gender, offence type and first offence to two probation groups and one group of incarcerated male offenders. The findings on reoffending are rather compelling. They show that RR offenders had a significantly lower rate of in-programme reoffending compared with probationers during 18 months of follow-up (Bonta *et al.* 1998: 25–7). Also, while the difference in reoffending between RR male offenders and male inmates was not statistically significant after 12 months, significantly lower reoffending rates for RR offenders were observed after two years.

A recent meta-analysis conducted in Canada (Latimer *et al.* 2001) renders the issue of reoffending somewhat perplexing. A meta-analysis is a quantitative analysis of prior quantitative analyses. One might think of a meta-analysis as a kind of quantitative literature review. Researchers analysed 32 'effect sizes' across 22 studies that compared a restorative justice intervention with other types of interventions on reoffending. The average effect size was 0.07, which means that restorative justice programmes yielded an average 7 per cent reduction in reoffending, compared with other non-restorative programmes. This outcome is encouraging for restorative justice advocates and seems to suggest that restorative justice programmes can reduce crime. However, when one considers that effect sizes ranged from -0.23 to 0.38, one may be less confident about the crime prevention potential of restorative justice. The range in effect sizes analysed by Latimer *et al.* (2001) demonstrates the highly variable nature of restorative justice programme effects on recidivism. Some programmes reduced reoffending by as much as 38 per cent, while other programmes led to increases in reoffending by up to 23 per cent.

These results are very similar to an earlier meta-analysis conducted in Canada (Bonta *et al.* 1998). Bonta and colleagues conducted a small meta-analysis of 14 restorative justice and reoffending studies, which produced 20 effect sizes. Studies were chosen if they included a comparison group. The average effect size was .08, which indicates that the restorative justice programmes yielded an average 8 per cent reduction in reoffending compared with traditional interventions. However, the range of effect sizes was substantial. Most of the effect sizes (15) indicated reductions in reoffending (between 1 and 29 per cent), but some effect sizes indicated increases in reoffending among restorative justice offenders (between 2 and 45 per cent). Stepping back, results from this meta-analysis seem encouraging and suggest that restorative justice has crime reduction potential. Nevertheless, Bonta *et al.* (1998) caution readers about placing too much faith in these research outcomes, as they noted several methodological shortcomings associated with the studies they analysed.

In the UK, Miers *et al.* (2001: 1) assessed seven restorative justice schemes across England to learn 'which elements, or which combination of elements, in restorative justice schemes are most effective in reducing crime'. They conducted a 'retrospective study' and compared the reconviction rates for offenders referred to the restorative justice schemes with a group of similar offenders who were not referred to restorative justice. A significant difference in reconviction was noted for only one of the restorative justice schemes (West Yorkshire victim–offender mediation). Approximately 44 per cent of offenders referred to restorative justice were reconvicted after two years, compared with 56 per cent of offenders in the control group. However, when the researchers also took into account offenders' risk of reconviction (measured with the Offender Group Reconviction Scale), they found that restorative justice was more effective in reducing reoffending for the lowest-risk offenders (Miers *et al.* 2001: 44–6). No differences in reconviction were noted in comparisons with restorative justice offenders and control group offenders for the remaining six schemes.

Also in the UK, researchers recently conducted a very large comparative analysis of restorative cautioning (Wilcox *et al.* 2004). This study followed from a smaller, qualitative field study of 51 offenders receiving a 'scripted' restorative caution (Hoyle and Young 2002). For the smaller study, the researchers concluded that the Thames Valley restorative cautioning scheme was 'generally successful in achieving its many short-term aims, such as helping offenders to understand the effect of the offence on the victim, encouraging symbolic reparation (e.g. verbal apology) and answering victims' questions about the offence' (Wilcox *et al.* 2004: 2). The researchers also examined the offending behaviour of these offenders for the year preceding and following their restorative caution and found that approximately 25 per cent registered no new offences or 'reduced their offending at least in part because of what happened within the restorative justice encounter' (2004: 2).

The larger study aimed to confirm the findings of the smaller one with the examination of a much larger sample of offenders receiving a restorative caution between April 1998 and March 2001, as well as the inclusion of a comparison group of similar offenders receiving a traditional caution.[7] Wilcox *et al.* (2004) gathered reconviction data for nearly 20,000 offenders receiving restorative[8] and traditional cautions for 24 months post-intervention. In addition to confirming that offender characteristics (such as age at first conviction, age at caution, gender and offending type) were associated with post-caution reconviction, they compared the reconviction rates for offenders receiving a traditional or restorative caution. Controlling for offender characteristics associated with reconviction, they found no difference in the reconviction rates for offenders receiving traditional and restorative cautions[9] and thus concluded that 'there was no evidence to suggest that restorative cautions or conferences had any *statistically* significant impact on overall resanctioning rates or that they were more effective for particular subgroups of offenders' (Wilcox *et al.* 2004: 16, emphasis in original).

Finally, in New Zealand, Maxwell and Morris (2002) report reoffending outcomes for adult offenders participating in two community panel pre-trial diversion pilot programmes, compared with matched samples of adults appearing in court. The community panels consisted of community members, and offenders were referred to the panels by the courts. Offenders met with panel members (as well as police and victims in one programme – Project Turnaround) to confront the consequences of their offending and establish a reparative plan. Following 200 adult offenders participating in the community panel pre-trial diversion programmes (100 offenders from each programme), they found that offenders participating in the restorative justice programmes were significantly less likely to be reconvicted, compared with adult offenders dealt with by the courts. For example, after 12 months, only 16 per cent of Project Turnaround offenders were reconvicted compared with 30 per cent of offenders in court. Also, fewer offenders in the second panel programme (Te Whanau Awhina) were reconvicted (33 per cent) compared with offenders in court (47 per cent). Furthermore, survival analyses showed that the estimated rate of reconviction for offenders in the two panel programmes was significantly lower compared with estimated reconviction rates for court offenders (Maxwell and Morris 2002).

The studies summarized above aim to show how the effects of restorative justice on reoffending compare with traditional justice. Scanning across these studies, we see that the outcomes are mixed. Many comparative analyses show no differences in post-intervention offending; however, some do. That some studies highlight that restorative justice has no effect on reoffending may discourage some restorative justice proponents. However, if one considers that many restorative justice encounters are relatively brief (e.g. restorative justice conferences typically last 60–90 minutes), it may be unrealistic to think that such encounters will lead to radical changes in offenders' behaviour. As Umbreit has commented: 'it is naïve to think that a time-limited intervention such as mediation by itself ... would be likely to have a dramatic effect on altering criminal and delinquent behaviour' (1994: 117, cited in Bonta *et al.* 1998). Thus, we might assume that a restorative process (e.g. a conference) in itself will have less crime reduction potential compared with more comprehensive approaches that combine restorative justice processes with other practices that address the causes of crime (e.g. restorative justice plus aftercare, such as counselling or rehabilitation).

How are the variable effects of restorative justice related to post-intervention offending?

Turning to those studies which aim to assess the variable effects of restorative justice on reoffending, we see more consistency in outcomes. To date, four variation analyses have been conducted. These are in New Zealand and Australia. Results from the first variation analysis of family group conferencing in New Zealand became available in 1999, after a 6.5-year follow-up study of several young offenders (Maxwell and Morris 1999). In New Zealand, when young offenders are apprehended by police and when police take action (i.e. do not issue a warning) and when young offenders choose not to deny allegations, they attend a family group conference. Thus, the universality of family group conferencing in New Zealand renders comparative analyses problematic (Braithwaite 2002). Nevertheless, some interesting results have emerged from this jurisdiction. Maxwell and Morris (1999, 2001) followed 108 young offenders attending a family group conference for 6.5 years and found that, in addition to prior negative life experiences and what happened to offenders after their conference (e.g. unemployment), things that happened during the conferences were related to reoffending. Some of these included offenders not being made to feel a bad person, conferences being memorable for offenders, offenders agreeing to and complying with conference agreements, and offenders meeting with and apologizing to their victims (Maxwell and Morris 2001). When these things were present in conferences, reoffending was less likely.

In a more recent analysis of family group conferencing in New Zealand, Maxwell and colleagues also obtained encouraging results. They analysed case file and offending data for 1,003 young offenders who were between the ages of 15 and 17 at the time of their family group conferencing in 1998. They also interviewed a subgroup of 520 offenders from this larger 'retrospective sample' during 2000 and 2001 (Maxwell *et al.* 2004). They estimated a model of reoffending that controlled for several offender characteristics associated with reoffending (e.g. gender, ethnicity, prior offending). Their results showed that reoffending was less likely when family group conferences were seen as 'inclusive, fair, forgiving, allowing [offenders] to make up for what they had done and not stigmatising or excluding them' (Maxwell *et al.* 2004: 214). They conclude that 'quality' family group conferences go some way to reducing reoffending, but other factors also are important. In addition to a good conference, reoffending is less likely when anti-social behaviour is detected early and effectively managed, when young people have adequate access to schooling, when programmes are established that assist in the effective reintegration of young offenders into their communities (e.g. assistance with access to education and employment) and when severe (i.e. punitive) responses to offending are avoided (Maxwell *et al.* 2004: 213–5).

In Australia, variation studies have been conducted in South Australia and Queensland. In South Australia, Hayes and Daly (2003) analysed data collected for the SAJJ (South Australian Juvenile Justice) project (Daly *et al.* 1998; Daly 2001) to examine how features of family conferences, as well as offender characteristics known to be associated with reoffending (such as age, gender, race and prior offending), relate to future offending behaviour. Drawing on observations of 89 conferences convened in early 1998 and the offending history data for the primary offenders[10] in these conferences, they found prior offending, sex and race to be highly predictive of post-conference offending.[11] Beyond these variables, however, they also found that, when young offenders were observed to be remorseful, and when conference decision-making about outcomes (agreements) was observed to be consensual, reoffending was less likely. These results were remarkably similar to those obtained by Maxwell and Morris (1999, 2001), which showed that remorseful offenders who perceived fairness in their family group conference were less likely to reoffend.

With respect to the ways that offender characteristics are associated with future offending among conference offenders, similar results were obtained in a recent variation analysis in Queensland. Hayes and Daly (2004) followed 200 young offenders for three to five years following their youth justice conference to assess the variable effects of youth justice conferencing and offender characteristics on reoffending. Findings suggest that offender characteristics such as age, gender and prior offending remain highly predictive of future offending. In addition to this, another important finding emerged in relation to age at first offence and age at conference. Hayes and Daly (2004) found that reoffending was *less likely* among the youngest group of offenders (10–12 years of age) at the conference. Their expectation (consistent with the recidivism literature (e.g. Blumstein *et al.* 1986)) was that 10–12-year-old offenders at conference would have had a higher risk of reoffending, compared with older offenders. To understand this finding better, they separated very young offenders at conference into two groups: those with a prior offence who would have received a formal caution or appeared in the youth court;[12] and those with no prior detected offending whose first offence met with a youth justice conference. Comparing the estimated probably of reoffence for these two groups showed that those very young offenders with no prior detected offending were significantly less likely to reoffend than young offenders with prior detected offending. This finding suggests that 'conferencing may be a more effective intervention for very young offenders who have a high risk of reoffending, compared to cautioning or court' (Hayes and Daly 2004: 181).

Unlike outcomes for South Australia, however, no features of conferences were associated with future offending. Analysing survey data collected from the 200 young offenders in their sample, they found little to no variability across offenders on common measures of restorativeness (e.g. 'People seemed to understand my side of things', 'Doing the conference means I can now make a fresh start') and procedural justice (e.g. 'Overall, I thought the conference was fair', 'I got to have my say at the conference'). Very high proportions of reoffenders and 'desisters' agreed to survey items such as these. For example, to 'People seemed to understand my side of things', 98 per cent of offenders agreed. Of these, 56 per cent reoffended.

To summarize, recent research on the restorative justice and reoffending demonstrates the following:

1 Offenders, victims and supporters have positive experiences in restorative justice. They perceive restorative processes as procedurally fair and are generally satisfied with outcomes.

2 Studies that have examined the variable effects of restorative justice conferences on reoffending show that conferences have the potential to reduce offending. When offenders are remorseful and when decision-making about conference agreements is consensual, reoffending is less likely.[13] However, what young offenders bring to their conferences (e.g. prior offending, age at conference, age at first offence and gender) remains highly predictive of what they do afterwards.

3 Studies that compare the effects of restorative justice with other interventions show that restorative justice interventions may reduce crime, may have no effect on crime or may increase further offending.

The reoffending question answered: concluding remarks

One observer recently commented: 'The honest answer to the reoffending question is "we'll probably never know"' (Daly 2002: 71). While I prefer to look to the future of restorative justice and reoffending research with more optimism, I do agree that our current knowledge base offers insufficient evidence about how restorative justice is linked to future offending. There are a few reasons why this is so. First, and perhaps foremost, restorative justice is a concept that refers to many and varied ways of responding to crime and conflict. Restorative justice includes a broad range of justice activities and processes. Some aim to divert offenders away from traditional justice processes and others run in conjunction with traditional processes. Restorative initiatives also may be placed at various levels of the criminal justice process: pre-court diversion (e.g. restorative cautioning and conferencing), pre-sentence or post-sentence, and they may appear in juvenile justice, child protection and criminal justice. They also come with various labels: reparative justice, transformative justice, republican justice, informal justice (Daly and Immarigeon 1998). With so many varied forms, it is understandable that restorative justice has varied effects on reoffending. Thus, it should not surprise us to learn that restorative justice effects reductions in reoffending in some sites, increases reoffending in some sites, or has no effect on reoffending in some sites, especially when the forms of restorative justice being assessed are diverse (see, for example, Latimer *et al.* 2001; Miers *et al.* 2001).

Another factor driving the variation in research outcomes on restorative justice and reoffending has much to do with how reoffending is assessed. As we look across the several studies conducted to date, we see a wide variety of working definitions of reoffending (ranging from post-intervention (or post-assignment) arrest to reconviction). Variation in outcome measures is surely related to variation in research outcomes. While there is no sound methodological argument for one outcome measure over another, critics and advocates alike should be mindful of the limits that certain methodological choices place on one's ability to answer the reoffending question.

So, what is the answer to the persistent reoffending question? Rather than claiming 'we'll never know', I propose that the evidence amassed to date now renders us more confident in claiming that restorative justice 'works' to reduce crime. Despite results that show restorative justice effects no change (e.g. Sherman *et al.* 2000; Wilcox *et al.* 2004) or in some cases is associated with increases in offending (e.g. Bonta *et al.* 1998; Latimer *et al.* 2001), the weight of the research evidence on restorative justice and reoffending seems tipped in the positive direction to show that restorative justice has crime reduction potential. I am not making a definitive claim about restorative justice's ability to prevent crime because, at this stage, we simply do not know enough about *how and why* restorative justice is related to offenders' future behaviour. I am, however, suggesting that, on balance, restorative justice 'works'.

On reflection, one might consider why the reoffending question is important. Advocates remind us over and over again that crime reduction is not a primary aim of restorative justice (Morris 2002). Rather, restorative justice aims to hold offenders accountable and offer offenders and victims better (e.g. fairer and more satisfying) justice experiences than traditional methods provide. Reoffending remains important, however, because restorative justice remains theoretically linked to future offending. Recall advocates' claim that if restorative justice processes meet the key aims of holding offenders accountable, encouraging offenders to accept responsibility for their wrongdoing and make amends (e.g. apologize), not stigmatically shaming offenders, providing a forum that promotes forgiveness and achieving reintegrative and rehabilitative outcomes, reoffending *should be* less likely (e.g. Johnstone 2002; Morris 2002). Thus, we expect that 'successful' restorative justice processes will effect reductions in future offending.

Rather than focusing empirical scrutiny squarely on reoffending, perhaps researchers should attempt a better understanding of the complex of possible outcomes of restorative processes. As several observers have pointed out, a 60–90-minute restorative intervention is unlikely to lead to radical changes in post-intervention offending, especially for very active young offenders. Governments and researchers should consider what restorative justice is able to achieve both theoretically and realistically. That is, while restorative justice ought to reduce crime, empirical researchers should consider and measure other outcomes to learn, for example, how restorative interventions affect offenders' sensitivities and understandings of wrongfulness. In addition, when empirical attention turns to reoffending, governments and researchers should work to understand how restorative justice works to reduce crime given the myriad of factors that work against crime reduction (e.g. negative post-intervention life experiences such as chronic unemployment, drug dependency and abuse). Some work in this direction has been attempted

(Maxwell and Morris 1999 2001, 2002) and we learnt that restorative justice can work to reduce crime but post-intervention experiences are important.

While learning how restorative justice affects young people's ways of thinking about crime should be a key feature in future research, it nevertheless remains important to assess the theoretical link between restorative justice and reoffending. Today, we can confidently say there is a link, but the nature of the link is still not fully understood. As we continue to subject restorative justice to analytical scrutiny, we should attempt to devise better ways of learning *how and why* restorative justice renders change in offenders. This will likely entail a move away from large-scale comparative evaluations of restorative justice and traditional justice methods, and a move towards more detailed qualitative assessments of what offenders in restorative justice *understand* about the process and how this affects them and their future behaviour.

Selected further reading

Hayes, H. (2005) 'Assessing reoffending in restorative justice conferences', *Australian and New Zealand Journal of Criminology*, 38: 77–101. This article considers the ways researchers have assessed the effects of restorative justice processes on further offending. It reanalyses data from the Bethlehem Restorative Policing Experiment to examine how restorative justice conferences compare with traditional court interventions, as well as how variation within court and conferences affect future offending.

Latimer, J., Dowden, C. and Muise, D. (2005) 'The effectiveness of restorative justice practices: a meta-analysis', *Prison Journal*, 85: 127–44. Expanding on their 2001 report, the authors summarize the results of a meta-analysis of 22 studies that compare a restorative justice process with traditional non-restorative responses to criminal behaviour. Results indicate that, on average, restorative justice interventions yield reductions in future offending behaviour.

Maxwell, G. and Morris, A. (2001) 'Family group conferencing and reoffending', in A. Morris and G. Maxwell (eds) *Restorative Justice for Juveniles: Conferencing, Mediation and Circles*. Oxford: Hart Publishing. Summarizes results from a 6.5-year longitudinal study of family group conferencing in New Zealand. The results suggest that reoffending was less likely when conferences were memorable, when young offenders were not stigmatically shamed, when offenders felt involved in conference decision-making and agreed to conference outcomes, and when offenders met victims, offered apologies and felt they had repaired the damage caused by their offending.

Notes

1 This draws on a recent paper (Hayes 2005), in which I explore key issues in restorative justice and reoffending research.
2 An alternative to the field experimental approach is retrospective comparison, in which offender records are used to compare outcomes for conference and court. Using this approach, researchers match (or equalize) offenders on key variables

associated with reoffending (e.g. prior record and gender) and examine offender behaviour during a specified post-intervention period. This approach was taken in a recent study in Australia (Luke and Lind 2002) and the UK (Wilcox *et al*. 2004).

3 While the origins of restorative justice initiatives may be traced back to victim–offender mediation trials in Canada in the mid-1970s (Johnstone 2002), legislatively based restorative justice programmes have emerged only within the past 15 years.

4 Offenders include drink drivers, youth violence offenders (29 years or younger), juvenile property offenders (17 years or younger) and juvenile property-security offenders (17 years or younger who shoplifted from stores employing security staff).

5 The Type 1 error probability associated with this outcome was 0.16, which exceeds the conventional alpha level 0.05.

6 During this evaluation of the programme, victims and offenders met in only 10 per cent of cases.

7 This study adopted a 'retrospective quasi-experimental' design. That is, offenders were not randomly assigned to traditional or restorative cautioning groups. Thus, the degree to which outcomes were affected by police discretion could not be directly assessed.

8 Where a victim attended the caution, it was termed a 'restorative conference'. Victims were present in only 14 per cent of all restorative cautions.

9 This also was true when the restorative caution group was separated into two groups: one in which no victim attended the caution and another where victims were present (the 'conference' group).

10 In conferences where there were multiple offenders, research observers sought advice from conference convenors regarding whom they felt was the main (or 'primary') offender. Observations were keyed to primary offenders.

11 Reoffending was measured for 8–12 months following the conference.

12 The young offenders included in this study were the first to process to a youth justice conference in Queensland. Because none of the offenders in the study had attended more than one conference, any prior detected offending would have met with a formal caution or referral to the youth court.

13 That remorsefulness is associated with reductions in post-conference offending has been observed in only two studies (Maxwell and Morris 2001; Hayes and Daly 2003), both variation analyses. While several comparative projects have examined the ways that remorsefulness or 'restorativeness' features in diversionary conferences, none has linked this to reoffending. In RISE, for example, comparative analyses showed that significantly more restorative justice was observed in conferences than in court across all four experiments. Also, significantly more participants in conferences perceived restorative justice compared with participants in court (Strang *et al*. 1999). There were no significant differences in observed levels of remorse among court and conference offenders in the property and violent experiments. Thus, remorse did not seem to be associated with future offending in the RISE reoffending analysis (Sherman *et al*. 2000). Meta-analyses of restorative justice and reoffending have not directly assessed how remorsefulness or restorativeness is linked with future offending. Rather, the aim has been to learn how 'programme characteristics' (e.g. administrative features of restorative justice programmes) and 'participant characteristics' (e.g. prior offending, age, gender) are associated with future offending (Latimer *et al*. 2001).

References

Blumstein, A., Cohen, J., Roth, J. and Visher, C. (1986) *Criminal Careers and 'Career Criminals'*. Washington, DC: National Academy Press.

Bonta, J., Wallace-Capretta, S. and Rooney, J. (1998) *Restorative Justice: An Evaluation of the Restorative Resolutions Project*. Montreal: Solicitor General.

Braithwaite, J. (2002) *Restorative Justice and Responsive Regulation*. Melbourne: Oxford University Press.

Daly, K. (2001) *SAJJ Technical Report No. 2: Research Instruments in Year 2 (1999) and Background Notes*. Brisbane: School of Criminology and Criminal Justice, Griffith University.

Daly, K. (2002) 'Restorative justice: the real story', *Punishment and Society*, 4: 55–79.

Daly, K., and Immarigeon, R. (1998) 'The past, present, and future of restorative justice: some critical reflections', *Contemporary Justice Review*, 1: 21–45.

Daly, K., Venables, M., McKenna, L. and Christie-Johnston, J. (1998) *South Australian Juvenile Justice (SAJJ) Research on Conferencing, Technical Report No. 1. Project Overview and Research Instruments*. Brisbane: School of Criminology and Criminal Justice, Griffith University.

Gendreau, P., Little, T. and Goggin, C. (1996) 'A meta-analysis of the predictors of adult offender recidivism: what works!', *Criminology*, 34: 575–607.

Hayes, H. (2005) 'Assessing reoffending in restorative justice conferences', *Australian and New Zealand Journal of Criminology*, 38: 77–101.

Hayes, H. and Daly, K. (2003) 'Youth justice conferencing and reoffending', *Justice Quarterly*, 20: 725–64.

Hayes, H. and Daly, K. (2004) 'Conferencing and reoffending in Queensland', *Australian and New Zealand Journal of Criminology* 37 (available online at http://www.aic.gov.au/rjustice/docs/hayes.pdf).

Hayes, H., Prenzler, T. and Wortley, R. (1998) *Making Amends: Final Evaluation of the Queensland Community Conferencing Pilot*. Brisbane: Centre for Crime Policy and Public Safety, Griffith University.

Hoyle, C. and Young, R. (2002) *Proceed with Caution: An Evaluation of the Thames Valley Police Initiative in Restorative Cautioning*. York: Joseph Rowntree Foundation.

Johnstone, G. (2002) *Restorative Justice: Ideas, Values, Debates*. Cullompton: Willan Publishing.

Kurki, L. (2003) 'Evaluating restorative justice practices', in A. von Hirsch *et al.* (eds) *Restorative Justice and Criminal Justice: Competing or Reconcilable Paradigms?* Oxford: Hart Publishing.

Latimer, J., Dowden, C. and Muise, D. (2001) *The Effectiveness of Restorative Justice Processes: A Meta-analysis*. Ottawa: Department of Justice.

Luke, G., and Lind, B. (2002) 'Reducing juvenile crime: conferencing versus court', *Crime and Justice Bulletin: Contemporary Issues in Crime and Justice*, 69: 1–20.

Marshall, T. (1999) *Restorative Justice: An Overview*. London: Home Office.

Maxfield, M. and Babbie, E. (1998) *Research Methods for Criminal Justice and Criminology*. Boston MA: Wadsworth.

Maxwell, G. Kingi, V., Robertson, J., Morris, A. and Cunningham, C. (2004) *Achieving Effective Outcomes in Youth Justice: Final Report*. Wellington: New Zealand Ministry of Social Development.

Maxwell, G. and Morris, A. (1996) 'Research on family group conferencing with young offenders', in J. Hudson *et al.* (eds) *Family Group Conferences: Perspectives on Policy and Practice*. Annandale, NSW: Federation Press.

Maxwell, G. and Morris, A. (1999) *Understanding Reoffending: Full Report*. Wellington: Institute of Criminology, Victoria University of Wellington.

Maxwell, G. and Morris, A. (2002) 'Restorative justice and reconviction', *Contemporary Justice Review*, 5: 133–46.

Maxwell, G. and Morris, A. (2001) 'Family group conferences and reoffending', in A. Morris and G. Maxwell (eds) *Restorative Justice for Juveniles: Conferencing, Mediation and Circles*. Oxford: Hart Publishing.

McCold, P. and Wachtel, B. (1998) *Restorative Policing Experiment: The Bethlehem, Pennsylvania Police Family Conferencing Project*. Pipersville, PA: Community Service Foundation.

McGarrell, E. (2001) 'Restorative justice conferences as an early response to young offenders', in *Juvenile Justice Bulletin*. Washington, DC: Office of Juvenile Justice and Delinquency Prevention, US Department of Justice.

McGarrell, E., Olivares, K., Crawford, K. and Kroovand, N. (2000) *Returning Justice to the Community: The Indianapolis Juvenile Restorative Justice Experiment*. Indianapolis, IN: Hudson Institute.

Miers, D. (2001) *An International Review of Restorative Justice*, London: Home Office.

Miers, D., Maguire, M., Goldie, S., Sharpe, K., Hale, C., Netten, A., Uglow, S., Doolin, K., Hallam, A., Enterkin, J. and Newburn. T. (2001) *An Exploratory Evaluation of Restorative Justice Schemes*. London: Home Office.

Morris, A. (2002) 'Critiquing the critics: a brief response to critics of restorative justice', *British Journal of Criminology*, 42: 596–615.

Morris, A. and Young, W. (2000) Reforming criminal justice: the potential of restorative justice', in H Strang and J Braithwaite (eds) *Restorative Justice: Philosophy to Practice*. Aldershot: Ashgate.

Sherman, L. W., Strang, H. and Woods, D. J. (2000) *Recidivism Patterns in the Canberra Rintegrative Shaming Experiments (RISE)*. Canberra: Centre for Restorative Justice, Research School of Social Sciences, Australian National University.

Strang, H., Barnes, G., Braithwaite, J. and Sherman, L. (1999) *Experiments in Restorative Policing: A Progress Report on the Canberra Reintegrative Shaming Experiments*. Canberra: Australian Federal Police and Australian National University.

Umbreit, M. (1994) *Victim Meets Offender: The Impact of Restorative Justice and Mediation*. Monsey, NY: Criminal Justice Press.

Umbreit, M. (1996) 'Restorative justice through mediation: the impact of programmes in four Canadian provinces', in B. Galaway and J. Hudson (eds) *Restorative Justice: International Perspectives*. Amsterdam: Kugler.

Umbreit, M. (1998) 'Restorative justice through victim–offender mediation: a multi-site assessment', *Western Criminology Review*, 1: 1–29.

Wilcox, A., Young, R. and Hoyle, C. (2004) *Two-year Resanctioning Study: A Comparison of Restorative and Traditional Cautions*. London: Home Office.

Part 6

The Global Appeal of Restorative Justice

Gerry Johnstone and Daniel W. Van Ness

For a number of reasons, the majority of the chapters in this *Handbook* are based upon developments in the theory and practice of restorative justice in North America, the UK, Australasia and parts of western Europe. Although most of these chapters draw upon advancements in all these regions and beyond in order to say something general about restorative justice, what they say is inevitably influenced strongly by the specific context with which the authors are most familiar. Yet, although much more developed in some places than others, restorative justice is a global phenomenon. In order to capture this, however imperfectly, Part 6 of the *Handbook* is devoted to a review of the global appeal of restorative justice and attempts to indicate the ways in which restorative ideas and practices have been taken up and applied in different parts of the world.

In Chapter 23, David Miers compares and contrasts different ways in which restorative justice has been taken up in a number of countries. This is a far from straightforward task, given the sheer diversity of practices that are – or could be – identified as restorative justice, the lack of a common language with which to talk of these practices and other factors. Then, focusing on schemes in Belgium, England and Wales, New Zealand and the USA, this chapter distinguishes a number of dimensions along which we may differentiate between usages of restorative justice and also identifies and explains the different intervention models which have evolved. The chapter concludes by pointing to the necessity of comparing restorative justice programme design and delivery across countries for understanding the local, national and international development of restorative justice as well as for realizing a number of policy goals, such as the enforcement of international standards and protocols for victim–offender engagement.

Chapter 24 supplements Miers' analysis of the international growth of restorative justice by offering regional reviews of the development of restorative justice: Ann Skelton on Africa; Ping Wang, Xiaohua Di and

King Hung Wan on Asia; Jolien Willemsens and Lode Walgrave on Europe; Pedro Scuro on Latin America; Daniel W. Van Ness on North America; and Gabrielle Maxwell and Hennessey Hayes on the Pacific region. Each author reviews the historical growth of restorative justice within their regions, offers a brief survey of its current use and identifies unique features of the field. The chapter concludes with a section by Dobrinka Chankova and Daniel W. Van Ness identifying recurring themes within the regions. It is shown, among other things, that part of the appeal of restorative justice is its resonance with older ways of resolving conflicts; unsatisfactory functioning of the criminal justice system motivates interest in alternative approaches; global exchanges of information, research and programme ideas are critical; it is important to understand the legal and social context in which restorative justice is attempted; and the interaction between theory and practice is vital to the successful development of restorative justice.

One clear lesson to emerge from the reviews in Chapters 23 and 24 is that restorative justice conceptions and schemes – like the criminal justice systems they seek to supplement, reform and partially displace – are strongly conditioned by the wider cultures within which they emerge, even while they challenge certain aspects of those cultures. This lesson is amplified in Chapter 25, in which Jan Froestad and Clifford Shearing present a case study of conflict resolution in South Africa. The project in which they have been involved – in Zwelethemba, a poor community near Cape Town – is one which seeks to govern security through local micro-level institutions that mobilize local capacity and local knowledge. This can be understood as an application of restorative justice principles and values, but one which consciously seeks to develop restorative justice in a somewhat different direction from that it has taken in many programmes in Australia, Europe and North America. In an effort to meet the challenges encountered by the restorative justice movement, as it shifts from being an innovative assortment of ideas and experiments to being a rationale for officially sponsored programmes and practices, the Zwelethemba experiment seeks to direct the focus of restorative encounters towards options for future peace, to extend channels for referral of 'cases' beyond the criminal justice system, to forge stronger links between the management of individual conflicts and the approach to general problems, and to organize restorative forums in such a way that responsibilities and resources are moved to local communities.

Chapter 23

The international development of restorative justice

David Miers

Introduction

This chapter reviews the development of restorative justice in a number of selected countries, comparing and contrasting the diverse ways in which it has been deployed. Following this introduction, the chapter comprises three substantial sections, each of which both makes some general comments about key aspects of its development and refers in more detail to four particular jurisdictions that may be considered representative of international practice or otherwise of particular interest internationally. These are Belgium, England and Wales, New Zealand and, in the USA, the Balanced and Restorative Justice project.

Counting restorative justice provision

It is probably impossible to say with certainty how many restorative justice schemes, programmes or other forms of intervention are, at the time of writing, in operation, even in those countries where it is a well established practice. But it may be possible to obtain close approximations that, in aggregate, give some idea of its salience and its growth. In the USA, Umbreit and Greenwood (1998) identified, in 1996, 289 victim–offender mediation (VOM) programmes but very few involving juvenile restorative conferencing. Five years later, Schiff and Bazemore (2002: 180) were able to approximate 773 of these conferencing programmes. A 1998 survey identified over 200 Canadian programmes (Griffiths 1999), and Roberts and Roach (2003) give a number of examples of specific programmes. But as they note, there remains, despite the Criminal Code obligation placed on the judge to consider restorative objectives when sentencing, and the Federal government's acceptance of their value, 'a dearth of empirical research in Canada on restorative justice' (2003: 239). Viewed globally, informed observers estimate that, by 2000, there were some 1,300 programmes across 20 countries directed at young offenders (Umbreit *et al.* 2001: 121). In Europe, a survey of 15 countries showed remarkable variations in the numbers of VOM services in European countries: France and Germany had around 200 and 300 victim–offender services respectively, while others such as Ireland (3) and Italy (8) had very few (Mestitz 2005: 13).

While we may notice its remarkable expansion over the past two decades (Braithwaite 1999; Miers 2001; McCold and Wachtel 2003; Miers and Willemsens 2004; Aertsen *et al.* 2006), much of it indexed on various websites,[1] it needs to be recognized at the outset that the task of tracking and accounting for the international development of restorative justice and its various analogues is beset with difficulty. There is a plethora of descriptors for the varying practices that could claim to fall within its ambit. These include informal mediation, victim–offender mediation, victim–offender conferencing, victim–offender groups, family group conferencing, restorative conferencing, restorative cautioning, community conferencing, sentencing circles, tribal or village moots, community panels or courts, healing circles and other communitarian associations.[2] These descriptors naturally disguise the varying political and legal philosophies that underlie a society's or a group's preference for one type of engagement to another. It is not this chapter's purpose to capture or to comment on those preferences, which are dealt elsewhere in this book. But if reviewing the international development of restorative justice is to be a meaningful exercise, its diversity of theory and practice must be accommodated, lest the exercise does not become merely a matter of counting heads.

Counting heads may tell us something, but it does not tell us very much. For example, the countries Mestitz identified as having a low number of victim–offender mediation centres includes Austria, which has one of the most well developed and successful programmes within Europe, and is widely regarded as a model. As Chapter 24, this volume, recounts, legislatively based conferencing schemes exist in all Australian states except Victoria. But that recognition of itself tells us very little about the salience of conferencing within those states. For that, as Maxwell and Hayes demonstrate, it is necessary to have regard at least to the numbers of conferences that are held (see also Daly's cautionary remarks (2001: 62)). So much depends on how any particular intervention may be classified as more or less restorative, and on what is meant by 'in operation'. In their attempt to capture the prevalence of restorative conferencing for juveniles in the USA, Schiff and Bazemore (2002: 178) relied on a programme's self-identification as restorative, but could not claim to provide an exhaustive count of all conferencing programmes then operating. 'In operation' can capture the spectrum from the well established, well funded and robust programmes that have already been through periods of evaluation and reform, to pilot projects that have yet to generate a meaningful referral and outcome profile: 'Some states may have a variety of programmes in several jurisdictions, while others – including some densely populated states may have one or two small projects operating within a single locality only' (Schiff and Bazemore 2002: 181). Writing of the Canadian programmes, Griffiths commented that they 'vary appreciably in the types of offences and offenders processed, the procedures for hearing cases, reaching dispositions, and imposing sanctions, and the extent to which justice system professionals are involved' (1999: 281). Generalization, a necessary step in comparative analysis, is compromised by the diversity of actual experience.

Even if we approach the exercise of trying to provide an admittedly time- and jurisdiction-limited picture of the international prevalence of restorative justice, there are many reasons why we need to be cautious about its comparative value. Three of these are mentioned here (see further, Miers and Willemsens 2004: 155–60). First, there is no obvious, exact or agreed way in which we can be clear on *what* we are counting, even if we rely only on self-identification. Given the accessibility of published laws, we could say that a jurisdiction has restorative justice provision where its specific or general laws permit or require a criminal justice official to direct given cases (whether adult or juvenile offenders) to a particular restorative intervention. In a unitary state, such as England and Wales, we could count the five new statutory procedures for juveniles introduced since 1999 as just that: five types of restorative justice intervention. Or should we focus on just one of those five, the referral order, and try to audit how it operates in the 155 local authorities that are statutorily responsible for its management? At issue is the level of generality at which that count should take place. The higher the level, and where it is focused on published legal documents, the easier the exercise, but at the expense of important nuances in its operation. In Belgium, court-ordered mediation between juvenile offenders and their victims has been authorized by the federal Juvenile Justice Act 1965, but its operation differs between the Flemish and the French provincial communities (Lemonne and Vanfraechem 2005).

The second reason is that we need also to know the *purpose* for which the count is undertaken. If this were to identify instances in which an official is mandated to refer a young offender to a restorative justice intervention, then there is only one example of such provision in England and Wales: the referral order. In New Zealand, the provisions of the Children, Young Persons and their Families Act 1989 equally mandate such referral, though this is the only form of intervention and specifies only family group conferencing. By contrast, the Belgian law is permissive; interventions may be a matter of prosecutorial or court discretion, according to the particular modality. Another purpose for which a count might be undertaken is to identify the point of time at which an intervention may occur (post-arrest, pre-trial, trial, sentencing or post-sentencing); or, again, the locus of decision-making: police, prosecution, court or correctional services. Each permutation produces a different count, and for the purpose of comparing how programmes work, it is its basis that is a key but by no means the only component.

Thirdly, many jurisdictions have poor or non-existent national registration or data collection arrangements (Lauwaert and Aertsen 2001). It may be difficult or even impossible to identify key aspects of the programmes that do exist – for example, the number of mediators available to provide victim–offender mediation services, or the number of referrals. Even where figures are available, there remain questions concerning their robustness. In Germany for example, despite the combined efforts of seven major institutes, the figures remain partial and themselves reflect only the data provided by those victim–offender mediation services that have agreed to co-operate. As this example illustrates, these lacunae can exist in longer-established programmes; nor have they necessarily been addressed in those that have been introduced more recently. This is notably the case in the European Union, where there has been a rapid development of victim–offender mediation programmes among its new and applicant member states (Miers and Willemsens 2004: 135–53). It is essential that such data are systematically gathered, preferably according to common templates, if programme evaluation and comparison are to have any value.[3]

The diversity of restorative justice provision

Many of the analyses published in recent years recognize three levels of diversity affecting the programmes under review. Comparing provision across 25 European countries, Miers and Willemsens commented that the overall picture in 2004 remained as it had been in a review conducted three years earlier (Miers 2001), one of considerable heterogeneity. They analysed and present in tabular form the programme characteristics of 17 of these European countries' provision, distinguishing its application to juvenile and adult offenders. These characteristics include details of its legal base, scope and implementation. The variations they noted between these countries' provision of victim–offender mediation continue to display, in Peters' memorable phrase, 'a diversified landscape of competing visions' (2000: 14).

If restorative justice provision varies among countries, it also varies within them. In 2004 Wilcox and Hoyle reported on the survey they had undertaken of 46 projects funded by the Youth Justice Board (YJB) in England and Wales. The projects reviewed had bid for funding and in their applications had not been directed to promote any particular restorative justice theory or model. The YJB's aim, 'to let a thousand flowers bloom', was indeed a success: the funded projects were 'a heterogeneous group in terms of types of intervention offered, method of delivery, size of project and type of training received by staff' (Wilcox and Hoyle 2004: 15). Plurality is not a vice (Daly 2003a), but it is important that when one comes to compare provision as a means of determining whether one particular restorative justice model is more or less effective than another, there is baseline agreement about those models' restorative components. This is no more than a sound prudential principle, but real dangers arise where diversity is so marked that it becomes 'almost impossible to identify what each of the programmes selected for review have in common that can be called restorative' (Roche 2001: 342; see also Daly 2002). One of the primary research obstacles that needs to be overcome when conducting programme evaluations is the presence of 'dramatically different intervention models' within the jurisdiction under review (McCold 2004).

Finally, even where clarity as to a programme's focus is established, it is necessary to mind the gap between design and delivery (Daly 2003b). Diversity in its implementation can be as much a feature of a given programme as it can be of different programmes within the same jurisdiction, and between different countries. This is so notwithstanding that they may share the same names and declared restorative objectives.

The development of restorative justice practices

National and international perspectives

As noted above, the phrase restorative justice 'means different things to different people' (Weitekamp 2002: 322). At the most general level, it is probably idle, when charting its international development, to do much more than remark on the variety of impulses that have prompted its introduction in any one country or region, even if some resonate with developments elsewhere. In Canada the first victim–offender reconciliation programme was established in Kitchener, Ontario, in 1974, when, instead of being channelled down the conventional path, arrangements were made for two teenagers who had committed a series of criminal damage offences to meet their victims, with apparently beneficial results. The Royal Canadian Mounted Police (RCMP) became closely involved in family group conferencing (FGC) with young offenders, a model later adopted as community justice forums with adults. By contrast, the Canadian aboriginal sentencing and healing circles that developed in the 1980s and 1990s sought to devolve criminal justice services to the communities affected by the offending behaviour, as part of their wider political empowerment.

Aboriginal models likewise informed New Zealand's adoption of FGC for all young offenders as a mandatory referral in nearly all instances of serious youth offending (detailed in Chapter 24, this volume). This initiative for young offenders was introduced as a deliberate attempt to relocate the collective response to juvenile offending outside the criminal justice system and within the community most closely concerned with the young person – the family. As a process whereby conflict is returned to those most directly affected by it, FGC has ideological affinities with Christie's thesis (1977), and, in its particular manifestation, 'was strongly influenced by traditional Maori concepts of conflict resolution' (Morris and Maxwell 2000: 208). The Act was a radical departure from the existing models of youth justice, a radicalism shared, but not to the same extent, by developments in Belgium and more recently in England and Wales, where, as in New Zealand, the growing victims' movement has been influential.

It is difficult to generalize the many restorative justice initiatives that have been introduced in the USA over the past 30 years. Many originated in informal, indigenous or faith-based groups, such as the Mennonites and Quakers in the 1970s, largely operating outside the formal criminal justice system. A summary of these and other victim–offender reconciliation programmes, which note the spread of victim–offender mediation and of conferencing, including police-based initiatives (McCold and Wachtel 1998), may be found in McCold (1998). Together with the descriptive and evaluative narratives of other leading authorities (Bazemore and Umbreit 2001; Bazemore and Schiff 2005), these provide a rich and extensive overview.[4]

This chapter's focus is the Balanced and Restorative Justice project (BARJ). This is an initiative of the Department of Justice's Office of Juvenile Justice and Delinquency Prevention (OJJDP). In contrast to the specific provisions of the other three jurisdictions highlighted in this chapter, BARJ 'is first and foremost a blueprint for juvenile justice reform' (Bazemore and Schiff 2004: 43). It contemplates the development within state jurisdictions of policies and practices for juvenile justice 'founded on the belief that justice is best served when the community, victim and youth receive balanced attention'.[5] The public has a right to a safe and secure community and should be protected while offenders are under juvenile justice supervision. Victims and communities should have their losses restored by the offender's actions, and victims should be empowered as active participants in the juvenile justice process. Offenders should leave the system more capable of being productive and responsible to the community. These goals are to be met through its 'balanced approach', in which these three clients – victims, offenders and communities – are treated as equal co-participants in decision-making. BARJ also differs from these other jurisdictions by the fact that restorative practice is not one of its goals, but only a contingent means of realizing them. It may be that 'there is a more or less restorative way of accomplishing juvenile justice goals' (Bazemore and Schiff 2004: 44), but that does not make BARJ a vehicle for achieving restoration. It is both wider than restorative justice in that it addresses juvenile justice as a whole, but narrower in that it addresses only part of the restorative justice agenda.

In addressing juvenile justice systems throughout the USA, BARJ has a panoptic vision of change (Bazemore and Schiff 2001). But there are many other programmes in the USA that more explicitly seek to secure restorative principles as a central element in the state's responses to youth offending (Bazemore 1999); nor does it have any application to adult offending. The survey by Schiff and Bazemore (2002: 181) reports that 48 states 'currently have some form of conferencing/dialogue programme in place' for young offenders, but as they caution, the level of activity is very variable.

Within Europe there are two striking points of similarity in the growth of restorative justice and VOM, at least in the context of youth offending. These are that its development has largely been driven by 'bottom-up' rather than 'top-down' initiatives, which also explains the fact that much of the initial activity has taken place in the absence of specific enabling laws (Mestitz 2005: 8–10). But there are, equally, important points of dissimilarity.[6] Some of these flow from the implications of the subsisting legal culture, in which the role of the prosecutor varies significantly as between the common and civil law traditions. Others flow from motives underlying its growth. In some instances, such as Norway and Sweden, the impetus sprang from ideological assumptions about the nature of unwanted conflicts and the way in which communities should respond to them (Christie 1977). In Belgium the spur for the current arrangements for juvenile mediation lay in the state's desire to manage juvenile delinquency more effectively. These arrangements entailed both theoretical reflection and the introduction of some innovative mediation models. Over the past decade or more, Belgium has developed a range of interventions that focus on diversion, reparation and attitudinal change among adult prisoners, and on alternative approaches to youth offending. But it is difficult to generalize its approach, as much depends, as noted earlier, on whether one is speaking of the provisions in the Flemish or the French communities (Lemonne and Vanfraechem 2005; Aertsen 2006).

As we will see shortly, at a pan-European level it is customary to distinguish victim–offender mediation (VOM) from restorative justice; as Miers and Willemsens (2004) show, it is only England and Wales that routinely categorizes its provision as restorative justice, even though VOM is a preferred means to its achievement. The drive behind the present range of practices directed at young offenders and introduced in the late 1990s was to create a response to youth offending that held greater promise in terms of reductions in reoffending than a system that had evidently failed in this key respect. A central element in the new regime is an emphasis on victim reparation. Each of the five new non-custodial responses (final warnings, reparation orders, action plan orders, supervision orders and referral orders) is intended to include communication between the offender and the victim, and reparation for the victim. Final warnings are managed by the police; the other four are court ordered and managed by local-authority youth offending teams, whose operating principles are generated by a new statutory body, the Youth Justice Board (see further Miers and Semenchuk 2005).

By contrast, restorative justice with adult offenders has until recently been less well developed. The Home Office is committed to its more explicit use (Home Office 2003 2005), and is currently supporting programmes that are being evaluated as random trials (Shapland et al. 2004). Conditional cautioning, introduced as a pilot project in July 2004 following the major changes to sentencing law in the Criminal Justice Act 2003, is another example of the burgeoning use of restorative justice as part of the Home Office's wider efforts to address and reduce crime.

Creating a common language

These brief and very general observations remind us that in tracking the international development of restorative justice (or of VOM), 'the greatest danger is the illusion of a common language' (Peters 2000: 15). It has sometimes been remarked that mediation is a continental European, and restorative justice an Anglo–American, concept and it has also been observed that for some European jurisdictions there is no linguistic equivalent of the Anglo–Saxon phrase 'restorative justice' (Kemény 2000: 83). But even within these broad jurisdictional preferences, there are variations. North America has traditionally been associated with the development of VOM, and within the civilian tradition, it is not the case that all jurisdictions sign up to victim–offender mediation. In Germany the provision is for offender–victim mediation, a fundamentally different value orientation.

It is not possible here to explore all the variations and their refinements in the use of these terms, but it may be useful to distinguish four dimensions along which we may distinguish their different usages: understanding, values, modalities and implementation.

By *understanding*, we may seek to capture what it is that its proponents believe or wish their preferred restorative justice provision to achieve. This may range across a wide spectrum: from the restoration of individual victims by their offenders by means of an approved modality, to the offender's reintegration in his or her community, via (measurable) changes in behaviour or attitude on the part of either offenders or victims (or both) to each other, to their self-image or to their place in the world. By *values*, we may likewise wish to identify what social, moral, ethical or legal values its proponents consider underpin or are reinforced by particular restorative interventions. Here too, as other chapters in this book illustrate, there is no single answer.

Modalities refer to the forms that restorative justice assumes, whether directly sanctioned by law or indirectly by administrative practice that conforms to the legal culture. Reparation orders, restorative cautioning, family group conferencing and the other familiar forms described in this book all need to be distinguished, as do the understanding and the values that underpin them if, first, the development and, secondly, the effects (good or bad) of restorative justice interventions are to be evaluated. By *implementation*, we mean the means by which given modalities are delivered. This includes the institutional and financial context in which the modalities' gatekeepers operate, the identification of who is responsible for the individual application of given restorative interventions, under what conditions, with what objectives and with what results.

Structure

This section comments on the two structural elements of any restorative justice programme: its design and its delivery. Design principally implies such matters as whether the authority for intervention arises from specific legal provision or the exercise of law enforcement agencies' routine discretion (legal base), and to what types of offence, offender and victim the programme applies (scope). Delivery concerns responsibility for initiating and implementing the programme in any case, together with the establishment, funding, practice and intervention types (modalities) of the responsible agencies. I begin with some general observations before turning to an analysis of the particular jurisdictions reviewed in this chapter.

Why structure matters

Reflecting the variety of restorative justice practice, there is a variety of analyses that attempt to map the degree to which that practice might be considered restorative. McCold and Wachtel (2003), for example, present a continuum across fully, mostly and partly restorative, and allocate particular practices to those headings. Thus family group conferencing is classified as 'fully', victim–offender mediation as 'mostly' and compensation as 'partly' restorative. This classification is debatable, but that is not a debate to be pursued here. The point is that to understand the development of restorative justice it is necessary to have *some* analytical grasp if the diversity of practice is not to overwhelm the observer.

Another attempt to exert that grasp is Van Ness's (2003) presentation of a number of tests by which we might choose to evaluate restorative justice programmes. These tests relate to their degree of 'restorativeness' as demonstrated by their adherence to four value dimensions: encounter, amends, reintegration and inclusion. For each, there is a continuum, from a greater to a lesser degree of adherence to that value. One programme may be equally strong or weak across all four, another strong in one value but weak in another. These four dimensions can be conceived as ideal types whose possible correspondence to particular forms of restorative design and delivery Van Ness presents diagrammatically. On the basis of this analysis, he develops maximal and minimal restorative justice systems. These have explanatory, normative and evaluative force, in terms both of their design and their delivery.[7]

In terms of design, it becomes possible, first, to explain how any one system conforms to what its proponents might regard as optimal restorativeness, according to their understanding and their values. Secondly, that explanation can be used to demonstrate, for example to a jurisdiction looking for advice, how to design a system that yields (assuming effective delivery) that particular level of restorativeness. Lastly, this analysis can evaluate those design elements in any one system that are likely to impede or inhibit restorativeness.

Well chosen and well constructed design will not yield the preferred outcomes if the delivery is wanting. In the same way as design can be analysed, delivery can be explained, presented as a model or evaluated in terms of its potential to meet the preferred understanding. In addition, delivery (effective or ineffective) can be mapped against design (well or badly chosen and constructed); again to the same purposes, to explain, to evaluate or to recommend a particular combination. 'Ensuring programme integrity is vital for researchers if they are to avoid concluding restorative justice has "failed", when the blame may rightly lie with faulty design and implementation' (Wilcox and Hoyle 2004: 15).

National perspectives

While we may keep in mind Van Ness's heuristic, comparative analysis of the programme characteristics of provision for restorative justice and victim–offender mediation discloses features both of homogeneity and heterogeneity along each dimension of design and delivery. Whether the generalizations that can be drawn are sufficient to inform, for example, the EU Council's drive to realize its universal provision by all member states is a matter of conjecture (European Union: 2001). This has not, however, dissuaded countries without such provision from seeking to explain, model and evaluate what elements of design and delivery that are currently on offer are more likely than not to meet the desired restorative values in their own case. We now turn to consider in detail the structure of restorative provision in the four jurisdictions under review.

Belgium

In the case of their design, the legal base for court-ordered mediation between victims and young offenders is indirectly authorized by the Juvenile Justice Act 1965. This gives the court power to impose a 'philanthropic or educational service' as a condition of placing a young offender under the supervision of the social services. Mediation is assumed to fall within this power. However, mediation as a diversionary measure appears to have no legal base, save as an exercise of the discretion that the public prosecutor enjoys in respect of any case referred for prosecution. In 2005 the Belgian federal government introduced modifications to the Juvenile Justice Act, which, while maintaining the traditional youth protection rationale, give prominence to restorative approaches such as mediation and conferencing.

The scope of the interventions directed at young offenders in Belgium has embraced both offences against property and against the person, but their orientation has varied: some agencies have sought to pay equal attention to the needs of victims and those of young offenders; most have been more offender oriented. Delivery of interventions is provided by a number of different services. These include special youth care, co-operative initiatives by public services, non-governmental organizations (NGOs) and judicial institutes, and services set up specifically to start alternative measures for juveniles. Mediators are employed by the special youth care services, local public service or by autonomous organizations. For juvenile offenders, the mediation process is much the same for all projects and follows the universal protocols concerning contact and consent. By contrast, the content of the agreements that result from mediation varies markedly. They can contain elements of financial reparation, symbolic reparation (e.g. apologies) and direct forms of reparation (e.g. work for the victim).

In the case of adult offenders there are four possible types of mediation, which, in contrast to the earlier position, all now have a legal basis. In respect of penal mediation the specific legal regulation comprises Article 216 of the Code of Criminal Procedure (introduced by law in 1994), a Royal Decree of 1994 concerning its implementation and two departmental circulars issued by the Ministry of Justice in 1994 and 1999. In June 2005, a new, more generally oriented law on mediation in criminal cases was enacted. This regulates the three other types: mediation for redress, mediation at the police stage and mediation during detention. It is useful to focus on one of these, by way of example. The law on mediation for redress is based on a clear restorative justice philosophy, defining mediation as a communicative process and guaranteeing the principles of confidentiality and voluntariness. Mediation is conceived as an offer or service to victims and offenders, not merely as a judicial measure, although it is established in each judicial district. Criminal justice officials have to inform parties and to make the offer available at all stages of the process, including after sentence. Only with the explicit consent of both victim and offender can information on the mediation process and outcome be communicated to the prosecutor or the judge. In the latter case, the judge must mention this in his sentence (see generally Aertsen 2006).

The form of mediation (direct and or indirect) and the intended outcomes likewise vary as between the four modalities. Two of the adult interventions (mediation at the police stage and penal mediation) are diversionary in nature. Mediation at the police stage is less oriented to the process of mediation than to the outcome of the negotiations between victims and offenders who typically know one another. Its purpose is also often intended to produce financial compensation for the victim. Penal mediation is available to the public prosecutor as a condition of the formal dismissal of the case against the offender. Despite its name, penal mediation does not necessarily involve any mediation. Its most common outcome is reparation, often linked with community service. It comprises a mix of punitive, rehabilitative and restorative elements, is 'institutionally embedded in the criminal justice system and predominantly focused on the offender' (Aertsen 2000: 174). Mediation for redress is aimed at more serious offences in which a decision to prosecute has been taken. It involves neither case dismissal nor waiver; sentencing will always follow in which the outcome of the mediation is a relevant factor. Mediation during detention is focused on establishing a process of in-depth communication between victim and offender. This modality is often used in cases where the victim and offender knew each other before the conflict had taken place; agreement on how they are to manage their relationship after release from prison is therefore an important element for discussion next to reparation.

Whether the mediation service is managed by private (mediation for redress, mediation during detention and mediation with juveniles) or public bodies (mediation at the police stage and penal mediation), the service itself is typically located in another organization. Mediation is in all cases carried out by professional mediators. The 1999 departmental circular specifies standards of good practice for penal mediation. Mediation for redress in each judicial district is based on protocols agreed by the partner agencies. But training is neither uniform nor structured. In 1998, two NGOs were established (one in Flanders and one in Wallonia) as umbrella organizations for the support and development of victim–offender mediation and restorative justice. In 2003, there were about 60 victim–offender services available throughout Belgium.

England and Wales
Since the 1970s non-custodial sentences have been available to the courts whereby offenders may be ordered to compensate or make reparation to their victims, or to perform community service, such as maintaining public property. These various options have until recently not been conceived in restorative justice terms. Other possibilities include work with prisoners and offenders on probation, but with the exception of the very recently introduced conditional caution (Criminal Justice Act 2003, s. 22), there is no specific legal basis for the use of restorative justice with adult offenders.

In the case of young offenders, the legal basis for restorative justice interventions, almost entirely diversionary in nature, was simply the discretion that police officers may lawfully exercise when deciding what action to take in the face of an offence and an identified offender. The absence of any legislative basis might have been regarded as having an enabling effect. Provided that they did not act in contravention of any court order affecting or legislation protecting the young person, these schemes could also be used in the time between a (guilty) plea being entered at court and the sentence being passed, or during a custodial or community sentence.

Restorative interventions are now governed by statute. Sections 65 and 66 of the Crime and Disorder Act 1998 introduced reprimands and final warnings, replacing the caution. They are a tiered response to first-time offending. Young offenders who receive a final warning from the police are immediately referred to a youth offending team (YOT) for the purpose of fixing with the young person a rehabilitation or 'change' programme. This must contain either an element of direct reparation to the victim or community, or victim awareness input.

Referral orders, introduced by s. 1 of the Youth Justice and Criminal Evidence Act 1999, are mandatory for most young offenders pleading guilty at their first youth court appearance.[8] The court must refer the young person to the local YOT. Its purpose is to agree on a programme of behaviour with the young person, whose aim is to prevent reoffending. The programme of behaviour is formalized as a youth offender contract. The terms and conditions of the agreement with the young person are to be guided by the principles of restorative justice. Its terms may require the offender to attend mediation sessions with the victim or 'other person' who appears to be affected by the offence, or any of the offences, for which the offender was referred.

Reparation, action plan and supervision orders are used where the young person has previous convictions. They are provided for in the Crime and Disorder Act 1998. They reflect lesser (reparation orders) to the more serious offences (supervision orders) that do not warrant a custodial sentence, but the court can require the offender to make reparation directly to the victim or indirectly to the community. An aspect of the order is designed to help young offenders understand the consequences of, and take responsibility for, their offending.

A new statutory body, the Youth Justice Board (YJB), created by s. 41 of the 1988 Act, is responsible for these options, and it has statutory oversight of youth offending teams. Also introduced by the Crime and Disorder Act 1998, YOTs are among the most far-reaching of these reforms to youth justice, replacing the earlier reliance on local authority social services departments. There is a YOT in every local authority; they are responsible for the delivery of the restorative interventions. Each has a dedicated manager and representatives from each of the police, social services, Probation Service, health and educational services. They are multi-agency organizations, which may co-opt others (for example from the voluntary sector). The final piece of the new statutory arrangements is the youth offender panel (YOP). These panels operate only in respect of referral orders. Introduced by s. 6 of the Youth Justice and Criminal Evidence Act 1999, it is the YOP that devises the exact nature of the 'contract' arising from the order. It should consist of the young person and his or her family or carers, the victim(s) if they wish to attend and a panel consisting of at least two lay members of the community advised by a YOT officer. It is hoped that the victim and his or her family or supporters will attend, but there is no obligation to do so.

Where the response is to include victim–offender mediation, it will be almost always necessary to engage one of the voluntary organizations offering mediation services. There is no state agency in England and Wales appointed or contracted for the purpose of carrying out mediation work. It has always been an activity provided by the voluntary sector and, in some areas, commercial organizations. Mediation UK, a national voluntary organization 'dedicated to developing constructive means of resolving conflicts in communities', identifies 222 mediation providers on its website.[9] Where it is undertaken within the statutory framework, restorative justice activity is funded from the budget allocated to the local YOT, itself funded by the local authority.

The YJB's guidance document on reparation orders describes the various forms that reparation may take, singly or in combination. These include a letter of apology, a meeting or restorative conference at which the nature and consequences of the offence are discussed and the offender apologizes directly to the victim, or several hours per week of practical activity which benefits the victim or the community at large. Where possible, the nature of the reparation should be linked to the offence or type of offence for which the reparation is to be made. In 2004 the Home Office published new best practice guidelines for restorative justice practitioners (Home Office 2004).

New Zealand

The restorative justice practices for young offenders provided by the 1989 Act are the responsibility of the Department of Child, Youth and Family Services. The Act's underlying principle is to encourage and support the family as the principal arbiter of decisions affecting its members. This section of this chapter focuses on the FGC arrangements for young offenders accused of offences falling within the conferencing programme's remit (see Maxwell and Hayes, Chapter 24, this volume).

The referral to the FGC is made by the police or by the court. For the offender, attendance at the conference is mandatory; for the victim, voluntary (over 90 per cent do participate). The obligatory nature of the referral for the offender, which it shares with the referral order in England and Wales, is unusual among restorative justice programmes. What it achieves is the elimination of the exercise of a variable discretion by restorative justice gatekeepers – in this case, the police (Roche 2003: 161). 'One of the distinctive features of the New Zealand model is that provision is made for a number of professionals to attend' (Roche 2003: 241). The conference is convened by a youth justice co-ordinator (from the Department of Social Welfare) in the role of facilitator. The participants include the offender, the victim and, in each case, their supporters (family, friends) and a police representative. Often a social worker or a youth advocate (a lawyer appointed by the court in the case of young persons who are arrested) may also be present.

The conference is required to focus on the young person's offending behaviour and the matters related to its surrounding circumstances. In particular offenders are encouraged to accept responsibility for their actions. The Act also requires the conference to take account of the victim's interests and to try to persuade the offender to make amends. These objectives are sought through a meeting that is intended to be inclusive, flexible and sensitive to changes in the victim's and offender's response to the offence and to each other. There may be breaks during the conference to enable the victim's and the offender's family to discuss privately what outcomes to propose. Agreements may include apologies, work in the community, reparation or participation in an offender-oriented programme. The first two outcomes are the most common; financial reparation, by reason of young offenders' limited means, is the least common.

The conference may be followed by an appearance at the Youth Court if the participants agree that there should be a prosecution. This may also occur where, since no young person can be arrested unless there was at the time of the offence a danger that he or she would abscond or interfere with witnesses or evidence, the offender was in fact arrested. In these two cases the court has a duty to review, confirm (or amend) and monitor compliance with the conference outcome. In other cases, this last duty falls to the Department for Social Welfare.

The USA: the Balanced and Restorative Justice (BARJ) project

BARJ was initially funded by an Office of Juvenile Justice and Delinquency Prevention (OJJDP) grant to the Florida Atlantic University, which in 1994 engaged also the Center for Restorative Justice and Mediation at the University of Minnesota. The project team is led by Gordon Bazemore and Mark Umbreit. In this respect, the academic management of the project echoes the pioneering work undertaken by the Catholic University of Leuven in Belgium, albeit that was on a smaller scale.

As noted, BARJ is not a jurisdiction-specific programme, but an action-oriented vision of an alternative community justice response to juvenile offending that its proponents encourage juvenile justice systems throughout the USA to adopt. It is emphatically not intended to be an addition to existing practices and policies, but a replacement for them. In this respect it is prescriptive, but its proponents recognize that, within its framework for strategic planning, implementation should be guided by the needs of each jurisdiction and its community members. The project team facilitates conversion by discussing model development and the reorientation of existing systems to embrace the BARJ philosophy, and by a programme of national training and technical assistance. These engagements are in turn supported by a suite of training materials. By 2005 the BARJ project had worked with some 50 juvenile justice systems across 35 states.

The BARJ website has advocated three 'programme trends',[10] of which perhaps only the first would be immediately recognized by restorative practice practitioners elsewhere as firmly located within that tradition: restitution, community service and victim–offender mediation. The other two focus, first, on providing opportunities for offenders to improve their employment prospects so they can in turn earn a wage from which, for example, compensation to the victim can be deducted. This reordering of the offender's life into gainful employment is one means by which this 'programming trend' (work experience, active learning and service) serves to locate the offender in civil society, able publicly to demonstrate a commitment to competent and productive behaviour. The second, intermediate, community-based surveillance and sanctioning systems, maintains this theme. The 'intensive structuring' of the offender's time towards productive activities having value for the community, such as building shelters for the homeless or redecorating the homes of those unable to wield their own paint-brushes, is intended to reinforce the young person's competency development and accountability to the community.

The activities that are engaged by these last two of BARJ's three 'practices and priorities' would in practice be recognizable within other jurisdictions as longstanding instances of community-based sanctions. They would also recognize them as being contemplated by more recent initiatives designed to achieve reparation of the victim or the community. What they might not recognize is the explicit focus of restorative-community justice on the broader re-education of the offender. In mobilizing 'informal social control and socialisation processes' (Bazemore and Schiff 2001: 5), the balanced approach places considerable emphasis on the offender's social, moral, educational and workplace improvement. This may include the development of competencies in computing and communication skills, and awareness of the value of good health and nutrition, exercise and safe sexual practices. In seeking to remedy deficiencies in the young person's development to date, this recalls aspects of some of the Belgian provision for young offenders, but is remote from the aspirations of the restorative justice interventions prevailing in England and Wales as well as in New Zealand.

Intervention models

Theory

A number of models have been advanced that aim to situate a country's restorative justice provision within or alongside its conventional criminal justice structures. We focus here on two of these, proposed by Groenhuijsen (2000) and Van Ness (2003). These models may be used both for normative and for descriptive purposes. Where they are normative, they represent an ideal to which a society should aspire: typically, that the conventional criminal justice system should be replaced both in its design and its delivery by a restorative ideology. This is Van Ness's 'unified model', in which 'the restorative system is the only option. It is capable of handling all eventualities, including situations in which parties refuse to co-operate voluntarily' (Van Ness 2003: 16). It is probably true to say that no restorative justice provision is of this kind; certainly not known to this author. By way of a variation on this extreme, Van Ness identifies a 'safety net' model, in which the orientation is towards unification, but the criminal justice system is engaged where the restorative approach will not work, for example where the offender disputes guilt. Others, most notably Braithwaite (1999) and Dignan (2003), have proposed models in which restorative principles are used as a first point of entry for the majority of offences for tractable offenders. Resort to the conventional pathways is reserved for the recalcitrant offender and cases where the public interest requires a system response that is not entirely determined by the wishes of victims and offenders. It is fair to say that, while many jurisdictions' provision in practice resembles this configuration, it does not yet appear to be the result of a conscious policy decision as to how the state should respond to offending behaviour.

Most common is what Van Ness calls a 'dual track' and Groenhuijsen 'integrated' provision. Under a dual-track model, 'the criminal justice and restorative systems operate side-by-side with occasional co-operation' (Van Ness 2003: 16). This co-operation occurs, in Groenhuijsen's analysis:

> when at a certain stage of the criminal procedure the case is referred to a mediator charged with reaching an agreement between victim and offender. If this is accomplished successfully, it will have an impact on the outcome of the public proceedings: either the charges will be dropped, or the agreement will affect sentencing (2000: 71).

This relationship may not be aptly described as 'integrated', which implies a greater harmony of interests, closer to but not identical with each other, as would be the case in a unified model.[11] Conversely, what amounts to 'occasional' co-operation may vary substantially as between the many countries where this 'in and out' relationship can be seen. 'Occasional' may in fact be routine for certain modalities, but one of the obvious limitations of these generalizations is that they cannot readily capture the variations within a jurisdiction. Allowing for that, this does in gross terms describe the provision to be found in the majority of European countries, including some of the modalities in Belgium and in England and Wales.[12]

Both writers identify models in which the restorative intervention operates independently of the criminal justice system, though each of them conceives this independence in somewhat different terms. Groenhuijsen identifies 'alternative' provision, and the example he gives 'happens when a case is at a very early stage diverted from the criminal justice system. Victim–offender mediation then altogether replaces any penal response to the crime committed' (2000: 72). This echoes Van Ness's 'hybrid' model, in which parts of the system exhibit strong restorative, and others, strong conventional criminal justice values. He exemplifies this independence by reference to cases where 'the typical adversarial approach applies until sentencing, and then a restorative approach is taken' (2003: 16). For Groenhuijsen this kind of independence does not comprise an alternative to the conventional approach, but an addition to it, 'used as is a complementary device, often used after the criminal trial has run its course. Usually this type of intervention is employed in instances of the most serious crime and in the prison context' (2000: 72). Specific examples are mediation during detention in Belgium and a similar programme that has operated for adult prisoners in parts of England and Wales (Miers *et al.* 2001: 42–8).

Application

In terms of understanding its international development, what value might we derive from these efforts to model the relationship between restorative justice provision and the criminal justice system of the relevant country? Van Ness was concerned to develop tools for tracking the progress of restorative programmes in achieving 'restorativeness'. Unified, safety-net, dual-track and hybrid models provide macro-level instruments by which the relationship between restorative and criminal justice systems can be described, and the potential or reality of each to realize restorative values measured. Similarly, and at a less elevated level of generality, such measures can be identified by analysis of the design and delivery characteristics of particular programmes (and, as we have seen, there may be many varieties in any one jurisdiction).

Groenhuijsen was concerned to identify the legal and procedural safeguards that ought to accompany the introduction of restorative interventions, whether as integrated, alternative or additional features of the criminal justice system. That concern prompts other possibilities. As noted earlier, there is a powerful drive to a convergence of standards, both within Europe (Council of Europe 1999; European Union 2001; Aertsen *et al.* 2004) and internationally (United Nations 2000, 2002; Porter 2005). These share a common purpose, even if their particular expression varies in its detail. They all require their member states to promote mediation in criminal cases, and to ensure that any agreement between the victim and the offender reached in the course of such mediation in criminal cases can be taken into account.

In the case of the European Union's directive, there follow a set of guidelines on which member states may construct such opportunities, or against which they may evaluate those that they have already created. These guidelines concern the legal basis of and operation of the criminal justice system in relation to mediation services, their operation and development.[13] It is plain that both the development of international standards (for example, concerning protocols for victim and offender engagement), and the subsequent mapping of individual countries' compliance with those standards are tasks that assume the clear identification of how programmes are designed and delivered. The capacity to compare restorative justice programme design and delivery across countries according to common dimensions is a necessary condition of an understanding of its local, national and international development. It is also essential if substance is to be given to such recommendations as the United Nations, for example, made in 2005, that 'states should increase the use of restorative justice processes where appropriate and consistent with international guidelines and standards' (United Nations 2005: 21).

Selected further reading

Aertsen, I., Daems, T. and Robert, L. (2006) *The Institutionalisation of Restorative Justice in a Changing Society.* Cullompton: Willan Publishing. This book comprises a theoretical analysis of the development and adoption of restorative justice set in the context of shifting and conflicting criminal justice agendas in a range of Australasian, European and North American jurisdictions.

Aertsen, I., Mackay, R., Pelikan, C., Willemsens, J. and Wright, M. (2004) *Rebuilding Community Connections: Mediation and Restorative Justice in Europe.* Strasbourg: Council of Europe Publishing. This describes and evaluates the action that the member states of the Council of Europe have taken to give effect to its 1999 recommendation for the provision of mediation in criminal cases.

Miers, D. and Willemsens, J. (eds) (2004) *Mapping Restorative Justice: Developments in 25 European Countries.* Leuven: European Forum for Restorative Justice. This text contains detailed accounts of restorative justice and VOM provision in Europe, together with an analysis of the similarities and dissimilarities between their principal characteristics.

Acknowledgements

I would like to thank Ivo Aertsen, Gordon Bazemore and Kathleen Daly for their comments on drafts of this chapter. The usual disclaimer applies.

Notes

1 In particular, http://www.voma.org/; http://www.realjustice.org/; http://www.restorativejustice.org/resources/world/; http://www.restorativepractices.org/Pages/redirect.html. A major repository of information and research is the Center for Restorative Justice and Peacemaking located at the School of Social Work, University of Minnesota. Its website (http://2ssw.che.umn.edu/rjp/) gives access to a large number of documents describing and evaluating programmes in the USA and Canada.

2 Roche (2003: Appendix A) contains a useful overview of a number of different programmes in Australia, Canada, England and Wales, New Zealand and the USA.

3 For example, that used by Roche (2003: Table 3.1); and see Mestitz (2005: 7). Within Europe, the development of such templates is particularly associated with the work of the European Forum for Restorative Justice (http://www.euforumrj.org/; see Aertsen and Willemsens 2001) and COST Action A21 (Restorative Justice Developments in Europe, http://www.euforumrj.org/projects.COST.htm).

4 The reader is advised to consult the Center for Restorative Justice and Peacemaking website for further references.

5 http://www.barjproject.org/.

6 See Miers and Willemsens (2004: 160–9) for a more detailed discussion.

7 Hayes and Daly (2003: 729) note that the South Australia Juvenile Justice project 'is exploring the dynamics of "restorativeness" among victims, offenders and their supporters'.

8 These provisions were consolidated in Part 3 of the Powers of Criminal Courts (Sentencing) Act 2000.

9 http://www.mediationuk.org.uk/.

10 http://2ssw.che.umn.edu/rjp/BARJ.htm.

11 Nor does it follow that 'dual track' or 'integrated' provision means that the working relationship between the two pathways will be smooth. Reporting on the first year of their evaluation, Shapland *et al.* (2004: viii) commented that these three new initiatives funded by the Home Office, 'working without statutory backing, have found it hard to insert themselves into the existing arrangements and cultures of criminal justice agencies' and criminal courts' patterns of working'.

12 See also Ghetti (2005: 372–3).

13 See also Department of Justice Canada, *Values and Principles of Restorative Justice in Criminal Matters* (http://fp.enter.net/restorative practices/RJValues-DOJCan.pdf) and *Restorative Justice Program Guidelines* (http://fp.enter.net/restorative practices/RJValues-DOJCan.pdf).

References

Aertsen, I. (2000) 'Victim–offender mediation in Belgium', in European Forum for Victim–offender Mediation and Restorative Justice (ed.) *Victim–Offender Mediation in Europe*. Leuven: Leuven University Press.

Aertsen, I., (2006) 'The intermediate position of restorative justice: the case of Belgium', in I. Aertsen *et al*. (eds) *The Institutionalisation of Restorative Justice in a Changing Society*. Cullompton: Willan Publishing.

Aertsen, I., Daems, T. and Robert, L. (eds) (2006) *The Institutionalisation of Restorative Justice in a Changing Society*. Cullompton: Willan Publishing.

Aertsen, I., Mackay, R., Pelikan, C., Willemsens, J. and Wright, M. (2004) *Rebuilding Community Connections: Mediation and Restorative Justice in Europe*. Strasbourg: Council of Europe Publishing.

Aertsen, I. and Willemsens, J. (2001) 'The European Forum for Victim–Offender Mediation and Restorative Justice', *European Journal on Criminal Policy and Research*, 9: 291–300.

Bazemore, G. (1999) 'Crime victims, restorative justice and the juvenile court: exploring victim needs and involvement in the response to youth crime', *International Review of Victimology*, 6: 295–320.

Bazemore, G. and Schiff, M. (2001) *Restorative Community Justice: Repairing Harm and Restoring Communities*. Cincinnati, OH: Anderson Publishing.

Bazemore, G. and Schiff, M. (2004) 'Paradigm muddle or paradigm paralysis? The wide and narrow roads to restorative justice reform (or, a little confusion may be a good thing', *Contemporary Justice Review*, 7: 37–57.

Bazemore, G. and Schiff, M. (2005) *Juvenile Justice Reform and Restorative Justice: Building Theory and Policy from Practice*. Cullompton: Willan Publishing.

Bazemore, G. and Umbreit, M. (2001) 'A comparison of four restorative justice conferencing models', *Juvenile Justice Bulletin*. Washington, DC: Office of Juvenile Justice and Delinquency Prevention.

Braithwaite, J. (1999) 'Restorative justice: assessing optimistic and pessimistic accounts', in M. Tonry (ed.) *Crime and Justice: A Review of Research. Vol. 25*. Chicago, IL: University of Chicago Press.

Christie, N. (1977) 'Conflicts as property', *British Journal of Criminology*, 17: 1–15.

Council of Europe (1999) *Mediation in Penal Matters*. Recommendation R(99)19 adopted by the Council of Ministers of the Council of Europe on 15 September 1999.

Daly, K. (2001) 'Conferencing in Australia and New Zealand', in A. Morris and G. Maxwell (eds) *Restorative Justice for Juveniles: Conferencing, Mediation and Circles*. Oxford: Hart Publishing.

Daly, K. (2002) 'Restorative justice: the real story', *Punishment and Society*, 4: 55–74.

Daly, K. (2003a) 'Making variation a virtue', in E. Weitekamp and H.-J. Kerner (eds) *Restorative Justice in Context*. Cullompton: Willan Publishing.

Daly, K. (2003b) 'Mind the gap: restorative justice in theory and practice', in A. von Hirsch *et al*. (eds) *Restorative Justice and Criminal Justice*. Oxford: Hart Publishing.

Department of Justice Canada (2000) *Restorative Justice in Canada* (available online at http://www.justice.gc.ca/en/news/conf/rst/rj.html).

Dignan, J. (2003) 'Towards a systemic model of restorative justice', in A. von Hirsch *et al*. (eds) *Restorative Justice and Criminal Justice*. Oxford: Hart Publishing.

European Union (2001) *Standing of Victims in Criminal Proceedings*. EU Council, Framework Decision, OJ L82/1 22 March 2001 (available online at http://europa.eu.int/comm/justice_home/doc_centre/criminal/victims/doc_criminalvictims_en.htm).

Ghetti, S. (2005) 'Juvenile offenders and the legal system: what we have learned from victim–offender mediation', in A. Mestitz and S. Ghetti (eds) *Victim–Offender Mediation with Youth Offenders in Europe*. Amsterdam: Springer.

Griffiths, C. (1999) 'The victims of crime and restorative justice: the Canadian experience', *International Review of Victimology*, 6: 279–94.

Groenhuijsen, M. (2000) 'Victim–offender mediation: legal and procedural safeguards. Experiments and legislation in some European jurisdictions', in European Forum for Victim–offender Mediation and Restorative Justice (ed) *Victim–Offender Mediation in Europe*. Leuven: Leuven University Press.

Hayes, H. and Daly, K. (2003) 'Youth justice conferencing and reoffending', *Justice Quarterly*, 20: 725–64.

Home Office (2003) *Restorative Justice: The Government's Strategy*. London: Home Office Communication Directorate (available online at: http://www.homeoffice.gov.uk/justice/victims/restorative/index.html).

Home Office (2004) *Best Practice Guidance for Restorative Practitioners*. London: Home Office Communications Directorate.

Home Office (2005) *Restorative Justice: Helping to Meet Local Needs: A Guide for Local Criminal Justice Boards and Agencies*. London: Home Office Communications Directorate.

Kemény, S. (2000) 'Policy developments and the concept of restorative justice through mediation', in European Forum for Victim–Offender Mediation and Restorative Justice (ed) *Victim–Offender Mediation in Europe*. Leuven: Leuven University Press.

Lauwaert, K. and Aertsen, I. (2001) 'Restorative justice: activities and expectations at European level.' Paper presented at a conference on restorative justice, Belfast, Northern Ireland.

Lemonne, A. and Vanfraechem, I. (2005) 'Victim–offender mediation in Belgium', in A. Mestitz and S. Ghetti (eds) *Victim–Offender Mediation with Youth Offenders in Europe*. Amsterdam: Springer.

McCold, P. (1998) 'Restorative justice: variations on a theme', in L. Walgrave (ed.) *Restorative Justice for Juveniles: Potentialities, Risks and Problems for Research*. Leuven: Leuven University Press.

McCold, P. (2004) 'Protocols for evaluating restorative justice programmes in a European context.' Paper presented at the *COST Action A21: Research on Restorative Justice in Europe Conference*, National Institute of Criminology, Budapest.

McCold, P. and Wachtel, B. (1998) *Restorative Policing Experiment*. Pipersville, PA: Community Service Foundation.

McCold, P. and Wachtel, T. (2003) 'Restorative justice theory validation', in E. Weitekamp and H–J. Kerner (eds) *Restorative Justice: Theoretical Foundations*. Cullompton: Willan Publishing.

Mestitz, A. (2005) 'A comparative perspective on victim–offender mediation with youth offenders throughout Europe', in A. Mestitz and S. Ghetti (eds) *Victim–Offender Mediation with Youth Offenders in Europe*. Amsterdam: Springer.

Miers, D. (2001) *An International Review of Restorative Justice. Crime Reduction Research Series* paper 10. London: Home Office.

Miers, D., Maguire, M., Goldie, S., Sharpe, K., Hale, C., Netten, A., Doolin, K., Uglow, S., Enterkin, J. and Newburn, T. (2001) *An Exploratory Evaluation of Restorative Justice Schemes. Crime Reduction Research Series* paper 9. London: Home Office.

Miers, D. and Semenchuk, M. (2005) 'Victim–offender mediation in England and Wales', in A. Mestitz and S. Ghetti (eds) *Victim–Offender Mediation with Youth Offenders in Europe*. Amsterdam: Springer.

Miers, D. and Willemsens, J. (eds) (2004) *Mapping Restorative Justice: Developments in 25 European countries*. Leuven: European Forum for Victim–Offender Mediation and Restorative Justice.

Morris, A. and Maxwell, G. (2000) 'The practice of family group conferences in New Zealand: assessing the place, potential and pitfalls of restorative justice', in A. Crawford and J. Goodey (eds) *Integrating a Victim Perspective within Criminal Justice.* Aldershot: Ashgate.

Morris, A. and Maxwell, G. (2003) 'Restorative justice in New Zealand: assessing the place, potential and pitfalls of restorative justice', in A. von Hirsch *et al.* (eds) *Restorative Justice and Criminal Justice.* Oxford: Hart Publishing.

Peters, T. (2000) 'Victim–offender mediation: reality and challenges', in European Forum for Victim–Offender Mediation and Restorative Justice (ed) *Victim–Offender Mediation in Europe.* Leuven: Leuven University Press.

Porter, A. (2005)'Restorative justice takes the world stage at United Nations Crime Congress' (available online at http://realjustice.org/library/uncrimecongress. html).

Roberts, J. and Roach, K. (2003) 'Restorative justice in Canada: from sentencing circles to sentencing principles', in A. von Hirsch *et al.* (eds) *Restorative Justice and Criminal Justice.* Oxford: Hart Publishing.

Roche, D. (2001) 'The evolving definition of restorative justice', *Contemporary Justice Review,* 43: 341–53.

Roche, D. (2003) *Accountability in Restorative Justice.* Oxford: Clarendon Studies in Criminology.

Schiff, M. and Bazemore, G. (2002) 'Restorative conferencing for juveniles in the USA: prevalence, process and practice', in E. Weitekamp and H.-J. Kerner (eds) *Restorative Justice: Theoretical Foundations.* Cullompton: Willan Publishing.

Shapland, J., Atkinson, A., Colledge, E., Dignan, J., Howes, M., Johnstone, J., Pennant, R., Robinson, G. and Sorsby, A. (2004) *Implementing Restorative Justice Schemes (Crime Reduction Programme): A Report on the First Year.* Online report 32/04 London: Home Office.

Umbreit, M., Coates, R. and Vos, B. (2001) 'Victim impact on meeting with young offenders: two decades of victim–offender mediation practice and research', in A. Morris and G. Maxwell (eds) *Restorative Justice for Juveniles: Conferencing, Mediation and Circles.* Oxford: Hart Publishing.

Umbreit, M. and Greenwood, J. (1998) *National Survey of Victim Offender Mediation Programs in the United States.* Minneapolis, MN: University of Minnesota, Center for Restorative Justice and Peacemaking.

United Nations (2000) *Commission on Crime Prevention and Criminal Justice Report on the Ninth Session (18–20 April 2000). Economic and Social Council Official Records, 2000 Supplement No. 10* (E/2000/30 E/CN.15/2000/7) (available online at http://www.un.org/documents/ecosoc/docs/2000/e2000-30.pdf).

United Nations (2002) *Economic and Social Council Official Records (1–26 July 2002)* (E/2002/INF/2/Add.2) (available online at http://www.un.org/special-rep/ohrlls/ldc/Pages%20from%20N0252842.pdf).

United Nations (2005) *Eleventh United Nations Congress on Crime Prevention and Criminal Justice: Workshop 2: Enhancing Criminal Justice Reform, Including Restorative Justice.* (A/CONF.203/10).

Van Ness, D. (2003) 'The shape of things to come: a framework for thinking about a restorative justice system', in E. Weitekamp and H.-J. Kerner (eds) *Restorative Justice: Theoretical Foundations.* Cullompton: Willan Publishing.

Weitekamp, E. (2002) 'Restorative justice: present prospects and future directions' in E. Weitekamp and H.-J. Kerner (eds) *Restorative Justice: Theoretical Foundations.* Cullompton: Willan Publishing.

Wilcox, A. and Hoyle, C. (2004) *Restorative Justice Projects: The National Evaluation of the Youth Justice Board's Restorative Justice Projects.* London: Youth Justice Board.

Chapter 24

Regional reviews

Editors' note: David Miers' chapter on the international development of restorative justice (Chapter 23, this volume) offers an important global perspective on the field. This chapter will supplement that by offering regional reviews of the development of restorative justice in Africa, Asia, Europe, Latin America, North America and the Pacific. The authors of each section review the historical growth of restorative justice, offer a brief survey of its current use and identify unique features of the field within their regions. The chapter concludes by identifying recurring themes within the regions.

Section A
Africa

Ann Skelton

Introduction

A sunny hillside in Arusha, Tanzania was the setting of Christie's 1977 article 'Conflicts as property' (1977). The article includes a description of a traditional conflict resolution process. Using this anthropological example for comparison, Christie described modern law procedures and institutions as remote from the daily experience of the average person. Christie said that conflicts, whether civil or criminal, ought to belong to the participants but they had been stolen by lawyers and other professionals. Christie argued that this theft of the conflict by the state deprives the community of 'opportunities for norm-clarification'. He proposed a conflict resolution process similar to the Tanzanian model that would be victim oriented, with appropriate reparation by the offender.

During the 1960s and 1970s there was a rediscovery of African traditional justice by Western mediation practitioners (Wright 1991: 50), with linkages being made between the modern development of mediation and the African models of conflict resolution such as the traditional moots of the Kpelle (Gibbs 1963), the Barotse (Gluckman 1967) and the Tiv (Bohannen 1957). With the development of the theory of restorative justice the connection continues to be made. Bishop Desmond Tutu has said that '[r]etributive justice is largely Western. The African understanding is far more restorative – not so much to punish as to redress or restore a balance that has been knocked askew. The justice we hope for is restorative of the dignity of the people' (Minow 1998: 51).

This chapter aims to explore the linkages between restorative justice and African traditional justice, and to provide some case study examples of restorative justice in African countries. It does not aim to describe the traditional justice systems in all African countries but, rather, to capture common themes in the many systems that do exist. The examples are illustrative and not intended to be an audit of all the restorative justice projects and processes that may be underway.

The links between restorative justice and African traditional approaches to conflict resolution

Several writers around the world have underscored the fact that restorative justice accords well with indigenous conflict resolution approaches (Yazzie and Zion 1996; Consedine 1999, Lilles 2001). Traditional courts still operate in many parts of Africa today, mostly in rural areas. With the emphasis on 'problems' rather than offences, these structures hear the stories of the parties involved and then make decisions regarding outcomes. These outcomes aim to heal relationships, and they ensure restitution or compensation to victims. Symbolic gestures, such as sacrifice of animals and the sharing of a meal, indicate that the crime has been expiated and the offender can now be reintegrated (Kgosimore 2002: 69).

African traditional justice is widely underpinned by a philosophy known as *ubuntu* or *utu*. Mafeje has said that the term is not translatable into English, but identifies the core qualities of the concept as 'human sympathy, willingness to share and forgiveness' (2000: 2).

Penal Reform International identifies the salient features of African non-state traditional justice systems as follows:

- The problem is viewed as that of the whole community or group.
- There is an emphasis on reconciliation and restoring social harmony.
- Traditional arbitrators are appointed from within the community.
- There is a high degree of public participation.
- Customary law is merely one factor considered in reaching a compromise.
- The rules of evidence and procedure are flexible.

- There is no professional legal representation.
- The process is voluntary and the decision is based on agreement.
- There is an emphasis on restorative penalties.
- Enforcement of decisions is secured through social pressure.
- The decision is confirmed through rituals aimed at reintegration.
- Like cases need not be treated alike (2001: 22).

All these features accord with the modern understanding of restorative justice, although recent developments concerning minimum standards may raise some issues for debate.

Examples of African traditional approaches influencing restorative processes at a national level

The link between traditional justice and restorative justice processes is not only relevant in relation to crimes or disputes between individuals. There are two prominent examples in which African traditional approaches have formed the basis of processes to resolve the harms arising from conflicts at a national level.

The first of these is the Truth and Reconciliation Commission (TRC) in South Africa. The spirit of *ubuntu* (humanity to others) has been described as having been at the heart of the decision to go the route of the TRC in South Africa (Boraine 2000: 425). An interim constitution was drafted by the negotiating parties in 1993, which set out the rationale for the TRC. The post-amble to the interim constitution claimed that the constitution provided a foundation for South Africans to transcend the divisions of the past, which had generated violations of human rights and had led to a legacy of hatred, fear, guilt and revenge. The post-amble goes on to say: 'These can now be addressed on the basis that there is a need for understanding but not for vengeance, a need for reparation but not for retaliation, a need for ubuntu but not for victimisation.'

The second example is the use of *gacaca* in Rwanda. *Gacaca* means grass and refers to a traditional 'meeting of neighbours seated on the grass for the purpose of settling litigation between the inhabitants of the neighbourhood' (Penal Reform International 2001: 73). *Gacaca* in post-conflict Rwanda is based on that old practice, but has been resurrected to address a number of genocide-related crimes. Having realized that it would take many decades to bring all the accused to trial in Western-style courts, the government set up new tribunals based on the traditional system of justice in Rwanda, in which elected members of the public ('people of integrity') participate in deciding on the appropriate penalties.

Although neither of these processes is fully restorative (Zehr 1997: 6), they both indicate an inclination on the part of African countries to find their own solutions to conflict, based loosely on traditional approaches, in order to promote healing in their countries.

Law reform and practice examples of the application of restorative justice in African juvenile justice systems

The following juvenile justice systems in sub-Saharan Africa provide examples of the application of restorative justice to law and practice.

Uganda

Uganda was one of the first countries to bring its laws in line with the Convention on the Rights of the Child. The Children's Statute, passed in 1996, includes both child protection and child justice issues, and its general approach is to ensure that families and communities are involved, with the formal system coming in only as a last resort.

In 1987, 'resistance committees', which had developed as informal dispute resolution structures, were given formal recognition as part of the legal system and renamed 'local council courts'. The Children's Statute gave jurisdiction to the local council courts at village level regarding civil matters and criminal matters where children are accused of affray, common assault, actual bodily harm, theft, trespass and malicious damage to property. The local council courts can use the following remedies: reconciliation, compensation, restitution, apology, caution or a guidance order of up to six months.

Legal recognition of the local council courts is an important starting point for making the child justice system in Uganda more restorative, because it brings the victim and offender together in a forum that is managed by the community. The outcomes permitted under the statute are very typical of restorative justice outcomes and focus on healing and restoring rather than on punishment.

A limitation of the system is the limited jurisdiction of the local council courts, as they can only deal with rather petty offences. All other cases must go to the family and children's courts, and capital cases such as murder, rape and defilement end up in the mainstream system.

The Ugandan model is one in which a separate restorative justice track is linked to, or interdependent with, the formal juvenile justice system. The linkage is seen in two ways – the formal system has predetermined which cases the restorative track can handle and, secondly, cases handled by the local council courts at village level can be appealed through the formal system, all the way up to the Supreme Court.

South Africa

Family group conferencing
Despite the fact that there has been no legal framework to allow for family group conferencing (FGC), there have been various pilot projects. An important one was set up by the Inter-ministerial Committee on Young People at Risk in 1996. The project was evaluated and the findings published in a document that is both a practice research study and an implementation manual (Branken and Batley 1998).

In this project, FGCs were established as diversionary alternatives for juveniles. The project sought to divert cases involving offending deemed to be relatively serious, such as assault, theft of and out of motor vehicles, house-breaking and robbery. The research study raised interesting issues, which are particularly relevant to the South African context, and perhaps to some other African countries. For example, the project experienced difficulties regarding interpretation when the victims and offenders spoke different languages. Where interpreters were used it was found that the facilitator's role was weakened. Nevertheless, the stories which emerged from the project richly illustrated the healing possibilities of FGCs. Furthermore, the implementation manual from the project has been used for training probation officers running FGCs. The National Institute for Crime Prevention and the Reintegration of Offenders (NICRO) has also used it to train its employees, who are running about 400 FGCs per year as a diversion option around the country.

Child Justice Bill

Lessons learnt from this use of FGCs were incorporated in the Child Justice Bill (B-49 of 2002), which was introduced into Parliament in 2003 (at the time of writing it has been debated in Parliament but not yet passed). The bill includes an objectives clause that focuses on *ubuntu* and restorative justice. Children can be referred to restorative justice processes during the pre-trial phase, during trial or as part of the sentencing process. In addition to the possibility of referral to a family group conference, the bill also allows for referral to a 'victim–offender mediation or other restorative justice process'. This is to allow for creative or indigenous models of restorative justice procedures to be developed or to re-emerge (Skelton 2002: 503).

Namibia

The child justice system in Namibia is also undergoing change. A bill has been drafted based on principles of restorative justice, but at the time of writing the bill has not been placed before Parliament.

Despite the lack of an enabling legal framework, however, there has been substantial work done in the area of diversion. The Juvenile Justice project of the Legal Assistance Centre offers a diversion option called 'consensus decision making,' which is described by Schulz as follows:

> This is a therapeutic process which is used at the pre-trial stage, following a referral by a prosecutor. The victim, the offender and their families are brought together to discuss the offence, their feelings, and the restorative effort that each party can make. A Juvenile Justice Project staff member, who acts as a mediator, facilitates the meeting between the parties. It is designed to allow the victim and offender an opportunity to reconcile and mutually agree on reparation (2002: 363).

Ghana

Ghana's Children's Act (Act 560 of 1998) makes provision for the establishment of child panels at the district or community level. The panel is intended to assist with victim–offender mediation (VOM) in minor criminal matters involving the child, the outcomes of which may include an apology, restitution or service to the victim. The regulations to the Act were published in 2002, and thus far there are only ten children's panels operating (Sloth-Nielsen and Gallinetti 2004: 90).

Lesotho

Qhubu (2005) speaks of restorative justice being 'revived' in Lesotho 'because it is a common feeling in our country that only the name is new to Basotho while the practice has always been there'. The probation services began to pilot FGCs and VOMs as diversion programmes for young offenders in 1999, with very positive results. Consequently, probation is using restorative justice strategies with adult offenders as part of community-based sentencing, 22 principal chiefs have been trained in restorative justice and a draft bill has been prepared (Child and Protection Welfare Bill 2004) containing restorative justice features.

General examples of the restorative justice programmes or processes

Victim–Offender mediation and conferencing

NICRO was the first organization in South Africa to begin VOM, in 1992. This followed a trip by a NICRO employee to the USA where he was hosted by the Mennonite Central Committee. From the outset, the conferencing was described as 'restorative justice' and NICRO employees were trained to facilitate the conferences in all provinces (interview with Lukas Muntingh 2004).

In 2001, a group of South African non-governmental organizations (NGOs) under the banner of the Restorative Justice Initiative established a victim–offender conferencing (VOC) project, which focused on the resolution of disputes between parties that were criminal in nature. This operated in a partnership with three community-based organizations in township areas (Dissel 2003).

The aims and objectives of the project were to enable people affected by a crime to enter into dialogue about the event and what had led up to it, and to develop a plan for dealing with the consequences of the act and the harm caused to any of the parties. The project also sought to develop a model that drew on the experiences and principles of African customary traditions. The principles underpinning VOC are described as follows:

- *Acknowledging the injustice*: the offender needs to acknowledge responsibility for the offence before being referred to VOC.

- *Restoring the equity*: a delicate process of levelling the power imbalances that exist between offender and victim as a result of the offence or the nature of the relationship between them.

- *Addressing the future*: developing an appropriate and concrete plan of action acceptable to all parties concerned.

The project was set up by selecting and training mediators from each of the communities associated with the VOC partners. Cases were referred to the VOC partners by the courts, the police and community-based organizations. In all cases the mediators undertook screening and preparation of the parties (Dissel 2003).

The Community Peace programme

The Community Peace programme's first project was in a local community in Zwelethemba, a township 120 km from Cape Town. The peace committees are made up of local township residents who undertake both peace making and peace building. *Peace making* focuses on resolving specific conflicts, while *peace building* aims to address the underlying problems in the community, such as poverty and lack of access to services. Peace-making activities deal with a range of legal disputes – including civil as well as criminal matters. Most of their referrals come directly from the community, not from the police or courts. Furthermore, there is no requirement that anyone should make admissions up front, which makes these forums different from most modern forms of restorative justice processes, but similar to more traditional structures. Outcomes of the peace-making meetings are restorative in nature: apologies, restitution and compensation. But the peace-building initiatives take the process even further by looking at the wider issues affecting the community and trying to resolve these problems in an attempt to avoid a reoccurrence of conflict (Shearing 2001; Roche 2002). (For more information on this project, see Chapter 25, this volume.)

African Transformative Justice project

The Prisoners Rehabilitation and Welfare Action (PRAWA) was founded in 1994. One of its objectives is the implementation of restorative justice practices that are sensitive to African cultural traditions. Their African Transformative Justice project has set up pilot projects in Nigeria, Gambia and Ghana. These projects have two phases: education and training in victim–offender mediation followed by the opening of mediation centres in each country. In Gambia, local chiefs participated in the training, and mediation and peace centres opened in two Gambian cities in June and August 2002. In the opening ceremony at Brikama, the acting Deputy-Solicitor General described the project as being very similar to African traditional practice.

Restorative justice and penal reform

> African countries have been giving serious thought to alternatives to imprisonment arguing that the more traditionally accepted measures of restitution, compensation and (affordable) fines be adopted as the main penal measures in place of imprisonment, particularly as the African cannot appreciate a treatment like imprisonment which, if it benefits at all, is benefiting only the government, in total disregard of the victim and the African need to maintain social equilibrium (Adeyemi 1994).

The Kampala Declaration and Plan of Action on Prison Conditions in Africa

An important conference took place in Uganda in September 1996 at which 40 African countries drafted the Kampala Declaration on Prison Conditions in Africa (and the plan of action linked thereto), which was officially noted by the Economic and Social Council of the United Nations on 21 July 1997 (Resolution 1997/36). Some of the commitments were as follows:

• Petty offences should be dealt with according to customary practice or mediation without recourse to the formal system.
• There should be recompense to the victim.
• There should be a study of successful African models and a feasibility study about using them in other countries.

The Ouagadougou Declaration and Action Plan on Accelerating Prison and Penal Reform in Africa

A second pan-African conference on prisons was held in Ouagadougou, Burkina Faso, in September 2002. It was attended by 123 delegates from 38 countries. The objectives were to assess the progress made since 1996 and to explore further new African models for dealing with offenders and ways of influencing policy at national and international levels. The conference drafted the Ouagadougou Declaration and Action Plan on Accelerating Prison and Penal Reform in Africa, which was adopted by the African Commission on Human and People's Rights, in its 34th Ordinary Session held in Banjul, Gambia, 6–20 November 2003.

The work of Penal Reform International (PRI) in Africa on community service schemes

Much work has been done by Penal Reform International on the introduction of community service as an alternative to imprisonment. While community service falls short of being fully restorative due to the fact that it generally lacks an 'encounter' between the offender and the victim, it can be said to focus on reparation to the community, and sometimes the work is done directly for the victim.

PRI support of community service schemes in Africa started with its close association with the Zimbabwe Community Service scheme from its inception in 1992. By December 2000, 41,000 offenders in Zimbabwe had been sentenced to a community service order instead of to prison (Penal Reform International 2001). On the strength of this success, PRI obtained further funding from the European Union to help with the implementation of community service schemes in Kenya, Malawi, Uganda, Zambia, Burkino Faso, Congo-Brazzaville, the Central African Republic and Mozambique.

In 1997, a conference entitled 'International conference on community service orders in Africa', organized by PRI, in collaboration with the Zimbabwe National Committee on Community Service, issued the Kadoma Declaration and Plan of Action on Community Service, together with a Code of Conduct for National Committees on Community Service.

Conclusion

It is undeniable that traditional African justice systems have many features that can be characterized as restorative. Many of these systems have been weakened or over-ridden because of colonization, and modern African states are grappling with questions of how to harmonize these systems with the statutory and common law legal framework (Schärf and Nina 2001). It has become evident, however, that the rich history of conflict resolution offers fertile ground for restorative justice, and restorative initiatives are being enthusiastically embraced throughout the region.

References

Adeyemi, A. (1994) 'Personal reparations in Africa: Nigeria and Gambia', in U. Zvekic (ed.) *Alternatives to Imprisonment in Comparative Perspective*. Chicago, IL: Wadsworth.

Allott, A. (1977) 'The people as law makers: custom, practice and public opinion as sources of law in Africa and England', *Journal of African Law*, 1: 21–39.

Bohannen, P. (1957) *Justice and Judgment amongst the Tiv*. London: Oxford University Press.

Boraine, A. (2000) *A Country Unmasked: The Story of South Africa's Truth and Reconciliation Commission*. Cape Town: Oxford University Press.

Braithwaite, J. (2002) 'Setting standards in restorative justice', *British Journal of Criminology*, 42: 563–77.

Branken, N. and Batley, M. (1998) *Family Group Conferences: Putting the Wrong Right*. Pretoria: Inter Ministerial Committee in Young People at Risk.

Christie, N. (1977) 'Conflicts as property', *British Journal of Criminology*, 17: 1–19.

Consedine, J. (1999) *Restorative Justice: Healing the effects of crime*. Lyttleton: Ploughshares Publications.

Dissel, A. (2003) 'Giving a face to crime: report on the second phase of the RJI initiative victim offender conferencing' (Unpublished paper available online at www.csvr.org.za/papers/htm).

Gibbs, J. (1963) 'The Kpelle Moot', *Africa*: 1–10.

Gluckman, M. (1967) *The Judicial Process among the Barotse of Northern Rhodesia*. Manchester: Manchester University Press.

Kgosimore, D. (2002) 'Restorative justice as an alternative to dealing with crime', *Acta Criminologica*, 15: 69–82.

Lilles, H. (2001) 'Circle sentencing: part of the restorative justice continuum', in A. Morris and G. Maxwell (eds) *Restorative Justice for Juveniles: Conferencing, Mediation and Circles*. Oxford: Hart Publishing.

Johnstone, G. (2002) *Restorative Justice: Ideas, Values, Debates*. Cullompton: Willan Publishing.

Mafeje, A. (2000) 'Africanity: a combative ideology', *Codesria Bulletin*, 1: 1–5.

Minow, M. (1998) *Between Vengeance and Forgiveness*. Boston, MA: Beacon Press.

Parker, L. (2002) 'African NGO works for transformation in the justice system' (available online at http/www.restorativejustice.org/editions/2002/nov02/africanngo).

Penal Reform International (2001) *Access to Justice in Sub-Saharan Africa*. London: Penal Reform International.

Penal Reform International (2003) 'PRI support to community service programmes in Africa' (available online at www.penalreform.org).

Petty, C. and Brown, M. (1998) *Justice for Children: Challenges for Policy and Practice in Sub-Saharan Africa*. London: Save the Children.

Qhubu, N. (2005) 'The devlopment of restorative justice in Lesotho.' Paper presented at the Association of Law Reform Agencies for Eastern and Southern Africa conference, Cape Town, 14–17 March.

Roche, D. (2002) 'Restorative justice and the regulatory state in South African townships', *British Journal of Criminology*, 42: 514–33.

Schärf, W. and Nina, D. (2001) *The Other Law: Non-state Ordering in South Africa*. Lansdowne: Juta.

Schulz, S. (2002) 'Juvenile justice in Namibia – a system in transition', in J. Winterdyk (ed.) *Juvenile Justice Systems*. Toronto: Canadian Scholars' Press.

Shearing, C. (2001) 'Transforming security: a South African experiment', in H. Strang and J. Braithwaite (eds) *Restorative Justice and Civil Society*. Cambridge: Cambridge University Press.

Skelton, A. (2002) 'Restorative justice as a framework for juvenile justice reform: a South African perspective', *British Journal of Criminology*, 2: 496–513.

Skelton, A. and Frank, C. (2001) 'Conferencing in South Africa: returning to our future', in A. Morris and G. Maxwell (eds) *Restorative Justice for Juveniles: Conferencing, Mediation and Circles*. Oxford: Hart Publishing.

Sloth-Nielsen, J. and Gallinetti, J. (eds) (2004) *Child Justice in Africa: A Guide to Good Practice*. Cape Town: Community Law Centre.

South African Law Reform Commission. (2000), *Report on Juvenile Justice* (project 106). Pretoria: South African Law Reform Commission.

Wright, M. (1991) *Justice for Victims and Offenders: A Restorative Response to Crime*. Milton Keynes: Open University Press.

Yazzie, R. and Zion, J. (1996) 'Navajo restorative justice: the laws of equality and justice', in B. Galaway and J. Hudson (eds) *Restorative Justice: International Perspectives*. Monsey, NY: Criminal Justice Press.

Zehr, H. (1997) 'When justice and healing go together', *Track Two*, 6: 20 (available online at http://ccrweb.crr.uct.ac.za/two/6-34).

Section B
Asia

Ping Wang, Xiaohua Di and King Hung Wan

The term 'restorative justice' is new in Asia, but the concept is deeply embedded and rooted in Asian heritage. In the past, village people preferred peaceful, informal ways of resolving disputes, and resorted to court only as last resort. That was true at one time in the West, of course, but over time Europeans and Americans began to prefer courts and criminal justice (Zehr 1990). This preference reflects the attitudes of the respective cultures towards conflict resolution. Figure 24.1 depicts the perspectives of both cultures on conflict.

Conflict avoidance gossip forebearance termination of relationship	Informal discussion problem-solving	Negotiation and conciliation	Mediation	Arbitration	Judicial or legislative decision	Non-violent direct-action	Violence

		ASIA					Last resort
Last resort		WESTERN					

Private/relational-based decision-making by parties	Private third-party decision- making	Legal (public) authoritative third-party decision-making	Extra-legal coerced decision-making

Figure 24.1 Asian and Western perspectives on conflict resolution
Source: Adapted from Duryea and Grundison (1993: 1)

Several Chinese proverbs reflect the Asian philosophy of conflict resolution: 'If you have not fought with each other, you do not know each other'; 'Sacrificing your little self for the greater self; it is better to have less trouble than to create more.' Regarding the justice system, the classical motto is 'avoid the official gates in this life and you will avoid the gates of hell in the next life' (Augsburger 1992). Traditional orientals would be very surprised if family members or acquaintances reported a crime committed by a relative or friend to the police. They would conceal the crime because of their beliefs in family honour, the family name and family face-saving. It should be noted that Westerners and the Chinese mean something different when they use the term 'mediation' (Clarke 1991: 245–96). For the Chinese in the People's Republic of China (PRC), some mediators explain the intentions behind laws and government policies and try to persuade the disputants to comply. They sometimes educate, criticize and effectively persuade disputants to accept a solution (Cloke 1987: 73–4). One has to understand that the traditional Chinese concept of mediation is highly malleable. It may be characterized, at one and the same time, as a flexible procedure of concessions and compromises, and as a coercive aspect of adjudication (Moser 1982: 2). This coercive, arbitrative nature of traditional Chinese mediation is sometimes inconsistent with mediator neutrality as professed in Western practice (Chan 2003: 4). Further, in a collectivist tradition, hierarchy is important: 'Male and female roles are defined differently in Asia than in the West. Our [Anglo-Saxon] mediation model with its emphasis on "empowering" the less assertive party may be inappropriate or ineffective in the context of People's Republic of China' because traditional Chinese tend to expect mediators to be active and directive in giving advice (Duryea and Grundison 1993: 19; Yeo 1993: 30). Furthermore, venting one's feelings and interests publicly in a way that makes one vulnerable does not accord with the values of harmony, self-control, and collectivity that are important to Asians (Duryea and Grundison 1993: 21). Other examples of differences between the two cultures are given in Table 24.1 (Cartledge 1996: 94–5, 99).

Table 24.1 Differences between Asian and Western cultures

Asian	Western
Restraint is internalized according to family values. Feelings of guilt or shame can be a powerful means of social control	Restraint comes from external sources. Both achievement and failure are attributed to the individual
Harmony is the basic rule guiding interaction with others	Sincerity is emphasized
Self-expression or feelings that may cause conflict are not encouraged but are restrained in the interest of harmonious relationships	Self-expression and feelings are encouraged, with emphasis on the value of the individual
Individualism is seen as selfish or inconsiderate towards other family members	An individual-centred society; individualism, independence and self-sufficiency are stressed
A collectivistic and affective perspective	An individualistic and rational perspective
A soft attitude towards resolving conflicts	A less tolerating and compromising attitude towards resolving conflicts
Rigid social norms	Less rigid and more flexible norms
Person-oriented government and loose legal system. Emphasis on affection (*qing*) and reasoning (*li*). Law is but human affection	Constitutional government and public institutionalized law. Emphasis on law
Saving face is a priority in order to avoid personal or group embarrassment, loss of dignity and harmony. Individuals may avoid giving direct criticism, disagreeing, or offering unsolicited suggestions. Prefer flight to fight. Could leave or avoid a situation of conflict, confrontation or embarrassment. Interpret criticism, offers of advice, direct confrontation and expression of emotion as lacking maturity, subtlety, respect	Confrontation, embarrassment, conflict and loss of dignity may be temporarily acceptable in order to correct a situation and resolve a problem. Individuals may accept and use direct criticism, disagree or offer unsolicited suggestions. Prefer fight to flight in situations of confrontation. Expression of emotion. Interpret aversion to confrontation and criticism, to giving advice and suggestions or to showing emotions as lack of commitment, motivation, confidence, enthusiasm or knowledge
An individual may consider it inappropriate to elaborate or volunteer information when asked a question. Consider it more respectful to answer exactly what was asked and wait for a more detailed question, especially with persons in positions of authority	An individual may expect to provide all relevant information in answer to one question only

Table 24.1 continues opposite

Table 24.1 continued

Asian	Western
Hierarchical – people do not see themselves as having social and political equality	Egalitarian – people see themselves as having social and political equality
Interdependence is highly valued. Everyone has clear expectations for his or her relationships with others	Independence is highly valued
Relationships are more important than time	Punctuality is important
Communication is indirect and roundabout	Messages are direct and explicit

Of course, one should be careful when stereotyping or generalizing about a culture because of the internal differences that are likely within that culture.

The links between restorative justice and Asian approaches to dispute settlement

Three basic forms of dispute resolution in Asia are linked to restorative justice in theory or practice.

Customary/indigenous law

Customary law (*hokum adat*) is still used in many communities in Indonesia, although not in all. While it is principally applied in civil matters, it is also used in instances of malicious mischief, theft of religious facilities, defamation, incest and adultery. Its use is also permitted for purposes of maintaining peace and order in a country that has hundreds of different ethnic groups. The mayor (or another public figure) facilitates the informal dispute settlement process between offenders, victims and community. Pakistan and the Philippines recognize *Hudood* laws (which are given directly in the Qur'an) and the *Shari'a* law, in addition to their modern criminal law (Ota 2003: 32–3). Both Bangladesh and the Philippines have numerous cultural minorities whose non-state justice systems (NSJSs) coexist, sometimes uneasily, with those of the state:

> Much of the civil law system in Bangladesh could be seen as NSJS (Non-State Justice System) in origin, in that it applies Muslim and Hindu laws to these respective majority and minority religious groups. The Philippines also has special state Shari'a courts in parts of its Muslim south, which incorporate previously non-state laws into processing of certain disputes within that religious group (Golub, 2003, 2).

In China, PRC, customary law practice is still prevalent among 8 per cent of Chinese ethnic minorities (Gao 2003: 12). This customary law (in criminal matters) pertains to murder, manslaughter, assault causing bodily harm, theft, rape, adultery, property damage, breach of public interest, robbery, kidnapping, etc. (Gao 2003: 162–87). Penalties and mediation are executed by means of indigenous practices.

Mediation outcomes differ from tribe to tribe, with examples including mediating tea, wine *(ganbei)* and feasting; poultry restitution; gifts; removal of genealogical name; fine; lash *(bianchi)*; public ignominy; labour service; re-education; letter of repentance; banishment; imprisonment; death penalty; spiritual practices *(shenming)*; and war *(siedou)* (Gao 2003: 187–216). Some of the foregoing practices are still in use, but others are forbidden by current criminal law, such as burying the murderer alive with the deceased victim.

In addition, there is a strong connection between Confucianism and restorative justice (Jiang and Yang 1990: 56–8). Strongly influenced by Confucianism, traditional Chinese people are predominantly introverted, meek, self-respecting, contented with reality, seeking harmony, honest, friendly, modest, self-sacrificing, benevolent, sympathetic and kind. These virtues have influenced the development of restorative justice in three ways: 1) they increase the willingness of parties to settle their disputes through mediation; 2) they encourage third parties to assist as voluntary mediators; and 3) they make the settlement of the dispute more likely (Di in preparation; Wang in preparation).

Community mediation (both informal and formal)

In the Philippines, the Barangay (i.e. Neighbourhood Community) Justice System (BJS) is a non-governmental organization whose purpose is to provide access to justice and to empower communities to participate in justice reform. Since it is connected to local jurisdictions, the BJS limits itself to neighbourhood and family disputes, including criminal cases where the possible penalty is imprisonment not exceeding one year or a fine not exceeding 5,000 pesos (Golub 2003: 12; Parker 2004: 1).

In Taiwan this system is referred to as municipal mediation *(xianzhenshi tiaojie)*. A committee of 7–15 lay people is authorized to mediate victims' complaints, such as certain types of sexual offences, simple assault, negligence resulting in injury, defamation and malicious mischief. According to Ota:

> The difference between barangay justice in the Philippines and municipal mediation in Taiwan is that the former has primary jurisdiction over certain types of small disputes but the latter is one option available to parties of disputes, who otherwise can make a formal complaint or private prosecution to the authorities (2003: 35).

In Japan, an NGO, Presbyterian Support Otago, has initiated a court-referred restorative justice pilot project. This is a social agency with a variety of initiatives, including advocacy; budget advice; food assistance; social work support; counselling; group programmes; child and youth mentoring; elder abuse and neglect prevention; and supported employment for young people. New Zealand's experience with restorative justice has impressed a group of Japanese academics, who are exploring ways to initiate restorative justice in Japan. Tetsuya Fujimoto has noted: 'Restorative justice is not used in the Japanese criminal justice system, [it] is seen as a new concept in Japan. A form of restitution – whereby offenders can get reduced sentences by paying compensation to victims – is used in Japan, but we don't call it restorative justice' (Department for Courts 2003: 2).

In China, PRC, there are many forms of mediation, which might be categorized as follows (Wang in preparation):

- The mediator's status. Mediation can be divided into non-governmental mediation and official mediation. Non-governmental mediation includes people's mediation councils (PMCs), colleagues, relatives, friends, neighbours, lawyers and those who are present when the dispute takes place (volunteer mediators). The most extensive and effective programme is the PMC.

- The status of litigation. Mediation can be divided into 'mediation during litigation', which is done by the court, and 'mediation without litigation', which is not.

- Enforcement of the agreement. Finally, mediation can be divided into mediation with legal effect and mediation without legal effect. Mediation presided over by the court or an arbitration council is with legal effect, whereas mediation presided over by others is without.

PMCs are NGOs subordinate to the neighbourhood committee, and they are instructed by the local government and court. As one of the most extensive non-governmental organizations, PMCs in different parts of the country have established networks to ensure that there are sufficient mediators so that disputes can be settled at any time and in any place in a flexible way. The councils have no guarantee from the government, nor do they have judicial or administrative oversight or power – they are totally self-governed. They can mediate all kinds of disputes related to rights and interests, conflicts between family members, neighbours, colleagues and residents. In short, they mediate disputes about personal rights, marriage, property and damages.

Family group conferencing/victim–offender mediation

Family group conferencing (FGC) is an organized programme of restorative justice in Singapore and Thailand. It aims at making juvenile offenders aware of the effects of crime on each party and thus helps them to admit responsibility, clarifies the family's and community's responsibilities, prevents future recidivism and makes amends for the victim's losses (Lim and Liew 1997; Boonsit et al. 2004).

Hong Kong has a common law system, and the police have discretionary power to act in the public's interest after an arrest, which means they can apply the most appropriate measure available. When a juvenile offender below 18 years of age commits a minor offence and is cautioned by the police superintendent, social workers-mediators decide whether the case will go to mediation and, if so, will make arrangements accordingly. This programme has focused primarily on theft cases, such as thefts from stores, bicycles and stealing in schools. More recently it has expanded to handle individual conflicts among juveniles.

Restorative justice development in Asia

There is a continuum of restorative practices in use in Asia, ranging from the restitution/compensation order, to reconcilable offences, community service, mock tribunals and repatriation, letter mediation, victim–offender reconciliation and family group conferencing (Hong Kong, Macau, Singapore and Thailand) (Chuk and Wan 2003: 131–46; Ota 2003: 7–16). In addition, institutions have been established to promote and support restorative initiatives.

People's Republic of China (PRC)

Restorative justice is relatively new in in PRC. However, In Beijing, Hong Kong, Macau, Nanjing and Yunan, PRC, there have been important developments.

Beijing, PRC

The Centre for Restorative Justice at China University of Political Science and Law in Beijing was founded in June 2004. Its programme focuses on restorative justice and the reform of criminal justice in China. Its first programme is to translate and publish 16 books written or edited by authorities on restorative justice outside China.

Hong Kong, PRC

From 1999 to 2001, the first indigenous mediation model in Hong Kong was undertaken by the Evangelical Lutheran Church of Hong Kong (Social Services). It utilized the Police Superintendents' Discretion Scheme plus family group conferencing to mediate 28 cases involving a total of 40 offenders and 31 victims (Chuk and Wan 2002). The programme was based on the reintegrative shaming theory of John Braithwaite (1989). The term 'mediation' (*hejie*) was used instead of 'reconciliation' because mediation means both peace (*He Ping*) and doubt resolution (*Jie Yi*) in Chinese.

In the intervening years, restorative conferencing training was offered to educators, social workers, teachers and counsellors. Recently, three academics (two from Hong Kong and one from New Zealand) have proposed legislation that includes restorative processes for adolescents who have committed minor offences (Lo Wong *et al.* 2004).

Macau, PRC

The Social Work Council of the Macau Special Administrative Region is currently considering the creation of a diversionary programme for juvenile delinquents that would incorporate police cautioning and family group conferencing (Lo Cheng *et al.* 2004).

Nanjing, PRC

Restorative justice is virtually unknown in China and is only now being investigated by academics, judges, policy-makers and programme administrators. In 2003, the Research Institute of Crime Prevention and Control at Nanjing University conducted a symposium on the integration of criminal justice and restorative justice. Since then, the institute has published a number of papers on restorative justice and is due to publish a book entitled *Theoretical Introduction to Restorative Justice* (Di in preparation).

The institute has also co-operated with local organizations to promote the use of restorative justice in cases of young offenders charged with minor offences. Finally, it is conducting research on the use of restorative justice in dealing with minor offences committed by juveniles (Di in preparation).

Yunan, PRC

In 2004, Save the Children UK, in collaboration with the Ministry of Justice, PRC, started a pilot restorative justice project for juvenile delinquents.

Bangladesh

A community-based, largely informal non-state dispute settlement practice known as *shalish* is operated in three forms: by local influential leaders (traditional *shalish*), by a local government body (the union *parishad*) and by non-governmental organizations (non-governmental organization-facilitated *shalish*) (Golub 2003: 1–30).

Shalish means 'calm deliberation': all the parties patiently put forward their perspectives and impartial mediators soberly sort through the issues. However, the actual implementation may depart from this ideal, with 'bursts of shouting and even laughter or tears ... often with the noise of other community activities filtering in from outside' (Golub 2003: 4). Due to personal biases, power imbalances, corruption, political patronage and manipulation that too often characterize the traditional shalish and government-facilitated shalish, non-governmental organization-faciliated shalish is preferred for settling civil disputes and petty criminal offences. These are governed by the Muslim Family Laws Ordinance 1961, the Village Court Ordinance 1976 and the Conciliation of Dispute Ordinance 1979 (Golub 2003: 4–7).

Japan

Japanese officials and culture place a high value on confession, repentance, remorse and apology, and often reward these through pardon and leniency (Haley 1994: 249–372). Victim impact classes and victim awareness programmes for juvenile offenders have been launched. These programmes take place before court proceedings or while the juveniles are on probation (Haley 1994; Van Ness 2005: 7–8).

Nepal

Alternative methods of punishment, such as community service, have been introduced through the Prison Act (2nd Amendment) Ordinance 2004. The newly introduced community service is a community-based sentence for those who are imprisoned for terms of three years or less. Offenders can undertake their community service in such organizations as schools, hospitals, temples or old folks' homes. However, they remain under the supervision of the prescribed officer until their sentence expires (Ojha and Chapagai 2003: 3–4).

Pakistan

Gandhara University and the Federal Investigation Agency of the Islamic Republic of Pakistan jointly organized the first International Seminar on Restorative Justice in Peshawar, Pakistan in 2003. Forty-eight official participants attended the presentations. Many agreed that the traditional *jirga* and *panchayat* dispute resolution systems had much in common with restorative justice principles.

Philippines

Although the Barangay Justice System (BJS) had handled almost 280,000 disputes by 1998 with a settlement rate of 84 per cent, it has been criticized for gender bias, favouritism, pressure from significant others and for its low transparency to the general public. In response, the Barangay Justice Service System (BJSS) was set up in 1998 to provide mediation training for community leaders, including female BJ advocates (Golub 2003: 13–14; Parker 2004: 1). BJSS is an indigenous, inexpensive, non-state justice initiative that began in Panay and and Guimaras Islands and is now a nationwide community justice programme of the Manila-based Gerry Roxas Foundation (Gerry Roxas Foundation 2003: 3). The programme has been expanded to include the Muslim *Mindanao* (under the name 'Dalan sa Kalinaw', meaning 'Road to peace'). 'Dalan sa Kalinaw' aims to promote community peace by applying *Shari'a* law in the implementation of Barangay justice (Gerry Roxas Foundation 2003: 1).

The USAID-funded BJSS has employed more than 2,000 volunteers since 1998, with 85–95 per cent of the 1,512 cases being resolved (Gerry Roxas Foundation 2003: 1; Garong 2005: 1). Research has shown that, from 1998 to 2002, there was a reduction in the backlog of court cases, financial savings, increased harmony among the various stakeholders and the mutual empowerment of the parties involved (Salvosa 2002).

Singapore

Restorative justice is not a new concept to Singapore since its origins lie in the Singaporean *kampong* (village) system (Wan 2001). FGC has been formalized under the Children and Young Persons Act, and conferences have the legal authority to demand compensation for damages.

Thailand

In the past, Thai villagers resolved their problems through a form of community justice. Both parties to the dispute were involved in arriving at an apology, compensation and some form of community discipline. This approach is being resurrected: in 2003 the Juvenile Observation and Protection Department instituted FGC for juvenile delinquents. These offenders are juveniles who have been charged with minor offences carrying a penalty of less than five years' detention. Diversion to FGC can take place at any stage of the justice process. It has been estimated that 9,000 out of 35,000 juvenile delinquents participate in FGC each year (Parker 2003: 1).

In addition, the Justice Ministry's Department of Probation is nearing the completion of a pilot project for the use of restorative processes in adult cases. It has also established community committees in economically deprived areas of Bangkok. These committees provide a range of services in crime prevention and also mediate in certain cases involving juveniles (Van Ness: 2005).

Conclusion: the future of restorative justice in Asia

When considering how restorative justice might continue to develop in Asia, it is important to remember that Asia is increasingly pluralistic and multicultural (Wan 2003: 71–6). In these circumstances, an indigenous system of joint conciliation with shuttle diplomacy (Duryea and Grundison 1992), FGC (Chan 2003; Boonsit *et al.* 2004; Lo, Cheng *et al.* 2004; Lo, Wong *et al.* 2004), satellite mediation and surrogate mediation (Wan 2003) is particularly suitable to Asian dispute resolution. Asian mediators should therefore preferably be individuals who are well respected, multilingual and multicultural.

Further, in the future more Asian countries are likely to consider restorative justice as an alternative or supplement to their traditional criminal justice systems. In 2001, 37 countries responded to a United Nations' draft set of basic principles on the use of restorative justice. Ten of those were Asian countries. In that same year, 18 experts gathered in Canada to review the submissions. Two of these were from Asia. These demonstrations of interest (combined with the significant number of recent initiatives noted in this chapter) suggest that restorative justice may one day play an important role in Asia.

Acknowledgements

We are indebted to Daniel W. Van Ness, who provided valuable critique of this article and mediated international exchange about restorative justice in China and overseas. We would also like to thank Ms. Lynette Parker, who provided us invaluable materials from PFI International Centre for Justice and Reconciliation as well as the Restorative Justice Online: www. restorativejustice.org.

References

Augsburger, D.W. (1992) *Conflict Mediation across Cultures: Pathways and Patterns*. Louisville, KY: Westminster/John Knox Press.

Boonsit, A., Claassen, R. and Suwatchara, P. (2004) 'Restorative justice and domestic violence resolution in Thailand', *VOMA Connections*, 17: 9–16 (available online at http://voma.org/docs/connect17.pdf).

Braithwaite, J. (1989) *Crime, Shame and Reintegration*. New York, NY: Cambridge University Press.

Cartledge, G. (1996) *Cultural Diversity and Social Skills Instruction: Understanding Ethnic and Gender Differences*. Saline, MI: McNaughton & Gunn.

Chan, L.-W. (2003) 'The cultural dilemmas in dispute resolution: the Chinese experience.' Paper presented at the conference, Enforcing Equal Opportunities in Hong Kong: An Evaluation of Conciliation and Other Enforcement Powers of the EOC. University of Hong Kong, 14 June.

Chan, W.-C. (2003) 'Victim–offender mediation, making amends and restorative justice in Singapore', in T. Ota (ed.) *Victims and Criminal Justice: Asian Perspective*. Tokoyo: Keio University.

Chuk, W.H. and Wan, K.H. (2002) 'Restorative justice: a way forward in Hong Kong.' Paper presented at the international conference, Offender Rehabilitation in 21st Century, Hong Kong, 1–5 December.

Clarke, D.C. (1991) 'Dispute resolution in China', *Journal of Chinese Law*: 245–96.

Cloke, K. (1987) 'Politics and values in mediation: the Chinese experience', in J.A. Lemon (ed.) *Developing Family Mediation*. San Francisco, CA: Jossey-Bass.

Department for Courts (2003) 'Te Ava Whakatika', *Newsletter of the Court-referred Restorative Justice Project*, 17: 1–4.

Di, X. in preparation (2005) 'Theory and practice of restorative justice in Nanjing, China.'

Duryea, M.L. and Grundison, J.B. (1993) *Conflict and Culture: Research in Five Communities in Vancouver, British Columbia*. Vancouver: Uvic Institute for Dispute Resolution.

Gao, Q.B. (2003) *Research on Chinese Customary Law of Ethnic Minorities*. Beijing: Tsinghua University (in Chinese).

Garong, E.A. (2005) 'Improving the Philippine justice system' (available online at http://www.usaid.gov/stories/philippines/fp_philippines_justice.html).

Gerry Roxas Foundation Development Team (2003) 'Access to Justice for Families and Communities' (available online at http://ns.roxas-online.net.ph/grf/BJSS.html).

Golub, S. (2003) 'Non-state justice systems in Bangladesh and the Philippines.' Paper presented at workshop, Working with Non-state Justice Systems, Institute of Development Studies, 6–7 March (available online at http://www.ids.ac.uk/ids/law/pdfs/golub.pdf).

Haley, J.O. (1994) 'Crime prevention through restorative justice: lessons from Japan', in B. Galaway and J. Hudson (eds) *Restorative Justice: International Perspectives*. Monsey, NY: Criminal Justice Press.

Jiang, W. and Yang, R. (1990) *Introduction to People's Mediation*. China: Law Press (in Chinese).

Lim, L.Y. and Liew, T.L. (1997) *Court Mediation in Singapore*. Singapore: FT Law & Tax Asia Pacific.

Lo, T.W., Cheng, H.K., Wong, S.W. and Ching, A.L.S. (2004) 'Community prevention for deviant adolescents in Macau: a blueprint for deviant adolescents and social service development', in P. Chan Yan Yan (ed.) *The Collection of the Symposium: The Judicial Protection for Juvenile Delinquents*. Macau (in Chinese).

Lo, T.W., Wong, S.W. and Maxwell, G. (2004) *Measures Alternative to Prosecution for Handling Unruly Children and Young Persons: Overseas Experiences and Options for Hong Kong*. Hong Kong: Youth Studies Net, City University of Hong Kong.

Moser, M.J. (1982) *Law and Social Change in a Chinese Community: A Case Study from Rural Taiwan*. London: Oceana.

Ojha, G. and Kiran, C. (2003) 'In absence of restorative justice', *Kathmandu Post*, 18 August: 3–4 (available online at www.nepalnews.com/contents/englishdaily/ktmpost/2003/aug/aug18).

Ota, T. (2003) 'Introduction: the development of victimology and victim support in Asia', T. Ota (ed.) *Victims and Criminal Justice: Asian Perspective*. Tokyo: Keio University.

Parker, L. (2003) 'Responding to juvenile crime in Thailand' (available online at http://restorativejustice.org/rj3/Feature/2003/August/Thailand.htm).

Parker, L. (2004) 'Using traditional practices to improve the justice system', (available online at http://restorativejustice.org/rj3/Feature/2004/June/traditional.htm).

Salvosa, R.D. (2002) 'Incorporating a restorative justice approach in the Philippine juvenile justice system: a case study.' Paper presented at the Third International Conference, Conferencing, Circles and other Restorative Practices, Minneapolis, 8–10 August.

Van Ness, D.W. (2005) 'An overview of restorative justice around the world.' Paper presented at the International symposium, Latest Developments on Criminal Justice Reform, Shenzhen, 19–20 August.

Wan, K.H. (2001) 'Alternative rehabilitation: assessing the effectiveness of complainant respondent mediation at the Mediation Services of Winnipeg and the Community Mediation Centre of Singapore', in P. Chan Yan Yan (ed.) *The Proceedings of the Symposium of the Juvenile Criminal Judicial Policy*, Macau (in Chinese).

Wan, K.H. (2003) 'Mediation Services of Winnipeg, Canada and Community Mediation Centre of Singapore: a comparative study', in *Research on Crime and Rehabilitation*. Beijing: Ministry of Justice (in Chinese).

Wang, P. (in preparation) 'Restorative justice in China.'

Yeo, A. (1993) 'Counseling in Singapore: development and trends', in A.H. Othman and A. Awag (eds) *Counseling in the Asia-Pacific Region*. Westport, CI: Greenwood Press.

Zehr, H. (1990) *Changing Lenses: A New Focus for Crime and Justice*. Scottdale, PA:

Section C
Europe

Jolien Willemsens and Lode Walgrave

Introduction

While there may be difficulties in finding a commonly accepted definition of restorative justice, there is in fact little debate about its participatory philosophy, its objective of repairing harm caused by crime and its basic practice models. But how restorative justice becomes operational varies throughout the world – even within regions. In Europe, for example, the

British countries have more in common with North America than with continental Europe because of their common cultural and legal heritage.

Even on the continent great internal differences exist. Countries in the south of Europe reflect Latin culture, influenced by French traditions and literature. Germany, the Netherlands and the Scandinavian countries have been influenced by Anglo-Saxon literature and culture (as has Great Britain), but their institutions are continental. This diversity is even found within such countries as Belgium, where Northern Flanders is linked culturally to Northern Europe, while Southern Wallonia is French oriented.

Nevertheless, we believe that there are some observations that may be made about the development and operation of restorative justice in Europe.

Restorative justice on the European continent

In this section, we describe the development of restorative justice on the European continent.[1]

The emergence of restorative justice

While the current restorative justice movement in Europe emerged at the beginning of the 1980s, the ideas underlying victim–offender mediation practices were not new. Already in the late 1960s there was debate on how victims and offenders might be given an opportunity to confront and resolve issues related to crime. During the 1970s and 1980s, critical criminologists devoted their attention to the counterproductive effects of criminal justice and its incapacity to assure peace in social life. Abolitionists argued for scrapping or phasing out the criminal justice system, in order to replace it with a bottom-up, deliberative model of dealing with conflicts (Christie 1977; Bianchi 1994). Hulsman, for example, stressed the importance of the conflict settlement function of criminal justice and thereby influenced public policy in the Netherlands. As a result, the mediation of conflicts has become part of the regular debate in the Netherlands, particularly as a way to improve the position of the victim (Aertsen 2001). In 1977, Nils Christie described how the state 'stole' conflicts from people and often deprived them of any possibility to reach a resolution independently. Beneficiaries of these critiques have proposed restorative justice-like alternatives (De Haan 1990; van Swaaningen 1997) or have turned to restorative justice as the mainstream alternative to criminal justice (Blad 1996) or youth justice (Walgrave 1995).

In the 1980s and 1990s pilot projects and initial legislation were introduced in many European countries. Norway took the lead in 1981 with a diversionary project aimed at first-time young offenders. By 1989, 81 of the 435 Norwegian municipalities offered mediation. A series of circulars issued by the Attorney-General extended its scope to certain adults and repeat offenders. In 1991, the Municipal Mediation Service Act came into effect (Bolstad 2004). The first Finnish pilot project began in 1983 and Austria followed in 1984–85. By 1998 there were more than 900 mediation programmes (Lauwaert and Aertsen 2002).

A diversified landscape of complementary visions

Tony Peters has described the restorative justice scene in Europe as a 'diversified landscape of competing visions' (2000: 14). We would rather describe it as a diversified landscape of complementary visions.

In some countries (for example, Finland, France and Norway), volunteers play an important role in mediation practice, whereas in other countries (for example, Austria, Germany and Belgium) the intervention is highly professionalized. There is similar diversity concerning the relationship of mediation services to the criminal justice system: it varies from being exclusively system based (for example, 'penal mediation' in Belgium, functioning under the authority of the public prosecutor) to being primarily community based (certain initiatives in, for example, France, Germany and Belgium; in Belgium, for example, mediation during detention is organized by two NGOs). There has also been diversity in the role played by criminal justice institutions in the adoption of restorative justice programmes. In Norway and Finland, for example, mediation arose quite autonomously alongside the neighbouring fields of probation and victim support. In other countries, such as Austria, Germany, the UK, France and the Czech Republic, probation or victim support have played a central role. In Belgium, the needs of the victim were the point of departure for the mediation for redress model in response to more serious crime (Lauwaert and Aertsen 2002).

Mediation as the predominant restorative justice model in Europe

Victim–offender mediation has for a long time been almost the sole model of restorative practice on the European continent. The term 'restorative justice' was for a long time unknown to practitioners so that, for example, the European Forum for Victim–Offender Mediation and Restorative Justice only recently deleted 'Victim–Offender Mediation' from its title.[2]

Mediation has a legal basis in most European countries, especially (but not only) for juveniles (Schelkens 1998). Most mediated cases involve relatively minor crimes committed by (first time) offenders. Serious and violent crimes are not excluded, and some programmes focus especially on these cases. A current tendency in many European countries expands the scope of mediation to more serious crimes.

Mediation mostly is a way to divert cases from the criminal justice process. Most referrals are made by the public prosecutor or the police. A positive outcome will often lead to dismissal. But mediation can also run parallel to prosecution, especially in more violent offences. In these cases the judgment will take the result of mediation into account. Finally, several projects deal with mediation after the sentence has already been passed. In a few countries, mediation can take place during the execution of the prison sentence. Under the auspices of the Belgian Ministry of Justice, for example, a nationwide restorative justice programme has been established in the prison system. Each Belgian prison now has a restorative justice adviser whose main task is to introduce a 'restorative culture' into the prison system.

It must be said that the official and legislated structure of several European mediation programmes sometimes runs counter to the restorative quality of the practices. Some programmes are called mediation but are in fact little more than an unofficial warning or an imposed judicial obligation. Others, however, obviously operate under a clear restorative justice philosophy, while accepting necessary compromises with the judicial system.

Community service is a common practice in European juvenile justice systems, and is often explicitly seen as a kind of symbolic reparation to the community (Schelkens 1998). In the rehabilitative tradition of juvenile justice systems, however, many consider community service more as an alternative treatment model.

Conferencing is just beginning on the European continent. In the Netherlands, the so-called Wagga Wagga model is applied to less serious delinquency, as well as in schools and in welfare cases. In Belgium, an experiment with the New Zealand conferencing model has led to very encouraging results when dealing with serious youth offending (Vanfraechem and Walgrave 2004).

The case of Central and Eastern Europe

Although a number of countries in Central and Eastern Europe already have well established victim–offender mediation practices (for example, Poland, the Czech Republic and Slovenia), others are still struggling to take the first steps.

As the old regimes collapsed, so did also the highly politicized police and judicial institutions, resulting in a continuing movement to build new institutions. Most of the reforms are based on Western civil law, but the new institutions are relatively provisional, flexible and willing to consider renovation. Contrary to Western Europe, for example, where restorative philosophy and practices have to compete with rigid institutions founded upon long-established power, restorative justice ideas may find more of a welcome in Central and Eastern Europe.

Practitioners, academics and officials do seek contact with their Western European colleagues in the restorative justice field, and many have set up their own approaches, whether or not supported by official politics. So, restorative practices are increasingly being implemented in many countries, not only for dealing with traditional offences but also for postwar situations, as in Serbia or in Croatia.

Nevertheless, many counter-forces are also active. Through the AGIS2 project, 'Meeting the challenges of introducing victim–offender mediation in Central and Eastern Europe', the European Forum for Restorative Justice is trying to make an inventory of these problems and is looking for possible solutions.[3] Interviews with Eastern European experts have revealed a number of possible obstacles:

- A highly punitive attitude among the public and policy-makers.
- An uncritical reliance on incarceration.
- Strong resistance within the police, prosecutors and judges, who fear competition from alternatives.
- A passive civil society and weakened public legitimacy of the state and its institutions.

- Limited trust in NGOs and in their professional capacities.
- Lack of information about restorative justice and of restorative justice pilots.
- Low economic conditions, making it difficult to set up projects.
- No tradition of co-operation and dialogue in several sectors and professions.
- A general loss of trust in a better future, and a mood of despondency and cynicism.
- Forms of nepotism and even corruption in parts of the criminal justice system.
- Heavy administrative and financial constraints on the agencies, preventing investment in qualitative work.

Many of the elements mentioned also apply to Western European and other countries, but they might affect life more in Central and Eastern Europe. The loss of power by the predominant institutions may lead to transitional confusion. Its flexibility may offer great opportunities for the profound renovation restorative justice stands for, but it may also cause fear of the unknown and lead to harsher rigidity in attempts to keep the old traditions alive. The direction the institutions are going to take will probably partly depend on the support provided by external forces.

Supranational developments

Since the end of the 1990s, several international and supranational organizations have encouraged the development of restorative justice practices. In 1999, the Committee of Ministers, the decision-making body of the Council of Europe, adopted Recommendation No. R(99)19 concerning mediation in penal matters. This sets out the principles of victim–offender mediation as guidelines for member states. Among other things, the recommendation encourages member states to provide mediation as a voluntarily accepted and confidential service at all stages of the criminal justice process. It also provides that legislation should be adopted, as well as appropriate working principles, for the operation of the criminal justice system and the mediation services themselves.

In 2002, a follow-up study showed that this recommendation had been remarkably influential. In a number of countries it had contributed to the introduction of mediation and, in others, it had helped shape legislation or national restorative justice policy (Pelikan 2003). The recommendation was also used in drafting a declaration on the use of restorative justice adopted by the United Nations in 2002.[4]

In 2004, the Council of Europe, as part of its integrated project 'Responses to violence in everyday life in a democratic society', commissioned the European Forum for Restorative Justice to write a guide further to support policy development on, and the implementation of, restorative justice (Aertsen *et al.* 2004). The Council of Europe has also regularly supported the training of mediators in Central and Eastern Europe.

In 1999 the European Commission of the European Union made a plea for additional research and experiments in victim–offender mediation in the

Communication on Crime Victims in the European Union: Reflections on Standards and Actions.[5]

Two years later, it issued a framework decision on the standing of victims in criminal proceedings.[6] This framework decision obliges the member states of the European Union to adapt their national laws so as to afford victims of crime a minimum level of protection. It also provides that member states must promote mediation in criminal cases for appropriate offences. Furthermore, the European Union has supported financially a number of (research) projects in the field of restorative justice.

On 19 September 2002, the Belgian government officially introduced a proposal for a European Council decision setting up a European network of national contact points for restorative justice.[7] The idea behind this initiative is to create a network of higher civil servants responsible for restorative justice. This network would support the effective implementation of restorative justice through national policies and by criminal justice agencies. During the April 2003 plenary session of the European Parliament, the initiative was discussed, slightly amended and approved.[8] Since then, the dossier awaits further consideration by the Council of the European Union.

European co-operation

Until a few years ago, European victim–offender mediation projects had little contact with one another. To remedy this, the European Forum for Restorative Justice was created as a not-for-profit organization, based in Belgium, in December 2000. Its general aim is to help establish and develop restorative justice throughout Europe. It does this by promoting the international exchange of information and mutual help; by exploring and developing the theoretical basis of restorative justice; promoting the development of effective restorative justice policies, services and legislation; stimulating restorative justice research; and assisting with the development of principles, ethics, training and good practice. Its members now consist of 200 individuals and organizations from more than 37 (mainly European) countries.[9]

Over the last few years there have been many European research projects. One of the bigger is the COST Action A21 on 'Restorative justice developments in Europe'. In late 2002, this resulted in creation of a European network of researchers from 20 countries. The main objective of Action A21 is to enhance and deepen knowledge on theoretical and practical aspects of restorative justice in Europe, with a view towards supporting implementation strategies in a scientifically sound way. The scientific programme of the action is divided up into evaluative, policy-oriented and theoretical research.[10]

Finally, in addition to these large-scale initiatives, there have been a number of bilateral or regional collaborations between countries. Germany, for example, has provided support for the development of mediation and the training of mediators in Poland. Norway has supported a project to promote the development of restorative justice in Albania. The Nordic countries (Norway, Sweden, Finland and Denmark) have engaged in regional consultations.

In search of European particularities

The preceding section may have made it clear that restorative justice developments on the European continent have been both similar and different when compared with other regions of the world. While Europeans also ground their view on a participatory philosophy and on the priority to repair the harm caused by crime, they sometimes have a considerably different way of making it operational. This seems to be especially true when considering the degree of institutionalization.

We will now try to explain the forces that may have influenced the development of these particularly European characteristics of restorative justice.[11]

Common law vs. civil law

Restorative justice promotes the inclusion of the parties with a stake in the response to the offence. This is basically a challenge to the traditional state monopoly in the reaction to crime. Changing this situation is most difficult when this monopoly is strongly centralized and consolidated, as in civil law regimes.

The opportunity principle prevails in common law, while the legality principle is central in the civil law systems on the European continent. All agents in the common law system – the police, prosecuting agencies, judges – have been given the *opportunity* to exercise broad discretionary powers in deciding how to act in the 'public interest' and in imposing measures they feel are most appropriate in response to the crime committed. This is not the case in civil law countries, where the *legality* principle prevails, obliging the police, for example, to inform the public prosecutor about all cases (mandatory prosecution). Moreover, the public prosecutor has only very limited power not to refer cases to court if there is sufficient evidence.

As a generalization, it might be said that Anglo-Saxon judges focus more on concrete conflicts than on abstract judicial rules. The legal professionals in common law countries think in a more inductive way, while continental judges reason in a more theoretic-deductive way and support their judgments using abstract legal rules (Aertsen 2001).

The flexibility of common law brings it closer to the reality of public life and to the attitudes of the 'community'. It risks, however, populist influences and offers weak legal safeguards. Civil law, on the other hand, provides stricter legal safeguards but is also more rigid and sometimes unworldly.

The flexibility of the common law system can play an important role in the development of restorative justice. This is true not only because of the space it allows for the running of experiments but also because flexibility is a crucial element in restorative practices themselves. It is therefore easier to carry out mediation or conferencing outside the justice system (within the 'community', for example) or to include these practices in judicial procedure (as is the case in 'cautioning'). The outcome of a restorative process is not as strictly weighed against legal checks as would be the case in civil law regimes. To put this somewhat bluntly: in a common law system, the judiciary 'adapts' the legal rules in order to make possible a socially constructed solution whereas, in a civil law system, the solution must fit the existing legal framework, even if, thereby, it would become less socially constructed.

It is, therefore, not coincidental that most restorative practices have been 'invented' in common law countries, and that Europeans are more concerned with the legal basis of these practices when they are introduced into their countries. Despite the legality principle, however, many civil law countries have found creative ways to make mediation possible, usually by using an article that allows for the discontinuation of the process under certain conditions. For example, s.12 of the former Austrian Juvenile Justice Act gave the state prosecutor power (except in more serious cases) to drop a charge when there were reasons to expect further law-abiding behaviour on the part of the young perpetrator. Compensating the victim directly was interpreted as one such reason.

More than most other common law countries, many European continental countries have legislated detailed plans for the procedural phase and for which cases restorative schemes can be implemented. For some prominent European scholars, the legal concerns are a reason to be very sceptical of restorative justice (Groenhuijsen 2000; Albrecht 2001). For others, these legal concerns are reason to explore a possible legal framework for restorative justice, as they consider them to be almost a condition *sine qua non* in order to be able to extend the scope of restorative justice (Walgrave 2002; van Stokkom 2004; Claes *et al.* 2005; Aertsen *et al.* 2006).

Community v. citoyenneté

While a European discussion about restorative justice is focused on the legal perspective and the role of the state, in North American discourse the concern is with the community. Community is often presented as a network of informal interactions based on spontaneous human understanding, as opposed to a formal institutionalized society (the 'government' or the 'state') with its rules and rigid communication channels. Restorative interventions, of course, require a minimum of 'community' support: the victim and offender must feel at least some common interest in settling the aftermath of the crime through constructive dialogue and reparation.

Indeed, the re-emergence of restorative justice has boosted communitarian concerns to revitalize (local) communities as the bedrock of informal mutual support and control. The community literature in restorative justice is predominantly Anglo-Saxon (more specifically, often American), where there is a tendency to see restorative justice as community justice (Bazemore and Schiff 2001).[12]

Most Europeans have great difficulty coming to grips with the term 'community'. There is no doubt that an informal climate of mutual understanding is crucial for restorative practices, but the European perspective is that confidence in community seems rather naïve, and perhaps even dangerous. Communities are not always available, nor are they always good (Pavlich 2001; Crawford 2002).

In the European perspective, power is concentrated in the authorities, who are viewed as the holders of the *vox communi*. People are supposed to be represented fully by the state. The state is the formalization of the community, or the community of communities. Criminal law is a part of the state's system of control over its citizens. Strict legalistic civil law offers state protection against the abuse of power by the state and by the most powerful in the community.

Anglo-Saxons have a more sceptical view of state power. In the USA in particular, the state is often presented as a bureaucratic taxing machine, an opponent to freedom, at an unbridgeable distance from real life. The state's provisions with regard to education, medical care, social services and allowances are impoverished. Communities based on religion, territory or ethnicity, however, very often compensate for this lack of provision (Hastings and Bailleau 2005) by providing private schools, local private care or community support. This may explain the reason why Americans embrace the idea of community as opposed to 'government' and are less sensitive to the exclusionary anomalies contained within many communities. Criminal justice in Anglo-Saxon countries is not there to defend the state's interests but to preserve individual citizens' needs for justice and peace so that they can live their lives as they wish. Common law can more flexibly respond to these individual needs and can individualize problem situations.

Europeans are, of course, also sensitive to the state's bureaucratic and formalist excesses, but they see the state as something useful that can be improved. The state is a safeguard against abuses of power by the most powerful. The *citoyenneté* ('citizenship'), as the French call it, is a crucial good, including all the rights and protections offered by the state as well as its obligations. Decentralization does not send matters to the community, as in North America, but to the municipalities (Hastings and Bailleau 2005). Communitarianism often has a pejorative meaning in French society because it is suspected of promoting the selfish interests of a particular community to the detriment of the general citizens' interests. It is not that Europeans love paying taxes; basically, they consider it as a contribution to collective life.

This is probably why many Anglo-Saxons, especially Americans, see restorative justice primarily as a way to extend the reach of the 'living' community in dealing with the aftermath of an offence and as a way to push back the interference of formal state power. Europeans try to include restorative practices in a judicial frame and look for models that locate restorative schemes under state-guaranteed supervision, while at the same time preserving the benefits of informal deliberation.

First nations and other indigenous people

Indigenous populations currently have a strong voice in Canada, the USA, Australia and New Zealand. Their traditional practices have energized the debates on criminal justice and have influenced deeply thinking and practices on restorative justice.

Unlike other regions of the world, Western Europe has not had a driving force for restorative justice eminating from the ethnic and cultural diversity of its populations. This is undoubtedly due in part to the low numbers of non-Western European populations. However, it certainly also has to do with these populations' status as immigrants. The white population is the 'First Nation' in Europe. White Western society and culture have their territorial roots on the European continent, and this fact positions ethnic and cultural minorities as 'visitors'. According to mainstream opinion, these visitors must simply 'integrate' into Western culture – they must accept Western values and institutions. Muslim or African traditions do not really penetrate European social institutions. They are accepted only at the margins, in so far as they do not challenge the Western society model. This is also the case for criminal justice. Furthermore, a centralized civil law system is not flexible enough to be influenced to the same extent as the common law systems in Anglo-Saxon countries.

Conclusion

Despite a common philosophical foundation and comparable practices, each region of the world, each country, develops its own way of implementing restorative justice. One should be aware of this since differences provoke questions, assure flexibility and help avoid rigidity. Comparisons can help to improve practices.

Europeans might, for example, learn that a more flexible judicial system (such as the common law system) does not lead to the collapse of democracy. Furthermore, it is important that all social institutions (including criminal justice) remain aware of developments in the concept of community. Knowledge of the common law context helps those working in a civil law regime to resource criminal justice as a servant to the quality of social and public life. Many European criminal law actors and theorists, however, often have the tendency to see criminal law as the ultimate criterion.

Anglo-Saxons might also learn from the Europeans how restorative practices can be combined with legal guarantees, while preserving the quality of deliberation and reparative outcomes. Finally, those who have confidence in the community should not be naïve when they use community processes and volunteers. If the community is not well defined and its representation is not regulated, legal and civil rights do matter.

Notes

1 See further European Forum (2000), Aertsen *et al.* (2004), Miers and Willemsens (2004).
2 This change took place on 28 October 2005. Throughout this chapter, the forum will be referred to by its new name, even when referring to its activities prior to that date.
3 For more information about the AGIS2 project, see http://www.euforumrj.org/projects.AGIS2.htm.
4 *Basic Principles on the Use of Restorative Justice Programmes in Criminal Matters*, United Nations, E/2002/INF/2/add.2.

5   COM (1999) 349 final.
6   Council framework decision of 15 March 2001 on the standing of victims in criminal proceedings (2001/220/JHA).
7   *Official Journal*, C 242/20, 8 October: 20. The Belgian government consulted the European Forum for Restorative Justice during the preparatory phase of this initiative.
8   *European Parliament Legislative Resolution on the Initiative by the Kingdom of Belgium with a View to the Adoption of a Council Decision Setting up a European Network of National Contact Points for Restorative Justice* (11621/2002-C5-0467/2002-2002/0821 (CNS)).
9   For detailed information about the European Forum, see http://www.euforumrj. org
10 For more information and progress reports, see http://www.euforumrj.org/ projects.COST.htm
11 This section is based on Walgrave (2004).
12 Not all American restorative justice advocates are happy with this development. See for, example, McCold's (2004) heavy opposition.

References

Adler, C. and Wundersitz, J. (eds) (1994) *Family Conferencing and Juvenile Justice: The Way Forward or Misplaced Optimism*? Canberra: Australian Institute of Criminology.

Aertsen, I. (2001) 'Slachtoffer-daderbemiddeling: een onderzoek naar de ontwikkeling van een herstelgerichte strafrechtsbedeling.' Doctoral thesis, K.U. Leuven.

Aertsen, I., Daems, T. and Robert, L.   (2006) *Institutionalising Restorative Justice*. Cullompton: Willan Publishing.

Aertsen, I., Mackay, R., Pelikan, C., Willemsens, J. and Wright, M. (2004) *Rebuilding Community Connections – Mediation and Restorative Justice in Europe*. Strasbourg: Council of Europe Publishing.

Albrecht, H.J. (2001) 'Restorative justice. Answers to questions that nobody has put forward', in E. Fattah and S. Parmentier (eds) *Victim Policies and Criminal Justice on the Road to Restorative Justice*. Leuven: Leuven University Press.

Bazemore, G. and Schiff, M. (eds) (2001) *Restorative Community Justice: Repairing Harm and Transforming Communities*. Cincinnati, OH: Anderson Publishing.

Bianchi, H. (1994) *Justice as a Sanctuary: Towards a New System of Crime Control*. Bloomington, IN: Indiana University Press.

Blad, J. (1996) *Abolitionisme als strafrechtstheorie (Abolitionism as Penal Law Theory)*. Amsterdam: Gouda Quint.

Bolstad, T. (2004) 'Norway', in D. Miers and J. Willemsens (eds) *Mapping Restorative Justice: Developments in 25 European Countries*. Leuven: European Forum for Victim–Offender Mediation and Restorative Justice.

Christie, N. (1977) 'Conflicts as property', *British Journal of Criminology*, 17: 1–15.

Claes, E., Foqué, R. and Peters, T. (eds) (2005) *Punishment, Restorative Justice and the Morality of Law*. Antwerp and Oxford: Intersentia.

Crawford, A. (2002) 'The state, community and restorative justice: heresy, nostalgia and butterfly collecting', in L. Walgrave (ed.) *Restorative Justice and the Law*. Cullompton: Willan Publishing.

De Haan, W. (1990) *The Politics of Redress*. London: Sage.

European Forum for Victim–Offender Mediation and Restorative Justice (ed.) (2000) *Victim–Offender Mediation in Europe. Making Restorative Justice Work*. Leuven: Leuven University Press.

Groenhuysen, M. (2000) 'Victim–offender mediation: legal and procedural safeguards. Experiments and legislation in some European jurisdictions', in European Forum for Victim–Offender Mediation and Restorative Justice (ed.) *Victim–Offender Mediation in Europe. Making Restorative Justice Work*. Leuven: Leuven University Press.

Hastings, R. and Bailleau, F. (2005) 'Socio-legal regulation in a multi-ethnic society: assessing the shift to the local in France or the community in Canada', in N. Queloz *et al.* (eds) *Délinquance des jeunes et justice des mineurs (Youth Crime and Juvenile Justice)*. Berne and Bruxelles: Staempfli/Bruylandt.

Lauwaert, K. and Aertsen, I. (2002) 'Restorative justice: activities and expectations at European level', *ERA – Forum*, I-2002: 27–32.

McCold, P. (2004) 'Paradigm muddle: the threat to restorative justice posed by its merger with community justice', *Contemporary Justice Review*, 7: 13–35.

Miers, D. and Willemsens J. (eds) (2004) *Mapping Restorative Justice: Developments in 25 European Countries*. Leuven: European Forum for Victim–Offender Mediation and Restorative Justice.

Pavlich, G. (2001) 'The force of community', in H. Strang and J. Braithwaite (eds) *Restorative Justice and Civil Society*. Cambridge: Cambridge University Press.

Pelikan, C. (2003) 'Follow-up study of Recommendation R(99)19 of the Council of Europe', *Newsletter of the European Forum for Victim–Offender Mediation and Restorative Justice*, 4: 6–7.

Peters, T. (2000) 'Victim–offender mediation: reality and challenges', in European Forum for Victim–Offender Mediation and Restorative Justice (ed.) *Victim–Offender Mediation in Europe. Making Restorative Justice Work*. Leuven: Leuven University Press.

Schelkens, W. (1998) 'Community service and mediation in the juvenile justice legislation in Europe', in L. Walgrave (ed.) *Restorative Justice for Juveniles: Potentialities, Risks and Problems for Research*. Leuven: Leuven University Press.

Vanfraechem, I. and Walgrave, L. (2004) 'Restorative conferencing in Belgium. Can it decrease the confinement of young offenders?', *Corrections Today*, December: 72–5.

Van Ness, D. and Strong, K.H. (2002) *Restoring Justice* (2nd edn). Cincinnati, OH: Anderson Publishing.

Van Stokkom, B. (ed.) (2004) *Straf en Herstel. Ethische reflecties over strafdoeleinden (Punishment and Restoration. Ethical Reflections on the Purposes of Punishment)*. Den Haag: Boom Juridische Uitgevers.

Van Swaaningen, R. (1997) *Critical Criminology: Visions from Europe*. London: Sage.

Walgrave, L. (1995) 'Restorative justice for juveniles: just a technique or a fully fledged alternative?', *Howard Journal*, 34: 228–49.

Walgrave, L. (2002). *Restorative Justice and the Law*. Cullompton: Willan Publishing.

Walgrave, L. (2004) 'Restorative justice in comparison', in J. Winterdyk and L. Cao (eds) *Lessons from Comparative Criminology*. Toronto: De Sitter.

Winfree, T. (2002) 'Peacemaking and community harmony: lessons (and admonitions) from the Navajo peacemaking courts', in E. Weitekamp and H.J. Kerner (eds) *Restorative Justice: Theoretical Foundations*. Cullompton: Willan Publishing.

Section D
Latin America

Pedro Scuro

Justice: hard and soft

A meeting of the Restorative Justice group of the School of Magistracy (City of Porto Alegre, Brazil) watched a man's account of how two assailants stole, at gunpoint, his only valuable possession – an old car. One of the offenders was an adult and the other a juvenile. The courts to which each was sent dealt with the case quite differently. The minor, accompanied by his mother and girlfriend, was invited to take part in a restorative procedure. In the video, the victim described how relieved he was with the chance to tell the juvenile how badly the incident had affected his life and family, and he was delighted with the resulting agreement that the offender would pay restitution. The story was rather different for the adult offender, however. 'In the other courtroom', the victim said, 'I had less than five minutes to give evidence, and the mugger left the room mocking me, convinced that he would be given just a light prison sentence.'

After viewing the videotape, the public prosecutor (who was also present at the meeting) said:

> All of us in this room seem to be very pleased with restorative justice and the benefits it has for victims. But we should not forget that we are middle-class professionals, members of the justice system, unable to address ordinary citizens in terms other than the language and symbols *everybody understands*.

In other words, he was referring to the way justice is carried out, communicating familiar messages, in 'hard' and 'soft' ways to offenders, victims and the community (see Table 24.2).

'Hard' and 'soft' messages are incorporated into justice systems everywhere, and they are expressed in ways that try to demonstrate their superiority to all other forms of justice. In Latin America, for instance, penal codes claim that the courts do not inflict a penalty as a 'punishment' but as a condition for the granting of freedom, which wrongdoers earn through good behaviour and by demonstrating social responsibility. This is, in fact, merely judicial relativism that aims to camouflage serious structural problems. In Latin America and sub-Saharan Africa (the two worst regions of the globe in so far as criminal justice and law enforcement are concerned), badly managed systems are misused or are simply unavailable because the penal codes and procedures are labyrinthic and there is too much reliance on state power, imprisonment and court rulings. The consequences of this are alarming, as is easily demonstrated through homicide statistics (see Table 24.3).

Table 24.2 Retributive justice: messages

	'Hard'	'Soft'
Sanction	Punishment	Compulsory treatment
Offender	You're bad and will be punished in proportion to the evil you caused	You're sick and quite irresponsible. We're going to take care of you, for your own good
Victim	You benefit when the offender is punished	Your needs are less important than the requirements of justice and the offender's necessities
Community	Intimidation is the best way to control offending behaviour and to make one understand what behaviour is not tolerated	Rehabilitation is a job for experts exclusively

Table 24.3 Homicide rates by region (1990s)

Region	Homicide per 100,000	No. of countries
Arab states	1.7	12
Western and Southern Europe	1.9	18
Southern Asia	2.2	7
Eastern Asia	5.5	4
Southeastern Asia	5.6	9
North America	6.1	2
Eastern Europe	8.6	16
Sub-Saharan Africa	13.0	17
Latin America and Caribbean	19.8	20

Source: Scuro (2005)

Crime, punishment and US foreign policy

Commentators normally look at figures such as these and deduce that, in Latin America and sub-Saharan Africa, the problems of crime and law enforcement are 'too complex and multidimensional', a matter of human nature in 'crime-inductive societies' in which 'masses of starving offenders are made reckless by indifference and chronic deprivation' (Kahn 2001: 38, 42). That is to say, these are problems no criminal justice system can resolve or possibly control, particularly when law enforcement is 'perverse' – in other words, it works exclusively 'the way resources allow' (AJUFE 2001). So, the argument goes on, one can understand why policing in Latin America (and, for that matter, also in sub-Saharan Africa) is so poor: it 'depends on resources much superior than public coffers can allocate', thereby tarnishing 'the image of criminal justice as whole because court judges simply cannot concoct convictions or contrive forms of punishment' (AJUFE 2001).[1]

The picture is made even more complex when it is observed that, in Latin America more than in any other part of the world, homicide rates arguably depend on the way individuals resolve what they see as grievous personal differences.[2] A recent police survey in the city of Sao Paulo, for example, revealed that, in murder cases, 80 per cent of the people involved knew one another or even loved each other. Nevertheless, murder figures are coming down steadily in large Latin American cities at a consistent rate of 4–6 per cent a year – even though experts say that this has nothing to do with a single social or economic factors, such as relative improvements in living conditions or reduced migratory flows. What seems to be making a difference is *mano dura* – that is, hard-line law enforcement that results in soaring rates of incarceration, prohibition, firearm control and, above all, *mano superdura*, extreme measures against drug dealers and 'dangerous' offenders.

Mano dura and *superdura* strategies are in keeping with the US Department of State's notion of how to 'create a more secure, democratic, and prosperous world for the benefit of the American people and the international community' (Farrar 2005). The primary agency promoting this is the INL, the Bureau of International Narcotics and Law Enforcement Affairs, whose meta-discourse[3] is to maintain 'security', 'democracy' and business interests in balance with a doctrine centred on anti-corruption and strong hemispheric commitment against narco-trafficking. Hence the need to establish criminal justice systems that are not only stable[4] but also competent in the identification, investigation and prosecution of offenders and criminal organizations. One of the key strategic thrusts of this doctrine is to disrupt the overseas production of illicit drugs and trafficking in close co-ordination with Latin American governments, intergovernmental groups (such as the G8 'Lyon Group') and international organizations (the UN and OAS).

So far US foreign policy in the region has been topically focused. For many years it was preoccupied with the 'war on drugs' (Scuro 2002: 295) so intensely that it failed to address most of 'the deep-seated institutional problems that kept partner-nation police forces from being effective in combating crime in all of its forms, including drug trafficking' (Farrar 2005). More recently, topical interests have been expanded and now include financial crime and terrorist fundraising; arms trafficking; smuggling illegal migrants and trafficking in human beings; cyber-crime; and intellectual property-rights theft, etc. Along with the enlarged focus came more strategies so that, rather than simply trying to build 'capable institutions to complement near-term operations-driven programming', US policy now also seeks to augment 'public engagement in improved law enforcement, anti-corruption, and rule of law [to be seen] as a basis of democracy and as a deterrent to terrorism' (Farrar 2005). The intention is to balance near-term operational support and longer-term alternative institution building, on the one hand, with 'soft side' crime prevention and education, on the other. In other words, the mission of INL is to promote 'top down' reform while endorsing grassroots-level initiatives to uphold a 'culture of lawfulness' – which includes using restorative justice as an ingredient to soothe deep civil-war wounds in Colombia with a three-year, 1.7 million dollars programme (US Embassy 2004).

Restorative justice: between the will of masters and shared responsibility

Instead of being understood as a new mode of justice with radically different messages for victims, offenders and the community (see Table 24.4), restorative justice in Latin America is in danger of being confused with the 'soft side' of retributive justice. In this respect, even though there are quasi-official documents stating that community and government may work together to change local conditions 'toward a more restorative system' (NIJ 2000), the US government's position is, in fact, hardly favourable to restorative justice. In 2002 the USA refused to collaborate with the small group of nations that drafted the UN's (2002) *Basic Principles on the Use of Restorative Justice Programmes in Criminal Matters*. More recently, Desmond Tutu's proposal to apply restorative justice in cases of terrorism was ruled out by a high-ranking State Department official. Today, at least as far as policy in Latin America is concerned, the US government's attitude to restorative justice has changed, but it still fails to differentiate restorative justice from the almost infinite list of alternative means to widen admission to legal facilities (Sen 1999) in 'weak states vulnerable to terrorist networks and drug cartels within their borders' (Farrar 2005). At the same time, Latin American officials and international organizations present restorative justice as a 'hope' for the region's problems with crime, violence, and judicial inefficiency (De Vitto *et al.* 2005: 13).

Given these limitations, is there any possibility that restorative justice in Latin America can mean anything different from what foreign and domestic 'masters' say it means? If so, can it become a tool for resolving issues that focus not only on individual responsibility but also on collective pledges and for contributing to building a cohesive society based on such values as respect, participation, inclusion, empowerment, consensual decision-making, repair of harm and the reintegration of society as a whole (Toward a Restorative Society 2005)? These problems, however, are less conditioned by the political cynicism of the masters than by the teething troubles in the

Table 24.4 Restorative justice: messages

Actor	Compromise
Offender	What you did caused damage and had consequences. You're responsible and capable of straightening things out
Victim	You are entitled to have your losses restored
Community	Members of the community must help victims and offenders to take on their responsibilities and to fulfil their commitments

selection of appropriate restorative practices, in the operation of these as interventions with a broad impact and, finally, in the evaluation of these processes' integrity ('restorativeness') and social and political relevance.

The status of restorative justice

In Latin America, as in other countries, attention has focused on the legal status of agreements reached in restorative processes. In this sense, the first and foremost obstacle for restorative justice relates to the technical grounds that condition its uses and results in relation to justice 'everybody understands'. The realistic way to bypass this is to say that all 'may be resolved by *finding a means* for taking agreements reached in conferences [*cámaras restaurativas*, in Spanish] into account in judicial sentencing' (Strang 2002: 203, emphasis added).

Problems, however, begin with the notion of 'crime' as a voluntary or reckless action (or fact) that causes injury to a person or damages a thing protected by law. Thus, whether the system is adversarial or inquisitorial (as in Europe and Latin America),[5] crime is a *public* wrong punishable by the state in criminal proceedings. The word 'public' here conveys law's irresistible concern with social behaviour; more precisely, one's 'fair' conduct in relation to 'others'. Therefore, prototypical crimes (such as homicide, theft and violation to personal physical or moral integrity) are offences against fundamental human rights, and individual action by the person wronged to sue for damages, injunction, decree of specific performance or declaration fails to redress the public dimension of the wrong. Only criminal justice can do that, but it leaves the victims with little in the way of remedies, particularly when the courts are overworked and law enforcement is badly managed.

In other words, social changes influence penal legislation and criminal codes, which are rapidly modified to answer to new realities. As a result, criminal classification and proceedings must adjust, not only because crime is increasingly more complex and inter-related but also in view of the transformation of criminal justice systems into gigantic administrative apparatuses affected by contemporary institutions' massive loss of legitimacy. Furthermore, the evolution of fundamental rights is setting limits to penal processes and making the search for judicial certainty progressively more unrealistic – most noticeably when courts do not admit evidence that is crucial for the determination of truth because of how it was obtained (Muñoz Conde 2000).

Restorative justice thinking could, arguably, have marched into this conceptual and procedural 'no-man's land'. However, efforts to offer it as a robust legal theory have been meagre and have been limited by an emphasis on *results*.[6] To prevent restorative definitions from becoming a 'hostage of laws and written norms', they are classified as resulting from 'shared judgements of the community affected by the offence' (Korte 2005). In truth, international findings that could have given substance to new definitions of crime are promising and encouraging, particularly in view of the success of restorative programmes in terms of 'victim satisfaction', 'restitution agreements completed without state supervision' and 'lesser amounts of reoffending'. None the less, procedures that achieve those results are seldom applied. For example, among hundreds of restorative programmes in progress in the USA, the vast majority prefer to use 'victim–offender mediation and dialogue' (50 per cent) or 'neighbourhood accountability boards' (30 per cent) instead of *cámaras* (just 12 per cent) – arguably the procedure that fits best the threefold Van Ness and Strong perspective of 'repairing harm', 'stakeholder involvement' and 'transformation of the community/government relationship' (Bazemore and Schiff, 2005).[7]

However, the idea that really gives force and direction to effective procedures is that people can come together to do more than resolve conflict: they can also consider preventive action. So, if strengthened with testable theories, restorative procedures may become powerful tools for rescuing the influence of the community and for reversing the demand for more police and more formal controls – thereby changing our conventional perspective on *crime*. Those procedures would then help participants to realize that accountability is a *communal virtue* and that they may 'become more involved in social justice issues' (Bazemore and Schiff 2005: 294). This increases the chances of success and enhances individual and collective capacity to build cohesive and newly reintegrated societies – something that criminal justice seldom does.

This opportunity exists everywhere, but notably in Latin America where restorative interventions have just been implemented. Uncompromising restorative thinkers are persuaded that, 'if conferencing networks must be put in operation to decide on judgements and prescriptions that differ from social objectives', the existing, inefficient systems of justice will be replaced (Korte 2005). If so, and if based on principles and verifiable theories, restorative practices will offer 'new opportunities for governments and communities' to attend to the needs of those affected by crime, and also to provide for 'positive changes throughout society' by stimulating 'macro-level changes to address corruption, access to justice, and generalised violence' (Parker 2005).

Restorative justice can, indeed, be approached as the 'soft side' of punishment or simply as a mechanism for delegalizing certain kinds of conflict. But its potential will be thereby limited for, if it is truly a new vision of justice (Zehr 1990: 180), it should serve as an official framework for an entirely original understanding and response to *all* forms of crime. The structural integrity of inquisitorial law may help to accomplish this task,[8] provided that *jurisdiversity* is preserved. Furthermore, in view of the widespread lack of confidence in current legal approaches and structures, there is a chance in Latin America to explore restorative justice as an alternative model of justice. However, if globalization of the rule of law continues to give the 'Americanization' of criminal justice systems a central role 'throughout Europe and (most substantially) Latin America' (Nadelmann 1997: 126), the most probable result will be a 'common-ization' of inquisitorial law.

Prospects for restorative justice in Latin America

A plan to reform systems of justice from a restorative point of view is already in hand (Bazemore and Walgrave 1999: 65–6). To begin with, this plan, outlined in a daring three-part agenda, proposes broad changes that shift the focus of criminal justice, currently centred on responses to crime, towards 'community solutions'. Once this is accomplished, the messages, performance objectives and methods used by the system to bring about its goals would be changed. Finally, participative structures would be developed from the bottom up, so that the system moves away from its conventional bureaucratic standards. To undertake these tasks, restorative justice adherents must implement programmes from *inside* the structure of the state, which means taking as theirs some of the most important challenges faced by the system today. Building a restorative justice system therefore means facing squarely current burdens, such as judicial log jams, which are arguably the worst and most singular warning sign of ailing justice in Latin America.

In Colombia, for example, during the 1990s the time required to conclude a legal matter in the lower courts averaged 3.2 years in civil matters and 3.9 years in criminal cases. Experts reckoned that, to deal with the backlog of cases completely, the 'courts would have to close to new suits for at least nine years' (Mercado 2005). Congress men therefore voted to implement 'alternative methods of dispute resolution' (Law no. 23/1991) and provisionally allowed citizens to administer justice without a court claim or ruling. Subsequently, again to 'unfasten court logjams, reduce costs, make proceedings run quicker and increase society's involvement in conflict resolution', the new constitution provided a role for private referees and facilitators in the performance of judicial functions.

However, despite increased legislative support, the use of conciliation (and arbitration) in Colombia remains modest and inconsistent (except in the case of some labour conflicts and in youth courts). The reason is that they were adopted simply as *dejudicialising tools* good for:

1 devolving jurisdictional competence to administrative organisms (such as the 'Casas de Justicia', created with support from USAID and international agencies, to place under one roof several agencies that can enforce law extra-judicially);
2 persuading citizens not to use the gargantuan judicial apparatus;
3 reducing log jams (with bonuses for 'outsourced' legal services); and
4 promoting traditional or community ways for minor dispute settlement.

So, despite its richness and potential, conciliation remains *informal* – a somewhat permanent gadget used only in limited, uncomplicated circumstances. This is generally true of judicial informality all over Latin America, which fosters:

1 poorly institutionalized programmes run by a mass of practitioners or small organizations not fully prepared for the job,

2 almost no investment in training or research (which means there is little connection between practices and immediate and intermediate outcomes and to longer-term changes in the well-being of 'clients');[9]

3 the implementation of programmes only as 'compensatory policy' for underprivileged segments of society; and

4 work done mostly on a voluntary basis by individuals and groups, with no consistent methodologies (Sinhoretto 2005).

Such problems can only be dealt with adequately if restorative procedures are introduced into the routines of justice systems. In Argentina, for instance, Law 24.573/1995 made mediation and conciliation quasi-integral aspects of the system, but they are used on a very restricted basis (Alvarez 2005). So, the best chances for a Latin America model of restorative justice integrated into the justice system and free and readily available to all are the Brazilian *special courts* – a nationwide system created in 1982 and manned by magistrates and (not everywhere) professional conciliators. The system works according to the principles of 'simplicity', 'informality' and 'swiftness', and it seeks agreements 'whenever possible' via conciliation. Its strength rests on the magistrates' much-enlarged power to decide more freely than in ordinary courts – standards of proof are commonsensical so that decisions are 'fairer' and closer to the 'common good' and the 'social objectives of law' (Nalini 2005).

On the other hand, this enhanced magistratal power indicates that, when the system was conceived, the lawgivers were less concerned with *how* it would function than with *who* would make the decisions. Thus, despite the fact that hundreds of special courts now function that have frequently absorbed half the demand made of the traditional judiciary, the rate of agreements through conciliation is falling markedly. System executives (that is, magistrates) say this has been caused by external factors, such as escalating social litigiousness, lawyers' resolve to litigate instead of trying to conciliate and, mostly, by 'contamination', and by the penchant of special court judges and conciliators to pass over the principles of 'informal, flexible, negotiated justice' to surrender to the bureaucratic ways of inquisitive justice (Schmidt 2005). This problem is illustrated in Figure 24.2, which shows the evolution in the first Brazilian state so to do of the building of a special court system. The number of facilities grew from two in 1986 to 169 in 2004 and there were 20 professional conciliators in 1986 whereas now there are almost 2,000 but, in spite of this growth, the percentage of agreements reached has fallen from 58 per cent (1986) to just 28 per cent (2004).

The problems of Brazilian special courts do indeed have to do with 'building a new juridical culture', but uncontrollable external factors are not the 'independent variable' (Scuro 2005). What the system needs is organizational change by means of a commitment to quality from those at the top – that is, the magistrates themselves. To achieve this, strategic human resource management should replace the fragmentary 'informal' and 'flexible' routines for recruiting conciliators – a process based on human resource planning, job analysis and performance appraisal, on feedback consistent with system goals and organizational structure and, above all, on

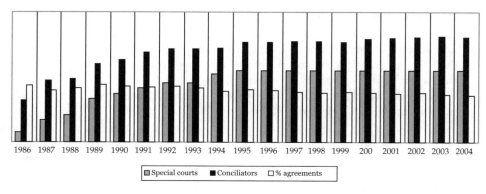

| | Special courts | ■ Conciliators | □ % agreements |

Figure 24.2 Agreements: Brazilian (State of Rio Grande do Sul) special civil courts, 1986–2004

the idea that special courts are effective, decisive and indispensable elements of the justice system.

The saga of Brazilian special courts suggests that the system is the natural ground for the further, definitive development of restorative justice, as part of a process that aims towards a new juridical culture. To achieve this, the system must elaborate a clearer notion of 'conciliation', not just in view of the needs of those directly involved in conflicts but also of the institutions' requirements for further evaluation criteria. Thus, depending on case complexity, restorative justice procedures should be added to present routines, focused not on legal guilt but on the uncovering of truth, on identifying responsibilities and on generating grounds for accord, amends, reintegration and inclusion. This requires maturity from restorative justice advocates and researchers in combining political awareness with understanding and rigour so that they can face domestic institutional resistance to change and heavy-handed foreign interference in the creation of 'capable institutions', and so that they can shape a genuine 'public commitment to the rule of law as basis of democracy and deterrent to terrorism' (Farrar 2005).

Notes

1   In truth, in some Latin American countries, law enforcement is among the most subsidized of public sectors. In Brazil, for example, it receives on average 10 per cent of the states' budgets. Brazilian police staffs are also among the largest in the world (278 officers per 100,000 population), behind only China, India, USA and Russia (sources: UN and Crime Trends, 1997).

2   Brazilians, for example, four times more than Americans, seem to have 'a startling propensity to shoot each other' (Rohter, *The New York Times*, 20 October 2005).

3   Meta-discourses are grandiose narratives with moral and pragmatic elements that societies use for self-interpretation and to assert their goals as the civilizing deeds of a chosen people who 'should shew forth the praises of him who has called you out of darkness into his marvellous light' (*The New Testament*, I Peter, 2: 9) (Scuro 2002: 293–4).

4 Institutional stability is precisely a factor that makes Latin American justice systems so impervious to change (Wheatley, *The Financial Times*, 15 November 2005).

5 The basic difference between inquisitorial and adversarial systems is that judges in the former actively determine the facts of a case whereas, in the latter, they act mainly as impartial referees.

6 The dynamics of justice systems is not conveyed by results alone, but mainly through processes involving regular, successive decisions – measured not only by numbers but also by the energy and inclinations of system members (Scuro 2004: 203).

7 According to the authors of the survey, in every programme there could have been instances of either 'horrible encounters' or provision for 'maximum healing', for 'often the most restorative encounters [happen] outside of any kind of programme' (Gordon Bazemore, pers. comm., 2005).

8 Daniel Van Ness (pers. comm., 2005).

9 Also a feature of restorative practices in the USA and elsewhere; see Bazemore and Ellis (Chapter 21, this volume).

References

AJUFE (Brazilian Federal Judges' Association) (2001) *Informativo AJUFE* (available online at www.ajufe.org.br).

Alvarez, G.S. (2005) *Estudio de Experiencias Comparativas en Resolución Alternativa de Disputas*. OAS/Department of Legal Affairs and Services (available online at http://www.undp.org/surf-panama/docs/resolucion_disputas.doc).

Bazemore, G. and Schiff, M. (2005) *Juvenile Justice Reform and Restorative Justice: Building Theory and Policy from Practice*. Cullompton: Willan Publishing.

Bazemore, G. and Walgrave, L. (1999) 'Restorative juvenile justice: in search of fundamentals and an outline for systemic reform', in G. Bazemore and L. Walgrave (eds) *Restorative Juvenile Justice: Repairing the Harm of Youth Crime*. Monsey, NY: Criminal Justice Press.

Braithwaite, J. (2004) *The Evolution of Restorative Justice*. Tokyo: United Nations Asia and Far East Institute for the Prevention of Crime and the Treatment of Offenders.

De Vitto, R., Sklamon, C. and Gomes Pinto, R.G. (eds) (2005) *Justiça Restaurativa*. Brasília, DF: Ministério da Justiça/Programmea das Nações Unidas para o Desenvolvimento (PNUD).

Farrar, J.D. (2005) *Transparency and the Rule of Law in Latin America*. Washington, DC: U.S. Department of State (available online at http://www.state.gov/p/inl/rls/rm/46913.htm).

Kahn, T. (2002) *Cidades Blindadas. Ensaios de Criminologia*. São Paulo: Conjuntura.

Korte, G. (2005) 'Derecho Restaurativo: campo de conocimientos de prácticas restaurativas.' Paper, Santo Domingo de Heredia, Costa Rica, 20–23 September.

Mercado, H.H. (2005) *Estado de los Metodos Alternativos de Solucíon de Conflictos en Colombia*. OAS/Department of Legal Affairs and Services (available online at http://www.oas.org/juridico).

Muñoz Conde, F. (2000) *La Búsqueda de la Verdad en el Proceso Penal*. Buenos Aires: Hammurabi.

Nadelmann, E.A. (1997) 'The Americanization of global law enforcement: the diffusion of American tactics and personnel', in W.F. McDonald (ed.) *Crime and Law Enforcement in the Global Village*. Highland Heights, KY: ACJS/Anderson.

Nalini, J.R. (2005) *Juzgados Especiales en Brasil*. OAS/Departament of Judicial Affairs and Services (available online at http://www.oas.org/juridico).

NIJ (National Institute of Justice) (2000) *How to Change your Local System*. Washington, DC: National Institute of Justice (available online at www.ojp.usdoj.gov/nij/rest-just/ch6/chg_sys.html).

Parker, L. (2005) 'Developing restorative practices in Latin America.' Paper presented at the Eleventh United Nations Congress on Crime Prevention and Criminal Justice Ancillary Meeting, Bankok, 21 April.

Schmidt. R.P. (2005) *Jornal da AJURIS*, March.

Scuro, P. (2002) 'Justiça, Controle Penal Transnacional e "o mais frio de todos os monstros"', *Revista da EMARF*, 2: 291–308.

Scuro, P. (2004) *Sociologia Geral e Jurídica*. Sao Paulo: Saraiva.

Scuro, P. (2005) *Os Juizados Especiais Cíveis do Rio Grande do Sul*. Porto Alegre: Escola Superior da Magistratura.

Sen, A. (1999) *Nuevo Examen de la Desiguald*. México, DF: Alianza.

Sinhoretto, J. (2005) *Acesso à Justiça por Sistemas Alternativos de Administração de Conflitos. Mapeamento Nacional de Programmeas Públicos e Não-governamentais*. Brasília, DF: Ministério da Justiça.

Strang, H. (2002) *Repair or Revenge: Victims and Restorative Justice*. Oxford: Clarendon Press.

Toward a Restorative Society (2005) Conference. Wellington, New Zealand, 10–11 October.

US Embassy (Colombia) (2004) 'Restorative justice, coexistence and peace' (available online at http://bogota.usembassy.gov/wwws0065.shtml).

Zehr, H. (1990) *Changing Lenses: A New Focus for Crime and Justice*. Scottdale, PA: Herald Press.

Section E
North America

Daniel W. Van Ness

The beginning of the modern restorative justice movement might be traced to two young men in Elmira, Ontario, and their 22 vandalism victims.[1] With the cautious approval of a sentencing judge, the probation officer and a community volunteer organized meetings with each victim for the offenders to apologize and work out restitution agreements (Kelly 2004). The probation officer was so impressed with the relational impact of the meetings that he developed it into a project called the Victim Offender Reconciliation Program (VORP) and within a few years had started an NGO in nearby Kitchner, Ontario to provide and promote the programme. Interest in the programme spread within Mennonite networks into other parts of Canada, and similar programmes began to develop. In 1978, a VORP programme opened in Elkhart, Indiana, directed by Howard Zehr, also a Mennonite. In his subsequent efforts to explain why victims and offenders who went through VORP were more satisfied than those handled in ordinary court proceedings, he suggested that they represented different forms of justice. Retributive justice was found in court; restorative justice emerged in VORP.

Other restorative justice processes in North America

Descriptions of restorative processes typically focus on three approaches: victim–offender reconciliation/mediation, conferences and circles. The North American connection to the first has been presented above, but this region has connections with the other two as well.

Conferences developed in New Zealand in 1989, where the meetings were facilitated by social workers. Shortly thereafter a local jurisdiction in Australia, Wagga Wagga, adapted the New Zealand model for use by the police. Part of the adaptation consisted of preparing a short script that conference facilitators could use in leading the conference. In 1994, this approach was presented to audiences in North America. One result was the creation of an NGO to promote conferencing now known as the International Institute for Restorative Practices, which has not only conducted widespread training in North America but also around the world. In that year it also began sponsoring annual conferences that alternate between North America and Europe and that have provided a vehicle for networking among practitioners and researchers (Wachtel 2002).

The third model, circles, grew out of first-nations practices in Canada. In these communities, harmonious relationships and problem solving approaches to justice are part of the tradition. Circle processes were one of the vehicles for training the council of members of the community in how to address community issues. In 1992, a Yukon Territorial Court Judge, Barry Stuart, agreed to use a circle to help him determine the sentence for a member of the Na-cho-Ny'ak Dun First Nation (*R. v. Moses*, 1992). The resulting agreement was so much more comprehensive and appropriate than what Judge Stuart could have devised himself that he began using circles on an increased basis and training other judges to do the same. Over time, awareness of circles spread across Canada and the USA. Circles are used to determine sentences, but they are also used to address conflict and to assist victims and offenders in their reintegration (see Pranis *et al.* 2003; Chapter 4, this volume).

The roles of community-based organizations in the early development of restorative justice

Initial VORP programmes were small and funded both privately and, to varying degrees, by government. Most were pilot projects, and one of their common problems was to attract case referrals. Most worked with juvenile offenders only, although in Canada adult offenders were also included. When people running these programmes got together, they not only discussed practical issues such as funding and case referrals, but they also sought to deepen their understandings of restorative values. There was a significant bias towards community-based programmes in the early days, although this changed over time as system-based participants joined them. Community-based practitioners worried about how to avoid co-option by the government, even as they also struggled to be noticed by local governments (Van Ness 2002: 130).

NGOs played an important role in advancing restorative programmes and ideas throughout the continent. Initially these groups were primarily religious. In the late 1970s and through the 1980s, the Mennonite Central Committee (MCC) publicized VORP programmes and restorative justice generally through its newsletters, a series of pamphlets and training events and manuals. Howard Zehr is the best known restorative justice leader to have played key roles in the MCC, but there were others as well. The Criminal Justice Programme of the Presbyterian Church, USA, took a strong interest in restorative justice during the 1980s, and among other things commissioned study guides on the topic for adults. The Church Council on Justice and Corrections in Canada made submissions on restorative justice to a parliamentary law reform commission, compiled a compendium of restorative options available in Canada and elsewhere, co-sponsored a national symposium on restorative justice, and developed and sponsored the highly regarded Collaborative Justice Project, which focused on serious crimes and on meeting the needs of the victims, offenders and communities. The USA-based Justice Fellowship, a branch of Prison Fellowship Ministries organized in the early 1980s to advocate for sentencing reforms, developed a series of public policy proposals based on restorative justice that it promoted to state and federal officials. Because it was part of an evangelical religious organization, its advocacy gave credibility to restorative justice among politically and theologically conservative communities and public officials.

Over time, non-religious NGOs emerged to provide leadership as well. The Victim Offender Mediation Association grew out of informal gatherings of restorative justice practitioners in the 1980s, and continues to play a significant role in North America and internationally through annual conferences, newsletters and its website. The PACT Institute of Justice was created in 1981 to provide training and research on restorative justice programmes; this work moved to the University of Minnesota School of Social Work in 1990, which established a research and training centre now called the Center for Restorative Justice and Peacemaking. Other academic institutions began to take active roles in researching and developing restorative initiatives. Examples include the Community Justice Institute at Florida Atlantic University, the Conflict Transformation Programme at Eastern Mennonite University in Virginia, the Center for Peacemaking and Conflict Studies at Fresno Pacific University, the restorative justice concentration at Queen's Theological College in Ontario and the Centre for Restorative Justice at Simon Fraser University in Vancouver.

However, perhaps the most profound community influence came from the indigenous populations of North America. In both the USA and Canada, the justice processes of these people had been suppressed as part of a policy of containment and Westernization. But many within those communities retained memories of practices and a way of living that resonated with and informed restorative justice thinking. Elders and leaders within those societies began to incorporate older understandings of peace-making into their justice systems and, when possible, to use older processes within the Western criminal justice system (for an excellent collection of articles on this topic, see McCaslin 2005). Two very important contributions of those nations to restorative justice are the peace-making circle mentioned above (Pranis *et al.* 2003; Chapter 4, this volume) and the development of healing lodges for incarcerated aboriginal men and women in Canada. In addition, first-nations peoples worked with Corrections Service of Canada (CSC) and the national parole board to develop elder-assisted parole hearings for aboriginal offenders.

One significant consequence of community-based participation in the development, expansion and evaluation of restorative programmes is that restorative justice in North America has had a strong community emphasis, as opposed to parts of Europe, for example, where restorative programmes have been largely initiated and funded by government agencies (see Section C, this chapter).

The growth of governmental support

Almost from the outset, some government officials became interested in the potential of restorative justice. But in the late 1980s and the 1990s, this interest turned into significant system support and endorsement. While there were too many initiatives to review, the following examples will illustrate the variety of ways through which that support was expressed.

Legislation

In 1987, the Canadian House of Commons Standing Committee on Justice and Solicitor General began a review of criminal justice and corrections in the aftermath of a national debate on the death penalty. In the course of the review it became acquainted with the concept of restorative justice and heard testimony from practitioners from across the country. Its 1988 report, *Taking Responsibility,* included a discussion of restorative justice and made recommendations for sentencing reform that would encourage offenders to take responsibility for the harm they had caused, and to make victim–offender reconciliation programmes available when requested by the parties. After experiencing a dramatic increase in the prison population, and following consultations between the federal government and provincial and territorial officials, the government adopted a new sentencing code in 1995 that articulated restorative purposes for sentencing along with the conventional purposes of retribution, deterrence and incapacitation. Four years later, the Supreme Court of Canada upheld the legislation and endorsed the increased use of restorative justice that the legislation called for. The Youth Criminal Justice Act, which became effective in 2003, added a number of restorative approaches for use with juvenile offenders (Daubney 2005: 1–8), and the Correctional and Conditional Release Act 1992 created restorative options for aboriginal offenders and their communities.

In the USA, responsibility for criminal justice and corrections has rested more with states than with the federal government. A survey of state juvenile justice policies found that only six states did not explicitly refer to restorative justice in statutes, policy statement, mission statement, programme plans and/or evaluation measures (O'Brien 2005: 4). Much of the impetus for this reform came as a result of the BARJ project mentioned below.

Leadership

In both countries, significant support for restorative initiatives has come from individual officials and agencies that have championed restorative reforms.

During the early 1990s, the CSC worked with aboriginal peoples and community partners (such as the Task Force on Federally Sentenced Women, 1990) to pioneer restorative approaches and healing lodge facilities for female and aboriginal offenders. A revised internal grievance process for offenders developed by the CSC in 1995 led to more mediation/dialogue options for inmates and also to the creation of a restorative justice position and later a branch in the CSC. The branch provides training to staff, offenders and volunteers within prisons and education to the broader public. With the CSC's Chaplaincy Branch, it has sponsored Restorative Justice Week since 1996, providing resources for events across Canada and internationally. The CSC pioneered with community partners the application of restorative processes to serious crime cases. It has been a supporter of such innovations as inmate–community restorative justice coalitions, victim surrogate/empathy programmes and restorative living units in prisons. The CSC Community Chaplaincy developed circles of support and accountability, which link trained community members and sex offenders being released from prison to create a safe and secure living environment for the ex-offender and for the surrounding community (see CSC 2002). The CSC has offered an annual Restorative Justice Award since 1999 and supports various community based restorative and victim advisory committees.

Another example of this sort of championing at the state government level occurred in Minnesota. In 1994, the Department of Corrections created the position of restorative justice planner and hired Kay Pranis to fill that position. This initiative was designed to promote restorative justice and to assist the Department of Corrections, local corrections, community organizations, legislators and other policy-makers, educators and law enforcement in considering how it might be implemented throughout the state. The initiative provided education, technical assistance and networking to these constituencies. As a result, several restorative practices were adopted in schools to deal with conflict there, family group conferencing was piloted by police, community corrections departments began offering restorative processes to victims and offenders, victim empathy programmes were begun in prisons and neighbourhood groups began providing circles for young offenders from those communities (Pranis 1998).

The final example is of local officials who launched a series of restorative programmes in Batavia, New York, just ten minutes away from the notorious Attica Prison. Beginning in the early 1980s and continuing through the 1990s, sheriff Doug Call, his successor Gary Maha, Judge Glenn Morton and a sheriff's employee, Dennis Witman, have built something they call 'Genesee Justice' (after the name of their county). The sheriff's department offers victim–offender dialogue meetings, community service, intensive victim assistance, child advocacy and domestic violence programmes (among others), each focused on offender accountability, victim support and reparation and, when possible, restorative encounters among the stakeholders (Swift 1996).

Pranis points out that restorative justice must ultimately be designed and implemented locally, but that state and federal officials can provide leadership in presenting and legitimizing a restorative vision, by facilitating the search by local jurisdictions for resources, ideas, networking and training, and by ensuring that the resulting programmes are fair and appropriate (Pranis 1998).

Model building, training and assessment

A third role that governments have played is to support the creation of models, training and evaluations. This was the role that the US Justice Department played during the late 1980s under the leadership of Attorney General Janet Reno. Three departments became involved in significant projects related to restorative justice. One was the Office of Juvenile Justice and Delinquency Prevention which, in 1993, began an initiative called the Balanced and Restorative Justice project. The purpose of the project was to work locally to advance reforms in juvenile justice policy and practice by providing training and technical assistance (Bazemore and Umbreit 1998: xi). The project was active in 50 jurisdictions and 35 states, and was the impetus for much of the legislative reforms noted above. The second department was the National Institute of Corrections, which sponsored demonstration projects, created a training curriculum on restorative justice, delivered training at regional symposia and through national videoconferencing, and supported research (Dooley 1997). The third department was the Office of Victims of Crime (OVC), which has sponsored and published the results of projects focused on the interests of victims.

Anomalies within the region

Michael Tonry has observed that there are now four competing conceptions of sentencing in the USA: indeterminate, structured sentencing (e.g. guidelines), risk-based sentencing and restorative/community justice. He explained his reasons for including restorative justice in this way: 'A fully elaborated system exists nowhere,' he points out, 'but there is considerable activity in many States, and programmes based on community/restorative principles are beginning to deal with more serious crimes and criminals and to operate at every stage of the justice system, including within prisons.' It is 'spreading rapidly and into applications that a decade ago would have seemed visionary. These include various forms of community involvement and emphasise offender accountability, victim participation, reconciliation, restoration and healing as goals (though which goals are emphasised and with what respective weights vary widely)' (Tonry 1999: 1–4) If this is true in the USA, it is certainly true in Canada, whose Supreme Court has recognized restorative justice as one of the country's primary sentencing philosophies.

Nevertheless, if one looks at US and Canadian justice systems through a 'restorative lens,' two anomalies present themselves. The first is the strained relationship that often exists between restorative justice proponents and victim support proponents. The second is the almost schizophrenic political climate that has both invested in restorative justice programmes and in increasingly harsh criminal justice penalties for offenders. The first challenges the claim that restorative justice is victim centred. The second raises questions about the politics of restorative justice.

Restorative justice and victim advocates

The focus on repairing harm done to victims, on inclusion of all parties and on accountability of offenders to victims suggests that victims play a prominent role in restorative justice theory and practice. It is not unusual to hear that 'victims are central' in restorative justice, implying that, in contrast to the offender-oriented criminal justice system, restorative justice begins and ends with victims. In light of these stated values, it is surprising to discover that the support of many victim assistance providers is lukewarm at best towards restorative justice.

It has been observed that victim advocacy in the USA and, to a certain extent in Canada, has focused on the rights of victims, whereas in Europe the emphasis was on the needs of victims for support services (Strang 2002: 28–33). An early (and continuing) effort in North America was to insist that law enforcement agencies and courts take more seriously crimes such as sexual violence, drunk driving and domestic violence. To the extent that restorative justice appears to undo these hard-fought gains, some victim advocates have resisted it. Furthermore, if restorative justice is a process designed to facilitate confession, forgiveness and reconciliation between the parties, it could be easily misused to perpetuate domestic violence syndrome.

Victim assistance practitioners have raised a number of more generalized concerns about restorative justice. In actual practice, many restorative programmes seem to be driven by the demands of the criminal justice system so that those programmes are actually far more offender oriented than victim oriented. Secondly, to the extent that victims feel restorative justice promises genuine offender apologies and a significant degree of repair, victims may feel harmed again if they do not receive these. Thirdly, to the extent that offenders participate in order to receive more lenient sentences, victims are likely to mistrust their motivations, words and even actions. Further, to the extent that victim supporters believe that this is why offenders participate, they will be unlikely to recommend victims participate (Mika *et al.* 2002; Achilles 2004).

From 1999 to 2002, the Institute for Justice and Peacebuilding at Eastern Mennonite University co-ordinated a 'Listening project' whose purpose was to stimulate increased understanding among victim support and restorative justice advocates about their common and diverse perspectives. The final report had recommendations for both, and five common recommendations. The first was to continue and expand structured dialogue between the two communities in order to agree on terminology, refine models, develop evaluation criteria and so forth. The second was to form teams of both restorative justice and victim proponents with national perspectives in their areas of expertise to offer feedback locally. The third was to develop a series of short publications developed by a consortium from both groups that offer guidance to restorative practitioners, courts and other justice officials. The fourth was to develop collaborative training programmes that could be offered nationally and locally. The final recommendation was to develop collaboratively standards and evaluation measures that could be used not only to evaluate restorative programmes but also more accurately to distinguish between the values and vision of restorative justice and its actual performance and outcomes (Mika *et al.* 2002: 18–19).

Restorative justice and an increasingly harsh criminal justice system

There were 2.3 million people imprisoned in the USA at the end of 2004; 1.5 million were in federal and state prisons, and the rest primarily in local jails. The US incarceration rate in that year was 724 inmates per 100,000 residents. This means that one in every 138 US residents was in prison or jail at the end of 2004 (Harrison and Beck 2005). Although data collection differences make it impossible to make firm comparisons, a 1981 survey reported that there were 329,122 prisoners in state and federal prisons (US Department of Justice 1981). These figures underscore an important public policy reality in the USA, at least: expanding prison populations have overwhelmingly overshadowed any growth in the use of restorative justice.

Canada's experience has been different. The prison population was actually lower in 2003 than in 1997 (32,327 compared with 34,041; this includes combined federal and provincial prisoners and those awaiting trial or sentence) (Public Safety and Emergency Preparedness Portfolio Corrections Statistics Committee 2004: 37). Furthermore, its incarceration rate of 116 prisoners per 100,000 residents, while higher than many Western European countries, is much lower than in the USA (Walmsley 2005: 3).

There are several explanations for why restorative justice, in spite of its claims of being a new paradigm of justice, could be embraced in the USA along with expanded use of imprisonment. One is that while restorative justice has captured the imagination of some, it has not significantly permeated criminal justice policy in the way hoped for by its advocates. The converts within and outside the system have successfully obtained support for restorative initiatives, but these have been marginalized and not become mainstreamed into the criminal justice system (Roche 2003). A second and related explanation is that arguments for restorative justice programmes have frequently been framed in terms of conserving finite prison space for the more serious offenders without sacrificing accountability of less serious offenders. This argument may be politically useful in that it appeals to liberals as well as conservatives, but it fails to confront the public fear and hopelessness, or the vested interests, that fuel the drive for longer sentences (Shelden 2004). Whatever the reason, the dramatic expansion of imprisonment in the USA is an anomaly when contrasted with the (at least verbal) acceptance of restorative justice.

Conclusion

North American NGOs have been important participants in the development of restorative justice processes. While in Canada it appears that restorative principles have taken root in legislation and official government endorsement for both minor and serious crimes, it appears to have been largely reserved for minor crimes in the USA, with harsher and harsher sanctions being imposed on violent, repeat and drug offenders. This represents both a challenge and an opportunity for restorative justice.

Acknowledgements

I wish to thank David Daubney, Jane Miller-Ashton and Annie Warner Roberts for their advice and suggestions on this section of this chapter, some of which I was wise enough to take.

Notes

1   There were programmes in North America that brought victims and offenders together to pay restitution, but these were merely reparative in intent, and not focused on the relationship between the victim and offender, as was VORP (Umbreit 1985: 1).

References

Achilles, M. (2004) 'Will restorative justice live up to its promise to victims?', in H. Zehr and B. Toews (eds) *Critical Issues in Restorative Justice*. Monsey, NY: Criminal Justice Press.

Bazemore, G. and Umbreit, M.S. (1998) *Guide for Implementing the Balanced and Restorative Justice Model*. Washington, DC: US Department of Justice, Office of Justice Programmes, Office of Juvenile Justice and Delinquency Prevention.

Correctional Service of Canada (2002) *Circles of Support and Accountability: A Guide to Training Potential Volunteers*. Ottawa: Correctional Service of Canada.

Daubney, D. (2005) 'Establishing a framework for the use of restorative justice in criminal matters in Canada.' Paper presented at workshop 2, *Enhancing Criminal Justice Reform Including Restorative Justice*, at the eleventh United Nations congress on Crime Prevention and Criminal Justice, Bangkok (available online at http://www.icclr.law.ubc.ca/Publications/Reports/11_un/DAUBNEY%202005%final%20paper.pdf.

Dooley, M. (1997) 'The NIC on restorative justice: a brief history of the NIC's involvement in community justice', *Corrections Today*, 59: 110–19.

Harrison, P.M. and Beck, A.J. (2005) 'Prisoners in 2004', *Bureau of Justice Statistics Bulletin*, October.

Kelly, R. (2004) 'The Elmira story – Victim Offender Reconciliation Programme (VORP)' (available online at http://www.cjiwr.com/resources_article_6.html).

McCaslin, W.D. (ed.) (2005) *Justice as Healing: Indigenous Ways*. St. Paul, MN: Living Justice Press.

Mika, H., Achilles, M., Halbert, E., Stutzman Amstutz, L. and Zehr, H. (2002) *Taking Victims and Their Advocates Seriously: A Listening Project*. Akron, PA: Mennonite Central Committee.

O'Brien, S.P. (2005) 'National survey looks at states' development and implementation of restorative justice policy', *Kaleidoscope of Justice: Highlighting Restorative Juvenile Justice*, 1: 4–5.

Pranis, K. (1998) 'The Minnesota Restorative Justice Initiative: a model experience', in National Institute of Justice (eds) *Restorative Justice: On-Line Notebook* (available online at http://www.ojp.usdoj.gov/nij/rest-just/ch1/mnrjmodel.htm) (originally published in *The Crime Victims Report*, May/June 1997).

Pranis, K. and Stuart, B. and Wedge, M. (2003) *Peacemaking Circles: From Crime to Community*. St. Paul, MN: Living Justice Press.

Roche, D. (2003) 'Review article: gluttons for restorative justice', *Economy and Society*, 32: 630–44.

Shelden, R.G. (2004) 'It's more profitable to *treat* the disease than to *prevent* it: why the prison industrial complex needs crime.' Center on Juvenile and Criminal Justice (available online at http://www.cjcj.org/pdf/treat.pdf).

Strang, H. (2002) *Repair or Revenge: Victims and Restorative Justice. Clarendon Studies in Criminology*. Oxford and New York: Oxford University Press.

Swift, R. (1996) 'A way out', *New Internationalist*, August (available online at http://www.newint.org/issue282/awayout.html).

Tonry, M. (1999) 'The fragmentation of sentencing and corrections in America.' Paper presented at the Executive Sessions on Sentencing and Corrections, National Institute of Justice: Washington, DC, September.

Umbreit, M.S. (1985) *Victim Offender Mediation: Conflict Resolution and Restitution*. Washington, DC: National Institute of Corrections.

US Department of Justice, Bureau of Justice Statistics (1981) 'Prisoners in 1980', *Bureau of Justice Statistics Bulletin*, 3 (May).

Van Ness, D.W. (2002) 'Creating restorative systems', in L. Walgrave (ed.) *Restorative Justice and the Law*. Cullompton: Willan Publishing.

Wachtel, T. (2002) 'Dreaming of a new reality: welcoming remarks.' Paper presented at the Third International Conference, Conferencing, Circles and other Restorative Practices, 8–10 August, Minneapolis (available online at http://www.iirp.org/library/mn02/mn02_wachtel.html).

Walmsley, R. (2005) *World Prison Population List* (6th edn). London: International Centre for Prison Studies, King's College London.

Section F
Pacific

Gabrielle Maxwell and Hennessey Hayes

Introduction

The Pacific region is of particular interest to students of restorative justice for two important reasons. It is in many senses the cradle of modern restorative justice processes within Western justice systems: the developments of the last 15 years in New Zealand and Australia demonstrate a variety of ways in which restorative theory can be effectively translated into formal processes and general practice within the structure of legislative frameworks and modern urban societies. At the same time, in the islands of Polynesia and Melanesia, a variety of examples of older indigenous forms of restorative practice are still operating. Thus this section provides a picture of both the old and the new. And it enables us to examine the strengths and weaknesses of both and their very different impact on participants.

The Pacific Islands

Most Polynesian and Melanesian cultures report the widespread use of extended family and village processes of meeting to resolve disputes and heal conflict. In this part of the review, we first present a case study of the *ifoga* of Western Samoa drawn primarily from Consedine (1995: 120–31) and then provide a more general account of practices in Melanesia drawing largely on Dinnen (2003).

Western Samoa: a Polynesian example

In most of Polynesia, traditionally there was a clear power structure in both the family and the tribe. In Samoa, *matai* (family elders) make up the village *fono* (council) that is responsible for all major decisions, including judicial decisions, through a process of negotiation, debate and compromise. It is the *fono* that makes the laws of village and decides how breaches should be punished; traditionally this could be by exile or beatings but, also, through the offending party offering compensation (*ifoga*). *Ifoga* literally means 'to bow down', an act that signals humbling and apology. In the case of individual offenders, they and the families will sit outside the home of a victim with their mats over their heads in a display of reconciliation. They will continue sitting until the victims come out. There will then be a process of negotiation that usually ends in the acceptance of compensation, forgiveness and reconciliation.

The introduction of a Western system of justice has led to conflict with the system of *fono* decision-making and the settlement of disputes through *ifoga*. The differences lie not only in the source of authority and the nature of punishments but also in the different roles given to the group and the individual. Ownership and responsibility traditionally lie with the group in Samoa but in the Western legal system the individual is paramount. There has been intense debate over the many cases where the two systems demand very different outcomes and the consequences of these for both the collective and the individuals.

Currently the *fono* operate under the Village Fono Act 1990 and remain responsible for maintaining order and customs, although now outcomes usually consist of fines that can be paid with money, food or fine mats. Over recent years, the courts have taken into account any restorative role played by *ifoga*, and new options for formalizing restorative practice within the justice system are being considered.

Melanesia

In Melanesia there are a variety of informal traditional structures for managing conflict and delivering justice. But, unlike the situation in Western Samoa, power is widely diffused, although mostly confined to adult males, rather than located in a single authority. Notions of reciprocity and equivalence are crucial to redressing wrongs and most approaches typically entail a strong element of bargaining and compromise. Any particular settlement reflects the current distribution of power. The powerful interpret *kastom* (customary rules, practices) to their advantage and the interpretation of *kastom* changes with shifts in the balance of power.

Settlements, both within and between different groups, take the form of ornate peace and reconciliation ceremonies involving the payment of compensation or the exchange of gifts. The main purpose of settlement is the restoration of stable relationships. Solutions are likely to be restorative when the parties are bound together through kinship or other forms of social or economic relationships. Punitive and retributive approaches are more likely for the most serious breaches of social norms or in situations where there is no morally binding relationship between the parties. Cycles of warfare and peace-making have characterized relationships between many groups. Asymmetrical encounters where men were killed or dispersed, women captured and land occupied have existed alongside relationships determined by long-term conceptions of balance.

As in Western Samoa, the impact of colonial administrations has been to introduce Western justice systems while at the same time there has also been some attempt to integrate local systems of *kastom* within the new structures. Examples include the 'island courts' in Vanuatu and the Fijian Constitution in force between 1990 and 1998. Informal methods of dispute resolution within local communities continue in many areas. Indeed, the informal justice system remains the most accessible and commonly used system for most of the people in Papua New Guinea, the Solomon Islands and Vanuatu, where 85 per cent of the population live in rural areas.

Many tensions arise from the differences in expectations due to the multiple systems, and this has led to the re-emergence of older patterns, such as the tribal fighting in Papua New Guinea. *Kastom* is no longer always effective in the face of lessening social cohesion and increased Westernization of values and social and economic relationships. There is also a tension in relation to human rights. *Kastom* concentrates power in the hands of a few and often fails to recognize the equal rights of women, children and men. Women have been imprisoned for adultery while their male partners have gone unpunished, and children have been treated harshly for minor offences.

Western justice, too, has problems. There have been complaints about the mistreatment of children by the police, and about the lengthy delays and high costs of court processes that fail to fix problems and restore peace to communities. As a result, within Melanesia there has been increasing diversity in approaches to crime and conflict, and growing calls for developing restorative justice as an alternative to both Western law and customary processes.

New Zealand[1]

Origins and legislation

New Zealand society is influenced importantly by the Polynesian cultures of a large number of its people[2] and particularly of Maori, the indigenous people. Within Maori society, conflicts and problems were traditionally dealt with in family and community meetings. Calls to return to these processes, together with Maori concerns about the institutionalization of their children, exerted a strong influence on the values and processes set out in the current child welfare and youth justice legislation. The Children, Young Persons and their Families Act 1989 emphasizes the responsibility of families and family groups for decisions about children, in partnership with and with the support of the state, through the process of the family group conference (FGC). In addition, concerns over victims led to their recognition and inclusion in decision-making.

Since then, the Sentencing Act 2002 and the Victims Rights Act 2002 were adopted to allow judges in the adult criminal courts to refer matters to a restorative justice conference; the judges are required to take into account any outcomes of such a conference in *all* cases in which one has been held.

Values

The principles and objectives of the youth justice system emphasize the protection of rights of the children and young people and the importance of ensuring that responses to offending are diversionary, timely, fair and just. Such values are consistent with those in many other jurisdictions. Other principles, which can now be identified as consistent with restorative justice theory, emphasize participation, repair, healing and reintegration. The Act requires that offenders, their families and victims are to be involved in decisions, young people are to be made accountable by making amends to their victims, and plans are to be put in place to respond to young people's needs and to reintegrate them in society. The family group conference is now recognized as the first example of a mechanism within a traditional Western system that makes a restorative justice solution central to determining the response to offending, while still enabling the sanctions of the court to be available when necessary.

Processes

Family group conferences

In the youth justice system, the family group conference is the key decision-making procedure for the top 25 per cent of offenders,[3] including all serious offending except for the few cases of murder and manslaughter dealt with in the adult courts. Conferences may originate from either a direct referral by the police or a referral from the Youth Court to a youth justice co-ordinator employed by the social welfare department. Normally, those who attend include the young offenders, parents, extended family members and supporters, victims, a police youth-aid officer, a youth advocate in court cases and the facilitator.

The conference begins with introductions, moves to discussion about what happened and canvasses options for responding. The family then retires to develop a plan after which the conference reconvenes to discuss, modify and agree on the final plan. Actual conference arrangements with respect to venue and process can vary widely depending on the participants' wishes. Outcomes will usually involve apologies, some measures that aim to repair the harm to the victim, work in the community (if possible related to the offending) and/or referral to an appropriate rehabilitative or reintegrative programme for the young person and/or his or her parents.

Restorative justice conferences

Most restorative justice conferences are arranged by one of the 19 community programmes on contract to accept judicial referrals. In addition, programmes accept self-referrals from offenders, victims or other members of the community. Most are guided by core values similar to FGCs in the youth justice system, but they are different from FGCs in terms of offence seriousness, referral source and in the requirement that both victim and offender agree to participate before a conference is held. There are, additionally, important differences in practice and effectiveness between the various programmes.

Police youth diversion

Only about a quarter of young offending cases are considered serious enough for referral to an FGC or youth court. The rest are dealt with by police youth-aid officers through the use of warnings or diversionary plans.

After investigating officers make their reports about the circumstances and impact of the offences, youth-aid officers meet with the young offenders and their parents to decide on a plan that is consistent with the restorative values set out in the legislation. Victims and schools may also be consulted. The resulting plans are similar in type to those for more serious offenders but usually contain fewer elements, smaller financial contributions (usually less than $50) and fewer hours of work in the community (usually less than 30 hours).

Research

New Zealand has been fortunate to have considerable and varied research on all aspects of the system. Data are drawn from files, interviews and observation. Studies have often included large samples, and some have covered all those involved in an intervention. Further, a variety of designs and comparison strategies have been used in conducting the research. Consequently, the conclusions from those studies have become increasingly reliable and influential in affecting policy and practice.

In summary, results of these studies demonstrate that the outcomes of the processes described above are largely restorative rather than retributive, that for the most part the parties are actively involved in the processes and agree with decisions, and that the resulting outcomes primarily focus on repairing harm and reintegrating offenders rather than on punishing and restricting them (Maxwell and Morris 1993, 1999; Maxwell *et al.* 2004a, 2004b). Furthermore, these results confirm the worldwide findings of greater satisfaction of all parties with restorative processes when compared with traditional court processes (Law Talk 2005).

Key features of best practice identified by research include fair and respectful treatment of all participants, an absence of stigmatic shaming and retributive outcomes, and processes that enable young people to understand what is happening, to feel supported, forgiven, remorseful and able to repair the harm they had caused, and to determine not to reoffend (Maxwell *et al.* 2004a, 2004b).

In general, research shows that when those involved in restorative processes have committed moderately serious or serious offences, when plans are carried out and when those plans include reintegrative elements (i.e. support programmes and vocational or educational opportunities), there is evidence of reduced reoffending and improved positive life outcomes. On the other hand, processes and plans that are restrictive or punitive, or that result in stigmatic shaming of offenders, are associated with increased reoffending (Maxwell *et al.* 2004a, 2004b).

Research has also been done on the impact of preliminary screening of cases, and of the presence of victims. Both programme elements significantly reduce the number of cases that qualify for a conference, but it appears that conferences that proceed with no screening and without the presence of the victim will nevertheless often result in constructive and effective outcomes (Maxwell *et al.* 2004b).

Finally, the research shows that there are financial savings to the justice system when adult offenders are handled through restorative processes rather than court, particularly with more serious offences. This is largely because of the lower costs of keeping offenders in the community compared with the costs of extensive court processes and penal responses (Maxwell *et al.* 1999).

Australia[4]

Like New Zealand, Australia is a world leader in restorative justice conferencing, and legislatively based conferencing schemes are in place in all but one Australian jurisdiction (Victoria). The rise of restorative justice in Australia was largely influenced by developments in New Zealand. Below, we summarize current developments in restorative justice conferencing in Australia by jurisdiction and follow with a summary of indicative research findings on conferencing processes and outcomes.

South Australia (SA). SA is the jurisdiction with the most experience in conferencing and it was the first Australian jurisdiction to implement a statutory conferencing scheme. SA conducts conferences for approximately 1,650 young offenders each year for offences ranging from minor property offences to serious person offences, including serious assault and sexual assault. SA, like several other Australian jurisdictions, has adopted the 'New Zealand model' of family conferencing. This means that conferences are managed and run by professionals other than the police.

New South Wales (NSW). Restorative justice conferencing was trialled in Wagga Wagga NSW as a police-run scheme that was largely informed by reintegrative shaming theory (Braithwaite 1989). A statutory scheme, based on the New Zealand model, was introduced in 1998 and today youth justice conferences are available throughout NSW. Approximately 1,370 conferences are convened per year.

Queensland (QLD). QLD began trialling New Zealand model conferences in 1997 in two sites in the state's southeast (Ipswich and Logan). In 2002, conferencing services expanded throughout QLD and referrals have climbed from an average of 250 per annum in 1997 to approximately 2,000 by 30 June 2005.

Australian Capital Territory (ACT). Conferencing in the ACT first began in 1994 as a police-run scheme, also largely influenced by Braithwaite's theory of reintegrative shaming. Both police and civilians now convene conferences in the ACT. Only young offenders charged with or convicted of less serious offences are currently eligible for restorative justice conferencing. However, both young and adult offenders charged with or convicted of all types of offences are expected to become eligible for conferences in 2006.

Tasmania (TAS). Conferencing in TAS has been used since 1994 as a police-run scheme. Since 2000 a dual system has been operating with the police using the conferencing to administer formal cautioning and the Tasmanian Department of Health and Human Services (DHHS) conducting conferences following police referral. The police use specially trained police officers to facilitate their conferencing process and DHHS uses external contracted facilitators. Conferencing has been available state-wide since inception within both the police and DHHS.

Western Australia (WA). Conferencing was implemented following proclamation of the *Young Offenders Act 1994* in WA. Young people charged with minor offences can be referred to a conference (convened by 'juvenile justice teams') as a diversion from court processing. Restorative justice conferencing is available throughout WA, and referrals (averaging approximately 3,000 per year) come from the police and the youth court.

Northern Territory (NT). The courts established conferencing in August 1999 for young offenders as an alternative to custody. Court-referred conferencing is available throughout the state only to second-time property offenders between 15 and 17 years of age. Given the eligibility limitations for court-referred conferencing, only a small number of conferences are convened annually (fewer than 20 per annum). In addition, the NT police have operated a pre-court diversion conferencing scheme since August 2000 for non-serious young offenders. Approximately 70 young offenders are conferenced per year.

Victoria. Victoria is the only Australian jurisdiction without statutory provisions for restorative justice conferences, although legislation is currently being drafted. In 1995, Anglicare Victoria commenced a group conferencing programme targeting more serious offenders at risk of further penetrating the justice system. A small number of cases (fewer than 50 per year) were referred from the children's court for group conference. In 2001 group conferencing was expanded to all of metropolitan Melbourne, as well as two rural areas (Gippsland and Hume regions).

Research

There has been sustained research activity in Australia following the introduction of conferencing in the early 1990s. In this part we review key findings by jurisdiction.

South Australia. The SAJJ (South Australian Juvenile Justice) project began in 1998 with the aim of examining the degree to which participants experienced 'restorativeness' and procedural fairness, and how their conference experiences affected them afterwards. Results from SAJJ analyses show that most participants judge family conferences as procedurally fair and they are largely satisfied with outcomes (agreements). Furthermore, a reoffending study of SAJJ offenders shows that family conferencing has the potential to reduce offending (Hayes and Daly 2003). However, fewer participants were 'restored'; that is, there was notably less 'positive movement between offender and victim' (Daly 2002: 70).

New South Wales. In 2000, Trimboli undertook a comprehensive evaluation of the NSW youth justice conferencing scheme. Trimboli (2000) surveyed nearly 1,000 young offenders, victims and supporters immediately following their youth justice conference to gauge participants' judgements of satisfaction and fairness with the conference process. She found that very large proportions of offenders, victims and supporters rated the conference process as fair, they perceived they were treated with respect and they were satisfied with outcomes. In addition, Luke and Lind (2002) recently assessed the impact of youth justice conferencing on reoffending and found that conferencing resulted in a 15–20 per cent reduction in the estimated rate of reoffence, compared with court.[5]

Queensland. In 1998, the trial conferencing programme was evaluated (Hayes *et al.* 1998). Results showed that very high percentages of offenders, victims and supporters reported being treated fairly and respectfully and being satisfied with outcomes. In 2002 Hayes and Daly (2004) assessed reoffending to learn how variable features of conferences and offender characteristics related to future offending. They found that offender characteristics, such as age at conference, age at first offence, gender and prior offending, were associated with post-conference offending. However, no features of conferences were associated with further offending.

Australian Capital Territory. The Re-integrative Shaming Experiments (RISE) began in 1995 to assess the effects of conferencing compared with court. Researchers found that significantly more offenders assigned to conferences felt they were able to make up to society and the victim for the offence compared with those in court (Strang *et al.* 1999: Tables 5-41 to 5-44). They also found that reoffending rates were lower for young violent offenders in conferences compared with those in court (Sherman *et al.* 2000).

Western Australia. Only one evaluation study of restorative justice conferencing in WA has been undertaken. In a study of 265 restorative justice conference participants in Perth during 1996–7, the vast majority reported fairness and satisfaction with the process (Cant and Downie 1998).

Northern Territory. In a recent study of the NT police pre-court diversion conferencing scheme, Wilczynski *et al.* (2004) gathered operational data from NT police for the first three years of the scheme. In addition, they gathered juvenile court statistics for the 12 months preceding and three years following commencement of the conferencing scheme. Key findings include high levels of satisfaction with juvenile diversion registered among victims, as well as a substantial impact on reoffending. After 12 months following initial apprehension, only 29 per cent of offenders diverted to a family conference or victim–offender conference reoffended, compared with 57 per cent of young offenders who went to court (Wilczynski *et al.* 2004: Table C12).[6] After 24 months, only 38 per cent of young offenders diverted to family conference and only 37 per cent diverted to a victim–offender conference were reapprehended, compared with 61 per cent who went to court (Wilczynski *et al.* 2004).

Victoria. Some indicative results on the effectiveness of conferencing in Victoria were obtained from an evaluation of the group conferencing scheme initially administered by Anglicare Victoria (1995–97). The study generally found that offenders and victims had positive experiences. Victims reported that the programme had been 'helpful and healing' and young offenders felt that group conferencing had made a beneficial impact on them (Markiewicz 1997: vii). A more extensive evaluation of group conferencing in Victoria is currently underway.

Conclusion

A review of the extensive development of restorative justice options in the Pacific raises important questions. First, the examination of customary practice in the Pacific shows that indigenous justice processes, while they can be respectful and restorative, can also be unfair and punitive. Secondly, in contrast with the modern systems in Australia and New Zealand, they focus on the well-being of the group rather than the individual and that has both advantages and disadvantages.

The New Zealand youth justice example is the first and remains the only fully legislated example of a system that requires restorative values at all levels of the system and provides for restorative processes for all relatively serous offences. Its success owes much to the existence of clearly stated values and mandatory requirements about the use of restorative processes. To the extent that similar values and processes are used in Australia, similar positive outcomes for victims, offenders and the state can be observed but the restriction of restorative processes to only minor offences appears to limit the potential impact of the new development. Comparisons of the results from different conference models, for example scripted and unscripted, victim present or absent, screened and unscreened, suggest that it is not the model used but the values underpinning the process and adherence to the aspects of best practice identified by the research that is the critical factor in determining quality outcomes.

Finally, the combination of clearly stated values, enabling legislation, clear guidelines about best practice, and the use of research findings to identify critical factors in effectiveness has enabled restorative justice to become a valued part of mainstream justice systems within both New Zealand and Australia. Many of the Pacific Island nations may not be long in following suit, adding information on the effectiveness of their own unique focus based on different customary practices.

Notes

1   Primary sources are Maxwell *et al.* (2004a, 2004b), Crime and Justice (2005), Maxwell and Paulin (2005) and Maxwell and Hayes (forthcoming).
2   Approximately one in five in 2001.
3   About 100,000 or more since 1989.
4   Information for this section is drawn mainly from Maxwell and Hayes (forthcoming).
5   Chapter 22, this volume, provides more details. See also Chan *et al.* (2004) for a detailed analysis of the system impacts of the implementation of the NSW Young Offenders Act 1997.
6   Offenders were not randomly assigned to conference or court. Therefore, the authors of the report note that re-offending rates are likely higher for the court group because their offending was typically more serious and they were more likely to have had a record of prior detected offending.

References

Braithwaite, J. (1989) *Crime, Shame and Reintegration*. Cambridge: Cambridge University Press.

Cant, R. and Downie, R (1998) *Evaluation of the Young Offenders Act (1994) and the Juvenile Justice Teams*. Perth: Social Systems and Evaluation.

Consedine, J. (1995) *Restorative Justice: The Healing Effect of Crime*. Christchurch: Ploughshares Publications.

Crime and Justice Research Centre (2005) *New Zealand Court-referred Restorative Justice Pilot: Evaluation*. Wellington: Ministry of Justice.

Daly, K. (2002) 'Restorative justice: the real story', *Punishment and Society*, 4: 55–79.

Dinnen, S. (2003) *A Kind of Mending: Restorative Justice in the Pacific Islands*. Canberra: Pandanus.

Hayes, H. and Daly, K. (2003) 'Youth justice conferencing and re-offending', *Justice Quarterly*, 20: 725–64.

Hayes, H. and Daly, K. (2004) 'Conferencing and re-offending in Queensland', *Australian and New Zealand Journal of Criminology*, 37: 167–91.

Hayes, H., Prenzler, T. and Wortley, R. (1998) *Making Amends: Final Evaluation of the Queensland Community Conferencing Pilot*. Brisbane: Centre for Crime Policy and Public Safety, Griffith University.

Law Talk (2005) 'Partial success for restorative justice programmes', Issue 642: 5.

Luke, G. and Lind, B. (2002) 'Reducing juvenile crime: conferencing versus court', *Crime and Justice Bulletin: Contemporary Issues in Crime and Justice*, 69: 1–20.

Markiewicz, A. (1997) *Juvenile Justice Group Conferencing in Victoria: An Evaluation of a Pilot Programme, Phase 2 Report*. Moorabin, Victoria: Anglicare Southbridge Youth Services.

Maxwell, G.M. and Hayes, H. (forthcoming) 'The past and the future of restorative justice: a review of indigenous and modern processes in the South-West Pacific.'

Maxwell, G., Kingi, V., Robertson, J., Morris, A. and Cunningham, C. (2004a) *Achieving Effective Outcomes in Youth Justice: An Overview*. Wellington: New Zealand Ministry of Social Development.

Maxwell, G., Kingi, V., Robertson, J., Morris, A. and Cunningham, C. (2004b) *Achieving Effective Outcomes in Youth Justice: Final Report*. Wellington: New Zealand Minstry of Social Development.

Maxwell, G. and Morris, A. (1993) *Family Victims and Culture: Youth Justice in New Zealand*. Wellington: GP Print for Social Policy Agency Ropu Here Kaupapa and Institute of Criminology, Victoria University of Wellington.

Maxwell, G. and Morris, A. (1999) *Understanding Reoffending: Full Report*. Wellington: Institute of Criminology, Victoria University of Wellington.

Maxwell, G., Morris, A. and Anderson, T. (1999) *Community Panel Adult Pre-trial Diversion: Supplementary Evaluation*. Wellington: Institute of Criminology, Victoria University of Wellington.

Sherman, L., Strang, H. and Woods, D. (2000) *Recidivism Patterns in the Canberra Reintegrative Shaming Experiments (RISE)*. Canberra: Centre for Restorative Justice, Research School of Social Sciences, Australian National University.

Strang, H., Barnes, G., Braithwaite, J. and Sherman, L. (1999) *Experiments in Restorative Policing: A Progress Report on the Canberra Reintegrative Shaming Experiments*. Canberra: Australian Federal Police and Australian National University.

Trimboli, L. (2000) *An Evaluation of the NSW Youth Justice Conferencing Scheme*. Sydney: New South Wales Bureau of Justice Statistics and Research.

Wilczynski, A., Wallace, A., Nicholson, B. and Rintoul, D. (2004) *Evaluation of the Northern Territory Agreement*. Canberra: Urbis Keys Young.

Section G
Themes

Dobrinka Chankova and Daniel W. Van Ness

The preceding regional reviews offer an opportunity to identify themes related to the global adoption and expansion of restorative justice. In this brief conclusion we would like to note some of the important similarities and differences in the growth of restorative justice.

Theme one: part of the appeal of restorative justice is that it resonates with older or informal methods of resolving disputes

This has certainly been true in the Pacific, North America and Africa, where programmes identified with restorative justice (conferencing, circles and

South Africa's Truth and Reconciliation Commission) emerged as adapted forms of indigenous processes. But in all regions (excepting Europe), an effective argument for considering restorative justice has been that it reflects values of precolonial justice processes.

Restorative justice values and grounds, although expressed in modern language, resonate with memories of the older ways. The crime victim is central (Zehr 1995; Wright 1996, 1999; Umbreit 2001). Restorative justice is not done because it is deserved by the offender but because it is needed by the victim, the offender and the community (McCold and Wachtel 2003). Amends plays a key part in restoring the parties and, while often that is the extent of the restoration, reconciliation of relationships remains a possibility (Zehr 1985).

Theme two: dissatisfaction with current criminal justice problems provides motivation for societies to consider other approaches

The unsatisfactory functioning of the criminal justice system has led to openness to alternative approaches, and provided the context in which old responses to crime and conflict have been rediscovered. In New Zealand, concerns about the treatment of Maori children led to the development of family group conferences. In North America, the search for more meaningful alternatives to imprisonment led to the development of victim–offender mediation. Expectations that justice should solve problems and not simply punish have motivated African, Latin American, Asian and Pacific countries to examine alternatives to Western justice. Concern about the 'theft' of crime from victims and offenders resulted in experiments in victim–offender mediation in Europe.

That dissatisfaction has motivated restorative innovations is underscored by the fact that what we now call restorative justice sprang up independently in different parts of the world. European experiments with victim–offender mediation were unknown to the people who developed those programmes in North America. Family group conferencing emerged in the Pacific and only after its development was it connected to restorative justice theory. The South African Truth and Reconciliation Commission grew out of *ubuntu* and not a restorative justice textbook.

Theme three: global exchanges of information, research and programme ideas have been critical to the expansion of restorative justice

The strength of restorative justice as a global reform dynamic is based on more than local dissatisfaction with criminal justice. The recognition that new approaches were being adopted, expanded and evaluated in different parts of the world has encouraged and equipped local practitioners and given them credibility with policy-makers. Air transportation makes it possible for people to visit one another, but even more significant has been the growth of the Internet, which allows people around the world to communicate with, learn from and share information with others. Furthermore, regional and global networks, such as the Victim Offender Mediation Association and the European Forum for Restorative Justice, together with international conferences sponsored by academic institutions and NGOs, have made face-to-face interaction possible.

Theme four: there is significant diversity in the understanding and use of restorative justice

This comes as no surprise, certainly, but it bears noting, none the less. The three best known restorative processes (victim–offender mediation, family group conferences and circles) started independently of restorative justice thinking, and have been linked to one another and to restorative justice because of their common values. This point was emphasized in the Pacific review, but it is implicit in the linkage between restorative justice and older and informal practices. Furthermore, as was emphasized in the European review, this diversity is not only between regions, but exists within regions as well.

Theme five: the legal and social context in which restorative justice is attempted is significant, and contributes to the global diversity

As was underscored in the North American and European reviews, in some parts of the world restorative justice relies very much on community involvement, based on a belief that such involvement is positive. Emphasis is placed on the capacity of communities to restore and rehabilitate the victim and offender. It is sometimes viewed as a cheap resource that can be used to solve problems state institutions are unable to address (Brown 1994). The challenge in those places is how to respond to fragmented societies in which there is a deficit of community identification and commitment. A more fundamental question is whether communities are ready and able to take on this role (McCold 1996).

In other regions, the legal and social context is much more supportive of the government playing a more central role. This brings stability and protection from potential abuses by communities, but the risk is that governments may have other priorities, as noted in the Latin American review. Those priorities may be internally set or be the result of outside pressure, such as the influence of the USA on criminal justice policy in that region. Related to this is the degree of confidence that officials and citizens have in the justice system itself. To people living in a polarized society, restorative justice may seem to be a luxury, or something belonging to the future and not the present.

Each of the reviews has underscored the importance of civil society in the development and expansion of restorative justice. NGOs and academic institutions have been significant actors within countries and regions, and it may be that these serve to bridge gaps that may exist between governments and their communities. These institutions deserve much of the credit for introducing restorative justice into their countries and into intergovernmental organizations such as the United Nations, the Council of Europe and the European Union.

However, the influence of civil society bears watching as well. There are signals that some consider restorative justice a new sort of business, with funding coming from foundations or governments. These institutions fill an important need, particularly in new democracies in which government's role in society has been reduced. Nevertheless, replacing the state's monopoly of justice with that of one or two NGOs closely related to the government should not be confused with authentic community empowerment.

Theme six: the legal status of restorative justice programmes is significant

In some instances, particularly when starting up, restorative justice programmes have no specific legal authorization. According to the European review, this has even been true in countries subject to the legality principle. However, most countries eventually adopt legislation governing the programmes, and they take one of two stances: either they *allow* justice officials to divert cases to restorative programmes, or they *require* them to do so. The difference is important.

If restorative justice is to become the presumptive disposition, then legislation should and will provide for that. In those instances, use of the relevant mechanisms of the criminal justice system would be exceptional, reserved for cases where restorative justice has failed (Braithwaite 1999). The description of how New Zealand deals with young offenders in the Pacific review is an example of this.

More common is legislation that permits the use of restorative justice. A risk here is that vested interests in the criminal justice system will seek either to prevent or delay the use of restorative justice in an attempt to marginalize it (Davis 1992; Fattah 2004). But this also offers an opportunity for practitioners to maintain the restorative integrity of the programmes because they may refuse to accept cases that they do not consider suitable. Where restorative justice is mandatory, such as in New Zealand, programmes must be prepared to operate without all the elements that make it most restorative (such as the presence of the victim). There is a tension, then, between the desire to offer restorative justice to as many people as possible (with all the necessary compromises) and the desire to maintain a fully restorative programme that may handle only a small percentage of cases.

This is why the government's motivation in adopting restorative practices is important. If the government wants to divert offenders from courts and/ or custody (an offender-centred objective), then its legislative provisions are likely to be mandatory. If the policy is to offer victims an opportunity to meet with their offender (or vice versa), then legislation will be permissive.

Theme seven: the interplay between practice and theory continues to be important

The restorative justice field continues to be in an ongoing process of development. New practices emerge as do new insights concerning the theory of restorative justice. In this fertile ground, evaluation is particularly important as a means of testing the assumptions of restorative justice theory as well as the effectiveness of programme elements in reflecting restorative values and achieving restorative outcomes.

Acknowledgements

We are most grateful to Martin Wright, who read an early draft of this section, gave advice and made some helpful comments and suggestions.

References

Braithwaite, J. (1999) 'A future where punishment is marginalised: realistic or utopian?', *UCLA Law Review,* 46: 1727–50.

Brown, J. (1994) 'The use of mediation to resolve criminal cases: a procedural critique', *Emory Law Review*, 43.

Davis, G. (1992) *Making Amends: Mediation and Reparation in Criminal Justice*. London: Routledge.

Fattah, E. (2004) 'Gearing justice action to victim satisfaction: contrasting two justice philosophies: retribution and redress', in H. Kaptein and M. Malsch (eds) *Crime, Victims and Justice. Essays on Principles and Practice*. Hampshire: Ashgate.

McCold, P. (1996) 'Restorative justice and the role of community', in B. Galaway and J. Hudson (eds) *Restorative Justice: International Perspectives*. Monsey, NY: Criminal Justice Press.

McCold, P. and Wachtel, B. (1998) 'Community is not a place: a new look at community justice initiatives', *Contemporary Justice Review*, 1: 71–85.

Umbreit, M. (2001) *The Handbook of Victim-Offender Mediation. An Essential Guide to Practice and Research*. San Francisco, CA: Jossey-Bass.

Wright, M. (1996) *Justice for Victims and Offenders: A Restorative Response to Crime* (2nd edn). Winchester: Waterside Press.

Wright, M. (1999) *Restoring Respect for Justice: A Symposium*. Winchester: Waterside Press.

Zehr, H. (1985) *Retributive Justice, Restorative Justice. Occasional Paper 4. New Perspectives on Crime and Justice Series*. MCC Canada Victim–Offender Ministries Programme and the MCC US Office on Crime and Justice.

Zehr, H. (1995) *Changing Lenses: A New Focus for Crime and Justice* (2nd edn.). Scottdale, PA: Herald Press.

Chapter 25

Conflict resolution in South Africa: a case study

Jan Froestad and Clifford Shearing

Introduction

During the 1990s many countries around the world introduced statutory goals more supportive of restorative justice and restorative programmes received greater recognition by the formal justice system. Internationally, the movement for restorative justice became more acknowledged. The 'Tenth UN Congress on the Prevention of Crime and Treatment of Offenders', held in Vienna in May 2000, called on all governments to expand their use of restorative justice (Van Ness *et al.* 2001: 11). In spite of significant and evidential achievements on a range of fields and despite its recent national and international recognition (or may be because of that), many writers seem to think that restorative justice is now confronting a range of new challenges. Under the headings of 'model qualities', 'model drift', and 'model ownership', the following sections deal with some of the themes, trends and challenges in restorative justice as they are currently discussed among scholars. In the last section we present a model that has consciously been designed as a response to those challenges.

Model qualities: essential elements.

Restorative justice rejects, at least in principle, the retributive logic of 'balancing a harm with a harm'. This, however, does not necessarily mean abolition of the concept of crime. Braithwaite (2003a: 62) argues that 'In restorative justice rituals, being able to call wrongdoing a crime can be a powerful resource in persuading citizens to take responsibility'. While restorative philosophy rejects the idea of responding to crime merely by punishment ('inflicting pain, as pain'), it remains preoccupied with the notion that an act of crime offsets a balance that in some way must be reset or restored. As Brunk (2001) and Barton (1999) (both cited in Zehr 2002: 29) have observed, philosophically both retribution and restoration seek to vindicate through reciprocity; where they differ is in how the balance is assumed to be righted. In the words of Pavlich (2002: 97): 'Restorative justice may avoid the state's emphasis on legal guilt, but it still assumes that some wrong has occurred, that there is a responsible offender and a receiving victim/community.'

A potential problem with this understanding is that it does not always fit well with empirical realities, where thin and frayed boundaries may exist between offending and victimization. Parties to conflicts of some duration are often in long-lasting relationships where roles frequently alternate; the offender today might have been yesterday's victim, and vice versa. Putting the blame where it belongs becomes a more complicated matter than thinking about crime as isolated instances of harmful behaviour. Christie (1977) once argued that Borotse law, which allows 'the conflicting parties to bring in the whole chain of old complaints and arguments', can be a good instrument for norm-setting and problem-solving on such occasions. This suggests that a process of seeking to uncover the chain of causation that has nurtured and intensified a conflict, and of debating the consequences thereof for the parties involved, might be significant elements of restorative problem-solving. Christie seems to suggest that conceiving of the conflict as a one-incident encounter with clearly defined roles might sometimes constrain the collective attempt to search for fair and reasonable outcomes.

According to John Braithwaite (2003b: 159), the most forceful critique of restorative justice has been a feminist one regarding the oppression of women and children in domestic relationships. In such relations of acute power imbalances, the concern is that restorative practices may 'privatize' the response to domestic violence and thus trivialize offences that the feminist movement only recently has managed to get recognized as particular and serious forms (Dignan 2005: 169). Some scholars hope that imbalances of power between battered women and their abusers can better be bridged through restorative interventions, and bring evidence that conferences confronting family violence are sometimes quite effective (Braithwaite and Strang 2002: 11–12). The position that restorative justice has much to offer in dealing with family violence is clearly controversial, however. It begs the question of what is likely to be restored by such conferencing processes (McLaughlin et al. 2003: 12). Busch (2002: 223–48) argues against the use of restorative justice for the vast majority of domestic violence cases, claiming that in most instances better choices and safer forms of interventions can be made, with less risk of undermining the victims' sense of security. The feminist critique seems to call into question the basic premise of restorative justice that the most fundamental obligation of the approach is to repair the harm between victims and offenders and restore social relationships (Cunneen 2003: 187).

Some note that it actually remains quite unclear in restorative justice literature what is meant by the idea of 'restoring' or 'reintegrating' into communities (Crawford and Clear 2003: 221). Cunneen (2003) points to the fact that cultures frequently make use of a variety of other interventions to prevent or solve conflicts, such as 'permanent exile, withdrawal from and separation within the community' (2003: 188). While 'restoration' and 'reintegration' may be good things if and when they happen, such outcomes may not be preferred solutions to all instances of conflict and violence. According to Buruma (2004: 23), 'what victims want, even before redress, is the freedom from fear and from the threat of future victimization'. He seems to indicate that transforming a conflict from a situation of violence and fear to one of non-violence and security might sometimes take priority over the concern for 'restoration' or 'reintegration'. Bazemore and Walgrave (1999a: 61), concurring with this line of reasoning, highlight the commitment of restorative justice not only to 'make things right', but also more broadly to preserve the future peace between victim and offender. Moore (2004: 88) suggests that it might actually be more fruitful to think of conflicts and relationships as 'managed', than as resolved or restored.

In recommending a more future-oriented way of thinking, Moore claims that 'There may be less transformation as a result of the process, and more transformation as a result of the outcome. Change comes from an action plan that is put into practice' (2004: 89). Within such a future-oriented approach to justice, the primary objective might be to offer disputants hope for a better and more peaceful tomorrow, but not necessarily in the form of socially integrated, peaceful coexistence. The reasoning of these scholars seems to indicate the possibility of a more open-ended experience of justice, beyond the common assumptions of either legal or restorative practices (Pavlich 2002: 98).

Model qualities: micro–macro connections

As underscored by James Dignan, much of restorative justice's initial appeal had to do with its conceived 'transformative potential'. The restorative agenda, however, continues to be shaped by criminal justice due to the fact that the latter system remains in control of case selection and case definition. Some scholars point to the fact that distinctions between responses to crime and a variety of other community problems are often artificial (Walgrave and Bazemore 1999: 377). As noted by Feld (1999: 38), 'Youths who are homeless, hungry, pushed out of school, ill, or just desperately poor and disadvantaged seemingly would have greater claims to "restoration" than those who simply offend'.

Based on this background, scholars argue that there may be greater similarities between restorative and criminal justice than is usually acknowledged. They point to the fact that many restorative practices have a strong reactive orientation, processing instances of conflict already defined as 'cases of crime'. As such it is conceived as a reform 'profoundly traditional in the location of its effort' (Crawford and Clear 2003: 215).

An important focus in restorative justice has been on handling singular cases of crime as part of a reactive response, focusing on the need to repair the harm and restore relationships. A potential problem with such an orientation is that an undue focus might be put upon particular instances of behaviour understood as violating laws or social norms and that conditions that beget such actions in the first place may not be subject to appropriate scrutiny (Mika and Zehr 2003: 141). Processing individual cases, however, is also 'a window of opportunity'. Conflicts can be utilized as fuel for positive action that strengthens local communities (Christie 1977). Each new 'case' is an opportunity to build local knowledge about causes and conditions that make violent conflicts emerge, and to develop ideas of how generic problems, collective disadvantages and issues of social inequalities can be approached. According to Braithwaite (1994: 201), experiences in Wagga Wagga show that restorative conferences do have a potential for strengthening communities' concern with wider institutional problems such as unemployment, schooling, patriarchy and the like. An increasing number of scholars express concern, though, that restorative justice programmes show little concern for or have demonstrated limited capacity to forge such a link between individual cases and more structural problems (Mika 1992: 563; White 1994: 183–5; Levrant *et al.* 1999: 14; Crawford and Clear 2003: 224). There is an increasing awareness among scholars of the need to 'increase the compatibility and resonance between the emphasis on repairing prior harm and these more future-oriented transformative efforts' (Bazemore and Walgrave 1999a: 56).

Model drift

Restorative justice has become popular and 'mainstreamed' during a decade in which the support for punishment has gained new legitimacy, as evidenced by the rise in popularity of just-desert philosophy (von Hirsch 1993). Rather than facing overt resistance, a major challenge for restorative justice now seems to be that it is pulled in different directions, and not necessarily in those that are more restorative.

Early observations of restorative justice practices in New Zealand showed that conferences did not lead to less punitive outcomes for offenders (Lemly 2001: 49). Evaluations in Australia led researchers to conclude that 'at least for property cases, offenders were agreeing to harsher outcomes than they would have received in court' (McCold and Watchel 1998 cited in Young 2001: 217).

In the UK the tendency has long been to regard compensation by the offender and various forms of community service as forms of punishment rather than as new measures superseding punishment (Wright 1992: 531). Morris and Gelsthorpe (2000 cited in Ashworth 2003: 168) argue that newly institutionalized restorative practices in England and Wales seriously distort the fundamental elements of the approach, placing power and control with the professionals, and not with the key parties to the offence. According to Dignan and Marsh (2003: 113–4), the focus is increasingly on reducing offending and increasing levels of victim satisfaction, sacrificing a concern for broader restorative objectives and locking new projects into a pragmatic concentration on crime reduction.

In Canada and the USA redress to victims seem to have prevailed over every other restorative consideration; the popular US nomenclature 'balanced and restorative justice' seeks to promote victim needs and interests in particular (Thomas *et al.* 2003: 142). The goal of victim–offender reconciliation has clearly become secondary to the objective of ensuring restitution by the offender to the victim, as indicated by the altering of nomenclature from 'victim–offender reconciliation programmes' to 'victim–offender mediation programmes' (Fattah 2004: 27). The objective of restitution prevailed to such an extent that, according to Fattah (2004: 27), programmes used to be described as 'collection agencies' for the victims. Brown (1994 cited in Roche 2003: 39) observed that some victim–offender mediation programmes in the USA allowed offenders to participate only to the extent that it was likely that they would be able to make restitution payment to victims. The 1990s also saw an exponential growth in community-based family group conferencing initiatives in the USA, but the vast majority of them are reported to depart from accepted standards of such practice (Merkel-Holguin 2000: 225–6). Schiff and Bazemore (2002), basing their observations on a national survey of restorative justice programmes in the USA that included family group conferencing, conclude slightly more optimistically that 'programmes are conscious of and are, at least in theory, making an effort to integrate restorative principles in their day-to-day work' (p.197).

In continental Europe restorative justice programmes are still less developed and more weakly institutionalized, especially in countries with strong victim support systems (Weitekamp 2001: 149). In Germany, mediation schemes seem to be implemented with a strong educational bias. According to Trenczek (2003: 276); 'educative solutions' are frequently being forced upon youths to close down a case 'successfully'– of course always in their 'best interest'. Advocates for restorative justice recently presented it as an approach in criminal justice which meets 'the punishment purposes and the need of the victim as well or even better than a traditional sanction alone' (2003: 280).

Observations like those above might indicate that a new coalition of criminal justice strategies is forming, within which restorative practices increasingly are being included as an element alongside rather punitive and repressive interventions (Cunneen 2003: 182). One is reminded of Daly's (2002) insistence on not confusing ideal descriptions of restorative justice models and values and real restorative justice practices.

Even though restorative justice programmes show evidence of significant achievements, particularly in relation to parties' subjective experiences of procedural fairness, restorative justice may still fail to ensure equitable and fair outcomes for particular groups, or communities (Cunneen 2003: 191). The most disappointing observation from Australian conferencing practice, according to Braithwaite (2003b: 160), is the small proportion of Aboriginal young persons attending. The programmes have failed to reduce Aboriginal imprisonment rates in Australia. What this indicates is that, despite their progressive underpinnings, restorative justice programmes may have unintended class and racial biases that disadvantage poor communities (Levrant et al. 1999: 16). Restorative justice programmes in Australia have become embedded in a development towards a more bifurcated approach to juvenile offenders, dividing clients according to their 'suitability' for restorative justice, channelling some into more punitive processes of incapacitation (Blagg 2001: 237; Cunneen 2003: 184). In Canada, LaPrairie (1999 cited in Roche 2003: 39) reports the same tendency: offenders well known to the system and most vulnerable to imprisonment due to criminal records may be systematically excluded from participation in alternative restorative approaches. Observations like these seem to testify to a real danger that restorative justice could become what it opposes: a practice which closes, limits and excludes some individuals and groups to the advantage of others (Cunneen 2003: 183–6).

Instances of 'model drift' towards more punitive practices and unintended distributional outcomes negating core restorative values suggest that restorative practices ought to be evaluated in a broad social and political context. A key future challenge might be the issue of 'ownership'; the question of who will have the power to design, implement and monitor programmes intended to promote core restorative values.

Model ownership

As noticed by Cunneen (2003: 189), a key criticism against the way restorative justice programmes have been introduced has been a lack of negotiation and consultation with indigenous and minority communities. Most programmes have continued to be state directed and state controlled. Especially in family conferencing, a lasting tendency has been to use public officials as convenors and facilitators. Research after a few years of operation of the schemes did indicate a tendency for professional dominance (McCold 2001: 45–6). The Wagga Wagga model of police-led conferencing, in particular, has been very controversial. Braithwaite has frequently expressed his preference for this model on the bases that it is cheap, that fewer social control agents of the state get involved in the life of the offenders because cases are not referred to other agencies, and that police officers can be trained to be 'competent, empowering conference coordinators' (1994: 211). He assumes that the typical police concerns of legal/responsibility and victim/harm give lesser risk of professional domination and stigmatization than the professional discourses of social work or psychology (p.211). An inquiry into children and the legal process in Australia, however, concluded that 'the level of police involvement in most conferencing models is particularly problematic for Indigenous youth' (cited in Blagg 2001: 231). Blagg (2001: 230) argues that the restorative justice movement has tended selectively to appropriate certain elements of traditional Maori practice without an acknowledgement of the wider cultural universe that gave these elements their purpose and significance for the actors involved. He claims that, while the Maori conference model in New Zealand was designed to reduce the degree to which the police intervened in the lives of Maori youth, the Australian model 'has led to the supplement and extension of already significant police powers over young people' (Blagg 1997 cited in Wood in press). Observations by Young and Goold (2003: 94–104) on restorative police cautioning in England also seem to contradict Braithwaite's assumptions. Their study measured police dominance during the conferencing, and found that young offenders frequently perceived outcomes as being disproportionately severe. Furthermore, when an offender criticized the investigating officer, the typical reaction of the police facilitator was defensive (Young 2001 cited in Roche 2003: 234). Young concludes that all facilitators can be expected to reproduce strategies that chime with their particular professional mind-sets (2001: 220). Based on a review of 25 restorative programmes in six countries, Roche (2003: 233) strongly warns against police and judge-led convening and facilitation in restorative justice, due both to the degree of authority they wield as experts and state officials, and because the 'Police simply cannot be held accountable themselves if they convene meetings' (2003.: 233).

The New Zealand alternative of locating restorative conferences in social work/social welfare has not worked particularly well either, for a number of reasons. Morris and Maxwell (2001: 271) observed that many families had previously had negative experiences with social welfare; urgent child abuse and neglect cases tended to be given priority over youth justice cases; that while the youth justice co-ordinators were supposed to be independent they were usually supervised by social work managers; and social welfare and restorative justice values were not always reconcilable. In concluding they suggested that 'to the extent that family group conferences in New Zealand have reflected restorative objectives, this has happened despite being placed in social welfare rather than because of it' (2001: 271). A general conclusion in evaluations of family group conferencing in New Zealand seems to be that professionals tend to overtake, distort and undermine proceedings (Roche 2003: 37).

Regarding circle sentencing, Cunneen (2002: 45) casts serious doubts as to whether this form of restorative justice really represents a shift in power structures, due to the obligation that is still imposed on the judges to impose a 'fit and proper' sentence within the sentencing guidelines of the Canadian Criminal Code. He refers to observations that tensions remain between the participants of the circle and the role that the judge must perform (Green 1998). Cunneen concludes that the practice 'is still very much trapped within the confines of the Canadian justice system' (2002: 45).

As a solution to the problem of state and professional dominance, Morris and Maxwell (2001: 272–3) argue that the responsibility for convening conferences should be 'delegated to local conference convenors who are not public servants and who live in the communities in which the offenders and victims also live'. They see a number of advantages with such a solution: first, it would limit the role (monopoly) of the state and transfer power to those most directly involved in the offence and its consequences; secondly, in finding solutions the voluntary sector is likely to be seen by victims and offenders as more independent than a statutory organization and less likely to be contaminated by competing values; and, thirdly, it would increase the likelihood of receiving referrals from victims who do not want to have their victimization dealt with within the criminal justice system but still want some resolution (2001: 272). In addition, experience in restorative justice practices has indicated that the best results are obtained when the characteristics of the mediator or the facilitator do not differ markedly from those of the disputants themselves (Grönfors 1992: 419).

What these scholars seem to suggest is that a more radical redistribution of resources and power in restorative justice from the state and the public sector to civil society and local communities might be required. Two opposite objections are frequently mounted, however, against such an argument for strengthening the 'private governance' of security.

On the one hand, some scholars argue that the ascendancy of neoliberal ideology and forms of governance and the simultaneous rise and popularity of restorative justice practices are not accidental. Modern states are confronted with the dual pressures of globalization and localization/pluralization of security governance. Recognizing their limited capacity to deliver security, states are increasingly becoming more inclined to mobilize and enrol individuals, families, groups, corporations and other collectivities into their own governing agenda (Crawford and Clear 2003: 215). This new development might open a space for marginalized or disadvantaged groups to increase their say in the shaping and implementation of forms of security governance tuned to their needs and experiences. The trajectory so far, however, seem to indicate a growing 'governance disparity' in the field of security as rich and powerful groups take advantage of the opportunities to become included within the new forms of 'co-governance', while the poor and the disadvantaged remain excluded and continue to be exposed to more traditional and hierarchical forms of security governance that frequently are quite punitive in their orientation (Johnston and Shearing 2003).

To the extent that new responsibilities for the governing of security are delegated to local communities, there is a real danger that they will become 'responsibilized' for implementing a governance agenda established by others, in other places. If a core element of neoliberal governance is to design governing arrangements that allow for 'ruling at distance' (Rose and Miller 1992), the obvious risk is that government maintains its monopoly to do the 'steering', limiting the role of local 'security partners' to finding good ways of doing the 'rowing'. Within such an arrangement the likelihood is great that the governance of security will be based on expert knowledge and the premises of the state's own policy agenda, and will not reflect how security problems are experienced and perceived in local communities. The real challenge might be, however, as suggested by Rose (1996: 353), 'not simply to condemn the injustices and disadvantages entailed by the de-socialization of government, but also to engage inventively with the possibilities opened up'. Accordingly, a key question is how new ways of governing can be designed that make selective use of neoliberal ideas about governance so that the self-direction of poor communities is enhanced.

The opposite objection to devolving both the steering and the rowing of security governance to local communities is less concerned with the risk that such forms of governance will be integrated into governing networks in which the state remains the dominant node, and more preoccupied with the dangers posed by the community itself. Proponents of this position claim that restorative justice has been as naïve in its conception of 'community' as it has been in its conception of the state (Walgrave 2002). Pavlich (1999) argues that the image of community adhered to by many advocates of restorative justice assumes an 'identifiably, shared and integrated community capable of being restored and reintegrated'. Communities, however, are often hierarchical formations, structured upon lines of power, dominance and authority, frequently defining themselves through strong identities of 'we' and 'others' and engage in practices of exclusion (Crawford and Clear 2003: 221).

Due to such problems some scholars argue that restorative justice should offer as many safeguards against 'bad practice' as the traditional criminal justice system (Braithwaite and Parker 1999; Ashworth 2003). The argument seems to be that to avoid the danger that restorative justice may be utilized to defend sectional interests or may deteriorate into practices making an undue use of their powers, like vigilantism, due limits must be set as to how local knowledge and capacity are mobilized and made use of. How might such safeguards be constructed? How can restorative justice be developed as a form of 'empowerment with process control' (Braithwaite 2003a: 61)? A predominant tendency among writers is to look to the state for answers. Crawford and Clear (2003: 224) insist that restorative justice must recognize the crucial role of the state 'as power-container and norm-enforcer'. Braithwaite and Parker (1999: 204) emphasize the need to constrain restorative justice in a way that puts upper limits on permissible punishment. Braithwaite (1994: 204) proposes a ban against incarcerative orders and also against orders more punitive than those typically imposed by the courts for particular offences. Some critics of restorative justice claim that legalism is the only viable means of doing justice in individual cases in a way that guarantees enough accountability. Ashworth (2003: 164–77), in particular, emphasizes that empowering communities might be to sacrifice the 'rule of law' values. He proposes that restorative justice ought to be forwarded within a firm legislative framework, with respect for individual legal and human rights and within the bonds of proportionality.

Roche's (2003) study, however, reveals a range of accountability mechanisms already at work in restorative justice. He argues that critics of restorative justice have typically overlooked the presence of such informal accountability in the deliberations of restorative meetings. When restorative encounters work at their best, the process of negotiation and collective problem-solving contains its own in-built form of immediate and mutual 'deliberative accountability'. In such settings, people have to give reasons for whatever they propose, and in encountering a plurality of legitimate needs, viewpoints and interests, they have to accept that some arguments are more powerful than others: 'When decision-makers are required to explain their actions – or proposed actions – and have those explanations scrutinized, they are more likely to made better decisions, and their eventual decisions are more likely to be regarded as fair and legitimate' (Roche 2003: 228).

Reading Roche's study leaves a strong impression that such internal systems of rules and principles, standard operating procedures and arrangements for review and monitoring are the stuff that largely determine what restorative programmes actually are doing on a day-to-day basis – including, probably, even their ability to avoid 'model drift' in different contexts. Restorative values guide behaviour to the extent that they are expressed through systems of rules and procedures enabling encounters to take place with a minimum of domination and a maximum of mutual respect and dialogue. Roche seems to suggest that such internal systems for 'governing conduct' may be of greater importance for keeping restorative programmes tuned towards particular values than what any assistance the state and the formal system of law might be able (and willing) to offer. For 'respectful dialogues' not to collapse, it must be nurtured by substantive and procedural rules, systems of review and internal incentive schemes.

Restorative potential: the need for new innovative designs

Some scholars suggest that what makes processes more or less 'restorative' is the *intent* with which they are imposed, seeking reparative outcomes instead of the use of punishment as a deliberate infliction of 'pain' to balance the harm (Bazemore and Walgrave 1999a: 48–9). Others strongly oppose such a simple dichotomy between restorative justice and the formal criminal justice system, arguing that restorative outcomes frequently lead to obligations for offenders which are experienced as unpleasant (Duff 1992; Daly 2002; Roche, Chapter 5, this volume). Whatever might be the correct philosophical position of this debate we find little value in using intention as a measure of 'restorativeness', due to such practical problems as deciding who constitutes the punisher or the 'good doer', who is privileged to interpret his or her intention and, in particular, who decides what these intensions actually are (Crawford and Newburn 2003: 46).

Four other dimensions seem to offer a more fruitful and practical way to assess the restorative capacity of restorative practices. First, McCold (2000) has produced a typology that can be used to measure the restorative potential of different practices depending on the degree to which people who have a stake in the conflict are engaged. Programmes' *degree of inclusiveness of stakeholders* thus appears to be a useful criterion to evaluate restorative processes. We assume that programmes that 'broaden the circle', allowing a plurality of voices to be heard, will normally have a greater restorative and problem-solving capacity than programmes that limit participation.

Secondly, Dignan (2005: 8–9) and Van Ness (2002: 10) suggest that significant differences between restorative practices have to do with *variations in the restorative agenda or aspiration* of different practices. Some programmes define their goals rather narrowly, such as repairing the specific harms that are caused by particular offences, while other schemes have goals that extend far beyond that to approach structural problems and social inequalities that cause instances of domination and conflict to emerge, or that aim at the re-empowering of the community itself to increase its capacity of conflict management and peace-building. It seems reasonable to assume that programmes of the last category might have greater restorative potential, aiming beyond 'crises intervention' towards a genuine governance of conflicts and their causes.

Thirdly, Mika and Zehr (2003) argue convincingly that restorative justice programmes can be distinguished by *their locations relative to bases of power and control.* They suggest that restorative practices might be arranged along a continuum 'from programmes that are community based where the responsibility, resources and control of services are vested in the local community and its citizens, to those programmes that are promulgated, underwritten and controlled by the state' (2003: 139). The restorative justice movement has been based on the idea of 'conflicts as property' (Christie 1977), aiming to redistribute power and disperse decision-making, reducing system interventions and increasing community interventions. Restorative justice is about restoring the balance between state and civil society to the advantage of the latter. Therefore, programmes that are locally based and driven by non-governmental associations ought to have greater restorative potential than centrally managed, state-driven projects.

Our fourth evaluative dimension of restorative potential is based on Braithwaite's (2002) identification of 'respectful dialogue' and 'non-domination' as core restorative values. We suggest that honouring these values might require not only that the voices of significant 'conflict-owners' are heard, but also that the resolution of problems be based primarily on how local stakeholders experience and conceive of conflicts. This resonates with Christie's (1977) argument that 'Specialisation in conflict solution is the major enemy'. Therefore, to the extent that conflicts are predefined by the criminal justice system and then referred to restorative programmes as 'cases of crime', the capacity of such programmes to search for outcomes in an open, non-constrained manner will be reduced. Also, to the extent that professionals, or trained volunteers, dominate restorative meetings, the parties to the conflict lose some of their ownership of the problem. For that reasons, programmes that *prioritize decision-making based on local knowledge and capacity* might have greater restorative potential than programmes in which problem-solving is circumscribed by definitions and categories formulated in other places, or that rely more heavily on the skills of professionals or semi-experts to reach solutions.

As a way of summing up the discussion under this and the previous sections we suggest that there is a need for new and more innovative strategies in restorative justice. Based on our analysis of contemporary trends and challenges, and of what factors seem to determine the restorative potential of different programmes, we suggest that restorative practices adhere more strongly with the following principles:

- Focus attention on options for future peace more than on issues of restoration or reintegration.
- Extend channels for referral of 'cases' beyond the criminal justice system.
- Forge stronger links between the management of individual conflicts and the approach to generic problems.
- Organize restorative forums so that responsibilities, resources and control are moved from state-sponsored restorative professionalism to local communities and laypeople.
- Establish systems of rules and procedures, and review mechanisms that are required to keep local practice within limits and tuned towards core values.

In the next section we present a model that adheres to such principles and that has been consciously designed to strengthen the position of poor and marginalized communities in the governance of security.

A South African innovation: the Zwelethemba model[1]

In South Africa the work began quite literally by one of us going, with a couple of colleagues, to a poor community near Cape Town and holding several general community meetings. At these meetings we proposed the idea of working in an 'experimental' trial-and-error fashion with members of the community to build a method for governing security through local micro-level institutions that mobilized local capacity and local knowledge. This suggestion was accepted and what has come to be called the 'Zwelethemba model' for local capacity governance was born. 'Zwelethemba', the name of the community, is a Xhosa word that means 'place or country of hope'.

This work began at the end of 1997 after the first democratic government in South Africa had been elected. During this post-election period the Truth and Reconciliation Commission was actively engaged in its work and there was a widespread desire to find ways of making governance more responsive and more deliberative so as to resonate with African culture and values. At the same time there was a mood of dissatisfaction with the various 'popular' governance forums that had emerged within 'townships' during the apartheid era to provide governance outside discredited state structures. A central feature of this dissatisfaction was a widespread rejection of the often brutal and autocratic features of these 'popular' institutions. A further feature of the mood, reflected very strongly at the early Zwelethemba meetings, was a frustration with the slow pace of change within government delivery mechanisms. Associated with this was the feeling that to gain a rapid improvement in the delivery of services, more effective and controlled local or popular mechanisms would have to be developed. This mixture of partially consistent and partially inconsistent local analyses might be summed up as a combination of considerable hope and high expectations concerning the transition to democracy coupled with pessimistic realism.

This hope that deliberative democratic processes that resonated with African values would deliver better governance, combined with a scepticism concerning government priorities and the ability of existing agencies to realize the hopes of a better life, established a relatively fertile ground in which to plant the seed of experimentation with local capacity governance. This ground was nurtured by the sensibilities of both the Justice Minister at the time, who was willing to give his endorsement to this line of exploration, and a national commissioner of police who was willing to do the same.

Following two years of experimentation a set of governance processes had been developed that was sufficiently robust and well articulated to be thought of as a model for managing conflict. While some six years later there have been many adjustments to this model (as the experimentation has continued in Zwelethemba and other similar townships), its essential features have remained remarkably intact.

Peace-making

The Zwelethemba model is built around a process that came to be called 'peace-making' because it is concerned with establishing peace in the face of conflict. This idea of peace resonates with a widespread transitional sensibility that had developed around the notion of a peace process. Peace-making refers to the objective of reducing the likelihood that the particular conflict will continue. According to the Zwelethemba model, individuals directly involved in the conflict are considered 'participants' or 'parties' rather than 'victims' and 'offenders'. The victim/offender dichotomy is viewed as serving to separate, exclude and prejudge.

In practice, it is commonplace for a 'case' brought to the attention of peace-makers (organized in the South African case as 'peace committees') to be regarded as no more than a single slice in time that can be traced back to a history of conflict between the parties concerned. In such cases the 'offending' party and the 'harmed' party may, and probably do, change over time — today's 'offender' may have been yesterday's 'victim'. Central to the model is the argument that the language of 'victim' and 'offender' structures the meaning of what happened in the past in ways that make it difficult for parties involved to understand and articulate their own reality or lived experience.

A future orientation

The goal of peace-making gatherings is the establishment of a future-oriented solution to a conflict, agreed to by most and ideally all parties, that will 'make for a better tomorrow'. In this regard, the model stresses a deliberative approach that promotes consensus building (Shearing and Wood 2003) – an idea that has strong cultural as well as contemporary resonances. The model is designed, in LaPrairie's (1995: 80) phrase, 'to return the conflict to its rightful owners' (see also Christie 1977). During a peace-making gathering, or at its termination, considerable affect (anger, sadness, remorse, etc.) may be displayed, but emotional transformation is not the goal of the process. Instead, the goal is instrumental. The key question guiding the peace-making process is: 'how do we make a better tomorrow?' This focus on the future and the 'nice if it happens' stance towards emotional transformation has its roots in the life experience of poor people who are required daily to get on with the business of living. With its instrumental focus on the future, the process may produce the outcome of reintegration as described by Braithwaite (1989) but once again reintegration is a 'nice if it happens' consequence, not a goal.

The term 'reintegration', however, is not the most appropriate one to use in characterizing this local capacity model, as it suggests that there existed a prior collectivity (small or large) to which an individual or individuals were bound or with which they were integrated. This is certainly not always or even usually the case. In other words, the notion of reintegration implies that a certain relationship or 'bundle of life' needs to be 'restored'. If this was indeed the case, such a restoration may indeed be the outcome of a gathering. However, living in peace and making a better future may simply involve an agreement between parties to ensure that a particular conflict will not happen again, or at the very least, to ensure that participants at the gathering will abide by the particular plan of action established.

An example from Zwelethemba serves to illustrate this. One of the conflicts brought to the Zwelethemba Peace Committee was by neighbours of a family who were worried that the ongoing conflict between the daughter-in-law and her husband's mother would escalate into serious violence. A gathering was convened of the persons regarded as most likely able to contribute to a resolution of the conflict. The invitation to the gathering was to persons who were regarded as being in a position to be helpful in an instrumental sense, not simply to be there as 'supporters' of the conflicting parties. The gathering quickly concluded that the chances of restoring a 'happy family', if there had ever been one, were minimal. The agreed plan of action involved moving the son and the daughter-in-law's informal house to another part of the township far from the mother-in-law.

The uniqueness of the Zwelethemba model, compared with both retributive and restorative justice arrangements, is that the matters of dispute are not addressed through a backward-looking process that seeks to balance wrongs with burdens but through a forward-looking one that seeks to guarantee that the disputants' moral good will be respected in the future. Contrary to what one might expect from the discourses of many moral philosophers with a deontological approach, this is experienced by the parties to the dispute, and by members of the community, as both a just and an instrumentally effective outcome. Justice, as a moral outcome, is given meaning within a future-focused framework (Shearing and Johnston 2005).

In over 96 per cent of the 9,000 peace-making gatherings that have been convened in some 20 sites in South Africa to date, simple plans of action to reduce the likelihood of the conflict in question have been formulated. People at the gatherings commit themselves formally in writing to play their part in each plan of action.

Regulating peace making

Although it stresses the importance of local knowledge and capacity, the model does not propose that the knowledge and capacity gathered together should be unfettered. The peace-making gathering enacts processes of deliberative democracy at the local level, but must do so within limits. This conclusion was reached in Zwelethemba by its people, who were very familiar with the often brutal and autocratic excesses associated with popular forums.

Accordingly, the Zwelethemba model includes, as an essential component, a regulatory framework in the form of a 'Code of Good Practice'. This code operates as a 'constitutional framework' that guides and limits what takes place. It also establishes a language and a set of meanings that are used in constituting cases and subsequently acting on them. The code, along with peace-making steps that set out how a gathering is to be organized, structures the actions of peace committee members in such a way that they are enabled to 'act out' the restorative values these standards express.

The code requires that force should never be used to solve a problem as a consequence of a peace gathering. If the conclusion is that a coercive solution is required, this is grounds for referring the matter to the police or some other state agent. Secondly, the code requires that the members of the peace committees should never engage in adjudication. They are not judges but facilitators of the peace-making process, assisting both parties in searching for a plan of action that they will accept. The focus is on discovering what can be done to reduce or eliminate the problem or problems identified as root causes of the conflict.

Sustainability: corporate governance

The issue of sustainability proved to be both a crucial and a difficult one. During the pilot phase, participants in peace-making forums often raised the 'free rider' problem, saying: 'we do all of this work for which the community benefits; but we get no compensation; the members of our households would prefer us to spend the time earning some money instead'. However, the project team, and community members involved in the Zwelethemba 'experiment', were very aware that the 'obvious' solution to the problem – paying participants a salary for their work – might merely replicate the failures of previous reform programmes undertaken by governmental and non-governmental organizations in South Africa. It was clear, for example, that turning the work into paid employment though giving people jobs would eventually give rise to another layer of 'experts', divorced from the community, and create divisive status distinctions between different groups.

The approach to getting around this problem was to recognize both the material value of the committees' work to its members and to the community as well as the administrative costs associated with carrying it out. To achieve these aims a payment-for-outcome structure has been built into the model. Committees earn a monetary payment for every peace gathering held and facilitated according to the Code of Good Practice. Part of the money obtained in this way is ploughed back into local development projects, linked to the generic problems identified during the peace-making process. These generic interventions, known as peace building, address such issues as public health, education, childcare, playgrounds for children, support for the elderly, environmental protection, etc.

The income-generating mechanism ensures that the peace committees have access to resources that they 'own' both as direct income and as funds to be used in community development. Seen in this light, peace committees may be conceived as small businesses responding to local demands for conflict management, earning money as they demonstrate a capacity to fulfil this function that they then spend on themselves and others as part of their 'social responsibility'. These businesses operate, however, in a market that is regulated by the code and the steps of peace making, which means that these businesses and their business relationships are conducted in a particular manner.

An essential principle is that members of local peace committees, 'organizers' (who assist in arranging gatherings) and 'co-ordinators' (who have a wider mandate) are paid strictly on an outcome basis, and their work is subject to audit. The stance of the model has been to blend features of market-based governing mechanisms with a feature of Keynesian economics – namely, the use of tax resources from local governments to promote economies for enhancing self-direction and 'thickening' of collective capital in poor communities. The focus on output is important since the model aims to ensure that peace-making and peace-building processes are funded in a manner that conforms with the effective use of tax resources, thus preventing the growth of costly bureaucracies. The model is predicated on a 'no product, no support' mentality. The importance of the Keynesian element is to ensure that the programme does not succumb to the tendency of many programs of 'empowerment' that have been developed under the neoliberal approach to pass on the work of governance without a corresponding shift of resources.

Accountability and transparency

The model includes safeguards. The over-riding principle is that collectivities have a right to undertake peace making and peace building as long as what they do is within the law and is undertaken in a transparent manner so that the legality of their actions can be assessed. A similar principle is applied at a political level: the position the model takes is that no political approvals are necessary or required as long as the process is legal. This is true for governments, political parties and for the 'community'. Political support is, however, regarded as desirable.

Peace committees are typically formed after general community meetings in which the peace making and peace building are introduced to a group of residents. In the initial stages, external coaches (typically from neighbouring peace committees) help novice committee members to develop facilitative skills. Soon, however, internal coaches are identified within the committee so as to ensure that learning is both localized and continuous. To ensure transparency the committees attempt to make known, to as many people as possible within a collectivity, what procedures will be used by, for example, publicizing widely the Code of Good Practice and the peace-making and peace-building steps. This is also done at the outset of peace gatherings.

An essential part of the model involves the collection of data. This takes place as part of a review process in which audit teams analyse the range of problems arising and also monitor what happens in every gathering. In addition to analysing the reports of gatherings, the audit team may interview a sample of those attending in order to generate an independent source of information about the validity of the reports they receive. In addition to data gathering and analysis, surveys are used to assess the nature of community problems and steps which people take to resolve them. By these various means transparency is ensured and feedback given to peace committees and to their coaches.

Zwelethemba and State Governance

The Zwelethemba model promotes local governance of security through forms of self-direction which comply with state law and which make no attempt to challenge the state's claim to monopolize the use of force. On the other hand, the model is not equivalent to a state-led strategy of 'responsibilization' in which people are mobilized to act in accordance with state objectives, and where the community merely provides human and other resources for the delivery of state agendas. To put it another way, the Zwelethemba model does not subscribe to a neoliberal strategy of governance whereby the state 'steers' and the community 'rows'. On the contrary, the model assumes a devolution of both the 'steering' and the 'rowing' as a way of strengthening the capacity for local self-directedness in poor communities.

A new innovative state/civil society partnership – Project Themba – was launched in the township of Nkqubela in October 2002, in the Boland town of Robertson. The partners are the Community Peace Program, the Boland District Municipality, the Boland Region of the South African Police Service and the Nkqubela Peace Committee. The experiment was precipitated by a request from a poorly serviced residential area to have the local police station, closed for several years, reopened. Negotiations between the South African Police Service, Boland Region and the Community Peace Programme resulted in a plan to reopen the building, not as a police station but as a 'Community Peace Centre', with input both from the police and from the programme. Through this project the police gain increased access to, and respect from, communities who for historical reasons tended to be hostile, sceptical and unco-operative, as well as relief from dealing with matters for which they are less suited, thus saving time, money and unnecessary frustration all round. An objective of the peace committees and the Community Peace Programme is to gain further recognition that opens doors to sustainable financial support from agencies such as the national police force and local governments, and access to an existing network of police districts into which peace committees can expand through the creation of new community peace centres.

The partnership with the police is based in a model of role differentiation at the level of service delivery, with the assumption that the police will refer the majority of cases, depending on the consent of the parties to the conflict, to the peace committee. At the time of writing there are three community peace centres in operation, with plans to open at least three more. The partnership is also seen as an opportunity to explore the conditions under which the local forms of knowledge that the models generate will impact on larger policy networks concerned with issues of crime, policing, poverty reduction and local governance generally.

Conclusion

Participatory governance has had a chequered history, sometimes producing limited change, sometimes being hijacked for repressive ends. However, the main strength of a governance model that takes a 'nodal' approach, such as the Zwelethemba model, is that it enables us – indeed requires us – to situate debates about security governance within a strategic and normative framework. As argued by Johnston and Shearing (2003), there are two main reasons for this. First, the model refuses to prioritize any particular locus of power, seeing governance as a relationship contained within a shifting network of alliances rather than as a product of the realization of governing 'interests'. Secondly, the model refuses to posit any correspondence between mentalities, institutions and technologies associated with them, and governmental 'outcomes'. What the Zwelethemba model seems to indicate is that with demonstrative evidence of nodal governance becoming more and more apparent, opportunities may arise to transform networked relations in ways that could, under the right conditions, advance just and democratic outcomes; and do so in a way that uses as little force as possible.

Selected further reading

Roche, D. (2002) 'Restorative Justice and the Regulatory State in South African Townships', *British Journal of Criminology*, 42(3): 514–33. Discusses how the South African peace committees reflect restorative processes and values, yet at the same time are quite different to most restorative justice programmes in England, Australia, New Zealand, Canada and the United States.

Shearing, C. (2001) 'Transforming Security: A South African Experiment', 14–34 in Strang, H. and Braithwaite, J. (eds) *Restorative Justice and Civil Society.* Cambridge University Press. Discusses the Zwelethemba peacemaking and peacebuilding agenda and its implications for thinking about changes in the nature of governance and the project of restorative justice.

Shearing, C. (2001) 'Punishment and the Changing Face of Governance', *Punishment and Society*, 3(2): 445–73. The article explores the implication of shifts in the way in which security and justice are being conceived. It argues that the emergence of a logic of risk is refiguring the way in which punishment is being used as a tactic of governance.

Note

1 This part is primarily based on earlier presentations of the Zwelethemba model by Shearing (2001), Johnston and Shearing (2003), Shearing and Wood (2003) and Shearing *et al.* (in revision).

References

Ashworth, A. (2003) 'Is restorative justice the way forward for criminal justice?', in E. McLaughlin *et al.* (eds) *Restorative Justice: Critical Issues.* London: Sage/The Open University.

Barton, C. (1999) *Getting Even: Revenge as a Form of Justice.* Chicago, IL: Open Court.

Bazemore, G. and Walgrave, L. (1999a) 'Restorative juvenile justice: in search of fundamentals and an outline for systemic reform', in G. Bazemore and L. Walgrave (eds) *Restorative Juvenile Justice: Repairing the Harm of Youth Crime.* Monsey, NY: Willow Tree Press.

Bazemore, G. and Walgrave, L. (1999b) 'Reflections on the future of restorative justice for juveniles', in G. Bazemore and L. Walgrave (eds) *Restorative Juvenile Justice: Repairing the Harm of Youth Crime*. Monsey, NY: Willow Tree Press.

Blagg, H. (1997) 'A just measure of shame? Aboriginal youth conferencing in Australia', *British Journal of Criminology*, 37: 481–501.

Blagg, H. (2001) 'Aboriginal youth and restorative justice: critical notes from the Australian frontier', in M. Morris and G. Maxwell (eds) *Restorative Justice for Juveniles. Conferencing, Mediation and Circles*. Oxford: Hart Publishing.

Braithwaite, J. (1989) *Crime, Shame and Reintegration*. Cambridge: Cambridge University Press.

Braithwaite, J. (1994) 'Thinking harder about democratising social control', in C. Alder and J. Wundersitz (eds) *Family Conferencing and Juvenile Justice: The Way Forward or Misplaced Optimism?* Canberra: Australian Institute of Criminology.

Braithwaite, J. (2002) *Restorative Justice and Responsive Regulation*. Oxford: Oxford University Press.

Braithwaite, J. (2003a) 'Restorative justice and a better future', in E. McLaughlin *et al.* (eds) *Restorative Justice: Critical Issues*. London: Sage/The Open University.

Braithwaite, J. (2003b) 'Restorative justice and social justice', in E. McLaughlin *et al.* (eds) *Restorative Justice: Critical Issues*. London: Sage/The Open University.

Braithwaite, J. and Parker, C. (1999) 'Restorative justice is republican justice', in G. Bazemore and L. Walgrave (eds) *Restorative Juvenile Justice: Repairing the Harm of Youth Crime*. Monsey, NY: Willow Tree Press.

Braithwaite, J. and Strang, H. (2002) 'Restorative justice and family violence', in H. Strang and J. Braithwaite (eds) *Restorative Justice and Family Violence*. Cambridge: Cambridge University Press.

Brown, J.G. (1994) 'The use of mediation to resolve criminal cases: a procedural critique', *Emory Law Journal*, 43: 1247–309.

Brunk, C. (2001) 'Restorative justice and the philosophical theories of criminal punishment', in M.L. Hadley (ed) *The Spiritual Roots of Restorative Justice*. Albany, NY: State University of New York Press.

Busch, R. (2002) 'Domestic violence and restorative justice initiatives: who pays if we get it wrong?', in H. Strang and J. Braithwaite (eds) *Restorative Justice and Family Violence*. Cambridge: Cambridge University Press.

Christie, N. (1977) 'Conflicts as property', *British Journal of Criminology*, 17: 1–15.

Crawford, A. and Clear, T.R. (2003) 'Community justice: transforming communities through restorative justice?', in E. McLaughlin *et al.* (eds) *Restorative Justice: Critical Issues*. London: Sage/The Open University.

Crawford, A. and Newburn, T. (2003) *Youth Offending and Restorative Justice: Implementing Reform in Youth Justice*. Cullompton: Willan Publishing.

Cunneen, C. (2002) 'Restorative justice and the politics of decolonization', in G.M. Weitekamp and H-J. Kerner (eds) *Restorative Justice: Theoretical Foundations*. Cullompton: Willan Publishing.

Cunneen, C. (2003) 'Thinking critically about restorative justice', in E. McLaughlin *et al.* (eds) *Restorative Justice: Critical Issues*. London: Sage/The Open University.

Daly, K. (2002) 'Restorative justice: the real story', *Punishment and Society*, 4: 55–79.

Dignan, J. (2005) *Understanding Victims and Restorative Justice*. Maidenhead: Open University Press.

Dignan, J. and Marsh, P. (2003) 'Restorative justice and family group conferences in England: current state and future prospects', in E. McLaughlin *et al.* (eds) *Restorative Justice: Critical Issues*. London: Sage/The Open University.

Duff, R.A. (1992) 'Alternatives to punishment – or alternative punishments?', in W. Cragg (ed.) *Retributivism and its Critics*. Stuttgart: Franz Steiner.

Fattah, E. (2004) 'Gearing justice action to victim satisfaction: contrasting two justice philosophies: retribution and redress', in H. Kaptein and M. Malsch (eds) *Crime, Victims and Justice: Essays on Principles and Practices*. Aldershot: Ashgate.

Feld, B.C. (1999) 'Rehabilitation, retribution and restorative justice: alternative conceptions of juvenile justice', in G. Bazemore and L. Walgrave (eds) *Restorative Juvenile Justice: Repairing the Harm of Youth Crime*. Monsey, NY: Willow Tree Press.

Green, R.G. (1998) *Justice in Aboriginal Communities: Sentencing Alternatives*. Saskatoon, Canada: Purich Publishing.

Grönfors, M. (1992) 'Mediation – a romantic ideal or a workable alternative?', in H. Messmer and H.-M. Otto (eds) *Restorative Justice on Trial. Pitfalls and Potentials of Victim–Offender Mediation – International Research Perspectives*. Dordrecht, Boston, MA and London: Kluwer Academic.

Johnston, L. and Shearing, C. (2003) *Governing Security: Exploration in Policing and Justice*. London: Routledge.

LaPrairie, C. (1995) 'Altering course: new directions in criminal justice and corrections, sentencing-circles and family group conferences', *Australian and New Zealand Journal of Criminology*, December: 78–99.

LaPrairie, C. (1999) 'Some reflections on new criminal justice policies in Canada: restorative justice, alternative measures and conditional sentences', *Australian and New Zealand Journal of Criminology*, 32: 139–52.

Lemley, E.C. (2001) 'Designing restorative justice policy: an analytical perspective', *Criminal Justice Policy Review*, 12: 43–65.

Levrant, S., Cullen, F.T., Fulton, B. and Wozniak, J.F. (1999) 'Reconsidering restorative justice: the corruption of benevolence revisited?', *Crime and Delinquency*, 45: 3–27.

McCold, P. (2000) 'Towards a mid-range theory of restorative criminal justice: a reply to the maximalist model', *Contemporary Justice Review*, 3: 357–414.

McCold, P. (2001) 'Primary restorative justice practices', in M. Morris and G. Maxwell (eds) *Restorative Justice for Juveniles: Conferencing, Mediation and Circles*. Oxford: Hart Publishing.

McCold, P. and Wachtel, B. (1998) *Restorative Policing Experiment: The Bethlehem Pennsylvania Police Family Group Conferencing Project*. Pipersville, PA: Community Service Foundation.

McLaughlin, E., Fergusson, R., Hughes, G. and Westmarland, L. (2003) 'Introduction: justice in the round – contextualizing restorative justice', in E. McLaughlin *et al.* (eds) *Restorative Justice: Critical Issues*. London: Sage/The Open University.

Merkel-Holguin, L. (2000) 'Diversion and departures in the implementation of family group conferencing in the United States', in G. Burford and J. Hudson (eds) *Family Group Conferencing: New Directions in Community-centered Child and Family Practice*. New York, NY: Aldine De Gruyter.

Mika, H. (1992) 'Mediation interventions and restorative justice: responding to the astructural bias', in H. Messmer and H.-M. Otto (eds) *Restorative Justice on Trial. Pitfalls and Potentials of Victim–Offender Mediation – International Research Perspectives*. Dordrecht, Boston, MA and London: Kluwer Academic.

Mika, H. and Zehr, H. (2003) 'A restorative framework for community justice practice', in K. McEvoy and T. Newburn (eds) *Criminology, Conflict Resolution and Restorative Justice*. New York, NY: Palgrave Macmillan.

Morris, A. and Gelsthorpe, L. (2000) 'Something old, something borrowed, something blue, but something new? A comment on the prospects for restorative justice under the Crime and Disorder Act 1998', *Criminal Law Review*, 18, 27.

Morris, A. and Maxwell, G. (2001) 'Implementing restorative justice: what works?', in M. Morris and G. Maxwell (eds) *Restorative Justice for Juveniles. Conferencing, Mediation and Circles*. Oxford: Hart Publishing.

Pavlich, G. (1999) 'The force of community.' Paper presented at the Restorative Justice and Civil Society conference, Australian National University, Canberra.

Pavlich, G. (2002) 'Deconstructing restoration: the promise of restorative justice', in G.M. Weitekamp and H.-J. Kerner (eds) *Restorative Justice: Theoretical Foundations*. Cullompton: Willan Publishing.

Roche, D. (2003) *Accountability in Restorative Justice*. Oxford: Oxford University Press.

Rose, N. (1996) 'The death of the social? Re-figuring the territory of Government', *Economy and Society*, 25: 327–56.

Rose, N. and Miller, P. (1992) 'Political power beyond the state: problematics of government', *British Journal of Sociology*, 43: 173–205.

Schiff, M. and Bazemore, G. (2002) 'Restorative conferencing for juveniles in the United States: prevalence, process and practice', in G.M. Weitekamp and H.-J. Kerner (eds) *Restorative Justice: Theoretical Foundations*. Cullompton: Willan Publishing.

Shearing, C. (2001) 'Transforming security: a South African experiment', in H. Strang and J. Braithwaite (eds) *Restorative Justice and Civil Society*. Cambridge: Cambridge University Press.

Shearing, C. and Johnston, L. (2005) 'Justice in the risk society', *Australian and New Zealand Journal of Criminology*, 38: 25–38.

Shearing, C. and Wood, J. (2003) 'Governing security for common goods', *International Journal of the Sociology of Law*, 31: 204–25.

Shearing, C., Wood, J. and Font, E. (in revision) *Nodal Governance and Restorative Justice*.

Thomas, J., Capps, J., Evans, T., Lewin-Gladney, W., Jacobson, D., Maier, C., Moran, S. and Thompson, S. (2003) 'Critiquing the critics of peacemaking criminology: some rather ambivalent reflections on the theory of "being nice"', in K. McEvoy and T. Newburn (eds) *Criminology, Conflict Resolution and Restorative Justice*. Basingstoke: Palgrave Macmillan.

Trenczek, T. (2003) 'Within or outside the system? Restorative justice attempts and the penal system', in G.M. Weitekamp and H.-J. Kerner (eds) *Restorative Justice in Context. International Practice and Directions*. Cullompton: Willan Publishing.

Van Ness, D.W. (2002) 'The shape of things to come: a framework for thinking about a restorative justice system', in G.M. Weitekamp and H.-J. Kerner (eds) *Restorative Justice: Theoretical Foundations*. Cullompton: Willan Publishing.

Van Ness, D., Morris, A. and Maxwell, G. (2001) 'Introducing restorative justice', in M. Morris and G. Maxwell (eds) *Restorative Justice for Juveniles. Conferencing, Mediation and Circles*. Oxford: Hart Publishing.

Von Hirsch, A. (1993) *Censure and Sanctions*. New York, NY: Oxford University Press.

Walgrave, L. (2002) 'From community to dominion: in search of social values for restorative justice', in G.M. Weitekamp and H.-J. Kerner (eds) *Restorative Justice: Theoretical Foundations*. Cullompton: Willan Publishing.

Walgrave, L. and Bazemore, G. (1999) 'Reflections on the future of restorative justice for juveniles', in G. Bazemore and L. Walgrave (eds) *Restorative Juvenile Justice: Repairing the Harm of Youth Crime*. Monsey, NY: Willow Tree Press.

Weitekamp, E.G.M. (2001) 'Mediation in Europe: paradoxes, problems and promises', in M. Morris and G. Maxwell (eds) *Restorative Justice for Juveniles. Conferencing, Mediation and Circles*. Oxford: Hart Publishing.

White, R. (1994) 'Shame and reintegration strategies: individuals, state power and social interests', in C. Alder and J. Wundersitz (eds) *Family Conferencing and Juvenile Justice. The Way Forward or Misplaced Optimism? Australian Studies in Law, Crime and Justice Series*. Canberra: Australian Institute of Criminology.

Wood, J. (in press) 'Research and innovation in the field of security', in J. Wood and B. Dupont (eds) *Democracy, Society and the Governance of Security*. Cambridge: Cambridge University Press.

Wright, M. (1992) 'Victim–offender mediation as a step towards a restorative system of justice', in H. Messmer and H.-M. Otto (eds) *Restorative Justice on Trial. Pitfalls and Potentials of Victim–Offender Mediation – International Research Perspectives*. Dordrecht, Boston, MA and London: Kluwer Academic.

Young, R. (2001) 'Just cops doing "shameful" business? Police-led restorative justice and the lessons of research', in M. Morris and G. Maxwell (eds) *Restorative Justice for Juveniles. Conferencing, Mediation and Circles*. Oxford: Hart Publishing.

Young, R. and Goold, B. (2003) Restorative police cautioning in Aylesbury – from degrading to reintegrative shaming ceremonies?', in E. McLaughlin *et al.* (eds) *Restorative Justice: Critical Issues*. London: Sage/The Open University.

Zehr, H. (2002) 'Journey to belonging', in G.M. Weitekamp and H.-J. Kerner (eds) *Restorative Justice: Theoretical Foundations*. Cullompton: Willan Publishing.

The Future of Restorative Justice

Gerry Johnstone and Daniel W. Van Ness

Impending challenges facing the restorative justice movement is the theme of part 7. Chapter 26 is by Lode Walgrave, well known in the restorative justice movement for his view that restorative justice should be conceived less as a complement to the traditional punitive justice system and more as a philosophy which should penetrate and modify the criminal justice system itself. Walgrave addresses the challenge emerging from the erosion of the belief – which was prominent in the early development of the restorative justice movement and which still lingers – that there is a crystal-clear distinction between restorative justice and more conventional conceptions of criminal justice. As restorative justice has expanded its scope, many proponents have concluded that there may be challenges that restorative responses are incapable of addressing, thus necessitating use of conventional criminal justice processes and philosophies. Walgrave does not agree, and in this chapter he addresses four of those challenges: how to deal restoratively with the public dimensions of criminal wrongdoing; how to deal restoratively with non-cooperative offenders; how to ensure that wrongdoing is adequately (and restoratively) censured; and how to how to ensure that outcomes of restorative processes are just.

In Chapter 27, Ann Skelton and Makubetse Sekhonyane explore in detail the fundamental question of how the risks that restorative interventions might pose to human rights can be managed. Simply addressing this issue requires engagement with an idea, still prevalent in the restorative justice movement, that the sorts of procedural protections of rights found (however imperfectly) in criminal justice systems are not appropriate for restorative justice – which is voluntary and non-punitive – and may actually obstruct the sort of engagement which is necessary in order to achieve restorative outcomes. Others, sensitive to this concern but less willing to assume that benevolent intentions of programme sponsors and facilitators are sufficient protection for human rights, have sought to develop official guidelines and standards that are more consistent with the idea of restorative justice and that, if followed, should minimize the dangers of human rights violations in restorative justice. Skelton and Sekhonyane, after reviewing the concerns about rights which have been raised (not only by those hostile or sceptical about restorative justice, but also by many who are quite sympathetic to the idea), examine debates about how standards should be set and what they should contain. Importantly, they also point to the need to incorporate into the debate broader ways of thinking about human rights and their protection.

Some of the foremost critical perspectives on restorative justice are reviewed by Gerry Johnstone in Chapter 28. Critics have argued that descriptions of restorative justice are vague and incoherent, that exaggerated claims are made about the achievements and potential of restorative justice, that restorative interventions fail to provide an effective deterrent to crime and can also result in a failure to deliver justice, and that restorative justice is actually dependent on much of the criminal justice framework to which it seeks to be an alternative and hence may end up extending rather than reducing the size of the penal control apparatus. Chapter 28 elucidates these criticisms and also attempts to define their implications and scope, and to survey the different ways in which proponents of restorative justice might respond constructively to the critics.

One way of understanding what the restorative justice movement is about is to see it as an effort to reintroduce people's ethical values and understandings of justice into a criminal justice process which has become 'over-rationalized' – i.e. dominated by professionals' concerns with smooth and effective management of a people-control system. In Chapter 29, George Pavlich focuses upon this dimension of restorative justice and cautions against recent efforts to ascertain foundational and universally applicable restorative principles which can be used to identify and guide genuinely restorative practices. Such efforts to ground justice practices in universal ethical principles are dangerous, he argues, and should be refused. As an alternative, Pavlich argues, we should understand ethics as itself an essentially contestable discourse. Hence, we should conceive of restorative justice as an open ethical forum that is valuable precisely because it enables people to struggle with the ethical limitations of a past, unjust, way of being with one another and collectively to imagine better ways.

Chapter 26

Integrating criminal justice and restorative justice

Lode Walgrave

Introduction

Based on victims' concerns, communitarianism and critical criminology (Van Ness and Strong 2002), restorative justice in recent decades has developed a socially more constructive philosophy, in order to reorient the response to crime towards being more satisfying for the victim, more peace-assuring for the community and more reintegrative for the offender. Its new philosophy is also based on dissatisfaction with the traditional criminal justice system. Initially, restorative justice advocates presented restorative justice as being opposed to, and better than, the traditional punitive criminal justice response to crime. A number of interconnected factors distinguished restorative justice from criminal justice (Barnett 1977; Zehr 1990; Walgrave 1995; McCold 2000; Van Ness and Strong 2002):

- Crime in restorative justice is defined not as a transgression of an abstract legal disposition, but as social harm caused by the offence.
- In criminal justice, the principal collective agent is the state, while collectivity in restorative justice is mainly seen through community.
- The response to crime is not ruled by a top-down imposed set of procedures but by a deliberative bottom-up input from those with a direct stake in the aftermath.
- Contrary to formalized and rational criminal justice procedures, restorative justice processes are informal, and include emotions and feelings.
- The outcome of restorative justice is not a just infliction of a proportionate amount of pain but a socially constructive, or restorative, solution to the problem caused by the crime.
- Justice in criminal justice is defined 'objectively', based on legality, while justice in restorative justice is seen mainly as a subjective-moral experience.

In recent years, however, the oppositional view of the relationship between restorative justice and criminal justice has increasingly been questioned. Restorative justice is leaving its 'infancy', and its potential is being recognized increasingly by policy-makers, the judiciary, practitioners, academics and by the population in general. It is becoming obvious that a clear-cut distinction between restorative justice and criminal justice cannot be sustained as was originally proposed. Restorative justice-in-action is confronted with questions for which partial answers may be found in the criminal justice model.

How do we include the public dimensions of the offence?

Crime is not only a matter of conflict between two (groups of) citizens. Criminalization intrinsically means that public life is considered to be at stake by certain behaviour. While traditional criminal justice responses have addressed too exclusively its public dimension, some restorative justice practices have not included it at all, and restorative justice philosophy as a whole seems not really at ease with it. Some refuse to recognize the public aspect of a crime and reconsider offending as a tort, as if it were part of a civil law settlement. But if the needs of collectivity are to be addressed in the response, many questions arise. How do we define these collective entities (local communities, community, state), and how do we understand their interests in the response to the concrete crime? Who will represent the collective entities? Which processes and procedures can assess the harms and interests? How do the collective interests relate to the needs of the concrete victim? Criminal justice responses to these questions are unsatisfying from a restorative point of view. It would be unwise, however, simply to reject the criminal justice procedures without even considering the possible lessons restorative justice may learn from them.

How do we deal restoratively with non co-operative offenders?

Restorative justice prioritizes voluntary deliberative processes. It is, however, not always possible to reach an agreement with all the protagonists. Usually offenders simply want to get away with the least possible sanction. Some victims do not want to meet the offender, and/or want to try to maximize, unreasonably, the benefits of their victimship. For many restorative justice proponents, the absence of a deliberative process marks the limits of restorative justice. They hope to increase the feasibility of such processes, but leave the remaining cases to the traditional criminal justice procedures. This would, however, reduce restorative justice to being a marginal addendum to the criminal justice system. Others try, therefore, to conceive a reparation-oriented form of coercion within the restorative justice scope. In any event, to be acceptable to a democratic constitutional state, restorative justice has to provide safeguards based on legal standards. Criminal justice has a traditional set of constraints to try to guarantee the civil rights and freedoms of the offender and the victim. These may serve as a starting point, but they can probably not be transferred unchanged to restorative justice.

Do we need to punish?

Accepting coercive sanctions after a crime may leave no or very few differences with the traditional punishments. This is why a number of restorative justice advocates refuse to accept coercivity. Others consider punishment after a crime indispensable, and try to reformulate restorative justice as an alternative punishment. Criminal justice advocates advance several arguments to justify the punitive a priorism in the response to crime, and often consider it indispensable. Close inspection may however, undermine the validity of many of these arguments. Other arguments, on the other hand, such as the need for censuring norm transgression or the need for some kind of retribution, seem valid. But are these arguments linked with a need to punish? Perhaps the fundamental justifications for a criminal justice system do apply a fortiori for a restorative justice system.

How do we ensure that the outcomes are just?

By giving priority to voluntary deliberation, restorative processes aim at a consensus on how to resolve the problem created by the offence. At the beginning of the process, the participants usually hold different views about the problem and about possible solutions. Such processes do not, evidently, therefore result in a balanced outcome. If the power balance is unequal – the offender is not co-operative, the victim is too revengeful, the community is too exclusionary and/or the facilitator is too interventionist – restorative justice processes may yield very unjust outcomes. This is why restorative justice needs a system of checks and balances based on controllable standards. Current criminal justice provides such a system. While it is too intrusive for potentially constructive problem-solving at the bottom, its principles may give rise to a strong model of rights and freedoms that shields restorative processes from abuses of power.

Restorative justice thus cannot simply rule out criminal justice: a number of principles, models and concerns within criminal justice must be taken seriously. The basic question about the relationship between restorative justice and criminal justice is how to combine informal flexibility (crucial in the participatory approach of restorative justice) with the formality necessary to maintain the balances demanded by the principles of a democratic state.

Some scholars (for example, Ashworth, Albrecht, Duff, Dumortier and Eliaerts, Feld, von Hirsch and others) are sceptical that such a combination is really possible. They recognize the social value of restorative practices but focus on the possible threats to legal safeguards. Restorative practices are accepted only at the margins of the traditional criminal justice system. For these scholars, the mainstream response to crime must remain a punitive one, for principled retributive reasons and for the safeguarding of legal standards and controls.

Most restorative justice advocates now understand that an exclusively deliberative response to crime is not possible, and that at least a minimal juridical framework is needed, including a coercive element. There is no consensus on how this should be developed. Several authors (Braithwaite 2002a; Dignan 2002; Van Ness 2002b; Walgrave 2002b; Zehr 2002) have reported provisionally how they would see it develop. A 'diversionist' version attempts to extend the deliberative approach as broadly as possible but leaves the 'untreatables' to the punitive system. The so-called 'maximalist' version tries to change the criminal justice system itself so that it is mainly a restorative criminal justice system that would possibly include coercive sanctions with a view towards reparation.

The public dimension of crime in restorative justice

One of the main objectives of restorative justice against traditional criminal justice is that it focuses too exclusively on the public aspects of crime; restorativists, on the contrary see crime primarily as harm to people. This conception of crime has caused some to reconsider the response to offending as a 'civilization thesis' (Hulsman 1982) or as a system based on the rules of the civil law of torts (Barnett and Hagel 1977). In practice, many restorative processes based on meetings with offenders and their victims clearly prioritize the private dimensions of the harm and sufferings caused, and tend to neglect the public dimension. However, the public dimension of a crime remains essential (Johnstone 2002; Bottoms 2003).

Crime is also a public event

After a burglary, restitution or compensation for the victim's losses could be a private matter, possibly arranged by civil law. However, we all are concerned to see the authorities respond to a burglary. Imagine that the authorities did nothing or limited their intervention to registering the crime and identifying the offender, and then inviting the offender and victim to try to find a solution, without exerting any pressure on the offender. In such a scenario, most burglaries would probably remain unresolved, provoking private actions to 'make things even', which could lead to an escalation in mutual revenge and could drag down the security of the community as a whole. Such a disinterested attitude by the authorities would also damage all citizens' trust in public rules, their trust in the right to privacy and property, and their trust in the authorities' power and willingness to preserve order and justice. Not only would the community peace be lost, but also order and justice in society as a whole. 'While the government is responsible for preserving a just public order, the community's role in establishing and maintaining a just peace must be given special significance' (Van Ness and Strong 2002: 42). Order and peace are both threatened by crime, and both demand a public response. Consequently, restorative justice should include not only the community dimension but also the state dimension (Walgrave 2002a).

How can we make this more concrete? Traditional criminal justice lists in its laws the types of acts that are punishable. It has been established that public order is threatened by burglary, physical violence, fraud and other forms of criminalized behaviour. Other possibly wrongful behaviour is not included as this seems not to represent such a threat to public order. There are good reasons to avoid over-criminalization, especially when this would intrude on private life or be based on purely moral or religious beliefs. Over-criminalization would represent ethical absolutism, leading to a kind of 'Talibanization' of society. Public order and norm enforcement must be limited to what is needed for the quality of public life. Possible harm to social life is the only reason for criminalizing behaviour. There still remains, however, a grey area. Why, for example, is it debated whether criminal justice should intervene in some types of sexual behaviour among consenting adults, in the use of (currently illegal) drugs or in abortion? The reason is that, while there may be a large majority who consider such behaviour undesirable, there is no agreement on whether such behaviour is sufficiently harmful to social life to justify the authorities' intrusion into individual rights and freedoms.

Assurance in dominion

The social dimension of the harm caused by crime is reflected in Braithwaite and Pettit's 'republican theory of criminal justice' (1990). For them, an offence consists of an intrusion into dominion. 'Dominion' (or 'freedom as non-domination')[1] can be defined as a set of assured rights and freedoms. It is the mental and social territory of which we freely dispose, as it is guaranteed by the state and the social environment. The assurance aspect of rights and freedoms is crucial in the theory. I am assured only if I trust that my fellow citizens and the state will take my rights and freedoms seriously.[2] It is only then that I will fully enjoy my mental and social domain.

The assurance element is the crucial distinction between the social concept of 'freedom as non-domination' and the liberal concept of 'freedom as non-interference'. In the latter, the rights and freedoms of another individual citizen end where the rights and freedoms of the other citizen begin. Rights and freedoms are conceived as stable givens, to be distributed as justly as possible. Other citizens are possible interferers in my freedom and rivals in my struggle to expand my freedom. In the republican view, however, rights and freedoms are a collective good. Dominion is a value to be promoted and expanded by individual and collective action. Fellow citizens are allies in trying to extend and mutually assure dominion.

A good state, Braithwaite and Pettit suggest, seeks to extend and deepen dominion by promoting equality through increased democracy, education, equitable socioeconomic policy, welfare policy and the like. Criminal justice is the defensive institution. Crime is an intrusion upon dominion, and criminal justice must act to repair this intrusion (Walgrave 2000). This intrusion mostly damages the assurance in dominion. In the example of the burglary, the act does not strictly diminish the actual legal rights of privacy and property because they still exist legally, but it does diminish the extent to which the victim and the citizens are assured of them. The burglary not only hurts the individual victim's trust that his or her privacy and possessions are respected by his or her fellow citizens, but also all citizens' trust. If the authorities did nothing, it would undermine all citizens' trust in their right to privacy and possession. Their dominion is at stake.

Public intervention after a crime is not primarily needed to rebalance the benefits and burdens or to reconfirm the law, as retributivists would suggest. It is needed to restore assurance by issuing the message that the authorities take dominion seriously. The intervention must reassure the victim and the public of their rights and freedoms, and restore these rights and freedoms into being an assured, fully fledged dominion. This happens when the intrusion is clearly censured and when the offender, if possible, is involved in reparative actions. The offender's voluntary co-operation can only restore assurance if it is backed up by public institutions. Indeed, assurance comes not only from the individual offender's repentance and apologies but also from the authorities' clear determination to take the assured set of rights and freedoms seriously.

Restorative justice thus reformulates the public aspect of a crime as an intrusion upon dominion and reframes the public dimension of the response as an attempt to restore the general assurance of rights and freedoms, which is essential for restoring the intruded dominion. In principle, this is not contrary to traditional criminal justice. Locating it explicitly in a restorative justice context, however, helps to make it more concrete.

The restorative reformulation of crime in terms of an intrusion upon dominion can lead to a reconsideration of the acts that are criminalized. Would the criminalization of certain behaviour not be counterproductive for dominion? It also affects the response to crime. Its main purpose is the clear communication to the public at large that rights and freedoms are taken seriously by the authorities. The most effective way to achieve this is possibly not punishment but the determination to guarantee reparation. This has an important consequence. In dominion, the contradiction between repairing private and public harm is less evident than is sometimes suggested. A system that prioritizes punishing the offender makes reparation for the victim difficult. But authorities committed to guaranteeing reparation of individual harm and suffering also issue to the public the strongest possible message that dominion – the assured set of rights and freedoms for all citizens – is the central concern of the authorities' intervention.

Coercion in restorative justice

After the occurrence of a crime, voluntary encounters between the victims and offenders cannot always take place. The victim and the offender may have (good) reasons to avoid deliberate contacts, or these contacts may not result in an agreement. Social pressure may fail to convince the offender to co-operate. Some crimes are so serious that a mere encounter seems insufficient. The exertion of coercion or force must then be considered. Restorative justice proponents do not agree on what should happen at this point. 'Purists' in the restorative justice field exclude the use of force. They try to extend as broadly as possible the reach of these encounters, but they leave the case to the traditional justice system if encounters are unfeasible (Marshall 1996; McCold 2000). So-called 'maximalists', on the other hand, try to develop restorative justice into a fully fledged alternative to the traditional system (Bazemore and Walgrave 1999). They do, therefore, include coercion under the restorative justice umbrella, arguing that, under some conditions, imposed sanctions can serve a reparative goal.

The options are based on different views. Many 'restorativists', for example, adhere to a process-based approach: 'The essence of restorative justice is not the end, but the means by which resolution is achieved' (McCold 2004: 15). These scholars rightly promote informal voluntary deliberation with the direct stakeholders so that restoration is achieved maximally. The communicative potential of mediation, family group conferences or circles indeed favours the authentic assessment of the harm suffered and may more easily yield a genuine agreement on how to repair the harm or to compensate for it reasonably. The offender's recognition of the harm caused and his or her willingness to apologize express his or her understanding of the wrongs committed and his or her compliance with the social norms. This is much more restorative for the victim, the community and the offender than if the offender simply receives a sanction.

Nevertheless, restorative justice cannot be reduced to such a process. First, no process can be defined and valued without referring to the purpose for which it was undertaken. The process is valued not because of the deliberation on its own, but because of the outcomes it helps to achieve. A deliberative process is more 'restorative' because the expressions of remorse, compassion, apology and forgiveness it facilitates may readily yield feelings of being respected, of peace and satisfaction. These feelings are outcomes, even if they are not written down in the agreement.

Secondly, restricting restorative justice to voluntary deliberations would limit its scope drastically (Dignan 2002). The mainstream response to crime would remain coercive and punitive. The criminal justice system would probably refer only a selection of the less serious cases to deliberative restorative processes, thus excluding the victims of serious crimes who need restoration the most. Moreover, it would hand over a category of citizens to the punitive reaction (including its problems), a matter we shall come back to. There is no reason to give up a principled restorative response in cases of non-cooperative offenders.

Process-based definitions therefore confuse the means with the goal and limit the possible means to achieve (partial) restoration. Deliberative processes have the highest potential for achieving restoration but, if they cannot be accomplished, coercive obligations in pursuit of (partial) reparation must be included in the restorative justice model. Possible examples of such reparative sanctions are formal restitution or compensation, a fine or doing work for the benefit of a victims' fund, or community service. Such sanctions, of course, do not achieve completely the potentials of the restorative paradigm. Restorative justice is an option that may penetrate different actions to different degrees. Between fully restorative programmes and minimally restorative ones, graduations of moderately restorative approaches exist (McCold 2000; Van Ness 2002a; Zehr 2002).

This position is a challenge for restorative justice in its relationship with traditional criminal justice. Coercive restorative sanctions can only be imposed under a system of controllable legally based rules and procedures. Questions then arise as to how the priority for informal processing will be related to the formal judiciary; as to how far reparative sanctions will remain distinct from punishment; and as to whether the legal principles of traditional criminal justice will apply to a system that would be oriented primarily to reparation.

Restoration, punishment and retribution

Accepting enforced restorative sanctions, imposed according to judicial procedures that assessed accountability for the consequences of wrong behaviour, raises questions about the remaining differences between restorative sanctions and punishments.

McCold (2000), for example, does not accept coercive judicial sanctions as being potentially restorative, because these would shift restorative justice back to being punitive. For others, a punitive response to crime is needed, even though restorative responses may be socially constructive. Such adherents try to integrate restorative schemes into the punishment philosophy (Duff 1992; Daly 2000). Duff (1992), for example, calls restorative justice interventions not 'alternatives to punishment', but 'alternative punishments'.

Much depends, of course, on how punishment is understood. If every painful obligation after committing a wrong is called 'a punishment', most reparative impositions will indeed be punishments. But such a position overlooks some critical differences between punishment and restoration (see also Walgrave 2003).

Intentional pain infliction v. awareness of painfulness

A punishment is composed of three elements: hard treatment, the intention of inflicting it and the link with the wrong committed (von Hirsch 1993). If one of these elements is lacking, there is no punishment. Painful obligations that are not imposed with the intention to cause suffering are not punishments. Taxes, for example, are not punishments.

In this view, punishment is the intentional infliction of suffering (Wright 2003). Pain is imposed for the sake of pain and not as a coincidental side-effect of an obligation. It is the punisher who considers the action to be wrong and who wants the wrongdoer to suffer for it. If a juvenile, for example, sees a punishment as a reason for pride among his or her peer group, it still remains a punishment. Conversely, if the juvenile called a reparative obligation 'a punishment', it is not a punishment if the judge's intention was not to impose pain but to request a contribution to reparation.

However, not taking into account the hardship a request may cause could lead to draconian results. If, for example, a juvenile was obliged to pay back the full amount for the Jaguar he had stolen and crashed, he would in fact be condemned to a lifetime of repayment and poverty. Even if there is no intention to inflict pain, there must be an awareness of the painful effects, and these must be taken into account. The juvenile's contribution to reparation will probably transcend the material repayment, which will be limited in view of the boy's financial, mental and social capacities and his future. The remaining material damage should be repaid by the insurance company or by a victims' fund.

Taking the acknowledged hardship into account is not the same as intentionally inflicting pain. Pain in restorative justice is a possible reason to reduce the obligation, never to augment it. In retributive punishment, the painfulness is the principal yardstick, and its amount can be increased or decreased in order to achieve proportionality.

Punishment as a means, restoration as a goal

In truly democratic societies and in the most dictatorial regimes, punishment is a means used to enforce legal and political systems. It is an act of power to express disapproval, possibly to enforce compliance, but it is neutral about the value system it enforces. Restoration, on the other hand, is not a means but a potential outcome. The broad scope of harm considered for reparation demonstrates inherently restorative justice's orientation towards the quality of social life. Restorative justice, therefore, is not morally neutral.

Traditional criminal justice conceives of punishment as the a priori means of the intervention, and punishment aims to achieve a variety of goals. A long tradition of criminological research has lead to the overall conclusion that punishment is not socially effective (Tonry 1995; Sherman 2003). In contrast, restorative justice advances restoration in its broader sense as the objective and chooses among a diversity of possible means. Punishment is not an appropriate means for achieving restoration. The a priori option for punishment may even be an obstruction. The procedure involved in determining a proportionate punishment often obscures the harm done to the victims: the threat of punishment prevents genuine communication about the harm and possible reparation; the penalty hampers the offender's efforts to repair and compensate.

The communicative potential of punishment is very limited. Disapproval expressed through the sentence may communicate a clear message to the public, but it fails to communicate adequately to the other key actors: the victim and the offender. Good communication needs an adequate setting. This is not the case in court, where confrontation prevails over communication, and where it is the judge who will in the end decide upon the hard treatment (Wright 2003). The offender does not listen to the moralizing message but tries to get away with as lenient a punishment as possible. He or she does not hear the invitation to improve his or her behaviour, but merely experiences the threat.

While censure is needed, hard treatment is not the only way to express it. In daily life, disapproval is routinely expressed without punishment. Morally authoritative people who have no power to punish are more effective in influencing moral thinking and behaviour than are those who do have the power to punish. After a crime has occurred, a restorative setting is more appropriate for communicating moral disapproval and for provoking repentance than punitive procedures and sanctions. Most offenders are open for communication if they themselves experience respect and a basic understanding. In a climate of respect and support, victim–offender mediation or family group conferences position the harm and suffering centrally. This presents victimization as the focal concern, and provides huge communicative potential.[3]

Punishment is thus a means, based on the intentional infliction of pain, whereas restorative justice is an objective, for which the intentional infliction of pain is an obstacle. More crucial still is that the intentional infliction of pain poses serious social ethical problems.

Ethical problems with punishment

Penal theories can be divided into consequentialist and retributivist theories (von Hirsch 1998). According to consequentialist reasoning, the evil associated with punishment is needed to achieve a greater social good: social order and peace. Besides the principled difficulties that limit consequentialist interventions, empirical research has shown clearly that instrumentalist ambitions are not fulfilled (Braithwaite 1989; Sherman 2003). On the contrary, there is an increasing awareness that relying on punishment for dealing with crime leads to more imprisonment, more human and financial costs, less morality and less public safety (Skolnick 1995; Tonry 1995).

The different versions of retributivism all basically go back to the Kantian principle that punishing the wrong is a categorical imperative. It is inherent in morality that wrongdoing must be redressed by imposing hard treatment on the wrongdoer. Contrary to consequentialism, retributivism does not primarily ask questions about the possible targets or effects of punishment. The reasons for pain infliction are sought in a vision of equality (by rectifying the illegitimate advantage gained by the crime) or in the expression of blame. The amount of pain inflicted depends on the amount of illegitimate advantage or the degree of blameworthiness of the crime (von Hirsch 1993).

The censuring aspect of retributivism is easy to accept. No community can survive without norms, which are to be enforced. But does censure require punishment – i.e. the intentional infliction of pain? This is an important question because most ethical systems consider the deliberate and coercive imposition of suffering on another person as unethical (de Keijser 2000). Why should punitive pain infliction be an exception? Retributivist theories advance several arguments:

- Punishing evil is a deep human need; it overcomes our resentment (Moore 1995/1987) or expresses our adherence to the good.
- Evil can only be defined through punishing it. It is a categorical imperative that norm transgressions must be responded to by punishment.
- Retribution refers to the wrongs committed in the past, which provide a controllable yardstick for constructing proportionality in the degree of pain delivery (von Hirsch 1993).
- Good societies must issue clear norms, enforce them and unambiguously disapprove of law breaking so that all citizens understand these norms and so that law breaking is reduced in the future.

These arguments are discussed in this volume and elsewhere (Walgrave 2003, 2004). What is retained is that censuring wrongful behaviour, as proposed in the last argument, is essential. But does censure necessarily include intentional pain infliction? Censuring is a matter of communicating disapproval and, as we have just seen, the communicative potential of penal justice is limited. There may be better ways of condemning wrongful behaviour effectively.

Penal theories thus do not resolve the ethical problems concerning punishment as the intentional infliction of suffering. Moreover, punishment is counterproductive. For society at large, penal criminal justice intervention may offer a strong confirmation of legal order, but it carries with it the seeds of more social discord and unwell-being, and thus of more crime and criminalization. Victims are principally used as witnesses but then left alone to deal with their losses and grievances (Dignan 2005). For the offender, the sanction is a senseless infliction of suffering, which does not contribute to public safety nor to the victim's interests. It is a counterproductive, ethically highly doubtful intrusion into the offender's freedom.

In fact, the evidence concerning accepting punishment as the mainstream response to crime is in itself ethically doubtful. This is why ways of expressing blame without punishment must be thoroughly explored.

Censure and retribution in restorative justice

In retribution: 1) the blameworthiness of the unlawful behaviour is expressed clearly; 2) the offender's responsibility is indicated; and 3) the imbalance is supposed to be repaired by paying back to the offender the suffering he or she has caused. Restorative justice can fulfil the same functions (Walgrave 2004).

Restorative justice clearly articulates the limits of social tolerance because restorative processes express disapproval of the wrongful act. What distinguishes restorative censure from punitive censure is that restorative censure does not refer to an abstract legal rule but to the obligation to respect the quality of social life. The wrongfulness disapproved of is causing harm to another person and to social life.

As in punitive retribution, restorative justice holds the offender responsible. Punitive retribution is based on the passive concept of responsibility: the offender is confronted with his or her responsibilities and must submit to the consequences imposed by the criminal justice system. Restorative justice, on the other hand, is based on the concept of active responsibility: the offender must take active responsibility by contributing positively to repairing the negative consequences of his or her offence (Braithwaite and Roche 2001). Whereas passive responsibility is merely retrospective, active responsibility is both retrospective and prospective.

The 'pay back' principle is also evident in restorative justice. Punitive retribution restores the balance (whatever that balance may be) by paying back the offender for the harm he or she has caused. However, 'balancing the harm done by the offender with further harm inflicted on the offender ... only adds to the total amount of harm in the world' (Wright 1992: 525). The amount of suffering is doubled but spread equally.

In restorative justice, the 'pay back' principle is reversed. The offender must pay back him or herself by repairing, as much as possible, the harm and suffering he or she has caused. Instead of doubling the total amount of suffering, the balance is now restored because suffering is taken away. Retribution is achieved, but in a constructive way. Such reversed, restorative retribution also contains a proportionality principle. Proportionality, however, is not based on a 'just desert' principle but on a principle of 'just due' – what the offender can reasonably be expected to 'pay back' for the losses he or she has caused.

Restoration and retribution have thus much in common (Zehr 2002): clear censure of reprovable behaviour, an appeal to responsibility and an attempt to restore a balance. Restorative justice scholars, however, should accept the necessity of using coercive power when deliberative processes are impossible. Not to do so obscures restorative justice's commonalities with retributivism and makes it difficult to point out the essential differences. The concept that intentional pain infliction is indispensable when censuring wrongful behaviour is, in my view, a principle that restorative justice cannot encompass.

Justice in restorative justice

Constitutional democracies guarantee a set of rights and freedoms for all citizens. These rights and freedoms cannot be infringed unless by legally well defined exceptions and according to clearly defined procedures. The criminal justice system safeguards rights and freedoms through a complex of formal rules and conditions, and by the involvement of lawyers who check whether these rules and conditions are being respected. For most restorative justice proponents, criminal justice procedures and outcomes may lead to legal justice but they may not accord with what is considered to be just: 'The right punishment, according to some retributive theory will almost always be the wrong solution to the problem. By wrong I mean less just' (Braithwaite 2002b: 158). At first, many restorative justice advocates avoided state control, fearing the state's power to invade the process to the detriment of its informal, humane and healing potential. At times, however, the scales were tipped so far from state control that legal guarantees were also lost.

It is now almost generally accepted that a state-controlled legal framework is needed to locate restorative justice within the principles of a constitutional democracy. However, a broad range of interpretations remain, between the minimalist option, which sees the state as a marginal safeguard far removed from the restorative justice process, and the traditional criminal justice position, which locates the state as the central actor and stakeholder in the procedure. The state's position as a sort of victimized stakeholder was discussed above; the following section considers the function of the state as a (possibly coercive) safeguard.

Need for the state's commitment

An offence victimizes an individual citizen and his or her community of care, and intrudes upon dominion. The response must address the individual as well as the public dimensions of the harm. As noted above, these dimensions are complementary because restoring dominion necessarily includes responding to the individual citizen's needs. Moreover, the response must itself respect, as much as possible, the set of assured rights and freedoms. As we shall see, the dominion concept suggests that, whenever possible, priority must be given to the less intrusive responses steered by the most direct stakeholders.

In restorative responses, genuine encounters are crucial: meetings where all the stakeholders tell their stories, express their emotions, come to understand one another and perhaps conclude an agreement (Van Ness and Strong 2002). It is now clear that a large proportion of crimes can be resolved in this way (Latimer *et al.* 2001; Braithwaite 2002a; Kurki 2003; McCold 2003; Sherman 2003). These outcomes should become more commonplace as the monitoring agencies become more skilled and more widely available, and as the public becomes more acquainted with problem-solving deliberations. But the state cannot withdraw completely, not even from deliberative processes.

First, if it was not possible to invoke corrective state power, mediation or conferencing could risk uncontrollable abuses of power. These processes take place in private and are confidential and include intense personal commitment. A high degree of 'deliberative accountability' is needed in conferences and other restorative processes (Dignan 2002; Roche 2003). But this does not always occur and, as a result, such meetings may turn into serious abuses of informal power, and may impose unreasonable and excessive punitive outcomes. The authorities must therefore act as guarantors for the power balance in deliberations and for the reasonableness of the outcome.

Secondly, a complete absence of the state in the process would leave the parties alone to find a solution. The state authorities would not be able to guarantee respect for rights and freedoms, and would thus not be able to assure dominion. For assurance to be given, the state must be present, at least in the background, to make sure that the deliberation actually takes place and results in an acceptable outcome. It provides an opportunity for the parties to turn to the traditional judicial response if one of them feels their interests are not adequately acknowledged in the deliberative process. The authorities then demonstrate their commitment to dominion, not only regarding the victim's rights and freedoms but also guaranteeing the offender's rights, thus safeguarding the collectively assured set of rights and freedoms.

Thirdly, though voluntariness is crucial in restorative processes, one must not be naïve: offenders do not ask to participate in a conference or in mediation. The great majority probably want to get away with the least possible sanction. They agree to participate because they are pressured to do so by their families, by other members of their community of care or even by the threat of being referred to court (Boyes-Watson 2000). Restorative justice processes offer the space for free deliberation, but social pressure is always present. Above all, the threat of being referred to court may convince some offenders to accept deliberation with the victim. Such offenders do not present the best possible starting position for restorative encounters, but even meetings such as these appear to deliver more satisfying outcomes than traditional court proceedings.

Respecting rights and freedoms in dominion

The principle that civil rights and freedoms are to be safeguarded in a restorative settlement is not easy to operationalize. The problem is to find a way of respecting and extending as far as possible the space for deliberative processes that has the maximum decision power for those with a direct stake in the aftermath of a crime, while at the same time safeguarding human and legal rights.

Traditional criminal justice is guided by a set of procedural rules that ensure citizens' rights are not restricted illegitimately. These rules represent a top-down approach and are too intrusive for the bottom-up vision of restorative justice. The 'dominion' concept, the set of assured rights and freedoms, provides a means of defining the limits to justice interventions from a restorative justice perspective (Walgrave 2000, 2003). The intervention used to assure dominion must itself show respect for rights and freedoms. Braithwaite and Pettit (1990, 2000) list four constraints: parsimony, the checking of the authorities' use of power, the reprobation of crime, and the reintegration of victims and offenders.

The 'parsimony' constraint means that judicial power should be limited to what is absolutely necessary. It requires an active search for non-coercive ways to restore dominion. The more voluntary restorative processes lead to satisfying and balanced outcomes, the less appeal to coercive judicial interventions is needed, and, thus, the more the parsimony principle is achieved. A restorative justice system should fulfil its parsimony obligation whenever possible by leaving space for, and diverting to, voluntary processes.

The 'checking of power' constraint is derived from the assurance aspect of dominion. Citizens must be assured that they cannot be subjected to arbitrary power by the powerful or by the authorities. Therefore, the top-down power of the courtroom must be decentralized as much as possible towards the bottom-up deliberative meetings of those most directly concerned. Controllable rules must also be provided to hold the authorities accountable (Roche 2003) and to check whether dominion has not been unnecessarily intruded upon. The traditional deontological principles that guide criminal justice can serve as a basis for this, but they must be revised in view of restorative justice principles.

The 'reprobation' constraint includes the clear rejection of the criminal offence, but the 'reintegration' constraint means that it must not be unnecessarily exclusionist. Dominion, indeed, must be maximized for all, victims and offenders included. Together, both these constraints lead to responses that clearly reject the act, while avoiding the exclusion of the actor and even favouring his or her reintegration. Therefore, traditional punitive a priorism is rejected and restorative possibilities are explored maximally.

Some procedural reflections

Some scholars have investigated whether restorative justice practices fulfil the traditional standards for criminal justice – such as presumption of innocence, due process, the right to defence and proportionality (Ashworth 1993; Warner 1994; Feld 1999). Can these standards, however, be applied unchanged to restorative justice? If restorative justice is another paradigm with a different definition of crime, different objectives, different schedules, different roles and different actors, traditional criminal justice standards may not be applicable to it without significant revision and reformulation, in line with restorative justice philosophy. The deontological juridical questioning must be turned around. Instead of trying to insert restorative justice into the traditional criminal justice principles, the legal criteria must be adapted to restorative principles. How that would look has only recently been examined (Braithwaite 2002a; Dignan 2002; Walgrave 2002c; Roche 2003; von Hirsch *et al.* 2003; Van Ness 2004).

A justice system that is primarily oriented towards restoration has some commonalities with and some crucial differences from the traditional criminal justice system. Both the criminal justice system and the restorative justice systems have clear limits on social tolerance, hold the offender responsible for his or her behaviour, attempt to restore a kind of justice balance and use, if necessary, coercion according to legal standards.

In traditional criminal justice sentencing, two questions are asked (Ashworth 1986): have the facts been established? Has the (degree of) guilt been established? Sentencing in line with reparation adds a third question: which sanction contributes best to reparation? This question is not asked in punitive justice because of the a priori option for punishment, and because punitive justice is not prospective. Restorative justice, on the other hand, aims at repairing the harm and is therefore prospective also.

How these principles would influence concrete procedural rules may be clear from the following options:

- Because of the parsimony constraint, procedures should, at all stages, allow the easy diversion of cases to voluntary, informal, deliberative processes. Diversion is obligatory wherever possible. The decision to prosecute in court must be justified with positive arguments, and not simply because the law has been broken.
- Because of the reparative orientation, procedures must allow opportunities for input by victims and others affected by the crime. This is crucial in defining the kind and amount of harm and in finding the best possible restorative outcome. Victims have no decisive power in judicial sentencing because such sentencing must, of necessity, transcend the victim's option and needs.
- Criminal investigation is not only focused on establishing the facts and guilt but also on the harm caused by the offence and on the potential for deliberation, and thus for 'diversion' and for possible restorative sanctions if diversion is not possible.
- The sanction should not link the seriousness of the crime to a proportionate punishment; the seriousness and kind of harm should be linked to the maximum restorative effort possible.

Towards a restorative criminal justice system?

Several scholars have recently outlined how they see the ideal legal framework for restorative justice (Braithwaite 2002a; Van Ness 2002b; Dignan 2003; Walgrave 2003). They have all taken, as their priority, the need for voluntary deliberative processes, which are assumed to resolve the (increasing) majority of cases. They then provide several variations of coercive interventions by courts, while still maintaining opportunities for (partial) reparation. Finally, security concerns may make the incapacitation of the offender inevitable. These levels roughly represent different degrees of restorativeness.

The models give priority to voluntary deliberation with decisive participation by the stakeholders, but they also accept coercion and even public security as indispensable elements, and a legal system to frame the entire construction. Distinguishing restorative from punitive criminal justice does not, mean rejecting coercion and legalism. I strongly believe in the necessity to retain a criminal justice system which must, however, be oriented primarily towards doing justice through restoration, not through punishment. In the longer term, the criminal justice system should evolve towards being a fully fledged restorative criminal justice system.

The possibility of increasing pressure and coercion gradually must be provided. Even at the lowest level, coercion should implicitly be present. Understanding that, even for a minor act of vandalism, for example, the community of care, the local community, the public authorities and, finally, the criminal justice system, may expect, demand and ultimately enforce a gesture of reparation has an influence at the most freely accepted deliberative level. For the victim, it is reassuring that the victimization is not tolerated and must be repaired. For the offender, it makes it clear that he or she will not escape from his or her responsibility. For both it is reassuring and moderating to know that the legal framework maintains the action within bounds (Braithwaite and Parker 1999). After all, such a deliberation is never completely free of pressure, and it would be unrealistic to expect that it could be so.

But even the most powerful and coercive intervention systems must be permeated by the parsimony constraint. Wherever and whenever favourable for restoration and in line with public security, 'de-escalation back down the pyramid' (Braithwaite 2002b: 167) is needed. When the offender appears to represent a lesser danger to public security than originally feared, when he or she finally agrees to comply with reparative sanctions, when the victim and offender agree to try to find a constructive outcome, each time, the case should be left to, or given back to, the less coercive levels. This presupposes a moderated attitude in the coercive agencies, and especially in the justice system. The rule of law must not only penetrate into restorative justice, but restorative justice concerns must also guide legal discourse and procedures (Braithwaite and Parker 1999).

Conclusion: restorative justice and the sociology of institutional inertia

In this chapter, a maximalist approach to restorative justice has been taken. Restorative justice is not seen as a complement to the traditionally punitive criminal justice system but as a philosophy that should penetrate and modify the criminal justice system itself. The kind of justice it aims at is not achieved through punishment but through reparation. Wherever possible, priority must be given to participative deliberations in view of restoration. If needed, coercive justice interventions must serve as far as possible reparative objectives.

The arguments presented here are based on social, ethical and juridical principles. But changing a traditional institution like the criminal justice system is not possible through principles and rational arguments alone. Choices in the responses to crime are a matter of criminal policy, which is part of policy in general. That is why reflections on restorative justice must include a sociological analysis of the rise of restorative justice within the broader social and societal context (Bottoms 2003). The sociology of the current criminal justice system is one of the main subjects for investigation, because criminal policy is strongly influenced by it and because opportunities for restorative justice are largely dependent on the space allocated to them by that very system. Is it possible to imagine that restorative justice philosophy could penetrate the criminal justice so deeply that the system would itself become a restorative justice system? Or would some reparative practices receive additional value only within the bureaucratic-administrative approaches that are dominant in the criminal justice system (Bottoms 2003)?

All institutions display some form of institutional inertia, a kind of resistance against change, based on fear of the unfamiliarity of the proposed innovation and on the perceived risk of loss of power and influence. This inertia is still stronger in institutions with a long tradition in the centre of society – powerful institutions that have high social authority (Faget 1997; Fabri and Langbroek 2000). Matters of belief are transformed into irrefutable truths, juridical interpretations become coercive realities, complex human relationships and experiences are reconstructed as facts. The system is highly hierarchic, with many levels between the top and the fieldworkers, strict role definitions and internal sanctions. The distance from reality is great, so that changes in needs, problems and opportunities reach the top only in a filtered way. Hierarchy functions as the guard of conservative ideology within the organization. It controls compliance with the rules and seeks to confirm its power. No wonder that Sessar, for example, found that professionals in the criminal justice system stuck much more to the punitive tradition than ordinary people (Sessar 1995). The opposition to restorative justice by some penalists may disguise this sociological basis of resistance. Indeed, based as it so often is on a superficial knowledge of the restorative justice approach, this resistance cannot be grounded on open-minded reflection.

Restorative justice advocates should be aware of such dynamics, and should try to maximize the possibilities to penetrate the criminal justice system by including scientific strategic change processes (Mintzberg and Quinn 1991) in their deliberations towards criminal justice.

Selected further reading

Contemporary Justice Review, 3 (4) (2000). A special issue. A symposium on the debate between the 'purist' and 'maximalist' versions of restorative justice, where the relationship between restorative justice and coercion and punishment is one of the key issues.

Braithwaite, J. (2002) *Restorative Justice and Responsive Regulation*. Oxford: Oxford University Press. This volume explores the potentials of restorative justice as a philosophy for all kinds of conflict handling, and it presents a state concept that could promote the achievement of these potentials.

von Hirsch, A., Roberts, J., Bottoms, A., Roach, K. and Schiff, M. (eds) (2003) *Restorative Justice and Criminal Justice: Competing or Reconcilable Paradigms?* Oxford: Hart Publishing. A selection of chapters written by prominent scholars on how restorative justice and criminal justice could (should) relate to each other.

Walgrave, L. (2002) *Restorative Justice and the Law*. Cullompton: Willan Publishing. This volume presents a series of contributions by prominent scholars on how restorative justice can be inserted into the legal principles of a constitutional democracy.

Notes

1 In later publications, 'dominion' has been renamed by Braithwaite and Petitt as 'freedom as non-domination'. It may make it easier to oppose it to the liberal concept typified as 'freedom as non-interference', but I see no other advantage in complicating the wording. I will therefore stick to the 'old' naming, 'dominion'.

2 See what Putnam (1993) called 'trust' in social capital. Putnam does not limit trust to 'thick trust' based on strong ties with family, friends and close neighbours. The strongest social capital lies in the generalized trust based on weak ties with the social organisations and with the generalized other. It is this trust which constitutes our assurance of rights and freedoms.

3 Understanding the communicative poverty of traditional criminal justice sentencing, Duff has tried to combine his retributivist position with a punitive communication through what he calls a 'criminal mediation' (Duff 2001, 2003). I have elsewhere criticized this interesting development (Walgrave 2003)

Bibliographic references

Albrecht, H.J. (2001) 'Restorative justice. Answers to questions that nobody has put forward', in E. Fattah and S. Parmentier (eds) *Victim Policies and Criminal Justice on the Road to Restorative Justice*. Leuven: Leuven University Press.

Ashworth, A. (1986) 'Punishment and compensation: victims, offenders and the state', *Oxford Journal of Legal Studies*, 6: 277–99.

Ashworth, A. (1993) 'Some doubts about restorative justice', *Criminal Law Forum*, 4: 277–99.

Barnett, R. (1977) 'Restitution: a new paradigm of criminal justice', *Ethics*, 279–301.

Barnett, R. and J. Hagel (eds) (1977) *Assessing the Criminal*. Cambridge, MA: Ballinger.

Bazemore, G. and Walgrave, L. (1999) 'Restorative juvenile justice: in search of fundamentals and an outline for systemic reform', in G. Bazemore and L. Walgrave (eds) *Restorative Justice for Juveniles. Repairing the Harm by Youth Crime*. Monsey, NY: Criminal Justice Press.

Bottoms, A. (2003) 'Some sociological reflections on restorative justice', in A. von Hirsch *et al.* (eds) *Restorative Justice and Criminal Justice: Competing or Reconcilable Paradigms*? Oxford: Hart Publishing.

Boyes-Watson, C. (2000) 'Reflections on the purist and the maximalist models of restorative justice', *Contemporary Justice Review*, 3 (4): 441–50.

Braithwaite, J. (1989) *Crime, Shame and Reintegration*. Cambridge: Cambridge University Press.

Braithwaite, J. (1999) 'Restorative justice: assessing optimistic and pessimistic accounts', in M. Tonry (ed.) *Crime and Justice: A Review of Research*. Chicago, IL: University of Chicago Press.

Braithwaite, J. (2002a) *Restorative Justice and Responsive Regulation*. Oxford: Oxford University Press.

Braithwaite, J. (2002b) 'In search of restorative jurisprudence', in L. Walgrave (ed.) *Restorative Justice and the Law*. Cullompton: Willan Publishing.

Braithwaite, J. and Parker, C. (1999) 'Restorative justice is republican justice', in G. Bazemore and L. Walgrave (eds) *Restorative Justice for Juveniles. Repairing the Harm by Youth Crime*. Monsey, NY: Criminal Justice Press.

Braithwaite, J. and Pettit, P. (1990) *Not Just Desert: A Republican Theory of Criminal Justice*. Oxford: Clarendon Press.

Braithwaite, J. and Pettit, P. (2000) 'Republicanism and restorative justice: an explanatory and normative connection', in H. Strang and J. Braithwaite (eds) *Restorative Justice: Philosophy to Practice*. Aldershot: Dartmouth.

Braithwaite, J. and Roche, D. (2001) 'Responsibility and restorative justice', in G. Bazemore and M. Schiff (eds) *Restorative Community Justice. Repairing Harm and Transforming Communities*. Cincinnati, OH: Anderson Publishing.

Daly, K. (2000) 'Revisiting the relationship between retributive and restorative justice', in H. Strang and J. Braithwaite (eds) *Restorative Justice. Philosophy to Practice*. Aldershot: Dartmouth.

de Keijser, J. (2000) 'Punishment and purpose. From moral theory to punishment in action.' PhD thesis: University of Leyden.

Dignan, J. (2002) 'Restorative justice and the law: the case for an integrated, systemic approach', in L. Walgrave (ed.) *Restorative Justice and the Law*. Cullompton: Willan Publishing.

Dignan, J. (2003) 'Towards a systemic model of restorative justice: reflections in the concept, its context, and the need for clear constraints', in A. von Hirsch *et al.* (eds) *Restorative Justice and Criminal Justice: Competing or Reconcilable Paradigms*? Oxford: Hart Publishing.

Dignan, J. (2005) *Understanding Victims and Restorative Justice*. Maidenhead: McGraw Hill, Open University Press.

Duff, A. (1992) 'Alternatives to punishment or alternative punishment?', in W. Cragg (ed) *Retributivism and its Critics*. Stuttgart: Steinder.

Duff, A. (2001) *Punishment, Communication and Community*. Oxford: Oxford University Press.

Duff, A. (2002) 'Restorative punishment and punitive restoration', in L. Walgrave (ed) *Restorative Justice and the Law*. Cullompton: Willan Publishing.

Eliaerts, C. and Dumortier, E. (2002) 'Restorative justice for children: in need of procedural safeguards and standards', in E. Weitekamp and H.J. Kerner (eds) *Restorative Justice. Theoretical Foundations*. Cullompton: Willan Publishing.

Elias, N. (1994) *The Civilizing Process*. Oxford: Blackwell.

Fabri, M. and Langbroek, P.M. (2000) *The Challenge of Change for Judicial Systems. Developing a Public Administration Perspective*. Amsterdam: IOS Press.

Faget, J. (1997) *La Médiation: essai de politique pénale*. Ramonville Saint Agnes: Erès.

Fatic, A. (1995) *Punishment and Restorative Crime-Handling*. Aldershot: Avebury.

Feld, B. (1999) 'Rehabilitation, retribution and restorative justice: alternative conceptions of juvenile justice', in G. Bazemore and L. Walgrave (eds) *Restorative Juvenile Justice: Repairing the Harm of Youth Crime*. Monsey, NY: Criminal Justice Press.

Hulsman, L. (1982) 'Penal reform in the Netherlands. Part I. Bringing the criminal justice system under control', *Howard Journal on Penology and Crime Prevention*, 20: 150–9.

Johnstone, G. (2002) *Restorative Justice: Ideas, Values, Debates*. Cullompton: Willan Publishing.

Kurki, L. (2003) 'Evaluating restorative practices', in A. von Hirsch *et al.* (eds.), *Restorative Justice and Criminal Justice: Competing or Reconcilable Paradigms?* Oxford: Hart Publishing.

Latimer, J., Dowden, C. and Muise, D. (2001) *The Effectiveness of Restorative Justice Practices: A Meta Analysis*. Ottawa: Department of Justice.

Marshall, T. (1996) 'The evolution of restorative justice in Britain', *European Journal of Criminal Policy and Research*, 4: 21–43.

McCold, P. (2000) 'Toward a holistic vision of restorative juvenile justice: a reply to the maximalist model', *Contemporary Justice Review* 3: 357–414.

McCold, P. (2003) 'A survey of assessment research on mediation and conferencing', in L. Walgrave (ed.) *Repositioning Restorative Justice*. Cullompton: Willan Publishing.

McCold, P. (2004) 'Paradigm muddle: the threat to restorative justice posed by its merger with community justice', *Contemporary Justice Review*, 7: 13–35.

Mintzberg, H. and Quinn, J. (1991) *The Strategy Process: Concepts, Contexts, Cases*. London: Prentice-Hall.

Moore, M. (1995) 'The moral worth of retribution', in J. Murphy (ed.) *Punishment and Rehabilitation*. Belmont, CA: Wadsworth, (reprint from F. Schoeman (ed.) (1987) *Responsibility, Character and Emotions*. Cambridge University Press).

Putnam, R. (1993) *Making Democracy Work. Civic Traditions in Modern Italy*. Princeton, NJ: Princeton University Press.

Putnam, R. (2000) *Bowling Alone*. New York, NY: Simon & Schuster.

Roche, D. (2003) *Accountability in Restorative Justice*. Oxford: Oxford University Press.

Sessar, K. (1995) 'Restitution or punishment. An empirical study on attitudes of the public and the justice system in Hamburg', *Eurocriminology*, 8: 199–214.

Sherman, L. (2003) 'Reason for emotion: reinventing justice with theories, innovations, and research', *Criminology*, 41: 1–37.

Skolnick, J. (1995) 'What not to do about crime. The American Society of Criminology 1994 Presidential Address', *Criminology*, 33: 1–15.

Tonry, M. (1995) *Malign Neglect: Race, Crime and Punishment in America*. New York, NY: Oxford University Press.

Van Ness, D. (2002a) 'The shape of things to come: a framework for thinking about a restorative justice system', in E. Weitekamp and H.J. Kerner (eds) *Restorative Justice: Theoretical Foundations*. Cullompton: Willan Publishing.

Van Ness, D. (2002b) 'Creating restorative systems', in L. Walgrave (ed) *Restorative Justice and the Law*. Cullompton: Willan Publishing.

Van Ness, D. (2004) *Restorative Justice City* (available online at www.restorativejustice. org).

Van Ness, D. and Strong, K.H. (1997) *Restoring Justice* (1st edn). Cincinnati, OH: Anderson Publishing.

Van Ness, D. and Strong, K.H. (2002) *Restoring Justice* (2nd edn). Cincinnati, OH: Anderson Publishing.

von Hirsch, A. (1993) *Censure and Sanctions*. Oxford: Clarendon Press.

von Hirsch, A. (1998) 'Penal theories', in M. Tonry (ed.) *The Handbook of Crime and Punishment*. New York, NY and Oxford: Oxford University Press.

von Hirsch, A. and Jareborg, N. (1991) 'Gauging criminal harm: a living-standard analysis', *Oxford Journal of Legal Studies*, 11: 1–38.

von Hirsch, A., Roberts, J., Bottoms, A., Roach, K. and Schiff, M. (eds) (2003) *Restorative Justice and Criminal Justice: Competing or Reconcilable Paradigms?* Oxford: Hart Publishing.

Walgrave, L. (1995) 'Restorative justice for juveniles: just a technique or a fully fledged alternative?', *Howard Journal*, 34: 228–49.

Walgrave, L. (2000) 'Restorative justice and the republican theory of criminal justice: an exercise in normative theorising on restorative justice', in H. Strang and J. Braithwaite (eds) *Restorative Justice. Philosophy to Practice*. Aldershot: Dartmouth.

Walgrave, L. (2002a) 'From community to dominion: in search of social values for restorative justice', in E. Weitekamp and H.J. Kerner (eds) *Restorative Justice. Theoretical Foundations*. Cullompton: Willan Publishing.

Walgrave, L. (2002b) 'Restorative justice and the law: socio-ethical and juridical foundations for a systemic approach', in L. Walgrave (ed.) *Restorative Justice and the Law*. Cullompton: Willan Publishing.

Walgrave, L. (ed.) (2002c) *Restorative Justice and the Law*. Cullompton: Willan Publishing.

Walgrave, L. (2003) 'Imposing restoration instead of inflicting pain: reflections on the judicial reaction to crime', in A. von Hirsch *et al.* (eds) *Restorative Justice and Criminal Justice: Competing or Reconcilable Paradigms?* Oxford: Hart Publishing.

Walgrave, L. (2004) 'Has restorative justice appropriately responded to retribution theory and impulses?', in H. Zehr and B. Toews (eds) *Critical Issues in Restorative Justice*. Monsey, NY and Cullompton: Criminal Justice Press/Willan Publishing.

Warner, K. (1994) 'Family group conferences and the rights of the offender', in C. Alder and J. Wundersitz (eds) *Family Conferencing and Juvenile Justice: The Way Forward or Misplaced Optimism?* Canberra: Australian Institute of Criminology.

Wright, M. (2003) 'Is it time to question the concept of punishment?', in L. Walgrave (ed.) *Repositioning Restorative Justice*. Cullompton: Willan Publishing.

Zehr, H. (1990) *Changing Lenses. A New Focus for Crime and Justice*. Scottsdale, PA: Herald Press.

Zehr, H. (2002) *The Little Book of Restorative Justice*. Intercourse, PA: Good Books.

Chapter 27

Human rights and restorative justice

Ann Skelton and Makubetse Sekhonyane

Introduction

What do we understand when we speak of human rights? We are used to thinking in slogans that begin with the words 'freedom of' as in 'freedom of expression', or 'the right to' as in 'the right to remain silent' or beginning with the word 'no' as in 'no person shall be subjected to cruel or inhuman punishment'. Theorists differ about whether rights should be viewed as a positive or negative construct. The positive construct theorists see rights as requiring a duty that society or the government must deliver. A negative construct views rights as protecting people from harm that might be imposed on them by the state or by the community. Dworkin's theory of rights is that they are 'trumps', which can be used to protect individuals from being exposed to the risk of a utilitarian approach according to which the least harm to the greatest number prevails (Waldron 1993). Human rights are derived from accepted principles, or are required by accepted societal ends such as peace and justice, and individual ends such as human dignity, happiness and fulfilment (Henkin 1990).

A number of restorative justice writers have sought to show that, although retributive crime control dominates in the West, if we look back far enough in our collective history we will find a time when disputes belonged to the people and restitution was the normal resort (Christie 1977; Jacob 1977; Zehr 1990; Bianchi 1994; Van Ness and Strong 1997). Though this version is not uncontroversial (Daly 2002; Johnstone 2002), it forms a good basis for understanding how rights protection for suspects developed. Following the invasion of Britain by the Normans the monarchy gradually took over the role that had previously been occupied by the victim, as crimes became offences against the crown (Jacob 1977). This method of dealing with crime developed into the criminal justice system we know today in which the state and the suspect are the sole parties. The imbalance of such a system, the might of the monarch or the state on the one side and the puny individual on the other, led the system gradually to develop protections for suspects. This was necessary, largely because the consequences of such a system are harsh. These protections came to be referred to as the principles of a fair trial, and later, due process rights. In this chapter we will address the standard protections that exist in the criminal justice system, as well as broader human rights issues, and consider what implications restorative justice has for the rights of both victims and offenders.

Restorative justice processes have consequences, even though they appear to be less harsh than the usual response of the criminal justice system. We need to remember that 'as the punitive characteristic of criminal justice measures is diminished, so too is the perceived need for strong procedural protection' (Barnett 1980: 119). Johnstone (2002) points out that advocates for restorative justice tend to neglect procedural protection for suspects, and even see strict procedural rules as a stumbling block to achieving restorative outcomes. This may be because many proponents of restorative justice see the process as being non-punitive, focused on restitution and reparation, rather like a civil law compensation claim. Johnstone warns that this approach is dangerous, because in most systems the wider context against which restorative justice operates is essentially one of crime and punishment. The process is organized around a 'criminal' wrong. The terms 'offender' and 'victim' are used, and the police or prosecutors are often involved. An offender who fails to fulfil his or her obligations will return to the criminal justice system. In this chapter the risks restorative justice may pose to human rights are explored, as well as some ideas about how we might minimize or manage those risks. We will also be proposing that the discourse about rights needs to be broadened beyond the Western legalistic focus on individual rights.

What rights are protected in the criminal justice system?

The right to a fair trial

The principles of a 'fair trial' or 'due process' include legal principles that protect the suspect, which are common to all Western legal systems, irrespective of whether the procedure is adversarial or inquisitorial, as both have been influenced by the ideology of enlightenment (Damaska 1975). The essential difference between the two systems is that in the adversarial model the onus is on the litigants to present their cases before a passive judicial officer, while in the inquisitorial system the judicial officer plays an active role by conducting the proceedings throughout. The principles of a fair trial are included in international instruments, bills of rights, statutes and common law. They are briefly enumerated in the following paragraph.

A person charged with a crime has the right to a public trial by a competent and impartial court. The presumption of innocence is considered a primary element from which flows the right to remain silent (Schwikkard 1999). The suspect has a right to be present and to participate at the trial, and should have adequate notice and time to prepare. Any punishment handed down should not be cruel, inhuman or degrading, and should be proportionate to the crime (Akester 2003). Any judicial decision which affects a defendant's rights should be open to review, and there should be mechanisms to apply for appeal from the decisions made by the court. A person must not be tried twice for the same offence. The adversarial system is party based, and the defendant has a right to be placed on an equal footing with the prosecutor. The right to legal representation is thus considered to be very important (Steytler 1988).

The rights of victims

The fair trial principles focus on the defendant, but in the past 25 years the rights of victims have come to the fore. Strang (2001) records how the victim movement developed differently in different parts of the world. She describes the model that developed in the USA as a rights-based one, whilst the European model has been more support focused, and this may be linked to the differences in the adversarial and inquisitorial approaches to criminal justice.

The rights movement has concentrated on reforming laws that are detrimental to victims, such as cautionary rules that prejudice victims, particularly women and children, and which weaken the impact of their evidence. The victims' rights movement has also fought for the right of victims to be informed about the developments in their cases. Greater participation in the criminal justice process is something that the victims' rights movement has lobbied for, particularly the opportunity to make victim impact statements. The rights of victims to participate at the sentencing stage is controversial, as some fear that their subjectivity may tip the scales heavily against the offender. Ashworth, for example, says that crime is a matter for 'public interest' and that this goes beyond whether the victim considers that action should be taken against the offender, or how the offender should be punished (2002). He cites the cases of *Clotworthy*[1] and *Nunn*[2] to illustrate that courts are reluctant to give victims the last word on sentence. Braithwaite (2002a) has pointed out that cases such as these prove that victims tend to demand less harsh punishments than just deserts theorists expect.

Is it necessary to protect rights in restorative justice processes?

Risks specific to victims

The risks to the rights of victims within restorative justice processes include coercion to participate, threats to personal safety through participating, offender-biased proceedings and a lack of information about what to expect from proceedings. Restorative justice processes may leave victims without a remedy if there is a failure by offenders to follow through on agreements, especially with regard to restitution. Given the value placed on restitution by victims (Umbreit *et al.* 2001), this kind of failure may result in overall distrust in the potential of these processes to respond to victims' particular needs. One of the attractive aspects of restorative justice is that restitution or compensation can be dealt with in the same forum as the offence. There has been minimal discussion about the victim's right to bring civil proceedings being compromised by taking part in a restorative justice process. Can we ask victims of crime to forfeit their right to use the civil process as a prerequisite to participating in a restorative justice process? If we do not do so, what about the risk to offenders who may be asked to pay compensation through a restorative justice process, and later be sued through the civil process (Skelton and Frank 2004)? It is clear that legislated mechanisms are necessary to manage these risks, and such regulations are already in place in some jurisdictions.

Risks specific to suspects

The risk of coercion to acknowledge responsibility

Most restorative justice processes, such as victim–offender mediation or family group conferencing, start from the position that the offender must acknowledge responsibility, and it may be argued that this effectively removes the presumption of innocence and the right to silence from the suspect. An obvious answer to this concern is that the suspect is voluntarily relinquishing these rights in order to benefit from the restorative justice option. However, are such decisions really voluntary? It depends on how the options are put to the suspect. Furthermore, it must be said that this problem of the risk of coercion is not unique to the situation where suspects are offered the opportunity to participate in a restorative justice process. Police cautioning and plea bargaining are options in many formal criminal justice systems, and when accepting such an opportunity the suspect gives up the rights to be presumed innocent and to remain silent in order to benefit from a diversion or a reduced sentence. Improving the manner in which the options are put to the suspect can reduce the risk of coercion, and proper training of the officials who are responsible for putting the option to the accused is necessary.

Legal representation

The right to legal representation is considered an intrinsic part of the right to a fair trial in adversarial criminal justice proceedings. While some restorative justice processes do allow parties to have legal representatives present, there are indications that lawyers who have not been trained in mediation or restorative justice tend to hinder rather than help the process. Braithwaite (2002b: 566) points out that restorative justice is intended 'to transcend adversarial legalism', and he therefore does not support a legal right of the accused to be represented by a lawyer at such proceedings, although he considers it reasonable to allow suspects to seek the advice of a lawyer on whether they should participate in the programme. However, a useful model has emerged in New Zealand, where youth advocates assist young people in family group conferences. They are specially selected and trained for this work, and therefore they assist with the process while ensuring rights protection.

Outcomes

The principle of proportionality is a major factor in deciding on a particular sentence in a criminal trial. Warner (1994) asserts that in a criminal trial a sentence cannot be increased beyond a limit appropriate to the severity of the offence, on the grounds of possible future offending, nor on the grounds of the need to treat the offender. However, these considerations may tend to influence outcomes of restorative justice processes.

Another concern relates to disparities in outcomes. Restorative justice outcomes may be outside the range of penalties usually imposed by courts. Thus there is a risk that not only will there be internal inconsistency in restorative justice outcomes, but in addition there will be disparity between restorative justice outcomes and court outcomes for similar offences.

In most criminal justice systems, if a convicted person is of the view that his or her sentence is disproportionate to the offence, or if it is not consistent with sentences in similar cases, a remedy lies by way of an application for leave to appeal. This option is not always available in restorative justice processes.

Double jeopardy

A fair trial includes the right not to be tried twice for the same offence. This is known as double jeopardy, or as 'autrefois acquit, autrefois convict'. The risk of double jeopardy in restorative justice may arise where an offender complies with the agreement to a certain point, and then fails to complete all the terms of the agreement. Warner (1994) points out that this situation is not true double jeopardy, because it does not involve having previously been convicted of a crime. Nevertheless there is risk, because the offender may have done months of community service, or paid over a substantial sum of money, only to find him or herself back in the criminal justice system when he or she breaches the conditions towards the end of the period. Warner gives an example of legislation that prevents the outcome of the mediation being presented back to court. This approach, however, may leave the victim with no remedy.

The risks of 'net widening'

It is broadly understood by criminal justice reformers that efforts to find alternatives to the criminal justice system sometimes have the unintended consequences of drawing a larger number of people into the new processes and this is referred to as 'net widening'. Net widening can appear in different guises. Cases where there is insufficient evidence to sustain a conviction may end up being 'dumped' on the restorative justice pile, along with petty cases that the prosecution considers not worth taking to trial, school cases that could have been dealt with in school and family issues that could have been dealt with in the family. However, a restorative justice approach may consider that solving conflicts in schools or neighbourhoods while these are still 'small' amounts not only to peace-making but also to peace-building, thus contributing effectively to crime prevention.

Risks to child defendants

Due to their lack of experience children are highly suggestible, and are more likely to be coerced into making false admissions to avoid 'more trouble'. Dumortier (2003) has recorded research that indicates that children are often excluded from mediation due to their inability to pay material reparation, and that once in a process they may concede agreements that they cannot in reality fulfil. Haines (1997) has warned against a situation in which a child is 'upbraided' by a room full of adults. When dealing with child offenders, special care must be taken to ensure that the process does not result in domination, or in outcomes that are disrespectful or humiliating. Morris (2002) has pointed out that these risks are minimized if the child is properly supported throughout the process.

Broader human rights issues

Social justice

A critique often levelled at restorative justice has been its inability to resolve questions relating to social justice (White 2000). This question looms large when assessing the rights of participants in restorative justice interventions. Economic, social and racial inequalities are deepening globally. It is likely that the rights of those who are disempowered, excluded and vulnerable due to these inequalities will be at risk in restorative justice processes. While it is not suggested that the criminal justice system is any better an arbiter of these social justice concerns (Ashworth 2002), the broader ambitions of restorative justice dictate that these concerns be brought to the centre of the discourse relating to both theory and practice (Skelton and Frank 2001).

Power imbalances

Researchers and observers have raised many concerns relating to the effects of power imbalances that frustrate the intentions of restorative justice interventions (Daly 2002; Dumortier 2003). These disparities, arising from differences such as race, class, culture, age and gender, pose a substantial threat to the protection and promotion of rights in restorative justice programmes. Razack (1994: 910, 907) has observed that 'community has not been a safe place for women' and that 'culture, community and colonialisation can be used to compete with and ultimately prevail over gender based harm'. Mbambo and Skelton (2003) have raised concerns about children suspected of crimes in South African communities being victimized, sometimes violently, by communities that are angry about crime. Issues of race and culture play themselves out in different, though equally problematic ways (Umbreit *et al.* 2001).

Given the power imbalances discussed above, coercion and the degree of voluntariness remain a concern (Zehr 1990; Boyes-Watson 2000). The assumption that coercion disappears once there is consent to participate in a restorative justice process is dangerous and denies the nuances relating to power that are present in all human interactions (Skelton and Frank 2004).

Protection of rights in non-state forms of justice

Informal justice systems or non-state forms of justice are those that do not rely on or are not linked to the formal justice system. These take many forms but can broadly be divided into three categories.

First, in some countries with indigenous populations, traditional or customary courts are still part of informal systems to which people take their disputes directly, rather than going to the police. Secondly, in some countries there are popular forums that have been modelled on traditional systems, but have grown out of a lack of faith in the colonial or imposed systems (Penal Reform International 2001). Thirdly, there are instances when communities take the law into their own hands and mete out punishments which are not restorative.

In the first category, it must be noted that the existence of non-state forms of justice in many communities poses a different set of challenges than those presented by restorative justice processes linked to the criminal justice system. African traditional courts, for example, often do not follow the principles of a fair trial. In such systems a person is often presumed guilty until proven innocent and the right to remain silent is not recognized. The patriarchal nature of traditional society means that the justice system is sometimes prejudicial towards women and children (Bennett 1999; Tshehla 2005).

On the other hand, the practice of these traditional courts can be described as restorative in many respects (Elechi 2004). Through the traditional court system, the perpetrator must apologize to the victim and compensate for stolen or damaged property either by restitution, or by repairing damage, or paying for losses. When Lesotho piloted their restorative justice approach in rural villages it took root very quickly, largely due to the fact that elements of restorative justice already existed in the traditional justice practices (Qhubu 2005).

With regard to the second category of non-state forms of justice, Ashworth (2002) identifies two countries, Northern Ireland and South Africa, as examples where the legitimacy of the state and its apparatus had suffered a serious collapse, giving rise to non-state forms of justice (Schärf and Nina 2001; McEvoy and Mika 2002). The failure by the state to provide legitimate systems and the failure of many states to deal with social inequalities are acknowledged as reasons why many restorative justice advocates call for the state to play a residual rather than prominent role in the criminal justice process. However, Ashworth (2002) is of the view that the state should maintain control over crime and punishment, and one of the reasons he advances for this is that human rights must be protected. His rationale is that values such as impartiality, proportionality and consistency are of vital importance to human rights protection, but that in restorative justice they are in tension with other values such as participation, involvement of the victim and empowerment. Strang and Braithwaite (2001: 13) summarize the balance needed: 'We come to see the restorative justice agenda not as a choice between civil society and state justice, but as requiring us to seek the most productive synergies between the two.'

The third type of non-state justice arises where high levels of crime and the resulting fear have caused many communities to administer harsher measures (Mistry *et al.* 2004). This, coupled with the perceptions that the criminal justice system is weak, has seen the rise of vigilante activity in some countries. Some communities in South Africa, tired of crime in their areas and feeling that the police and courts have failed to curb the scourge, are taking the law into their hands, assaulting and even killing suspected criminals. From media reports and research conducted by a number of civil society organizations and academics, there is a general consensus that vigilantism exists because the state fails to provide security for the people, especially the poor and marginalized. The other argument advanced heavily is that the criminal justice process is perpetrator friendly. Proponents of vigilantism argue that criminals get off lightly because sentences are lenient and bail is granted easily, and they therefore feel it is justified when communities take action to remedy this weakness in the criminal justice. *Mapogo a Mathamaga*, a vigilante-based private security organization in South Africa, refers to the remedial action required as 'medicine administered to criminals'. The medicine involves severe corporal punishment of the suspect until he or she confesses to the crime (Louw and Sekhonyane 2002). The situation is exacerbated by rapid urbanisation, which creates communities of strangers. Restorative justice works best in a functional community founded on the principles of good neighbourliness. However, in communities of strangers such principles do not necessarily exist.

It is important when considering non-state forms of justice to separate out those that are restorative in nature from those that are not. Traditional justice systems are generally restorative, although they may fail to include women and young people adequately and in some cases may use corporal punishment. While the systems do not hold up to a critique of due process rights protection that Western legal practitioners expect from the criminal justice system, the processes are generally protective and healing and aim at restoring harmony in communities.

The second category of community-driven alternatives to justice that operate independently of the criminal justice system are less steeped in tradition and are more likely to allow full participation of women and young people. In the South African Community Peace Programme, for example, it has been noted that women are at the forefront of the peace-making and peace-building work (Roche 2002). This programme has its own code, part of which states that those involved will abide by the rights set out in the South African Constitution. Similarly, the restorative justice alternatives in Northern Ireland have developed their own sets of standards for rights protection. The history of non-state forms of justice in South Africa, however, demonstrates that people's courts can become a negative force, particularly in times of conflict, and can ultimately lean towards the third category, vigilantism.

Sachs has observed, in the Foreword to a book on non-state forms of justice in South Africa, that 'there can be neither an in-principle acceptance nor a categorical rejection of this Other law … The Other law would function not outside of or in opposition to the constitutional realm, but in the spaces acknowledged by the Constitution itself' (Schärf and Nina 2001: vi).

Standards setting

There appears to be fairly broad agreement that rights should be protected in the operation of restorative justice. Setting of standards both internally (within the project or programme) and at a national or even international level has now become part of restorative justice discourse (Van Ness 2003).

Points for and against standard setting

Braithwaite (2002b: 565) has identified some of the dangers of standardization:

> While it is good that we are now having debates on standards for restorative justice it is a dangerous debate. Accreditation for mediators that raises the spectre of a Western accreditation agency telling an Aboriginal elder that a centuries old restorative practice does not comply with the accreditation standards is a profound worry. We must avert accreditation that crushes indigenous empowerment.

He also fears that standardization may inhibit innovation, as we are still learning how to do restorative justice well. However, he concedes that there is some practice that is so obviously bad that we do need to act to eliminate it. He gives the example of a family group conference in Australia that required a boy to publicly wear a tee-shirt bearing the words 'I am a thief'. Braithwaite concludes that such practices may be an even greater threat to restorative justice than overly prescriptive standards.

The UN basic principles on restorative justice

At the eleventh session of the UN Commission on Crime Prevention and Criminal Justice, Canada put forward a resolution that encourages countries to draw from the *Basic Principles on the Use of Restorative Justice Programmes in Criminal Matters* in developing and implementing restorative justice. The commission approved the resolution, and the basic principles may be seen as guidelines to assist states and organizations in their work. The principles were developed by a UN expert group on restorative justice, drawing on previous recommendations and existing guidelines developed by practitioner groups (Van Ness 2003).

Section II of the principles is headed 'Use of restorative justice programmes' and includes the following principles:

- Restorative justice programmes should be generally available at all stages of the criminal justice process.
- Restorative processes should be used only with the free and voluntary consent of the parties. The parties should be able to withdraw such consent at any time during the process. Agreements should be arrived at voluntarily by the parties and contain only reasonable and proportionate obligations.

- All parties should normally acknowledge the basic facts of a case as a basis for participation in a restorative process. Participation should not be used as evidence of admission of guilt in subsequent legal proceedings.
- Obvious disparities with respect to factors such as power imbalances and the parties' age, maturity or intellectual capacity should be taken into consideration in referring a case to, and in conducting, a restorative justice process.
- Where restorative justice processes and/or outcomes are not possible, criminal justice officials should do all they can to encourage the offender to take responsibility vis-à-vis the victim and affected communities, and reintegration of the victim and/or offender into the community.

Section III of the basic principles has the title 'Operation of restorative justice programmes'. Guidelines and standards and fundamental safeguards should be applied to restorative justice programmes and processes, and these include the parties' right to legal advice before and after the restorative justice process, parties being fully informed of their rights and protection from being induced by unfair means to participate. Confidentiality of the proceedings is flagged as a principle, with the discussions not to be disclosed subsequently, except with the consent of the parties. Judicial discharges based on restorative justice agreements should preclude prosecution on the same facts.

The basic principles include guidelines on what should happen when the parties fail to reach agreement, and when there is failure to implement an agreement that has been made. The remainder of the basic principles deal with the recruitment of facilitators and guidelines for how they should carry out their functions, as well as the continuing development of restorative justice programmes, the promotion of research on and evaluation of restorative justice programmes.

International and regional standards are not specific to the particular country context. Therefore the possibility of standards being set in a more detailed manner in individual countries is also a consideration. This is sometimes done through legislation, or through codes of conduct. The more prescriptive such standards become, however, the more there is a danger that they begin to destroy the essence of what restorative justice sets out to achieve.

Categories of rights and values

The Universal Declaration of Human Rights adopted in 1948 by the United Nations General Assembly was the first attempt to universalize human rights. Rights that are universal do not all enjoy the same standing, however. Some rights, such as the right to life and the right to human dignity, are inalienable or entirely non-derogable. The South African Constitution, for example, prizes the values of human dignity, equality and freedom above all others, and these three values, in addition to being in the list of rights themselves, are also used as values to test the other rights contained in the Bill of Rights. It is apparent, therefore, that there is some congruity between rights and values. The right to human dignity has proved to be a touchstone for the interpretation of the South African Bill of Rights, and the interesting thing about this value is its applicability across both Western and African legal systems.

Braithwaite (2003) has offered a list of values relevant for restorative justice, which he divides into three different categories. The first list he describes as constraining values, which are fundamental procedural safeguards that take priority where any serious sanction is at risk. They include empowerment, honouring legally specific upper limits on sanctions, respectful listening, equal concern for stakeholders, accountability, appealability and respect for the fundamental human rights specified in international instruments. A second group of restorative justice values is proposed by Braithwaite (2002a), which he describes as 'maximizing standards', meaning that they should be promoted and encouraged. These values relate to healing and restoration. They include very basic kinds of restoration such as returning property, and more abstract ones such as the restoration of dignity, compassion, social support and the prevention of future injustice. The third group of standards is described as 'emergent standards'. They are remorse over injustice, apology, censure of the act, forgiveness of the person and mercy. Unlike the second category, participants should not be actively encouraged to bring these standards to the fore, they should simply be allowed to emerge. Braithwaite recognizes the usefulness of the UN standards, which he describes as 'top down'. However, he stresses the importance of 'bottom-up value clarification'. Those working at local level must consider how to ensure effective quality assurance and accountability in restorative justice. This can be done by taking a list of values, such as those Braithwaite has proposed, and beginning a debate about the standards to which they want their programmes to conform.

Are restorative justice processes dependent on the state legal system for protection of due process?

Zehr (1990) describes three 'system' possibilities for the operation of restorative justice. The first is the possibility of 'civilizing' the criminal justice system – by replacing the entire adversarial criminal justice system with one in which the victim and offender are central. The second possible system is a parallel track, which runs alongside, but is independent of, the mainstream criminal justice system. The third system described is a parallel but interdependent or interlinked track.

Walgrave has described a version of restorative justice in which the overall aim is to deal with offenders and victims in a restorative way. Such a system would include coercive sanctions in addition to voluntary processes. While such a restorative justice system should prioritize the voluntary processes which involve face-to-face meetings between offenders and victims, if these are not possible or appropriate then the formal criminal justice system will need to take over, but it should still aim for restorative justice outcomes (Walgrave 2001).

Although there are models that accord with Zehr's parallel track approach (Shearing 2001), the majority of restorative justice programmes currently operating appear to adhere to Zehr's third system possibility – linked to the state system, and in many ways dependent upon it (Skelton 2002).

Ashworth (2002: 581) points out that, although communities have a greater stake in the resolution of criminal justice matters through restorative justice, the state nevertheless retains a responsibility to impose a framework that guarantees rights and safeguards for suspects and offenders, because restorative justice processes still involve public censure and the imposition of obligations on offenders. He remarks: 'The State surely owes to offenders to exercise its power according to settled principles that uphold citizens' rights to equal respect and equality of treatment.'

Even among writers who take a more relaxed view of the need for procedural rules, there is agreement that certain protections are nevertheless required. Braithwaite, for example, believes there should be protection against what he calls 'domination' or power imbalance, and that restorative justice processes must never be able to impose a punishment beyond the maximum allowed by the law for that kind of offence, nor to impose a punishment that is degrading or humiliating.

Braithwaite would agree that there is a need for standards, but he would disagree with Ashworth that the state should 'impose' such a framework. He would favour a more democratic process of participation by community stakeholders in the development of certain practice principles in order to ensure that rights are protected.

Broadening the discourse around human rights

Human rights protection must be part of developing restorative justice practice. The criminal justice system emphasis on due process rights is, however, a rather narrow construct of rights. It is possible to give up the right to be presumed innocent through acknowledging responsibility and have one's human rights remain intact. Indeed, human rights such as dignity and equality may be enhanced through acknowledging responsibility in a restorative justice process, notwithstanding concerns about the limitations of restorative justice to deal with issues of social justice and power differentials.

The interdependent relationship between the state and restorative justice programmes is part of the reason for this narrow discourse, as comparisons with the standard criminal justice process are more likely to be made. Systems that run parallel and are not interdependent are more likely to set up their own rules for practice that promote restorative justice and human rights, and do not as easily fall into the trap of creating a set of narrow rules designed to meet the needs of a criminal justice trial. A project in South Africa, for instance, has set up a code of good practice for their peace-making process, which transcends details like whether a person is presumed innocent or is entitled to legal representation. It promotes instead concepts such as 'we create a safe and secure environment in our community, we do not gossip about our work or other people, we are consistent in what we do, our aim is heal, not to hurt' (Shearing 2001: 21).

Humbach (2001: 41–61) has offered a fresh perspective on rights. He is of the view that depersonalized rights and rules cannot mediate the intricacies of interactions among human beings. Humbach refutes the idea that justice is achievable through the protection of individual rights. He believes that what we should be striving for is 'a justice of right relationships'. He contrasts this with the justice of rights, which he characterizes as 'a justice of entitlements'. A justice of rights relationships, on the other hand, arises out of the human attachments and connections that people form: 'At its core, the justice of right relationships is the intrinsic good that inures to persons who live in interaction with others whose fundamental concern is to maintain the quality and mutual worth of their relationships, instead of insisting on their rights'(2001: 42).

The way forward may lie in broadening the discourse around rights. The confines of the due process conceptualization of rights will tie the field down to providing a mirror of the standard criminal justice process. Human rights encompass a broader view but are still, as reflected in international instruments, based on a very individualized approach. In countries that have a history of indigenous conflict resolution a more communitarian approach to rights is evident (Skelton 2004).

In an essay on the ethics and values needed for peace in the twenty-first century, Horace Campbell asserts that the world has been organized according to the views of Western male leaders who have relied on conceptions such as the importance of the individual as espoused by John Locke, the free market as propounded by Adam Smith and the survival of the fittest as described by Charles Darwin. Campbell suggests that it may be possible to provide alternatives to this approach of maximizing self-interest by focusing on other values such as peace, reconstruction and reconciliation (2002).

The starting point of this alternative ideation is the moral ethic of collective unity. While Western ideation is premised on individualization, African ideation is based on a theory of collective living, which finds voice in a number of key African concepts. The philosophy of *ujamaa* (familyhood) is used by Julius Nyerere to describe the kind of life he believed Tanzanians should live. This was a simple life in which people lived in harmony with their close families. Wealth belonged to the family as a whole, and no one could use wealth as a way of dominating others. 'We want the whole nation to live as a family', was how Nyerere explained the idea. He recognized that this approach was akin to socialism, but he used the term *ujamaa* because he wanted to root the concept of socialism in the African philosophy of collectivism, and because he wanted to be sure that no one would act as 'master over servant' in the system that he was promoting (1998: 78). The importance of people living together at the same level, recognising differences but not allowing domination or discrimination, was further illustrated by Nyerere in his promotion of the concept of *ndugu*, meaning brotherhood or sisterhood. In South Africa it has been argued that the ethic of collective unity is captured in the concept of *ubuntu* (humanity for others) (Mokgoro 1998; Tutu 1999).

African philosopher Kwame Gyeke (1998) asserts that a communitarian ethos underpins African social structures. He believes that, although the general thrust of this ethos emphasizes duties towards the community, it does not do so to the detriment of individual rights, the existence and value of which should be recognized by the community. Restorative justice theorists and practitioners may need to move beyond the focus on the individual which characterizes the Western approach to human rights, and begin an evaluation of the rights of the individual within a more communitarian approach (Skelton and Frank 2004).

Conclusion

Restorative justice writers differ in their opinions about the importance of rights protection. There are those who are of the view that due process rights need to be strictly enforced in restorative justice processes and programmes, while others take the position that such an approach is not necessary, and may even hinder or impede restorative justice outcomes. It has been observed that:

> in an attempt to be sensitive to human rights protection, restorative justice practitioners appear to be getting drawn into a confined discourse about due process rights, in which restorative justice processes are being expected to provide the same protections as courts. The protections relating to due process were designed to deal with the specific dangers inherent in the criminal justice trial process, particularly adversarial trials. It is not particularly logical, therefore, that the rules designed for those processes must be mirrored in restorative justice processes (Skelton and Frank 2004: 209).

It is likely that those restorative justice processes that are interlinked with the formal criminal justice process will be under particular pressure to conform to due process standards commonly found in the criminal justice system. Restorative justice processes that are less closely linked to the criminal justice system may be able to find informal and individual ways of ensuring rights protection. In general, it appears that there is a consensus that there should be standards or guidelines in the practice of restorative justice, although on the issue of how these standards should be set and what they should contain there is, and should continue to be, much debate. This chapter has aimed to show that there are different ways of looking at rights, and that these different ways should be factored into the debates about how to ensure human rights protections within restorative justice practice.

Selected further reading

Ashworth, A. (2002) 'Responsibilities, rights and restorative justice', *British Journal of Criminology*, 42: 578–95. Ashworth takes a critical view of restorative justice in this article, highlighting the risks of the process and questioning the extent to which the victim's view should play a role in sentencing.

Braithwaite, J. (2002) 'Standards for restorative justice', *British Journal of Criminology*, 42: 563–77. Braithwaite's article highlights the dangers of over-regulating restorative justice, but concedes that the risk of bad practice requires standard setting, which should be developed through a bottom-up rather than a top-down process.

Braithwaite, J. (2003) 'Principles of restorative justice', in A. von Hirsch *et al.* (eds) *Restorative Justice and Criminal Justice: Competing or Reconcilable Paradigms?* Oxford: Hart Publishing. Braithwaite takes his standards analysis further, setting out a framework of values in three categories: constraining, maximizing and emergent standards.

Skelton, A. and Frank, C. (2004) 'How does restorative justice address human rights and due process issues?', in H. Zehr and B. Toews (eds) *Critical Issues in Restorative Justice*. Monsey, NY and Cullompton: Criminal Justice Press/Willan Publishing. Skelton and Frank suggest that debates about standard setting in restorative justice need to be broadened to encompass communitarian values.

Notes

1 R *v.* Clotworthy (1998) 15 CRNZ 651 (CA).
2 R *v.* Nunn [1996] 2 Cr. App. R (S) 136.

References

Akester, K. (2003) 'Restorative justice, victim's rights and the future' (available online at www.restorativejustice.org.uk/article 1. html).

Ashworth, A. (2002) 'Responsibilities, rights and restorative justice', *British Journal of Criminology*, 42: 578–95.

Barnett, R. (1980) 'The justice of restitution', *American Journal of Jurisprudence*, 25, 117–32.

Bennett, T.W. (1999) *Human Rights and African Customary Law*. Cape Town: Juta.

Bianchi, H. (1994) *Justice as Sanctuary*. Bloomington, IN: Indian University Press.

Boyes-Watson, C. (2000) 'Reflections on the purist and maximalist models of restorative justice', *Contemporary Justice Review*, 3: 441–51.

Braithwaite, J. (2002a) 'In search of a restorative jurisprudence', in L. Walgrave (ed.) *Restorative Justice and the Law*. Cullompton: Willan Publishing.

Braithwaite, J. (2002b) 'Standards for restorative justice', *British Journal of Criminology*, 42: 563–77.

Braithwaite, J. (2003) 'Principles of restorative justice', in A. von Hirsch *et al.* (eds) *Restorative Justice and Criminal Justice: Competing or Reconcilable Paradigms?* Oxford: Hart Publishing.

Braithwaite, J. and Strang, H. (2000) 'Connecting philosophy to practice', in H. Strang and J. Braithwaite (eds) *Restorative Justice: Philosophy to Practice*. Dartmouth: Ashgate.

Campbell, H. (2002) 'The ethics, qualities and values necessary for leadership and peace in the twenty-first century', in G. Wildschut (ed.) *Emerging African Leadership: Opportunities and Challenges for Peace and Development*. Cape Town: Desmond Tutu Leadership Academy.

Christie, N. (1977) 'Conflicts as property', *British Journal of Criminology*, 17: 1–15.

Coward-Yaskin, S. (2002) 'Restorative justice', *Horizons*, 15: 22–9.

Daly, K. (2002) 'Restorative justice: the real story', *Punishment and Society*, 4: 55–79.

Damaska, M. (1975) 'Structures of authority and comparative criminal procedure', *Yale Law Journal*, 84: 480–532.

Dumortier, E. (2003) 'Legal rules and safeguards within Belgian mediation practices for juveniles', in E. Weitekamp and H.J. Kerner (eds) *Restorative Justice in Context: International Practice and Directions*. Cullompton: Willan Publishing.

Elechi, O. (2004) 'Human rights and the African indigenous justice system.' Paper presented at the 18th International Conference of the International Society for the Reform of Criminal Law, Montreal, 8–12 August (available online at http://www/isrd.org/papers).

Gyeke, K. (1998) 'Person and community in African thought', in P. Coetzee and A. Roux (eds) *The African Philosophy Reader*. London: Routledge.

Haines, K. (1997) 'Some principled objections to a restorative justice approach to working with juvenile offenders', in L. Walgrave (ed.) *Restorative Justice for Juveniles: Potentialities, Risks, and Problems for Research*. Leuven: Leuven University Press.

Hamilton, D. (1988) *Foul Bills and Dagger Money*. Oxford: Professional Books.

Henkin, L. (1990) *The Age of Rights*. New York, NY: Columbia University Press.

Humbach, J. (2001) 'Towards a natural justice of right relationships', in B. Leiser and T. Campbell (eds) *Human Rights in Philosophy and Practice*. Dartmouth: Ashgate.

Jacob, B. (1977) 'The concept of restitution: an historical overview', in J. Hudson and B. Galaway (eds) *Restitution in Criminal Justice*. Lexington, MA: Lexington Books.

Johnstone, G. (2002) *Restorative Justice: Ideas, Values, Debates*. Cullompton: Willan Publishing.

Mbambo, B. and Skelton, A. (2003) 'Preparing the South African community for implementing a new restorative child justice system', in L. Walgrave (ed.) *Repositioning Restorative Justice*. Cullompton: Willan Publishing.

McEvoy, K. and Mika, H. (2002) Restorative justice and the critique of informalism in Northern Ireland', *British Journal of Criminology*, 42: 534–62.

Mistry, D., Burton, P., Du Plessis, A., Leggett, T., Louw, A. and Van Vuuren, H. (2004) *National Victims of Crime Survey*. Pretoria: Institute for Security Studies.

Mokgoro, Y. (1998) 'Ubuntu and the Law in South Africa', *Buffalo Human Rights Law Review*, 4: 15–24.

Morris, A. (2002) 'Critiquing the critics: a brief response to critics of restorative justice', *British Journal of Criminology*, 42: 596–615.

Morris, A., Maxwell, G. and Robertson, J. (1993) 'Giving victims a voice: a New Zealand experiment', *Howard Journal*, 32: 304–21.

Nyerere, J. (1998) 'Leaders must not be masters', in E.C. Eke (ed.) *African Philosophy: An Anthology*. Oxford: Blackwell.

Penal Reform International (2001) *Access to Justice in Sub-Saharan Africa*. London: Penal Reform International.

Qhubu, N. (2005) 'The development of restorative justice in Lesotho.' Paper presented at the Association of Law Reform Agencies for Eastern and Southern Africa Conference, Cape Town, 14–17 March (available online at http://www.salrc.org.za).

Razack, S. (1994) 'What is to be gained by looking white people in the eye: culture, race and gender in cases of sexual violence', *Signs: Journal of Women in Culture and Society*, 19: 894–923.

Roche, D. (2002) 'Restorative justice and the regulatory state in South African townships', *British Journal of Criminology*, 42, 514–32.

Schärf, W. and Nina, D. (eds) (2001) *The Other Law: Non State Ordering in South Africa.* Cape Town: Juta.

Schwikkard, P.J. (1999) *Presumption of Innocence.* Cape Town: Juta.

Sekhonyane, M. and Louw, A. (2003) *Violent Justice, Vigilantism and the State's Response.* Pretoria: Institute for Security Studies.

Shearing, C. (2001) 'Transforming security: a South African experiment', in H. Strang and J. Braithwaite (eds) *Restorative Justice and Civil Society.* Cambridge: Cambridge University Press.

Skelton, A. (2004) 'For the next generations: remaking South Africa's juvenile justice system', in E. Doxtader and C. Villa-Vicencio (eds) *To Repair the Irreparable: Reparation and Reconstruction in South Africa.* Claremont: David Philip.

Skelton, A. (2002) 'Restorative justice as a framework for juvenile justice reform: a South African perspective', *British Journal of Criminology*, 42: 496–513.

Skelton, A. and Frank, C. (2001)'Conferencing in South Africa: returning to our future', in A. Morris and G. Maxwell (eds) *Restorative Justice for Juveniles: Conferencing, Mediation and Circles.* Oxford: Hart Publishing.

Skelton, A. and Frank, C. (2004) 'How does restorative justice address human rights and due process issues?', in H. Zehr and B. Toews (eds) *Critical Issues in Restorative Justice.* Monsey, NY: Criminal Justice Press and Willan Publishing.

Steytler, N. (1988) *The Undefended Accused on Trial.* Cape Town: Juta.

Strang, H. (2001) 'The crime victim movement as a force in civil society', in J. Braithwaite and H. Strang (eds) *Restorative Justice and Civil Society.* Cambridge: Cambridge University Press.

Strang, H. and Braithwaite, J. (eds) (2001) *Restorative Justice and Civil Society.* Cambridge: Cambridge University Press.

Tshehla, B. (2005) *Traditional Justice in Practice: A Limpopo Case Study.* Pretoria: Institute for Security Studies.

Tutu, D. (1999) *No Future without Forgiveness.* London: Rider.

Umbreit, M., Coates, R. and Vos, B. (2001) 'Victim impact of meeting with young offenders: two decades of victim offender mediation practice and research', in A. Morris and G. Maxwell (eds) *Restorative Justice for Juveniles: Conferencing, Mediation and Circles.* Oxford: Hart Publishing.

Van Ness, D. (2003) 'Proposed basic principles on the use of restorative justice: recognising the aims and limits of restorative justice', in A. von Hirsch *et al.* (eds) *Restorative Justice and Criminal Justice: Competing or Reconcilable Paradigms.* Oxford: Hart Publishing.

Van Ness, D. and Strong, H.K. (1997) *Restoring Justice.* Cincinatti, OH: Anderson Publishing.

Waldron, J. (1993) *Liberal Rights: Collected Paper 1981–1991.* Cambridge: Cambridge University Press.

Walgrave, L. (2000) 'How pure can a maximalist approach to restorative justice remain?', *Contemporary Justice Review,* 3: 415–32.

Walgrave, L. (2001) 'On restoration and punishment: favourable similarities and fortunate differences', in A. Morris and G. Maxwell (eds) *Restorative Justice for Juveniles: Conferencing, Mediation and Circles.* Oxford: Hart Publishing.

Warner, K. (1994) 'Family group conferences and the rights of the offender', in C. Alder and J. Wundersitz (eds) *Family Conferencing and Juvenile Justice: The Way Forward or Misplaced Optimism?* Canberra: Australian Institute of Criminology.

White, R. (2000) 'Social justice, community building and restorative strategies', *Contemporary Justice Review,* 3: 55–72.

Wright, M. (1991) *Justice for Victims and Offenders: A Restorative Response to Crime.* Milton Keynes: Open University Press.

Zehr, H. (1990) *Changing Lenses: A New Focus for Crime and Justice.* Scottsdale, PA: Herald Press.

Zehr, H. and Toews, B. (eds) (2004) *Critical Issues in Restorative Justice.* Monsey, NY: Willan Publishing.

Chapter 28

Critical perspectives on restorative justice

Gerry Johnstone

Much of the literature of restorative justice is written by proponents, ranging from fervent enthusiasts to more cautious sympathizers. They portray it as an approach to wrongdoing which is both ethically better and more effective than conventional methods used to respond when someone 'has harmed another, namely, methods based in punishment' (Sullivan *et al.* 1998: 8). However, alongside the literature of proponents, there are other writings which provide more critical perspectives.[1] These raise doubts about the credibility of proponents' claims about restorative justice and about the ethics and effectiveness of the approach itself. This chapter introduces some critical perspectives found in this literature and looks briefly at their implications.[2]

The critical perspectives introduced here can be summarized as follows:

1 Proponents' descriptions of restorative justice are vague and incoherent.
2 Proponents make exaggerated claims about what restorative justice can achieve.
3 A significant move away from punishment towards restorative justice will undermine the policy of deterrence.
4 A significant move away from punishment towards restorative 'justice' will result in a failure to do *justice.*
5 A significant move away from punishment towards restorative justice will result in systematic departures from axiomatic principles of justice.
6 While presented as a radical alternative to conventional approaches to wrongdoing, restorative justice actually shares a great deal with conventional approaches and its introduction will simply extend the reach of conventional systems of penal control.

Vagueness and incoherence

A frequent complaint about proponents of restorative justice is that they fail to provide a coherent account of what restorative justice is and what it seeks to achieve. According to Andrew von Hirsch *et al*. (2003: 22–3), this failure is exhibited in at least four ways. First, advocates of restorative justice propose simultaneously a variety of restorative justice goals which are 'vaguely formulated' and which are not ranked in any order of priority. The goals include 'the victim be "restored"; the offender be made to recognise his wrong; the "conflict" between victim and offender be healed; the breach in the community's sense of trust be repaired; the community be reassured against further offending; and fear of crime be diminished' (von Hirsch *et al*. 2003: 22). Secondly, restorative justice advocates fail to identify – except in the vaguest of terms – precise methods of achieving any of these goals, save to state that they will be achieved through deliberative processes in which victims and offenders take part (von Hirsch *et al*. 2003: 23). Thirdly, advocates offer 'few or no dispositional criteria' for decision-making bodies (such as participants in a restorative conference) in restorative justice; rather, within very wide bounds, decision-makers seem free to pursue any aim and to choose nearly any means of achieving such aims (2003: 23). Finally, restorative justice advocates have 'dangling standards of evaluation' and fail to explain how the criteria used to evaluate restorative justice programmes relate to the goals to be achieved. For instance, criteria used to evaluate programmes almost invariably include 'participant satisfaction' and 'impact on recidivism', yet it is seldom explained why these are appropriate or meaningful criteria (2003: 23).

It should be noted that for von Hirsch and many of his colleagues, these objections arise because of their experience with benevolent-sounding programmes that ended up being unjust in practice. Von Hirsch's work with the deserts model of sentencing grew out of deep concern about the injustice of indeterminate, rehabilitative sentences that resulted in grossly disparate sentences being imposed on and served by similar offenders convicted of similar crimes. In other words, the objection to vagueness is not merely aesthetic; it is made because of the belief that incoherent goals can lead to unjust sentences.

Von Hirsch *et al*. clearly think that, in order to have a sensible debate about the pros and cons of any particular alternative model, that model must provide precise and consistent answers to a number of questions: what is the exact objective of intervention? If there is more than one objective what is the relative importance of each? What methods are to be used to achieve each objective and why are these methods appropriate? Precisely what constraints are decision-makers subject to – i.e. what objectives and what methods are they not permitted to pursue and use? By what criteria is the success of any particular intervention or scheme to be evaluated and how do these criteria relate to the goals of intervention?

The general difficulty which von Hirsch *et al*. (2003) have with proponents' accounts of restorative justice is that they fail to provide careful answers to such questions. Rather, they suggest, the literature promoting restorative justice tends to be 'aspirational' in character (2003: 24). It presents us with a range of *ideals* that they think we should aspire to in responding to offenders, ideals such as healing victims, reintegrating offenders, reconciling people in conflict and empowering communities. However, according to von Hirsch *et al.*, such expressions of ideals are of little value as guides to action for those who are *serious* about reforming our ways of dealing with criminal offenders. Rather, what serious reformers require is a conceptually coherent model in which the precise objectives of intervention, the methods of achieving these objectives, any limiting principles and evaluation criteria are clearly and consistently specified.

It is important to be clear about the implications of this critique. Von Hirsch *et al.* are not suggesting that there is no role for something like restorative justice in our responses to criminal wrongdoing (indeed, they themselves present us with a 'making amends' model which they think might play a role within a just sentencing system). Their critique is best understood as being aimed – not at restorative justice *per se* – but rather at advocates for failing to provide a conceptually coherent model of restorative justice. Proponents, they indicate, tend to confuse exhortations and expressions of ideals with useful models of intervention, and offer us the former as if they were the latter.

It follows that, schematically, there are a number of different ways in which restorative justice proponents could respond to this critique: 1) they might accept von Hirsch *et al.*'s claim about what is required – i.e. a conceptually coherent model of intervention – and also concede that they have failed to provide it and proceed to construct such a model;[3] 2) they might accept von Hirsch *et al.*'s claim about what is required but claim that they have already provided it; and 3) they might reject altogether von Hirsch *et al.*'s claim about what is required, arguing that an 'aspirational' approach has more going for it than von Hirsch *et al.* realize.

Exaggerated claims

Restorative justice proponents frequently make significant claims about what restorative justice does achieve or has the potential to achieve. Sometimes these claims are made directly, as when promotional literature (which includes scholarly books and papers, magazine articles, information leaflets and films) makes explicit claims about the capacity of restorative justice to achieve outcomes such as the prevention of reoffending, the recovery of victims from traumatic experiences, the creation of positive healthy relationships between people previously at loggerheads, the saving of public funds which can be diverted to constructive socializing and educating projects, and so on. At other times, these claims are more implicit, as when restorative justice proponents tell stories about particularly successful restorative interventions and (perhaps not consciously) create the impression that the outcomes in these cases are representative of those of well run restorative justice interventions in general.

Not surprisingly, more critical writers have pointed to significant gaps between these claims and the actual achievements of restorative justice. A prominent example is Kathleen Daly (2003). While quite sympathetic towards restorative justice, Daly is also concerned to debunk certain 'myths' about it, myths propagated by what she would see as overenthusiastic proponents. Some of these 'myths' are to do with the way restorative justice is represented as the opposite of retributive justice, as the norm in all pre-modern societies or as a feminine response to crime. However, Daly also takes restorative justice proponents to task for suggesting that restorative justice interventions typically result in remarkable transformations of people and relationships: perpetrators of harm experience and express genuine remorse and improve their behaviour; victims experience healing; and enmity between perpetrators and victims of harm is transformed into mutual empathy and even friendship. Daly accepts that such changes hardly ever result from traditional courtroom proceedings and that they can and do result from restorative justice proceedings. However, proponents of restorative justice seriously mislead, she argues, when they suggest or imply that such outcomes are typical. Empirical evidence, argues Daly, suggests what we would in fact expect: the effects of restorative justice on participants are usually far less dramatic.

Again, it is necessary to be clear about the precise implications of this critique. Daly is not arguing against investment in and use of restorative justice. Indeed, she also points to positive benefits of restorative justice which have been detected in empirical research but tend to be underemphasized by proponents. In particular, she points out that victims and offenders tend to view both the process and outcomes of restorative justice as fair and that, in this respect, restorative justice compares favourably with traditional courtroom processes. Daly's critique (like von Hirsch et al.'s) is directed at *proponents* of restorative justice rather than the approach itself and her charge is basically one of over-selling. She suggests that, while this overselling can be useful in attracting people to the restorative justice movement, and in persuading policy-makers, it is ultimately counterproductive. It can result in despair, when people realize that restorative justice does not usually have the promised magical effects, and withdrawal of support from what is – for Daly – an approach that does have much value.

How might restorative justice proponents respond to this critique? 1) They can take up Daly's challenge, which is to stop making exaggerated claims; to 'be courageous and tell the real story of restorative justice' (2003: 377); 2) they might, as some apparently have, deny that they ever propagated such myths (2003: 372); or 3), of course, they might accept that they have indeed made strong claims for restorative justice and argue that there is evidence in support of these claims (perhaps arguing that Daly's evidence is drawn at least partly from interventions which are not truly restorative; cf. Morris 2003).[4]

Undermining deterrence

One of the main reasons usually given for the practice of punishing lawbreakers is that is necessary in order to deter them – and other potential lawbreakers – from committing wrongs in the future. The underlying assumption is that many people in our society either lack discipline or are insufficiently disposed to obey the law because it is the right thing to do.

Hence, in order to obtain their compliance, it is necessary to make them believe that if they are caught breaking the law they will be 'punished' – i.e. they will suffer unpleasant consequences. Accordingly, many people assume that any significant move away from punishment towards restorative responses to crime will undermine the policy of deterrence and hence lead to an increase in lawbreaking.[5]

Restorative justice proponents, anticipating this concern, have answered it in a variety of ways. A common retort is that punishment actually does not work as a deterrent and frequently – for a number of reasons – increases rather than reduces the chances of further crime. It is of course true that the deterrent effects of punishment tend to be greatly overestimated and its tendency to re-enforce criminality underestimated. However, the average citizen will probably find this response unconvincing (Wilson 1983: 117– 44), because the idea that without penal sanctions for lawbreaking many people will succumb to temptations to break the law seems self-evident to most people.

Another retort from proponents is that restorative justice is far from the soft option many assume it to be – i.e. many offenders find it much tougher than the punishment they would normally receive. However, this tends to be the perception *after* completion of the restorative process rather than before; before going into the process most offenders have elected to do so because it seems preferable to prison. Furthermore, that argument does tend to concede the very point of the critique: that it is necessary to create fear of unpleasant consequences in order to ensure compliance with laws.

A third response is to point out that the critique applies only to those who assume that restorative justice is capable of handling virtually all criminal wrongdoing and hence argue for a purely restorative system (Llewellyn and Howse 1998). In fact, many restorative justice proponents accept that there are many cases which cannot be handled through restorative justice and that these will need to be dealt with through normal criminal processes (although these could be reformed to make them as restorative as possible). Hence, the more common argument is that restorative justice should be the 'presumptive' response to crime, but there should also be a 'background system' of deterrent and incapacitating sanctions in place for cases which are unsuitable for restorative justice or where restorative justice repeatedly fails (Braithwaite 1999a). To the extent that this meets concerns about deterrence, it does seem to do so by conceding more ground to those who see punishment as a social necessity than some restorative justice proponents are comfortable with. Also, as Andrew Ashworth argues, it raises a whole host of fresh questions, including that of how this background system can be justified (2003: 431–3).

Failure to deliver 'justice'

Is restorative justice a form of punishment or something entirely different? Many proponents of restorative justice vehemently deny that restorative justice is a form of punishment, arguing that the purpose of restorative interventions is to repair harm caused by criminal wrongdoing, not to punish the wrongdoer. Although repairing harm may be burdensome for the wrongdoer, this does not mean that it constitutes punishment since other essential elements of punishment – in particular the aim of making things unpleasant for offenders as an objective in its own right – are missing (see Chapter 26, this volume).

The question of whether or not restorative justice should be understood as a form of punishment is a thorny one (see Fletcher 1998: 25–42). Walgrave is surely correct in his contention that we often impose burdens upon people that are not properly characterized as punishment. He gives the example of taxes, but a much more pertinent example is our imposition of a liability to pay compensation upon those who commit wrongs which are not defined as criminal – i.e. wrongs that are torts but not crimes (e.g. defamation of character in English law). Here, we impose a burden upon wrongdoers, but it is not classed as punishment because the core purpose is to compensate the victim, not to make things unpleasant for the wrongdoer. Hence, it would be inappropriate to object if somebody other than the wrongdoer – such as an insurer or a sympathizer – pays the compensation. As long as the victim is compensated, the purpose of intervention is accomplished. This suggests that 'purposes' must be taken into account when deciding whether an intervention is punishment.

One important question, then, is whether the purpose of intervention in restorative justice is *only* to make things better for the victim or if it is *also* to impose a burden upon the offender (on this, see Barnett 2003; Johnstone 2003: 8–14). In other words, the goal of restorative justice is not what Randy Barnett calls 'pure restitution' but is what he calls 'punitive restitution'. For example, it *would* be regarded as inappropriate if a young offender agreed to contribute 10 per cent of her wages each week for six months towards the cost of repairing property she had wilfully damaged, and then her parent simply paid the whole amount for her in a lump sum. If the goal were purely to compensate the owner of the property, this would be unobjectionable. But restorative justice has other goals, such as bringing offenders to make amends for wrongdoing, which would make payment by somebody other than the offender unsatisfactory.[6]

But perhaps this is going too far? We might require that offenders undergo something burdensome, but still not be punishing them. For instance, we compel young people to undergo education, which many find extremely burdensome and even unpleasant, but do not classify it as punishment. Perhaps restorative justice should be thought of then as akin to – or even a form of – education rather than punishment. This is the view of at least some proponents (Moore 1993). The problem with this argument is that it ignores the way in which the context in which an intervention takes place helps determine its meaning, both for the participants themselves and for the wider society. In the case of criminal justice interventions following criminal wrongdoing, it is usually quite clear that what is happening is taking place within the framework of criminal law and punishment. Indeed, this is even the case when – as sometimes happens – restorative conferencing takes place in buildings which are not the usual location for criminal justice (such as schools, community centres or churches). Even then, the fact that one party is called 'the offender' and will have been processed by the police tends to create the impression in the minds of almost everyone involved that what is taking place – no matter how constructive – is the punishment of the offender.

This debate continues within the restorative justice field (perhaps contributing to the perception of critics that it is vague and ill-defined). However, both possible answers (restorative justice is non-punitive or restorative justice accomplishes punitive purposes) raise two further criticisms. The first, directed to those who argue that it is not punitive, is that restorative justice cannot therefore be considered *justice*. The second (discussed in the next section) is directed to those who agree that there is a punitive dimension to restorative justice. In that case, the critics argue, restorative justice fails to offer fundamental protections that must be provided to anyone facing punishment. Let us turn to the first criticism.

This critique argues that even if its (arguably) exaggerated claims were true, if restorative justice is not punitive then it fails to perform one vital function: providing *justice*. The critique suggests that, in order to provide justice in the aftermath of serious wrongdoing, punishment of wrongdoers is necessary (Robinson 2003). Hence, it is argued, while restorative 'justice' might have a very useful role to play as a *supplement* to punishment (since justice is only one of the things that we need to achieve in the aftermath of wrongdoing) the idea of *replacing* punishment with restorative 'justice' is unacceptable because justice requires punishment.

Where proponents of restorative justice would disagree with critics such as Robinson is over what precisely is necessary to achieve justice. For proponents, offenders can make amends by demonstrating a clear understanding of the magnitude of the wrong they have committed and the harm they have caused and by doing all that is reasonably possible to put things right and to repair the harm (such as listening respectfully to their victims, answering any questions the victim has, apologizing, agreeing to undertake reparative work and making serious efforts to change whatever it was about themselves or their situation that led them to wrongdoing). Provided what they do is acceptable to their victims – i.e. provided victims are satisfied that their offender has made amends – then justice has prevailed.

Critics would surely agree that many wrongs can be *corrected* in this way, and that reparations are therefore a route to justice. However, they would argue, for *serious* forms of wrongdoing – wrongdoing serious enough to label 'crime' – correction is not enough. In order to achieve justice in the aftermath of crime, they argue, punishment of the offender is necessary. Indeed, some suggest, in order to treat the offender justly, our response must be punishment.

The underlying idea here is that there is something special about *criminal* conduct and that this calls for a qualitatively different response from that we use to correct other wrongful and harmful behaviour. Criminal behaviour, properly understood, is behaviour in which persons cause harm to others *intentionally* or *recklessly*. Hence, it is not so much the 'material harm' it results in which makes behaviour criminal (indeed, non-criminal behaviour can often cause much greater material harm than results from crime). Rather, what makes behaviour criminal is the *hostile attitude* of the wrongdoer towards other people at the time of the conduct (e.g. the criminal wrongdoer wants to harm others or is completely indifferent about whether they are harmed).[7] The harm resulting from crime consists of the harm resulting from displaying such an attitude, as well as the material harm.

For many, punishment is necessary in order to communicate a particular social attitude towards such behaviour: an attitude of censure (see von Hirsch 1993; Duff 2001). If we fail to use punishment in redressing such serious wrongdoing, we imply that it is on a par qualitatively with less serious wrongdoing (e.g. where people cause harm to others through careless behaviour) which can be redressed through reparations alone. The critique, then, is that by seeking to abolish or marginalize the use of punishment, restorative justice proponents treat criminal wrongdoing as essentially no different from less hostile conduct that causes harm.

There are a number of ways that restorative justice proponents might respond. First, Christopher Marshall (2001) has argued in a quite sophisticated way that it is possible to conceive of justice in the aftermath of wrongdoing in a way that does not entail punishment as conventionally understood, but instead would involve something he calls 'restorative punishment':

> While it makes sense to repay good deeds with further good, it makes little sense, morally or pragmatically, to repay evil deeds with further evil. Far better … is to requite evil with a counteraction that seeks to redeem and restore. Such counteraction may need to be imposed by society and may be painful, and hence may legitimately be regarded as punishment. But the intention of the punishment is to reclaim the offender, restore relationships, and bring healing to the victim (p. 139).

In other words, we need not choose between punishment and restoration, because restoration accomplishes what punishment seeks to achieve, but it does so in a way that repairs harm rather than creates new harm (see also Duff 2003).

A second response would be to argue that, while there may be many wrongs for which punishment is a necessary ingredient of redress, they are arguably far fewer than those for which we currently use punishment. In other words, restorative justice can replace punishment in some criminal cases. Thirdly even in those cases where punishment is deemed necessary, proponents could argue that punishment is seldom sufficient, and that for a fully just response restorative justice must be added to punishment. Fourthly, as Paul Robinson himself contends, it can be argued that justice may even require that in deciding what punishment offenders deserve we take into account not only the offenders' wrongdoing but also their subsequent attitude and response and especially efforts at redress through material and symbolic reparation. Hence, 'a rich desert theory would take account of many facets of what can happen during restorative processes. Genuine remorse, public acknowledgement of wrongdoing and sincere apology can all … reduce an offender's blameworthiness – and, thereby, the amount of punishment deserved' (Robinson 2003: 380).

Departures from principles of justice

The next critique takes as its point of departure the assumption that, however benevolent its intentions, restorative justice *does* indeed involve the punishment of offenders. As such, legal scholars such as Andrew Ashworth argue, it should comply with principles which have been developed – especially in liberal-democratic societies – to ensure that punishment is allocated in an equitable manner. According to Ashworth (2005: 71–2), among many others, the most important sentencing principles include the following:

- Responsibility for the allocation of punishment belongs to state institutions, rather than victims or other individuals.
- Decisions on punishment should be taken by independent and impartial tribunals.
- Decisions should be based upon settled principles.
- Chief among these principles is that the severity of punishment must be in proportion to the seriousness of the offence committed.

Ashworth (2003) argues that restorative justice *systematically* departs from such principles. For instance, under the mantle of returning conflicts to their rightful owners, it removes decisions about the punishment of offenders from state agencies and places them in the hands of groups of private citizens. Moreover, it is not even clear whether such decisions are to be reviewable by state agencies or, if so, what the terms of such a review would be (cf. Roche 2003). Further, the decision-makers are not just any private citizens, but people who are selected precisely because they have a stake in the case and its outcome. This departs from the principle of a fair hearing by an independent and impartial tribunal. Ashworth regards the involvement of victims as particularly problematic:

> Everyone should have the right to a fair hearing 'by an independent and impartial tribunal', as Article 6.1 of the European Convention on Human Rights declares. This right expresses a fundamental principle of justice ... Do conferences and other restorative processes respect the right? Insofar as the victim plays a part in determining the disposition of a criminal case, is a conference 'independent and impartial'? The victim cannot be expected to be impartial ... conferences may fail to meet the basic standards of a fair hearing, insofar as the victim or victim's family plays a part in determining the outcome (2003: 429).

The lay decision-makers in restorative forums are not, of course, expected to know about the range of sentences available or the principles for disposition of criminal cases. Hence, they are unlikely to be able to follow settled principles of sentencing. Moreover, they are positively encouraged not to look to external guidelines in reaching decisions, but to think of what will meet their own needs – i.e. to devise creative ways of repairing the harm resulting from offences that are subjectively satisfying. This makes it probable that at least one settled principle, the principle that like cases be treated alike, will be contravened.

According to Ashworth, the involvement of victims in restorative forums not only makes an independent and impartial tribunal unlikely, but it also makes breach of the proportionality principle likely:

> Some victims will be forgiving, others will be vindictive; some will be interested in new forms of sentence, others will not; some shops will have one policy in relation to thieves, others may have a different policy. If victim satisfaction is one of the aims of circles and conferences, then proportionate sentencing cannot be ensured (2003: 428).

If attempts to answer the criticism of Ashworth and others by defining restorative justice as non-punishment do fail, are there other options for restorative justice proponents? One would be to develop restorative justice in a way that *does* make it quite distinct from criminal punishment. This might be done, for instance, by providing restorative justice services outside the criminal justice system, making them available on a purely voluntary basis, making it clear that compliance with any agreements made is also voluntary, and refusing to employ within them any of the vocabulary of criminal justice. They would then be forums to which people involved in disputes with each other (even disputes arising from 'criminalizable events') could go (if all agreed) instead of seeking state intervention in the form of criminal justice.[8] It is difficult to know whether such services would thrive and there are also questions about how they would be funded. But, in principle, such services would avoid the critique of unprincipled punishment.

An alternative would be to continue to develop restorative justice as a practice within – or closely connected to – the criminal justice system but to argue nevertheless that it should not be judged by the sentencing principles proposed by Ashworth and others. This would involve arguing that what is presented by Ashworth as *universal* principles of justice are in fact much more *contingent*. It could be argued that Ashworth's sentencing principles have emerged in conjunction with a particular practice – i.e. state punishment – in order to regulate that practice. If the practice of punishment is changing radically, then – it might be argued – we should also rethink the principles that should regulate it.[9]

The conservativeness of restorative justice

Proponents of restorative justice see themselves as in the business of revolutionizing our society's response to wrongdoing (Wachtel 1997). However, some critics – while not denying that the methods of restorative justice differ significantly from those conventionally used to sanction wrongdoing – question just how revolutionary it is. George Pavlich, for instance, writes: 'while positing itself as a distinct alternative, restorative justice also predicates itself on key concepts within the criminal justice system. As an alternative, it is presented as a separate and autonomous entity; yet its foundational concepts derive from the very system it claims to substitute' (2005: 13–4).

The main thrust of this critique is that what restorative justice schemes provide is a different *method* of responding to situations conventionally defined as 'crime' and that this method takes for granted much of our conventional way of thinking about these situations. A true alternative, the critique suggests, would challenge prevailing ideas about the sorts of conduct that are harmful enough to warrant being deemed criminal, and would also think about these situations in a radically different way. In what follows, I will try to convey something of the flavour of this critique.

First, let us look at the sorts of conduct into which restorative justice typically intervenes. A fairly standard list would include things like store theft, vandalism, stealing from employers, personal assault, arson and bullying.[10] It is undeniable that these forms of conduct cause significant harm and trauma and that they call for some intervention. It is also plausible to argue that existing forms of intervention do little to repair that harm and trauma and indeed often add harm to harm, and that they should therefore be replaced (where the right circumstances exist) by restorative interventions. However, one would expect a genuine alternative to conventional criminal justice – and especially one which attempts to put *harm* at the centre of attention – to start by asking whether (for whatever reason) the conventional criminal justice system is blind to the harm, or underestimates the seriousness of harm, caused by other activities which are seldom effectively 'criminalized' and concomitantly overstates the relative harmfulness of behaviour that is conventionally deemed criminal. This is a routine move by 'critical criminologists' who tend to point to things like 'corporate wrongdoing' as typical examples of harmful behaviour which often avoids criminalization (Hillyard and Tombs 2004).[11] This would suggest that, to be a true alternative, the restorative justice movement would need to take serious notice of Dennis Sullivan and Larry Tifft's (2001) proposal that it adopt 'a radical perspective on crime and social harm'.[12]

Secondly, let us look at the way of thinking about criminal conduct that underpins restorative interventions. Conventional criminal justice operates on the basis that the harm emanating from criminal conduct can be attributed to one person or at most a relatively small group of people (the actual perpetrators and those who directly aid and abet them). Arguably, an important effect of such attribution is to exonerate anyone outside this small group from blame for the harm resulting from crime. Some restorative justice writers question this conventional way of attributing responsibility for criminal harm. Rupert Ross (1996), for instance, in his study of sexual abuse in Hollow Water, demonstrates persuasively that sexual abuse and other crimes in Hollow Water are caused by a sense of powerlessness that in turn stems directly from various governmental policies towards aboriginal peoples in Canada. This disturbs any simplistic process of attribution and exoneration. Moreover, Ross also shows that – in the context of Hollow Water at least – any attempt to divide people up into perpetrators and victims (as hard-and-fast categories and identities) would be completely mistaken. In Hollow Water a large number of people are both perpetrators and victims of sexual abuse and other crimes. In order to understand and deal with the problem, Ross suggest, it is necessary to think in terms of 'a whirlwind of sexual abuse'.

The 'healing path' described by Ross, as Hollow Water's response to its problems, does appear to be a distinct alternative to conventional criminal justice. Granted, it does involve a different process or method of dealing with 'criminalizable events'. But, crucially, this process is just one element in a much broader reconstruction of the whole problem of sexual abuse, one which disturbs conventional practices of attribution and allocation of responsibility. However, the restorative justice movement, as a whole, has not tended to act upon the full implications of the Hollow Water experiment with 'justice as healing' and similar experiments. Rather, arguably, it has tended to 'borrow' processes – such as 'circle sentencing' – and utilize them in an attempt to deal with problems that have been constructed in a much more conventional manner.[13]

Many other examples of how restorative justice incorporates the vocabularies and assumptions of conventional criminal justice could be provided. However, the main thrust of this critique should now be clear. The suggestion is that, in the main, restorative justice has been developed as a new social technique for dealing with criminal wrongdoing, but it remains rooted in the very same domain assumptions as more conventional techniques.

To the extent that this critique is correct, it suggests a very different reading of the relationship of restorative justice to conventional systems of penal control from that suggested by its own rhetoric. Proponents and supporters envisage a future in which the practice of punishment plays a relatively marginal role in our societies, and restorative justice replaces it as the routine way of approaching wrongdoing (Braithwaite 1999b). The critique suggests that restorative justice might instead replace or supplement conventional *processes* of punishment. This gives rise to a familiar pattern which has been described by Stanley Cohen (1985), among others. Formal legal processes and professionally administered penal sanctions – which are costly and painful – will continue to be used, but will be more strategically targeted on what are regarded as serious cases. Less serious cases will be diverted to informal restorative processes and sanctions. But, because they are less formal and regarded as more benign, these processes will be extended to cases which previously would not have given rise to penal interventions. Overall the reach of the system of penal control will be extended rather than cut back.

Some restorative justice proponents are well aware of this danger. Howard Zehr, for instance, has long warned about the dangers of restorative justice being co-opted and diverted from its original vision, about new language being used to clothe ideas that are not new, and about restorative justice serving interests and goals which are different from those projected (Zehr 1990: 222). To prevent this from happening, he proposes continuous questioning of fundamental assumptions and careful thinking about the implications of proposed changes, including difficult-to-foresee consequences. George Pavlich's critical work actually seems close in spirit to that of Zehr. Pavlich (2005) points to the paradox inherent in any attempt to transform social practices or institutions: in order to transform a social practice or institution it is necessary to invent an alternative which is both similar to and different from the existing practice or institution. The problem then becomes one of keeping the emphasis on breaking with the past, rather than allowing the past to swamp and incorporate what is new. To this extent, reformative efforts are always ongoing, rather than something that could ever be finished.[14]

Conclusion

Since its emergence, restorative justice has encountered a range of criticisms. This chapter has presented a brief and highly selective account of these critical perspectives.[15] One important observation which emerges from this is that many criticisms are directed, less at 'restorative justice itself' (whatever that is), and more at proponents' representations of and claims about restorative justice. Such critiques call for responses which either revise the way restorative justice is represented and promoted, or which justify existing descriptions and claims. Those critiques which focus more on 'restorative justice itself' tend to point to limitations and dangers, rather than dismissing the approach *per se*. Their implication is that restorative justice needs to be combined with other approaches rather than offered as a 'stand alone' response to wrongdoing and that certain checks need to be in place to ensure that restorative justice is developed in a way consistent with other things that are valued (such as fairness or freedom from an over-intrusive society or state).

As noted in the last section, it is unclear whether these limitations are endemic to restorative justice, or simply the consequence of restorative justice as currently understood being far more conventional than the rhetoric of its proponents. If it is the former, then it would be appropriate for proponents to tone down their rhetoric. If, however, the rhetoric and aspirations of proponents point to something genuine, then far more attention should be given to the revolutionary, transformational potential of restorative justice.

It is extremely important that the restorative justice movement listens carefully to this critical discourse, heeds it and adjusts its proposals, claims and language in its light. This will strengthen rather than weaken the restorative justice movement, although it might also involve a painful rejection of familiar and much loved themes. What is most interesting is that even the most fervent critics tend to regard restorative justice – suitably reformulated and modified – as an extremely valuable contribution to the ongoing debate about how we should understand, relate to, and handle the problem of wrongdoing.

Selected further reading

Morris, A. (2003) 'Critiquing the critics: a brief response to critics of restorative justice' in G. Johnstone (ed.) *A Restorative Justice Reader*. Cullompton: Willan Publishing. Describes a list of criticisms of restorative justice and defends it from these criticisms.

Johnstone, G. (ed.) (2003) *A Restorative Justice Reader*. Cullompton: Willan Publishing (Part E). Contains essays or excerpts from critical interventions into the debate about restorative justice, including works by Ashworth and Daly discussed in this chapter.

Pavlich, G. (2005) *Governing Paradoxes of Restorative Justice*. London: Glasshouse Press. A short book, critiquing the assumptions of restorative justice while also acknowledging its strengths and importance.

Acknowledgements

I am grateful to Daniel Van Ness for advice and assistance which went well beyond the usual 'comments and suggestions'. A conversation with Kathleen Daly while I was thinking through the aim and scope of this chapter was extremely helpful. Jarem Sawatsky provided useful criticism of an earlier draft.

Notes

1 See Morris (2003) for an account of – and response to – a list of criticisms of restorative justice.

2 A few brief words about the purpose and scope of what follows: first, I will provide a highly selective account of critical perspectives on restorative justice (one which focuses upon what are in my view the most interesting and important critical perspectives rather than one which attempts a comprehensive survey of everything critical that has been said about restorative justice). Secondly, even so, what is presented is more of a survey than an in-depth account. Thirdly, it is not my intention to take sides in debates between proponents and critics; rather, my purpose is to facilitate constructive and sophisticated debate.

3 As Daniel Van Ness and I argue in the first chapter of this book, one of the difficulties is that restorative justice proponents do not agree among themselves about how restorative justice is to be conceived; rather there are multiple and competing conceptions of restorative justice. Nevertheless, it should be possible for proponents of each conception (the encounter conception, the reparative conception and the transformative conception) to specify precise models that would satisfy the Von Hirsch *et al.* standard.

4 A quite different response would be take Daly to task for the way she uses the concept of myth (she uses it to indicate stories which are incredible and demonstrably untrue). This usage arguably blinds us to the possibility of an interesting inquiry into the use of mythology within the discourse of restorative justice (see, for instance, Van Ness and Strong 2006, who use myths to explain certain restorative justice ideas; on broader and more positive understandings of myth, see Armstrong 2005). Daly has little to say about the functioning of

classic mythological themes which clearly exist just below the surface of much restorative justice discourse (cf. Sylvester 2003; Acorn 2004).

5 Surprisingly, although this is probably the most commonly encountered objection to restorative justice, it is difficult to find it expressed in scholarly work. Concerns about deterrence are discussed very briefly in Llewellyn and Howse's (1998) review of restorative justice and in my own work (Johnstone 2002: 27–9). As we shall see, proponents of restorative justice are often at pains to point out that it is more effective than punishment as a means of containing crime.

6 The issues here are actually more complex. For instance, if the offender were ordered to pay a fine – which we would regard as a straightforward punishment – there would be no objection if the parent paid the fine. This could suggest that restorative justice is perhaps *more* concerned that the offender suffer something burdensome than are some parts of conventional criminal justice (cf. Duff 2003).

7 I should make it clear that much of what is legally defined as crime in contemporary societies does not fall within the narrow confines of such a definition. However, a frequent criticism of the criminal law is that it is now far too expansive as the criminal sanction is used as a convenient way of regulating behaviour which would be better regulated by other means; for one discussion see Husak (2004).

8 Of course, the fact that a 'victim' of crime chooses not to seek state intervention into the life of the perpetrator does not in itself mean that such intervention will not occur. One of the principles of criminal justice is that the decision on whether to charge or prosecute is one for the state, and to be made by considering the public interest, rather than one for the victim to be made only by reference to the victim's 'private' interest.

9 Declan Roche's book, *Accountability in Restorative Justice* (2003), might be read in this light.

10 These examples come from a random browse though Ted Wachtel's (1997) book, *Real Justice* – but they could have been drawn from dozens of other sources.

11 John Braithwaite (2002) has of course developed restorative justice as a response to corporate wrongdoing. Arguably, however, the mainstream practice of restorative justice – because it is so dependent on referrals from conventional criminal justice agencies – has not tended to follow suit.

12 For example, one might suggest that the restorative justice movement in North America ought – in order to be true to its own rhetoric and logic – align itself significantly with the movement in the USA for reparations for slavery. Roy L. Brooks (2004) depicts slavery as an atrocity against an innocent people, for which the US government has an obligation to apologize and provide reparations. This is a crucial precondition, for Brooks, for forgiveness and racial reconciliation. Brooks makes explicit use of the term 'restorative justice' in this respect, but would not conventionally be regarded as part of the restorative justice movement. Radicals might point to fairly direct historical links between slavery and Jim Crow and contemporary penal policy in the USA.

13 This critique is being developed by Jarem Sawatsky in his doctoral research into what it is that sustains notions of healing justice in traditional communities; see also Sawatsky (2005).

14 See Mathieson (1974) on 'the unfinished'.

15 Inevitably, in the space of a short chapter it has not been possible to discuss critiques which others regard as far more important than those discussed here. For instance, some think that restorative justice is mistaken to focus on crime (and analogous forms of wrongdoing) to the neglect of 'social structural violence'

(Sullivan and Tifft 1998; cf. Johnstone 2002: 8–9). Some argue that – although an improvement on conventional criminal justice – restorative justice still fails to meet critical needs of crime victims (Herman 2004). Some aboriginal critics suggest that any 'justice' based within the current nation-state model will be a system of injustice (Alfred 1999). Annalise Acorn (2004) has criticized restorative justice's aspiration to reconcile love and justice. Others contend that restorative justice leaves power imbalances untouched, encourages vigilantism and lacks legitimacy (discussed by Morris 2003). The list could go on and on.

References

Acorn, A. (2004) *Compulsory Compassion: A Critique of Restorative Justice*. Vancouver: UBC Press.

Alfred, T. (1999) *Peace, Power and Righteousness: An Indigenous Manifesto*. Toronto: Oxford University Press.

Armstrong, K. (2005) *A Short History of Myth*. Edinburgh: Canongate.

Ashworth, A. (2003) 'Responsibilities, rights and restorative justice', in G. Johnstone (ed.) *A Restorative Justice Reader*. Cullompton: Willan Publishing.

Ashworth, A. (2005) *Sentencing and Criminal Justice* (4th edn). Cambridge: Cambridge University Press.

Barnett, R. (2003) 'Restitution: a new paradigm of criminal justice', in G. Johnstone (ed.) *A Restorative Justice Reader*. Cullompton: Willan Publishing.

Braithwaite, J. (1999a) 'Restorative justice: assessing optimistic and pessimistic accounts', *Crime and Justice: A Review of Research*, 25: 1–127.

Braithwaite, J. (1999b) 'A future where punishment is marginalized: realistic or utopian?', *UCLA Law Review*, 46: 1727–50.

Braithwaite, J. (2002) *Restorative Justice and Responsive Regulation*. New York, NY: Oxford University Press.

Brooks, R. (2004) *Atonement and Forgiveness: A New Model for Black Reparations*. Berkeley, CA: University of California Press.

Cohen, S. (1985) *Visions of Social Control: Crime, Punishment and Classification*. Cambridge: Polity Press.

Daly, K. (2003) 'Restorative justice: the real story', in G. Johnstone (ed.) *A Restorative Justice Reader*. Cullompton: Willan Publishing.

Duff, R.A. (2001) *Punishment, Communication, and Community*. New York, NY: Oxford University Press.

Duff, R.A. (2003) 'Restorative punishment and punitive restoration', in G. Johnstone (ed.) *A Restorative Justice Reader*. Cullompton: Willan Publishing.

Fletcher, G. (1998) *Basic Concepts of Criminal Law*. New York, NY: Oxford University Press.

Herman, S. (2004) 'Is restorative justice possible without a parallel system for victims?', in H. Zehr and B. Toews (eds) *Critical Issues in Restorative Justice*. Monsey, NY: Criminal Justice Press and Cullompton: Willan Publishing.

Hillyard, P. and Tombs, S. (2004) 'Beyond criminology?', in P. Hillyard *et al.* (eds) *Beyond Criminology: Taking Harm Seriously*. London: Pluto.

Husak, D. (2004) 'The criminal law as a last resort', *Oxford Journal of Legal Studies*, 24: 207–35.

Johnstone, G. (2002) *Restorative Justice: Ideas, Values, Debates*. Cullompton: Willan Publishing.

Johnstone, G. (2003) 'Introduction: restorative approaches to criminal justice', in G. Johnstone (ed.) *A Restorative Justice Reader*. Cullompton: Willan Publishing.

Llewellyn, J. and Howse, R. (1998) *Restorative Justice – A Conceptual Framework*. Ottawa: Law Commission of Canada.

Marshall, C.D. (2001) *Beyond Retribution: A New Testament Vision for Justice, Crime, and Punishment*. Green Rapids, MI and Cambridge: Eerdmans.

Mathieson, T. (1974) *The Politics of Abolition*. London: Martin Robertson.

Moore, D. (1993) 'Shame, forgiveness and juvenile justice', *Criminal Justice Ethics*, 12: 3–25.

Morris, A. (2003) 'Critiquing the critics: a brief response to critics of restorative justice', in G. Johnstone (ed.) *A Restorative Justice Reader*. Cullompton: Willan Publishing.

Pavlich, G. (2005) *Governing Paradoxes of Restorative Justice*. London: Glasshouse Press.

Robinson, P. (2003) 'The virtues of restorative processes, the vices of "restorative justice"', *Utah Law Review*, 1: 375–88.

Roche, D. (2003) *Accountability in Restorative Justice*. Oxford: Oxford University Press.

Ross, R. (1996) *Returning to the Teachings: Exploring Aboriginal Justice*. Toronto: Penguin Books.

Sawatsky, J. (2005) 'The ethic of traditional communities and the spirit of healing justice', *Justice as Healing: The Native Law Center of Canada*, 10: 1–12.

Sullivan, D. and Tifft, L. (1998) 'The Transformative and Economic Dimensions of Restorative Justice', *Humanity and Society*, 22:1, pp. 38-53.

Sullivan, D. and Tifft, L. (2001) *Restorative Justice: Healing the Foundations of Our Everyday Lives*. Monsey, NY: Willow Tree Press.

Sullivan, D., Tifft, L. and Cordella, P. (1998) 'The phenomenon of restorative justice: some introductory remarks', *Contemporary Justice Review*, 1: 7–20.

Sylvester, D. (2003) 'Myth in restorative justice history', *Utah Law Review*, 1: 471–522.

Van Ness, D.W. and Strong, K.H. (2006) *Restoring Justice* (3rd edn). Cincinnati, OH: Anderson Publishing.

von Hirsch, A. (1993) *Censure and Sanctions*. Oxford: Oxford University Press.

von Hirsch, A., Ashworth, A. and Shearing, C. (2003) 'Specifying aims and limits for restorative justice: a "making amends" model', in A. von Hirsch *et al.* (eds) *Restorative Justice and Criminal Justice: Competing or Reconcilable Paradigms?* Oxford: Hart Publishing.

Wachtel, T. (1997) <u>*Real Justice: How We Can Revolutionize our Response to Wrongdoing*</u>. Pipersville, PA: Piper's Press.

Wilson, J. (1983) *Thinking about Crime* (2nd edn). New York, NY: Basic Books.

Zehr, H. (1990) *Changing Lenses: A New Focus for Crime and Justice*. Scottsdale, PA: Herald Press.

Chapter 29

Ethics, universal principles and restorative justice

George Pavlich

'You think you know what is just and what is not. I understand. We all think we know.' I had no doubt, myself, then, that at each moment each one of us, man, woman, child, perhaps even the poor old horse turning the mill-wheel, knew what was just: all creatures come into the world bringing with them the memory of justice. 'But we live in a world of law,' I said to my poor prisoner, 'a world of the second-best. There is nothing we can do about that. We are all fallen creatures. All we can do is uphold the laws, all of us, without allowing the memory of justice to fade' (Coetzee 1980: 139).

Introduction

Proponents of community mediation, community justice, victim–offender mediation, alternative dispute resolution and, recently, restorative justice have consistently championed the ethical bases of their proposed initiatives. They advocate a foundation in restorative values and through associated practices seek to deploy a justice different from that offered by criminal justice arrangements. The quest for alternative visions of justice places their discourse squarely within an indeterminate realm of ethics that Grayling summarizes as, 'thinking and theorizing about what is good and bad, and how people should live' (2003: ix). However, when focusing on justice *per se* one is specifically concerned with what Plato, all those years before, understood as the branch of ethical knowledge where we learn how to live virtuously as harmonious selves who are equally in harmony with others in society (*The Republic, Part 5, Book 4*). Combining such ideas, one might identify a framing context for the discussion of this chapter as a rather specific area of ethics – i.e., thinking and theorizing about 'how people should live' in order to restore just relations with one another after experiencing an injustice (see also Sharpe 2004).

This chapter focuses initially on restorative justice proponents' concern to develop programmes out of a distinctly 'values based' foundation of justice (see Johnstone 2004). Their emphasis on values and ethics serves as a counterpoint to 'criminal justice' and its failure to grapple with primordial philosophical questions of justice. The state's approach to crime focuses narrowly on identifying and punishing individual offenders proved guilty of offending against its interests and laws (Walgrave 2004). It also subordinates the concerns of victims and communities to state interest; as well, justice is defined in procedural or administrative terms, and is even mistakenly rendered synonymous with a day in the courtroom. The worry repeated in restorative justice discourses is the degree to which ethical values and principles of justice become quite peripheral to the state's dealings with crime (e.g. Walgrave 2002; Zehr 1990, 2002). In a somewhat different context, but stating the gist of the critique succinctly, Douzinas and Warrington ponder:

> how was it that the law had managed to establish its credentials by the very act of eliminating most, if not all, substantial considerations of justice? (1994: 10).

Responding to this curious predicament, restorative justice advocates actively distinguish their versions of justice from a 'repressive' criminal justice. They focus restorative discourses on developing essential, foundational and universal ethical principles that would differentiate the two forms of justice (e.g. Morris 2000: ch. 1; Umbreit 2001: 4ff.; Van Ness 2002; Zehr 2002: app. 1; Braithwaite 2003a, 2003b; Sharpe 2004: 19ff.). At the outset, one should note that the restorative principles proffered vary considerably throughout the discourse, with little agreement on what uniquely defines this justice. Yet, there is a remarkable consistency in the advocates' call for universal restorative principles to define justice and provide guiding values for practical restorative initiatives. The ethical work here involves declaring idiosyncratic restorative principles before formulating maxims to gauge how 'restorative' a given programme of justice might be (Van Ness 2002; Van Ness and Strong 2002).

In what follows, I shall argue that the emphasis placed on universal principles by leading proponents is misplaced and even serves to counter restorative justice's laudable quest for a new calculation of justice that does not seek solutions to crime in abstracted laws or universal procedures. More than this, a universal approach to justice endorses an increasingly anachronistic modern ethical frame of reference that is difficult to sustain in late modern contexts. Perhaps one could frame the problem in this way: *is an approach to ethics that seeks universal principles of restorative (as opposed to criminal) justice viable given the broader intellectual milieu facing us today*? I will argue that achieving agreement on principles supposedly able to prescribe, universally, how to live justly with others is difficult to imagine in an intellectual ethos, such as our own, beset by an obdurate uncertainty. As well, the very idea of ethical certainty is problematic, for ethics is a domain intrinsically shaped by indeterminacy, unpredictability and the absence of regular law. Therefore, it may be timely to confront the difficult task of recasting ethics and images of such virtues as justice. It may also be important to refuse a modern intellectual blackmail that commands us to come up with founded, universal ethical principles to guide our actions, or be condemned as unethical, immoral and even just plainly irrational.

Why refuse the extortion? Aside from the question of whether universalizing approaches are sustainable in current epistemological climes, one might recall that despite the past century's illusory claim that universal moral principles could secure social advancement, peace and justice, our ways of being together have still not closed the book on immense slaying and blood-letting. The tragedies of recent genocides, social catastrophes (Nazism, apartheid, communist purges) and unprecedented world wars have, at best, not been avoided by general ethical precepts; at worst, they have been purveyed in the name of some or other supposedly universal principle. If we now have good reason to question the validity of the extortion, we also have an opening to envision other possible grammars of ethics, other ways of thinking about how to live with one another. What follows draws on different figures (Derrida, Levinas, Bauman) to suggest that the allegory of a host welcoming a received guest might help to frame a grammar of ethics for restorative justice that does not defer to fixed, universal principles. The task is, of course, far greater than it might be possible to accomplish in this chapter, but one could at least reference issues that are impossible so long as the reign of universal principle usurps the field of ethics in the context of restorative justice discourse.

Principles of restorative *v.* criminal justice?

> the holes in our criminal justice system are so glaring, it doesn't take long for any open-minded person to come across them, and before long, I was giving talks about what was wrong with the existing system. My favorite line was: 'There is nothing wrong with our existing justice system except that it is an expensive, unjust, immoral failure' (Morris 2000: 5).

As indicated by Morris's statements above, restorative critiques of the criminal justice system are extensive and wide-ranging. Furthermore, they are issued from diverse socio-political and cultural vantage points. However, for my purposes here, I want to focus exclusively on ethical critiques of the state's so-called 'repressive' visions of justice. In this respect, proponents clearly seek to distinguish restorative justice's compassionate 'restitutive' approach, and the radically different 'paradigm shift' that this entails (see Zehr 2003: 81). They see the shift as so significant that it requires a change of theoretical 'lenses' (Zehr 1990), as well as ethical orientation (Van Ness 2002; Sharpe 2004). Such altered grids of thinking about justice challenge several foundations of state criminal justice approaches. Specifically, restorative justice proponents contest: the definition of crime as a state/law violation; the adversarial courtroom process geared towards establishing individual guilt and dominated by lawyers; the focus on passive offenders at the expense of victims and community; the importance of punishing guilty parties so that they can repay debts to state/society; the use of punishment to deter future crimes (Walgrave 2004); the emphasis on individual cut-throat values; and so on (e.g. Umbreit 2001: xxxi; Zehr 2002: 21). Consequently, the main thrust of the ethical critique is levelled at the repressive, coercive, individualistic and adversarial values of the criminal justice system that embrace the *lex talionis*, a law of retribution.

Against this retributive approach, the new restorative justice paradigm works around a different ethics of justice. Its orientation, as the name betrays, is restorative because of its framing values and principles. These valued principles enjoy a privileged status in the discourse since they specify core features of restorative justice. In context, this is especially important because many fluid processes claim to be operating in the name of restorative justice; as such, no particular process is considered capable of defining what such justice entails (Sharpe 1998). Restorative justice offers, that is, a largely contextually defined response to the aftermath of crime; the harms and the needs generated by a criminal act are to be defined by affected parties. Proponents thus hold out underlying values and principles to serve as an anchor point, charged with framing specifically restorative practices. Just how much a given practice is restorative depends on how far it reflects underlying restorative justice principles (see generally Zehr and Toews 2004).

This approach reflects a particular kind of ethics: establish the foundational and universally applicable restorative principles, and use these to guide the deployment of particular, contextually nuanced practices (see Johnstone 2003, 2002; Wachtel and McCold 2001). Even without broad consensus on precisely what such overarching principles might entail, there is a general commitment to establishing their content and using them to guide particular practices. As Braithwaite and Strang note, ferment 'over values suggests that many more books will be written before there is consensus on any list of restorative values' (2001: 12). Nevertheless, commitment to principle continues to serve as a means of demarcating a distinctive *restorative* justice, and to guard against a proverbial lynch-mob, kangaroo court, justice (Roche 2003).

In keeping with a well entrenched modern belief in the significance of generating universal ethical maxims derived from an authoritative source of value, restorative justice advocates look to various discursive traditions to frame their visions of justice. First, there are those who embed restorative principles in theological roots (e.g. Consedine 1995; Consedine and Brown 1999; Batley 2004) or moral philosophy (e.g. Cooley 1999; Hadley 2001; Zehr 2002). The qualities of compassion, forgiveness, healing and caring tend to come to the fore in such conceptions. Secondly, some frame principles around political and social theory (e.g. Strang and Braithwaite 2001; Braithwaite 2003b), in which governmental regulation in civil society designed to secure republican democracy provides a guiding orientation. Thirdly, other proponents frame restorative principles around evaluations of specific practices (e.g. Bonta *et al.* 1998; Umbreit 2001; Wachtel and McCold 2001: 126). The principles here tend to be directives for best practice. Finally, there are those who develop restorative justice principles out of various shades of communitarian thinking. For instance, some champion the background of transformative social science (e.g. Bush and Folger 1994; Morris 2000); others look to extract ideals from communitarian philosophy (e.g. Bazemore and Schiff 2001; Kurki 1999, 2003); still others turn to derivative fields such as peace-making (Sullivan *et al.* 1998; Sullivan and Tifft 2004). In general, deriving principles from communitarianism tends to focus attention on how best to repair collective relational fabrics disrupted by crime.

Although this list is by no means exhaustive, it is sufficient to indicate some important features of the ethical landscape at hand. To begin with, there is no clear consensus of values or principles deemed to define a specifically restorative justice. Even so, there is a common assumption that essential principles are discoverable and so one finds a corresponding commitment to locate these.

In this respect, Zehr's work (e.g. 2002: 21; 2003: 81) is both influential and illustrative of the point at hand. Here, restorative justice is regarded as distinctive to the extent that it commits to universal moral principles – such as, criminal harms ought to be healed by addressing underlying individual (victim, offender) and communal needs, or the best society is an ordered, harmonious, consensually driven relational complex that must be preserved and/or restored through the active participation of its members. As well, when a crime has been committed, justice involves finding ways to address needs, allow offenders to make meaningful amends, reconcile parties, heal broken relations, reintegrate offenders and – when appropriate – reach levels of forgiveness.

These principles provide a framework for defining crime as a generator of harm, as a violation of 'one person by another' that disrupts peaceful interpersonal relations between victims, offenders and communities. Crime's harm creates needs and obligations, both of which are canvassed and addressed through active dialogue between the above-named participants. If the aim of this dialogue is to focus attention on victim needs as well as the attendant responsibilities of offenders/communities, it also emphasizes future-directed solutions to specific events. From this one discerns that universal values (principles) are used to anchor and enunciate a community-based, victim-centred approach to crime that promotes active 'dialogue and participatory decision-making' while encouraging offenders to take responsibility for their actions (Zehr 2002: 55). Such maxims license commonly deployed restorative justice practices: family group conferences, victim–offender mediations, sentencing circles, community mediation and panels, reconciliation commissions and various informal tribunals (see McLaughlin *et al.* 2003; Roche 2003: 6).

While Zehr's approach gives a sense of how the ethical landscape is crafted in context, it also begs a question that Zehr and Toews have recently directed to the whole discourse: 'Is it a problem that there is no agreed upon definition or set of principles? Should there be? Could there be? How restrictive should such a definition be?' (2004: 405). These questions strike at the heart of the above-noted problem facing us in contemporary ethical realms – whether the quest for consensus on the fundamental principles of how to live with one another is even remotely possible given the uncertain intellectual milieu facing us nowadays. That restorative justice protagonists should now be open to such fundamental questions is important; yet the discourse simultaneously falls into modern ethical traps with consequential effects in epistemological environments unable to support universalizing principles of justice. Let us explore this issue further.

Universal principles in uncertain conditions

Bauman (1992, 1993) describes our current cultural milieu as one in which modernity appears to be terminating in a self-critical, self-effacing and 'self-dismantling' moment. For him, a pervasive – 'ambient' – uncertainty has gripped our ethical lives to the extent that we no longer place any faith in reason's ability to secure agreement on a valued social end, a *telos*, and of its ability to formulate universal maxims. For example, there is little agreement on what social progress might amount to, or what a just society would look like. But more than this, there is little agreement on whether one end-point is even desirable, or that justice is singular. As Lyotard (1984) over two decades ago and in another context so forcefully put it, there is simply an 'incredulity' towards any metanarratives that claim an ability universally to declare one version of emancipated, restored, just, peaceful, etc., social relations.

I have elsewhere argued that the seeming disjunctions of this complex situation produce a watershed ethical ethos in which people continue to think about how to live with others *as though* nothing had changed (Pavlich 2002). As the remnant columns of a modern ethical ethos centred on grand principles crumble, and as competing grammars of ethics stake new ground, ethical agents try to make their ways through ruins that are as ambiguous as they are uncertain. In the remains of a particularly influential modern ethics, many continue to evoke a universal ethical grammar even though they are unable to point to a universally common *telos*, or even a widespread belief in the intrinsic value of declaring universal maxims.

Consequently, even through advocates of restorative justice may recognize a fundamental dissensus rocking the ethical foundations of their endeavours, many – as we have seen – continue to speak and act as though there were some underlying consensus. The *as though* is even more complicated because the very reference frames for declaring universal principles – theology, philosophy, science, communitarianism, etc. – offer competing and disparate ethical precepts without an agreed-upon method for deciding between these. The sheer diversity of restorative principles and maxims, without any certain way to decide between competing values (e.g. restoration *v.* transformation, maximalist *v.* minimalist alternation, etc.), leads to a dissonant chorus of ethical voices (Pavlich 2005a: ch. 5). One effect of this dissonance is to sustain and enhance disaffection with the very grammar of an ethics that revolves so centrally around universal principles.

The problem thus identified echoes in wider debates about justice that surfaced over two decades ago. To take but a few selected examples, one could refer to Walzer's (1983) recognition that pursuing universal principles of justice is fraught from the outset. Rather than being a singular universal, justice operates in incommensurable 'spheres'. These distinct 'spheres of justice' operate independently of one another and do not permit the sort of crossovers that are necessary to reach agreement on what is essential to all of them. MacIntyre (1988) even wonders whether it is remotely possible to demarcate spheres of justice, since we do not have the conceptual or ethical tools to decide between competing images and definitions of justice (thus his title, *Whose Justice? Which Rationality?*). Although MacIntyre laments the passing of a time where an agreed upon *telos* for social relations might be possible, Young (1990) celebrates the diversity and difference unleashed by refusing to surrender to the dictates of overarching (universal) moral principles. She sees this as a victory over the narrow constraints produced by universalist approaches to justice. Adding to these analyses, one could point to the deconstructive formulations of Lyotard and Thebaud (1979) and Derrida (1992), for whom there is no such thing as justice *per se*. These analysts recognize the indeterminate, incalculable horizon within which justice serves as a mirage-like promise of how life with others might be. It is an infinite idea only ever approached from finite ethical contexts, and this somewhat impossible, highly aporetic, structure invites a unique response.

For one thing, the above examples challenge the very auspices of an ethical grammar that takes as its point of departure the need for absolute, universal principles. They underscore the radically unfounded, open-ended character of ethics, exposing the imperious silencing involved with any attempt to universalize specific ethical precepts over others. An ethos that recognizes its ethics as fundamentally groundless is only ever able to produce what Bauman records as an 'ethically unfounded morality': 'whatever morality there is or there may be in a society which has admitted its groundlessness, lack of purpose and the abyss bridged by just a brittle gangplank of convention – can be only *an ethically unfounded morality*. As such, it is and will be uncontrollable and unpredictable' (1995: 18).

The stakes of this unpredictable ethical predicament are high, for we are no longer concerned with finding ways to decide between this or that ethical principle; instead, the chief matter concerns an ethical grammar hell-bent on deriving maxims from unshakeably universal principles. What might this all mean for understanding ethics in the context of restorative justice?

Extortion refused

To begin with, we might refuse the previously noted blackmail requiring one either to work from founded universal principles, or simply flee the field of ethics. This is an old blackmail, and one that was used to great effect by the champions of modern morals. However, in view of the radically uncertain predicaments in which ethical grammars now operate, it may be timely to refuse the arrogant extortion that has impeded attempts to imagine a different grammar of ethics. We who live either amidst, or in striking memory of, nightmares that eventually transpired from modern dreams narrated through an ethical grammar of universal principle, and associated images of necessity, must surely question that grammar on experiential grounds alone. As noted, there are many tragic cases – the holocaust, apartheid, global warfare, Stalin's purges, the Gulag archipelago, ongoing genocides and so on – all of which defy claims that ethical principles can provide guarantees against evil, tyranny, terror or injustice.

Bauman is again perceptive here:

> The foolproof – universal and unshakeably founded – ethical code will never be found; having singed our fingers once too often, we know now what we did not know then, when we embarked on this journey of exploration: that a non-aporetic, non-ambivalent morality, an ethics that is universal and 'objectively founded', is a practical impossibility; perhaps also an *oxymoron*, a contradiction in terms (1993: 10).

Why a 'contradiction in terms'? Well, let us recall that ethics is a domain that by its very precept deals with what is indeterminate, or never absolutely fixed. Were its domains subject to unyielding laws of regularity and determinacy, then it might be apposite to employ ontological grammars expressly designed to discover essential (universal) laws of being. However, ethics is possible precisely in terrains that are not predetermined, in circumstances (such as how best to live with one another) where there are many different, and fundamentally indeterminate, courses of possible action. To approach its subject matter as if it were determinate (making it possible to exact absolute, essential, universal principles) is a contradiction in terms.

Confronting this austere realization puts a specific onus on ethical discussions, but simultaneously suggests it may be timely to develop indeterminate languages of ethics that do not rely upon anachronistic modern grammars. An alternative grammar might confront the enormity of recasting an ethics without the comforts of determinate thinking. I have elsewhere used Derrida's (1999; Derrida and Dufourmantelle 2000) work on hospitality to explore this point further, and so need not repeat the argument here (see Pavlich 2002). Suffice to say that one way to think of ethics and how to be with others is to draw analogies with the case of a host welcoming a stranger at the threshold of what will be negotiated ways of being with each other in the immediate future. The reference to Derrida's work on hospitality provides, that is, a possible way to conceptualize a grammar (and thus language) of ethics that conceives of its ethical subjects around the idea of a hospitable welcome.

This vision of restorative ethics does not claim to be universalizable, nor does it assume a naturally defined ethical subject (e.g. victim, offender, etc.). Rather, it acknowledges its aporetic and ambivalent character, reminding us always of our ethical situation: like the welcoming host, restorative justice participants are required to calculate how to be with others in the future, for which they are profoundly responsible. Yet, no one can predict the outcome of any given – ultimately incalculable and never determinate – ethical decisions. If nothing else, this should serve as a stinging reminder of our mortal finitude and make us ever vigilant of any ethical decision – no matter how clear-cut it may appear. There are no ethical absolutes (the 'self-contradiction' argument); as well, no ethical decree is free from potentially dangerous institution. In the modesty such a realisation inevitably demands, one might think of ethical calculation as needing to be attached to a permanent ethos of critique that continuously enables us openly to reflect on the life courses initiated by previous ethical demands (see Pavlich 2000, 2005a). Furthermore, if ethics is formulated as an attempt to think about how to be with others using a grammar inspired by the analogy of a host welcoming a guest at the threshold to his or her home, city, country, a family group conference and so on, it may be possible to develop an open ethical language without universal principles.

Ethics and the critical night watch

What does this host–guest grammar of ethics imply for thinking about how to exist justly with others? We have seen that it demands modesty to the extent that ethics cannot provide unshakeable principles, nor is a principle-based approach capable of dictating unqualified social advancement. As Badiou notes, this means that we should acknowledge 'There is no ethics in general. There are only – eventually – ethics of processes by which we treat the possibilities of a situation' (2001: 16). There are processes, that is, through which we can explore the local possibilities; the idea of hospitality provides a guide for this. However, we should quickly add that this does not mean ethics involves a nihilistic sort of language of 'anything goes'. Rather, although we cannot escape ethical decisions in local contexts, there is no reassuring, and ultimately delusional, apparatus of certainty at our disposal.

If nothing else, this imposes an immense responsibility upon us for every one of our ethical decisions and actions. We must calculate the 'possibilities of a situation' and to reflect/decide on an ethical course of how to be with others. Yet without universal certainties to found our ethical decisions, it is mandatory that we establish reflective review practices to provide a constant vigil over ethical life. This takes seriously the contention that few decisions or courses of action are free from dangerous possibilities:

> Few choices … are unambiguously good. The majority of moral choices are made between contradictory impulses … The moral self moves, feels and acts in the context of ambivalence and is shot through with uncertainty … uncertainty is bound to accompany the condition of the moral self forever (Bauman 1993: 11–12).

If this is so, then we should understand ethics as a fundamentally contestable discourse. Its life-blood is precisely those incalculable, undecided and undetermined moments of being which nevertheless require calculation, decision and determinate actions. However, ethically inspired action can never claim to be necessary and so demands a grammar that enables us to make decisions, etc., and yet hold out the *continuous* possibility that these be subject to critical scrutiny. In this sense, fundamental critique remains inextricably yoked to ethics.

More specifically, critique is central to the structure of ethical life, as the all-important night watch that must never doze. For ethics to remain loyal to its fundamentally contestable foundations, there should be continuous opportunities for critique to wrest open past ethical calculations, decisions and actions. This is a crucial element to avoid any of these from declaring themselves as necessary, certain, universally, absolute, etc. (and so spawning the possibility of totalitarian thinking). Let us recall that in the indeterminate realm of ethics, there are no certain necessities, no situation in which alternative calculations or decisions are impossible. In other words, ethics is always deconstructable, and critique (or at least a certain kind of critique) provides one way to dissociate and open given ethical formulations to their intrinsic dangers, possibilities, alternatives, etc.

In parentheses, one might also note that the grammar of critique appropriate to this task is unlikely to be found in dominant judgemental grammars of critique that work by establishing founded criteria and then judging given contexts against these to determine future actions. To embrace this approach to critique would be to adopt a very similar style of thinking to that of principle-based ethics. There is, however, a far older (philological) grammar of critique, which is not judgemental in orientation, but has more to do with 'separating out', dissociating and opening lines of thought. I have elsewhere described in detail the possibilities of such a deconstructive grammar of critique (Pavlich 2000), and more recently reflected on how the experience of hospitality may too be associated therewith (Pavlich 2005b). Suffice here to note that a grammar of critique appropriate to ethical analysis might seek to expose the contingent structure of any given ethical formulation; open up decisions and actions about how to be with others in future; focus reflective attention on specific ethical injunctions and actions by thinking about how things might be done differently (i.e. dissociating existing lines of thought); work with the 'possibilities of given situations'; and emphasize the inherently aporetic, paradoxical and contradictory elements of ethical injunctions. Such critiques acknowledge that while ethical enunciations are inevitable, they are also inevitably indeterminate and require – by virtue of that impossible structure – constant alertness to premature definitional closures.

An ethics of restorative justice

So much for the meta-theory, but how might this *critical* ethics (way of thinking about how to be with others) work in the context of restorative justice? No doubt, specifying a universal format for such thinking would rescind the preceding; yet that does not mean we cannot consider the sort of ethical work involved in seeking to address injustice outside the state's courtrooms. The remaining text serves as a game opening to this difficult, but potentially important, area of analysis. A caveat, however: I do not for one moment pretend that the following is anything more than illustrative and tentative, and should not in any way be considered a general blueprint. To be sure, the closures that enable me to communicate this possibility to a reader should themselves permanently remain amenable to future critiques, discernments, deconstructions, openings, developments and so on. Such is more than fatuous modesty; it is – on the strength of the positions adopted before – integral to non-essential grammars of critique and ethics.

Let us imagine a case in which a contextual politics has successfully enunciated a given event as an injustice requiring restorative remedies. As such, let us suppose that those concerned to regulate the event outside state criminal justice institutions find themselves in a context that declares itself to be operating in the name of restorative justice. From our vantage, the ethical work at hand is specific because it is primarily about restructuring relations so that all parties may live justly with others in future. Whatever the precise form of the gathering (e.g. family group conference, community panel, victim–offender mediation or some yet to be instituted practice, etc.), the ethical subjects assemble in consequence of, and as a response to, the injustice. How might an ethics that allegorically refers to images of hospitality approach the situation?

To begin with, it will be noted that the restorative assembly is hosted and that the host, as host, retains degrees of mastery over the place where guests are received. However, to be hospitable is also always to welcome, to open up to the stranger who appears on the threshold. Through the welcome, host and guest open up to a future way of being with one another. Elements of critique appear at this very moment because, if the hosting relationship is to continue, both host and guest must open up a past injustice to exist differently in an emerging relational complex. In so opening up, dissociating, past ways of being, the ethical subjects can begin to negotiate the contours of the unjust events, perhaps name them in precise ways, and contemplate the promise of future (just) relations.

It is important to note that it would be wrong to consider the ethical subjects as immutable, pre-existing absolutes who confront one another as isolated iconoclasts. To do so would be return ethics to ontology (the absolute being of natural subjects, or even of universal rights), and so eclipse the distinctively indeterminate realm of ethics. Levinas's (1998) perceptive work on the face and other clarifies that the ethical self does not exist as such (i.e. as an ethical subject), before being involved in specific types of ethical practice. The subject is not simply a natural, pre-given entity (as enshrined in human rights) capable of suffering (as a victim) and encountering the world of others. Instead, the subject is, or rather comes to be, by responding to the other (or rather an amorphous, indefinite and generalized 'face' of the other). That is, the 'I' comes to exist only through processes of responding to being with others. In that sense, any subject is primarily a response to others in given encounters, and so is profoundly responsible to them. Its very being, if anything, depends on such a response. Bauman puts it this way: 'moral responsibility – being *for* the Other before one can be *with* the Other – is the first reality of the self, a starting point rather than a product of society'

(1993: 13). Derrida's work on hospitality echoes the point, noting that a host's identity is as much 'hostage' to the guest as the latter is (in part at least) response to the host's welcome. The contextual identities assumed by host and guest emerge in response to each other, and the welcome issued in a finite context. Such ethical subjects, assembled in the name of justice, are in a profound sense *responsible* to and for their respective identities, as are they to the significant others that have shaped their past ethical orientations.

Therefore, returning to the example, let us note that a restorative welcome (i.e. what precise type of practices restorative justice assumes) directly shapes the kinds of ethical subjects that can emerge in context. If the elected process vehemently obliges participants to retain the identities of 'criminal offender' or 'victim', it also radically narrows the range of possible ethical responses and subjects; it may even end up imitating the criminal justice system (see Pavlich, 2005a). This indicates an important issue: it is crucial continuously to devise open ethical forums that enable fundamental questions, deconstructions and dissociations of past events and practices. The more these forums see their roles in that fashion, the more likely they are to open themselves to name and challenge the structured auspices that have shaped past injustices.

Furthermore, if the contours of a given injustice are negotiated through critical dialogues between responding subjects that call upon all present to respond to a welcome that seeks a just future, then the stage is set for grappling with some limitations of a past, unjust, way of being with each other. Conflict in all likelihood will be crucial to such dialogue. In this context, the host is not required to give up all mastery of the social space, but equally cannot dictate the guest's response. All responses are themselves conditioned by an ethical subject's previous responses to the 'face', to past images of social calls of the others, as well as from the welcome offered at a given restorative justice event. For example, the welcome at a threshold to new life may be curt, or an elaborately inviting one, etc., just as the response to that from guests could assume many different forms. In all cases, response and negotiation shape the identities of emerging ethical subjects, and all draw on the ethical resources brought to the context by their past experiences (responses?).

Through concrete dialogue, ethical subjects might be implored to dissociate the mode of being that they define as unjust, to puncture its meaning horizons and so lay the groundwork for contemplating new, future modes of being. Such contemplations, in context, are driven by the promise of an incalculable and infinite justice that is nevertheless calculated as a finite way to be just with one another in immediate, future relations. The promise of just relations is key here; justice serves as an infinite call that is sent forth from given, finite, modes of being as a way to bridge what is envisaged as possible future ways to be. The moment of critique occasions possibilities for ethical subjects to *become,* to develop out of the injustices of a past into the promise of future just ways of being with one another. The promise of being differently is all that remains; justice is the promise to live without the named injustices of a particular instance.

No doubt this brief indication, faint illustration, of an ethical imagination allied to critique that strives to bypass the deceptions of universal principle is little more than a trace; it requires the flesh and bones of a given context to exact fully the 'possibilities of a given situation'. However, I have attempted at least to provide a tracing of a grammar that might be evoked when re-imagining ethics and restorative justice beyond modern formulations of ethics and indeed justice. That trace, too, is present in restorative justice discourses, but it remains underdeveloped and even silenced by attractions to formulate universal ethical principles in a modern mode.

I am well aware that the preceding will be disquieting for those intent on continuing the search for a universal justice, despite all the horrors that attend when a finite calculation of justice is allowed to masquerade as necessary, essential, inevitable or indeed universally applicable. Stalin had his absolute justice, as did Hitler, Verwoerd and countless other promulgators of one (totalitarian) vision of the just. Perhaps it is simply that justice and ethics, by virtue of their indeterminacy, are of a different order – they do not lend themselves to essential, absolute and universal declaration without direct enforcement and often massively destructive consequences. Whenever justice operates under the subterfuge of an undeconstructable universal principle, one finds the deathly silence of imposed necessity that in one stroke voids resistance and its claim to ethics. In the aftermath of that decisive stroke, there is just no telling what atrocities will surface in the name of justice. We should perhaps recall that the promise of justice always also occasions a response from ethical subjects. And that response, too, is not without its paradoxes, succinctly captured through the following lines of Cavafy's poem, *Waiting For the Barbarians*:

> 'What are we waiting for, assembled in the forum?
> The barbarians are due here today.
> Why isn't anything happening in the senate?
> Why do the senators sit there without legislating?
> Because the barbarians are coming today.
> What laws can the senators make now?
> Once the barbarians are here, they'll do the legislating.
> Why did our emperor get up so early,
> and why is he sitting at the city's main gate
> on his throne, in state, wearing the crown?
> Because the barbarians are coming today
> and the emperor is waiting to receive their leader ...
>
> Why are the streets and squares emptying so rapidly,
> everyone going home so lost in thought?
> Because night has fallen and the barbarians have not come.
> And some who have just returned from the border say
> there are no barbarians any longer.
> And now, what's going to happen to us without barbarians?
> They were, those people, a kind of solution.'

Selected further reading

Bauman, Z. (1995) *Life in Fragments: Essays in Postmodern Moralities*. Oxford: Blackwell. Explores the implications of postmodernity for a new understanding of morality and ethics.

Derrida, J. (2001) *On Cosmopolitanism and Forgiveness*. London: Routledge. One of the most influential figures in contemporary philosophy explores the paradox of forgiveness.

MacIntyre, A. (1988) *Whose Justice? Which Rationality?* Notre Dame, IN: Notre Dame University Press. Outlines and examines a range of views on justice and practical rationality.

Pavlich, G. (2005) *Governing Paradoxes of Restorative Justice*. London: Glasshouse Press. Provides a constructive and original critique of the ethical promises of restorative justice.

Walzer, M. (1983) *Spheres of Justice: A Defence of Pluralism*. New York, NY: Basic Books. A major contribution to contemporary thinking about the concept of justice, which argues for a radical plurality of concepts.

Acknowledgements

The author wishes to thank Gerry Johnstone for his helpful comments on an earlier version of this paper.

References

Badiou, A. (2001) *Ethics: An Essay on the Understanding of Evil*. London: Verso.

Batley, M (2004) 'What is the appropriate role of sprituality in restorative justice?', in H. Zehr and B. Toews (eds) *Critical Issues in Restorative Justice*, Monsey, NY: Criminal Justice Press.

Bauman, Z. (1992) *Intimations of Postmodernity*. London: Routledge.

Bauman, Z. (1993) *Postmodern Ethics*. Oxford: Blackwell.

Bauman, Z. (1994) *Alone Again: Ethics after Certainty*. London: Demos.

Bauman, Z. (1995) *Life in Fragments: Essays in Postmodern Moralities*. Oxford: Blackwell.

Bauman, Z. (1999) 'The world inhospitable to Levinas', *Philosophy Today*, Summer: 151–167.

Bazemore, G. and Schiff, M. (eds) (2001) *Restorative Community Justice: Repairing Harm and Transforming Communities*. Cincinnati, OH: Anderson Publishing.

Bonta, J., Wallace-Capretta, S. and Rooney, J. (1998) *Restorative Justice: An Evaluation of the Restorative Resolutions Project*. Ottawa: Solicitor General Canada.

Braithwaite, J. (2002) *Restorative Justice and Responsive Regulation*. Oxford: Oxford University Press.

Braithwaite, J. (2003a) 'Restorative justice and social justice', in E. McLaughlin *et al.* (eds) *Restorative Justice: Critical Issues*. London: Sage/The Open University.

Braithwaite, J. (2003b) 'Principles of restorative justice', in A. von Hirsch *et al.* (eds) *Restorative Justice and Criminal Justice: Competing or Reconcilable Paradigms*, Oxford: Hart Publishing.

Bush, R. and Folger, J. (1994) *The Promise of Mediation: Responding to Conflict through Empowerment*. San Francisco, CA: Jossey-Bass.

Cavafy, C. (1864–1993) *Waiting for the Barbarians* (trans. E. Keeley) (available online at http://ccat.sas.upenn.edu/jod/texts/cavafy.html).

Coetzee, J.M. (1980) *Waiting for the Barbarians*. London: Penguin Books.

Consedine, J. (1995) *Restorative Justice: Healing the Effects of Crime*. Lyttelton, NZ: Ploughshares Publications.

Consedine, J. and Bowen, H. (1999) *Restorative Justice: Contemporary Themes and Practice*. Lyttelton, NZ: Ploughshares Publications.

Cooley, D. and Law Commission of Canada (1999) *From Restorative Justice to Transformative Justice: Discussion Paper*. Ottawa: Law Commission of Canada.

Derrida, J. (1992) 'The force of law: the "mystical foundation of authority"', in *Deconstruction and the Possibility of Justice*. D. Cornell *et al.* (eds) New York, NY: Routledge.

Derrida, J. (1997) *Deconstruction in a Nutshell: A Conversation with Jacques Derrida*. New York, NY: Fordham University Press.

Derrida, J. (1999) *Adieu to Emmanuel Levinas*. Stanford, CA: Stanford University Press.

Derrida, J. (2001) *On Cosmopolitanism and Forgiveness*. London: Routledge.

Derrida, J. and Dufourmantelle, A. (2000) *Of Hospitality*. Stanford, CA: Stanford University Press.

Douzinas, C. and Warrington, R. (1994) *Justice Miscarried*. London: Harvester Wheatsheaf.

Grayling, A.C. (2003) *What Is Good? The Search for the Best Way to Live*. London: Phoenix.

Hadley, M.L. (ed.) (2001) *The Spiritual Roots of Restorative Justice*. New York, NY: State University of New York Press.

Johnstone, G. (2002) *Restorative Justice: Ideas, Values, Debates*. Cullompton: Willan Publishing.

Johnstone, G. (ed.) (2003) *A Restorative Justice Reader*. Cullompton: Willan Publishing.

Johnstone, G. (2004) 'How, and in what terms, should restorative justice be conceived?', in H. Zehr and B. Toews (eds) *Critical Issues in Restorative Justice*. Monsey, NY: Criminal Justice Press.

Kurki, L. (1999) *Incorporating Restorative and Community Justice into American Sentencing and Corrections*. Washington, DC: US Department of Justice, Office of Justice Programs, National Institute of Justice.

Kurki, L. (2003) 'Evaluating restorative justice practices', in A. von Hirsch *et al.* (eds) *Restorative Justice and Criminal Justice: Competing or Reconcilable Paradigms*. Oxford: Hart Publishing.

Levinas, E. (1998) *Ethics and Infinity: Conversations with Philippe Nemo*. Pittsburgh, PA: Dusquesne University Press.

Lyotard, J.-F. (1984) *The Postmodern Condition: A Report on Knowledge*. Minneapolis, MN: University of Minnesota Press.

Lyotard, J.-F. and Thebaud, J.-L. (1979) *Just Gaming*. Minneapolis, MN: University of Minnesota Press.

MacIntyre, A. (1988) *Whose Justice? Which Rationality?* Notre Dame, IN: University of Notre Dame Press.

McLaughlin, E., Fergusson, R., Hughes, G. and Westmarland, L. (eds) (2003) *Restorative Justice: Critical Issues*. London: Sage/The Open University.

Morris, R. (2000) *Stories of Transformative Justice*. Toronto: Canadian Scholars' Press.

Pavlich, G. (2000) *Critique and Radical Discourses on Crime*. Aldershot: Ashgate/Dartmouth.

Pavlich, G. (2002). 'Towards an ethics of restorative justice', in L. Walgrave (ed.) *Restorative Justice and the Law*. Cullompton: Willan Publishing.

Pavlich, G. (2005a) *Governing Paradoxes of Restorative Justice*. London: Glasshouse Press.

Pavlich, G. (2005b) 'Experiencing critique', *Law and Critique* 14: 1–18.

Plato (1971) *The Republic*. Harmondsworth: Penguin Books.

Roche, D. (2003) *Accountability in Restorative Justice*. Oxford: Oxford University Press.

Sharpe, S. (1998) *Restorative Justice: A Vision for Healing and Change*. Edmonton: Edmonton Victim Offender Mediation Society.

Sharpe, S. (2004) 'How large should the restorative justice "tent" be?', in H. Zehr and B. Toews (eds) *Critical Issues in Restorative Justice*. Monsey, NY: Criminal Justice Press.

Strang, H. and Braithwaite, J. (2001) *Restorative Justice and Civil Society*. Cambridge: Cambridge University Press.

Sullivan, D. and Tifft, L. (2004) 'What are the implications of restorative justice for society and our lives?', in H. Zehr and B. Toews (eds) *Critical Issues in Restorative Justice*. Monsey, NY: Criminal Justice Press.

Sullivan, D., Tifft, L. and Cordella, P. (1998) 'The phenomenon of restorative justice', *Contemporary Justice Review*, 1: 1–14.

Umbreit, M.S. (2001) *The Handbook of Victim Offender Mediation: An Essential Guide to Practice and Research*. San Francisco, CA: Jossey-Bass.

Van Ness, D. (2002) 'The shape of things to come: a framework for thinking about a restorative justice system', in E.G.M. Weitekamp and H.-J. Kerner (eds) *Restorative Justice: Theoretical Foundations*. Cullompton: Willan Publishing.

Van Ness, D. and Strong, K. (2002) *Restoring Justice*. Cincinnati, OH: Anderson Publishing.

Wachtel, T. and McCold, P. (2001) 'Restoative justice in everyday life', in H. Strang and J. Braithwaite (eds) *Restorative Justice and Civil Society*. Cambridge: Cambridge University Press.

Walgrave, L. (ed.) (2002) *Restorative Justice and the Law*. Portland, OR: Willan Publishing.

Walgrave, L. (2004) 'Has restorative justice appropriately responded to retribution theory and impulses?', in H. Zehr and B. Toews (eds) *Critical Issues in Restorative Justice*. Monsey, NY: Criminal Justice Press.

Walzer, M. (1983) *Spheres of Justice: A Defense of Pluralism*. New York, NY: Basic Books.

Young, I.M. (1990) *Justice and the Politics of Difference*. Princeton, NJ: Princeton University Press.

Zehr, H. (1990) *Changing Lenses: A New Focus for Crime and Justice*. Scottdale, PA: Herald Press.

Zehr, H. (2002) *The Little Book of Restorative Justice*. Intercourse, PA: Good Books.

Zehr, H. (2003) 'Retributive justice, restorative justice', in G. Johnstone (ed.) *A Restorative Justice Reader: Text, Sources, Context*. Cullompton: Willan Publishing.

Zehr, H. and Toews, B. (eds) (2004) *Critical Issues in Restorative Justice*. Monsey, NY: Criminal Justice Press.

Glossary

Agreement
An arrangement between parties regarding a course of action; a covenant; the expected outcome of a co-operative process.

Best practices
The behavioural norms, skills, ideas, resources and traditions that have been proven to exhibit restorative justice principles and values successfully. Within the co-operative process their use is the principal way that stakeholders are assured of fair processes.

Circle
A format for facilitated dialogue. Circles include any combination of victims, offenders, communities of care, judges and/or court personnel, prosecutors, defence counsel, police, as well as interested community members. The circle is convened by a 'keeper of the circle' whose role is principally to oversee the process. Circles are used for different purposes. Common types are sentencing circles (to agree on a sentence), healing circles (to provide care and support for victims or offenders) and peace-making circles (to address conflicts that have not risen to the level of a criminal offence).

Circle of support and accountability
A support group formed around a person (usually a feared ex-prisoner, and

often a former sex offender) which supports and monitors the person in order to help achieve the twin goals of enabling the person to live safely in a neighbourhood, while enabling the neighbourhood to live safely with the person.

Coercion

Coercion means influencing a person through threat or guile to make a choice that he or she would not otherwise have made. A balanced presentation of options facing the person is not coercion.

Community

A group of people bound together by a common interest and willing to work together for that interest:

- *Local community*: the entire group of private citizens living in a given location.
- *Neighbourhood*: a group of individuals who live in close proximity to one another. Usually neighbourhoods include a couple of blocks of houses, although they can be smaller or bigger. Usually self-defined by those living in the neighbourhood, the neighbourhood boundaries may grow or shrink depending on the context.
- *Community of interest*: a group of individuals who gather together around a particular special interest or activity. Examples include those gathered by their faith, their job/vocation, sports, a particular life experience or problem, etc.
- *Community of care*: the group of people who are committed to care for, protect, support and encourage an individual. Frequently includes family members, faith community members, counsellors, teachers and/or friends. Some individuals do not have a strong or beneficial community of care, so these people may need help in recruiting a new one.
- *Relational neighbourhood*: the group of people with which an individual interacts frequently, to whom an individual feels connected or to whom the individual would go for help. Often includes families, friends, co-workers and neighbours, as well as faith or school community leaders.

Conference

A format for facilitated dialogue. Conferencing involves the community of people most affected by the crime – the victim, the offender and the community of care of both – in deciding the resolution of a criminal or delinquent incident. The affected parties are brought together by a trained facilitator to discuss how they and others have been harmed by the offence and how that harm might be repaired.

Confinement

Physical restriction of a person to a clearly defined area from which he or she is lawfully forbidden to depart. Departure is often constrained by architectural barriers and/or guards or other custodians. A subset of **incapacitation**.

Encounter
A face-to-face or indirect meeting of parties to discuss what took place, consider the impact of the offence on the parties and agree on how to make things right. An encounter may be facilitated or conducted by the parties alone; planned or spontaneous; large or small. See **mediation**, **conference** and **circle**.

Family
A group of people related by blood or law. For purposes of inclusion in restorative justice processes, can also be extended to include the group with whom an individual lives or those with whom one feels intimately connected and committed for life.

Force
Applying physical pressure or violence, or threatening to do so.

Formal
Refers to the degree of form within a programme. Formal programmes are those with structured accountability, fixed order and tradition. If a programme is established enough to have an address in the phone book, an official name or any kind of advertising, it may be considered formal. See **informal**.

Harm
The negative impact of an offence upon a person, group or community. Examples of direct harm include property loss, damage or destruction; physical and psychological injury; and death. Examples of indirect harm include rising fear in a neighbourhood or a growing general sense of lawlessness.

Healing
Restoring somebody who has suffered harm or trauma to a better condition than they are in.

Incapacitation
Steps or precautions to limit an individual's physical freedom. Examples include restrictions such as a curfew, probation, suspension of driver's licence or other privileges, time spent in a treatment facility, house arrest or imprisonment.

Informal
Informality refers to the degree of form within a programme. Informal programmes may be completely spontaneous, lacking any hierarchy, fixed order or tradition. Most informal programmes are community based; there may, however, be exceptions. See **formal**.

Integration
The process of being knitted into a healthy community. Both victims and offenders may need help with this, either because they have been estranged by their experience of crime (and the justice process, in some cases) and

others' reactions to that experience, or because they were never a part of a healthy community in the first place. See **reintegration**.

Mediation

A format for an encounter with facilitated dialogue. Also known as victim–offender mediation, the process involves an unbiased third person called a mediator or facilitator who assists the victim and offender in reaching a mutually acceptable and voluntary agreement. Decision-making authority rests with the parties.

Needs

Those things (material, physical, emotional, spiritual and/or relational) that are required in order to recover from the effects of experiencing or causing harm.

Negotiation

The process of creating an agreement between parties concerning how to resolve matters related to the offence. The negotiation may be conducted by the parties alone, with the assistance of a facilitator or by an intermediary working between the parties.

Offender

A person who has admitted, taken responsibility for or been convicted of an offence.

Prevention

The active process of creating conditions or individual attributes with an end result that the likelihood of criminal behaviour decreases. *Global* prevention approaches are directed towards a general population. *Selective* prevention approaches target groups at greater risk of developing or continuing negative behaviours. *Individual* prevention approaches target individuals who have known, identified risks for developing negative behaviours.

Public harm

That harm that is done to the community by a crime. Public harm is often due more to the collective influence of many crimes than to the influence of a single offence. Harm includes increased fear, distrust of the justice system and other state authorities, fragmentation of the community and the consumption of resources needed for other priorities.

Public interest

The interest of the community in its own welfare. This includes the need for safety, justice and confidence in the government.

Punishment

Punishment has two meanings:

1. A penalty imposed for wrongdoing with the intention of expressing the community's disapproval of the wrongdoing.
2. The entire process of criminalizing and penalizing conduct.

Rehabilitation

The process, programmes and support systems used to restore someone to a more healthy and useful place in society and life.

Reintegration

Re-establishment of people's practical and meaningful ties and relationships to their community of origin. See **integration**.

Reparation

The act of trying to repair the harm done. It may take many forms, such as payment of money to the victim or, if the victim wishes, to a charitable organization. It may involve work for the victim or, if the victim wishes, community service. For some victims the preferred form of reparation is that the offender will co-operate with whatever type of programme he or she needs to help avoid offending in the future, such as completing his or her education, acquiring skills, or attending treatment for addiction. Reparation involves compensation for an injury or insult.

Respect

Regarding people as worthy of particular consideration, recognition, care and attention simply because they are people.

Responsibility

Something one has a duty to do in response to crime. The duty may be determined by the one undertaking the responsibility (e.g., apology), by agreement of the parties (restitution agreement), or by order of a person in authority (restitution order).

Restitution

Monetary reimbursement to victims for loss of or damage to property or for other harm. Refers to the responsibility that offenders bear to their victims. Four restitution arrangements are possible:

1. Payments by the offender to the actual victim, perhaps through an intermediary.

2. Earnings shared with some community agency or group serving as a substitute victim.
3. Personal services performed by the offender to benefit the victim.
4. Labour donated by the offender for the good of the community.

Restorative justice

This term is sometimes used narrowly to refer to programmes that bring affected parties together to agree on how to respond to crime (this might be called the *encounter* conception of restorative justice). It is used more broadly by others to refer to a theory of reparation and prevention that would influence all criminal justice (the *reparative* conception). Finally, it is used most broadly to refer to a belief that the preferred response to all conflict – indeed to all of life – is peace building through dialogue and agreement of the parties (the *transformative* conception).

Rights

The term used to describe the protections owed to a stakeholder within the criminal justice system. Standards of freedom, dignity and respect to which every person is legally entitled in a certain situation.

Sanctions

A penalty, specified or in the form of moral pressure, that acts to ensure compliance or conformity with an agreement or order.

Sentence

An order for what an offender should to do make amends for the harm done by his or her crime. Should take into account the amount of personal and public harm done, the seriousness of the offence and the amount of pain caused to the offender by the sentence.

Seriousness of an offence

An evaluation based upon an assessment of 1) the degree of harm caused or threatened to victims by an offence (e.g. lasting impact, number of people affected, intrusiveness of crime into the lives of the victims, etc.); 2) the attitude of the harm-doer at the time of causing that harm (e.g. deliberately caused, recklessly caused, carelessly caused, caused despite exercising reasonable care); and 3) the attitude of the legislative and/or judicial authorities concerning the relative harm to society of this behaviour compared with other offences.

Services

The care that victims and offenders need to receive in order to integrate into healthy communities. Services are offered to the community at large. They can be community based or government based.

Victim (of crime)
A person who suffers from a destructive or injurious action or agency:

- *Direct victim (primary victim)*: people or groups or impersonal entities who experience the crime or its consequences first hand.
- *Indirect victim (secondary victim)*: people or groups or impersonal entities who also suffer emotionally or financially but are not immediately involved or injured.

Author Index

Subject Index